Building

Classic

Small Craft

Building
Classic
Small Craft

Complete Plans and Instructions for 47 Boats

JOHN GARDNER

INTERNATIONAL MARINE / McGRAW-HILL
Camden, Maine • New York • Chicago • San Francisco •
Lisbon • London • Madrid • Mexico City • Milan • New Delhi •
San Juan • Seoul • Singapore • Sydney • Toronto

Dedication to
Building Classic Small Craft

To all the boatbuilders gone before whom I have learned from, and to those yet to come
who may read this book, finding herein something of what I learned that they can use.

....

Dedication to
More Building Classic Small Craft

To Fred Dion, a good boss who knew boats; Kenneth Durant, a historian who wanted
the facts; Dave Getchell, editor, who always has given me scope; and Mystic Seaport
Museum, a haven for classic small draft and conservator of the skills that built them.

The McGraw·Hill Companies

4 5 6 7 8 9   QPD   QPD   9 0 9 8 7 6

Copyright © 1997, 2004 International Marine

Building Classic Small Craft, volume 1, copyright © 1977,
1991, International Marine; *More Building Classic Small
Craft,* copyright © 1984, 1990, International Marine.

All rights reserved. The name "International Marine" and
the International Marine logo are trademarks of The
McGraw-Hill Companies. Printed in the United States of
America.

Questions regarding the content of this book should be
addressed to: International Marine, P.O. Box 220, Camden,
ME 04843, www.internationalmarine.com

Questions regarding the ordering of this book should be addressed to: The McGraw-Hill Companies, Customer Service
Department, P.O. Box 547, Blacklick, OH 43004, Retail
customers: 1-800-262-4729, Bookstores: 1-800-722-4726

*The Library of Congress has cataloged the cloth edition as fol-
lows:*
Gardner, John, 1905–1995
    Building classic small craft : complete plans and in-
structions for 47 boats / John Gardner
        p.   cm.
    Rev. ed. of: Building classic small craft, c1997–c1984
and More building classic small craft, c1984–c1990.
    Includes bibliographical references (p.   ) and index.
    ISBN 0-07-022864-7
    1. Boatbuilding   I. Gardner, John, 1905–1995. Build-
ing classic small craft. More building classic small craft.
II. Title
VM351.G35   1996
623.8′202–dc20   89–24691
                                        CIP

Paperback ISBN 0-07-142797-X

Contents

In Memoriam

························•························

John Gardner died on October 18, 1995, at the age of 90. He was rich in the things that matter—a fortunate man—and all who have benefited and will benefit from his work are likewise fortunate. This volume, combining his *Building Classic Small Craft, Volume 1,* and *More Building Classic Small Craft*, is a memorial to his remarkable contributions as researcher, teacher, wordsmith, and craftsman.

It seems fitting to begin with a portrait of John. The sources we've drawn from include "Our Thanks to John Gardner" (*WoodenBoat* #90, September/October 1989); *The Ash Breeze*, Journal of the Traditional Small Craft Association, Vol. 17, No. 3, Summer 1995; "John Gardner in His Own Words" (an interview with Peter Spectre, *WoodenBoat* #40); and the letters of tribute submitted for *WoodenBoat* #129, March/ April 1996. To the contributors we express our sincere thanks. Thank you, too, to Matthew Murphy, Editor of *WoodenBoat*, and to Ken Steinmetz, Editor of *The Ash Breeze.*

We introduce John with four expressions of appreciation; then learn of his life through his own words, and close with a few remembrances—with apologies to the hundreds of other letter writers excluded by lack of space.

FROM "OUR THANKS TO JOHN GARDNER,"
WoodenBoat #90, September/October 1989

Quiet, reserved, terse in speech, at times almost shy, John Gardner seems the typical conservative New England boatbuilder, hardly the Marxist idealist he once was. But John's life has been long—now well into its eighth decade—and has spanned tumultuous and changing times. Complex better describes this unusual man whose gentle philosophy, centering on humanism and traditional values, has almost without intention influenced untold thousands.

I include myself among this multitude, for there is no way one could work closely with such a man for nearly a quarter of a century and walk away untouched. In fact, his influence has been pervasive, coloring with indelible dyes my thoughts on small boats, work ethics, the importance of independent thought, and tolerance for human frailties. For 23 years I edited nearly every one of hundreds of articles on boat design, construction, and nautical history that he wrote for the old *Maine Coast Fisherman* and *National Fisherman*. In addition, I read the scores of stories he wrote for the paper before I arrived and, best of all, carried on a long and richly rewarding correspondence that told me far more about him than his readers would ever know.

Soured by the excesses of capitalism in the 1920s and '30s, he became a union organizer enticed by the promises of Marxism, and when their emptiness became tragically obvious in the late '30s, the young intellectual turned inward, working in a boatyard by day and studying and writing on political history, woodworking, and eventually on boats, by night. It never entered his mind that he would one day become the guru of the traditional wooden boat scene, or that his influence in this field would extend worldwide, a much more impressive accomplishment than his purposeful attempts at political persuasion in the far distant past.

A brief comment of his remains etched in my mind and, I think, tells much about his instinctive logic. With no small trepidation, I was showing John my first attempt at housebuilding. He wandered around our new mountainside home, overlooking the obvious lapses in my limited woodworking skill and, as usual, saying little. Finally, he sat down in a chair, stretched his legs, and looked out a big picture window at the forested ridge climbing up the horizon.

"This project will add 10 years to your life," he said.

Given such reasoning, one understands why he remains so youthful in thought and deed.

DAVID R. GETCHELL, SR.
APPLETON, MAINE

David R. Getchell, Sr., was managing editor of National Fisherman, *founding editor of* Small Boat Journal, *and editor of* The Outboard Boater's Handbook.

Thirty years ago, there were only fairy tales of our historic small craft. Boatyards had closed or switched to the fiberglass bandwagon. The molds of the old classics were cut up for firewood. Chapelle's *American Small Sailing Craft* was the eulogy of this rich, varied part of our maritime past.

Then came the John Gardner articles in *Maine Coast Fisherman* (later *National Fisherman*), like a spark in the black hole of history.

Gardner wrote not only about historic boats and their builders, but about how to build them today, and who was still doing it. His articles were full of sound advice, encouragement, sources of hard-to-find gear. I can only guess at the zillions of letters and phone calls they generated.

The light grew brighter each month as the scattered tribe of classic small-craft nuts realized there was a contact point for information, a spiritual center for inspiration. From John we learned how to use hand tools again, even how to build them. He gave us consumer reports on the new goos, too, and lectured us sternly on protecting our health in the boatshop. He was our political watchdog on new rules that might stifle the resurrection of traditional small craft.

Then came the small-craft program he developed at Mystic Seaport Museum, and his books. The boat exhibits at Mystic, the yearly Small Craft Workshop at Mystic, and the books were the elements that transformed a bright light into a vital, popular movement. Traditional boat clubs and societies were formed. Regattas, rendezvous, festivals, conferences were conducted. Boatshops still bravely hanging onto wood were encouraged. New boatshops courageously started out. A small-craft museum was founded; even a magazine about wooden boats dared to begin. John had a hand in it all.

His communication skills match his encyclopedic knowledge, and that certainly has helped boost the movement along. John not only does impeccable scholastic preparation for his writings, but he lays it out in lean, crisp prose. His talks have all the above, plus a large dollop of Yankee droll. His grace, humor, and timing are skills that help the message of our small-craft heritage go down quite smoothly.

In the big picture, the message John has given us should deserve a Nobel Prize as service to humanity. Sure, John has made a detail-perfect Whitehall or Adirondack guideboat a legitimate prestige toy for some. But, beyond that, he has put small craft in the heritage hierarchy of museums. He has given them a permanent status and dignity that add "boat" to our cultural vocabulary. Because of Gardner, it's all right to have Henry Rushton and Thomas Eakins in the same sentence. And a whole rainbow of experiences in traditional small craft in between have sprung up due to Gardner. He's the Johnny Appleseed of our small-craft heritage.

DICK WAGNER
SEATTLE, WASHINGTON

Dick Wagner discovered John Gardner through his articles in Maine Coast Fisherman *in the late 1950s. The small craft Gardner wrote about were woven into a rich, complex fabric of technical, social, and historical issues. Gardner's inclusive views, elegantly told, inspired Wagner to create a living traditional boat museum, the Center for Wooden Boats.*

Unstinting generosity. That has been the constant in 17 years of treasured friendship with John Gardner. Never hesitation, never calculation, never "score-keeping."

There is an old legend—of the servant-leader, one whose leadership is quiet, unmarked by epaulettes, flag-waving, or side boys. Something there is so appropriate in having a craftsman lead a movement as broad, gentle, diverse, and *structurally* affirming in this Age of Information as the revitalization of small watercraft in North America, that one thinks of this 20-year movement more in terms of the *myth* than the historical. That that leadership has fused Word and Deed, to as great an extent as has characterized any movement of which I am aware, suggests a model outline for our times.

John chisels out clear, evocative prose with the left hand and distinctive American small craft with the right. He documents special boats in some of our most straightforward linestaking and drafting. He teaches, inspires, and informs a whole new population of builders, always having the grace to say quietly, "Let the tools teach you."

The degree to which he has helped me personally, in a sometime effort to set up institutions and programs centered on the perpetuation of the skills as distinct from the preservation of the boats—going beyond appreciation to apprenticing—is incalculable. A single incident and letter set a power train afire in me.

On the road home at midnight of the day in '72 when I first met John, drunks converted "Cutty Sark," my old London taxicab, to shrapnel. In a letter to John the next week, I mentioned this. He wrote back immediately, "We are all living on borrowed time."

Those words lent urgency to my efforts, then and ever since. They contain the will to embark on a chancy project; to go out on a fiscal limb; to embark on expeditions of all natures; to undertake the construction of distinctive watercraft, manuscripts, a new, three-story structure that serves the hunger-to-build lying latent in our youth—and then another and another.

Those words led me to ask John to write the introduction to a monograph devoted to precisely those stated ends. He wrote, and I treasure:

> *Trust youth, give them room, permit them to develop*
> *as whole persons; ask, and set no upper limits in asking,*
> *and they will rebuild the world.*

LANCE LEE
ROCKPORT, MAINE

Lance Lee is a sailor, boatbuilder, educator, and founder and president of the Atlantic Challenge Foundation, an international institute with apprenticeshops in several countries, including Canada, Mexico, the United Kingdom, Norway, and Russia. He is cofounder of the Apprenticeshop on the Neva in St. Petersburg, Russia, and is presently running his fourth apprenticeshop in the U.S. in Rockland, Maine.

FROM *THE ASH BREEZE,*
Vol. 17, No. 3, Summer 1995

The Dark Side of John Gardner
BY GREG FOSTER

The improbable heading above appears in my journal for 1994 following an entry labeled "Financial Options for an Aging Boatbuilder." That was a brief entry since the options I face at age fifty-five are few and far between. Where most people my age are faced with channeling income flow in a wide range of choices, my income flow is like catching drips from a leaky faucet, and there is only one choice for spending it: groceries. Under "B. Savings and Investments" the column is as bare as our cupboard. Nor does any prospect of retirement loom on the near or far horizon because there is no pension plan for self-employed boatbuilders in my income bracket.

I lay the blame for this predicament squarely at John Gardner's door. Back in the late 1960s and early 1970s, it was his enticing articles in *National Fisherman* that lured me away from a promising career in journalism with substantial financial benefits—at least more substantial than wooden boatbuilding. It couldn't possibly have been less.

You remember that campaign; it was the most clever and subversive tour de force ever perpetrated on an unsuspecting public. Articles like "Hearty Grandfather Cat Worth Careful Study," "Maine Peapod a True Double Ender," "Gardner Designs Sailing Whitehall to Be Built in a Number of Lengths," or "Rowing Workshop Soaked in Success," "Traditional Small Boat Sail Rigs Would Make Much Sense Today," and "Boatbuilders' Planes Are Many-Splendored Things."

It was relentless. For over a decade there was hardly an issue of this otherwise innocuous trade publication that didn't have buried in it somewhere one of these ironical subliminal messages that had nothing whatsoever to do with the modern fishing business or its awesome machines. When I should have been reporting on the local Chamber of Commerce or covering the Annual Begonia Festival, my nose was buried in "Ancient Pilot Gig Lines Offered for First Time," "14' Reach Boat is Obvious Maine Wherry Kin," or "A Smart Little Dory Tender."

John was listed as the Technical Editor, but as far as I'm concerned he was The Tempter. Back then I had never built a boat before. I was just a quivering bundle of expectancy. All unknowing I gobbled up "Determining Scantlings in Small Craft," "Stem Rabbet for a Skiff," and "No Mystery to Three Methods of Spiling."

It wasn't just the how-to that captured my curiosity. John snuck in insidious philosophy as well. Under "Feather-Weights Have Place in Modern Scene" he divulged a thinly veiled anarchistic program for enjoying nature. "What some may find surprising is that there are relatively untouched enclaves of wilderness not far distant from centers of urban congestion. It is not always necessary to travel half way across the continent to find nature much as it was a century ago."

Even more deadly was the seductive picture he painted of the past, the time when ". . . the engine had not yet replaced oars. Boats that rowed well and handled easily were at a premium." Technical Editor, forsooth, this was pure technological treason. I wonder that commercial fishermen didn't run him out of Dieselville on a rail. I don't think he was guilty of romanticizing the past; it's just that he referred to it in a way that made it sound so much more interesting than our present way of life. He had you beginning to suspect that we moderns had thrown out a very important baby with the bath water.

"Traditional Small Boat Rigs Would Make Much Sense Today." Does the marine industry subscribe to that? "Able Little 3-Master Was Popular among Gulf Coast Fishermen" made one wonder why the boats weren't still being used today.

John went so far as to fuel the fires of hope among the more naive imaginations (like mine) that he had already kindled. "Interest in Trades, Contrivances of Yesteryear at All-Time High" clearly noted that "Interest in the occupations of a bygone America is at an all-time high. *How the common man got his living on the farm, in the shop, and on the sea when this country was young is engaging the attention of Americans as never before"* (emphasis mine).

I never questioned such statements because they mirrored perfectly my own state of mind at that time. How *did* the common man get his living on the farm, in the shop, and on the sea? And if he did it once upon a time, why couldn't he do it again? It sounded like a healthy, self-reliant, close-to-nature kind of existence, one that had modern urban lifestyles beat seven ways from Sunday.

That was a quarter century ago. I did leave my comfortable ulcer-producing profession. I moved with my young family to a sea-girt rural island in British Columbia. I did try my hand at building not just one wooden boat but close to one hundred. How do you choose or stop when so many enticing designs from the past spring up to tempt you one after another?

By then John was writing books! We have worked at getting our living from the garden, in the shop, and on the sea. The first boat I built was meant to facilitate all three: a sailing cargo/fishing boat that supplied raw materials for the garden and boatshop on the same voyages that we brought back fish for the skillet, crab for the salad, and oysters for the stew. No engine, of course. By this time my curiosity was fully aroused to find out for myself just what kind of stuff those pre-engine farmer/builder/fishermen were actually made of. Better stuff was my ultimate conclusion.

That brings up another aspect of the dark side of John Gardner. Not only was his propaganda responsible for our hand-to-mouth existence and slim financial prospects, he never told the truth about oars and rowing. Just about all my friends have motor boats. They zip here and there, thumbing their noses at tidal currents, outrunning storms, covering distances in an hour or two that usually take me a day or two. Never mind that where my upwardly mobile friends see just another highway, I see waters filled with the mysteries of creation and the memories of noble ships and seafarers. At least my fast-moving friends get where they're going. After twenty-five years I'm somewhere in between—pulling on those crazy oars.

"Poverty sticks," they used to be called in the old days, I've since discovered. I don't think John ever mentioned that epithet. In a perverse way the name appeals to me since I've had a great admiration for poverty; it's the only sustainable life-style when you get right down to it.

Lately, with the onset of arthritis, I've realized that calling oars "poverty sticks" doesn't do them justice. They should be called "agony sticks." It hurts to row, and the further you row, the more it hurts. Anyone who belittles the agony of rowing is probably trying to sell you either a rowboat or oars or a membership in TSCA—maybe all three. I cringe when I think of the fate I've wished on so many boat customers through the years. But think of the widespread devastation John Gardner has caused, misleading an entire generation into believing that rowing is a good, perhaps even the best,

way to go on the water! I told you, he has a dark side. It's a wonder he can sleep at night with so many blisters, sore buns, and aching muscles on his conscience.

Doesn't John realize we don't do unpleasant or difficult things anymore? The modern good news is that nobody needs to experience pain or suffering or hardship or even inclement weather. Nowadays if there's any character-building to be done—to say nothing of soul-making—we can handle it with appropriate psychology or individualized attention or proper medication or the newest breakthrough in recreational clothing.

Now he's even taken to talking it up among the youngsters, giving the impression that rowing should be a family thing. I can see a whole new series of articles on the way: "A Nice Little Family Boat for the Northwest Passage," "The Family That Rows Together Grows Together," "Making Oars That Kids Can Handle."

Families beware! Consider what you may be getting your little darlings into. Consider me. By rights I deserve a secure and pampered old age surrounded by all the benefits that the comfortable society can provide. But do you think that will happen? Not a chance. I'll keep on making wood shavings, condemned to trying out different designs and wearing down the grips on my agony sticks until the day I drop—thanks to John Gardner.

I hope when he gets to the River Jordan, it's at the widest part with a stiff headwind blowing and the current strongly setting sideways, and I pray he has to row like the dickens every last inch of the way. Knowing John, he'll probably send back an article from the Pearly Gates: "A Jordan River Lifeboat You Can Build in Your Own Basement."

Greg Foster has been building and testing classic wooden boat designs from all over the world since 1970. Together with his sailmaking wife, Shay, he operates NW Historic Watercraft on Galiano Island, British Columbia, a private research facility dedicated to perpetuating crafty nautical technology and lore-powered boats.

John Gardner in His Own Words
BY PETER SPECTRE

This interview took place in the fall of 1980 at John Gardner's home in Mystic, Connecticut. The results of our conversation are published here without the questions so they will not get in the way of the story. What is worth reading is what he said, not what I asked him.

Unfortunately, the one thing this interview failed to reveal is Gardner's humor. On one level at least he is one of the wittiest people I have met, though the nature of his humor can only be understood on a person-to-person basis. He possesses the classical Yankee dry wit, which relies on understatement coupled with twinkling eyes or a wry grin, a style that cannot be conveyed by the written word. Take my word for it: he has the gift as few others do.

"My recollections go back to very early in the century. I was born in 1905 in Calais, Maine, which is on the St. Croix River at the head of Passamaquoddy Bay, where it forms the border between Maine and New Brunswick. I come from a long line of land surveyors. My great-grandfather was one, as was my grandfather and my father.

"We lived on a farm on the river about three miles below Calais. The farm ran down to the water and a mile back. As a boy I had boats on the river. There were great tides, twenty-six to twenty-eight feet, and the river at that point was about a mile wide, so when the tide was out there would be a half-mile of mud flats. Keeping a boat with tides like that took ingenuity. I had a pole about thirty feet long stuck in the mud flats and a square float—four boards nailed together—around the pole that would go up and down with the tide. I tied my boat to that. I also had a boat similar to the one Chapelle called the *Farmer's Daughter* with a wooden wheelbarrow wheel at the bow, which allowed it to be pushed over the mud flats.

"We built boats and used boats. My grandfather, before my time, had a pinky, which he used a great deal, and even while I was small he still went downriver in the fall to catch fish for the winter. In fact, there were many boats on the river at that time. There were lumber schooners, excursion boats, and steamboats. Calais was a thriving, enterprising, prosperous place, a center for the lumber industry.

"We cut our own boat lumber from our woodlot, usually at the same time we cut our firewood for the winter. We saved the good sawlogs and hauled them to a mill and brought the lumber home. My grandfather made everything. He made boats, he made hay racks and cart wheels, he built buildings and shingled roofs. He had been a carver's apprentice in Charlestown, Massachusetts, and was an accomplished woodcarver. I learned woodworking from him and my father as part of growing up.

"When I was young I used to spend quite a good deal of time at a nearby boatshop owned by the Whelan boys, so called although they were still called the Whelan boys when they were long past seventy. Jim and George were their names, though they were locally known as Pete and Repeat because they always repeated each other when they talked. They were Irish, Catholic, and Democrats, which put them apart to some extent in that area. They built all types of boats up to fifty or sixty feet for commercial or pleasure use, and all by hand. The shop had no power at all. Pieces were ripped out of rough-sawn lumber with handsaws and then planed. They used adzes and broad axes. I was influenced by these men. I was also influenced by a very skilled carpenter by the name of Tommy Webster, who lived up the road. He built my father's house with my father's assistance, without plans. The shelves and pantries were finished just like the interior of a vessel.

"I never apprenticed as a carpenter or boatbuilder, but I picked up the skills as I went along. My first attempt to rig my own boat came early on, when I took one of my great-grandfather's sea chests from the barn down to the brook and tried to sail it like a boat. From there I became a pretty good boatbuilder and built several craft before I got out of high school—rowboats, sailboats, nothing too difficult. Once I decided to build a dory and sent to the Maine State Library for a book with the lines of a pretty big dory. I scaled it down proportionally with the result that it was too tender. So to remedy the defect I built two airtight sponsons shaped something like crescent moons and attached them to the sides. The boat became very stable and rowed nicely but looked odd. I took it down to the Whelans, who scratched their heads but admitted the arrangement worked pretty good.

"I went to school in Calais, and after graduation I went to normal school in Machias. I took the standard two-year teacher-training course and then taught school for two years. I decided to become a teacher because I was encouraged to do so at home—both of my aunts were teachers—and it was the most convenient thing to do, I guess. Believe it or not, I was also motivated by football. Perhaps one of the most exciting moments of my life was when I made the varsity football team in my high school sophomore year at Calais Academy. In those days you had to supply your own uniform. I sawed and split and piled four cords of hackmatack wood to buy a pair of football pants. In my freshman year at Machias

Normal School I was one of the group that organized the school's first football team. But football wasn't the only thing. I had a lot of drive back then. I initiated and was editor of the *Washingtonia*, the school magazine, was president of the student body and did just about everything else.

"During one of my teaching years, I went to summer school at Columbia University in New York, which at the time was the leading teacher-training institution in the country. Only graduate courses were offered, but working teachers were permitted to take two years of graduate work that qualified them for a BS in education. So I stayed on at Columbia and took the two-year course, and then went on to get my master's degree in 1932.

"I got out of Columbia in the depths of the Depression. I was there in New York when they were selling apples on street corners and the financiers were jumping out of windows on Wall Street. It was a tough time to go to college and a tough time to get a job afterwards, even though I achieved honor rank.

"But in the meantime, in 1930, I had got a summer job as a counselor at Pine Island Camp in Belgrade Lakes, Maine. I worked there summers during the 1930s while I was at Columbia and afterwards when I was kicking around like most others during the Depression. I was in charge of the workshop, which was one of the features of the camp. We built model boats and yachts and sailed them. I also built several full-size boats there, such as a C. D. Mower sailing dinghy whose lines had been published in *Rudder* magazine. I was put in charge of the shop because of my background; I had the skills and the interest.

"I was also qualified because I understood both inland craft, like canoes, and saltwater craft. Calais, where I grew up, was intermediate between upriver—the woods—and downriver—the ocean. I understood both worlds. I found the camp to be a delightful experience and gained much inspiration from the work I did there.

"But full-time work eluded me. When I graduated from Columbia I had a first-class education. My expectations were that I would get a rather fancy job, but there weren't any. So I knocked about quite a bit and spent some time at home. I worked in the woods as a lumberman. I contracted and peeled pulpwood. I peeled a hundred cords of pulpwood one summer. I didn't teach at all—just knocked around at a lot of different things.

"My life as a boatyard worker began when World War II broke out. I happened to be in Lynn, Massachusetts, at the time and signed on at the Graves yard in nearby Marblehead because they were building Coast Guard picketboats as fast as they could and needed experienced workers. They never questioned my ability; I guess it was because I was from Maine and seemed to know what I was talking about.

"The picketboats were thirty-eight feet long and had been designed by Walter McInnis. We built seventy-two or seventy-three of them. I was on the night shift as a planker, since this was an assembly line operation. We were building two boats at a time, and I had two men who were hanging the planks and fastening them as fast as I got them out. Another crew was getting out the keel assemblies, lowering them on the forms and timbering them. Still another crew would finish them inside after they were turned over. We planked the boats upside down, and it was fast and furious work.

"When the picketboats were finished and things slacked off at Graves, I went over to Reed's Shipyard in Winthrop and went to work on a big, curious Navy barge, heavily built of Oregon fir. The yard was expanding like mad. I hung plank for a while and then was assigned to build a scale model of the craft for Washington. It was a typical government mess, with constant revisions to the full-size craft. I had to go out to the construction all the time and measure the changes and then rework the model. It was quite an elaborate job.

"Soon I got a call to go back to Graves, however. I returned to work on several different types of boats, and then started in on yachts because they were still trying to carry on with their yacht business even though there was a war on. I did yacht repair and other jobs; in fact, I built the tank-test model for the Hickman Sea Sled.

"It was wild over there in Marblehead at the beginning of the war. We had blackouts because the submarines were right off the coast, and a civil defense force was organized locally. We were all given guns; I had an old elephant gun that belonged to Graves's father-in-law. The foreman turned out billy clubs for blackout wardens in the joiner shop. We stopped work on several afternoons to go to the gravel pit and practice with our guns. We were given posts behind various rocks on the beach in case the submarines should land. It was completely wild.

"By then I had given up on being a teacher. I was doing what I wanted to do, and the job was over at four o'-clock on Friday. I had a great many intellectual interests that occupied me when I wasn't working. That was more or less the pattern until I went to work at Mystic Seaport in 1969. For example, I began to measure boats and take off lines. Some of those lines I put away until much later when I began to write. I then drew upon those resources that I gathered in Marblehead.

"I started taking off lines because I was interested in boats and their shapes, and I was interested in drawing them. I was also influenced by the people I worked with. I was working with a very fine boatbuilder, Charles Lawton, who was then considered to be the dean of his craft north of Boston. He was almost ninety at that time, still building boats at Graves. He had come down from St. John as a young man and had begun building boats in Boston as early as 1880. He worked at the Navy Yard before coming to Graves.

"World War II was the last hurrah of the old-time boatbuilders, many of whom came out of retirement for the duration. We had one boat joiner at Graves by the name of Dan Grant. He was a Nova Scotia Scotsman, an extraordinarily talented woodworker, sparmaker, carpenter. He could do anything. He made violins to pay the hospital expenses for one of his sons who had polio. He made very fine violins. He claimed he ruined his eyes working nights making them. He was a very ingenious man, and I count myself lucky for being able to work with people like that.

"I stayed at Graves until the end of the war; then I went to work for Simms Brothers in Dorchester, where they were building fine yachts for Sparkman & Stephens. Simms had formerly worked for Lawley, and his yard was sort of a home for old Lawley hands. We were double planking yachts fifty to sixty feet long. The outside layer was seven-eighths-inch African mahogany and the inside was three-eighths-inch white cedar with white lead between. The outside planking was so smooth and tight you couldn't see where the seams were. I finally left Simms in the late 1940s because it was too far from my home and the pay wasn't too good. I went to work at Dion's Boatyard in Salem. Relations there were very good. If you could do the work and you were reliable, Fred Dion didn't bother you. In fact, he gave me his youngest son so I could train him. I did all repair work—no new construction.

"From the late 1940s until 1969 I worked at Dion's, with the exception of two years during the Korean War when I worked at General Electric in the template room. I was essentially a patternmaker in the turbine division, though when business was slow I went out on the floor and tried my hand at welding and boilermaking. It was interesting work, but not too hard. I was generally done with my task in three or four hours, and for the rest of my shift I used to make things for myself or write.

"You have to understand that I was leading two lives. I was a manual worker to make a living but was engaged in intellectual pursuits the rest of the time. In the 1930s I had been doing a lot of reading in many fields, including boat design and building. I read the very fine articles in *Yachting* written by Howard Chapelle in the 1930s; they were quite definitely the foundation of all his work—those are the articles he contributed on the Friendship sloop and a series of other traditional American craft. I had Chapelle's book on boatbuilding, for example, which came out in 1941. I brought a copy in to work and showed it to Dan Grant. He said not to pay too much attention to it, because he had given most of the information to Chapelle, and it was old-fashioned.

"During this period I used to go to the Associates' meetings at the Peabody Museum of Salem, which group was very loosely constituted. We used to meet more or less regularly, and different people would talk and present papers—people like Samuel Eliot Morison and William Avery Baker. It was also during this time that I started to write about boats for publication. I wrote my first article for the *Maine Coast Fisherman* (which later became the *National Fisherman*) in 1951, and after my first piece on the Hammond dory appeared, I became acquainted with Howard Chapelle. We met and established a very close relationship, working together and exchanging information. For example, in the late 1950s I spent a week at his home in Maryland, where I learned much about Chesapeake Bay boat construction.

"Howard Chapelle was an extremely interesting man and had much influence on me and others. You hear occasional revisionist talk about him now, but I must say that he was an extraordinarily gifted man who made an enormous contribution. When I say gifted, I mean he could turn out prodigious amounts of work. He could draw boat lines, intricate boat lines, and carry on an animated conversation on an entirely different subject at the same time He was the first man in our field, a completely virgin field. There was an abundance of material scattered around just to be had for the asking, and he attempted to gather in so much that quite naturally he sometimes missed things. Sometimes he arrived at conclusions intuitively rather than from laborious digging. Sometimes his intuitions were not accurate, although they could be enormously brilliant. He read extensively but kept few notes. Occasionally his references are not to be trusted completely. Yet you have to give the man credit; he did a tremendous amount of work when no one else was paying any attention to it. He got the thing started, but some of what he did has to be refined.

"Marion Brewington, another pioneer, was a meticulous researcher, extremely fussy about the most minute details. He and Chapelle in the beginning were quite close friends, and I knew them both. Some of the slips that Chapelle made, Brewington couldn't take. On the other hand, Chapelle said he just couldn't understand Brewington.

Yet Chapelle was an extremely generous person, was always sharing his information. He was also argumentative, and his politics were quite conservative. You have to give Chapelle credit for what he did, and you need to be cautious about what you accept without checking. Incidentally, I believe that goes for all of us.

"But boats weren't my only interest. I was very much involved in Freudian psychology at that time and still have a whole Freudian library, which I don't read any more. I almost wrote a book on the Oneida Community. I still have the copious notes. I researched the obscure literature in the Widener Library at Harvard after getting special entree through a friend. I spent hours in the Boston Athenaeum, the Hart Nautical Library, and the Boston Medical Library.

"At the same time I was a contributing editor of *Contemporary Issues* magazine, which was published in England and has since gone out of existence. I wrote under the pseudonym of Clarkson. I did a long study of the Rosenberg case, one of the first analyses of what was going on. I did a very long analysis of the early background of atomic energy, with the mistaken notion that it was going to solve all our energy problems. Some of the others connected with the magazine thought otherwise. But I was wrong, and I know it now. I contributed to other publications as well, including *Balanced Living*, published by The School for Living. This was on ecology—back to the land, organic gardening—long before the present interest in that sort of thing. All this took quite a bit of time and research. I received no money at all; I did it just for the interest. I was making enough at the boatyard to get by on, but you might say it wasn't a life of luxury.

"Very early on in my writing for the *Maine Coast Fisherman* I did a series of articles on the Whitehall boat, which marked the beginning of the Whitehall revival. Previous to that the boat was pretty much forgotten except for a short article Captain Charleton Smith had done for *Rudder* back in 1943. About 1958 or 1959 Kenneth Durant, after retiring from journalism, became interested in Adirondack guideboat history. He started out with the idea that the guideboat might have developed from the Whitehall, and got in touch with me. From then until his death in 1972 we had a very productive working relationship. We shared research and boatbuilding knowledge. He was researching in Hanover, New Hampshire, Cambridge, and New York, and he had contacts abroad. We were together accumulating a great deal of boatbuilding background, both history and development. Durant was working in conjunction with the Adirondack Museum, and it was through him that I began to work on and off with that museum as a consultant. And

it was because of Ed Lynch, whom I worked with at the museum, that I came to Mystic Seaport in 1969.

"When Ed Lynch went to Mystic he decided he wanted to start a small-craft program. He arranged to have me hired. At the time I was still living in Lynn and working at Dion's in Salem, and it would be necessary for me to move to Connecticut. But it was a very promising job in many ways. I was getting older, and I could look ahead and see that the type of work that I was doing in the boatyard would be getting harder and harder for me. Although I liked the work at Dion's, it was fairly difficult, particularly in the wintertime, as we worked in unheated sheds. I was almost at retirement age. I came to Mystic for more money than I was getting in the boatyard, and it was a very interesting type of work, more or less a continuation, a culmination, of something that had been building up and growing for a long time.

"When I came to Mystic there was no small-craft program at all. I hunted around for a place and found an unoccupied corner of a storage shed where they had wagons and sleighs. I took that space and built a bench from materials I picked up around the seaport and started building a boat. I also started traveling around New England for the museum, buying up tools. There were many holes in the museum's collection. Tool collecting at that time had not quite reached the dramatic proportions that it has reached today, and I got a lot of good buys.

"That first year, 1969, I was invited to go to the Thousand Islands as a judge at the antique boat show, which was then in its fourth or fifth year. But there were no small craft. I saw St. Lawrence skiffs, which I had been interested in since I first went to work in Marblehead, and I suggested that they enlarge the program from one to two days and include small craft. The next year they did it. I got the idea from there that we should have some sort of small-craft meet at Mystic, with the result that in the summer of 1970, the following year, we had our first rowing workshop. That was the first meet of recreational small craft in this country, and it was the beginning of a continuing movement.

"That winter I decided to institute instruction in boatbuilding at Mystic Seaport, but not vocational boatbuilding. Ed Lynch had been toying with the idea of vocational instruction, but had discovered that there are all sorts of state regulations we would have to meet, which didn't seem feasible. It didn't seem to me that the regulations would prevent us from having instruction in recreational boatbuilding. We started our program in the winter of 1970–71. It was the first of its kind, to be followed later by Lance Lee's establishment of the Apprenticeshop in Bath, Maine, where he felt that boatbuilding could be used to mold character. He, too, succeeded, and the many other similar programs followed from those beginnings.

"As you can see, I have concentrated on small craft all of my life—unlike Howard Chapelle, for example, who studied the larger boats and ships as well—perhaps because that was what I was interested in as a boy, and in a certain way I am reliving my boyhood. I have always stressed practical experience in addition to theoretical study, perhaps because my father placed a high value on manual skills with woodworking tools. When I did a good job, I was praised for it. Maybe that's part of the reason I get satisfaction from using hand tools now. There is probably a psychological connection.

"Sure, I could have turned my efforts to recording the lines and details of larger vessels and luxury yachts, but my deeper interests lay with the smaller, simpler craft of my boyhood on the St. Croix River. And there were good examples of such craft still conveniently at hand in Salem and Marblehead thirty and forty years ago. I was drawn to them, as I was not to the larger craft, and it was easier, too. As it has turned out, there are many people now interested in building boats, and they do well to turn to the simpler, smaller craft of traditional design in making a start. My interests coincided with theirs.

"Traditional small craft are the field of my study and practical experience, but I have always been experimenting in new techniques within that framework. There are those who see this as something of a paradox—but innovation is traditional. If you will go back in the development of boatbuilding you will find that builders were innovative and always ready to adopt anything that came along that was good. In fact, boatbuilders seem to be more innovative than sailors, who tend to stick with what is tried and proven. There's a good reason for that. Sailors don't want to go out to sea in an experiment and drown.

"Boatbuilders, on the other hand, want to do the job as quickly as they can. One of the bywords of the trade is, 'Hurry up. The man wants his boat.' You hear that a dozen times a day around a professional boatshop. Sometimes it is said in earnest and sometimes it is said satirically, but either way the emphasis among boatbuilders is to use techniques and materials that will get the job done quickly, yet produce a satisfactory boat.

"Innovation has always made the difference. Without the type of wood screw with a point on it that we have today, a great many traditional boats would not have been built. We all consider the Adirondack guideboat to be traditional. Yet it could not have been built until self-tapping wood screws and small copper tacks came along. Those fastenings were just as much an innovation a hundred years ago as epoxy resins are today.

"There is misunderstanding of the meaning I give to traditional boats. I have explained the concept a number of times, but it still doesn't seem to sink in for many people. To me, traditional boatbuilding means the type of boat construction that blossomed toward the end of the nineteenth century. That period was one of immense technical progress in every area, and it was the culmination of refined and perfected boatbuilding techniques extending back over a period of centuries. There was a proliferation of small-craft types for sail and oar perfected to the ultimate for speed and convenience. The boats were quite different in the Chesapeake than they were in the Gulf of Maine or the swamps of Louisiana or San Francisco Bay or Boston Harbor. Boatbuilding was to some extent an ethnic melting pot, and this all came to a head, blossomed, so to speak, toward the end of the nineteenth century before the advent of the gasoline engine.

"Yet the end came very quickly. In ten years, between 1900 and 1910, all the Hampton boats in Casco Bay were converted to gasoline engines because they would no longer have to depend on the wind. Americans are prone to adopt new things even when it's not advisable to do so. They might be sorry afterwards, but it doesn't stop them from doing it. Given this climate, then, all the refinements, all these diverse boat types, were no longer in demand because you could stick a gasoline engine in any old tub. Such craft didn't have to be hydrodynamically perfect any more.

"Everything changed, the old boatbuilders were no longer needed, they died off, and boatbuilding to the standards of the late nineteenth century died with them. Such boatbuilding had never been recorded, as it had been carried on by rule-of-thumb methods. It was almost an illiterate trade until fairly recently. So with the advent of the gasoline engine, plus many other changes in American life brought on by the automobile, the bicycle, and the canvas canoe, we came to the end of an era.

"When I talk about traditional boats, I mean that perfection of design and technique for boats of oar and sail that came into predominance in the last decade of the nineteenth century. Yet I also believe that if the boatbuilding of that time had been allowed to progress naturally as it had before then, it would have evolved gradually, picking up new methods and techniques as it went. Therefore, I see no contradiction when plywood and epoxy are applied to the perfected designs of the late nineteenth century. Not at all. It's a mistake to think that all progress came to an end at a certain juncture, and that there was no chance for improvement after that. We must not restrict ourselves only to what was done in the past. Definitely not.

"What do I think about the future of wooden boat building? It seems to me at the present time in some areas it is taking on the characteristics of a fad, and I don't like it. A lot of people are jumping on a bandwagon. Some are doing it because they think it is a way to attract tourists or get some easy money from a foundation, and I wish it was not developing as fast, or along some of the lines that it is.

"I am also concerned about its vocational aspect. I have been making a certain amount of restrained comment concerning vocational programs, considering that there is little prospect that all who graduate will get jobs building wooden boats at wages they can live on. As you no doubt recall, I wrote a short piece for the fourth *Mariner's Catalog* advising young people interested in learning to build boats that perhaps the best way would be for them to teach themselves, while they held down a stopgap job of some sort to put bread on the table. Find a place to set up a bench, hang around boatshops and watch, read the books, start collecting hand tools, and begin with a simple boat with the idea of selling it. After a couple of years they will know if they want to build

boats for a living, and should have enough equipment to start out in business in a small way if they do. They will have supported themselves in the meantime, won't be out any tuition, and will have learned much of value on their own.

"I don't want to sound negative about this. That is farthest from my intention. I think I see a better future for wooden boat building than what we have today, even though it will be primarily in the recreational field. I have felt that way all along. There will always be people who will want wooden boats for recreation, and many won't want to build them themselves. Consequently, there will always be a place for a few commercial shops building a limited number of wooden boats. I hope that in the process the best that was developed in the past will be preserved and passed on, but I should expect this heritage to be reworked and even improved to some extent to meet the needs and preferences of future times. Our obligation is to make sure that the richness of our small-craft heritage is passed on intact to the generations that will come after us."

Peter Spectre is a longtime nautical writer and editor and a frequent contributor to WoodenBoat *magazine, where this piece first appeared.*

FROM *WOODENBOAT*
#129, March/April 1996

Dear *WoodenBoat*,

Unlike many historians, John Gardner had a clear, audience-based reason for researching and presenting historic material. It was not lines in a scholarly résumé, or a grant-hunter's demands, or preservation for its own sake that drove him. His interest was practical application to today's needs. John showed us how to involve people in the activities surrounding traditional watercraft, for the lessons of designing, building, and using these teach not only about the boats themselves, but about life.

John saw in the boats with which he grew up, and in the values and habits of their users, much of practical benefit. The craft were highly evolved, efficient, and economical; they could be developed further, in terms of both design and material, to become better adapted to their new recreational purposes; they could put people on the water in moderately priced, high-quality boats that they could build themselves.

The recreational benefit of going on waters great and small offers something arrestingly different from most peoples' daily lives. It offers, at once, beauty, pleasure, challenge, and risk. Building a finely crafted, complex object offers aesthetic benefit and a sense of accomplishment. Being on the water teaches values: self-reliance, teamwork, forethought, honesty, endurance, tolerance, modesty. Boating in traditional small craft leads naturally to an approach I call lean sailing or boating—a minimalist approach to sailing, and potentially to life.

Ultimately, John Gardner was a teacher who could see the value of boats as motivators. If we want John's work to continue, it is up to us to make our voice heard. So, invite a non-aficionado to your favorite maritime museum, to a boat meet, to a ride on your boat. Lend a boat. Spread the word.

BEN FULLER
CUSHING, MAINE

Dear Editors,

During a health crisis in my life I purchased and read "The Dory Book" and "Building Classic Small Craft," Volume 1, by John Gardner. As my health improved, I set about gathering the appropriate materials and began building a dory based on the plans in "The Dory Book." This was my first attempt at building *any* type of boat and so I followed John's instructions to the letter. After dabbling and attaching pieces together, I remember standing back and admiring the almost finished dory and saying, "By God John was right."

John's writings and drawings were from "one who knows," and can be understood very well by dabblers such as myself. The easy reading and clear instructions led me to shun the addiction of nicotine and become addicted to the construction of small boats. For this I owe John my life.

I reckon when John gets to heaven, St. Peter will welcome him with open arms, for I don't think that they have had a boat builder of John's caliber enter there since Noah. Thanks John.

FATHER ROBERT J. BARRY
PRINCE WILLIAM, NEW BRUNSWICK, CANADA

Dear *WoodenBoat,*

There is a saying, "When the student is ready, the teacher will appear." John Gardner appeared to me at the Small Craft Workshops in the late 70's at Mystic Seaport. I was there to assess the possibility of taking my place in the world of building small boats for fun & profit. Every time John spoke to us, I was more attentive than I had ever been to virtually anyone else involved in my more formal education. The nectar was not really about how to build boats, but why boats are built, and how small boats can take their rightful place in today's society. The lessons are just as clear to me today:

"Pleasure boating is a new idea; all the boats now being used for pleasure have their origins in working craft, so study them.

"Boats are built with the best materials geographically available to the builder, and should be built in a straightforward, workmanlike manner, for their intended use, on their intended waters, by their intended owners.

"The overall cost of the boat is related to the efficiency of the builder.

"The needs of seaworthiness, comfort, craftsmanship, style, and pride of ownership must be addressed by the builder.

"The fact that the wooden boat industry survives at all is because of the dedication of the amateur, or home builder."

I still have files of yellowed newsprint torn from the pages of *Maine Coast Fisherman,* wherein John acknowledged every new wooden boat being built, whether it was a dory, a steamboat, or a history lesson, a photo or two, a copy of a letter from someone. As his byline suggested: Comments Here & There. New materials, new tools, new goo, new ways & old ways. I considered those pages my correspondence course in boatbuilding.

Several years ago, I finally had my ratty copy of *Building Classic Small Craft,* a pencil, and John all in the same place, and I asked him to sign it. Pencil in hand, he said, "You know, I just heard about something you'd be interested in . . . ."

As a journeyman in this ancient trade of ours, I realize that one of the rewards for my years of fun & profit is to be able to pass along anything that will enable a good new boat to be built. Thanks, John.

KEN BASSETT
ONION RIVER BOATWORKS, N. HERO, VT

Dear Editor,

I was most grieved to hear of the passing of John Gardner.

Your magazine was the first print on which I came across the idea of wooden boat. The second were "Building classic small craft" and "More . . . ." of John Gardner.

His books opened the marvelous universe of wooden boat to me. The Common Punt, A Sharpie, Herreshoff Rowboat, The beachcomber-Alpha Dory, Pilot Gig, . . .

What lovely boats! What uniqueness! Every time I saw the photos, lines and illustrations, my imagination flied to Chesapeake Bay, Boston, Scilly Isles and so on.

At the same time, I was impressed by his sentences. They were so vivid that I strongly felt his personality and felt as if he was talking to me sitting side by side on the bench of small boat shop.

My cultural background is very different from John Gardner's. But his works strike me. This fact is the evidence that his knowledge, idea and enthusiasm for boat are universal. I hope many people here will read his works.

With deepest regret,

SHINICHIRO HORIGUCHI
TOKYO, JAPAN

Preface

Building Classic Small Craft, Volume 1

This is a book of small craft for amateur builders. It is comprised of a selection of material published in the *Maine Coast Fisherman* and later the *National Fisherman* over the last twenty-six years. Actually the material goes back farther than that, although it did not start getting into print until the spring of 1951.

In 1942 I was hard at it planking 38-foot Coast Guard picket boats on the second shift at James E. Graves's lower yard down at Barnegat off Front Street in Marblehead, Massachusetts. We were at war. German submarines were reported close offshore, so close, that, believe it or not, guns collected about town were brought into the yard, and the boatshop crew were assigned defense stations behind the rocks and ledges which skirted the waterfront. Upstairs in the joiner shop the foreman put someone at the lathe turning out billy clubs for the blackout wardens, although I never heard that these implements of persuasion were ever needed or used.

Young and old were caught up in the war effort, which brought together an assemblage of boatbuilding talent and experience that will not be seen again. Not only in Marblehead but all up and down the coast the oldtimers came out of retirement for one last hurrah, and for a brief interval the clock stood still while an era of wooden boat construction, which had all but passed away, was revived and renewed. Some of us who were younger sensed that we were involved in something special and absorbed as much of it as we could, but how special this was we did not realize then, and only came in time to know.

At his bench at the head of the stairs, Charlie Lawton, soon to be ninety, still did a day's work, and in odd moments snatched from the job turned out the prized planes for which he was famous, artfully shaped from selected chunks of ironwood, rosewood, lignum vitae, or native beech. As a young man in the late 1880's, Charlie had come down to Boston from Saint John, N.B., to work for the Partelows in their canoe factory at Riverside on the Charles River, building St. Lawrence River skiffs and fancy Whitehalls. Later at the Boston Naval Shipyard he made a name for himself, and as the years passed his reputation as a boatbuilder grew. When I got to know him his skill had become a legend, and he stood at the pinnacle of his trade. Dignified, self-assured, and crusty when crossed, Charlie did not hesitate to express his opinions in positive and forthright language, as he did on one well-remembered occasion when he gave L. Francis Herreshoff a dressing down over some differences involving the planking of a fancy yacht tender of Herreshoff's design. Herreshoff, who occasionally dropped in at the shop, cut an odd figure about town in those days with his beard and his dogs.

In 1941, H.I. Chapelle's *Boatbuilding* was published, and I wasted no time in getting a copy, which I read like a Bible, for although I had not yet come to know Chap in person, his ground-breaking studies of classic American small craft published in *Yachting* magazine during the 1930's had made me a devoted disciple. Sometime later on I brought my copy of *Boatbuilding* into the shop to show to the head joiner, Dan Grant, who had just returned to Graves from an interval as woodworking boss at the Robinson shipyard in Ispwich, Massachusetts, where Chapelle was the naval architect. Dan proceeded to take me down a peg. "The book is old fashioned and out of date," he told me, "and I ought to know," he continued, "for he got most of it from me." That may have been stretching it somewhat, but probably Chapelle did get quite a lot from Dan, as Dan had a lot to give. A Nova Scotia Scotchman who had come to the States as a young man to work at the carpenter's trade, Dan was a superb natural mechanic. As a joiner, patternmaker, and sparmaker, he was unexcelled. He had ruined his eyesight, he claimed, although it was not evident from his work, making violins at night, and very good ones, which he sold to defray the cost of medical treatment for a son crippled by infantile paralysis. In his old age when I knew him, his spare time was devoted to perfecting an elaborate machine that he had devised for turning out wooden lobster plugs by the bushel. The machine was kept out of sight in his attic because it would have been too costly to patent it.

Then there was Jess Hammond, an old-fashioned mechanic, who could do anything, it seemed, or almost anything. Jess, the last in a long line of independent Yankee artisans, had never worked for another man's wage a day in his life until he joined the Graves crew at the beginning of the War when he was nearing seventy. In his Danversport shop over the previous fifty years, Jess had turned out many fine boats, particularly power launches and dories, including some of the first power dories built around the turn of the century. In fact it was one of Jess Hammond's dories that was the subject of my first published article in the *Maine Coast Fisherman* in May, 1951, of which more later on.

There were others: Trim Robarts, rigger and splicer par excellence, whose domain was the spar loft, and his brother Jack, one-time yard boss for Sterns & McKay on Front Street, and a deep-water sailor in his youth. "Pot-lead" Conners who could plank circles around the best of them, and Ben Tutt, native of Marblehead, old Beachcomber sailor, and one-time hand at the ill-fated Burgess Plant where for a brief time wooden seaplanes designed by Starling Burgess were built during World War I.

About town there were still others. For a journeyman boatbuilder looking to learn, there was much to see and absorb. Captain Charleton Smith, then in his mid-eighties, sailor, author, and friend of W. P. Stephens, was still to be found at work in his shop, locally known as the Home of the Brutal Beast, after the little sailboat got up by Starling Burgess for youngsters to learn to sail in. And up at Fort Sewell in his shop in an ancient building once a fish house, Bill Brown built Yankee Sailing Dories designed by his brother, Sam, held in highest esteem by his fellow Marblehead townsmen as a naval architect.

Hauled out on the beach at Barnegat, where the lobstermen put in, lay an elegant double-ender, somewhat the worse for wear, it is true, and shabby of paint, but otherwise as trim and shapely as the day she was launched. She caught my eye from the first, and upon inquiry I learned that she had been Bill Chamberlain's own gunning dory built for winter duck hunting in the rough seas among the islands of the outer harbor. Nineteen feet, five inches over all, her rounded sides and graceful sheer made her, I thought, about the handsomest boat I had ever seen. Lightly built of cedar, she was hardly suited for the rough work of hauling lobster pots, the use to which Charlie Briggs had converted her.

As soon as work slacked enough in the shop for me to be spared for a Saturday, I took off the lines of the dory and carefully recorded the details of her construction in anticipation of the day when I should want to build another. It was a good thing I did. Too lightly constructed for lobstering and weakened by age, she went to pieces over the next few years and was broken up.

I did not build another right away, in fact it was over twenty years before I got around to building one myself. But in the meantime, in the February, 1960, issue of *Outdoor Maine*, a rival of the *Maine Coast Fisherman* that has long since folded, I had a story about the gunning dory, and her lines were published for the first time. Jim Rockefeller of Camden saw them and had Veli Holstrum of Vinalhaven build one for him for winter duck hunting in Penobscot Bay. He was more than pleased with the boat as was extensively reported at the time in several issues of the *National Fisherman*. Then Lew Dietz, one of Jim Rockefeller's duck-hunting companions, wrote a story about the boat for *Field & Stream*. So many inquiries about the boat ensued with requests for building plans that I got busy and put together four large sheets of building details and instructions for amateur builders, the same that you will find reproduced in this book. Since then, over 160 sets of these plans have been sold all over the United States and Canada, and some abroad. Just how many boats have been built from them I do not know, but there are gunning dories afloat today from the Gulf of Maine to Puget Sound, and from the Chesapeake to Alaska, and I have never had a bad report from the owners of any of them.

Also dating from these early years are the lines and details, reproduced herein, which were developed from the 19-foot surf dory, also built by Chamberlain. The boat I took them off was a life-saving dory that the Metropolitan District Commission used to keep on a cart at the entrance to King's Beach in Lynn, Massachusetts, during the summer season. Ten or twelve years later, in the mid-1950's, Dick Dion and I built one in Salem, Massachusetts, for the Texas Company to use in landing operations in the heavy surf off the west coast of Nicaragua. The boat worked out so well for this that more were

built later. At one time in Swampscott, George Chaisson also built surf dories of much the same model that were widely used along the coast as far south as Florida.

Plans for the Chamberlain dory skiff were likewise obtained back in the War years when I was working at Graves. I gained them from a former employee of Chamberlain who apprenticed at his Orne Street shop near the end of Chamberlain's career when he was going blind. Embittered by the loss of his sight, Chamberlain had begun to destroy his patterns and molds before giving up his shop. If the patterns of this fine skiff had not been copied at the time, they would probably have been lost forever. As it was they had been stashed away and forgotten until recalled to mind by my take-off of the gunning dory lines. In turn I filed them away and did not publish them until June, 1951. Since then, this skiff has been widely built on both coasts and for use on numerous inland lakes and rivers. Intended originally for rowing, various modifications of it have been successfully rigged for sail, particularly the widened version now in limited production at Mystic Seaport.

Over the past quarter of a century I have published my share of dories, but the first one to see print was special. This was one of Jess Hammond's, a 15-foot 10-inch LOA knuckle-sided Danversport dory, which I described in the May, 1951, issue of the *Maine Coast Fisherman*. Shortly after this appeared, I got a call from the Peabody Museum in Salem. Would I drop by on Saturday afternoon, there was someone interested in dories who would like to meet me? Drop by I did, and, gathered in Charles Copeland's office, I found a small group intently conversing with a tall man with thick, mussed hair and a wrinkled blue sport shirt. I was introduced to Howard Chapelle. For a long time I had admired the man and his work from afar, but unexpectedly to meet him, to be in the same room with him, and to talk with him was almost too much. The talk flowed on and was continued down the street at the Hawthorne Hotel where we went for dinner.

This was the beginning of a cordial relationship that lasted until Chapelle's recent death. His enthusiasm for boats and his encyclopedic knowledge of them, past and present, was equalled only by the generosity with which he spread this knowledge around, providing encouragement and inspiration for so many like myself who will always stand in his debt. For the wide-spread renewal in the use of traditional native watercraft that looms so large on the American boating scene today, Chap, more than anyone else, was directly responsible.

The small craft renewal that we are experiencing, the revival of traditional wooden boats, Whitehalls, peapods, St. Lawrence River skiffs, Rangeley Lake boats, wherries, Adirondack guideboats, sneakboxes, wooden sailing canoes, and all the rest, is something which to a large extent has taken place since the earliest of the articles reproduced herein were written. Whitehalls are no rarity these days; they are both amateur and commercially built. Indeed, Whitehalls are now numerous and popular for recreational boating on both the East and West coasts, but for several decades, until the 1960's, hardly any were to be found in use anywhere. In Marblehead in the 1940's, when I was eagerly absorbing all that old Charlie Lawton could tell me about the Whitehalls he had built in Boston before the turn of the century, my searches turned up only one lone surviving example of the type. Based on this boat, on what Charlie taught me and what I learned from Capt. Charleton Smith, I designed a 17-foot rowing Whitehall published in the *Maine Coast Fisherman* in 1953 in several issues and reprinted here. Except for the two Whitehalls in Chapelle's *American Small Sailing Craft,* 1951, these were the first detailed plans for a rowing Whitehall for amateur construction to be published, and in important respects the details were more complete than those furnished by Chapelle. A number of these Whitehalls have been built, one of the most recent is a clinker version launched last year by Bob Coe of Waldren Island, Washington, a boat that the owner cannot praise too highly.

Originally and primarily, Whitehalls were pulling workboats. Frequently a small sail laced

to a short mast was carried in the boat to be raised when the wind favored for running or reaching; but into the wind, a straight pull with oars was much faster than tacking. Practically none of the old working Whitehalls had centerboards, although Chapelle does show one in a boat with an uncharacteristic flat, plank keel. There is now, however, a growing demand in recreational boating for Whitehalls capable of sailing on all points. The 14-foot sailing Whitehall detailed herein was designed to fill this need. By changing the position of the molds, as used to be the practice, it is possible to build this boat in four lengths from 14 feet to 17 feet 3 inches. Installing a centerboard in a boat like this with its strip, or "scantling," keel instead of a flat, plank keel, presents some problems. One way of dealing with this is by the method detailed here. It is simple, does not weaken the hull, and requires only minimal changes to the basic structure of the boat.

Thirty years ago the working peapods of Maine lobstermen had been replaced in the fishing industry, to a great extent, by larger, motorized craft, and these fine sea boats seemed well on the way to extinction. Built by the fishermen themselves and in small boatshops along the coast, the lines and construction of these fishing pods had never been recorded and were unavailable to amateur builders. The first to put peapods in print, with the exception of a single isolated article in *Yachting* magazine in the 1930's, was Chapelle in *American Small Sailing Craft* in 1951. Two years later I followed in the *Maine Coast Fisherman* with more pods and building information, much of which is reproduced here. The following year I published the details for a 15-foot clinker-planked Matinicus Island peapod, selected for production twenty years later by the Apprenticeshop of the Bath Marine Museum at Bath, Maine, and successfully built and sold by them. Then just last year I worked out the details for another clinker pod and directions for planking it, which were published in the *National Fisherman* and are included here. My contention is that, for many small boats, pods included, it is simpler, easier, quicker, and less expensive to plank clinker rather than carvel, once the method is correctly understood and followed. Unfortunately, up to now clinker planking technique had remained largely a mystery to amateur builders, in part because little about it had been published, but in greater part because what had been written about it had not been explicit enough about basic clinker procedures. The detailed step-by-step explanation of essential clinker techniques included in this book in the sections on the Herreshoff pram, the Rangeley Lakes boat, and peapods, as already indicated, do together comprise, I believe, a fuller account of the clinker planking process, including lining, spiling, beveling, fitting, and fastening than is to be found elsewhere. It is complete enough for the inexperienced amateur to follow successfully. You will also find extensive explanations of clinker planking in the Appendix.

The details and directions for building a Rangeley Lakes boat are the only ones yet published, so far as I am aware, for this able craft developed for large, rough lakes. The section on the St. Lawrence River skiff is reproduced from articles written when this exceptional craft had all but dropped from sight, use, and memory, and helped, we like to think, in bringing about its current revival.

There are two small prams, one a 10-foot varnished cedar beauty after one by L. Francis Herreshoff, the other a 9-foot-plus plywood utility pram designed by me that has been widely built, proving sea-kindly, easy to row, and simple and inexpensive to build. For additional variety there is a 16-foot Sea Bright skiff rigged to sail, a New England wherry, a Barnegat Bay sneakbox of modified construction simplified and adapted for home building, and others as well.

Some boats had to be left out. Long-time readers of the *National Fisherman* may miss a favorite craft. It is not likely that the selection included will satisfy everyone in all respects. We regret this, but clearly not every one of the several hundred boating articles that I have contributed over the past twenty-six years to the *National Fisherman,* and earlier to the *Maine Coast Fisherman,* could be crowded between the covers of a single book. Yet we do believe that the selection is extensive enough and varied enough for nearly everyone looking for a small boat to build to find something worth his consideration, or at least to enlarge his knowledge and appreciation of our native small craft.

John Gardner
Mystic, Connecticut
1977

Introduction

Selecting and Building Classic Small Craft

························•························

If you were to discover that someone was attempting to teach the fine points of horsemanship with water buffaloes or camels for mounts, you might be amused or indignant, depending upon your feeling for horses and the extent of your regard for the equestrian art. A not entirely dissimilar situation now obtains in this country with respect to rowing. Thousands of youngsters each summer in a multitude of camps and recreational programs are being introduced to rowing in boats which were never designed or intended for this, and which, in fact, row abominably, even to the extent of being unsafe in rough water.

The net result is that, in all too many cases, the novice is conditioned against rowing for life. After tugging and sweating at leaden oars in order to move the clumsy and unresponsive hulk provided him in lieu of a proper rowboat, he soon decides that this is not for him, and he can hardly wait to throw away his oars and get in front of an outboard motor instead. To deduce from this any contrived and Machiavellian plot on the part of the outboard motor industry would be too absurd and verging on paranoia, yet outboard motors are the beneficiaries of poor rowboats.

Lacking suitable boats for rowing, people have forgotten how to row. They have forgotten that rowing, aside from any utilitarian application, is, or can be, a pleasurable and beneficial

form of recreation. Recreational rowing is a delightful, wholesome, relatively inexpensive outdoor sport that young and old, and all ages in between, can enjoy.

Recreational rowing is no competition to the use of the outboard motor for basic transportation. There are a thousand and one applications of the outboard to basic waterborne transportation in small boats; the outboard motor is supremely suitable for its proper use. No one, I think could reasonably argue its abandonment and the consequent return to oars, where it is simply a matter of getting something or someone over an expanse of water quickly and easily. Here, propulsion is merely a means to an end that is most effectively and economically accomplished by a machine.

Something more than mere transportation is involved in recreational rowing. Here, rowing becomes to some extent an end in itself. Ideally, the oarsman and his boat act together in a harmony of motion and balance not unlike a similar unity of response and action achieved by the equestrian and his mount. Indeed, not infrequently the old-time oarsman thought and spoke of his boat as a live thing.

Obviously, one must have the right sort of boat to feel this way, and unfortunately such are not easily obtainable at this time. The numerous mass-produced boats of aluminum or plastic now commonly available in the market are outboard boats and basically unsuited for rowing. Skilled handwork is so costly today that superior pulling types of traditional form and construction produced singly or on a limited scale would be far too expensive to compete with factory-produced craft now manufactured in great numbers for large-scale distribution.

This is not to say that good rowing boats, as well as outboard boats, could not be so produced, but this has not been done to any great extent. So far, there has been such a demand for outboard types that manufacturers have concentrated on these, thinking that such could also be made to do for rowing—at least, so it would seem. But these wide, shallow, broad-stern outboard hulls cannot be made to serve as rowboats with any degree of success, in spite of the rationalizations put forward in support of their versatility by those supplying them.

SAFETY AND STABILITY

First and foremost of the specious arguments for these ultra-wide, flat, outboard hulls is the claim for "safety." Thus a spokesman for the Boating Industry Association in a letter to Bulkeley Smith of Hamden, Connecticut, a life-long rowing enthusiast, a Scout leader since 1919, and a prime mover in the cause of better rowboats for beginners, concluded as follows: "The old wooden rowboats that slipped through the water so easily, just do not handle satisfactorily with the outboard motors people wish to use on boats of this size. They were also tippy (*sic*). The emphasis today on the part of all safety authorities stresses stability."

First off, it should be noted that the writer does not seem to realize that two distinctly different types of small craft might well be produced, one for outboards and the other for oars, and that there would probably be sufficient demand for the latter to make its production in quantity profitable. The Boy Scouts alone have around 5,000 rowboats in commission. Then there is the Red Cross, as well as hundreds of privately run summer camps using rowboats. The potential market for a superior,

mass-produced, general-utility rowing hull, whether in wood, metal, or plastic, easily reaches into the thousands.

But this is not the crux. The key is "stability." Apparently the BIA spokesman does not know very much about boats, at least about rowboats. He makes the fatal mistake of confusing stability, that is ultimate stability, with initial stability. There is a world of difference. I have used the word "fatal" in the previous sentence advisedly, for an ultra-wide, flat, light, shoal-draft outboard boat of great initial stability used as a rowboat, should it get caught in really rough water, might easily capsize or otherwise founder with the chance of drowning the unfortunate oarsman. Meanwhile, one of those "old wooden rowboats" characterized as "tippy," with a good man at the oars, would have a far better chance of coming through safely.

A large, rectangular box floating on the surface of a mill pond would have about maximum "initial stability," but that does not make such a safe boat. If the box is wide enough and the pond sufficiently calm, an occupant can stand up and walk around almost as if he were standing on terra firma. But start tipping the box to one side, and soon a point is reached where all of the initial stability is lost, and over she goes in a twinkling. Take the box into rough water. Heavy seas slam at its wide, flat bottom and square chine knuckles. If the box does not straightaway capsize or fill, it will nevertheless take a terrible pounding, so violent, in fact, as to make it nearly unmanageable. Some of the aluminum outboard hulls now passed off as rowboats are hardly different in shape from rectangular boxes, even though one end may be pointed.

The rounded hull of good design is treated much more kindly by the sea. For this reason naval architects often characterize such hulls as "sea kindly." There is nothing flat or square for surging seas to grab or slam against. Like the seasoned boxer, they "roll with the punches." The initial stability of such a hull may not be great because of the relatively sharp, easy lines of its underbody, so that it will start to roll quite easily. Yet, if competently designed with ample side flare, freeboard, and beam, as well as adequate overall length, it will rapidly pick up stability as it rolls down. Thus, it will go only so far and no farther, to pause briefly before starting to roll back. The ultimate stability of such a boat will, under almost all conditions, prove more than ample.

Safety in a small rowboat must not be judged by absence of motion, but rather by its control. Only a boat which responds freely, lightly, quickly, and easily to the motion of water can be considered safe. The sea is much too powerful to fight. Safety lies in being able to evade the sea. Like a sea duck riding the crests and dipping easily into the troughs, the superior small rowboat can take an amazing amount of weather.

A BOAT FOR ITS INTENDED USE

I must state categorically that there is just no such thing as the superior, all-purpose rowboat, just as there is no such animal as the superior, all-purpose dog. Border collies were bred for herding sheep, dachshunds for digging out badgers, malamutes for hauling sleds, Dobermans for police work, and Dalmatians for running after coaches.

Peapods are fine for setting lobster pots around rocky shores and ledges, guideboats for portaging through the Adirondack brush, salmon wherries for launching stern first into the surf, Whitehalls for fast taxi service across the bay before motors came into use—but swap these functions around at your peril! Whether a rowboat is any good or not depends to some extent on what it is used for and who uses it.

In former times, when men rowed boats in the course of their daily occupations, depended upon them for their livelihood and often for their lives, an intimate relationship existed between a man and his boat. Choosing a boat was a serious business, somewhat on the order of selecting a wife. There was a wide field to choose from, and many factors to take into account. Trim, smart lines were a consideration,

to be sure, but not the whole story, by a long shot.

It is no accident that such superlative watermen as Adirondack guides and Maine coast fishermen frequently built their own boats in bygone days. So much depended upon having a boat uniquely suited to their own individual needs and preferences that they did not trust the job to anyone else. To the city sport entering the North Woods for the first time, all guideboats must have looked pretty much alike. Not so to the guides. Likewise to the average summer visitor, all downeast peapods would have appeared double-ended, but precious little else besides. The uninformed eye simply cannot pick out all the little differences that add up to the Big Difference. To the fisherman, each boat had individuality, and each was as different in its own way as the man who owned it.

Even professional builders, formerly, did not always build all boats of the same model just the same. It is known that Bill Chamberlain in Marblehead never made any two of his famous dories exactly alike, but was always making slight changes and experimenting.

What it all comes down to is that if a man wants a really superior rowboat suited to his own needs and preferences, provided he knows what these are, he had best build it himself to his own personal specifications; and if he is not capable of this, he should have it custom built for him by a competent professional builder. This is to obtain the best. If he will be satisfied with something less, there are good stock rowboats to be had, from which he can probably choose one that will be adequate, provided he follows some fairly simple rules or guides.

Length is an absolute. Other factors being more or less equal, the longer boat (within limits) will always row faster and easier than the shorter one. But there is a perverse tendency today generally to make rowboats too short. The outboard motor can be blamed for this. Planing hulls for outboard power do not need length, and, as stated previously, most boats suitable for outboards are entirely unsuited for rowing.

In addition, traditional pulling types are

often ruined by scaling down their length. The automobile is partly responsible for this. People who know next to nothing about boats, but who want to haul one on top of a car, think they can take one of the better old types 16 to 18 feet in length, and scale it down to 10 feet or 12 feet, and still retain the superior qualities of the original. They could not be more mistaken. Disaster is almost always the invariable result. Some scaled-down "dories" are dangerous. They are anything but dories, and should not be labeled such under penalty of law.

The standard 16-foot guideboat is far superior to the 12-footer in all respects, except that the latter is lighter and easier to carry through the woods. Some well-designed yacht tenders of 12 feet and even 10 feet in length row fairly well, but the best of them cannot compare in speed or rowing ease with equally well-designed pulling craft 4 or 5 feet longer.

As for the greater safety of the longer boat, a boatbuilder and guide at Rangeley, Maine, once explained to me that rowboats under 17 feet in length were unsafe for treacherous lakes like those in the Rangeley chain, whose shallow water can grow dangerously rough in minutes when sudden winds whip down from the surrounding mountains.

Small pulling boats, mostly under 18 or 19 feet in length, such as are generally rowed by one man, are purely displacement hulls, never attaining planing speeds under oars. They cut through the water rather than skim over it. To knife along with as little fuss as possible at rowing speeds, the hull requires a sharp, thin entrance and an equally sharp exit, with long, easy flowing lines between. If the boat has a transom stern, this must sit high above the water for best results. To the extent that the transom is immersed, it will drag, cutting down rowing speed. This is a principal reason, of course, why boats with wide, low sterns to support outboard motors row poorly, or sometimes will hardly row at all.

While both the wherry and the Whitehall have transom sterns, they are both double-enders on the water. Likewise, the Banks dory, with its narrow "tombstone" stern, comes close to being a double-ender at the waterline.

A deep, sharp forefoot at the bottom of a perpendicular stem, such as is characteristic of the Whitehall, is excellent for holding the boat on a straight course, but a boat with such a forefoot turns slowly, tows badly, and is dangerous in surf. A more raking stem, and a rounder, more cut-away forefoot is required for quick maneuvering in broken water.

To gain displacement depth for stability in open water and rough seas, the bottom of the Banks dory is heavily "rockered" or cambered fore and aft. But in the shore fishery it is desirable for the dories used to ground out as high up on the beach as possible and out of the surf, so their depth of displacement is reduced to a minimum by building them perfectly flat on the bottom.

These are but a few of the many possible variations in underwater shape to be considered in choosing a rowboat, depending, as already mentioned, on what the boat is to be used for and who is to use it.

The portion of the hull above water must be taken into account. Windage, that is, the force of the wind against the topsides, can cut rowing speed markedly and make the boat difficult to manage, yet adequate freeboard is required to keep the boat from swamping. In racing shells confined to comparatively smooth and sheltered waters, freeboard can be minimal. Banks dories, on the other hand, operating in rough water and carrying tremendous loads of fish, are built high-sided. In a light condition they stick so far out of water that they are extremely difficult to handle in a wind. Contrary to the popular notion, the Banks dory for this, as well as for other reasons, is not a particularly easy boat to row. Quite the contrary. Yet it is well-suited on the whole to the purpose for which it was developed.

Wood and reinforced thermoplastic resin are the materials mainly considered in the boats discussed in this book. Construction combining both has come to be known as composite construction. When properly engineered, composite construction retains most, if not all, of the superior characteristics of wood with additional advantages derived from the plastic.

I have never seen an aluminum rowboat that I wanted any part of. This is merely my personal feeling, and it is true that aluminum does serve quite well for some inexpensive, light, cartop boats. Furthermore, I have seen few or no molded fiberglass rowboats that I considered equal to their wooden prototypes; most of them I judge to be quite inferior. Too often, changes in shape are made to make it easier to mold the boat, and while these changes may appear to be slight, the result can be serious.

Fiberglass is a much heavier material than cedar or pine. A hull thickness required to obtain a stiffness equivalent to wood means extra weight which, if added in the wrong places, can spoil the balance of the hull. One example of this is the fiberglass replica of a 10-foot yacht tender formerly planked with cedar by a famous Marblehead boatbuilder. The fiberglass replica is quite heavy, not a serious defect, if a defect at all, so far as rowing is concerned, but bad in a tender which must be lifted in and out of the water. This tender rows quite well for its 10 feet, yet it is definitely less steady than its wooden prototype. Apparently this is because of the additional weight of fiberglass concentrated in the topsides.

In some cases, to keep down weight, fiberglass hulls are made thin and flimsy, and the finish and general appearance of molded fiberglass small craft is still generally much inferior to first-class wood construction. Some of the small molded fiberglass prams and dinghies make adequate yacht tenders, but are not in a class with the rowing craft we are considering.

A boat that is framed with wood, although it may have a fiberglass skin, is not a fiberglass boat, strictly speaking. It is a composite boat. Furthermore, if weight is a consideration, it is far better to cover such a boat with polypropylene, which is only one-third the weight of glass, and tougher and more resilient, besides. As for molded fiberglass guideboats, at least two attempts to build them on a commercial scale have failed, because of the inferiority of the molded boats.

Except for extreme types, notably racing shells, moderate hull weight, if properly distributed, is an asset rather than a detriment in the rowing hull. This is particularly true in rough water where the inertia from moderate weight keeps the boat moving smoothly ahead between strokes of the oars. Only when boats have to be lifted frequently in and out of the water, or portaged, is moderate weight a liability.

The trouble is that today boats that are mediocre or worse are frequently passed off as excellent in all good faith, and accepted as such, because no one involved has ever seen a really superior rowboat or rowed one, or has any idea what such a boat is like. It is one thing to look at a picture or a model, or to read an account in a book. It is quite another thing to sit in an actual boat and to pull the oars. In this book are a number of designs and building instructions for boats that make superior rowing, and sometimes sailing, craft. They are intended for amateur construction, so if you want to feel what it is like to row a truly excellent boat, the realization of your wish is in your own hands.

AMATEUR CONSTRUCTION

Since our approach here is from the standpoint of the amateur builder rather than the professional, a few introductory words on building small craft are in order. The boats discussed in this book are not especially simple or easy to build, but, to the contrary, require careful and precise workmanship and some familiarity with tools and materials, none of which is beyond the reach of reasonable diligence on the part of the serious amateur.

The amateur has one immense advantage over the professional. His time is worth nothing, so he can be lavish in its expenditure. A simple model will suffice to explain why: Let us say it takes 200 man-hours to custom-build a varnished cedar pram in the old way; yet the factory can turn out molded fiberglass prams in lots of 100 or more at an average expenditure of only 20 man-hours or less per pram. At five dollars per hour for labor, plus whatever else the materials, advertising, marketing, and the rest come to, the fiberglass pram might be sold at a good profit for $500, while labor alone for the cedar pram has cost twice that much, or $1000. This is only a model, of course, yet if the figures are not precise, they are still close enough so that the picture given is in general a true one.

In all fairness to fiberglass, if you are going to buy a pram, the fiberglass one will probably serve adequately. While neither as handsome as a varnished cedar pram, nor as lightweight to lift in and out of the water, the glass job will row and tow almost as well (provided the model is the same), will stand more abuse and pounding on the beach, and has no seams to dry out and open up. Yet if you have the time and inclination to build your own pram, and especially the inclination, the advantages are all with the cedar one.

It would be next to impossible to produce a one-shot fiberglass pram in the home workshop; that is, one comparable in quality and finish to the factory-made product. However, as has been proved many times, the painstaking amateur can produce a superior wooden boat if he is willing to give it the required effort and if cost is any consideration. Materials for a cedar pram will stand him less than those required for glass.

The deciding consideration may very well be one of aesthetics. For some of us, the well-made wooden boat of superior traditional design is a thing of beauty, quite aside from its functional utility. Why it is would be difficult to explain, nor is it necessary to do so. It just is, and it is enough to recognize the fact and to acknowledge it.

The creation of beauty is more satisfying and joyous than mere possession. For the person who loves boats, and who has time on his hands, what better way to spend some of it than to build himself a boat that will please him every time he looks at it or uses it. It will take some pains, both in the figurative and the literal sense, for the creative process at levels of excellence is never easy, and often its demands are rigorous and its discipline is severe.

As others have often found in the building of boats, one is likely to come close to tears more than once before everything is shipshape and the job is finally and creditably done. But then that is life, and some travail would seem a nearly inevitable part of the accomplishment of any challenging and worthwhile aim.

In order to build successfully a boat like a cedar pram, and the others in this book, a number of requirements must be met. One prerequisite is a suitable place to work, with good light, bench room, and sufficient heat in winter for gluing. It is almost as essential to have a place where things can be left lying about without their being disturbed when the builder is absent—tools on the bench or lying under the boat waiting to be picked up when work is resumed.

Tools required: a large outlay for power tools is not necessary for most of the boats discussed here. Ordinary hand tools, provided they are of good quality, and the edged ones sharp, are all that are needed. But sharp they must be. Acceptable work cannot be done otherwise. One should have a grinder and oil stones and know how to get a keen edge.

Care and patience: Measurements must be exact. Fits close. To tolerate less is fatal. Just as the surgeon demands complete asepsis in the operating room, so the competent boatbuilder strives for precise and errorless measurement and layout in the shop.

Also, as the amateur builder is not driven by time, he need not be reluctant to discard pieces which he "spoils," or that otherwise are found to be defective in any way. Planks that do not fit should be put to the saw without hesitation, and new and corrected ones made.

Special knowledge of the type of craft abuilding, trade knowhow which is the fruit of practice, these we shall attempt to explain here, at least to an extent sufficient to guide the inexperienced builder over some of the hurdles and around some of the pitfalls.

SCANTLINGS IN SMALL CRAFT

The amateur boatbuilder frequently finds himself involved in problems of design that he is not prepared to handle. For instance, he may come across a set of lines that seem to be just what he has been looking for, but there is no construction plan or any scantling dimensions to speak of. If he is going to build the boat, he will have to work out construction details, and what he needs is not always to be found in books. There are no tables of standards for figuring the sizes and spacing of timbers for small wooden boats, the thickness of planking, size of gunwales and risers, width of thwarts, width of stem aprons, or a number of other values he will have to determine with some precision.

While it is obvious that the lighter the construction, the more critical the scantling dimensions, just how critical these may be is not easy to calculate. Sometimes it takes only a sixteenth of an inch plus or minus to make all the difference. There are a great many variables. The various species of wood show marked differences in strength, weight, and flexibility, not to mention durability, and even appreciable differences are sometimes found in various lots of boat timber from the same species. Another factor that must be taken into account is the complex structural interrelationships among the members that make up the hull fabric.

It hardly needs saying that the structural design of traditional wooden small craft has not been put on a scientific basis, and while it could be, no doubt, it is not likely to be. In the past, those who practiced boatbuilding as a trade in the small shops relied on imitation of previously built boats and on their boatbuilder's judgment, the latter largely a matter of accumulated experience and observation retained in part at the subconscious level. In most cases, also, the builder was more or less a specialist whose efforts were confined to a relatively few local types with which he was thoroughly familiar. When he ventured outside his specialty, it was generally with caution and reluctance. Sometimes the result was less than happy. I recall one instance when what was supposed to be a small round-bottom sailboat came out strangely like a dory when it was built by a dory builder.

We know very little about small craft in early America and how they were built. It does appear, however, that the earlier boats were rather standardized and quite heavily constructed. Timber sawn from root crooks and limb crooks seems to have been used exclusively, and screws and small sizes of machine-made copper and iron nails did not become available to boatbuilders until well along into the nineteenth century.

The nineteenth century was an era of continuous and rapid technological development and growth, which accelerated as the century advanced, and this was true in the area of small craft as elsewhere. Local diversification in boats took place on a broad scale, with progressive and marked refinements in structure, especially as older working types were taken over for recreational use. In almost all cases improvement took the same course: reduction in weight was sought without reduction in strength or durability. Generally the changes that were made came gradually.

Two of the most striking examples are the Adirondack guideboat and the yachts designed and constructed by the Herreshoff Manufacturing Company at Bristol, Rhode Island. In the 1840s or thereabouts the boats used by the trappers and market hunters in the Adirondack wilderness were heavily and crudely made. In the course of the next 40 or 50 years, by a process of gradual evolution, the hunter's and the guide's boat was transformed into a guideboat, a marvel of lightness with strength. The guideboat could never have happened except for the very small machine-made brass screws and tiny copper tacks which it required in great numbers. And its scantling sizes attained ultimate reduction by the removal of literally one shaving at a time.

In much the same way, the Herreshoff Manufacturing Company lightened yacht construction and revolutionized yacht design, although scientific calculations were used as well. Scantling sizes were gradually and daringly reduced until the ultimate combination of light weight with adequate strength was reached. Few since have even approached Herreshoff's mastery of lightweight yacht construction. That scantling reductions were not excessive is attested by the fact that a number of Herreshoff yachts built in the first decade of the present century are still sailing today.

In some cases the process of refinement was carried too far. This appears to have been the case for some of the later Great South Bay catboats to come from the Gilbert Smith shop in Patchogue, Long Island. While unexcelled for speed and appearance, some of his later catboats did not hold up too well in hard use over the years.

In the construction of light yacht tenders, reduction of weight was sometimes carried to an extreme to save what could hardly have been more than ounces, certainly not more than two or three pounds. Bent oak ribs were made so small in section that they broke quite easily. Here 1/16 inch, which doesn't amount to much in some places, might well have been critical.

How to know whether to leave on that final shaving or take it off? About the only way is to examine other boats of a similar nature whose history is known, before deciding. Essentially that is the way most yachts have been, and are still, designed. In one way or another, architects accumulate files of lines and structural data, which they draw upon when commissioned to design new boats.

It should be understood, of course, that there isn't any such thing, really, as a new boat. New boats are all combinations of old boats worked over. An occasional feature may be new, but that is all. Likewise, the old-time boat-builder accumulated a shop full of patterns, molds, and templates, and then whenever he was in doubt, he would go out on the waterfront with his rule to measure actual boats. The amateur builder can also go out on the water-front with his rule, and should do so by all means. In addition, he should have a notebook and camera with him.

A lot can be learned in boatyards, especially storage yards of the less exclusive sort where usually can be found numbers of old boats in various stages of decrepitude. In addition, there are also today a number of marine museums with extensive small craft collections, where they are beginning to make provision to assist amateur builders and antique boat buffs. One of these is Mystic Seaport, whose collection of small craft now totals over 200 and is still growing, the largest such collection in North America. While it is generally not expedient for a museum to permit all visitors to do their own measuring of boats in the exhibit collections, this is easily gotten around by having the museum staff do the measuring, beforehand, if possible, in anticipation of the public's needs. Already at Mystic Seaport, plans for a sizable selection of its small craft have been prepared by the museum staff, with prints furnished to the public for the cost of reproduction. In addition to various conventional exhibits of small craft at Mystic, a considerable number are now to be found in a separate building where they may be seen and studied upon request by persons with a particular interest in small craft.

Having made these several remarks about the choosing and construction of classic small craft, let us now go on to consider in turn a number of specific boats of good design. We will discuss a bit of their history and development, their form, and the details of their construction, together with something of their equipment and use.

1

The Common Punt

························•························

The simplest and easiest to build of all small workboats is what I learned to call a punt as a boy growing up in Maine on the St. Croix River. Names vary, however, both in time and place, so that some of our readers may be accustomed to designate this type of craft by another name, such as scow.

A punt has square ends and straight sides, giving it a rectangular shape in plan view. Its sides are vertical, and its bottom is quite flat athwartships, although fore and aft the bottom will show rocker, the amount varying from boat to boat. It has no sheer curve, being perfectly straight on top. In short, the shape is that of a rectangular box, except for the longitudinal curve of the bottom, which lifts the ends, cutting down resistance and making it easier to push the punt through the water. Some punts with well-proportioned sled-form bottoms offer surprisingly little resistance when moving, and, if lightly built, can be brought up to planing speeds by a high-speed outboard motor of sufficient power. (In fact, the extremely popular Boston Whaler is virtually a punt in form, although with secondary modifications which improve its appearance as well as its performance with an outboard motor.)

If my memory serves me, Punt is an ancient Egyptian name for a part of northern Africa; perhaps the name could be connected with the dugouts used on the River Nile and other African rivers and lakes from time immemorial. Indeed, the punt may be thought of as a replacement for the log dugout, more easily constructed of boards after sawn lumber became available.

However, what I am accustomed to call a punt, others call a scow, reserving the term punt for a slightly more sophisticated vessel. Thus, W. P. Stephens in his classic *Canoe and Boat Building*, published in the 1880s, designates the simplest and crudest form as a scow with a sketch of what is nothing more than a low, flat, rectangular box, somewhat wide and short in its proportions, and cross-planked on the bottom. This rises at the ends, not in a curve, but merely in a flat, straight incline, beveled back from either end about a quarter of the length of the boat.

Stephens's punt is a more shapely little vessel. The low side is still made of a single, wide board set on edge, but both sides are bent in plan view to give a slight but pleasing curve, and in profile they show a bit of sheer as well. The bottom is given considerable rocker fore and aft, and it is planked lengthwise. The ends are identical and square.

More frequently today the term scow is used for large vessels, while I can recall no instances in which punt is employed to designate anything larger than a rowboat. Some of the large sailing scows of the past were intricately

Stephens's punt (left) and Folkard's gunning punt (right).

developed and powerfully rigged craft. Howard I. Chapelle, in his *American Small Sailing Craft*, lists and describes a variety of sailing scows, including the New Jersey garveys.

In America, the term punt is most commonly applied to a small scow to be rowed, paddled, or poled; in England, it seems to cover round-bottomed boats as well. The English writer, H. C. Folkard, who was no less an authority in his country than was his contemporary, W. P. Stephens, in America, published in the sixth edition (1906) of *The Sailing Boat*, published in London in 1906, an engraving of a curious little double-ended, round-bottomed boat, which he calls a "gunning-punt," built "after the author's invention, suitable both for sailing and paddling in pursuit of wild-fowl." But only in sheltered waters. This English gunning punt has little freeboard or stability. Thus Folkard concludes: "The young wild-fowler is cautioned not to venture into rough water with the sailing-punt, for a sportsman's life is supposed to be of more value than that of a duck."

Another English authority, T. C. Lethbridge, in his *Boats and Boatmen*, suggests that the word punt is derived from the Latin *ponto*, in turn related to *pons*, a bridge. Webster substantiates this etymology, "ponto, punt, pontoon," defining punt as a "long, narrow, flat-bottom boat with square ends, usually propelled by a pole,—chiefly used in England." This last observation is probably not quite true, but the identification of punt with pontoon is highly significant. Flat, square-ended, wide boats of rough construction have been in use in Europe by the military since ancient times as pontoons to support bridges.

THE CHARLESTON BATEAU

Here, then, are the plans for what I would call a punt but which is called by its users a "Charleston bateau." It was brought to my attention for the first time by Richard H. Randall, chairman of the Maritime Committee of the Maryland Historical Society in Baltimore, whose friend, Hugh Benet, who grew up in Charleston, South Carolina, had one as a boy. His brother had one also. They bought them for 50 cents apiece secondhand from raft men who, after having delivered their logs, had no further use for the boats. As Mr. Randall explained:

At the turn of the century much logging was being carried on in that part of South Carolina. Rafts of timber and logs, roughly cut planks piled on log rafts, were floated down the rivers bound together as most log rafts were bound on the Delaware, Susquehanna, and other American rivers—a few angle irons driven into the outside logs, a few cross timbers through-bolted, again to the outside logs. These rafts were steered by a long oar, or sweep mounted on a raised Y-post securely braced. Usually two other sweeps were pinned on the port and starboard just ahead of midships.

Now, these raft men built at least one bateau per raft—frequently more. They were always the same, the hull was double-ended, with a punt-raised floor under the bow, so the bottom boards had to be shaped accordingly. The sides were nailed to the bottom boards, and cross cleats were likewise nailed to the bottom and sides, with seldom more than six cross cleats per boat. No thwarts or seats.

Occasionally a triangular piece at bow and stern helped to hold the sides in position. They were built of the cheapest pine and propelled by a paddle or two—

usually homemade by the purchaser, when the bateaux were sold at the end of the trip for no more than 50 cents apiece. Obviously these bateaux swamped easily.

Of course the rafters needed at least one to get ashore if the raft grounded, to help get tackle rigged to pull her out into the stream again, also to repair the raft if the logs slipped or got loose. Rafters used the paddle too.

The shores of the Ashley and Cooper Rivers at Charleston were muddy and swampy—still are at the southern entrance of the Inland Waterway. This swamp shore was called plough mud [pronounced pluff] and the boys had to dig into the mud with their paddles and slide the bateaux along to gain solid ground. Remember how terrible that mud smelled? And the Intercoastal still does!

With no caulking the seams would dry out overnight and these boats were not taken from the water, so the kids sank them every time they came home, and emptied them the next time they were used.

Charleston was settled by many French Huguenots, so perhaps that is how the name bateau became connected with this type of craft.

Following Hugh Benet's sketch closely, which he drew from memory, I made the drawings which accompany this description.

The lengthwise planking of the bottom is not what I am familiar with for small scows or punts like this. I believe that cross-planked construction is more usual, yet fore-and-aft bottom planking is probably better—certainly it would offer less resistance in sliding over mud, if there was much of this to be done. Also there would be fewer seams to open and leak. As we have already seen, W. P. Stephens designed his rather nicely modeled punt with the bottom planks running lengthwise.

There might be some difficulty in bending these bottom planks if the bottom curve or "rocker" were rounded too abruptly. The bottom curve I have shown in Profile 1 on the drawing closely reproduces the curve on Benet's sketch, and in my judgment might require steaming the planks. In Profile 2, I have eased this curve enough so that I think that softwood boards (pine, cedar, cypress), if not too dry, could be sprung in place without steaming. In a second sketch, I show the proper way of going about this: Nail one end securely, and then use the length of the board as a lever to spring the board down in place gradually, nailing securely as you proceed, both through the cross cleats of

1	VERTICAL SIDE CLEAT 3" x 1" PINE	4	BOTTOM PLANK 14' x 1'-3" x 1" PINE
2	BOTTOM CLEAT 2'-6" x 3" x 1" PINE	5	SIDE PLANK 14' x 1'-3" x 1" PINE
3	TOP CLEAT 2'-8" x 3" x 1" PINE	6	END CLEAT 2'-6" x 3½" x 1" PINE

GEORGIA PINE THROUGH OUT. CUT NAILS. NO SEATS. NO ROWLOCKS.

CHARLESTON BATEAU
PLANKING THE BOTTOM

NAIL
FIRST?

12" x 12" BLOCKING

CUT

J.G.

the bottom and through the side edges. Boards several feet longer than the bottom should be used in order to gain leverage and to get the other end down into place. When the planks are securely nailed, the excess is sawed off.

Boards as wide as were used originally, as shown in the drawings, are not necessary. The bottom can just as well be made of four boards instead of two, and the sides of two boards each instead of one wide one. The narrower boards will bend into place more easily.

Benet in his sketch did not show any cleats on the sides. Possibly these are not absolutely necessary and were not used for the cheapest construction, but I have put them in. They support the bottom cross cleats during construction when a lot of pressure is put on the cross cleats in springing the bottom boards into place. Also, side cleats brace the sides and help to keep the wide side planks from warping or splitting. If two planks were used for the side instead of one wide one, side cleats would, of course, be required.

This is a very easy and inexpensive boat to build, and either as it is, or with minor modifications, could prove a most useful craft under many different conditions and circumstances. It is capable of carrying heavy loads, is extremely stable in calm water, and will row or paddle more easily than might appear. It will take a lot of abuse and should not require much care or upkeep.

As a utility craft or small workboat on the waterfront—a river, lake, or ocean—this punt has real possibilities. It could be used with an outboard motor and would even sail with a few slight modifications. Its fore-and-aft bottom planking makes installation of a centerboard very easy.

This is a basic hull with which a great deal can be done for very little.

A UTILITY PUNT

Every boatyard needs one of these rugged punts. Likewise, summer camps and shore resorts, alongside fresh or salt water. This sturdy little vessel would more than earn its keep any place along the waterfront where work has to be done on or from the water. This punt would certainly give a good account of itself for a variety of jobs. For one thing, as it is roomy, fairly high-sided, and impossible to tip over, it would make a grand play boat for children in sheltered waters. Its flat bottom and sled bow are well adapted for beaching, although it would have to be built rather light to be pushed off the beach by children.

For a chunky, blunt-ended craft, this punt rows and handles remarkably well, and it is as steady as a small raft for carpenter work and painting. Its carrying capacity, for a boat not 12 feet long, is enormous. The original punt, from which the present design was faithfully copied, had as many as nine men aboard on occasion. Over its long career, it carried innumerable and varied heavy loads, such as hard pine blocking, lumber, sand, stone, and cement. Its main job was tending the two marine railways at F. J. Dion's yard in Salem, Massachusetts. The punt met its end recently when it got caught and crushed beyond repair in the larger railway. Fred Dion, who some thirty years before had designed and built the original, built a second punt copied from it. The lines, dimensions, and details are given herewith.

The idea for the first punt came from larger working punts developed on the Cape Cod cranberry bogs. These were sometimes dragged like sleds on the surface of the bogs by horses and were large enough to float a horse to parts of the bogs accessible only by water. Mr. Dion, in adapting the design, kept the general shape and proportions of the bog punt, but reduced the size to the requirements for a yard boat.

This punt, when properly handled, is surprisingly able in rough water. I witnessed its performance in the big hurricane of 1954, when the punt was used to put out extra dock lines. At the time it was blowing so hard that two men facing each other were required to hold one pair of oars in the water. At times the punt would drop nearly out of sight in the trough, and for long spells the boat seemed not to make an inch of headway. But finally the lines were set and secured, and the punt returned safely and completely dry to the float. This was a stiff test for any 12-foot boat, and some good yacht tenders could not have made it.

The construction shown in the accompanying drawings is extra heavy. This boat was built to take abuse of the heaviest and hardest sort and to last for many years. Since the boat was designed to remain in the water the whole

OFFSETS — FEET·INCHES·EIGHTHS — MEASURED TO INSIDE PLANE, BOTTOM & TRANSOM.																				
STATIONS MEASURED FROM BOW	+0	+1"	+2'	+3'	+6"	+9"	+12	1'-6"	+2'	+3'	3'-9"	+4'	+5'	+6'	+7'	7'-3"	+8'	+9'	+10'	10'-7⅞	10'-11¼
HALF BREADTHS — SHEER	1-2-6	1-7-7	1-8-0	1-8-1	1-8-3	1-8-6	1-9-0	1-9-5	1-10-2	1-11-1	1-11-5	1-11-6	1-11-7	2-0-0	1-11-4	1-11-5	1-10-0	1-9-7	1-8-4	1-7-4	1-7-0
BOTTOM	1-7-0	1-6-7	1-6-4	1-6-0	1-5-3	1-5-5	1-6-2	1-6-7	1-7-6	1-8-3	1-8-4	1-8-7	1-9-0	1-8-6	1-8-5	1-8-1	1-7-1	1-5-6	1-4-6	—	
HEIGHTS ABOVE BASE LINE — SHEER	2-4-0	2-3-7	2-3-6	2-3-4	2-3-3	2-3-1	2-2-7	2-2-4	2-2-0	2-1-4	2-1-1	2-1-0	2-0-7	2-0-6	2-0-7	2-1-0	2-1-2	2-1-7	2-2-5	2-3-1	2-3-3
BOTTOM	2-1-0	1-7-6	1-5-2	1-3-0	0-11-7	0-9-7	0-8-7	0-8-1	0-7-7	0-7-6	0-7-6	0-7-7	0-7-7	0-8-0	0-8-3	0-8-4	0-8-6	0-9-3	0-11-6	1-1-4	

DION 11-FT. WORK PUNT

season, from early spring to late fall, extra weight does not matter, as it would in a boat that has to be pulled in and out of the water frequently. For rowing, especially in rough water, considerable weight is an advantage, as it keeps the boat moving steadily between strokes once headway has been gained. Also, weight suppresses undue bobbing, jumping, and heeling, an important feature when a boat is to be used for carpenter work and painting, and as a tender around marine railways.

It would be easy, however, to make a much lighter boat to the same lines and general details. Such a boat would be amply strong for general use if the sides were made of marine fir plywood ½ inch thick, or even ⅜ inch thick if a very light

boat were desired. The ribs could be cut to 1¼ inches, the chines to 1¼ inches, the inwales and risers to 1½ inches, and the guards to 1¾ inches. Two of the inner bottom stringers could be eliminated, the size of the knees could be reduced by one third, and the thickness of the skeg could be reduced to ⅞ inch. The heavy oak bow stiffener could be eliminated, the stern outboard pad narrowed to 9 inches, and the oarlock pads shortened by one third. All in all, it would not be hard to reduce the total weight by 25 per cent and more without weakening the boat for ordinary use.

While marine fir plywood would make an excellent alternative material for the sides, plywood is not recommended for the bottom.

The white pine bottom cross plank should not be reduced in thickness to under a minimum of ¾ inch.

The boat shown here was fastened throughout with screws, except for the inwales, which were rivet-fastened through the topsides and timberheads with 20d copper wire nails headed over burrs. Screws used were mostly No. 12s and No. 14s, from 1½ inches to 2 inches long. To fasten the ends of the cross plank into the sides, No. 10s 2¼ inches long were used. The cross planks were also fastened into each stringer with two screws. Altogether, the fastening was extra generous. Galvanized nails could be used instead of screws if desired. Such would be cheaper, possibly quicker to drive, and sufficiently strong and lasting for all ordinary purposes.

Construction is quite simple. First, the two sides are made up in the flat. Comprised in this assembly are the side planks, inner chines, and ribs. The sides are then bent bottom up around the two molds, which are indicated in the lines plan. The fore and aft ends are hauled in with door clamps to the proper widths and secured with temporary stay-laths. After this assembly has been checked, horned, and plumbed for symmetry and conformity to the lines dimensions, and securely stayed with ample braces, the transom and bottom cross planking are put on.

The structure is next turned right side up. The inner bottom stringers, risers, bow stiffener, knees, inwales, etc., are installed. When all interior members are in and fastened, the boat is turned bottom up again to receive the outer bottom stringers and skeg. Before the stringers and skeg are fastened on, the bottom seams are caulked with a thread of cotton, payed with primer, and puttied. It is important to do a thorough caulking job on the ends of the cross plank where they meet the sides.

For yacht work, the continuous rubber bumper around the sheer and ends is a must.

Also, it should be noted that the sheer guard is well beveled on its lower edge so as not to catch on things when the boat settles in a swell. Heavy ring bolts are shown in each end, ample enough to be used as lifting rings; both are fitted with painters. The location of the rowlocks is indicated. These are galvanized iron of the Davis pattern that slip out of an upright position when not in use and hang down inside the boat. This also is a "must" for yacht work, as the ordinary rowlock can give a nasty dig on occasion in the overhanging counter of a yacht. Most of the rowing will be done from the forward center thwart, but the rowlocks are located so that a man can row pushing by facing forward from the after cross thwart. Thus two men can work at the same pair of oars in an emergency—one pushing and one pulling.

The thwarts and end seats are well braced and posted because men frequently have to jump from a height into the boat when working around railways. Also, heavy blocking is sometimes dropped into the boat. Such hard usage is one reason for the close stringers. In the old punt, thirty years of hard work had worn hollows in the pine cross planking exposed between the bottom stringers.

Finally, we should not forget the scull hole in the transom, although the art of sculling, as well as ordinary rowing, is fast being forgotten in this day of the ubiquitous outboard motor. An oak reinforcement suitable for mounting an outboard motor is indicated for the transom, but to my knowledge the old punt was never submitted to the indignity of an outboard. A motor would probably work all right, although the up-turn of the bottom aft is not suitable for efficient outboard performance. For best results with an outboard, the run of the bottom aft should be straight and flat. But this would drag water when the boat is rowed. "You pays your money and you takes your choice."

2

L. Francis Herreshoff's Pram

....................•......................

Along the waterfront these days prams are everywhere in evidence. Made of plywood and plastic, these snub-nosed craft now are probably our most popular and common type of small tender. Some are quite diminutive and boxy and can hardly be classed as sea boats, yet they serve quite adequately on calm days to negotiate the several hundred yards or less between the mooring and the float, which is about all that many require of a tender.

The advantages of such prams are several. They are light, compact, easy to handle and take aboard, and stow to advantage on deck, taking up a minimum of room. Some of the plastic ones are transparent, permitting them to be placed bottom-up over skylights or hatches without cutting off the light below.

Their form is such that they are relatively simple and easy to construct, and they are adapted, as well, for mass production. The lower building costs resulting sometimes carry over to the final selling price, although some of the more fancy plastic prams are priced about as high as the traffic will bear, and then some.

Yes, for fair weather use in sheltered harbors, most of these modern, mass-produced prams serve nicely enough, but if one is looking for something more in a tender—that is to say for a boat that will tow, that will pull easily over a distance, that will stand some rough water—

then the ordinary run-of-the-mill pram, as commonly seen today, just won't do.

But there are prams and there are prams. In Scandinavian waters, where prams originated long ago, they proved themselves fine sea boats, as some still are, and if properly designed, they tow beautifully. We have this from no less an authority than the late L. Francis Herreshoff, one of the greatest American yacht designers, sailor and yachtsman of wide experience, and in addition, one who knew small craft and the details of their construction as have few others. In addition to his other numerous accomplishments, Herreshoff was a proficient boatbuilder.

Back in the 1940s, Herreshoff wrote for *Rudder* magazine a long series of articles afterwards published in book form as *The Common Sense Of Yacht Design*, which has been reprinted by Caravan-Maritime Books, Jamaica, New York. The series was immensely popular. We waited with mounting anticipation for each new installment. We cherished the back issues—in fact, I have mine still, and they fill a rather large box. I well remember the appearance of the section on small craft, now Chapter XIX in the Caravan reprint, and how avidly I read it. Figure 362 of this section, reproduced here, is an undimensioned lines sketch showing the proportions of the pram that Herreshoff designed for the deck of the M boat he designed,

Racing tender designed by L. Francis Herreshoff for the deck of the M boat Istalena *(from* The Common Sense of Yacht Design, *Caravan Maritime Books)*

Folkard's praam.

the *Istalena.* I was so impressed with this pram at the time that I made a half model for a 10-foot pram developed from this sketch, working to the scale of 1½ inches to the foot. Here is what Herreshoff had to say about the design:

> After World War I yachts became smaller and smaller, so that a good dinghy (particularly for the deck of a racing yacht) became quite a problem, for when the usual models of dinghies are made too small they are not safe or comfortable. In England about this time the smaller yachts were using what is called a pram dinghy, that is, one with a transom both forward and aft. While somewhat similar models called square toes had been used in this country, as a general rule they were so poorly modeled that they were not a success.
>
> In 1921 when I was racing at Cowes in England, I had an opportunity to try one out in rough water on a day when the tide was setting up against a stiff breeze. I rowed one from Cowes Roads nearly to Southampton waters and back, and was so much impressed with the performance of that pram that ever since I have considered it the best model for a small tender. . . . These little prams tow as well as, if not better than, any other dinghy and on account of their low freeboard stow well on deck.

It is clear that the pram was known and used in England a considerable time before the period cited by Herreshoff. It was used as a rowing boat and as a sailboat in the larger sizes. In the sixth edition (1906) of *The Sailing Boat* by H. C. Folkard, London, there is printed a steel engraving, reproduced here, of a "large Sailing-Praam, adopted and rigged in British waters with two masts and lug-sails . . ." It is shown running before the wind with the foresail

or jib "hauled aweather," which, according to Folkard, was the usual method for steadying a boat in a seaway. What Folkard has in general to say about the pram is worth quoting here:

> The Praam (Praham) is also a boat of Norwegian contrivance, and of peculiar form. The Praams, like the yawls, are built of "Norway deal," but without nails, the planks being fastened to the keelson and timbers with hard wooden pegs; notwithstanding which they are very tight and secure, as well as strong and durable.
>
> The shape of the Praam is similar to a wooden boat scoop without a handle, having a broad, round shaped bottom; the greatest width of beam is at the stern, the head and bows gradually rising forward, and sometimes finishing with a carved figurehead. Small-sized Praams are used generally as rowing boats; it is only the larger size that are sailed.

Two characteristics of the Norway praam noted by Folkard call for comment. First is the manner of fastening with "hard wooden pegs." Treenail fastening was a common method for traditional Norse fishing small craft. Detailed drawings for shaping and wedging such treenails may be seen in the plans of a heavy, flat-bottomed boat of pram shape reproduced here from *Nordens Batar*, by Arne Emil Christensen, Jr. Treenail fastening, however, requires thick wood to be effective, and this, in turn, means relatively heavy scantlings. For a light tender, such as we are considering, construction of this sort is entirely unsuitable. Recommended for our purposes is white cedar planking, ¼-inch thick, fastened with small copper rivets. Instead

A heavy Scandinavian work pram shown in Nordens Bater. *Although of flat-bottomed construction, she is similar in shape to the 10-foot pram based on Herreshoff's lines.*

of heavy, hewn, natural-crook timbers such as were traditional with the Norwegian boats, our pram will be framed with slight, steam-bent ribs of white oak, closely spaced.

Second, according to Folkard's description, the praam's greatest breadth of beam came at the stern with the hull tapering forward to a small transom at the bow. The result was a somewhat pointed appearance combined with a marked amount of rocker. In the Herreshoff pram, although the stern is fairly wide, the greatest beam comes nearly amidships. The bow transom is not particularly small, nor is the profile curve of the bottom in any way excessive. In short, Herreshoff retained the characteristic pram shape, but without going to extremes in any particular. The result is an especially easy shape to plank without twists or hard bends of any sort. With proper lining, the strakes should run nearly straight, and none will require steaming.

From the half model of Herreshoff's pram that I made so many years ago, I have taken off the lines, which are reproduced here, along with the offsets. From these, an excellent tender can be made, I feel sure. It is a relatively easy one to build, a consideration not to be minimized by the inexperienced amateur. The pram is to be planked lapstrake or clinker, which is the way the Norwegians first built their praams, and the proper way of doing it still. Not only is clinker construction the easiest and strongest method for building this pram, and the lightest even, but also it makes a more stable boat, for the laps grab the water, helping to keep the boat from rolling, which this type of hull has a tendency to do.

The building process for this pram may be divided into four stages: (1) setting up, which

includes laying down the full-size lines, and
making the molds and setting these up with the
two transoms and the keel strip in place, ready
to receive the planking; (2) planking, which
comprises lining off the plank shapes on the
molds, spiling the shape of each plank in turn
and getting it out of planking stock, and finally
hanging it, that is bending and fastening the
plank on the boat; (3) timbering with white oak
frames, steamed and bent in, and riveted
through the laps after the planking is in place;
and (4) finishing, the addition of thwarts, rowlocks, gunwales, knees, and miscellaneous hardware.

Two Norwegian prams from
Norske Bater *by Arne Emil
Christensen, Jr. The pram at the
top is not unlike the Herreshoff
pram, although the latter's lines
are much less extreme. Note the
twin skegs that serve as both runners and keels.*

SETTING UP

The "ladder-frame" method I am proposing here for setting up is a bit unusual, and very likely the professional builder might do it differently to save time. But occasionally, as the old saying goes, "the longest way 'round is the shortest way home." The extra labor expended in making this ladder-frame setup will not be lost, let me assure you. Not only will it insure a fair shape, as well as an easy means of positioning the molds and holding them rigid, but also it will permit fastening the garboards without interference from posts or other kind of underpinning as might be in the way if the boat were set up on posts or a plank-on-edge, two of the more usual ways of doing this.

For the "ladder", two 12-foot 2 by 4s are required. These must be perfectly straight, otherwise the setup will not be fair. These are laid out side to side on edge on the bench or the floor, and the mold spacing from the lines plan is measured off on them and squared across both and marked. The two sides of the "ladder" are then separated so that they run parallel and are exactly 2 feet apart from outside to outside.

Cross cleats, previously prepared, are securely nailed on at the mold stations conforming exactly to the squared lines as

OFFSETS 10' HERRESHOFF PRAM

STATIONS		STERN	1	2	3	4	5	6	7	8	Bow
HEIGHTS	BOTTOM	0-6-4	0-4-7	0-3-5	0-3-1	0-3-1	0-3-5	0-5-6	0-10-1	1-0-7	1-2-5
	6" BUT.	0-7-1	0-5-4	0-4-0	0-3-5	0-3-4	0-4-2	0-6-5	0-10-7	1-1-5	1-3-6
	12" BUT.	0-9-3	0-6-6	0-5-1	0-4-3	0-4-4	0-5-5	0-8-0	1-0-7	1-4-3	1-9-3
	SHEER	1-7-1	1-6-7	1-6-6	1-7-0	1-7-2	1-7-6	1-8-4	1-9-5	1-10-0	1-10-6
HALF-BREADTHS	6" W.L	0-11-2	1-3-7	1-6-3	1-7-6	1-7-6	1-6-1	1-2-3	—	—	—
	9" W.L	1-3-1	1-6-1	1-8-2	1-9-3	1-9-3	1-8-1	1-5-1	0-10-5	—	—
	12" W.L	1-4-6	1-7-1	1-9-0	1-10-1	1-10-2	1-9-1	1-6-4	1-2-3	0-10-3	0-3-3
	SHEER	1-5-4	1-7-4	1-9-3	1-10-3	1-10-6	1-9-7	1-7-5	1-4-2	1-2-6	0-3
DIAGONALS	D1	1-7-6	1-10-6	2-0-0	2-1-1	2-1-2	2-0-1	1-9-5	1-6-0	1-4-0	1-1-3
	D2	1-9-3	1-11-7	2-1-5	2-2-6	2-2-6	2-1-4	1-11-0	1-6-6	1-4-1	1-1-4
	D3	1-9-0	1-11-2	2-0-5	2-1-3	2-1-3	2-0-3	1-10-5	1-5-6	1-2-7	0-0-7

BOTTOM HEIGHTS AT CENTER LINE OF HULL.
MEASUREMENTS TAKEN TO INSIDE OF PLANKING.

1	STERN TRANSOM ½" MAHOGANY PLYWOOD or ¾" MAHOGANY	11	THWART KNEE, AMIDSHIPS, NATURAL CROOK or LAMINATED, SIDED ½"
2	BOW TRANSOM " " " " "	12	BENT TIMBERS WHITE OAK ⅞ × 7⁄16
3	STERN POST ⅞" OAK	13	ROWLOCK SOCKET PAD OAK 10" × ½" × 1⅛"
4	KNEE, STERN QUARTER, NATURAL CROOK or LAMINATION, SIDED ⅞"	14	FITTED FLOORS SIDED ⅝
5	KEEL BATTEN, 2¼" × ½" OAK	15	THWARTS 7" WIDE ½" THICK MAHOGANY
6	TRANSOM REINFORCEMENT 1½" × ½" OAK SAWED TO SHAPE	16	FOOT WALK 7⁄16" TEAK
7	BOW KNEE ⅞" OAK	17	SEAT RISINGS 1¼" × ½" MAHOGANY
8	THWART KNEE, LAMINATED or NATURAL CROOK SIDED ¾"	18	CHANNEL, ROPE BUMPER GUARD 1⅝" × ⅝"
9	TURNED POST 1" SQUARE MAHOGANY	19	KNEE, BOW QUARTER, NAT CROOK or LAMINATED, SIDED ⅞"
10	INWALE OAK 1⅞" × ½" AMIDSHIPS, TAPERS TO ⅝" × ½" EITHER END	20	CLINKER PLANKING NORTHERN WHITE CEDAR ¼" TH'K.

STATION 7   6   5   4   3   2   1
9"——4"   7"——7"——7"   5"

FEET AND INCHES

previously marked. These cross cleats of 4-inch wide strips of one-inch spruce or pine boards must all be exactly 2 inches long with accurately squared ends. Not only will the sides of the ladder-frame when assembled be exactly parallel, but also the seven cross cleats at right angles to the sides will all be evenly spaced 15 inches apart and parallel with each other.

When the molds are located on this ladder-frame at their respective stations, their accurate positioning is virtually automatic. At the same time they are rigidly secured in place. The two beveled end cleats that hold the bow and stern transoms need not be fitted until the backbone assembly is put on the molds and fastened down.

The molds, to be located vertically, that is at their correct relative heights, are made with extensions which raise them the proper distance above the ladder-frame. The various lengths to make these extensions as required by different

molds are determined from a line added to the profile view of the lines drawing. It corresponds to the ladder-frame and is laid out parallel to, and 25 inches above, the baseline from which the offsets are measured. The molds are all extended to this line.

The keel batten, which provides backing for the garboards and to which they are riveted along their lower edges, is a strip of ½-inch by 2¼-inch oak. The molds must be notched to receive it, and, because it takes considerable bend, especially forward, some practicable means must be devised for holding it in position during the first stages of construction. This is accomplished by another batten, a temporary set-up batten, also oak and of the same dimensions except that it is shorter, extending from mold No. 1 to mold No. 7. This set-up batten is located inside, or rather, under, the keel batten, which rests on it and to which it is temporarily fastened by a number of one-inch No. 10 screws

1	STERN TRAN. ½" MAHG. PLYWOOD
2	BOW TRAN. ½" MAHG. PLYWOOD
3	STERN POST ⅞" OAK
4	SKEG ⅞" OAK
5	KEEL BATTEN. 2¼" × ½" OAK
6	TEMPORARY SETUP BATTEN 2¼ × ½" OAK
7	BOW KNEE ⅞" OAK.
8	MOLDS #2 COMMON PINE 1' (¾"NET)THK.
9	CROSS SPALLS PINE, SAME AS MOLDS.
10	CROSS CLEATS, LADDER FRAME PINE AS MOLDS.
11	LADDER FRAME SIDES. 2×4 SPRUCE OR D. FIR.
12	BEVELED END CLEATS. 2×3 SPRUCE
13	BRONZE DRIFT - 5" × ¼".
14	MOLD CLEATS PINE
15	EDGE REINFORCEMENT, STERN & BOW TRANS ½ × 1½ OAK
16	FORWARD KEEL STRIP, OAK ⅞ × 7 × ½.

"LADDER-FRAME" SETUP
10 FOOT CLINKER PRAM

put in from the inside of the boat and thus easy to get at when the molds are removed after planking.

Besides acting as a form to bend the keel batten on and to help hold the backbone in position for planking, the temporary set-up batten has another function: It serves to brace the molds and to hold them perpendicular to the ladder-frame and parallel to each other. The set-up batten is screwed securely into each mold, the keel batten notches in the molds having been cut an additional ½ inch deeper to receive it. With the tops of the molds secured to the ladder-frame cleats and the bottoms attached to the set-up batten, the result is quite rigid, as it will be absolutely immovable when the backbone

assembly is fastened on with the bow and stern transoms screwed to the beveled end blocks nailed to the ladder frame.

One thing to mention about the molds, lest it be overlooked: They are not located in the usual way either at one side or the other of the section lines, but directly over them, so that temporary fastenings into them through the plank may later be drawn and the same plank holes used to fasten through to the timbers, every third one of which will fall directly on a section line. Consequently, the end molds will have to be beveled slightly on one side or the other, but for only half the thickness of the mold.

Old-time builders of lapstrake boats frequently used only one mold, called the "shadow," which was set up amidships. Depending on this alone, they were able to control the shape of the boat as they planked, keeping it symmetrical and fair. But this method required a high order of skill attainable only through long practice, and, I dare say, even so, boats did not always shape out exactly as planned.

In this boat, two of the intermediate after molds, where the shape does not change quickly, could be left out, but for a beginner I would certainly recommend staying with all seven molds, although the 15-inch spacing between stations may seem pretty close.* There is a reason for spacing these molds exactly 15 inches apart on centers. The steamed white oak timbers, bent in place and riveted through the laps after planking is complete, are located 5 inches apart on centers. Thus, two timbers come between each two molds, and when the molds are removed timbers take their places, giving a uniform 5-inch timber spacing throughout the boat.

The timber "bays," that is, the spaces between the timbers, are divided to allow two riveted lap fastenings between every two riveted timber fastenings, so that the rivet heads on the outside of the laps are all spaced equally the length of the boat. The intermediate lap fastenings are put in and headed up tightly over roves or burrs as the planking goes on. This, of course, takes place before the molds are removed and the timbers bent in. Obviously, it is essential to space these intermediate lap fastenings correctly, leaving spaces for rivets which will fasten into the timbers later.

In this boat as laid out, it is easy to determine the location of the timbers by measurement from the molds, and thus to lay out the precise rivet spacing between timber locations as the planking proceeds. With the ladder-frame set-up, the molds are bound to be positioned right. With a little care the fastenings can be spaced perfectly. This is more important than might seem in a varnished boat where all the rivet heads will show, and any departures from a regular, uniform pattern will stand out like the proverbial "sore thumb."

Once the molds are in place, the bow and stern transoms are both got out with enough additional wood at their upper ends to allow them to be fastened to the end blocks on the ladder-frame. After the boat is planked and the molds have been removed, this excess is cut off and the ends are given their designed shape.

To save weight without loss of strength, ½-inch mahogany plywood of the best marine quality is suggested for the transoms. Solid mahogany could be used, but it should not be less than ⅝-inch thick. Perhaps ¾-inch thick would be better if weight were not too compelling a consideration. If plywood is used, it will be necessary to add a reinforcement around the inner edge to provide secure fastening for the screws which hold the ends of the planking. Such reinforcing pieces got out to the required curves can be either oak or mahogany and need not be more than ½-inch thick and 1½-inch wide. They should be nicely cut, well smoothed, and neatly beveled or rounded on the inside so as to look well when varnished. These pieces should be glued to the inner face of the transom with epoxy adhesive, in addition to being well fastened with ⅞-inch No. 8 bronze wood screws spaced not more than 2 inches apart, with the heads set just below the surface of the wood.

The side and bottom edges of the plywood transom will be covered with planking after beveling. The top edges of the plywood transoms need not be left exposed. There are various neat ways of protecting and hiding the end wood. One is by covering it with fiberglass tape set in epoxy, with the excess width trimmed off flush with the surface after the resin has hardened. Another is by the addition

---

*While it is nice to have plenty of molds to insure a fair and accurate shape, the spacing recommended would be pretty close when it came to riveting the laps of the bottom planks. Amidship, especially, it would be hard to reach in between molds set as close as this to get at the rivets conveniently in order to do the careful, painstaking job in heading them up which is so important and critical, as will be explained.

So on second thought I think it will be desirable (certainly for fat men) to make do with molds on the even numbered stations only, omitting molds on stations 1, 3, 5 and 7. Some might want to keep the mold at station 7 because of the greater bend in the plank close to the bow and the danger of getting a flat spot there.

of a thin strip or half oval of mahogany put on with epoxy adhesive and very fine brads.

The sternpost construction is typical of the best traditional design. It imparts strength and bracing action to the whole after end of the boat without adding extra weight. Note that it is shouldered to support the transom, and that it extends up the inside of the transom to brace it. The sternpost should be glued to the transom with epoxy adhesive, and fastened through from the outside with 1-inch and 1¼-inch No. 10 bronze screws 2 inches apart, with the heads carefully set just barely below the surface and with the slots lined the same way, which will look all right varnished. They should not be bunged, as the ½-inch plywood is not thick enough to take a bung and still retain its strength around the fastening.

The sternpost is of ⅞-inch thick oak like the skeg and the outer forward keel strip. It mortises snugly through the after end of the keel batten and comes down through the bottom of the boat to "marry," as the English boatbuilders say, with the skeg. Note how it is securely pinned with copper rod, and particularly how a small tenon on the inner side of the lower end fits into a mortise in the skeg and thus holds the two in perfect alignment, even though the tenon is only ¼-inch thick and ¼-inch deep. Note also how the end of the sternpost is fitted to the skeg with a raking joint in order to cover and to protect its end wood. By this arrangement the skeg is so solidly braced that it can sustain heavy shocks and even pounding on the beach without straining or moving or getting knocked sidewise, as would easily and most certainly happen if it were merely fastened on the bottom with a few screws through the keel batten. In such a case in a boat as lightly constructed as this one, even slight strain on the skeg might produce leverage enough to spring it sidewise, producing a split or a leak.

Where the sternpost mortises through the keel batten, outside strips of the batten ¹¹⁄₁₆-inch wide remain on each side. These should be fastened sidewise into the sternpost on each side with two 1¼-inch No. 8 bronze screws. The after ends of the garboard planks will be held in place by rivets driven through these cheek pieces.

Before planking starts, a ⅜-inch hole should be bored centering on the joint between the end of the skeg and the sternpost and just below the keel batten. Through this a tight pine stopwater is driven, and its ends trimmed off flush with the surface of the sternpost. The ¼-inch planking when it is on will not cover all the stopwater, but that does not matter. Better to have a stopwater too large than too small. The planking should fit tightly against it, but not so tightly that a thin thread of cotton cannot be driven in against this stopwater on either side. A bit of caulking may also be needed where the transom sits in its notch in the sternpost. No other caulking should be required in this boat.

After the mold assembly is completed on the ladder-frame, and the backbone assembly has been bent on and secured in place, the set-up is ready for planking, provided the molds don't require some final slight fairing. Of course this will be checked for and done if needed.

But before planking can start, the set-up assembly must be turned over and securely positioned in some manner at a convenient height for working, for in order for one man to rivet the laps of clinker planking as the several strakes go on up the sides starting from the garboards, the boat must sit right side up. This is so the planker can push against the rivet head on the outside with a weight in his left hand, perhaps assisted by his knee, while he heads up the rivet on the inside of the lap with his riveting hammer in his right hand. If riveting is attempted with the boat bottom up, two persons will be required for this operation, and even so they may not be able to coordinate their efforts to do it properly.

How to hold or suspend the set-up securely and at the correct position for planking to proceed? Possibly the extended ends of the ladder-frame can be supported by a couple of high horses. Or an arrangement of posts at either end may be substituted. Cleats nailed to a convenient wall could serve nicely to take one end of the ladder-frame, while a horse or posts hold up the other end.

Much will depend on the place serving for a

shop, and something needs be left to the builder's ingenuity. A few stay-laths, either pieces of strapping or long edgings, run from the set-up to convenient spots on the wall and/or ceiling and temporarily nailed, will steady the set-up wonderfully, and, after the garboards are on, a couple of light posts as props underneath will make things as solid as the Rock of Gibraltar. Several outside legs clamped to the outside of the wider molds and running to the floor will provide the finest kind of support without getting in the way of the planking enough to bother the builder excessively.

PLANKING AND TIMBERING

Though this 10-foot pram would admit construction by several methods using a variety of materials in different scantling sizes, the intention here is to build a fancy varnished tender, ultra light in weight, yet adequately strong and lasting if properly handled and cared for. For a quality tender of this sort nothing can equal clinker planking of northern white cedar.

J. H. Rushton of Canton, New York, one of this country's leading builders of small craft in the latter part of the nineteenth century, specialized in light lapstrake cedar boats. One of these, the "Nessmuk featherweight canoe," 10½ feet long and 27 inches in beam, was advertised in the Rushton catalog as weighing between 20 and 22 pounds. Rushton explained why he preferred northern white cedar:

Do not confound our White Cedar, which grows only in the most Northern States and Canada, with the White Cedar of New Jersey and Virginia. The former is the lightest known wood of this or any country that is suitable for planks for small craft. One cubic foot, air seasoned (not kiln-dried) weighs but eighteen pounds, while the White Cedar of New Jersey and Virginia weighs 28 pounds.

The Northern Cedar is soft, tough and durable. You can give it a vast amount of hard useage with but little injury, and time makes little impression on it, as I have known the Cedar planking in a boat to be sound and perfect after twenty years' constant use every summer, and having only such shelter winters as may be found in a woods camp.

In building clinker or lapstrake, thinner

planking can be used than is required for carvel, because the doubling at the laps in the former makes up in strength and stiffness for the slighter thickness. Besides, carvel planking generally must be thicker to hold caulking, which clinker does not require. Rushton built "Pleasure Row Boats" as long as 16 feet with a beam of 42 inches, planked lapstrake of northern cedar ¼-inch thick. For our 10-foot pram, a ¼-inch plank thickness will be quite adequate. We might use ⁵⁄₁₆-inch planking but little would be gained by it except a somewhat heavier boat. As old Charles Lawton used to say in this connection (Charlie was for many years the leading small-boat builder in Marblehead), "Three-eighths planking will smash just as quick on the rocks," meaning that for normal use ¼-inch planking was adequate for the small clinker tender, and that under conditions of extreme abuse, extra plank thickness availed little or nothing.

Of course, it should be understood that thin planking must be adequately reinforced and supported by suitable timbers or ribs. If these are made of choice white oak, they may be fairly small in cross section, but at the same time they should be rather closely spaced, as we shall see when we get to timbering.

The main event in building this pram is the planking. Setting up, and in general getting ready to plank, requires careful, accurate, methodical work, it is true, but is, in a sense, routine. Finishing the boat after planking is complete is not to be done haphazardly, but is anticlimactic and something of a letdown. It is the planking that separates the boatbuilders from the shoemakers, as they used to say in Marblehead. In planking, variables come into play requiring exercise of judgment. Aesthetics are involved to a critical extent. In fact planking is something of an art, perhaps one reason none of the boatbuilding books I have seen treat its mysteries adequately.

Fortunately, our pram has an easy shape to plank. Strakes can be lined out nearly straight, for the greater part, and go on without twist or sny. One advantage obtained from the pram's transomed bow is the elimination of twist in the fore ends of the lower plank, especially the garboard. In a comparatively short, wide boat with a sharp bow and nearly upright stem like the well-known Lawley tender, for instance, the hood ends of the lower plank, which land in the stem rabbet, require steaming and can prove vexatious to fit and hang even for experienced boatbuilders. With the pram, all this is avoided. The thin, narrow planks bend easily into place with a minimum of clamping and no forcing, if accurately spiled. No hollowing or rounding is required as with carvel planking.

To begin planking, the hull surface must be lined, that is divided up to best advantage with the widths and sweeps of the several planks marked off on the edges of the molds. Special devices employed in this operation, namely the lining batten and the diminishing batten, are described in the Appendix and need not be taken up here.

In lining plank, one of the first steps is to decide on the number of planks. For this pram I should think 10 strakes about right in order to give rather narrow widths, for narrow plank for a clinker boat of this sort are an advantage over wide planks, if not a necessity. Narrow planks

are not likely to split or rent. They do not move as much in swelling and shrinking as wider widths. They fit the curve of the sides better where the turn is sharp, and they are easier to get out of ordinary planking stock, where it is often desirable to dodge knots or other defects. Narrower planks mean more laps, however, and more riveting as well. An extra strake or two lengthens the building time somewhat, but this should not bother the amateur.

Plank shapes need to run in smooth, easy, continuous sweeps or curves, diminishing evenly in breadth from the wider mid-portion of the hull to its narrower ends. Not only is this necessary for appearance, so that the boat will "look right," but it would be difficult, if not impossible, to attain a watertight hull if the planks were of erratic shapes and made abrupt changes in contour.

Numerous considerations, sometimes conflicting ones, enter into the determination of plank widths. Compromise is often necessary. For one thing, hood ends must not be made so narrow as to preclude room for adequate fastening. As a general rule, plank should be fairly straight when laid out in the flat, both to avoid weak cross-grain and for economical utilization of planking stock. The apportionment of width in the strake has much to do with the amount of crook developed in its shape. Furthermore, in clinker plank, widths have a direct relationship to lap bevels and should correspond to the curvature of the frame, so that the sharper the rib bend, the narrower the plank will need to be.

The accompanying drawing shows tentative plank widths for three stations for the pram, for No. 3 in the mid-portion of the hull, No. 8 just abaft the bow transom, and for the stern transom. It should be noted that the planks are wider on the bottom and in the topsides next to the sheer, and narrower at the turn of the bilge and just above, where the most curve is found. The reason for such variation in plank width should be obvious.

As stated, these are "tentative" widths, which will need to be checked on the hull with the lining batten. Undoubtedly some adjustment in these preliminary widths will be required, although probably not much. There is no precise way of exactly determining plank widths in advance of building, except that it is possible to lay out close approximations on an accurate scale model.

In a lightly built clinker boat like this pram, it is desirable for strength to leave as much wood as possible in fitting the laps. The lap bevels can be controlled to some extent through plank widths. From the planking diagram for station No. 3 on the drawing, it will be found that the laps fit with little or no beveling. However, at station No. 8 the laps are beveled considerably more. This is because this station is close to the bow transom where the beveling must be increased to permit the hood ends of the plank to lie flat and smooth on the edge of the transom without any of the lap protruding.

This, of course, is what is also seen at the stern transom. Sometimes each of the meeting lap surfaces at the ends of adjoining plank are shaved to a sharp, or "feather," edge, so that they lie flush and continuous when brought together. The feather edge is more prone to break, so according to the best practice, as shown in the accompanying drawing, the edge of the outer lap is left a little blunt or "strong," so as to let in flush to a slight rabbet cut in the underpiece. This makes a neater and more secure job.

It must be admitted that the changing lap bevels required for this pram are fairly tricky and call for special attention. Yet they are nothing that cannot be handled, given care and a little study. For the novice who finds these bevels difficult or puzzling at the start, it might help to lay them out precisely and full-size on the drawing board, for several stations at different parts of the boat.

Incidentally, clinker plank may be finish-sanded on the bench before hanging. A small power belt sander, if available, serves famously for this, although the old fashioned sandpaper block run by potato power does just as good a job.

The planking may be got out of cedar boards even slightly thinner than one inch in the rough. A plank shape is laid out on such a board and cut out, and the edges are planed to the line. Then the piece is split in two lengthwise, giving two planks of identical shape, one for either side of the boat.

Copper rivets are indicated for fastening the planking laps of this boat, both through the timbers and between them, instead of clinched fastenings. Although rivets may mean a little more work, I believe they pull up tighter and are not so apt to work loose when properly put in. (For further information on this, including instructions on riveting, see the Appendix.) For the laps of this pram, a nail ¾-inch long is big enough. For riveting through laps and timbers together, a 1¼-inch nail is needed. For riveting the inwales and thwarts, a 2-inch nail is required.

Timbers in this pram run continuously from gunwale to gunwale and are spaced exactly on 5-inch centers. As previously indicated, the body sections in the lines have been laid out with this in mind, being drawn 15 inches apart, so that when timbers are located on the section lines, the spaces, or "bays," between will each divide evenly for two sets of timbers. Thus, it is easy and convenient to lay out on the inside of the planking, measuring from the molds, and using a thin, flexible batten for marking, the exact position to be occupied by each continuous timber or rib. The timbers are to be white oak. For instructions on steaming, placing, and riveting them, see the Appendix.

FINISHING OUT

After the boat is timbered, the finish work can begin. The fitted floors are scribed, cut to shape, and fastened in. Incidentally, these, while spaced approximately on 10-inch centers, should be shifted slightly one way or the other to miss fastenings already put in. The fitted floors add a little extra weight and some extra work, but are worth it in added strength. They must be well fitted, not less than ½-inch thick (molded thickness) where they notch over the keel batten. Don't forget the limbers to permit water to drain along the laps. The floors hold not only the inside walkway, but also the rubbing strips on the outside.

The walkway strips come next and should not be varnished, for more secure footing, and are best made of teak. Port Orford (Alaskan) cedar, or even ordinary white cedar could be used, however. The strips are fastened into the fitted floors with 1-inch No. 6 or No. 8 bronze wood screws. A round hole may be cut through these strips under the middle thwart for sponging out the boat. Strips, or "stretchers," are easily screwed on the walkway strips, to brace the feet when rowing.

Next, the seat risers can be installed, as well as the thwarts and thwart knees. The turned posts under the thwarts permit the thwarts to be made only ¾-inch thick, and thus save a great deal more than their own weight. The ¼-inch chamfer on the edges of the thwarts is for appearance, making the thwart look even thinner than it is. The thwarts, with their knees and center posts, or supports, are very important strengthening members. The bracing knees as shown are absolutely essential for strength.

The four quarter knees are installed next. These and the eight thwart knees may be made either of natural crooks or of laminations. In the past, the finest light tenders often had their knees made from apple limb crooks. These are still good, but not easy to obtain.

Laminated knees when properly made and finished look good and are very strong. A form should be made for bending and gluing thin strips (about 1/16-inch thick) to produce a blank of the right size from which to cut out the finished knees. The form is made in two parts, an inside and an outside part, which are drawn together, with the strip assembly between. Large C-clamps are most commonly used for clamping. All parts of the gluing form must be well waxed to prevent the glue from sticking to them. Strips are got out on the circular saw from stock 2-inches thick, let us say, so as to produce a blank that when glued will give two knees of 7/8-inch thickness, finished. Wood for laminated knees may be mahogany, ash, or Sitka spruce. Strips should not be too smooth for good results with epoxy glue—just as they come off the ordinary circular saw (*not* a planer-tooth saw) is fine.

Any good epoxy glue can be used but it should be rather heavy. The form should be arranged so the glue does not run out easily before it hardens. A proprietary epoxy glue may be used or any rather heavy epoxy resin mixed 50/50 with Versamid 140 as the hardener.

After the knees are in place, the oak inwale is fastened with rivets through the sheer plank and timberheads and through the ends of the quarter knees, bow and stern. Then the following items must be installed: rowlock sockets and pads; the outside channel strips to hold the cotton rope bumper; bronze eye bolt and ring for towing put in through the bottom of the bow transom into the bow knee, and lifting rings in the bottom, inside, if desired.

The final finishing includes sponging outside with hot water to take out dents, as well as inside around rivet heads, the final sanding, a coat of sealer, and three coats of varnish. Then the cotton rope bumper and painter is installed.

While 1/2-inch thick mahogany plywood with the edge reinforcement, as shown in the drawings, will make a strong, light transom without seams, the top edge will have to be protected in some way, possibly with a strip of solid mahogany securely fastened on with epoxy glue and 2-inch No. 6 or No. 8 bronze screws. Those who don't like the idea of plywood here can substitute solid mahogany 3/4-inch thick, but it will add a little to the weight of the boat.

Screws needed for the thwart knees, risers, fitted floors, and rub strips are No. 8 bronze 1-inch and 1¼-inches long. For the ends of the planking and the transom reinforcements, 7/8-inch No. 6 bronze screws will do, although those for the transom edge reinforcements might better be size No. 8. For the outside channel strips for the rope bumper, 7/8-inch No. 6 or No. 8 screws are needed to go through the sheer plank into the timber heads. For the sternpost, bow knee, outer keel strip, and skeg, assorted bronze screws of sufficient size and number will be required to give solid fastening. Plenty of fastenings are needed. Do not skimp.

Glue should be used throughout, especially for reinforcing knees and for securing the reinforcing strips around the edges of the transoms.

For flotation, six Styrofoam blocks may be affixed to the under sides of the thwarts. These may be made up the width of the thwarts to go on either side of the center posts, and covered with a thermoplastic coating of some sort for cleanliness and appearance. If fastened to a thin plywood backing, these flotation units may be secured with round-head screws so as to be removed easily if desired.

3

A Plywood Pram

This pram is all boat, and quite a vessel for less than 9½ feet of length. I took a lot of pains with my design, not only in the preliminary stage of gathering and comparing dimensions and other data, but in laying out trial lines and in making a working half model to see how the proportions looked in wood. After a year of use, it has more than met my expectations in all but one respect: the weight is slightly more than I had hoped. But weighing just under 100 pounds, the boat is not that heavy. Two persons can easily carry it. It could have been built lighter, but I chose to make it more than amply strong and rugged, and whenever it was a question of gaining extra strength by adding a little more weight or a slightly larger scantling, I decided for the extra strength.

The pram is very stiff and surprisingly seaworthy. It takes four adults easily, its bottom rocker and fairly deep vee give it a good grab beneath the surface, and its 55 inches of beam assure ample stability. Yet in spite of its exceptional width the boat is not tubby. It rows easily for a short boat and handles well. The considerable bottom rocker and vee plus the long slant of the bow transom largely account for superior performance here, I am inclined to think.

This pram builds easily according to the method devised for it, and it builds inexpensively, too. With the compartments under each of its three seats filled with Styrofoam, it is unsinkable, and no matter how long it lies hauled out in the hot sun it will not leak a drop.

The basic material is exterior fir plywood in ¼-inch and ⅜-inch thicknesses. The boat is glued throughout with epoxy resin, and its seams are reinforced with 3-inch fiberglass tape set in epoxy. The lengthwise reinforcing pieces, namely the inner keel strip or keelson, the chine strips, the risers, and the gunwales, are spruce, as are the beams and framing for the plywood seats. Spruce is used for the strips that frame the edges of the bow and stern transoms and those around the three interior plywood bulkheads, which serve both as building molds and fronts for the underseat compartments and as athwartship reinforcement for the boat. The skeg is likewise spruce, along with the four, long, outside bottom strips and the short, interior cross floors and stiffeners for the bottom. In short, all the wood in the boat other than the fir plywood is spruce got out of rough ⅞-inch Nova Scotia spruce ledger boards bought from a local lumber yard.

Spruce ledger boards used for building stagings are tough, light, and strong. They are moderately priced, going for a fraction of what Sitka spruce would cost. Yet by picking out good boards and getting a couple of extra ones, and in using care in splitting them on the circular saw, it is possible to dodge the knots, getting

STATIONS		S.T.	5	4	3	2	1	B.T.
HEIGHTS	Bottom	0-5-7	0-5-0	0-3-6	0-3-2	0-3-7	0-7-0	0-8-2
	Chine	0-10-2	0-9-4	0-8-5	0-8-2	0-8-7	0-10-6	1-0-0
	Sheer	1-8-5	1-8-4	1-8-3	1-8-6	1-9-2	1-10-6	2-0-6
HALF-BREADTHS	Chine	1-7-6	1-9-0	1-10-4	1-10-4	1-8-0	1-2-5	0-11-7
	Sheer	1-11-6	2-1-4	2-3-3	2-3-4	2-1-2	1-9-2	1-3-0

PRAM 9'-5" × 4'-7" × 1'-5½"

DIMENSIONS TO INSIDE PLANK – FEET, INCHES & EIGHTHS

clear wood throughout for the necessary strips. Although the boards I selected had been piled in the open, they were dry and thoroughly seasoned. Air-cured Eastern spruce like this is tough, glues well, and holds fastenings well. Wet, unseasoned stock should not be considered.

This boat is glued together with epoxy resin wherever wood meets wood. For the greater part, two-penny galvanized wire lath nails can be used to tack the joints in place and also to add mechanical reinforcement. Small screws might be used, but these will cost more and take longer to put in. Screws are employed only where special reinforcement is required, as for holding on the bottom strips and for fastening through the inner cross floors into the first of the outside bottom longitudinals. Screws are also used to tie the keelson and chines to the bulkheads and to reinforce the ends of the four laminated knees bracing the center thwart.

All outside plywood joints butting on the keelson, chines, and ends are bound with two layers of 3-inch fiberglass tape set in epoxy resin. This covering protects the plywood edges, ensures that the seams are perfectly and permanently tight, and binds the seams together with much additional reinforcement. Strips of fiberglass tape and epoxy are also used inside and out to bind and reinforce the corners where the ends of the sheer meet the stern and bow transoms. These tape strips are lighter and less bulky than the conventional wooden knees commonly used for reinforcement here.

One of the distinctive things about this pram is the easy method devised for setting it up for building. Two straight 10-foot 2 by 4s are laid level and parallel on horses and cleated together securely so that their inner edges are exactly 22 inches apart. The several stations shown in the plan are marked on them and squared across from side to side.

The end transoms are got out of ⅜-inch exterior fir plywood according to the dimensions furnished, and their edges are framed with glued spruce strips. Beveling may be postponed until after the boat is set up for planking. The three interior ¼-inch plywood bulkheads are cut out and prepared with spruce strips glued around their edges. Also made up are the two temporary molds that remain at stations 2 and 4 until the bottom and sides are on.

There are seven sub-assemblies in all; on each of them a pair of legs made from strapping or other strips of board is fastened parallel and equidistant to the centerline of the boat as marked on these molds and bulkheads, exactly 22 inches apart from outside to outside. These legs or posts are intended to fit between the horizontal 2 by 4s. Each pair is marked, according to the plan, so that the bulkheads, transoms, and molds will be located at the correct distance from the given baseline. When these marks are positioned to correspond with the top edge of the 2 by 4s, the sub-assemblies will be set at the correct height, and the legs can be clamped to the horizontal form or temporarily nailed. After the keel strip, the chines, and the risers are notched in and fastened, final adjustment may be made by moving the legs slightly up or down, if necessary, to remove any minor unfairness that might show up at this stage. Then the final fairing and beveling for the plywood bottom and sides is completed.

When the forms show fair throughout, with the keel strip, chines, and risers serving as longitudinal ribbands, the adjusted set-up is securely nailed and braced. All bevels should be checked and touched here and there with the plane if needed. Quite a bit of exacting beveling is required around the edges of the bow transom.

The bottom, in two pieces, is put on first. This is ¼-inch exterior fir, and a 4-foot by 8-foot sheet will suffice for the two panels. These must

be carefully fitted down their inner edges, which take a slight curve due to the rocker of the bottom. It doesn't matter if the outside edges of the two bottom halves project slightly beyond the chines; the excess is easily planed off after the bottom panels are glued and fastened in place. They will have to be faired to the correct bevels whether they project beyond the chines or not.

The side panels are put on next. They may be slightly larger for planing to exact shape after they are fastened and glued in place. One-piece sides require a 10-foot sheet of plywood, but they can be spliced up from shorter stock with an ordinary glued, tapered scarph, as I did on my own pram. Not much is saved, however, since the 10-foot sheet will yield besides the sides, enough extra plywood for the bulkheads and seats.

When the bottom and sides are on, the four lengthwise bottom strips may be glued and screwed on outside. These four strips running the whole length of the bottom are a distinctive and important special feature of this pram. They are needed to stiffen and to protect the wide, light bottom of ¼-inch plywood, and they help greatly in preventing the boat from slipping sideways in the water.

This is a good time to put on the bindings of fiberglass tape; installing the skeg should be left until later. The outside gunwales are not put on until the boat is turned over.

When the boat is turned over, most of the bracing and false work can be discarded, as can be the two temporary molds at stations 2 and 4. Then put in the low cross floors on either side of the bulkhead at station 3. These slight cross

(Left) The building jig completed and set up on horses. (Right) The chine and keelson in place. Note the temporary legs extending down from the frame and fastened to the 2 x 4 building jig.

Side plank going on. Note the splice in the plywood near the bow.

The boat has been turned over after the seams were taped. The risers are being installed.

The seats are almost completed. Note the Styrofoam in the compartment under the middle seat, which has yet to be fastened in place.

The completed pram.

floors add little weight, but strengthen and stiffen the thin plywood bottom wonderfully. They screw fasten into the keelson, through the bottom, into the first pair of outside longitudinal rub strips. Like all parts of the boat, the cross floors are glued with epoxy. Limbers next to the keel strips must not be forgotten. On top of the cross floors two strips of ¼-inch plywood are nailed; they should be narrow, but wide

enough to step on. Most of the stepping inside the boat can be done on these two strips.

The ¼-inch plywood bulkheads extending as high as the riser at stations 3 and 5 serve as foundations for the end seats and make compartments for Styrofoam flotation. Sufficient light spruce beams and cleats are put in to stiffen the thin plywood seats for sitting. Cleats are glued to the ends and the seats are screwed and glued to them and the risers, so the seats firmly brace the ends of the boat.

The middle seat, 11 inches in width, is strengthened with reinforcing strips underneath and tied to the sides of the boat at each of its four corners with knees laminated from thin spruce strips glued with epoxy. These four knees fasten securely with glue and screws to the sides and the gunwales, and to the thwart beams and the bulkhead underneath. The resulting structure forms a light but very strong and rigid truss at the center of the boat. In addition to the bulkheads and transoms at the ends, this framing makes a tremendously strong hull that would not smash or let go if dropped from a considerable height into the water. The space under the 11-inch middle seat is also packed with Styrofoam, having a capacity of at least three cubic feet.

Rowing is done from the middle seat facing the stern and pulling the oars in the usual way, or one may face the bow and push the oars from the stern sheets facing forward. The short cross floors, set 4 inches on centers in the bottom and tied together with their plywood strips, give good bracing for the oarsman's feet in all positions of rowing.

Rowlocks are located about 12 inches from either edge of the center seat on small pads glued to the inside of the plywood topsides and screwed through into the outside gunwale.

A novel feature to save weight is a number of ⅞-inch holes, in lieu of cleats and rings, which pierce the topsides just below the gunwales and through the stern and bow transoms close to the corners and just below the inside reinforcement of flat spruce the width of the outside gunwales. A special feature of these holes is to provide for lashing the boat to its cartop carriers. To strengthen the wood around these lashing holes and keep lines from wearing the plywood surface inside and outside, the edges of the holes are covered for a few inches on either side with epoxy and fiberglass.

Before any paint goes on the plywood and the spruce, the boat should be thoroughly soaked inside and out with a good wood preservative; it should also receive a coat of thinned and heated linseed oil if there is time for it to dry thoroughly. Oils will not harm the epoxy glue once it has set. It is of great importance to seal the wood, not only to forestall rot, but also to keep the boat from adding weight by taking up water, which will occur even though the edges of the plywood are all bound and sealed with epoxy and fiberglass. The preliminary oil treatment cannot be used if epoxy paint is to be put on later. When it comes down to hard choices like that, I'd rather forego the epoxy paint for a good preliminary treatment of oil-based wood preservative, followed by good, standard, oil paint.

4

A Sailing Flattie

As a sop to the traditionalists, let me point out at the beginning that the sailing flattie is an antique boat; that is, it is a modernized adaptation of an antique boat or type, and if there should be muttering in the background of less complimentary term, may I add that the old order changeth, and not always for the worse.

What is an antique boat? According to ground rules laid down several years ago by the Thousand Islands Antique Boat Show, it must have been built before 1930. Well, this flattie goes back to the 1890s and before. The lines and principal dimensions follow closely those of a racing flattie published by Charles G. Davis in *Rudder* in November, 1895, although the construction, rig, and sail plan are quite different. Davis mentions that his starting point in making up the design was a class of racing flatties on New York Bay at that time with a limit on the waterline length of 14 feet, which he thought was a good size.

Rudder magazine at the time had just completed its first five years of successful publication under its able editor and founder, Thomas Fleming Day, who inaugurated a pioneering department for amateur builders, titled "Designing" and presided over by Charles G. Davis. Davis, who was 25 years old at the time, had done considerable sailing in flatties. He had cruised in one with his brother, and had raced in them under conditions where crews of

three or four men were required to keep them on their feet. In introducing flatties to *Rudder*'s following of amateur builders in 1895, Davis made the following assertion: "For fifty dollars any man or boy can build a good, serviceable, flat-bottomed sloop, capable of carrying three or four men, and able if built to a proper shape to stand as heavy weather as anyone would care to be out in."

Davis's 14-foot flattie has a gaff and bowsprit. "Her rig," he explained, "is large, 238 square feet, 'but you can't fly unless you have wings,' and they are about as large wings as you can handle on such a boat, and then you want three or four fellows to hang out to windward for you." Should this sort of sailing appeal to you, I suggest you go back to Davis's original design. But for the less strenuous and chancy sailing, I have brought the rig entirely inboard with a sail area just under 100 square feet, which should be ample, although not excessive for a hard-chined boat with a waterline length of 14 feet and a beam of 5 feet.

The rig shown, however, is only one of a number of possibilities for this boat and is offered somewhat tentatively for consideration and experimentation. On a boat of this size it is not easy to tell how a rig will balance until it has been tried out. There are a lot of variables involved and no precise formulas for engineering this ahead of time. Some guesswork is involved,

and even educated guesswork is still guesswork. Consequently, I do not presume to guarantee that the rig as shown will prove entirely satisfactory without adjustment. Only trial on the water can give the final word.

The hull construction, on the other hand, is a different matter. This we can fully guarantee ahead of time, and, if directions are faithfully followed, a sturdy craft will result that is serviceable and tight. The weatherly qualities of a hull of this sort and its ability to carry sail hardly need extended comment. Flatties were a well known and proven type long before Davis's time. It is sufficient to say that when it gets too rough for a boat of this kind with a capable sailor at the helm, it is time to come in anyway. Naturally they are neither intended, nor offered, for crossing the Atlantic.

In choosing this particular boat, we were governed by a number of considerations. A lot of interest has been shown of late in small, easily built sailboats. To meet this demand, we at first cast about for a boat that could be both sailed and rowed, but these are distinctly different functions that do not combine with optimum effectiveness as a rule, although there are exceptions, like the St. Lawrence River skiff. But as particular interest seemed to be manifested in sail, we decided for this once to confine our efforts to sail.

General requirements decided upon went somewhat as follows:

1. Safe and seaworthy within reasonable limits for size and type.

2. Good performance under sail—while not the fastest boat on the bay, not the slowest either.

3. Sturdy, rugged, and able to take it, yet

STATIONS		1	2	3	4	5	6	7	8	9	TRAN
HEIGHTS	SHEER	2-4-2	2-2-6	2-1-4	2-0-5	2-0-0	1-11-7	1-11-4	1-11-7	2-0-5	2-2-0
	CHINE	0-10-3	0-8-6	0-7-4	0-6-6	0-6-1	0-6-6	0-7-0	0-9-2	0-11-5	1-2-0
	BOTTOM	0-10-0	0-7-7	0-6-3	0-5-4	0-5-0	0-5-3	0-6-5	0-8-0	0-10-4	1-1-0
WIDTHS	SHEER	0-7-3	1-2-4	1-8-5	2-1-2	2-4-4	2-6-1	2-6-1	2-5-0	2-2-4	1-11-5
	BOTTOM	0-3-0	0-10-3	1-4-7	1-9-5	2-0-7	2-2-4	2-2-5	2-1-4	1-11-1	1-8-4

MEASUREMENTS: INSIDE PLANK AND BOTTOM. OUTSIDE TRANSOM AND INNER STEM.

not too heavily built.

4. Pleasing appearance—must not look like a box or a tub.

5. Easy and inexpensive to build. This means, among other things, that materials should be standard and readily obtainable, and that no costly or unusual tools or building equipment should be required.

MATERIALS

Davis, in introducing his design, emphasized the necessity for light construction, that is, for not loading up the hull with unnecessary wood. For the two sides he recommended getting a white pine plank 18 inches wide, 1¼ inches thick, and 16 feet long. This was to be ripped into two boards to be dressed down to a finished thickness of ½ inch. The bottom, with the exception of an oak center plank ⅝ inch thick, was to be of ½-inch pine like the sides. Today,

select white pine of these dimensions would be prohibitively expensive, if it could be found. Fortunately there is an excellent substitute at hand, namely ⅜-inch fir plywood. It is a standard material, obtainable everywhere, and not expensive as compared with other materials today.

Fir plywood has several definite advantages over pine. It will not rent or split in wide widths, as sides made of single widths of pine boards are apt to do, and it ensures that there will not be any bottom seams to caulk or to open when the boat dries out. Plywood ⅜ inch thick is also somewhat lighter than pine ½ inch thick.

The two sides, the bottom and the foredeck can be got out of four standard 4-foot by 8-foot sheets, provided the half lengths are joined with glued splices or scarfs. Such splices are easily made. All that is required in the way of tools is a sharp, low-angle block plane. Glued splices in plywood are not difficult, except that they must be carefully done. (See the Appendix for specific instructions.) Success in building this boat will depend more upon painstaking attention to construction details than upon special woodworking skill.

Two additional 4-foot by 8-foot sheets of ⅜-inch plywood should more than suffice for gluing up the centerboard, rudder, and for the short afterdeck and the waterways, so the plywood inventory adds up to six 4-foot by 8-foot sheets in all. If need be, everything else can be got out of ordinary Douglas fir construction lumber, selected to obtain material as free from knots as possible. Standard sizes 2 inches and 4 inches thick can be stripped on the circular saw and glued without further smoothing just as they leave the saw. Chines and inwales can be built up by gluing together several thinner strips. Properly done, the result is stronger and stiffer than a single sawn strip.

For these reasons, it is desirable, if not almost essential, to have the use of a power circular saw in building this flattie. The boat could be built entirely with hand tools, but it would be harder to do and would take longer.

The inside keel batten, or keelson, as some might term it, is shown as 5 feet wide and 1 inch thick. This runs the length of the bottom and takes a considerable amount of curve. It would bend easier if glued together in place from two ½-inch layers, and the result would be both stiffer and stronger.

Deck beams should be laminated by gluing thin strips of spruce. For these, spruce staging boards or planks can often be found free or nearly free of knots. These come unplaned, but no planer is required to work them up for the boat, as a sharp saw blade will size them and smooth them enough for gluing.

If oak is available it can be used to advantage for the outer stem piece, for the fore and aft skegs, the outside rudder post and even for the keel batten. But oak is not required, and good quality Douglas fir will do nicely.

Material for the spars, as well as how to make them is covered later.

About fastenings: This boat is literally held together by glue, specifically epoxy glue. The metal fastenings are secondary, and in a number of places serve only to hold wooden members in position until the glue has hardened. With the glue now available, we can do things with wood today undreamed of when Charles G. Davis worked up his original design. For those uninformed about epoxy glue, and who want a detailed explanation plus a list of supply sources, I recommend the reprint of *National Fisherman* articles on this subject, *The Use Of Plastics In Boatbuilding*, which is available from International Marine Publishing Company, 21 Elm Street, Camden, Maine; the price is $3.00.

In building this flattie, it is recommended that all plywood edges which otherwise might be exposed be covered with epoxy-bonded polypropylene or fiberglass tape, and that the centerboard and the rudder blade, both of plywood, should be sheathed with epoxy-bonded Versatex PP fabric or fiberglass. Complete directions for a covering job of this sort can be found on the last page of *The Use of Plastics in Boatbuilding*.

BUILDING PROCEDURE

It is imperative to follow the correct building procedure or order of operations. This is as follows:

The boat is started upside down using the ladder-frame method of setting up. The 9-foot 6-inch plywood pram, whose construction is explained in Chapter 3, is built by this method. The ladder frame, made of two straight two-by-fours with spacers nailed across, serves as a base to locate and secure the building molds in position and at the correct height. Three molds plus the transom are sufficient for this boat. The molds are notched to take the keel batten, the chines, and the inwale strips or clamps.

It is not necessary to rabbet the stem, an operation that more often than not gives the novice trouble. The two-piece stem as shown in the drawing is just as strong, just as tight, and much easier to do than a one-piece stem. In this boat the inner stem piece is given the same bevel throughout and is attached to the keel batten by the stem knee with screws, but without any glue at first.

SECTION THRU TRANSOM

RUDDER

The plywood sides are then fastened to the inner stem both with glue and screws. The sides do not have to fit exactly, that is, they can project slightly, for after fastening, their outer ends will be faired with a sharp block plane to receive the outer stem piece, which can be prepared ahead of time at the bench. The outer stem is put on with glue and fastened with screws through the inner stem piece from the inside. To get screws through the bottom end, the stem knee must be temporarily removed, to be put back permanently afterwards with a liberal application of glue and the original screws. Before the hull is removed from the molds and ladder frame and turned right-side up, the fore and after skegs and outside stern post should be fitted and fastened. These can be only partly fastened from the bottom or outside of the boat. Fastening is completed as soon as the boat is removed from the molds and the ladder frame and turned right-side up to finish.

The frames, floors, and deck beams are fitted and glued in place with some nails and screws to reinforce the glue and to hold the various members in place until the glue has hardened. Pieces of board glued to the plywood sides of the boat and under the inwale stringer or clamp hold the chainplates, which are put on from the inside before the boat is decked; they extend through the deck. The mast step is nailed and glued to the inside keel batten or keelson. The ⅜-inch fir plywood deck is installed, and the fore-and-aft mast partners are fitted between the deck beams and glued to the underside of the deck.

The centerboard case (or trunk) and the centerboard are made up as a completed assembly apart from the boat, with bed logs carefully shaped to fit the curve of the keel batten where they are to go. Before the case is assembled, each bed log is set in place on top of the keel batten to test the fit and, if need be, planed until there is a touching fit throughout. When the centerboard case is assembled, the end posts are left long enough so that they will project through the bottom of the boat an inch or so when the case is bolted on. Later they are sawn off flush with the bottom. The sides of the case should be glued to the posts and through-riveted, if rivets are available, otherwise well screwed. The ends of the bed logs should be glued to the posts and through-bolted with two 5/16-inch bolts in each end.

The centerboard slot is not cut through the bottom until the case is made. The slot should be mortised carefully so the two end posts push through with a snug fit. It is best to locate and bore the bolt holes through the bed logs at the bench when the case is out of the boat. Then when the case is back in the boat and hauled down tight with a couple of door clamps through the slot, or some other clamping arrangement, the bolt holes are completed through the keel batten and bottom.

The bolts, which should fit their holes snugly, but not too tightly, are driven up from the bottom, but before this is done the logs are bedded in a generous application of thick glue.

Three-eighths-inch galvanized carriage bolts are used. The bottom plywood is countersunk just enough so that the bolt heads will be just below flush when the bolts have been set up tightly. These countersunk holes should not be deep enough to penetrate the keel batten. It will be noted that as the sided thickness of the bed logs is 2¼ inches, they will project 5/16 inches over the edge of the keel batten, which is 1 15/16 inches wide on either side of the 1⅛-inch centerboard slot. The bolts should be gradually tightened in turn until there is a firm, even strain on them all and their heads are pulled in just under flush, so they can be smoothed over with a plastic surfacer and painted.

MAKING THE SPARS

If fairly knot-free spruce ledger boards can be found at the local lumberyard to make the mast and boom, this is the material to use;

otherwise it should be clear Douglas fir stripped to size from a seasoned floor joist, four-by-four, or other similar piece of timber. Good quality fir is- excellent for spars, except that it is heavier than spruce.

It is not likely that a stick will be found that is long enough to get out the strips for the mast in one length, nor is it easy to handle timber of this length on the saw. It is perfectly admissible to splice the strips which form the mast, provided the scarphed joints are well separated.

The construction of the boom is so simple that it is perfectly obvious from the drawing. The procedure for assembling the mast is not involved, but needs to be briefly outlined. A pair of the A strips and a pair of the B strips (see drawing) are first got out on the circular saw. They will probably have to be spliced to get sufficient length; after the glue has set they are sized on the circular saw and dressed with a bench plane if necessary. The taper on their upper ends is put on at the bench with a hand plane. Then strip B is located on strip A, and the two are glued together. Small brads through B into A hold the two in position and together while the glue is setting. In the meantime, the seven solid-core blocks are made up from ¾-inch dry soft wood and glued together, but with a hole through the middle of each so there will be a passage for air to circulate inside the hollow mast after it is glued up. As soon as the center blocks are in and glued in place, the plywood sides can be fitted into place and glued. The brads shown in the drawing contribute some strength, but are mainly used to pull the D strips into place and hold them until the glue hardens.

If at all possible, a gluing jig should be set up on the floor or other suitable place to keep the mast straight while it is being assembled. A chalk line is snapped to give a straight line on which a series of blocks are set and temporarily nailed in place. These are used to clamp to or to brace against. The after side of the mast, which is perfectly straight the entire way, can be lined up and held against the row of blocks until the glue hardens. Otherwise the mast is likely to have kinks in it. Finally, the mast is lightly smoothed on all four sides, the corners rounded, the whole sanded, and then the various required fittings are installed.

Rigging details are straightforward and need not be elaborated on here. These can be closely similar to those for the 15-foot trailer sloop *Titmouse*, which can be found fully detailed starting on page 152 in S. S. Rabl's *Boat Building In Your Own Backyard*, Cornell Maritime Press, Cambridge, Maryland.

NUMBERED REFERENCES

1. Mast step. 1″ fir nailed and glued to the keel batten.

2. Coaming piece. Covers after end of the fore decking and braces the centerboard trunk. Notched over the trunk capping and screwed to cleat behind. Nailed and glued to deck beam.

3. Cleat. ¾″ fir or pine.

4. Side decking. ⅜″ fir plywood.

5. Side deck gusset. ⅜″ fir plywood glued and nailed to frame and deck beam.

6. Side deck carling. 2″ x ¾″ fir or pine.

7. Coaming. 3½″ x ⅝″ fir or pine.

8. Side frames. ¾″ fir, tapers from ¾″ molded width at top to 1½″ molded width at bottom end.

9. Floors. ¾″ fir sided thickness. Maximum molded depth 2½″, notched to fit over 1″ thick fir keel batten with limbers either side. Molded depth at outboard ends 1½″.

10. Keel batten. 1″ x 5″ fir.

11. Deck beams. Laminated from glued strips of spruce or fir. Sided thickness ¾″. Molded depth 1¼″.

12. Fore skeg. 1″ fir or oak, tapered to ¾″ at bottom edge. See drawing detail.

13. After skeg. 1″ fir or oak tapered to ¾″ at the bottom edge. Glued to bottom, spiked through keel batten from inside. Screwed from outside into keel batten where width permits. After end braced and secured by outside sternpost. Bore for spikes.

14. Sternpost. 1¾″ fir or oak. Molded 2¼″ at lower end, 1″ upper end. Glued and screwed to transom. Spiked and glued to skeg. Bore for spikes.

15. Transom framing. ¾″ fir to brace ⅜″ fir plywood.

16. Stern knee. Fir or oak sided 1½″.

17. Cap, centerboard case. ¾″ fir or pine.

18. Bed logs, centerboard case. Fir or pine, 2¼″ sided thickness. Maximum molded depth, 4″.

19. Bed log bolts. ⅜″ galvanized carriage bolts set on 8″ centers.

20. Knees. Fir or oak sided thickness 1¼″. Secure ends of floors to bed logs. Glued, nailed and/or screwed in place.

21. End posts, centerboard case. 1¼″ x 2½″ fir.

22. Lead weight in centerboard.

23. Centerboard. ¾″ thick glued up from two thicknesses of ⅜″ fir plywood. Recess for sheet lead cut before the two halves are put together. For best results, sheath with polypropylene fabric, Dynel, or fiberglass.

24. Rudder. Made the same as centerboard.

25. Rudder cheek pieces. Glued and through-fastened with copper rivets.

5

A Chamberlain Skiff

................•................

This 14-foot skiff is offered as one possibility to be considered in the selection of a general-purpose rowboat, one which will row easily and be a good sea boat, as well, within the limits of its size. It is a proven model, being a slightly altered and enlarged version of the 13-foot 6-inch dory skiff designed and formerly built in the early decades of this century by William Chamberlain of Marblehead.

From the load line as drawn in the lines plan, the depth of draft, including the thickness of the bottom, is 6¾ inches, and displacement at this depth is approximately 9 cubic feet, or something like 560 pounds. After allowing 150 pounds for the weight of the ⅜-inch marine fir plywood hull, the remaining displacement would be about equivalent to the combined weight of three medium-size persons. With this loading, the bottom of the transom would barely touch the water. There would be no stern drag. The entrance is fairly sharp—the additional 6 inches at the bow helped this—and with its somewhat narrow bottom and relatively steep deadrise in the sides, this hull is bound to row easily.

Because of the characteristics just noted, this boat's initial stability will prove somewhat tender, so that a landlubber stepping into her carelessly when she is light might get a start. Yet this is a stable hull where stability counts, and because of her ample side flare, beam, and length, a fair size boy could sit on her rail without putting it under.

In spite of its flat bottom, which of course is relatively quite narrow, this dory skiff has virtually a round hull, and for all practical purposes behaves as a round-bottomed boat. Indeed, this skiff closely resembles the old-time New England wherry, which was a fine sea boat. It is worth mentioning that this skiff fitted with a centerboard and a proper rig would sail smartly, but she is unsuited for an outboard.

For the utility rowing skiff, two building options in wood are open. One is classic dory construction planked with clinker strakes of sawn boards. The other is to use plywood for planking. The plywood strakes may be butted on internal seam battens to which the strakes are both glued and screwed. When such a seam is covered on the outside with a tape of either glass or synthetic fiber and cemented with epoxy thermoplastic, the result is both extremely strong and permanently watertight.

For this particular boat an alternate method for plywood is shown which omits the internal wooden seam batten, yet gives a construction that is adequately strong and watertight as well. This is a substantial simplification of building procedure. Sometimes inexperienced builders have difficulty with seam battens. They frequently find notching the battens into the frames as well as beveling the battens between frames to be a taxing and tedious operation. Besides, seam battens add nothing to the finished appearance of the boat, and frequently

OFFSETS — 14 FT. SKIFF							
STATIONS	STEM	1A	1	2	3	3B.	TRAN.
HEIGHTS SHEER	2-1-0	1-8-7	1-7-0	1-4-6	1-5-4	1-6-4	1-8-4
1st KNUCKLE	1-10-0	1-4-6	1-2-3	0-11-5	1-0-4	1-2-1	1-4-2
2nd KNUCKLE	1-6-4	1-1-2	0-10-4	0-7-4	0-8-4	0-10-4	1-1-0
INSIDE BOTTOM	0-3-0	0-2-2	0-1-1	0-0-0	0-1-1	0-3-0	0-5-4
HALF-BREADTHS SHEER	0-0-0	1-1-4	1-7-2	2-0-6	1-11-2	1-8-0	1-2-0
1st KNUCKLE	0-0-0	1-0-5	1-5-7	1-11-2	1-9-6	1-6-6	1-1-7
2nd KNUCKLE	0-0-0	0-10-4	1-3-6	1-8-2	1-7-0	1-4-0	0-11-6
INSIDE BOTTOM	0-0-0	0-2-4	0-5-4	0-9-3	0-7-4	0-4-4	0-1-0

LINES TO INSIDE PLANK, INSIDE BOTTOM, OUTSIDE TRANSOM AND STEM.

appear crude and clumsy. Leaving them out of this boat, as can be done without structural impairment, is a real gain, I believe. However, should anyone still prefer to retain the seam battens, there is nothing to prevent him from doing so.

Length of planking is no problem; glued splices will provide planking of any length. A properly made, epoxy-glued splice is practically as strong as natural unbroken lumber. This is the case for either sawn boards or plywood. (For splicing techniques, see the Appendix.)

As you can see, the strength of the planking seams is dependent on binding and reinforcing the seams with tapes set in thermoplastic resin. Because the plywood does not swell and shrink to any extent, comparatively inflexible tapes of glass fiber will serve adequately. Fiberglass tapes are much easier to obtain and to apply than a binding of synthetic fibers, particularly polypropylene. If there were much movement of the underlying wood as occasioned by swelling and shrinking with changes in the moisture content, then a flexible synthetic like polypropylene would be required.

A 3-inch-wide glass tape will do nicely. For covering the chine, that is, where the bottom edge of the garboard is nailed to the bottom, a 4-inch-wide glass tape would be better. When seam battens are omitted, two layers of tape over the seams between the large frames on the inside of the boat will be required. The short

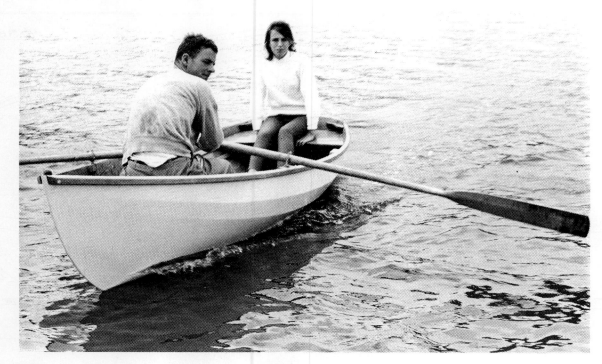

A 13½-foot Chamberlain skiff, similar to the one described here but slightly smaller. She was built of plywood and fiberglass.

SHEER BATTEN OAK ⅝" × 1½"
BATTEN TAPERS TO 1⅛" AT ENDS OF BOAT

CAPPING OAK 1" × 1⅞" TAPERED TO 1⅛" AT ENDS

PLANKING ⅜" MARINE PLYWOOD

1⅛"

INTERMEDIATE SHORT FRAMES
OAK-SIDED ½" MOLDED AS SHOWN
9 EACH SIDE - SPACING 1 FT.

SEAM BINDING: ONE 3" FIBERGLASS TAPE OUTSIDE. INSIDE - ONE 3" TAPE AND ONE 2" TAPE BUILT UP. TAPES SET IN EPOXY-VERSAMID.

1¼" #10 BRONZE W.S.

STANDARD DORY CONSTRUCTION

PLYWOOD PLANK ⅜" MARINE

1¾"

FRAMES OAK SIDED 13/16"

1½" PINE

STATION #2 AMIDSHIPS

OAK 13/16" × 2"

1¼" #10 BR. W.S.

⅞" PINE

BOTTOM KNUCKLE BOUND INSIDE AND OUT WITH 4" FIBERGLASS TAPE.

BOTTOM: TWO LAYERS ⅜" PLYWOOD SPRUNG TO CURVE OF BOTTOM ROCKER AND GLUED.

PROFILE CURVE 2×8 BOTTOM MOLD AND STRONGBACK

BOW

11' - 5"

BOTTOM: 2 LAYERS ⅜" PLYWOOD

2"×8" PLANK BOTTOM MOLD AND STRONGBACK

4½"

WAXED PAPER

WAXED PAPER

JIG FOR GLUING PLYWOOD SPLICE

SCARPH

4½"

8' - 0"

4' - 0"

GARBOARD SPLICED FROM TWO PIECES LAID OUT ON A 4×8 SHEET OF MARINE FIR PLYWOOD.

intermediate frames, extending down from the gunwales on the inside between the frames, go in after the interior tapes have been laid in place and saturated with epoxy adhesive. It is best to have these short intermediates fitted and bored for screws beforehand so that they can be put in and drawn tight with screws while the tapes over the seams are still wet.

There will be nine of these intermediate short frames on a side. They are to be spaced approximately on one-foot centers. Two will come aft of frame 3, two between frame 3 and frame 2, two between frame 2 and frame 1, and three forward of frame 1.

A siding of ½ inch will be ample for these intermediates, and they should not be made heavier because it is desirable to keep down weight. If they can be cut from oak with curved grain approximately the same as the curve of these members, they will be that much stronger, although actually these intermediates are fairly straight.

The three sets of main frames, which are located at stations 1, 2, and 3, are to be made of the best dry oak, of course, and are sided $^{13}/_{16}$ inch. For these, boards with curved grain would be highly desirable. It is of greatest importance to lay out the shape of the frames on the boards before cutting, taking care to get as little cross grain as possible; that is, the pattern should be placed so that the grain of the boards runs lengthwise on it and not crosswise, or at least with as little crosswise grain as possible. It will pay to go to some trouble in this respect not only in laying out the frames, but also in obtaining crooked boards to begin with. Boards for this purpose should not be straight-edged, but rather live-edged or flitch sawn, that is, sawn with the bark remaining on the edges.

The main frames can be made up like standard dory frames with metal clips through-riveted at the bottom knuckle to hold the side futtock to the bottom cross piece. For the plywood boat, a somewhat different arrangement is shown which might prove easier; if this is used, the limber for letting the water drain would not come in the bottom knuckle as is usual, but rather would be cut midway in the piece across the bottom.

The bottom could be made in the usual way of pine boards ⅞ inch thick and run lengthwise. Two or more boards would be required, and the seam or seams between would have to be caulked, and would open when the boat dried out. Besides, the rocker of the bottom is considerable aft, perhaps requiring more of a bend than the pine would take without steaming.

Rather than suggest pine boards for the bottom, I am going to suggest plywood, a double thickness, glued together of the same ⅜-inch plywood used for planking the sides. Both layers, top and bottom, will have to be spliced, and the splices in the two layers positioned so as not to come together. Plywood ⅜ inch thick will bend easily, and when two layers are bent over a form and glued, they will hold their curve after the glue has set. Here, the

gluing form will be the same strongback shaped from a 2-inch by 8-inch plank that will support the boat in an upside-down position while it is being planked. With care, both the bottom and the side plank for this boat can probably be got out of three 4-foot by 8-foot sheets. Of course, numerous splices will be required, which will take time. This would be expensive for the boatshop, but for the home builder who does not figure his time, splicing can mean real economy.

A few words about fastenings: Bronze screws are strong, lasting, pull up tightly, and generally are a pleasure to use, but they are very expensive. Nails can be substituted. Some of the modern annular nails (Anchorfast is one trade name) of bronze or monel have great holding power in dry oak. Galvanized nails also can be used, except that suitable galvanized nails are getting difficult to obtain.

If a plywood bottom is used, the garboards should be glued to the bottom as well as nailed. If this bottom knuckle is covered inside and out with a reinforcement of epoxy-bonded fiberglass tape, the garboard can be nailed to the bottom with eight-penny galvanized wire nails spaced 2½ inches to 3 inches apart. This will make a very strong job. It hardly needs saying that the nails are put in before the tapes are glued on.

If the sides are planked with plywood, there

is good reason for making the transom of plywood also, as is shown here. Three-eighths-thick
plywood is specified and is adequate, but some
might want to use ½-inch plywood instead.

The lines show the outside of the transom,
so that when the transom is laid out, extra
wood must be left for beveling. This also applies, of course, to the reinforcing strip or
frame which extends around the inside of the
transom to receive the fastenings for the ends
of the planking, and allowance must be made for
beveling here as well. This inner strip should be a
hard wood like oak or mahogany.

In a transom set on as much of a rake as is
found in the Chamberlain skiff, getting the
transom bevels can be a fairly tricky operation
for one not accustomed to it. Those given in the
sketch should be fairly exact as they were taken
from an accurately made half model. Notice that
they are taken "square" with the edge of the
transom, and should be so applied when

beveling. Transom bevels should not be taken in
the direction that the planking runs on the sides
of the boat. Let the stock of the carpenter's
bevel be placed flat against the outer surface of
the transom and at an angle of 90 degrees with
that portion of the transom edge where the
bevel is being taken. This is the procedure used
when bevels are taken and when applied, and
only by this method can one be sure of the
results.

This transom is not intended for an outboard motor; if it were, heavier internal bracing
would have been shown. However, additional
bracing, not indicated in the sketch, will be
obtained from the stern bench, which extends
aft to fit tightly against the transom. The bench
rests upon, and is fastened to, a cleat extending
across the inner face of the transom, and is glued
and screwed to it like the strips around the edges
of the transom. This arrangement adds greatly to
the structural rigidity of the stern.

6

A Modified Quincy Skiff

...................•....................

This modified Quincy skiff should row well, but build easily and cheaply. This is not a racing shell, obviously, nor is it intended for the open sea. This simple skiff should do well on lakes, large rivers, and sheltered waters along the coast. For someone interested in rowing for exercise, but only to the extent of committing a modest investment for this purpose, the Quincy skiff has much to offer.

Because of the length of the Quincy skiff, two can row together without crowding, as is not the case with most shorter boats, yet one person can handle the 18-foot version of this skiff by himself, without difficulty. The original Quincy was a rowing workboat capable of carrying heavy loads, but so lined as to move easily through the water either in a light or loaded condition. Her fine entrance and long, slim underbody offer a minimum of resistance. At the same time, her great amount of side flare picks up displacement fast, so even with heavy loads she does not become logy or drag water. It has been said that the old lumbermen's Quincys could take a thousand pounds of rafting chain in their stern sheets without settling unduly.

I judge that the Quincy skiff would show best with a moderate load, but that she might prove somewhat quick or "tiddly" in a light condition with only one occupant—not to an extent to give trouble, but requiring some attention to trim, nonetheless. While I have never

been in a Quincy, I base my surmise on the performance of the Quincy's eastern cousin, the bateau of the Maine lumberman, a craft with which I am quite familiar. These two boats have a great deal in common, but especially notable is their extreme, and nearly identical, amount of side flare, considerably more than is found in any other member of the dory family either in America or abroad.

There can be no doubt that the Quincy is a derivation of the bateau devised for western rivers and large lakes by New England watermen when lumbering moved westward during the nineteenth century. The form is definitely a modified bateau, except that the high, sharp, raking ends needed for shooting the roaring pitches of rapid eastern rivers, the Penobscot in particular, have been changed.

In construction the Quincy and the lumberman's bateau are basically identical, with sides and bottoms planked fore-and-aft with white pine boards on oak frames, preferably cut from natural root or limb crooks. But in appearance the basic similarity of these two boats is considerably disguised by the Quincy's plumb, rabbeted stem and cut-off, transom stern, features more normal in a general-purpose workboat not required to run the violent, rocky rapids of the eastern rivers.

Our knowledge of the classic Quincy skiff is derived from a plan by Allen D. Woods, N.A.,

18' QUINCY SKIFF

OFFSETS — INSIDE PLANKING and BOTTOM								
STATIONS		STEM	1	2	3	4	TRAN.
HEIGHTHS	SHEER	2-3-4	1-11-0	1-5-6	1-4-5	1-6-2	1-10-1
	BOTTOM	0-7-4	0-7-1	0-5-2	0-4-0	0-4-2	0-8-6
HALF-BREADTHS	SHEER	0-0-4	1-0-3	1-10-1	1-11-3	1-10-3	1-8-2
	BOTTOM	0-0-4	0-2-6	0-8-5	0-9-1	0-4-6	0-2-2

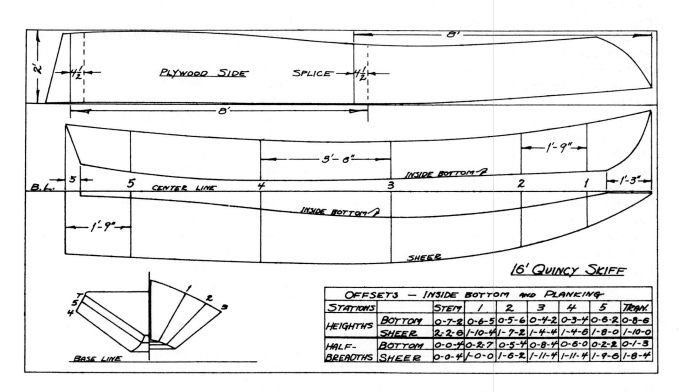

16' QUINCY SKIFF

OFFSETS — INSIDE BOTTOM and PLANKING								
STATIONS		STEM	1	2	3	4	5	TRAN.
HEIGHTHS	BOTTOM	0-7-2	0-6-5	0-5-6	0-4-2	0-3-4	0-6-2	0-8-6
	SHEER	2-2-6	1-10-4	1-7-2	1-4-4	1-4-6	1-8-0	1-10-0
HALF-BREADTHS	BOTTOM	0-0-4	0-2-7	0-5-4	0-8-4	0-6-0	0-2-2	0-1-3
	SHEER	0-0-4	1-0-0	1-6-2	1-11-4	1-11-4	1-9-6	1-8-4

who drew it from measurements made at Winona, Minnesota, in the summer of 1902 from a boat used in rafting operations on the upper reaches of the Mississippi River. I believe that the original plan or a copy of it is preserved at the Smithsonian Institution in Washington, D. C., from whence I obtained a blueprint copy a number of years ago. None of the original boats have survived to my knowledge.

The boat selected as typical by Woods was 18 feet long, and considering the boat's slim lines and comparatively shallow depth and light construction, this is not as big a boat as might appear, nor too large, I think, for one person to manage alone. Personally, I would favor the original 18-foot length. Nevertheless, I have also worked out a shortened version 16 feet long. Beam, depth, and other principal dimensions have not been changed. The shorter boat is not likely to row quite as well as the larger and possibly will prove slightly more tender, yet not enough to matter. It will prove a good boat and some may prefer it.

The original construction has much to commend it, but I shall not attempt to detail it here. I suggest that anyone interested take steps to obtain a print of Woods's drawing. If suitable materials were available, the experienced boatbuilder might want to follow the original plan. There is no doubt that the plumb, rabbeted stem adds considerably to the appearance. Ideally, this stem would require an oak or hackmatack knee and might tax the capability of the novice.

What I have attempted here is to simplify the building requirements, while retaining the lines and integrity of the original soundness of construction, so that the boat can be easily and inexpensively built with a minimum of specialized skill from stock materials readily obtainable from any ordinary local retail lumberyard or building supply firm.

MATERIALS

With one exception, the fastenings called for are galvanized common nails. No special tools or equipment are required. In fact this boat can be built entirely with a few common hand tools, although a power circular saw can be used to advantage and would speed up the job.

All lumber specified is standard dimensioned stock of species widely used for building construction and repair. Anyone able to do ordinary house carpentry should be able to put together this modified Quincy skiff without too much sweat. For those unfamiliar with the standard lumber sizes, "one-inch" boards, so called, come from the surface planer approximately ¾ inch thick. It is frequently possible, however, to obtain unplaned spruce ledger boards, which are actually 1 inch thick, or close to it. These can be bought in 8-inch and 10-inch widths, and usually can be selected so as to be free from large knots or other serious defects. In most cases if the buyer asks to pick out his own boards, he will be permitted to do so, especially where terms are cash and carry. Spruce is both stiff and strong, and such spruce boards are not only excellent for bracing the ladder frame and for making the molds, but are the finest kind for the rowing thwarts. This spruce can also be used for the inwale strips, the gunwales, and the capping strips.

When made a part of the structure of the boat, rough spruce will require a light brushing with a sharp hand plane (jack or smoother), otherwise these boards can be used as they come. Spruce is not recommended for planking the bottom, as it does not last too well in places where the water gets at it. For thwarts and gunwales and the like, if kept well painted, there is less danger of rot, so that spruce would be quite acceptable there.

In different parts of the country, the softwood species available from lumberyards will vary considerably. For planking the bottom, either pine or Douglas fir boards, or both, will generally be available. Northern white pine is excellent for bottom planking and need not be clear (select grade) as it is tougher and stronger with some sound knots of moderate size. Besides, the clear or select stock carried for interior finish is far too expensive. The short pieces required for cross planking can be cut from No. 2 common grade so as to avoid any bad knots or other serious defects. Southern pine, either long-leaf or loblolly, is good, but relatively heavy, so that its use for bottom planking will mean a somewhat heavier boat. The pines used for interior finish, in particular ponderosa pine and sugar pine, are not suitable, as these species rot easily when exposed to the weather.

Other softwood species that can be used for bottom planking include white cedar, western red cedar, and Alaskan cedar. The first two, while rot resistant and lasting, are quite soft. Alaskan or Port Orford cedar is superior in all respects, but generally expensive and not readily obtainable except in the Pacific Northwest. Cypress, another superior species, might be obtainable in a few southern localities but unobtainable elsewhere.

Oak might be used to advantage for the gunwale cap and for the stem, especially if a curved piece could be found to make laminating unnecessary. Oak could even be used for the chines but might be rather heavy in the size indicated.

CONSTRUCTION

No full-size lay down of lines is required. The drawings give exact dimensions for the molds, although these could be taken from the lines printed herewith. The molds are placed upside-down on a ladder form made of two 2 x 4's cross-braced at the mold stations with 1-inch boards well-nailed with 10d nails and set on two horses at a convenient height for working. The molds are securely braced and fastened to the ladder frame.

Next, attention is given to the chine logs. For these, standard Douglas fir 2-inch joists are recommended; in actual thickness they are slightly more than 1½ inches. To make the full-length log for either side, an 8-foot section of 2-inch by 8-inch joist and a 12-foot section of 2-inch by 6-inch joist are glue-spliced together as shown in the drawing. After the glue has cured, this assembly is cut to the contour required by the molds and beveled to conform to the slope of the sides.

The beveling operation probably can best be done, or at least finished, with the chine logs securely in place on the molds. The fore-and-aft curve or rocker of the bottom is so gradual there will be no difficulty in springing the logs down into place. The two side logs fit together at both ends of the boat and are glued together in the same manner in which they are spliced. The glue joints should be reinforced by nailing with 3-inch and 4-inch galvanized wire nails, or staging nails as explained in the Appendix, but not so as to come in the way of the beveling.

After the chine logs are in place and beveled, the stem and the stern transoms are fastened in place. After they have been secured and well braced, their bevels are checked with a batten laid across the molds, and if necessary, they are faired with a sharp plane.

CHINE LOGS - 18' QUINCY SKIFF

FORE-AND-AFT CURVE OF BOTTOM

The stem, that is to say the inner stem, is a glued-up lamination assembled from four layers, two of ⅜-inch fir plywood on the inside, covered on the outside, either side, with a layer of pine, fir, or other softwood, ¾ inch thick. Gluing pressure is applied with C-clamps, as well as with 2½-inch staging nails, later removed. When the glued-up stem is later sawn to the shape as shown in the drawing, but before it is attached to the bottom, it can be used as a form for gluing the laminated outer stem, made of ⅛-inch thick strips, bent to shape on the form and clamped to it.

The stern transom is also a glued-up lamination, consisting of one layer of ⅜-inch plywood on the inside and boards ¾ inch thick outside, put on horizontally. The outer boards are glued to the plywood underneath and are edge-glued to each other as well. This forms a transom which is both strong and tight, yet easily made. The plywood reinforcement is covered on the inside of the boat, and the short grain at the bottom of the outer layer is reinforced against splitting.

The last operation before the sides go on is to install the inwale strips, to which the upper edges of the plywood sides will fasten with glue and short nails. The inwales are strips of fir, pine, or spruce, 2¼ inches by ¾ inch in section and running the length of the boat.

To get one continuous length from bow to stern, these strips will probably have to be glue spliced. In making such a splice, the tapered scarph should be 12 times the thickness of the strip, or 9 inches. The forward end of the inwale strip is beveled to fit against the side of the stem to which it is glued and nailed. The after end of the inwale strip, which is let into a blind recess in the side of the stern transom, is also glued and nailed in place.

Where the inwale strip lies in the notches cut for it in the ends of the molds, it is held by a spot of glue. Glue is applied at the underside where it meets the mold; be careful not to get any on the lower edge. A staging nail holds the strip down in place until the glue has set, after which the nail is drawn to permit the plywood side to go on. After the boat is planked and has been turned right side up, a fine saw run between the inwale strip and the mold will separate the latter so that it may be removed from the boat. The inwales installed in this manner stiffen the plywood sides and hold them in shape until the thwarts are put in and the gunwales and capping strips are added.

The sides are panels of ⅜-inch exterior fir plywood, good both sides. In no place are the plywood sides wider than 2 feet and for most of their length they are appreciably less, so that the standard 4-foot-wide plywood panels used for planking can be cut in two lengthwise. These pieces will have to be spliced in two places to make a continuous length sufficient to cover the side.

The side panels are fastened both with glue and nails to the chine logs, the transom, the stem, and the inwale strips. The only frames required are those which support the rowing thwarts, and these are installed after the boat is

planked and has been turned right side up. But before this is done, the outside is finished; that is, the bottom is planked and the outer stem and stem band, the skeg, the sternpost, and the outside keel strip are put on.

At either end the bottom is too narrow for cross planking. Short lengths of board with the grain running fore and aft are used here. For the 18-foot boat, the bow section will require a 2-foot by 11-inch board; the stern section needs a 4-foot by 11-inch board. In the central portion of the bottom, cross planking serves to tie the chine logs together. The combined result is an extremely strong bottom, which is by far the strongest part of the entire structure. Further, a considerable part of the total weight of this boat is in the bottom, which makes for stability.

The ends of the cross planking as well as the edges of the end planks are not beveled but are left square to cover and to protect the edges of the plywood side planking. Cross planking should be under 5″ wide to prevent cupping, and to minimize opening at the seams through shrinkage. If the chine logs are liberally coated either with white lead or a good flexible bedding compound before the bottom planking is put on, no caulking of the garboard seam will be required. Screws need only be used for fastening the bottom; they should be 1¾-inch No. 12 galvanized flat-head wood screws.

Additional reinforcement for the bottom is secured from an outside keel strip 4 inches wide which runs the length of the bottom. The after end is slotted to fit around the skeg—this helps to keep the skeg from twisting.

The skeg must be well fastened from the inside of the boat with a ⅜-inch drift pin driven through the lower end of the stern knee and the bed logs. In addition the skeg is pinned through the lower end of the sternpost, which is bolted through the transom and the stern knee, as well as being screwed to the transom.

Once the outside of the boat is completed, it can be turned over. Before the molds are removed, two temporary cross spalls bracing the inwales apart are fitted. These remain in place until the thwarts are in and the gunwales and the cappings are in place (see detailed drawing).

Before the capping strip goes on, the surface underneath should be thoroughly sealed with thick paint. The usual breasthook and stern quarter knees are also installed.

Rowlocks are centered 12 inches aft of the after edge of the rowing thwarts. If the cap is to be bored for thole pins, it should be given a little additional width in the center portion of the boat.

With the boat sitting upright before painting, and provided the bottom has been caulked tight, it would be a good idea to pour in a gallon of linseed oil thinned with a pint of turps, allowing the bottom to soak up as much as it will take. While the bottom is soaking, frequently brush the oil on the upper surface of the bed logs and on the plywood sides.

A few words about caulking the bottom: The cross planking is wedged tightly on the inside, but is beveled so as to stand open on the outside about ¹⁄₁₆ inch to ⅛ inch. A double strand of soft caulking cotton is rolled into these seams

and set down with a caulking iron and mallet, but not hard enough to force it through the inside. The seams are thoroughly saturated with paint. After this is dry, the space remaining in the seam is filled with a flexible seam compound.

NUMBERED REFERENCES ON DRAWING

1. Fore end bottom. Runs fore and aft. Two widths of fir, pine or other glued together to give a maximum width of 13".

2. Cross planking, midsection bottom. Maximum width 5". Ends left square, not beveled to match the sides of the boat.

3. Bed logs from 2" fir joists. Neat thickness 1½". Molded width of bed logs changed from 4" to 4½".

4. Transom, glue laminated. ⅜" fir ply inside. "One-inch" (¾") fir or pine boards outside running horizontally.

5. Skeg, fir, hard pine, oak. Neat thick-

ness where it lands on the bottom, one inch tapering to about ¾" at the edge. Set down into slot in keel strip, No. 20.

6. Stern post. Materials and thickness to match skeg.

7. Strips running athwartships and let into bed logs to catch ends of the fore-and-aft bottom planks.

8. Stem. Glued lamination. Two thicknesses of ⅜" fir ply inside covered either side by one thickness "one-inch" fir or pine board.

9. Laminated outer stem covers ends of plywood side planking.

10. ½" brass half-round or half-oval.

11. Rowing thwarts. Thicker than a neat ¾" if possible, for stiffness.

12. Vertical frames or ribs either side of the rowing thwarts and supporting them. See detail in drawing.

13. Inwales. 2¼" strip of "one-inch" board glue-spliced to give continuous length from bow to stern.

14. Sides of ladder frame 2 x 4's butt-spliced to give continuous length.

15. Cross braces for ladder frame well nailed.

16. Cutouts in molds for inwale strips.

17. Reinforcement for side splice in ladder frame. Fastened with 3" nails.

18. Stern knee. Laminated like stem. Through fastened into skeg and stern post.

19. Stern sheets. Same wood as rowing thwarts. Fitted and screwed to cleats which are glued and screwed to plywood sides and transom. Braces stern. (Not shown on drawing.)

20. Outer keel strip. Slotted to take skeg. Screwed to bottom. Keeps cross planking amidships from working. Put on after bottom is caulked and puttied.

7

A Lowell Dory Skiff

•

Here we have a tried and tested dory skiff of large size. This substantial rowboat will give good service for fishing and general recreational use on all but the most exposed waters. This is a sturdy craft, built for rough treatment, and stout enough for a workboat. Its flat bottom and shallow draft make it easy to beach. Considering its weight and size, this skiff rows easily and handles well. But it should be well understood at the beginning that this skiff is not a model for the violent, open sea, and that in this respect it is not in a class with such rough-water types as the larger Banks and Swampscott dories, the peapod, or the Rangeley Lakes boat.

The flat, comparatively wide bottom of this skiff affords great initial stability, making it a steady, comfortable boat to fish from, and one that dogs and children cannot tip easily. The flat bottom draws little water even under a load, giving a craft well suited to extremely shallow water. While the boat would row easier with a narrower bottom, it would lose in steadiness.

A small outboard motor can be used to push this dory skiff along at moderate speeds, but considerable alteration of its lines would be required to make this boat suitable for large motors and high speeds. Features that make this skiff row easily and handle well under oars would need changing. The rocker would have to be taken out of the bottom, aft, to make a straight, flat run from amidships to the transom.

The transom would need widening and should be set more upright—by at least 15 degrees—to give a better angle for the motor. These are not difficult changes to make, and might well be considered if one were interested primarily in an outboard boat capable of a smart turn of speed. The resulting craft would be what is now frequently called a "semi-dory" (See Chapter 8). Boats of this type are now popular and widely used with large outboard motors. If one is mainly interested in rowing, however, the skiff is best left as she is.

The lines and the construction details in the accompanying drawing were taken from a boat owned by Mr. H. C. Riggs in Essex, Massachusetts. This boat was built for Mr. Riggs by Hiram Lowell & Sons, Amesbury, Massachusetts. The model was the old New York Yacht Club tender, so called, lengthened by two feet. Originally, this tender was designed and built by Toppan of Medford, Massachusetts, at one time a famous dory building concern, whose advertisements, incidentally, may be seen in the back files of *Rudder* of 50 years ago.

This boat could be built first-class, rather than with materials used in standard dory construction. You could use cedar planking, genuine white oak frames, and copper and bronze fastenings throughout, except for the lower edge of the garboard, which should be fastened to the bottom with 8d Anchorfast

The Lowell dory skiff owned by H.C. Riggs of Essex, Mass.

(Above and below, right) Two views of the construction of H.C. Riggs's Lowell dory skiff.

monel nails. It goes without saying that such materials make a boat of superior lasting qualities. Nevertheless, a good, serviceable boat can be constructed at considerably less expense with native pine planking and galvanized iron fastenings.

This need not be an expensive boat to build, nor should it be a difficult model for the amateur builder. There are no hard bends, and no steaming is required. Even fitting the laps is not hard, if the beginner will take time to study the operation. While some might find it easier to fasten the laps with copper nails riveted over burrs, the knack of properly clinching chisel point nails is not difficult to acquire with a little preliminary practice. When correctly turned and tightened, the chisel point nail is a good method of fastening. Planks spliced with epoxy glue can be got out economically from the shorter lengths of boards, which are cheaper and easier to obtain. If the amateur is interested in economy, and has plenty of time, he can build himself a good, serviceable boat of this sort, with a very moderate outlay of cash.

8

A Semi-Dory

This 14-foot semi-dory is a good boat for the beginning amateur boatbuilder. It is a tried and tested model, not too difficult to build, and a safe boat for children—one they can learn in and have a lot of fun with. It is also one that will take Dad fishing and that Mother can sail afternoons, if she has a mind to. While this semi-dory has proved to be an excellent family boat, it was not offered as such in the first place. The lines for this particular boat were drawn for a series on tabloid lobsterboats printed in the *Maine Coast Fisherman* in the spring of 1954. Considered in the series were a number of small fishing workboats suitable for outboard motors.

The semi-dory, sometimes called a half-dory, gets its name from its resemblance to the forward half of a large Swampscott dory, as if the after half of the dory had been cut away and removed. Of course, this is not the case. Rather, standard Swampscott dory lines are widened aft to give a stern section wide enough and powerful enough to support an outboard motor without settling or "squatting." In the semi-dory, the after part of the bottom is also changed somewhat by widening it and by taking out the rocker to produce a nearly straight run aft. Twenty or twenty-five years ago, semi-dories were a popular and much-used small craft type in New England, both for work and for sport.

Richard W. Hodgdon built the boat from the 1954 plans, and, as an outboard boat it more

than came up to expectations. Surprisingly, it rowed quite well, also; his young son, even, had no difficulty rowing it. This is exceptional for an outboard boat. Most are terrible under oars, as hardly needs saying. Enough of the Swampscott dory characteristics remain in the design so that this semi-dory would sail fairly well, also. A sail plan was worked out by Hodgdon's long-time friend E. D. McIntosh of Dover, New Hampshire, a well-known builder, designer, and sailing skipper. The result is not a racing machine, certainly, but a good sailing knockabout. Lifting out the mast and unshipping the rudder turns the boat back into an outboard boat as before. It performs well with motors ranging from 6 to 20 hp. The centerboard, when pulled up into its box, should not interfere with rowing.

As first designed in 1954, this semi-dory was intended for straight, old-time dory construction with sawn lumber. Since then, other methods of small craft construction have been worked out utilizing plywood, thermoplastic adhesives, and synthetic and glass reinforcements. I have therefore redesigned the boat for more modern wooden construction, and in the process I have made some changes to the sailing rig put in by Hodgdon.

Hodgdon's rig had a combined sail area of 115 square feet. This seems to me to be excessive, especially if the boat is to be sailed outside sheltered waters, where strong winds might

14-FOOT SEMI-DORY

J.G.

14 Foot Semi-Dory
SAIL CONVERSION PLAN
FROM SKETCH, R.W. HODGDON
PORTSMOUTH, N.H. APRIL 1970

RAKE
6"

17'-0"

18'-7"

14'-0"

88 SQ. FT.

35 SQ. FT.

13'-5"

9'-6"

5'-0"

2'-1"

1'-2"

1'-4"

3'-0"

1'-8"   4'-6"

J.G.

MODIFIED RIG
14 FOOT SEMI-DORY
CENTERBOARD MOVED
6" FORWARD

6"

15'-0"

16'-6"

10'-4"

11'-4"

60 SQ. FT.

90 SQ. FT.

90 SQ. FT.

8'-0"

8'-0"

5'-2"

be encountered. I have consequently reduced the sail area—the combined sail area for the alternate rig shown here has been reduced to 90 square feet, the mast has been shortened from 19 feet 2 inches above the deck to 17 feet 8 inches, and the boom has been raised high enough to clear the heads of those seated in the boat.

Hodgdon's drop rudder, convenient if the boat is beached frequently, has been retained. The details show one way of building it: not the only way, certainly, and not necessarily the best way, but it is one that will work.

The centerboard details, worked out some time ago for a slightly larger round-sided sailing dory, are typical, and are suitable for this semi-dory without any reduction in size.

The drawing showing how to set the boat up as well as how to proceed with the planking,

14-FOOT SEMI-DORY												
	HEIGHTS ABOVE BASE					HALF-BREADTHS						
	BOT.	GAR.	2	3	4	SHEER	BOT.	GAR.	2	3	4	SHEER
STEM		1-1-4	1-5-4	1-9-1	2-0-1	2-2-6	0-1-0	0-1-0	0-1-0	0-1-0	0-1-0	0-1-0
STATION 1	0-1-6	0-9-1	1-0-2	1-4-2	1-8-0	1-11-7	0-1-0	0-5-3	0-8-5	0-11-0	1-0-2	1-0-5
STA. 2	0-0-7	0-3-6	0-7-1	0-11-3	1-4-1	1-9-3	0-9-1	1-1-1	1-5-1	1-8-5	1-10-7	1-11-5
STA. 3	0-0-1	0-2-1	0-5-3	0-9-5	1-2-4	1-8-2	1-1-5	1-4-3	1-8-6	2-0-5	2-3-3	2-4-4
STA. 4	0-0-1	0-2-1	0-5-2	0-9-5	1-2-3	1-7-4	1-2-6	1-5-4	1-9-6	2-2-1	2-4-2	2-4-5
STA. 5	0-0-2	0-3-1	0-6-2	0-10-1	1-2-5	1-7-1	1-1-5	1-5-2	1-9-5	2-1-2	2-3-1	2-2-5
TRANSOM	0-0-6	0-4-6	0-7-3	0-11-0	1-3-4	1-8-2	1-0-0	1-5-0	1-9-1	1-11-3	2-0-4	2-0-0

OFFSETS IN FEET, INCHES, & EIGHTHS TO INSIDE PLANK, BOTTOM AND OUTER STEM PROFILE. STATIONS SPACED 30". TRANSOM AT SHEER 26¾" AFT STA. 5. RAKED 5°.

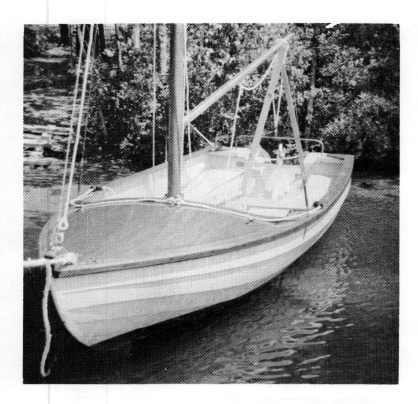

Richard Hodgdon's 14-foot semi-dory rigged for sail, oars, and even motor.

DETAILS FOR 16-FT. SEMI-DORY DRAWN FEB. 1960. APPLY EQUALLY WELL TO 14-FT. BOAT.

PLANK SPLICE

FRAME

5/8"

1/8"

LAPS BETWEEN FRAMES RIVETED EVERY 2" WITH 6d COPPER NAILS OVER BURRS

LAPS TO FRAMES No. 10 - 1 3/4" BRONZE W.S.

GARBOARD 3/8" PLY'D.

FRAMES DOUBLE AS MOLDS

CROSS SPALL ON CENTER LINE

2" EXTRA FOR SET UP

3"

MARK ℄ ON CROSS SPALL

3/8" PLY'D GUSSETS, GLUED AND SCREWED

LIMBER

BOAT SET RIGHTSIDE UP FOR PLANKING UPPER STRAKES GARBOARDS IN PLACE AND FASTENED

BOAT TEMP. SCREWED TO HORSES

16"

FLOOR

BOTTOM FASTENED TEMP. TO TRESTLES WITH SCREWS

GARBOARD IN PLACE

SHEER

TRESTLES SET LEVEL AND PLUMB

TEMP. BRACES TO FLOOR

FORM FOR BOTTOM CURVE TEMP. FASTENED WITH SCREWS

TOP EDGE   GARBOARD

TEMP. SHEER BATTEN

4'-6"

SET BOTTOM-UP FOR FAIRING & GARBOARDS ON TEMP. TRESTLES

STEM PLUMBED & CLEATED TO FLOOR

the manner of fastening the laps and so forth, was done for a 16-foot semi-dory, an enlargement of this 14-foot boat, so it applies equally well here. It will be noted that the 16-footer is a four-plank boat, while the 14-footer is a five-plank boat. In both cases the garboard and the next plank above are treated as a single plank, being made of plywood. This could not be done with natural lumber, as the width required would be too great, but is easily done with plywood, saving both labor and material. If one wanted to, however, this dory could be planked in the traditional manner with two bottom strakes of natural lumber replacing the one wide plywood strake as shown.

As can be seen, the various parts of the dory hull have been numbered. The numbers refer to the building descriptions, which follow:

1. Bottom. Northern white pine, Philippine mahogany, cypress, cedar. Pine preferred. Thickness ⅞". Make out of three or four boards. Fasten to bottom cleats with No. 12 or No. 14 wood screws, 1½" long; likewise to frames, stem, transom, and stern knees.

2. Bottom cleats. Oak, ⅞" thick, 2" wide. Install midway between frames to stiffen bottom.

3. Side plank. First two strakes from the bottom (garboard and broad) made as a single plank of ⅜" marine plywood. Glued to bottom, stem, and transom with epoxy, polysulphide caulk, or equivalent. Nailed to bottom with 8d or 10d monel Anchorfast nails, bronze Anchorfast, or galvanized wire nails, spaced approximately 2" apart. Fastened to stem with 1¼" No. 10 or No. 12 screws; to transom with 1½" No. 10 or No. 12 screws. Can also be made as two planks, lapped and fastened like the upper plank. The upper plank to be made of northern white pine, Philippine mahogany, cypress, or cedar ⁹⁄₁₆" thick and lapped 1⅛". Fasten through laps into frames with No. 10, 1½" or 1¾" screws. On the upper transom use longer screws in the end grain. Fasten laps between frames with copper nails riveted over burrs spaced approximately 2½".

4. Frames. Oak, ⅞" thick, molded approximately 2". Side futtocks joined to bottom cross frame with plywood gussets both sides.

5. Frame gussets. ⅜" marine plywood fastened to oak frames with glue and 1" No. 10 screws.

6. Risers. Same material as side plank, 3" wide amidships tapering at the ends to 2". Fasten to frames with No. 10, 1½" screws.

7. Stem. Oak 2" thick, molded 3". Grain to follow the curvature of the stem as much as possible.

8. Outer stem. Oak. Steam-bent strip applied after planking is complete. Fastened with No. 10, 1¾" screws, and faired to conform to the shape of the boat.

9. Deck beams. Oak or mahogany ⅝" thick, molded 2", and laid out to a curve rising 3" at the forward end of the deck.

10. Deck beam clamp. Same material as the thwart risers. Fastened the same. Molded 2". Fastened to the two forward frames and the stem to support the ends of the deck beams.

11. Breast hook. Oak, ⅞" thick. Grain runs athwartships. Fastened to stem with long screw or drift. Takes fastenings from the sheer strakes and the fore end of the deck.

12. Centerboard and centerboard box. Fully detailed in accompanying drawing.

13. Transom. Philippine mahogany 1" thick. Two or three pieces running athwartships glued and dowelled with ⅜" white oak dowels. Reinforced with stern knees and transom cleats.

14. Stern knees. Oak, 1¼" thick, 10" length of either limb. Molded and located as shown. Fastened through the stern with No. 12 or No. 14, 2" to 2½" screws bunged and plugged. Bottom fastenings may be longer than 1½".

15. Stern quarter knees. Oak, 1¼" to 1½" thick. 10" bearing on transom. Molded as shown. Fastening through transom same as stern knees. Sheer plank and inwale both screw into stern quarter knees with No. 10, 1½" screws.

16. Filler blocks. ⅞" oak, mahogany, pine, located as shown. Fastenings from sheer plank, inwales, and capping.

17. Mast. Spruce. 19'6" from step to head. 3½" diameter at deck, tapering to 2" diameter at head.

18. Mast step. Oak, 1¼" to 1½" thick. To overlap at least two bottom planks.

19. Mast hole cleat. ⅞" thick oak, 12" square. Underside of the center of the forward thwart, with grain running fore and aft, for reinforcement. Fastened with No. 12, 1½" screws bunged and plugged.

20. Thwart knees. Either side of the forward thwart to brace the mast. ⅞" thick. Preferably natural crooks of hackmatack, apple, oak, or other suitable hardwood. Can be glued laminations. Fasten to thwart, side planking, inwale, and capping.

21. Thwarts. Pine, Philippine mahogany, cypress, spruce. ⅞" thick. Notched around frames. Screwed to risers with No. 12, 1¾" to 2" screws bunged and plugged.

STEM OAK
SIDED 2"
MOLDED 3"

STATION
#1

SHEER

GARBOARD

6"
SQUARES

22. Side benches. Same material as thwarts. Between second and third thwarts either side. Fastened to thwarts by cleats on underside with 1½" No. 12 screws bunged and plugged. Fastened to risers, as well.

23. Side bench cleats. ⅞" oak, 3" wide.

24. Rowlock cleats. Oak strips, 11" x 2" x ⅞" beveled as shown and screwed into capping and filler blocks.

25. Fore deck. ⅜" plywood. Screwed to deck beams, sheer strake, and breast hook with 1¼" No. 8 wood screws. Filler blocks along the outside between the deck beams and fastened to the sheer strakes can be installed for added fastening and reinforcement. Can be covered with thin canvas laid in paint, with fiberglass or polypropylene, or can be merely painted. Outside edges may be covered with fiberglass or polypropylene tape under half oval trim.

26. Inwale. Oak or Philippine mahogany ⅞" thick, 2" wide amidships tapering to 1½" at ends. Fastened to stern quarter knees, frames, and filler blocks with No. 12, 1¾" to 2" screws.

27. Side capping. Pine or Philippine mahogany ½" thick. Forward end thinned slightly to fair into ⅜" thick fore deck. Put on in two pieces. Butt splice under after oarlock cleat. Fastened to stern quarter knees, inwales, filler blocks, and sheer strakes with No. 10, 1¼" to 1½" screws. Heads slightly countersunk and puttied.

28. Deck coaming. Philippine mahogany ⅝" thick. Finishes after end of deck, covering the after deck beam and projecting 2" above the deck. Rounded ends cover the joints between the deck and side capping and extend to the outside of the boat. Can be finished bright; if so, the inwales, side capping, and half oval trim can be made of Philippine mahogany to correspond and can be finished bright also. All fastenings through these members to be bunged and plugged.

29. Half oval trim. Philippine mahogany or oak 1" wide. Fore end approaching the stem tapered to ¾". Fastened with No. 8, 1" screws, bunged ⅜", and plugged.

30. Plywood garboard. (See No. 3.)

31. Bottom strip. Oak or Philippine mahogany ½" thick. To protect the lower edge of the garboard and to take wear on the bottom. Inside edge of bottom strip must be straight and parallel with the centerline of the boat, otherwise it will create drag and slow the boat. Thus these strips will be 8" wide at the center of the boat, dying out to a point about 6" forward of the second frame, slightly forward of the mast location. Fastened with No. 10, 1" screws bunged and plugged. Before the bottom strips are put on, and before any paint is put on the bottom, the lower edge of the garboard is to be reinforced with fiberglass or polypropylene tape 3" wide, equally lapped on bottom and up side. Tape to be bonded with epoxy-Versamid mix. A double thickness of tape to be applied at the base of the stem.

32. Frame cleat. ⅜" or ½" plywood glued and screwed to the two sides of the forward, or No. 1, frame.

33. Transom cleats. Oak strips ⅞" thick by 2" wide extending from the underside of the stern quarter knees to the bottom to reinforce the transom. Fastened with No. 12, 1½" screws bunged and plugged.

34. Bottom plate. Triangular piece of flat brass or bronze to cover lower end of false stem and fore end of bottom. Fasten with No. 8, 1" screws, countersunk.

9

A Car-Top Semi-Dory

• •

There is definitely a demand for a car-top boat. The requirements, when boiled down, are more or less uniform and quite specific:

1. It must be as light as possible for easy handling.

2. It should be large enough to carry at least three persons in moderately rough water with safety.

3. It must be tight, and must stay tight, even when exposed to drying winds and the direct rays of the hot summer sun when it is on top of a car.

4. It should be a model that rows at least moderately well, that will drive easily with a small outboard motor, and that can be adapted for sailing if the owner so wishes.

5. It must be capable of being built inexpensively and easily, that is to say its construction must come well within both the capability and the pocketbook of the average home builder.

This is asking quite a lot, yet not the impossible, by any means. A generation ago the fulfillment of all five requirements would have been impossible. A skilled professional boatbuilder taking pains and not sparing expense could probably have achieved the first four requirements, if he covered the hull with canvas. Few home builders could have made the grade. In attempting to make a permanently tight hull, the amateur would have likely built the boat too

heavy. In seeking to keep the weight down, he might have built it either too light or too flimsy.

Since the advent of thermosetting adhesives and reinforcements of glass and synthetic fibers in the last 15 to 20 years, it has become possible for amateur builders to build the kind of boat we are considering.

In the June, 1961, issue of *Outdoor Maine*, I offered the lines, construction details, and building directions for a car-top boat for the sportsman and amateur builder. In shape, the boat—12 feet LOA, 4 feet 2 inches beam, 1 foot 4 inches depth amidships—was that of a knuckle-sided semi-dory with four planks to a side. The planks, of 5mm Utile mahogany plywood (approximately 3/16 inches thick), were screwed and glued to Sitka spruce seam battens, with the joints covered on the outside with a narrow fiberglass tape bonded with epoxy resin. An entire covering of the outer surface of the hull with fiberglass was not advocated, as this would have added too much weight. The narrow tape was sufficient to waterproof and reinforce the planking seams, and was not too unsightly on the finished boat, if care was taken in putting on the tapes and in feathering out their edges by careful sanding before the final coats of paint were applied.

Such seam-batten construction, although it has proved quite successful, up to a certain point, is now obsolete. It is obsolete because the

CAR-TOP BOAT. LOA 12'-0. BEAM 4'-2". DEPTH 1'-4."
LIGHT OUTBOARD MOTOR OR OARS.

(Above and below) The plans for the car-top semi-dory as originally designed for four strakes per side. The five-strakes-per-side version appears on pages 74 and 75.

battens can be eliminated, giving way to a less expensive and much easier construction—one that permits a number of improvements in design.

Instead of wooden seam battens, an arrangement of Vectra polypropylene tapes bonded with epoxy can be used to join the edges of the strakes of plywood planking. The introduction of Vectra polypropylene has provided the amateur builder a fabric with flexibility, toughness, strength, and light weight—equivalent fiberglass reinforcement is approximately two and one-half times as heavy. (Note: if Vectra is unobtainable, then fiberglass tape may be substituted.)

The advantages gained by eliminating seam battens are worth considering. Seam battens must be fitted and beveled accurately, which sometimes calls for greater skill than the amateur can muster. If the edges of the plywood planks are screwed as well as glued to the battens, as is recommended, several gross of small brass or bronze screws are required, which add to the expense, take time to put in, and add weight. In addition, there are several objections to having seam battens on the inside of the boat.

LIGHT 12-FT. CAR-TOP BOAT

OFFSETS IN FEET, INCHES & EIGHTHS							
OUTSIDE TRANSOM & STEM. INSIDE PLANK & BOT.							
STATIONS	TRAN.	5	4	3	2	1	BOW
HEIGHTHS SHEER	1-4-0	1-3-0	1-2-6	1-3-5	1-5-4	1-8-3	2-0-4
1	0-11-4	0-10-2	0-9-4	0-10-1	1-0-1	1-3-5	1-8-5
2	0-7-7	0-6-2	0-5-2	0-5-6	0-7-7	0-11-6	1-5-3
3	0-4-1	0-2-7	0-1-7	0-2-4	0-4-2	0-8-1	1-1-2
BOT.	0-0-0	0-0-0	0-0-0	0-0-0	0-0-4	0-1-1	0-1-2
HALF-BREADTHS SHEER	1-6-2	1-10-2	2-0-6	2-0-0	1-7-3	0-11-3	—
1	1-6-2	1-9-7	2-0-0	1-11-2	1-6-8	0-10-7	—
2	1-5-3	1-8-2	1-10-0	1-9-1	1-4-5	0-9-2	—
3	1-3-0	1-5-0	1-6-0	1-5-0	1-1-0	0-6-5	—
BOT.	0-9-0	0-10-0	0-10-0	0-8-4	0-5-0	0-0-7	—

They look clumsy and add weight, they can catch water and dirt, and they prevent the use of bent frames, either steam bent or put in as laminations of thin, glued strips.

There is a further consideration, as well. The elimination of seam battens makes it easier to put more and narrower planks on a side. This

(Above and opposite page) The plans for the car-top semi-dory as newly designed for five strakes per side.

is no small factor. The original boat designed for *Outdoor Maine* had but four planks to a side. It would have been a better boat with five, but the number was kept at four in order to eliminate the additional labor and expense, not to mention weight, of an extra seam batten.

The original 12-foot car-top boat has now been redrawn for five strakes of plank instead of four as first laid out, and the revised lines and offsets are given herewith. The result is a more rounded hull with slightly increased displacement or capacity, which will be easier to plank because of its narrower strakes. The strakes can be cut out of standard 4-foot by 8-foot panels of ¼-inch marine grade fir plywood with very little waste, if the 12-foot strakes are spliced together from two or more shorter pieces. (See the Appendix for details on splicing.)

CONSTRUCTION

Following is a description of the method to be used in building this boat with Vectra reinforced seams instead of seam battens. It should be understood that this method of building is equally suited to a wide range of small craft, from kayaks to powerboats and sailboats up to 20 feet long, and even larger. Without altering the design to any significant extent,

many round hulls can be treated as if they were multi-chine or knuckle-sided and so built by this method easier than if standard carvel planking were used. To the inventive and resourceful amateur builder, this method of building offers a chance to experiment with novel and imaginative variations of traditional design. It should not be overlooked by the professional designer either; some of them, I must say, tend to be far too conservative in their approach to small craft.

To begin with, the lines, as always, must be laid down full size and faired. From these adjusted lines molds are made in the usual way with pine boards, so that they can be nailed into, and are set up carefully and checked and adjusted for fairness. They should not be too far apart, not more than 2 feet in any case, for there will be nothing between them to support the edges of the plywood strakes. If the molds were too far apart, the adjoining edges of the planks might not hold together tightly where there are hard bends or twists.

After each strake is shaped and fitted, but before it is nailed in place, a very shallow cut into the outer face is made along each edge. This is best done with a small, high-speed power hand router using a special gauge made for this purpose. The cut should be about one inch wide and not more than ⅟₃₂″ deep. The purpose of this cut is to allow the Vectra tape, which will eventually bind the seam, to lie flush with the surface of the plywood. Thus, when the final outer covering of polypropylene fabric is applied, the seams will not stand out from the rest of the hull as they otherwise would.

In planking, when the plywood strakes are fitted one to the other, the edges should be beveled to fit tightly on the inside, yet stand open on the outside, say about ⅛-inch for ¼-inch plywood planking. The strakes as they are fitted are nailed to the molds. As these nails are only temporary and must be drawn later when the hull shell is removed from the molds, some provision must be made for getting at the heads, although the nails must be set down with enough force to hold the strakes firmly against the molds. This can be done by putting washers of leather or thick cardboard under the heads, or by using a double-headed staging nail. The six-penny size should be large enough for ¼-inch plywood.

OFFSETS IN FEET, INCHES & EIGHTHS TO OUTSIDE OF TRANSOM AND STEM, INSIDE PLANK & BOT.								
STATIONS		TRAN	5	4	3	2	1	BOW
HEIGHTS	SHEER	1-4-1	1-3-4	1-3-2	1-3-6	1-5-7	1-9-0	2-0-3
	1	1-0-2	0-11-2	0-10-5	0-10-7	1-0-7	1-4-3	1-9-4
	2	0-8-2	0-7-0	0-6-2	0-6-4	0-8-6	1-0-5	1-5-7
	3	0-4-5	0-3-4	0-2-3	0-2-6	0-4-6	0-8-5	1-1-5
	4	0-2-3	0-1-4	0-0-6	0-0-4	0-2-4	0-5-4	0-8-6
	BOT.	0-0-0	0-0-0	0-0-0	0-0-0	0-0-5	0-1-3	0-1-4
HALF-BREADTHS	SHEER	1-6-3	1-10-6	2-0-7	2-0-0	1-7-4	0-11-4	—
	1	1-6-2	1-10-1	2-0-3	1-11-4	1-6-6	0-10-6	—
	2	1-5-5	1-8-5	1-10-6	1-9-4	1-5-2	0-9-4	—
	3	1-3-4	1-5-5	1-6-7	1-5-6	1-1-4	0-7-2	—
	4	1-0-6	1-1-6	1-2-3	1-0-6	0-9-2	0-4-2	—
	BOT.	0-9-0	0-10-1	0-10-0	0-8-2	0-5-3	0-0-7	—

After all the strakes are fitted and nailed in place on the molds, as well as permanently screwed to the transom and inner portion of the stem, the V-ed openings along the meeting edges of the strakes or planks are filled with a stiff epoxy-Thiokol caulk, which when it cures will be both strongly adhesive and somewhat resilient. It will not push through to the inside if the strakes fit tightly on their inner surface, but if they do not fit in some places, no matter, for temporary strips of masking tape applied on the inside will keep the caulk from oozing through.

After this caulk has cured and the excess has been cut or sanded away, 2-inch Vectra tapes are laid in the shallow depressions previously cut for them and are stapled or tacked where necessary to hold them in place. The tapes are then saturated with epoxy resin. When this has hardened (and it is best to let it cure at least a couple of days for full strength), all the nails through the planks into the molds are drawn. The shell can then be lifted clear of the molds and turned right side up.

Now the inside of the seams is reinforced. First a narrow tape of Vectra set in epoxy resin is applied straddling the inside of each seam. For width, 1½ inches is ample for this first tape. Over it, another and wider tape is glued. This one should be 2½ inches to 3 inches wide, extending equally on either side of the seam. After this double-tape reinforcement is in place and cured, the hull is ready for framing or timbering.

The builder can buy his polypropylene tape already cut, or he can cut it himself. For the one-shot builder who would not have need for polypropylene tapes except for this particular job, it might be simpler and no more expensive to buy his tapes all cut rather than cut his own from cloth. Polypropylene tapes in various widths can be bought from many marine suppliers. For the outside of this boat one 50-yard roll of the 2-inch tape would suffice. For the inside, a 50-yard roll each of the 2-inch and the 3-inch tapes will do.

If the builder wishes to cut his own, he can heat-cut his tapes from standard 4.3-ounce Vectra or Versatex polypropylene boat fabric. This can be done with an ordinary soldering iron with a sharp tip, but it is best and easiest done with the type of soldering gun commonly used today by sailmakers to cut the modern synthetic sailcloths.

Another possibility for the amateur builder is to stretch out 12-foot lengths of polypropylene fabric on a clean floor or on two sheets of plywood laid end to end. This could be the plywood he plans to use for planking, but before it is cut. A few ¼-inch staples here and there, later to be removed with ice pick and pliers, will hold the cloth in place and keep it taut. After the cloth is stretched out and the widths of tape marked on it with a soft pencil and straight edge, or even a chalk line, a thin application of flexible epoxy/Thiokol mix is sparingly applied in a narrow strip along each dividing line. When this has set, the tapes are cut apart with shears along the previously marked dividing lines. The thin edging of the cured epoxy/Thiokol prevents raveling, yet is flexible enough not to interfere with the application of the tape to the seams.

It should be mentioned here that polypropylene fabric creases easily, and such creases are hard to get out except with a warm iron, hence lengths of cloth should not be folded, but should always be rolled for shipment or storage.

It should be obvious, even without specific mention, that a stapling gun is almost an essential for working with synthetic and glass fabrics used for reinforcing thermosetting resins. In many cases it is possible to put on the covering fabric dry, stretching it in place and tacking it with staples to prevent blisters, and then saturating it with a low viscosity resin formulation thin enough to penetrate through the fabric to the bonding surface beneath. In most cases of this sort, the resin is best applied sparingly—just enough to achieve a bond, but not enough to run or sag. After the resin has hardened, subsequent applications can be made, as desired, to build up the surface. For this, the advantage of a formulation that does not run off, even on a vertical surface, can hardly be overestimated.

FRAMING

For framing the hull, there are three options:

1. Sawn frames of several sorts can be scribed in and fitted.

2. Steamed timbers continuous from gunwale to gunwale can be bent in. These will touch the center of each strake of plank and may be fastened through from the outside with either rivets or small bronze screws. The spacing and cross section of such steam-bent ribs, preferably select white oak from butt logs, will depend on the size and type of the hull. They need not be large to add greatly to the strength of the hull.

3. Instead of steam-bent ribs, glued laminated ribs make an excellent substitute. Perhaps substitute is not just the right word, for such laminated ribs if properly installed will be just as good or better than steamed ones. These are also put in continuous from rail to rail. Strips of spruce, or possibly ash, thin enough to bend easily to the shape of the hull, are used. Epoxy adhesive is applied to the number required to make up the desired thickness. These are bent in, forced down into place so as to fit snugly against the sides of the boat like steamed timbers, and the layered strips are lined up with several small wooden-jawed clamps until the lamination can be secured in place. The fastenings can be either rivets or screws, put in from the outside directly before the adhesive hardens, exactly as in the case of steamed frames. These fastenings will hold the laminations in place until the glue hardens.

In the drawing I have shown the frames as located on 6-inch centers. This spacing need not be followed exactly. Somewhat smaller frames could be put in closer together, and larger ones farther apart. I would not recommend frames smaller than ⅝-inch square in cross-section, and would judge that a width of ¾ inch might be better with a thickness or molding of 9⁄16 inch.

FINISHING OFF

After the ribs are fitted and in, the whole interior can be finished: risers, thwarts, breast hook, stern quarter knees, and inwales. When this work is complete, the boat is turned over.

The heads of rib fastenings and nail holes are faced with a stiff mix of epoxy resin and phenolic microballoons, or something equivalent. The Vectra strips covering the plank seams are also faced carefully. When this is hard, the whole outer surface of the hull is carefully sanded smooth and even in preparation for the outer covering of Vectra fabric.

The Vectra is put on dry, pulled tight, and

stapled where necessary to prevent wrinkling. After the first coat of resin has hardened, staples that show can be removed quite easily with an ice pick and pliers, but staples that come where the gunwales and outer stem are to be added may be left in, provided they are bronze or Monel.

The resin formulation for bonding the outside covering of Vectra should be quite thin and applied sparingly, yet there should be enough to penetrate the polypropylene fabric and to saturate it thoroughly. Any excess beyond this will tend to run and sag before it hardens, necessitating sanding and scraping in order to obtain a smooth surface before the second and final coat of resin is applied. Some may want to add an extra thickness of Dynel fabric on the bottom before the skegs go on, because of the superior abrasion resistance of Dynel. Instead of covering the outside with polypropylene fabric, Dynel fabric may be substituted with excellent results. Also, fiberglass

tapes may be used instead of polypropylene tapes without adding enough weight to matter.

Last of all, the gunwale strips, outer stem and skeg or skegs are fastened on. The outer stem is made the same as in the Rangeley boat and is fastened on through the inside stem with several long screws. It merely finishes off the bow—the boat is quite tight without it. Finally, enough foam flotation should be installed under the seats to support four persons easily.

A 12-foot boat built in this manner with ¼-inch fir plywood, marine quality, should weigh under 100 pounds, and even appreciably less, if care is taken not to make the scantlings larger than they need to be. Of course, the addition of a centerboard, should one plan to sail the boat, will add weight. The 12-foot boat as originally designed had a stern buoyant enough to support an outboard motor up to 7 hp or thereabouts.

1 0

The Dory

....................•....................

The common, straight-sided fisherman's dory, also known as the Grand Banks dory, is an old favorite with amateur builders. If you think you might ever want to build yourself a dory, here are a couple to consider.

Banks dories used to be designed by the bottom length; the two dories detailed here are dories with 12- and 15-foot bottoms, respectively. The 12-footer is about as small as is generally useful and safe, yet it is not too large to be handled easily by a single oarsman. The 15-footer can be rowed by one man, but it takes two good oarsmen to handle it in rough water. There are dories 16 feet on the bottom, and larger, but one with a 15-foot bottom is about as large as most people want, though if you must, it would be quite easy to make this 15-footer (19 feet 5 inches LOA) a few feet longer.

The lines and specifications for the 12-footer were worked out carefully by myself from study and comparison of numerous dories for an article on the dory published in *Yachting* in March, 1954. The plans for the 15-footer are those of a dory designed and built during World War II for the U. S. Coast Guard by Hiram Lowell & Sons, the famous Amesbury, Massachusetts, dory builders. For all-around general use it is probably the best Banks dory model ever worked out. It is less heavy and clumsy than some of the old fishing

models, which were generally made very deep to carry enormous loads of fish. Such deep models in a light condition are cranky and hard to handle. In making this dory shallower, it was possible to give the sides greater flare, all in all resulting in a boat much better suited for general use.

It goes without saying that the lines for either of these dories must be laid down full size. The lines are given to the inside of the plank, as is proper for lapstrake boats. The frames serve as molds.

Anyone who is building a dory for the first time, especially an amateur, should make a half model. The right scale is 1½ inches to the foot. On the half-model, the run, width, and laid-out shape of the plank can be found and taken off quite accurately if the model is carefully made. To get the run of the plank, one of the jobs that often gives the amateur trouble, use a thin strip of wood wide enough so that it cannot bend edgewise. Hold the strip or lining batten in position with thumbtacks. The straight sides of this dory make lining out the plank easy.

The first building operation is making the bottom assembly. The three or four pine boards that comprise the bottom are cut roughly to length, given straight edges with a slight caulking seam on the outside, and clamped together tightly; then the bottom cleats are put on. The frame stations are marked, and the stem and transom are fastened on.

The next step is to set up for planking. This can be done either upside down or right-side up. The latter way makes it easier to clinch the lap fastenings as the planking proceeds. The bottom-up method is better for fairing and beveling the frames, bottom, stem, and transom surfaces to receive the garboards.

This is difficult for beginners, and for that reason, the bottom-up method is possibly the best for the inexperienced.

When a dory is planked upside down, the bottom assembly is shored down and secured over a strongback, which is a wide, two-inch plank set on edge at a convenient height from the floor for working, rounded on its top edge to the curve of the rocker of the bottom, and notched out to take the frames and the bottom cleats. The strongback is set up over a centerline on the floor; this gives the location for the temporary cleating of the stem and transom of the floor while planking is in progress. The frame stations are squared out from the centerline, so that the frames can also be temporarily cleated to the floor, for which they are often left long to be sawed off when planking is finished.

After the bottom assembly with the frames attached has been set up as accurately as possible and secured, it is necessary to fair the framework for planking. This is a job that can't be hurried or slighted. It calls for patience and exactitude, and the final quality of the boat depends upon it. It is better to work over the whole boat several times, taking thin shavings sparingly here and there until the whole thing suddenly comes right all at once, than it is to attempt to do a finished fairing job a small piece at a time.

What is required for fairing is a thin, wide batten, say three or four inches wide, one-quarter or three-eighths of an inch thick, and long enough to reach across three or four frame stations. By bending this around the frames, bottom edge, and stem and transom bevels, it is easy to detect any lumps, unfairness, or wrong bevels.

The garboards must fit perfectly, that is, wood to wood along the entire length of the bottom and up on the fayed edges of the stem and transom. Otherwise, the boat will leak. The secret of a tight boat is to bevel the bottom and other parts so that the inside is a little strong, and the outside a little slack. Never the other way. Thus, when the fastenings are in and pulled up tight, the upper, inside edge of the bottom will press very tightly against the inside of the plank, or even dig into the soft pine or cedar a little. If the outside stands open slightly, no matter. A thin thread of cotton can be tucked in carefully, but never hard enough to force the plank.

The garboard is fastened to the bottom with 10d galvanized wire nails. It is best to drill a fine lead hole for the nail to follow, but not large enough to cut down the holding power of the nail. Try drilling in a scrap block of pine to get the right fit. To get the right angle for the drill, so as not to split out through the bottom, sight for the lead holes parallel to a piece of board laid flat across the bottom. Such directions may seem elementary, but fastening the garboards is critical, and the inexperienced builder had best take all the precautions necessary on this one to avoid mistakes. A little extra bottom thickness helps in construction; it also helps later when the boat is dragged over rocks and beached. For myself, I'd rather have the bottom of 1-inch-thick pine than the ⅞-inch dimension shown on the Lowell plan.

The laps are not hard to do on a straight-sided dory. If a person is not used to chisel-point nails, it is well to practice clinching a few before going on the laps. Please remember that they must be driven with their wide chisel edges cutting across the grain and shearing it, otherwise they will act as wedges, surely splitting the laps. In clinching, the thin points must be turned by the hold-on so that they return and re-enter the wood, drawing up tight with the finishing raps of the hammer. In place of chisel point nails, rivets may be used to fasten the laps. For rivets use 6d copper cut or wire nails headed up over burrs. Today, chisel point dory nails are all but impossible to obtain, so copper rivets will probably be used.

The planks should be fastened to the frames or ribs with a single fastening only, through the lap, as specially indicated on the detail for the 12-foot dory. Other fastenings into the frames through the middle of the planks, and especially in the middle of the garboards, will surely split the planks in time. The wider the dory planks, the more chance they need to come and go.

Standard dory fastenings are galvanized nails. But screws may be substituted throughout. Perhaps screws are easier for the amateur. I, myself, would not change the 10d galvanized wire nail fastening for the garboards in the bottom. Some are trying Monel Anchorfast nails for this. But ordinary galvanized wire nails hold well, and last as long as the wood.

White pine is the standard planking wood for dories. In New England, where the dory originated, good, country white pine is still fairly easy to come by, but not always in wide widths. A few knots, even loose ones, do no harm. In fact, they mean tougher lumber. Loose knots can be bored out and replaced by a tapered pine plug. The old dory builder often puts loose knots back, nailing them in with a small clinch nail going through one edge, bored for, of course. (See the next chapter, on the Swampscott dory, for more on dory lumber.)

The 15-foot dory is shown with three strakes. The boat might just as well be planked with five. The garboard need not be more than three inches wide at its narrowest part amidships. (See the typical dory garboard shape in the detail drawing for the 12-foot dory.) In fact, the garboards could be made of two pieces, spliced at the midpoint. The sheer strake can be spliced also, as was always done in the case of Swampscott dories whose shape gave a very crooked sheer strake.

If, as has been suggested, the planking is worked out first on a half-model, it may be planned to utilize available widths and lengths of boards, and real economy can be achieved in this day of scarce and expensive lumber. Actually, every strake in the boat could be spliced up out of two pieces, provided the splices were, with the exception of the garboards, kept at least within one-third of the length of the boat from the ends. Closer to the ends would be better, for the greatest strain is at the center of the boat. Also, splices would need to be alternated from one end to the other of the boat—one strake spliced near the bow, the next near the stern, and so on.

The straight sides of a Banks dory are easily covered with plywood in a single sheet. But with a little planning to utilize available and inexpensive lumber, standard planking is no doubt cheaper and better for the amateur.

After the dory is planked, the rest is easy, hardly requiring any special directions or comment. Finishing is adequately covered in the detail drawings.

Banks dories often carried a short, detach-

FISHERMAN'S DORY
AFTER LOWELL FOR
U. S. COAST GUARD, 1944.
SHEET 2

FEET AND INCHES

PARTS LIST

NO	NAME	MATERIAL	SIZE (FINISHED)
1	BOTTOM	WHITE PINE	7/8" OR THICKER
2	SIDES	WT. PINE	5/8"
3	TRANSOM	RED OAK	1 1/4"
4	STEM	RED OAK	2 1/16"
5	FRAMES	RED OAK	1 1/16" × 2" × 1 1/2" AT TOP.
6	FRAME GUSSET PLATES	16 GA. GAL. STEEL	
7	GUNWALES	RED OAK	1 1/4" × 1 1/2"
8	BOTTOM CLEAT	RED OAK	7/8" × 2"
9	CAPPINGS	RED OAK	5/8" × 2 1/8"
10	BANDS	RED OAK	.5/8" × 3"
11	SIDE CLEATS	RED OAK	5/8" × 2"
12	RISINGS	RED OAK	5/8" × 2 3/4"
13	SEATS	WT. PINE	7/8" × 10"
14	STERN KNEE	RED OAK	2 1/16"
15	STERN CLEAT	R. OAK	7/8"
16	BR. HOOK.	R. OAK	1 1/4"
17	FALSE STEM	R. OAK	5/8" × 1 3/4"
18	FRAME HEAD IRONS	14 GA. GAL. STEEL.	

ALL FASTENINGS GALVANIZED.
B. P. = BLUNT POINT BOAT NAILS.
C. P. = CHISEL POINT BOAT NAILS.
PLANK TO STEM & TRAN. 1 3/4" B. P. 1 1/2" APART.
PLANK TO FRAMES 2" B. P. 1 EACH LAP.
PLANK TO SIDE CLEATS 1 3/4" C. P.
BOTTOM TO CLEATS 2" C. P.
BOTTOM TO FRAMES 2" B. P.
BOTTOM TO STEM FOOT 2 1/2" C. P.
BOTTOM & TRAN. TO STERN KNEE 2 1/2" C.P.
CARBOARD TO BOTTOM 10d GAL. WIRE N. 2 1/2" APT.
CAPPING TO TOP STRAKE 6d. B. P. 2" APT.
CAPPING TO GUNWALES 4d. B. P. 2" APT.
BANDS TO GUNWALES 1 3/4" B. P.
FALSE STEM 1 3/4" B. P. 3" APT.
FRAME GUSSET PLATES 6 — 1 3/4" RIVETS.
FRAME HEAD IRONS 1" UNDER CAPPING —
   2 1/2" DOWN FRAME - 3 1/2" B. P.

LAPS CLINCHED FASTENED
WITH 1 1/2" CHISEL POINT
GAL. BOAT NAILS SPACED
2" APT.

3'-0"

5/16"
1 1/8"
5/8"

LAPS BEVELED TO
1/8" ON STEM &
TRANSOM. INCREASED
TO 5/16" 3' BACK FROM ENDS.

LINES TO INSIDE
PLANK & BOTTOM &
TO OUTBOARD SURFACE
TRANSOM & STEM.
BOT. #3 INSIDE W. 33"
BOT. #1 INSIDE W. 21 1/2"
BOT. #5 INSIDE W. 20 1/2"

FRAMES #1 & #5 - 55°
FRS. #2, #3, #4 - 53°
TRANSOM OUTSIDE
WIDTH AT SHEER - 15".
STEM SIDED 2 1/16"
BEVELED TO 1/8" EDGE
TO TAKE PLANK.

TRAN.

BASE LINE

STA. 3

B. L.

able mast and a small loose-footed sail, and were steered with an oar. It is easy with their flat bottom to install a centerboard. A modified Banks dory with centerboard and sailing rig can be found on page 91 of Howard Chapelle's *American Small Sailing Craft*, W. W. Norton, New York, 1951. Chapelle features a Cape Ann sailing dory from Annisquam, Mass., just outside of Gloucester.

11

A Modified Swampscott Dory

·······················•·······················

Here is a Swampscott dory that is not too large for one man, or even a strong boy, to handle, yet large enough to retain all of the excellent qualities for which the type is noted. Certain minor modifications have been made to adapt it for amateur construction and to permit the use of materials currently to be had at most retail lumber dealers. Its overall length is not so great as to require building space in excess of what is available in most home workshops.

This dory is much like a 17-foot model built in the Small Craft Boatshop at Mystic Seaport. By only slightly lifting the angle of the tombstone stern and at the same time raising the stem profile by a like amount, I have shortened the overall length of this boat by a foot without affecting its seakeeping qualities to the slightest degree. The waterline length remains almost the same.

Built as drawn, the modified model as measured on top from the extreme overhang of the transom to the fore edge of the false stem, will not exceed 16 feet by more than 3 inches. But if the spacing of the three frames is decreased from 34 inches to 32 inches, it is possible to bring the overall length a few inches under 16 feet.

First, let me say that I don't believe that shortening the boat in this way would affect its performance to any significant extent.

Actually, I doubt if any difference could be noticed under ordinary conditions of use. Perhaps the shortened model would be a few seconds slower in a race. I doubt if the boat's weatherly qualities would suffer at all.

However, this difference in length could be important in a situation where 16 feet of overall length has been set by statute or administrative edict as the cut-off point between regulation of various sorts. Some of the regulations applying to small craft are arbitrary, ill-advised, and in general nuisances well worth bypassing if possible.

Decreasing the frame spacing by only 2 inches will not require any significant alteration in the lines. They will still fair easily. The only adjustment called for will come in lining out the bottom, and this will hardly be noticeable, requiring only slight shifts in the batten to get a fair curve. The stem, stern transom, and frames will all remain exactly the same as presently drawn.

Shortening the dory will not affect her appearance in the slightest. This dory, by the way, is a really handsome model, as I was able to observe when I had completed the working half model on the scale of 1½ inches to the foot, made to prove the lines and to lay out the spacing and shapes of the planks.

The true Swampscott dory, of which this boat is a good example, is essentially a round-

Rowing craft in the harbor at Marblehead, Massachusetts, were photographed by Fred Preu shortly after 1900. The Swampscott dory in the middle foreground is similar to the one under consideration. (Photo courtesy of the San Francisco Maritime Museum)

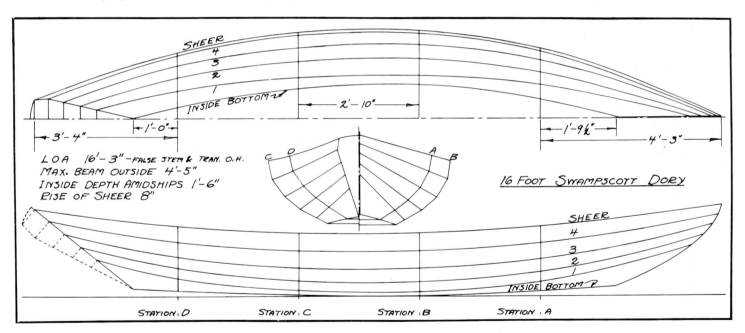

SHEER
4
3
2
1
INSIDE BOTTOM
2'-10"
3'-4"
1'-0"
1'-9½"
4'-3"
LOA 16'-3" - FALSE STEM & TRAN. O.H.
MAX. BEAM OUTSIDE 4'-5"
INSIDE DEPTH AMIDSHIPS 1'-6"
RISE OF SHEER 8"
C D A B
16 FOOT SWAMPSCOTT DORY
SHEER
4
3
2
1
INSIDE BOTTOM
STATION D
STATION C
STATION B
STATION A

bottom boat, yet with enough flat in its relatively narrow board bottom to sit upright on the beach when it grounds out. For a boat that is to be beached frequently, this is an especially desirable feature, particularly as it permits a double bottom, the outer layer of which is easily renewed when it wears thin from dragging over rocks.

These Swampscott boats are the aristocrats of the dory clan, and are not to be confused with their clumsier, more crudely built cousins, the heavy, slab-sided working dories of the Grand Banks fishermen. True, in some features of their construction Swampscott and Grand Banks dories are similar, but in performance there is a vast difference. Swampscott dories row and handle so much easier than the Banks model. Whether they are faster under oars remains open to argument, but certainly they are every bit as good sea boats. Their marked

16 FOOT SWAMPSCOTT DORY		STEM	STA. A	STA. B	STA. C	STA. D	STERN
HEIGHTS	BOTTOM	0-2-7	0-1-3	0-0-0	0-0-3	0-1-5	0-2-2
	1	1-2-5	0-4-1	0-1-2	0-1-6	0-5-2	0-10-7
	2	1-5-6	0-7-1	0-4-1	0-4-4	0-8-2	1-2-4
	3	1-8-7	0-11-0	0-8-0	0-8-2	0-11-4	1-6-2
	4	1-11-6	1-3-5	1-1-2	1-1-2	1-3-7	1-10-0
	SHEER	2-2-4	1-8-4	1-6-4	1-6-4	1-8-3	2-1-4
WIDTHS	BOTTOM	0-0-1	0-5-6	0-10-1	0-8-7	0-3-3	0-0-2
	1	0-0-1	0-10-1	1-0-6	1-0-2	0-8-3	0-2-4
	2	0-0-1	1-1-6	1-5-6	1-4-7	1-0-0	0-3-5
	3	0-0-1	1-5-2	1-9-6	1-8-6	1-3-5	0-4-7
	4	0-0-1	1-7-7	2-1-0	2-0-4	1-6-6	0-6-0
	SHEER	0-0-1	1-8-5	2-1-6	2-1-4	1-7-4	0-5-4

OFFSETS MEASURED IN FEET, INCHES & EIGHTHS TO INSIDE OF PLANKING & BOTTOM & TO OUTSIDE OF STEM & TRANSOM.

superiority over the Banks model for recreational use lies in their greater ease of handling. In normal conditions a youngster could manage the boat under consideration easily, but he definitely could not handle a Banks dory of the same size.

Yet, this is not a small boat by any means. With an inside depth amidships of 18 inches and a maximum inside beam of 52 inches, this boat could easily take six men or an equivalent load without undue reduction of freeboard. Because of its ample beam and depth, this boat would do well if rigged to sail, for which it can be adapted quite easily. Its flat board bottom makes the addition of a centerboard trunk easy.

MATERIALS

New England dories came into being when native lumber was plentiful and cheap, when beautiful clear boards of northern white pine 14 inches, 15 inches, and even 18 inches wide were to be had for a few cents a board foot. Dories were designed to be built with a few wide strakes, generally four to a side, in order to be planked up quickly and thus save labor and cut building costs. In all probability, neither the Banks dory nor the round-sided Swampscott dory would ever have taken form except for an abundance of wide pine boards.

Now that the supply of wide pine dory boards has almost run out, we have to find

other means of keeping these fine old heritage boat types alive. It is possible to build dories from plywood, but plywood has a number of disadvantages and has recently jumped sky-high in price. Besides, some people just don't like plywood in boats.

For this dory we have worked out an alternate method whereby pine can still be used for planking in the old way. This was done by relining the hull for five strakes of plank instead of four, and by specifying composite strakes made up of two or three short lengths joined by glued splices. This permits the use of ordinary No. 2 common white pine boards.

No. 2 common pine is still fairly reasonable in price, as present-day prices go, and generally available. Except for the garboards, which will take 10 inch widths, the boards required will only be 8 inches or less. When planks are pieced up from two or three short lengths, it is often possible to cut out and get rid of bad knots and other defects which otherwise would make the board unusable for a single-length strake. Sound, tight, round knots of small or medium size, when not too numerous and bunched too closely together, are quite acceptable. In fact, a few sound knots scattered through a plank strengthen rather than weaken it, making it less liable to split or "rent," as the boatbuilders say. In the old dories the wide ends of the garboards frequently split as the boat aged, especially if the boat was planked with clear, knot-free lumber. This was one of the weakest points of traditional dory construction, which now with narrower planks and knotty lumber, can be avoided all but completely. The size, number, placement, and type of knots that are allowable is a matter of judgment for which there is no hard and fast general rule. Common sense must govern.

Small, loose knots should be bored out and plugged. Holes reamed to take plugs should be slightly larger on the outside, and pine plugs must be carefully planed to the right taper to fit. These are driven tightly, but not so tightly as to split the plank. Glue should be applied to bond them securely, although in the past, before we had waterproof glue, plugs put in without glue held perfectly well.

The boards for the bottom, also pine, can have numerous sound knots, more than the side plank and larger, because the bottom boards are thicker, and because they don't have to withstand bending strains. In fact a pine bottom will be tougher and wear better with plenty of knots, but these should be kept away from the edges as much as possible so as not to interfere with the garboard fastenings. In both sides and bottom, "spike" knots, so called, which cut across a board and weaken it unduly, should be avoided.

The idea that one has to have clear lumber, and that a sound, serviceable boat, at least a dory, cannot be built without it, is a holdover from former times and is just not so. Of course as already noted, common sense must be used, but what is involved is not so critical that there is likely to be any trouble, if one observes the cautions and follows the directions given.

Splices, if properly made, are just as strong as the uncut board, and when planed smooth and painted cannot be detected. Their locations should be staggered, that is, the splices in any one strake should be separated by a couple of feet or so from those in the strakes directly above or below it.

In this boat the garboards might well be made up of three pieces of equal length, the plank above of two pieces spliced in the middle, the third plank of three lengths and so on. Of course, if full length boards for the straighter strakes should be available, so much the easier and better.

Curved strakes are better spliced up from several shorter lengths. They are frequently stronger than unspliced strakes because in the spliced strake, short, cross grain can be avoided. All of the strakes in the Adirondack guideboats were spliced from two and three shorter pieces for this reason; these strakes were plenty strong even though the builders did not have modern waterproof glue. In this dory the only strake besides the garboard that has any curve to speak of is the sheer, and the sheer planks in Swampscott dories were always spliced anyway, the splice coming about one-third of the way from the stern. In this boat two of the five strakes are nearly dead straight.

The planking layout or diagram given on page 88 for this dory was carefully spiled from an accurately made half model, and so the planking shapes and widths shown should be pretty close, close enough to use as a reliable guide in the selection and splicing of plank. By allowing a little extra width, the plank can be laid out and spliced up ahead of time. Of course the exact shape will have to be spiled directly from the planking set-up of the bottom frame assembly. So far as I know, this is the first time a dimensioned planking diagram has ever been worked out for a how-to design for building a dory. It will make the planking job simpler and easier, and should save a lot of time and lumber.

Plank splices could be fitted and glued on the boat as the planking operation proceeds, but I don't recommend this. It will be far better and easier to lay out the splices and glue them ahead of time. They can then be planed smooth and the full length plank spiled and laid out in one operation. There is much less chance of error.

To a great extent the strength of this hull will depend on its clinker construction, and good lap fastenings are of particular importance. Copper rivets should be used. I strongly recommend the heavier European dished roves and the square-section copper boat nails now available in this country from several suppliers. They are well worth the high price. The dished roves have greater holding power and grip the wood with greater compressive force when the rivet is made up, and are in every way far superior to ordinary flat roves or burrs.

I have shown the hood ends of the plank fastened into the stem with 2-inch galvanized boat nails; 1½-inch or 1¾-inch No. 12 screws could just as well be used.

First choice for the stem stock, sided 2

inches and molded 2½ inches, is dry white oak. Red oak is almost as good. If a plank can be found with a run of grain which favors the curve of the stem, so much the better. If not, straight grain will do, but the stem should be laid out so that the cross grain is equally distributed and does not come all in one end.

If oak is not to be had, any lasting hardwood can be substituted, preferably with a grain that favors the stem curve. Locust, although heavy, would be excellent; should locust be used, the stem could be molded slightly smaller, say 2¼ inches instead of 2½ inches. Apple wood also would be fine. In fact, there is nothing better for dory frames than sound apple limbs of the right bend or curvature.

In case suitable hardwood is not available,

good quality Douglas fir or even longleaf yellow pine may be substituted for the stem. When these softer woods are used, it would be wise to increase the molded dimension somewhat to compensate, say to ¾ inches or even as much as 3 inches. The extra weight would be negligible. Also if softer wood is used for the stem, the fastenings through the hood ends of the planking should be larger.

Another possibility is a glued-up stem using epoxy adhesive. This can be made of smaller pieces fitted together, if a single large plank of sufficient size cannot be found (see the Appendix for more on laminating).

The transom can be Douglas fir or yellow pine just as well as oak. If oak is used, it could be planed to 1¹⁄₁₆ inches thick to save weight. It is better to use red oak than white, because white oak is heavier and is more apt to pull out of shape in wide widths. A maximum width of 14 inches is required, which in most cases would mean making up the transom from two pieces. A heavy cleat across the inside face just below the sheer serves to tie the stern together, if the transom is made of two pieces, and to prevent splitting if it's got out of a single width of plank. The dimensions and bevels for the transom given in the drawing were derived from the lines layout and checked against the working half-model, which was accurately made to scale. They should be close. However, it would be prudent in beveling not to cut to the line at first, but to leave a little wood for final fairing after the set-up has been made, preliminary to planking. This goes for the stem as well.

CONSTRUCTION

The boat should be planked bottom up. The bottom is laid out first, cut to shape, and cleated together. Its edges may be beveled to receive the garboard planks, but for someone building a dory for the first time, it is probably best to leave this beveling operation until the completed frame and bottom assembly is secured bottom-up and in place on the strongback. When the bottom has been cut out and cleated, the stem, the frames, and the stern transom and knee, which have been made up separately, are put in position on the bottom and fastened. All of these members will have to be beveled.

Bevels can be taken ahead of set-up from the full-size laydown of the lines, which according to good boatbuilding practice should be made and faired before any woodwork is started. However, for the beginner who may not trust completely the bevels he takes from his laydown, it would be best, perhaps, not to cut the bevels down all the way to their lines until the boat has been set up and he can check these bevels with a batten. Wood is easily taken off when necessary, but it is much

A 17-foot swampscott dory in frame on a strongback at the Mystic Small Craft Boatshop. The boat is just about ready for planking. (Photo by Mary Anne Stets)

more difficult to pad out bevels that were cut too deep. Besides, in almost all cases it will be necessary to fair the bottom-and-frame assembly more or less extensively after it is set up and before planking starts.

The set-up is made over a strongback, which is a wide 2-inch plank secured on edge at working height, with its upper edge cut to the curve of the inner bottom and notched to receive the frames and bottom cleats. The ends of the strongback are likewise cut to receive the stern knee and the bottom end of the stem. The strongback supports the preliminary assembly of bottom, frames (which serve as molds), stem, and stern transom during the planking operation. After planking is completed, the planked-up shell is lifted off the strongback, turned right-side-up, and the laps are riveted in one operation. Of course, all the nails were previously in place, having been driven as the planks went on.

If the planks are carefully fitted and properly beveled, the riveting operation can be put off until the boat is turned over, when it is done all at once. Of course, the boat could be built right-side-up, and the laps riveted plank by plank, but it would be ever so much harder to bevel the bottom correctly to receive the garboards and to fit the changing lap bevels. The planking operation is far easier and surer when done bottom up over a strongback.

The accompanying drawings will bear some study. Comments and explanations for the numbered references follow:

1. Sheer plank, ½″ thick white pine. For a boat intended for extra hard use, a plank thickness of 9/16″ is recommended. The weight of the boat would not be greatly increased

thereby. This plank has some curve and could be just as well spliced from three pieces. The inwale and cap add extra reinforcement.

2. Frames sided ⅞″, molded 2″ to 3″. Approximately 2¼″ through the knuckles, tapering to 1½″ at the top. Oak should be used, although substitutes such as Douglas fir can be used with proportional increase in dimensions to give equivalent strength. As shown here, two halves are reinforced with a strip of ⅞″ oak across the bottom. Should be cut from natural-crook lumber to avoid cross grain.

There are a number of ways of making dory frames. They can be made in three sections cut out of ordinary oak boards spliced where bottom and sides come together with galvanized iron gusset plates on either side, through riveted. Instead of iron gusset plates, longer plywood gussets on either side, glued and screwed or riveted are acceptable. It is even possible to laminate continuous one-piece frames from thin strips glued on a form.

3. Reinforcing strip connecting to frame halves. Oak, ⅞″ x 2⅛″.

4. Also Nos. 16 and 17. Bottom ¹⁵⁄₁₆″ pine. To be not less than ⅞″ nor more than 1″. Can be two or three boards wide.

5. Outer or false bottom. ½″ thick. Pine, spruce, oak, elm, etc. Put on with screws to be removable and renewable. Function, to take wear from dragging over beaches and rocks.

6. Seat riser, ⅝″ pine, 3½″ wide tapering to 2½″ at ends. Same as No. 21.

7. Thwarts. Pine or spruce ⅞″ to 1″ thick, 8″ wide. Removable, notched to fit frames but not fastened to risers.

8. Inwale. Oak ⅞″ x 1½″ tapered to 1″ at bow, 1¼″ at stern.

9. Cap. Oak, ½″ thick by 2″ wide to cover inwale and top edge of sheer plank. Sawn to shape, not bent. Extends from forward to after frame. Replaced from after frame to stern, and from forward frame to stem, with a narrower strip, beveled on its inner edge, which covers the edge of the sheer planks and laps on the inwale about ¼″.

10. Note that the bottom edge of the garboard is not beveled off in line with the bottom, but is left square or approximately square for the false bottom to fit into.

11. At the ends of the boat where the bottom bevel is not suited to riveting, the lower edge of the garboard plank is fastened to the bottom with 10d nails, spaced 2½" to 3" apart. Nails can be galvanized iron common nails, bronze wire, or annular.

12. Limber to drain bottom of boat. When metal gussets are used to join frame futtocks, the joint in the frame is here.

13. The laps between the frames are fastened with copper rivets spaced 2½" to 3".

14. The laps are fastened into the sawn frames with 1¾" No. 10 bronze wood screws.

15. Plank splices are made 12 times the thickness of the plank—½" thick plank, 6" splice. Scarphs are not planed to a sharp or feather edge, but are left ⅟₁₆" thick on the ends. The splice clamps better this way, and the extra ⅟₁₆" is planed off after the glue has thoroughly set. Scarphs are planed fair and true with a sharp block plane or smoother. Either epoxy or resorcinol glue can be used. Pressure is applied with a piece of oak on either side of the splice, held by four C-clamps. Wax the oak pressure blocks to prevent sticking.

16 & 17. Bottom boards.

18. Frame, same as No. 2.

19. Intermediate bent frames, oak 1" x ½". Steam bent and copper riveted through laps.

20. Cant frames in the ends of the dory. Same as No. 19.

21. Seat riser, same as No. 6.

22. Thwarts, same as No. 7.

23. Bottom cleats. Oak. ⅞" x 2¼".

24. Frame reinforcement, same as No. 3.

25. Transom knee. Oak, hackmatack, or fir. 1¾" thick. 16" overall length.

26. Stem. Oak, 2" thick. Can be hackmatack or Douglas fir, laminated or solid.

27. Capping. Same as No. 9.

28. Inwale. Same as No. 8.

29. Transom cleat. Oak, ¾" thick by 4½" wide.

30. False stem. Oak, steam bent in place after planking is complete and plank ends faired.

31. Bronze strap to cover forward end of bottom and lower end of false stem.

32. Bronze strap, aft end of bottom and bottom of stern transom.

SAILING RIG

For those who would like to sail this Swampscott dory, as well as row her, I offer the following modifications. In adapting this dory for sail I have altered the interior arrangements of the rowing version in a few minor particulars. One of these was to raise the seat riser by one inch, which still leaves 6 inches between the surface of the rowing thwarts and the gunwales. One inch may seem a trivial amount, but it adds needed width to the centerboard without detracting from the rowing qualities of the boat. It is still comfortable to row. With the sail furled and the mast down and stowed in the boat, a single oarsman can row without interference from either thwart A or C, or both may be occupied at the same time with two men pulling. The thwart at station B can be left out entirely, and is not shown in the drawing. If desired, however, it could easily be installed in two pieces with the inboard ends supported by cleats screwed to the sides of the centerboard trunk.

As mentioned previously, the sailing balance of a small boat is affected by so many variables that it is difficult, and often impossible, to figure ahead of time just how the boat will behave in the water, and it is to be expected that adjustments will have to be made after launching and the first trial runs.

Charles G. Davis, who knew a great deal about small craft, both as a designer and as a sailor, was of the opinion that all too frequently in the design of a small sailboat the centerboard will be located too far forward. As it happens, this is especially true for some of the sailing dories, which in consequence have wicked weather helms.

Loading also has a lot to do with the sailing balance. Shifting weight forward or aft in a small boat can make a big difference under certain conditions, as is demonstrated by the behavior of the St. Lawrence River skiffs, which are sailed without rudders, steering being accomplished simply by moving back and forth in the boat to alter the trim.

In laying out the rig for this dory, I have done several things to enable adjustments in the sailing balance. For one thing, the centerboard has been made rather longer and larger than is usual for a boat of this size, and it is located well aft. By dropping it to different depths, or by raising it in the same manner, it will be possible to shift the boat's center of lateral resistance back and forth to some extent. To facilitate this, the oak board is given extra weight by adding a lead insert to give it positive drop, and it is raised by a rope pennant which makes fast to a cleat bolted to the oak capping of the centerboard trunk. In this manner the board is easily raised or lowered as desired.

In addition, there is a choice between two mast positions located 10 inches apart, which allows appreciable shift in the center of effort. By experimenting with mast position, centerboard depth, and weight placement in the boat, it should be possible to arrive at a combination giving satisfactory sailing balance, presumably with a slight weather helm, but not so much as to be tiring.

The indicated sail area is a moderate one with provision for reefing down in heavy weather. As there are no shrouds or stays, the entire rig as a unit is easily and quickly lifted out of the step for stowing in the boat. The spars are short enough to stow at one side, out of the way of the oarsman.

If desired, one might have one or more replacement rigs of smaller and/or larger size for different weather. This was a common practice early in this century at Marblehead, Beverly, and other towns on Boston's North Shore, where some dory fishermen had as many as three separate rigs—a large sail for summer racing, a medium working rig for the summer, and a small sail for winter fishing.

In the profile view on the next page showing a longitudinal section through the center of the boat, several features require additional com-

ment and explanation. The numbers in the explanation refer to the numbers in the drawing.

1. The forward thwart at station A is double width to permit two mast locations, and is braced and reinforced underneath with a fore-and-aft strip of oak 8 inches wide, and ⅞ inches thick. This should be well fastened from the top either with screws or rivets.

2. A pair of hanging knees is needed here for additional bracing. These should be oak, apple, or other hardwood, with a good run of grain—natural crooks, if available—and well fastened. As the riser is unsupported here for some 11 inches forward of the frame at station A, substantial knees at this location are a must.

3. The mast step with its two tapered sockets for the end of the mast is in one piece molded 3 inches deep and notched over the bottom of the frame at station A. Four-and-one-half inches should give sufficient sided width. Pine or Douglas fir will do as well here as oak. The holes to receive the end of the mast should be accurately tapered for a snug fit to grip the end of the mast with enough friction to prevent it from jumping out easily. For further insurance against sudden lifting on the part of the unstayed mast, a soft pine wedge with a long taper fits in a slot about 1½″ wide which is cut through the thwart on the forward side of the mast. If well fitted, a slight tap on top will secure the wedge against the mast, and it will be just as easily knocked out from the bottom in removing the mast.

4. Two fore-and-aft benches of the same stock as the cross thwarts and about 8 inches wide are fitted against the sides of the boat between the thwarts at stations C and D. These are for the convenience of the helmsman when the boat is sailing.

5. The oak blocks or cleats on the underside securing the ends of the fore-and-aft benches to the cross thwarts should be well fastened from the top with screws or rivets. The additional use here of epoxy glue would be desirable, as it would be elsewhere in the boat where members are fastened together in this way. Glue used in such places not only secures

the joint, but if liberally applied, waterproofs it as well. Otherwise, when moisture collects between the mating surfaces of a joint, rot tends to start.

6. The rudder is made of oak ⅞ inches thick, with the blade tapered and thinned somewhat at the bottom and toward the outside. It can be got out of a single width of 12-inch board, or from two narrow boards pinned together with 5/16-inch drifts.

7. A removable pin ½ inch in diameter goes through the transom and the transom cleat, serving as a stopper to keep the rudder from slipping out. A push fit will suffice for easy removal, and it need not be otherwise secured.

8. Either oak or ash will do for a tiller, sided 2 inches at its after end to mortise for the rudder head, ⅞ inch thick. The mortise should be cut long enough to allow the tiller to swing up or down easily. The tiller pivots on a ½-inch diameter pin through the rudder head with a washer and cotter pin to hold it in. The after end of the tiller is reinforced with a through rivet on either side of the mortise. The tiller will, of course, be thinned and tapered both for appearance and to lighten it.

9. The end posts for the centerboard trunk are oak, molded 3 inches and sided 1¼ inches. This should give sufficient clearance for the ⅞ inch thick centerboard. The lower ends of these posts mortise through the bottom for caulking, but are covered by the false, or outer,

bottom. The ends of the bed logs are fastened to the end posts and each other with bolts passing through from side to side. Glue should be used here as well, to insure a strong watertight centerboard trunk.

10. Bed logs for the centerboard trunk, sided 2 inches and cut to fit the rocker of the bottom from pieces 4 inches wide, can very well be pine. Oak is not necessary for strength because of the substantial thickness of these members, made so as to give ample wood for bolting and to secure a lasting watertight fit with the bottom. In cutting through the bottom cleats in the way of the centerboard trunk, keep the cleats long enough for them to be notched into the sides of the bed logs, as shown in the drawing. They should be put in with glue. The bottom of the frame at station B is cut to fit snugly against the bed logs and is secured to them either with a knee or a metal angle piece. The assumption is that the trunk assembly will be installed as a completed unit, having been put together outside the boat.

If the hole for the centerboard pin is accurately bored for a moderate drive fit, it can be cut to come flush with the outside of the bed logs and will stay in place when driven. It is easily driven out should it become necessary to remove the board for painting or repair.

Instead of making the centerboard of two widths of oak board pinned together as shown, you can make it from a piece of plywood ¾ inch thick, or from two thicknesses of ⅜-inch plywood glued together. A plywood centerboard should be covered with fiberglass. Before this is done, it may be tapered slightly and the edges rounded.

Spars should be spruce, if possible. Sitka spruce is hard to get and very expensive. Instead, we suggest the use. of the rough spruce now imported in large quantities from Canada for staging planks and boards. It is often possible to pick out pieces that are nearly clear. In cutting

out the narrow strips required for gluing up these small spars, it is generally possible to avoid any bad knots. An occasional small pin knot does not matter.

The sail could be laced to the mast, but the arrangement shown does just as well, and if it does not look quite as neat, it makes it much easier and quicker to bring down the sprit should it become necessary to reef. The two rolling hitches that secure the snotter to the sprit hold beautifully and are easy to tie and adjust.

1 2

A North Shore Surf Dory

· · · · · · · · · · · · · · · · · · · ●· · · · · · · · · · · · · · · · · · · ·

Getting a boat on or off the beach in running surf requires a knack—also a special kind of boat. Back in the mid-1950s, when the Texas Petroleum Company was in need of a small surf boat on the west coast of Nicaragua, they sent up to New England. The boat they picked was a double-ended, round-sided surf dory of the sort developed in the North Shore fishing towns of Marblehead and Swampscott, Massachusetts. It was essentially a refinement of the fisherman's beach dory, with a trace of whaleboat, perhaps, and something from larger lifesaving craft as well as from the general heritage of scores of double-ended lapstrake work boat types once found on the North Atlantic coast.

The 19-foot surf dory was designed to carry at least four men and several hundred pounds of equipment and lines. In heavy surf there is normally a helmsman with a steering oar and three men pulling single oars. Under less severe conditions, however, two men, rowing in the ordinary manner with a pair of oars each, can handle the boat nicely and show a fair turn of speed. The boat is by no means so heavy or cumbersome that one capable oarsman cannot manage under most conditions, outside of surf.

The last builder to construct any number of surf dories of this sort was the late George L. Chaisson of Swampscott, Massachusetts. In the 1920s, Chaisson made them for local use and also shipped them to various parts of the country. They are listed in his catalog of that time as "Life and Surf Boats." What he had to say about them in this old catalog is interesting and informative:

Small life-boats, suited for ocean-going yachts, or for surfboats to launch from the beach. Light, yet strongly built, and fitted with air tanks forward and aft. Cork sponsons on the outside. These boats have been adopted by the Metropolitan Park Commissioners as life-saving surf-boats along the New England Coast. Excellent sea boats and easily handled. Slightly flat on the bottom and will float in five inches of water. They have white oak frames, steam bent; cedar planking; oak bottom; gunwales and chafing strip, oak; cross seats, oak or spruce; copper fastened, and painted three coats of white, outside as in. Fitted with painter ring and hoisting bolts when required. Two pairs of ash oars and row-locks furnished with each boat. Built in lengths to suit the purchaser.

The Chaisson catalog also reproduced a letter from the Cummer Lumber Company of Jacksonville, Florida, dated October 10, 1923. After stating that a new surfboat, just received, had been placed in service, the letter went on to say: "Our beach is flat and naturally during high winds we have a very heavy broken surf to contend with. We succeeded in launching through a heavy northeaster two weeks ago, a feat which has never been accomplished on this beach before."

The surfboat built by Chaisson was certainly derived in large measure from the

(Left) Chamberlain's double-ended surf dory, built for the Metropolitan District Commission's Beach Patrol around 1900.   (Right) The 19-foot surf dory designed and built for use as an oil company beach tender.

distinctive, round-sided work dories developed by the fishermen on the flat, sandy beaches of Swampscott and Lynn. But William Chamberlain built these surfboats or lifeboats in his Marblehead boatshop before Chaisson. And it appears to have been Chamberlain who designed the model or derived it, rather, from the common round-sided work dory. Possibly Chamberlain was indebted also to the design of the larger (30 feet) lifeboats of the Old Massachusetts Humane Society, which in Chamberlain's day maintained

19-FOOT SURF DORY OFFSETS — FEET, INCHES, AND EIGHTHS					
STATIONS	STEM	7+8	5+6	3+4	1+2
HEIGHTS SHEER	2-10-1	2-4-6	2-1-2	1-10-7	1-9-2
KNUCKLE 4	2-7-2	2-1-1	1-8-6	1-5-1	1-2-6
" 3	2-3-0	1-8-4	1-3-5	0-11-4	0-8-4
" 2	1-10-5	1-4-6	0-11-6	0 8-0	0-5-2
" 1	1-5-7	1-1-8	0-8-6	0-5-3	0-3-2
IN. BOT.	0-2-4	STEM	0-2-2	0-1-4	0-1-2
HALF-BREADTHS SHEER	0-0-1	0-11-6	1-7-2	2-1-2	2-5-4
KNUCKLE 4	"	0-11-1	1-6-3	2-0-1	2-4-2
" 3	"	0-9-5	1-4-0	1-9-1	2-0-6
" 2	"	0-7-5	1-1-2	1-5-1	1-7-6
" 1	"	0-5-5	0-10-3	1-1-3	1-3-4
IN. BOT.	"	STEM	0-2-2	0-7-6	0-11-3

OFFSETS MEASURED FROM BASELINE TO INSIDE PLANK, TO INSIDE BOTTOM, TO STEM PROFILE.

its Lifesaving Station No. 10 at Marblehead. The Humane Society's lifeboats, in turn, show a definite whaleboat influence.

The boat built for the Texas Petroleum Company, the lines and offsets for which are reproduced here, follows closely the old Chamberlain 19-footer, except that the new boat was given slightly more depth and beam to increase its carrying capacity as a working boat. In this respect, the new boat reverts somewhat to the proportions of its ancestor, the round-sided Swampscott work dory.

The leaner, slimmer, Chamberlain model would possibly row easier than the boat drawn here, but would carry less and likely would be less stable. Chamberlain built a 19-foot gunning dory similar to a surf dory, except that it had

less sheer, was constructed lighter, and had four planks to a side instead of five as has the surf dory. (See Chapter 14). It was an exceptionally fast, easy-rowing boat even with only one man at the oars. But its exceptional lightness sometimes made it lively in rough water.

Several departures were made from Chamberlain's construction when the surf dory was built for the Texas Petroleum Company. Intermediate to the standard sawn dory frames, steam-bent white oak ribs were placed in the manner adopted by Chaisson, a structural feature of great importance in adding strength and stiffness to the hull. The garboards were made of 5-ply, ⅜-inch thick Douglas fir marine plywood, spliced in the middle. The garboards of this boat are so wide that suitable pine boards for them are nearly impossible to obtain today. (For more on plywood as a substitute for pine boards, see the Appendix.) Furthermore, plywood is stronger and does not split or rent, a common fault of old-style pine garboards. It was necessary, however, to take special measures to seal and to protect the edges of the plywood. A new method of locating the sawn frames up under the cross thwarts was employed to get a stronger frame and to avoid metal clips. An improved double bottom was adopted from one seen on a dory built by Fred Dion of Salem. For flotation, styrofoam was used instead of air tanks. Tanks can spring leaks. They are also difficult to make and expensive. Styrofoam is better in every way, and much cheaper. Instead of iron fastenings, bronze screws and copper rivets were used throughout. Modern waterproof glue as well as liquid rubber was employed. The inner bottom was made of mahogany, as mahogany gives a better hold for the garboard screws than pine, yet will not swell and shrink as much as an oak

bottom would in the extreme conditions of the tropics.

Certain features of the hull should be noted. Both ends are identical to meet breakers either way, and the inside arrangement is such that the boat can be rowed in either direction. The ends are sharp to cut through the waves, yet full enough to have lots of lift. They are also carried high enough to keep above the crests. This means more than an ordinary amount of sheer when the ends are swept down to a moderate freeboard amidships to permit a good rowing angle for the oars and to keep down wind resistance. The bottom is straight and flat, which gives the boat a good seat on the beach and a very shoal draft, permitting the boat to go high up on the beach before grounding out. The bottom is also exceptionally solid to take pounding on a rough beach. The flotation is placed quite high in the ends to make the boat right easily in the water, should it ever capsize.

1 3

The Chamberlain Gunning Dory

........................•........................

This boat is a Marblehead gunning dory of up-to-date construction and the most modern materials built for James S. Rockefeller, Jr., of Camden, Maine, by Veli Holmstrom in his Vinalhaven, Maine, shop with the owner assisting. The lines of the boat, with minor changes, are the same that I showed in the February, 1960, issue of *Outdoor Maine*. These were taken off by me in 1942 from William Chamberlain's personal gunning dory, since broken up and destroyed, but owned in 1942 by Charles Briggs of Marblehead who used it for part-time lobster fishing during the early 1940s.

Using a gunning dory for lobstering is like hitching a spirited horse to a dump cart. But this superbly beautiful double-ender of ultra-light construction stood the gaff for several years in spite of advanced age and the roughest sort of treatment. Even under huge loads of lobster pots it rode the waves lightly, with infinite grace and with only slight urging on the oars. The gunning dory as perfected in Marblehead by William Chamberlain is the queen of all dories, and one of the handsomest double-enders ever built anywhere, not to mention its easy speed under oars and its unexcelled rough-water ability with capable hands at the oars.

The fame of the gunning dory reached the ears of James Rockefeller, an enthusiastic duck hunter who finds gunning among the islands and ledges in lower Penobscot Bay around Vinal-

haven a fabulous and fascinating experience with a "certain mystique impossible to describe." He wanted to prolong the season into the first weeks of January, but that required a boat of unusual qualities, for as he observed, it can get quite nasty in a hurry on the offshore ledges in the winter time.

Rockefeller specified a boat large enough to hold two men with guns, decoys, and other gear, and to manage safely and comfortably in a bad chop. At the same time he wanted something that might double as a summer rowboat for his wife and two small children. And it must be light enough to drag up on the transom of his 36 foot lobsterboat with the aid of rollers.

In the beginning Rockefeller had not considered the possibility of sailing this boat, but when this was suggested he adopted the idea with alacrity. The original length of 19½ feet seemed excessive, particularly so, I suppose, in this decadent era of sawed-off, tubby outboard boats, but I held out for an overall length of nothing less than 18 feet and won my point.

The other changes in the lines were slight. I gave the modified version slightly more beam in proportion to length and widened the bottom a trifle aft. In lowering the deadrise angle just a bit, I attained a somewhat harder knuckle at the junction of the second and third planks with the object of giving stiffer bearing for sailing. In fact all changes in the lines, with the exception of

(Above) The 18-foot gunning dory under oars. The high bow, sharply raked ends, and low freeboard are key factors in the boat's exceptional rough water ability. (Left) The gunning dory under sail. The steering oar used can be replaced with the more efficient drop rudder described here.

Chapter 14). Otherwise we went about adapting this boat to sail cautiously and experimentally, starting out with a small sail area and an oar substituting for a rudder as originally used by the Swampscott and Marblehead lobstermen of 60 years ago when they sailed their working dories.

Even with meager canvas and the relatively clumsy steering oar, the new gunning dory sails surprisingly well. To some extent, this is certainly due to her exceptional lightness achieved without any sacrifice of strength by the use of a special seam batten construction utilizing laminated spruce framing, epoxy adhesive, and ¼-inch plywood planking reinforced with Dynel fabric set in epoxy resin. This is basically the same construction tested by me in the light pram described in Chapter 3. It combines lightness with great strength, insures perfect tightness, and obviates beveling for laps, which is generally a bugaboo for the inexperienced amateur builder.

shortening the length by about a foot under that of the original, were made with the object of making the boat stiffer under sail, yet without impairing her easy rowing qualities to any noticeable degree.

Originally the gunning dories carried a light, unstayed mast and a small sail for running before the wind. Naturally they required no centerboard. We had more ambitious plans for sailing, and borrowed the details for the centerboard and centerboard case from Chamberlain's famous 21-foot Beachcomber sailing dory (see

18' MARBLEHEAD GUNNING DORY
1965 REVISION — J. GARDNER
SHEET 3
INTERIOR DETAILS & MOTOR WELL

1. MARINE PLYWOOD ⅜" TH'K. CAN BE 2 LAYERS ¼" EPOXY GLUED
2. STEM (SEE SHEET 1)
3. FRAMES ⅞" OAK (SHEET 2)
4. SHEER BATTEN ⅝" x 1½" PINE OAK OR SPRUCE
5. PLANKING ⅜" MARINE PLYWOOD
6. SEAT RISER ⅞" x 3" x 2½" (KNOW) SPRUCE
7. THWARTS ⅞" x 9" SPRUCE, PINE
8. END DECKS PLYWOOD ⅜" – ½"
9. END DECK BEAM ⅞" SPRUCE, PINE
10. BREAST HOOK ⅞" PLYWOOD, LET IN FLUSH INTO SHEER BAT. & SH. PLANK. GLUED SCREWED
11. FALSE STEM ⅝" OAK. STEAM BENT SCREWED & FAIRED TO PLANKING.
12. BREAST HOOK REINFORCEMENT ⅞" PINE CURVED TO FIT UNDER EDGE OF BREAST HOOK
13. END DECK CLEAT ⅞" PINE SCREWED TO STEM
14. FLOOR GUSSET FR.3 ⅜" PLYWOOD (SHEET 2)
15. THWART KNEE. GLUED UP. CORE ⅞" OAK OR MAHOG. ⅜" PLYW. EITHER SIDE. WELL SCREWED FROM UNDERSIDE THWART & GLUED.
16. MAST STEP 3 LAYERS ⅜" PLYW. GLUED. SURFACE REINFORCED PLASTIC.
17. MAST STEP SUPPORT ⅞" OAK STRIP 2" HIGH TO MATCH FRAME. SCREWED THRU BOTTOM FROM UNDER SIDE.
18. THWART REINFORCEMENT UNDER SIDE AT MAST HOLE ⅜" PLYW. GLUED.
19. OARLOCK PLATE'S, 3 SETS. NO.1 DAVIS PAT.
20. FRONT END WELL BOX ¾" MARINE PLYWOOD OR 2 LAYERS ⅜" GLUED.
21. AFT END WELL BOX SAME AS FRONT.
22. MOTOR WELL BRACE ⅞" OAK. 2 PARTS BUTTED AMIDS. SCREWED TO BOX & THRU BOT. & SIDES OF BOAT.
23. SIDES WELL BOX PLYW. ¾" CLEATED SIDES & BOTTOM WITH 2" WIDE STRIPS ⅞" OAK. WELL SCREWED & GLUED.
24. WELL BOX CLEATS ⅞" OAK 2" WIDE
25. AFTER CLEAT MOTOR WELL ⅞" x 3" OAK, SPRUCE, PINE. SCREWED & GLUED TO BOX & UNDERSIDE OF THWART.
26. WEDGE, OAK. FOR CLAMPING MOTOR TO HANG AT CORRECT ANGLE WITH W.L. OR BASE LINE OF BOAT. ANGLE FROM 74° TO 78°.
27. THREE ⅝" RING BOLTS (I.D. 2") 2 INSIDE FOR PAINTERS. 1 OUTSIDE AT BOW FOR TOWING.
28. FOAM FLOTATION UNDER END DECKS AND UNDER THWARTS.
29. FILLER PADS BELOW SHEER BAT. TO CATCH LOWER SCREWS OARLOCK PLATES.

FRAME PATTERN OUTLINES
FRAMES SET ON NUMBERED STATIONS. THICKNESS OF BOW FRAMES FORWARD OF STATION LINES. THICKNESS OF AFT FRAMES AFT OF STATION LINES. THIS PERMITS BEVELING FRAMES FOR PLANKING FIT WITHOUT CHANGING SHAPE OR SIZE OF FRAME.

18' MARBLEHEAD GUNNING DORY
1965 REVISION — J. GARDNER
SHEET 1 — LAYOUT DIMENSIONS
FRAMES — STEM — BOTTOM

FRAMES OAK 7/8" THICK   MOLDED
DIMENSIONS AS SHOWN

FRAME 3

FRAME GUSSET 3/8" PLYWOOD

LIMBER

SIDES FRAME 3 JOINED WITH
PLYWOOD GUSSET RESTING ON
STEM. GLUED AND SCREWED WITH 1" #10'S.

BOW   SPLICE   SPLICE

PATTERN BOTTOM PLANK 3/8" MARINE GRADE FIR PLYWOOD. 2 SPLICES. FROM SCALE MODEL. ALLOW 2" EXTRA FOR FIT.

EPOXY

TEMPORARY SCREWS WHERE NEEDED TO DRAW TIGHT UNTIL EPOXY GLUE SETS — LATER REMOVE AND PLUG.

BOTTOM 2 LAYERS 3/8" M. PLYWOOD GLUED TOGETHER

BOTTOM SEAM BET FRAMES

BOTTOM REINFORCED OUTSIDE ONE LAYER POLYPROPYLENE EPOXY-BONDED COVERED WITH ONE LAYER OF DYNEL AND EPOXY RESIN.

SCREWS 1 1/8" #10 BRONZE 3" ON CENTERS BETWEEN FRAMES

6" POLYPROPYLENE STRIP INSIDE REINFORCEMENT EPOXY BONDED 2"

BOTTOM SEAM COMPLETED

1 3/4" #10 OR #12 BRONZE W.S. SPACED 3"- 4" ON BOTTOM

GLUED

1 1/2" #10 BRONZE W.S. SPACED 3" TO 4" ON SIDES OF FRAMES

LIMBER

FRAME 1

SIZE 'WALE REDUCED AT STEM GRADUAL TAPER STARTING AT FRAME 2

FASTENING BETWEEN FRAMES

FRAME 2

SIDES FRAME 2 BUTTED ON CENTER LINE OF BOTTOM JOINED WITH OAK 10" x 1 3/4" x 5/8" GLUED AND SCREW FASTENED WITH 1 1/2" #10'S OR #12'S.

FRAME 2

SIDES BUTT ON C.L.

2" #6 BRONZE W.S. IN SEAM BATTENS SPACED APPROX. 4" BETWEEN FRAMES NOT AT FRAMES TO AVOID WEAKENING BATTENS WITH TOO MANY FASTENINGS IN ONE PLACE.

PLANKING GLUED TO FRAMES AND BATTENS WITH EPOXY GLUE

FRAME 1

SHEER

EACH SIDE FRAME 1 MADE OF 2 PIECES TO GIVE STRAIGHTER GRAIN. JOINED WITH 3/8" PLYWOOD GUSSETS EACH SIDE. THESE COME UP FOR UNDER SIDE OF THWART TO REST ON.

TWO 3/8" PLYWOOD GUSSETS

BUTT

UNDER SIDE OF THWART

GUSSETS GLUED AND SCREWED WITH 1 1/2" #10'S

SIDES FR. 1 LAP BY EACH OTHER ON CENTER LINE.

SEAM BATTENS DIMINISH TO 1 1/4" AT BOW AND STERN. GRADUAL TAPER STARTING AT FRAME 2.

1   BOTTOM BOARDS 3 WIDTHS 7/8" WHITE PINE
2   BENT FRAMES BET. SAWN FRS. AND IN ENDS. WHITE OAK 1 x 7/8".
3   SAWN FRS. WH. OAK 3/8" TO 7/8" TH'C.
4   BOTTOM CLEATS OAK 2" x 3/8".
5   PLANKING 1/2" WH. PINE — CEDAR — CYPRESS.
6   SEAT RISER PINE 7/8" x 3" x 2 1/4"
7   GUNWALE OAK 7/8" x 1 1/4" AMIDS. TAPERED TO 3/4" AT ENDS.
8   GUNWALE CAP 3/8" TH'K RUNS TO LAST SAWN FRS.
9   GUNWALE TRIM AT ENDS 5/8" x 1/2"
10 BREAST HOOK 7/8" OAK.
11 FALSE STEM STEAM-BENT TO COVER PLANK ENDS & INNER STEM 3/8" OAK.
12 SHEER TRIM OAK HALFROUND 1" TAPERED TO 3/4" AT ENDS.

LAP FASTENED 2 1/4"- 3" ON CENTERS BETWEEN FRAMES

COPPER RIVET OR CLINCHED GAL. CHISEL POINT NAIL

SCREW OR BOAT NAIL THRU LAP INTO FRAME

GARBOARD TO BOTTOM 10 d. GAL. NAILS SPACED 2 1/2"- 3"

SECTION A-A

TRADITIONAL CONST. LAPSTRAKE PLANK. NATURAL LUMBER.

FIRST. CENTERBOARD AND C.B. TRUNK MADE UP AS A COMPLETE WORKING ASSEMBLY OUTSIDE BOAT.

SECOND FIT ASSEMBLY TO SLOT IN BOTTOM. SNUG WOOD-TO-WOOD FIT REQUIRED.

THIRD GLUE AND SCREW ASSEMBLY TO BOTTOM. 2 1/4" #16 BRONZE W.S. ON 3" CENTERS. PUT IN FROM OUTSIDE INTO BED LOGS.

LIFTING HANDLE

CLEAT

MAST HOLE

TOP STRIP PINE 5/8" x 1 1/2"

BED LOGS OAK 7/8" x 3"

GLUE

3/4" BRONZE PIN

BED LOGS

3/8" PLYWOOD SIDES

THWART

METAL STRAP LET IN FLUSH & RIVETED

SHOULDERED

GLUE

BOTTOM BOAT

END POST OAK 1" x 2" SHOULDERED THRU BOTTOM

CENTER BOARD 2 LAYERS OF 3/8" PLYWOOD GLUED WITH EPOXY AND ONE THICKNESS OF DYNEL IN THE JOINT. OUTSIDE COVERED WITH EPOXY BONDED DYNEL.

DYNEL

EPOXY AND DYNEL

EPOXY AND DYNEL

GLUED SPLICE 3/8" PLYWOOD. SCARPH RATIO 12 x THICKNESS

STRAPPING

TEMPORARY NAILS 2

WAX PAPER

EPOXY   SPLICE

PLYWOOD

WAX PAPER

TEMPORARY SUPPORT PLANK

FISHERMAN'S   LEG-O-MUTTON DORY RIG
ADAPTED FROM THE CHAMBERLAIN
"BEACHCOMBER"

PEAK LASHED

SHOULDER CLEAT

EYE SPLICE

BAND FOR SINGLE BLOCK

JIB HALYARD MANILA 1/4"

SWIVEL-EYE BOAT SNAP SHACKLED TO SINGLE BLOCK FOR MAIN HALYARD LINE 2

LUFF OF JIB SEIZED TO 3/32" YACHT WIRE. THIMBLE SPLICED IN EITHER END 2

JIB SHEETS 1/4" MANILA SPLICED INTO CLEW 4

SHACKLE AND SWIVEL-EYE BOAT SNAP INTO 3/8" RING BOLT.

HALYARD ONLY STAY CLEATS ON THWART

MAIN HALYARD MANILA 1/4"

SWIVEL BLOCKS TO SEAT RISER FOR JIB SHEETS

BOOM GOOSENECK BANDED TO MAST

BRIDLES 3/8" HEMP OR MANILA 1/4" DACRON. EYE SPLICE AT ENDS

LASHING

BRIDLE

MAIN SHEET 3/8" DACRON OR 1/2" COTTON

SWIVEL BLOCK

RING & SNAP

SWIVEL BLOCKS SHACKLED TO RING BOLT

SEE SEPARATE DETAILS FOR DROP RUDDER

SPARS SPRUCE. MAST 3" DIA. AT THWART. TAPERS TO 1 1/2" AT HEAD. MAST 14' LONG. BOOM AT GOOSENECK 1 1/4" 1 1/2" OUTER END 2 1/4" CENTER 12'-8" LONG. MAINSAIL LASHED TO SPARS WITH MARLINE THRU GROMMETS 10" ON CENTERS. SAIL NO.1 J. CLOTH.

GRATINGS TO FIT BOTTOM BETWEEN FRAMES

GRATING STRIPS 1/2" OR 3/8" PINE NAILED TO 3/4" PINE CROSS CLEATS

FRAME 3   FRAME 2   FRAME 1

	TOP STRAKE	TOP S.	TOP S.
	SECOND S.	SECOND S.	SECOND S.
	BOTTOM S.	BOT. S.	BOT. S.

SET THIS SIDE ON STATION LINE

STATION LINE SIDE

STATION LINE SIDE

APPROXIMATE FRAME BEVELS FOR PLANKING

The gunning dory partly planked, showing laminated stem, plywood planking, and seam batten construction.

THE DROP RUDDER

The boat sails well, but would obviously sail much better with a suitable rudder. For one thing, a rudder would permit the helmsman to place his weight where it would do the most good, and a well adjusted rudder of suitable size would give much surer control. But fitting a rudder to this double-ended boat, considering the curve and rake of its stern post or rather its "stern stem," if the term may be permitted, involves a few problems. For one thing a rudder hung on an excessive rake tends to lift and lose its bite in the water when it is turned. Besides, the slant is awkward for the tiller or the tiller yoke. Certainly it was not possible to borrow the Beachcomber dory's rudder, as we had its centerboard, for the Beachcomber's "tombstone" is straight and not raked excessively.

In addition to the problem of mounting the rudder on a curved and overhanging stern there are other things to consider. It is desirable that the rudder be easily removed. The drop rudder shown comes off by loosening a single nut; the hinged blade also swings up by itself to clear any obstructions, and lifts and secures above the bottom so that the boat may be drawn out on the beach without disengaging the rudder.

The drop rudder is not new. Who invented it and when is uncertain, but 85 years ago drop rudders were in general use in this country for sailing canoes and other small craft used at that time for cruising and racing. The one shown here is adapted from W. P. Stephens's *Canoe And Boat Building*, Fourth Edition, 1889. Stephens, canoeing editor of *Forest and Stream*, was a pioneer authority on American small craft and the boatbuilding practices of his period then at a peak of perfection unapproached today. His building manual for amateurs is a treasure house of detail and a standard source book in small craft design. The rudder that I have worked out for our modernized version of the Chamberlain gunning dory is taken directly from the drop rudder formerly made by Charles Piepenbrink of Albany, N. Y. Stephens recommended it as "one of the best," and has detailed it carefully in his book.

This drop rudder is really not as complicated as might appear from a quick glance at the drawings. Unfamiliar drawings of detail frequently give such an impression until they have been studied awhile. Actually this rudder is quite a simple contrivance, made entirely from standard, easily obtained materials, and it is not difficult to construct.

The rudder stock and the rudder port are made out of standard brass pipe. The only lathe work is the solid plug closing the upper end of the rudder stock, which can be shouldered and threaded in 15 minutes. The two cheek pieces and the rib that joins and stiffens them can be

cut out just as quickly from ordinary flat brass or bronze on a metal-cutting bandsaw. A few holes are bored on the drill press and assembly is made by brazing. There is nothing beyond the skill of the capable amateur or the ordinary equipment of most boatshops.

There is enough clearance between the interior diameter of the ¾-inch extra heavy red brass pipe specified for the rudder port and the outside diameter of the ⅜-inch extra heavy red brass pipe used for the rudder stock to give a loose working fit, but not too loose. In locating the rudder port enough off center, either to port or starboard, sufficient to clear the stern post, no loss in rudder efficiency or any other undesirable effect may be expected.

The rudder port pipe is threaded on its lower end so as to screw tightly into the ⅞-inch thick wood block reinforcing the hull where the port goes through. If the pipe is threaded in tightly and glued with epoxy adhesive, the connection should be perfectly rigid and tight. The rudder port is also braced and held by the 4-inch thwart at the sheer line. The pipe port must be strongly secured, for it holds the entire weight of the rudder on its upper end. The underside of the tiller or tiller yoke, which is reinforced by a brass plate, turns on the upper end of this pipe.

The cheek plates brazed to the lower end of the rudder stock or shaft must be rigid enough to resist any side leverage exerted by the blade. The ½-inch thick rib which separates them and to which they are brazed adds greatly to their rigidity. To provide for strength and rigidity here I have specified spring brass or hard bronze for these cheek plates. If there is any doubt or difficulty in getting proper materials, it would be better if these cheeks were made 3/16 inch thick instead of ⅛ inch.

Clearance of 1/16 inch is allowed between the cheeks and the blade to prevent the latter from binding. A metal bushing in the blade for the pivot pin to go through will prevent wear and decrease friction. The lower portion of the cheek rib and spacer acts as a stop to prevent the blade from dropping too low or swinging under the boat. The after edge of the blade is tapered to streamline it somewhat. It should be completely covered with fiberglass or, better, Dynel, set in epoxy resin. The finished surface should be sanded as smooth as possible.

The lanyard passing through the hole in the upper, outer end of the blade should be a piece of light cord, preferably nylon, but strong enough to lift several times the weight of the rudder. It should be long enough so that when the upper end is tied inside the boat, the blade of the rudder can swing freely and with no hindrance. This cord or lanyard serves two purposes. By means of it the blade may be drawn up and tied to clear the bottom. Or, with the cord tied inside the boat, the rudder may be safely dropped in deep water and hauled aboard.

Whether an ordinary stick tiller is used or a tiller yoke and tiller lines is a matter still to be settled. Yoke and lines are seldom seen today, but Chamberlain favored them for dories and rigged his famous racing Beachcomber in this way. With lines for steering, the helmsman could sit amidships and could place his weight wherever he wished. It is necessary for a boat so equipped to carry a slight weather helm to keep a taut steering line. Besides some of the sailing dories, many of the old sailing canoes were steered with yoke and lines. Some of these almost forgotten craft carried light rigs to nearly ultimate refinement.

14

The Beachcomber-Alpha Dory

It looks as though this fine dory, once popular in Marblehead and Salem, Massachusetts, and a product of the Beachcomber and Alpha Dory Clubs, could be in for a revival of sorts now that the pertinent data is available. The Beachcomber-Alpha dory is a good boat to learn to sail in. It is a safe boat for youngsters in their early teens, but no toy. In fact, sailed hard and to its capacity, this craft can provide thrills and a vigorous workout for most adult sailors. It can be rowed as well as sailed and handles easily under oars, like the working dories of the Massachusetts Bay shore fishermen of the late nineteenth century from which it was derived. With a full rig, 50 pounds of lead ballast on either side the centerboard trunk, and a crew of three hiked out on the rail, this boat will draw smartly to windward and handle like a spirited colt.

The Beachcomber-Alpha is also an economy boat. The standard rig, contrived to be lifted out of the boat and carried home at night in a compact roll on the skipper's shoulder, is just about as simple and inexpensive as it is possible for a workable rig to be. It would be misleading to say that the hull is an easy one to build, yet it is not so difficult as to be out of the reach of amateur capability. It looks harder than it actually is.

For those who do not feel up to beveling and riveting lapstrake planking, an easier seam-batten planking construction can be substituted. This modified construction has been very successfully used on other dory hulls of Chamberlain design. Strakes of marine plywood are butted and glued on longitudinal seam battens, and, for reinforcement, the joint on the outside is bound with fiberglass tape set in epoxy glue. The result is absolutely and permanently tight as well as extremely strong. The difficulties of fitting laps are bypassed, and the problems of finding suitable lumber are virtually eliminated—plywood is easily obtainable.

EVOLUTION OF
THE BEACHCOMBER-ALPHA

The Beachcomber-Alpha dories have had a long and interesting history. Central to their development was William Chamberlain, who was born in 1864 and who began building and racing dories sometime in the 1880s. Dory sailing was a coming sport in those days in Marblehead and neighboring North Shore towns, and boats like those that served the local fishermen on weekdays were raced on Sundays and holidays.

Chamberlain built superior dories, and won races and cups sailing them. Yet when the Beachcomber Dory Club was formed on the Marblehead waterfront sometime in the 1890s, Chamberlain may not have been sole builder of

21' BEACHCOMBER-ALPHA DORY
LINES REVISED NOVEMBER 1964 J.G.

	STATIONS	T	A	4	3	2	1	B	S
HEIGHTS ABOVE BASE-LINE	SHEER	2-4-1	2-0-5	1-10-6	1-9-2	1-9-4	1-11-1	2-1-5	2-7-2
	1ST KNUCKLE	2-0-5	1-7-4	1-5-0	1-3-2	1-3-3	1-6-1	1-9-7	2-5-7
	2ND KNUCKLE	1-9-5	1-3-0	1-0-2	0-10-2	0-10-1	1-1-5	1-5-7	2-2-6
	3RD KNUCKLE	1-5-1	0-11-4	0-8-4	0-6-6	0-6-7	0-10-2	1-2-5	1-11-2
	4TH KNUCKLE	0-10-6	0-7-4	0-5-2	0-4-2	0-4-2	0-7-0	0-11-4	1-7-4
	BOTTOM	0-3-2	0-2-7	0-2-3	0-2-1	0-2-0	0-2-6	0-3-3	0-3-4
HALF-BREADTHS TO INSIDE PLANKING	SHEER	0-6-7	1-7-2	2-1-1	2-5-3	2-6-0	2-1-4	1-6-2	0-0-0
	1ST KNUCKLE	0-7-3	1-6-3	2-0-0	2-4-2	2-4-4	1-11-5	1-4-7	0-0-0
	2ND KNUCKLE	0-6-3	1-3-4	1-8-5	2-0-3	2-1-2	1-8-5	1-2-4	0-0-0
	3RD KNUCKLE	0-4-6	0-11-6	1-4-1	1-7-3	1-8-1	1-4-6	1-11-7	0-0-0
	4TH KNUCKLE	0-2-6	0-7-0	1-11-2	1-2-3	1-3-0	1-0-5	0-8-5	0-0-0
		0-0-2	0-1-7	0-6-3	0-10-0	0-10-6	0-7-6	0-1-3	0-0-0

T = TRANSOM. STATION A. 3'-6" FRD. SHEER AT TRANSOM.
STATION B. 3'-7" AFT SHEER AT OUTBOARD STEM. S = STEM.
TOLERANCE, PLUS OR MINUS ⅛". REVISED NOVEMBER 1964. J.G.

club dories. There is evidence that, at first, members' boats and rigs were far from being uniform. But evidently Chamberlain's model soon became standard and had no competition until about 1912 when a young dory sailor by the name of Sam Brown, later to become a successful naval architect, designed the *Outlaw* for Ed Murphy.

The *Outlaw* was flatter on the sheer than Chamberlain's dory and faster around the harbor course. It constituted a further step in the evolutionary transition from the lobsterman's working dory to specialized racing class boats. As Ben Tutt of Marblehead once told me, the Outlaw "broke up the Beachcomber Club." Of course, the *Outlaw* actually didn't break up the Beachcomber Club or class there and then, for Beachcomber-Alpha dories were actively sailed and raced throughout the 1920s and even into the 1930s. But Tutt is right that the *Outlaw* started the evolution to larger, heavier, flatter, decked-over types with enlarged sail area and standing rigging that eventually replaced the lighter, slimmer, open dories directly copied from the workboats of the late nineteenth-century lobster fishermen.

After the *Outlaw*, it seems likely that Chamberlain may have modified the Beachcomber hull somewhat to increase its speed, but

we do not know and have no way of knowing. It has been credibly reported that Chamberlain sometimes adjusted the shape of his dories slightly to suit the planking boards at hand. We know that he liked to experiment. It is reasonable to assume some progressive evolution as well as random variation in the succession of Beachcomber-Alpha hulls that came out of Chamberlain's Orne Street shop over a space of more than 30 years.

We do know about changes in the Beachcomber-Alpha rig, however, which were both extensive and distributed throughout the life of the class. The development of the rig will be discussed further later on in this chapter.

A 21-foot Beachcomber sailing dory built by Ernest Tarr of Gloucester, Massachusetts. (Photo courtesy of Mystic Seaport)

LINES AND OFFSETS

The lines and offsets for the Beachcomber-Alpha dory have been rechecked and revised since they first appeared in *Outdoor Maine* in 1961. The sheer has been lifted one inch higher on the stem, and the hood ends of the planks below the sheer have been lifted and relined accordingly, so as not to alter appreciably their widths at the stem. This might not seem to be much of a change, yet it improves the appearance noticeably, as I discovered when I constructed the scale model of the Beachcomber-Alpha now in the Peabody Museum of Salem.

The sheer, as it now stands, is probably closer to the sheer line of the fishing dories from which the Beachcomber-Alpha class originally derived. Later on, the boats were flattened out on top somewhat in what seems to have been an attempt to increase speed by cutting hull windage.

It is important not to overlook that the lines are drawn to the inside of the planking. This is noted on the lines and offsets, but some readers, unfamiliar with dories and small craft building practice, might overlook it. To work from the inside of the planking is easiest and most accurate, especially for clinker-planked boats with knuckled sides. It permits laying out directly the shape of the frames which serve as building molds, without having to deduct plank thickness or to make an allowance for lap widths.

However, the planking lines as drawn do not represent the outside appearance of the hull after it has been planked. The finished plank lines will be lower by the width of the lap. This shows up especially in the width of the garboard, which will be reduced by the width of the lap, and in the sheer, which will be increased by the same amount.

The hood end of the sheer plank as it appears on the profile view of the lines might seem excessively narrow where it lands on the stem were it not understood that this is the inside view, less the lap, and that actually the end of the sheer plank will be wider by 1⅛ inches, which is the width of the lap. Even so, this makes the sheer plank quite narrow on the stem, but this is a characteristic of Chamberlain boats and one of the refinements by which he

achieved a hull of outstanding grace and beauty. Also by keeping the hood ends of the upper planks quite narrow on the stem, and likewise on the transom, it is possible to peak up the ends of the garboard and so to straighten out the garboard's upper edge (when laid out flat), as well as to straighten out the run of the plank above. This ensures less work in planking, more efficient use of lumber, and stronger planking because of straighter grain.

A note on the table of offsets specifies a dimensional tolerance of plus or minus one-eighth inch. This is about as close as it is possible to scale offsets from a drawing laid out to a scale of one and one-half inches equals one foot. Even greater corrections or adjustments may be required in making a full-size lay-down of these lines for building. But this is to be expected, and as long as changes are kept as small as possible, and the general proportions of the lines adhered to while all is made fair and true, the result will be satisfactory.

I believe that no two workmen, however skilled and careful, could ever achieve exactly the same lay-down, nor would there be any point in trying to. I am sure that Chamberlain never built any two Beachcombers exactly alike, although no hull ever left his shop that was not beautiful and true and that did not meet his very exacting specifications for the Beachcomber hull. Yet all Beachcombers were individuals, as alike as peas in a pod, and as different. This is the point where craft leaves off and art begins.

I would underline that lines and offsets alone are not enough for building this boat. They provide the raw materials for the fairing process, which, besides being a technical operation, is an artistic endeavor and a creative act.

MATERIALS

Originally the Beachcomber was built entirely of oak and pine lumber with the exception of hackmatack for its four sets of natural-crook sawn frames, and sometimes for thwart knees

and breast hook. It was fastened throughout with galvanized boat nails, and the fittings and hardware were all of galvanized iron. All in all, scantlings and fastenings were on the light side to give as light a hull as possible for fast sailing, and it is a tribute to the inherent strength of dory construction, and the careful workmanship by which these dories were put together, that they lasted as long and stood up as well as they did.

In some of the older boats, weakened by years of hard sailing or by collision, a brace in the form of a ⅜-inch iron rod with a turnbuckle in the middle ran from gunwale to gunwale just forward of the mast. This was not standard equipment, however, and I have not drawn it in the plans.

Today a lighter and stronger boat could undoubtedly be built by the judicious substitution of modern materials, including screws, plywood, glue, and resin-bonded fabric reinforcements. Safety flotation can be supplied by plastic foams. Undoubtedly, if Chamberlain were alive today and building dories, he would take advantage of the newer materials. As it was, I believe that screws had to some extent replaced nails in the last of the Beachcombers.

A list of "General Specifications" for the Beachcomber has been found among Chamberlain's papers. It is not complete, although nearly all items of importance are included. We shall use it as an outline, considering each of the headings in turn and adding such supplementary data as is needed.

Bottom. White pine, 7⁄8 inch in thickness, which is about a minimum bottom thickness for nailing on a garboard. Normally, either two or three boards will be required to make up a maximum bottom width of 21½ inches. Standard nailing for garboards into the edge of the bottom is with 3-inch galvanized wire nails spaced about 2½ inches. A fine pilot hole for each nail is carefully sighted and drilled to prevent the nail from entering at the wrong angle, causing it to split through either one face or the other. As a substitute, bronze of monel Anchorfast nails will hold equally well or better and will last longer; they'll also cost considerably more.

A bottom of plywood, ½ inch or even 3⁄8 inch thick, would be adequate, except that an internal chine strip would be required for fastening the edges of the garboards. For additional reinforcement and complete watertightness, this bottom edge, when plywood is used, should be bound with glass fabric or Dynel set in epoxy resin.

Bottom cleats. The several boards making up the standard pine bottom are cleated athwartships between frame stations and at the ends with 2-inch strips of oak 7⁄8 inch thick and laid flat. These are made short enough to let water run around the ends. They were originally fastened on from the outside with 2-inch galvanized chisel-point boat nails with the points turned back and clinched into the wood, but now it is generally easier to secure them with No. 12 or No. 14 screws, 1½ inches or 1¾ inches long.

Stern transom. Oak, 7⁄8 inch thick. If one board is used, a width of 16½ inches is required, which is probably wider than is commonly obtainable. Two boards will do, provided one is

quite wide and the two are solidly joined with No. 12 or No. 14 1½-inch screws into the stern cleat.

Stern knee. Oak, 1 7⁄8 inches thick like the stem, fastened to the transom with No. 14 or No. 16 screws, 1½ inches to 3 inches long. Originally this would have been fastened with galvanized blunt-point boat nails of approximately the same lengths.

Stern cleat. Oak, 7⁄8 inch thick. The molded width of 6 inches is sufficient to allow for through-bolting of the 3⁄8-inch eyebolt for the main sheet block.

Stem. Oak, sided 1 7⁄8 inches and molded 2¼ inches.

Outer or false stem. Oak, a strip about 2 inches wide by 1¼ inches thick, steam bent on the flat into place, nailed or screwed down tight, and finished to shape when cold.

Frames. Chamberlain lists: "4 sets hackmatack, sided 7⁄8 inch molded 2 inches between knuckles fastened to the bottom with galv. iron boat nails." Such natural-crook hack frames were crossed by each other across the bottom of the boat. More frequently, instead of such matched pairs of natural-crook frames, a three-part oak frame was substituted comprised of two side futtocks and a single piece across the bottom, the three joined together with riveted galvanized iron clips at the bottom knuckles. No. 12 or No. 14 screws 1¾ inches to 2 inches long fasten up through the bottom.

Stiffeners. Oak, 3⁄8 inch by 7⁄8 inch of tough, selected butt stock, steam-bent on the flat into place between the frame stations and in the ends to fit the shape of the boat, and fastened through the laps. Originally chisel-point boat nails were used with points turned back and clinched into the inside of the strip. Now that good chisel point nails are difficult to obtain, copper wire nails riveted over burrs make an excellent substitute.

Planking. Pine, 9⁄16 inch thick. Boards as wide as 16 inches are required for the garboards. Now that planks can be spliced with waterproof glues, great savings are possible by using pieced-out strakes glued up from shorter lengths of lumber. For the wide garboards (wide ends),

⅜-inch plywood may be substituted, scarphed and glue spliced from shorter pieces cut from 8-foot panels.

In fact, the boat may be planked entirely with plywood. Nor is it necessary to lap the plywood in the conventional way. The strakes may be butted and glued to internal longitudinal seam battens. In that case the joints may be bound with fabric tapes set in epoxy resin, or the whole surface of the hull may be covered with fabric set in epoxy.

In fastening conventional pine planking, No. 12 1¾-inch or 2-inch screws go through the laps into the frames, but only through the laps, for screws through the planks to the frames between laps are liable to split the planks. As previously mentioned, the lower edge of the garboards is nailed with 3-inch nails to the bottom.

The laps were fastened originally with clinched chisel-point nails spaced 2 inches to 2½ inches. Now, riveted copper wire nails would probably have to be substituted, but they are better and more lasting fastenings if properly put in. Incidentally, the 9/16-inch planking is beveled a width of 1⅛ inches.

Gunwales. Oak, ⅞ inch thick, and 1⅜ inches wide between frames, but tapering at the ends to ⅞ inch at the stem and stern. These are bent into place and fastened down into timberheads and through the sheer plank from the outside. Nails or screws may be used.

Capping. Oak, 9/16 inch thick and 2 inches wide, steamed, bent into place on the boat, and fastened down into the gunwales with nails or screws. The capping extends an inch or so past the frames at either end.

Beading. Oak, 9/16 inch thick by one inch wide, beveled on the inner edge, sprung to the shape of the boat at the ends, extending from where the capping stops to the stem and transom. It covers the top edge of the sheer plank and part of the gunwale, and can be fastened with screws or nails.

Breast hook. Natural crook hackmatack, apple, oak, ⅞ inch thick. It receives the ends of the gunwales, fastens to the stem, and takes fastenings through the sheer plank from outside.

Guard. Oak, half round, one inch wide. It should be planed so it tapers slightly at the ends for appearance. It can be nailed or screwed in place.

Thwarts. Pine, ⅞ inch thick by 9 inches wide. They are notched around the frames and screwed down to the seat risers with No. 12 2-inch screws.

Thwart knees. Hackmatack, apple, oak, ⅞ inch or ¾ inch thick. They are screwed where possible to the frames, thwarts, gunwale, and sheer plank, being fitted carefully against these.

Risers. Pine, ⅝ inch or ¾ inch thick and 3½ inches wide in the center, tapering to 2½ inches at the ends. They should be beveled on the top edge to receive the thwarts and screw fastened into the frames with 1½-inch No. 12 screws.

Centerboard trunk. Sides pine; lower half ⅞ inch thick, upper part can be 9/16 inch thick for lightness. The end posts, mortised through the bottom, are of oak, 1 1/16 inches thick by 1½ inches wide. The sides should be copper riveted through the posts.

Centerboard. Oak, finished ⅞ inch thick. It should be pinned with drifts of 5/16 inch rod and lead weighted.

Mast step. Oak block 4 inches by 4 inches by 6 inches notched over foot of No. 1 frame.

Mast hole reinforcement. Oak, ⅞ inch thick, by 9 inches wide.

Rudder. Oak, 1⅛ inches thick at the upper end of the stock, thinned to ¾ inch at the lower after edge. It should be pinned with 9/16-inch and ¼-inch rod.

Rudder yoke. Oak, ¾ inch thick.

Stern sheets cuddy. Pine, ¾ inch and 9/16 inch thick, fastened with No. 12 screws.

Gratings or racks. Pine, 9/16 inch thick, built to be removable.

Spars. Douglas fir, or spruce.

RUDDER AND CENTERBOARD

No surviving rudder or centerboard for the Beachcomber-Alpha is now to be found for copying, yet I have been able to get together enough reliable data from one source or another to reconstruct these essential accessories with substantial accuracy. Both are typical of sailing dories of the period. Their design and construction are quite simple, yet even so, pains must be taken in putting them together, and there are several things that the amateur builder should be sure he understands before he sets to work.

Even if a single board wide enough to make the rudder in one piece were obtainable, it is better to make it of two boards, as I show, as a precaution against warping. And with two boards, the lumber should not be slash sawn, but

as nearly rift sawn as possible, that is, with the grain of the annual rings running at right angles with the wide surface. Furthermore, when the two boards, or parts, are joined, they should be placed so that the grain in one runs opposite to the grain in the other. If warping takes place, the distortion in one part will tend to offset the distortion in the other, instead of adding to it, as happens when two or more boards are joined with their grain running in the same direction.

This precaution against warping is even more important in the construction of the

OAK
SECTION A-A'
FOR 3/8" PIN
132°
3 1/2"

TILLER YOKE 3/4" OAK
MORTISE
3/4" HALF OVAL BRASS
26"
13"
CENTER SECTION

SECTION B-B'
11 3/8"

TAPERED
9"
SECTION C-C'

3/8" #16 GAL. W.S.
5/16" OR 1/4" GAL. ROD
10"

21' BEACHCOMBER DORY
RUDDER AND TILLER YOKE
J. G. JAN. 1965

centerboard, for there, if even a small amount of warping or "dishing" takes place, the board will stick in its slot and will not be able to be put in or hauled out of its box. The cleats on the ends of the centerboard, like the cleat on the bottom of the rudder, are put there to stop warping or twisting, although they also help to hold the assemblies together.

For both rudder and centerboard, the lumber should be dry, well-seasoned oak. Green lumber—oak especially—is bound to twist and warp. Oak is specified because it is standard for New England dories, being what Chamberlain and other contemporary builders invariably used. A hard, solid grade of Philippine mahogany could be substituted. This wood keeps its shape and holds fastenings well, and costs

less, or is no more expensive, now, than a good grade of seasoned oak.

Plywood could also be substituted for oak for both rudder and centerboard, but if this is done, it would be best to cover the plywood with a skin of Dynel fabric bedded in epoxy resin. This covering serves both to waterproof the plywood and to reinforce it. By making up these parts from plywood, the need for pinning and cleating would be bypassed, for each could be made in a single piece. This would save a lot of labor and might more than offset the cost and trouble of adding the Dynel fabric and epoxy resin. Should the rudder be made of fir plywood, it would be necessary to reinforce the tenon that passes through the rudder yoke. With waterproof mahogany or birch plywood, such

113

reinforcement would not be required.

If oak is used, and pinned together as laid out in the drawings, the amateur should be briefed ahead of time as how best to go about this, for the operation is a fairly critical one that could easily be messed up for the want of the correct procedure. In boring for the pins, the uninstructed novice rarely gets his holes lined up accurately and too frequently puts his drill out through the side. Yet the operation is not essentially difficult. For detailed instructions on this, see the Appendix.

For the rudder, galvanized rod of $\frac{5}{16}$ inch diameter is recommended for pinning, although $\frac{1}{4}$-inch rod would do. Because the galvanizing adds slightly to the diameter, the drill should be the same size as the listed size of the rod. Even then it may be hard to drive without bending, especially the $\frac{1}{4}$-inch rod. A heavy hammer is better for driving than a light one.

For the centerboard, $\frac{5}{16}$-inch rod should be used. If the holes as laid out are drilled according to the method described in the Appendix, that is, from both sides of each piece separately, no bored depth would be greater than $4\frac{1}{2}$ inches, so there should be little danger of running off.

After the rudder is pinned, it is planed smooth and tapered, and the positions of the pintles and gudgeons are located. The top gudgeon is easily bolted through the transom cleat for extra strength. The pintles specified open $\frac{7}{8}$ inch between the straps. The straps of the top pintle will be let in slightly, for the rudder at that point is $1\frac{1}{8}$ inches thick. The straps of the bottom pintle will slip on without cutting, since there the rudder is tapered to $\frac{7}{8}$ inch. The pintle straps are fastened on with copper rivets.

The tenon on the rudder head must fit the mortise in the yoke snugly, so as not to wobble. A $\frac{3}{8}$-inch removable pin further secures it. Only the weight of the rudder itself is required to keep the pintles from slipping out of the gudgeons under most conditions. If the rudder should come unshipped, the tiller lines would keep it from getting away.

The only feature of the yoke that needs mention is the reinforcement of $\frac{3}{4}$-inch half-oval brass that binds and reinforces the center part of the forward edge where there would be some danger, otherwise, of breaking because of the short grain. Normally, this brass would be secured by screws.

The centerboard box is rather light, but that is the way Chamberlain's specifications show it. I, myself, do not think that much weight is saved by reducing the thickness of the upper half of the box to $\frac{5}{8}$ inch. In fact I would prefer that the sides of the box be $\frac{15}{16}$ inch or even one inch throughout. The end posts should always extend through the bottom, as shown, both to stiffen the box and to permit caulking the ends from the outside. Copper rivets are the best fastenings for the ends of the box, but these must be well headed over and set up tightly so that they pull into the wood. I would like to see the box put together and bedded with waterproof adhesive, preferably epoxy, for additional strength as well as watertightness. The old builders like Chamberlain used white lead, which gave a tight seal but did not make the construction any stronger.

The centerboard pivot pin is sometimes made of white oak or locust, in which case, it ought to be 1 inch in diameter. I have shown it as $\frac{3}{4}$-inch diameter brass or bronze. It must fit tightly, yet be removable in case it is desired to drop the board.

Sometimes a large screw eye or even an eye bolt was fastened to the top of the board for attaching the rod used for raising and lowering the board. I show a simple strap arrangement of $\frac{3}{4}$-inch by $\frac{1}{8}$-inch flat bronze, attached with copper rivets. The handle is easily formed of $\frac{3}{8}$-inch rod with an eye to hook into the strap on the board and a T-shaped outer end. This T-end or cross-bar rests on the top of the box when the board is down, preventing it from going farther. When the board is up, the T-end slips under a special cleat on the front end of the box, locking the board in the up position. This is a simple but effective device that was generally used on centerboard dories of the Beachcomber period.

One thing that should be mentioned is that

the lumber thicknesses given are quite critical in some cases and should not be reduced even if retail lumberyards attempt to argue otherwise. For instance, ⅞-inch thick pine for the bottom or the sides of the centerboard box should under no circumstances be less than ⅞ inch thick. Most "one-inch" pine boards as sold today are actually only ¾ inch thick. So you may have to have your pine planed up special, and if you do, I, myself, would specify a "plump" ⅞ inch, which, if it ran to ¹⁵⁄₁₆ inch, would be all the better.

THE RIG

In describing the Beachcomber-Alpha rig, we shall start at the bow. The luff of the jib is laced or seized to a length of ³⁄₁₆-inch, 7 by 7 galvanized yacht wire with thimbles spliced in either end. The tack end attaches by a ³⁄₁₆-inch screw-pin shackle to a no. 1 galvanized swivel-eye boat snap, which hooks into a ⅜-inch galvanized eye bolt through the stem head. The upper eye of the jib luff wire takes another no. 1 swivel-eye boat snap, which is shackled to a single block for ⅜-inch line. Another single block of the same size shackles to a 4-inch or 5-inch galvanized eye plate, which screws to the mast at the height designated on the rigging plan. Two ³⁄₁₆-inch screw pin shackles are needed for a fast eye block; one for a swivel eye block.

The jib halyard of ⅜-inch manila carries an eyesplice in the upper end just large enough to slip over the masthead, supported about 3 feet 6 inches below on a wooden shoulder cleat. The lower end reeves through the block snapped into the thimble at the head of the jib, back through the block fixed to the mast and is hauled down taut, passing through a leader on the port top forward edge of the mast thwart, and securing to a 5-inch cleat on the after side of the thwart. This arrangement makes a separate headstay unnecessary.

The halyard arrangement is simplicity itself, but effective and generally substantial, although weak snaps have been known to break under the strain of pounding into a heavy chop. While

⁵⁄₁₆-inch manila might be sufficiently strong here, ⁵⁄₁₆-inch dacron would be more than ample. Dacron, except for its higher cost, is to be preferred here as in every other part of the rig, not only for its great strength and long wearing qualities but also because it handles easily and does not stretch.

The twin jib sheets of ¼-inch manila are permanently spliced into the clew of the jib, although some Beachcomber sailors preferred to have them on snaps. These sheets lead aft through swivel-eye single blocks shackled to ¼-inch galvanized eye bolts through the seat risers, either side, 15 inches forward of station 2, and secure to a 4-inch cleat on the after slope of the centerboard box, above and forward of the second thwart.

The mast and boom are solid sticks of Douglas fir, according to Chamberlain's specifications, but Sitka spruce or eastern red spruce would be just as good or better. The mast is 3½ inches in diameter where it passes through the thwart and tapers to 2 inches at the head. It rises 16 feet above the thwart and extends 1 foot below, requiring a length of 17 feet in all. The gooseneck for the boom attaches about 5 inches above the thwart. The gooseneck was generally of brass or bronze of a type that attached to the end of the boom with side straps fastened by through rivets. The boom, 15 feet 6 inches long, is 2½ inches in diameter centrally, tapering to 2 inches at the inner end and 1¾ inches at the outer.

The mainsail is lashed permanently to the boom and mast with Italian hemp marline or suitable Dacron cord by a continuous series of half hitches passing through small grommets set close to the edges of the sail and spaced on 10-inch centers. Grommets of the same size and spacing are likewise pierced through the luff of the jib for its lashings.

Larger, heavier grommets in the corners of the sails permit lashings at the ends of the spars. The head and the tack of the jib are held taut by lashings through respective eyes in the ends of the luff wire. The tack of the mainsail is lashed to the gooseneck. The head, in absence of a main halyard, is pulled up by lashings passing

BEACHCOMBER DORY - 21'
ALPHA RIG

16'-6"

1"

15'

15'

8'-3"

9'-7"

4'-10"

13 12 11 10 9 8 7 6 5 4 3 2 1 0

FEET AND INCHES

J.G.

through a ⅜-inch hole bored through the top of the mast a couple of inches higher than the stretch of the sail. Likewise, a hole bored in the outer end of the boom allows a lashing from the clew that serves as an outhaul.

The two side stays or shrouds are ³/₁₆-inch 7 by 7 galvanized yacht wire (stainless steel would be better) with eye splices served and varnished at the upper ends of a size to slip over the mast-head and to lead neatly from ash shoulder cleats. Thimbles spliced into the lower ends allow lacing with light line to draw the stays taut. Turnbuckles are not used; instead, ⅜-inch galvanized iron eyebolts pass through the rail from 4 inches to 6 inches abaft the center of the mast. The eyes in the ends of the side stays hang about 6 inches above. A light line or lanyard threaded back and forth several times through these opposing eyes, secured with a couple of half hitches around the standing parts, puts sufficient tension in the stay. In an emergency two slashes with a knife will free the mast.

Formerly the main sheet was made of cotton line because it was softer on the hands than hemp or manila. Dacron would be best today, and for Dacron only ⅜-inch diameter line would be required, while cotton for this purpose should not be less than ⁷/₁₆ inch.

The main sheet requires two bridles on the boom. Old photographs show considerable variation in the length and location of these bridles. It is suggested that the outer one at the end of the boom, with the ring at its mid-point to take the snap in the end of the main sheet, should be 1½ feet to 2 feet long with a drop of 6 inches, and that the inner or center bridle, which carries the main sheet block, should be 3½ feet to 4 feet long with a 12-inch drop. Further, there should be about 6 feet between the center points of the two.

These bridles have eye splices in their ends of a size to slip over the boom, and are held in position by small ash stops fastened with two screws each. It is important that these bridles should not stretch; no doubt hemp was originally used. Dacron resists stretching well, and the ⅜-inch dacron recommended for the sheet would do nicely for these straps as well.

As previously mentioned, the outer end of the main sheet snaps into a ring tied in the outer bridle. Thence it leads down through a single block, preferably swiveled, which is shackled to a ⅜-inch eyebolt passing through the center of the transom and vertically located slightly below the bottom of the sheer strake. From this block the sheet leads forward and up through another swiveled single block secured at the mid-point of the inner and larger bridle. Thence it leads downward and forward to be secured when desired on a jam cleat of ash or white oak bolted to the after vertical post of the centerboard box.

In the past, a few well-heeled skippers had brass snatch blocks attached to swivel deck plates which bolted to the bottom of the boat about a foot aft of the centerboard box.

Since ⁵/₁₆-inch manila is ample for the two tiller lines, ¼-inch dacron will do nicely. One end of the tiller line snaps into a ¼-inch ring bolt or an equivalent screw eye set in the inner edge of the rail about 1 foot 5 inches aft of Station 3. The resulting two-part purchase is sufficient to work the rudder easily from almost any location in the middle of the boat. To secure the rudder, equivalent to lashing the tiller in other boats, the two lines are pulled tight thwartships and tied.

Rowlock sockets are set in the rail 12 inches aft of the after edges of the three forward thwarts so that the boat can be rowed from each of these thwarts if desired. When not in use, rowlocks are stored in the small after cuddy next to the transom. Here also could be stored the mooring line which was used without mooring chocks, being tied through the mast hole and lashed to the eye in the stemhead to hold it centrally.

A pair of 8-foot oars tied under the front thwart on either side, with the blades extending to the stem, were always carried in the old Beachcomber-Alphas. For rowing, some dories had a small hole through the upper part of the box through which a pin could be inserted to hold the board part way down to act as a keel for steadying the boat and holding it on course.

Now that we've seen how to rig the re-created Beachcomber-Alpha, let's look at the evolution of the rig.

HISTORICAL DEVELOPMENT OF THE RIG

The Beachcomber-Alpha sailing rig went through several evolutions over the years. We can trace the development of the rig from the recollections of those who owned and sailed these dories at various times. The features of the rig would be known and remembered by the dory sailor, while any precise apprehension of hull lines would not. Besides, numerous dated photographs of Beachcomber-Alpha dories have been preserved, showing comprehensive rigging details.

The committee representing the survivors of the Beachcomber and Alpha Dory Clubs, which recently presented to the Peabody Museum of Salem a scale model of a 21-foot Chamberlain Beachcomber-Alpha sailing dory constructed under their supervision and rigged to their specifications, diligently canvassed all former members of the two clubs that could be located concerning details of the rig as they recalled them. The secretary of the committee, Chesler L. Pattee, formerly of Salem, whose father helped organize the Salem club, and who, himself, had owned and skippered an Alpha dory from 1915 to 1924, headed up the rig research and furnished the sails for the museum model.

Pattee suggests that there were generally three eras of Beachcomber-Alpha evolution characterized by and, to some extent, caused by, marked departures in rig. He calls them:

1. The primeval period, extending from the class's inception in the 1890s through the first decade of this century.

2. The intermediate period, the second decade of the century with apogee circa 1915.

3. The sophisticated period, the third decade of the century and more precisely after 1925.

In the primeval period, side stays or shrouds had not appeared. The peak of the jib snapped into the eye of a short hemp pennant hung from the upper part of the mast. A piece of rope was spliced into the tack of the jib and was threaded through an eye in the stem head, pulled taut, and made fast. There was no jib halyard, so this arrangement was all there was to keep the mast from jumping out of its step.

An early modification and refinement of this first primitive arrangement is shown by photographs to have been the addition of a single sheave block to the end of the pennant that held the peak of the jib. This permitted the corresponding addition of a simple, single-purchase jib halyard. This was an important advance in the rig, for by changing the tension on the halyard, which served also as a headstay, the rake of the mast and the center of effort of the mainsail could be moved back and forth somewhat, better to suit the weather and to balance the rig.

The second or intermediate period was ushered in, Pattee is inclined to believe, not so much by the addition of side stays as by the adoption of a roached, "cross-cut" and battened mainsail, which rendered side stays necessary. Although no separate headstay appears at this time, the luff of the jib was beefed up with a length of rigging wire from the stemhead, and a second block was added to give extra purchase to the jib halyard, which doubled as forestay, permitting easy adjustment of tension for varying the rake of the mast.

The sophisticated, or final, stage brought permanent standing rigging, with metal turnbuckles replacing the simple lacings formerly used. Sails were enlarged and put on "runners," that is, track, necessitating another halyard. Heavier and more expensive fittings were added along with extras like mooring chocks. The rig was no longer capable of being lifted out at the end of a day's sailing to be carried home on the skipper's shoulder; now sails were furled and left on the boat. The boat was no longer rowed any more with the rig down, as was the lobsterman's dory from whence it evolved.

As the third decade closed, popular demand was for larger and more specialized racing types. In the ensuing competition with more powerful racing classes like the Massachusetts Bay Indian, also out of Chamberlain's shop, Sam Brown's Yankee Dory, the Marblehead Class, and the Alden O-Boat, the Beachcomber-Alpha rapidly lost ground, and after the death of Chamberlain in the early 1930s no more were built.

The ad hoc committee, set up in 1959 to

recover the Beachcomber-Alpha design and details to guide the construction of an authentic scale model, decided that the rig in general use circa 1915 was most representative. The committee researched this rig exhaustively. The immediate big difficulty that confronted the committee was that no specimen of the dories of the intermediate period had survived for measurement. Another vexing problem involved the dimensions of the sails.

A blueprint sail plan for the Beachcomber found among papers in possession of the Chamberlain family gave the dimensions as 15 feet equally on boom and hoist, 17 feet 11 inches on the leach, and a roach of 12 inches. But Chesler Pattee after inquiry and study, and from personal recollections, rejected the 17-foot 11-inch leach in favor of a 16-foot 6-inch leach dimension for the Alpha mainsail. His reasoning was as follows:

1. A mainsail for this dory with a leach longer than 16 feet 6 inches would drag excessively in the water when sailing on a broad reach in a stiff breeze.

2. The sail with the longer leach looks wrong when drawn to scale, and the lower boom angle does not correspond with contemporary photographs.

3. Recalling youthful experience, Pattee remembers it was quite a reach for a lad five feet tall to unsnap the main sheet from the bridle at the end of the boom when standing with one foot on the cuddy cover, which was about 12 inches above the bottom of the boat.

4. The helmsman on the third thwart would duck in coming about, more to dodge the main sheet pulley than to avoid being hit by the boom.

The late Samuel H. Brown, Jr., lifelong Marblehead doryman as well as a designer of successful sailing dories himself, in a letter to the committee in 1959, gave his recollections of the Alpha mainsail as 15 feet on boom and hoist, but failed to specify the distance across the leach. For the Beachcomber main, Brown recalled 16 feet 6 inches on the boom and hoist and 18 feet on the leach, which when laid out to scale gives approximately the same angle of rake

for the boom as the 15-foot by 15-foot by 16½-foot sail, and this accords with the local tradition that the Beachcombers carried more canvas than the Alphas. Finally in a list of "General Specifications, Beachcomber (Swampscott) Dory" (no date), sails are described and dimensioned as "leg o' mutton style, of No. 1 sailcloth, 15 feet on boom, 15 feet on mast, 16½ feet on leach with 12 inch roach. Jib of proper size."

So 15 feet by 15 feet by 16 feet 6 inches then are the dimensions for the main as finally adopted for this design. Naturally that doesn't prevent anyone from experimenting with canvas of larger or smaller measurements, should he so desire. It is said that some Marblehead skippers had three separate sizes of spars and sails for their dories: an oversize rig for racing, a medium rig for ordinary sailing, and a cutdown rig for heavy weather.

It will bear emphasizing that the Beachcomber-Alpha class did not enforce rigid uniformity. Considerable variation in rigs obtained from boat to boat. While we can't be sure about possible alterations in lines, there were some differences in internal hull arrangements. Instead of cross thwarts, some boats had benches along the sides aft of the centerboard box. Others left out the bottom gratings. Some carried 50 pounds of lead ballast on either side the centerboard. A few were reinforced with a ⅜-inch galvanized iron rod and turnbuckles running from side to side through the sheer strake just forward of the mast.

It is not suggested that the rig described in detail previously is the best one or the only one worth considering. But it is the rig most used when the class was at the peak of its popularity. It will do to set a norm, but a norm that a present-day builder would probably want to depart from to some extent. It does constitute a tried and tested rig that is probably the least expensive and the least complicated of any that are workable and safe. But some of the newer things like Dacron yacht rope, stainless steel wire, and some of the newer fittings are more than worth the extra cost.

15

A Sharpie

........................•........................

The 18-foot sharpie *Shag*, formerly owned by Charles H. F. Storrow of Stonington, Connecticut, is ideal for the home builder who wants a family boat of proven qualities, and one that is simple and easy to build and not too expensive. Of course, with the price of lumber what it is today, no boat is going to be cheap to build at this time, but even so, the cost and availability of materials for *Shag* will stack up favorably with those for any comparable craft.

Charlie Storrow has generous words for *Shag*: "She is a wonderful boat. She sails well and is easy to handle, is surprisingly able in a hard breeze, and is ideal for picnics, landing on beaches and similar activities. On a broad reach in a good breeze she is really fast. She is, in my opinion, strikingly handsome. . . . As a day sailer for a family with young children, there could be no better boat. She would also be a great boat for the home builder because of her extreme simplicity." Yet—and there always is a yet of some kind—Storrow suggested two possible improvements. One: more canvas, for as she is rigged, she is a bit slow in light airs. Two: less weather helm. Both of these will be discussed at length later.

Shag served the Storrow family well for almost seven years, but eventually their need for a bigger boat capable of extended cruising impelled them to buy a large catboat. *Shag* was sold, but not until Charlie had carefully measured and recorded her lines and details. As Storrow is an architect by profession and an amateur builder of some experience (he completed the boatbuilding course at Mystic Seaport), the job was well done.

We would have reproduced his drawings as Storrow did them, except that they were too large, and some of the details were too small to permit the reproduction required to fit these pages. The drawings printed here follow Storrow's plans closely without any essential changes. I have added, however, a larger sail plan for a longer version of this sharpie, as will be discussed, and additional plans for the centerboard.

CONSTRUCTION

A few remarks about the construction: There is nothing difficult or unusual involved in building this boat, nothing that any one of a half-dozen current boatbuilding manuals cannot explain quite handily. Only common species of lumber are required—pine, cedar, Douglas fir, hard pine, and oak. For the most part, fastening can be done with galvanized nails. Decks should be ⅜-inch exterior fir plywood; spars, Douglas fir, if need be, spliced with epoxy glue.

Comments on the numbered references on the construction plan follow:

1. Inner stem—oak, hard pine, Douglas fir.

2. Mast step—oak, hard pine, Douglas fir, 1½ inches thick. Makes a solid reinforcement at the bow into which the short cross planks are well nailed with 8d galvanized wire nails.

3. Centerboard—¼-inch steel. Better made of wood. Heavy logs bolted to the bottom for the centerboard trunk. Without a cross brace, thwart or other, to stay the forward end of the trunk, there is need for extra heavy logs. Left open forward so that two people can sleep on the bottom, one on either side of the trunk. (More on the centerboard and trunk later.)

4. Combination thwart, centerboard trunk brace, bridge deck—oak, Douglas fir, ash. Full inch thick, if possible, reinforce on underside in way of mast.

5. Two keelsons—oak, Douglas fir, hard pine. Run inside the whole length of the bottom. Set in paint. Well nailed or screwed into each cross plank from the outside of the boat in.

6. Vertical staving—white pine or cedar—like the longitudinal side planking. Cypress very good if obtainable.

7. Coaming.

OFFSETS - FEET, INCHES, EIGHTHS - OUTSIDE PLANK									
	STATION	0	1	2	3	4	5	5A	6
HEIGHTS ABOVE BASE LINE	SHEER	2-7-2	2-2-3	1-11-1	1-9-5	1-9-5	1-10-3	1-11-0	2-0-3
	CHINE	0-8-6	0-5-3	0-3-2	0-2-7	0-3-5	0-6-6	0-8-5	1-0-0
HALF-BREADTHS	SHEER	0-0-2	1-5-3	2-3-7	2-8-1	2-7-2	2-4-0	2-2-2	
	CHINE	0-0-2	1-1-3	1-10-4	2-2-1	2-1-2	1-10-6	1-9-3	

8. Deck, fore and aft—⅜-inch exterior fir plywood on slightly cambered deck beams, spruce, Douglas fir, oak.

9. Mast partners, also deck beams. Blocked under deck both sides.

The strength of this boat will be greatly increased by use of epoxy glue in all joints and on all contacting surfaces throughout.

THE SAILING RIG

Now let's go into the elements that could improve the boat. Charlie Storrow felt one of *Shag*'s weaknesses was light air performance. He experimented with a bowsprit and jib but the complication in rigging them did not seem worth the effort. But adding canvas will improve her performance. Together, we came up with a solution. In adding canvas, we felt that the essential character and proportions of the old rig should not be altered. As the main boom cannot be lengthened because of the location of the mizzen mast, the only way to increase the area of the mainsail would be to increase the height of the mast, but this was considered unwise, to the extent that would be required, for the obvious effect on stability.

There is a way to get more sail area without changing the character of the original rig. This is by lengthening the boat. *Shag*'s simple sharpie lines permit a 4-inch increase in station spacing—from 36 inches to 40 inches—without altering the basic shape, except for the increase in overall length of 2 feet. This allows longer booms as well as increasing stability somewhat to offset a greater area of sail, yet probably does not increase the wetted surface enough to slow the boat to any significant extent. I have included a sail plan for this longer hull. The same table of offsets can be used for both hulls—the 18-footer and the 20-footer—although it is recommended that, for the longer boat, these offsets represent the inside of the planking and the bottom, rather than the outside. This will simplify making the molds and frames, and will add a trifle to the beam and freeboard and, likewise, to stability.

As far as weather helm is concerned, Storrow felt *Shag* had an undue amount, which in his judgment slowed her down somewhat, even though she did not steer hard due to her balanced rudder. His suggestion was to move the centerboard aft, and possibly to increase its size. But how much to move it? As mentioned before in this book, there is no precise mathematical formula or reliable method for determining optimum balance for small craft rigs on the drawing board, before actual trials on the water. The calculations commonly resorted to are approximate and hit or miss. Often they don't even come close.

It will not be out of place here to review briefly the basic considerations underlying our problem. When a boat sails into the wind, the force of the wind on the sails tends to push the boat sideways in the water as well as to send her ahead. The effective force of the wind is concentrated at one point called the "center of effort." The resistance of the water against the side of the hull is likewise concentrated at one point, which is called the "center of lateral resistance." If the center of effort lies aft of the center of lateral resistance, the effect is to turn the bow into the wind. The rudder must counteract this turning force, and this is called weather helm. The greater the distance the center of effort is aft of the center of lateral resistance, the longer the lever arm turning the boat into the wind. The longer the lever arm, the more helm or rudder is required to keep the boat on course. But if the center of effort comes forward of the center of lateral resistance, the effect is the opposite. The bow seeks to turn away from the wind, and again the rudder must counteract. This is called lee helm. Lee helm is treacherous, and can lead to jibing and capsizing. A slight amount of weather helm, but not enough to drag, is desirable.

In rare instances, the force exerted by the wind and the counter force of the water against the hull will be so perfectly balanced that the boat all but steers herself. This does not happen

often. With small boats, too many changing variables are involved: ballasting, heel, wind velocity, sail trim. Other factors include the area and location of the sails, the underwater shape of the hull, the shape and location of the centerboard, and the size and location of the rudder.

All of our traditional small sailing types are the result of long processes of trial and error in which the many diverse factors affecting performance have been brought more or less into workable and harmonious balance. Changes are not to be undertaken lightly, nor is it easy when changes are made to predict the results before trying them out.

THE CENTERBOARD AND TRUNK

In the present instance, it would seem logical to seek to lessen the amount of weather helm in the 18-foot boat by moving the centerboard aft to bring the center of lateral resistance closer to the center of effort, but it must not be moved back so far as to result in lee helm. Yet the centerboard trunk in the 18-foot boat is already as close to the mizzenmast as it will go, and to move the latter aft any distance would radically change the rig. One way to get around this would be to put the centerboard case slightly offcenter and alongside the mast. Locating the centerboard offcenter should not affect sailing performance noticeably, and is to be seen in the No Man's Land boat, the Barnegat sneakbox, and other types.

How far to move the board back is another matter, and is, in fact, anyone's guess. If I were to do this, I do not think I would go back more than a foot, and to do this I would merely extend the present trunk by a foot, leaving the forward end as it is and increasing the length of the board by a foot. At the same time, the width of the board might be increased by several inches, perhaps three or four. This would be a relatively safe gamble and easily hedged. If the board proved too long, some could easily be cut off. This is all simple, straightaway construction, requiring no diagrams.

For the 20-foot boat, we have worked out

quite a different arrangement. Here we have devised a centerboard that is easily moved forward or aft until the best of several positions has been determined by trial. In addition, because of the size and shape of the board, its effectiveness can be adjusted to some extent by raising or lowering with the tackle convenient to the helmsman's hand. This arrangement, it should be noted, was adapted from one worked out in 1912 or thereabouts by H. Willyams for a 16-foot sailing dinghy recently redrawn by William Garden.

Before the two pieces of ⅝-inch plywood which make up the centerboard are glued together, recesses are cut into the inside surfaces to hold the steel plate which forms the lever arm, and also the lead insert for weighting the board. These should fit tightly, but if not, any slack places can be filled with epoxy surfacer or putty. A stiff mix of the epoxy adhesive used and phenolic microballoons is excellent for this.

After the centerboard is glued together, the edges are rounded and sanded, and the sides are planed and smoothed to a streamlined taper in preparation for sheathing either with polypropylene or glass fabric set in epoxy. Do not use a polyester resin for this. But before the centerboard is sheathed, rivets are put in along the forward edge through the wood and the steel insert from side to side as shown in the drawing. These may be copper, as there is no danger of electrolytic action between the copper and the steel because the plastic sheathing will seal them from contact with water. Holes for the rivets are most easily bored on a drill press, but an ordinary electric hand drill will do. Actually, these rivets are probably not needed if the assembly is properly glued with epoxy adhesive, but they should be put in nevertheless to be on the safe side.

The lever arm is cut out of ordinary steel plate ⅜ inch thick. In changing the position of the board in the boat, a short length of rod is put through the one-inch diameter hole in the end of the lever arm to hold on to. In this way, it is quite easy to support the board until the pivot bolt has been shifted from one hole to another. All that is required for a pivot bolt is an ordinary ½-inch carriage bolt (6 inches or 6½ inches long). The holes through the board and the sides of the trunk for this bolt are 9/16 inch to provide clearance.

The case or trunk for the 20-foot boat is made heavier and is more securely braced than that for the 18-footer to take care of the larger board. Bed logs for the trunk are easily available from Douglas fir construction lumber 1½ inches thick, floor joist and the like. The ¾ inch thick sides of the trunk are not rabbeted into the bed logs as is usually done, but are glued to them and extend all the way down to the bottom of the boat. When the trunk is bolted on as shown, through the cross-planked bottom and the fore-and-aft stringer or keel piece on the outside, the result can hardly help being solid and leakproof.

The trunk end posts are morticed all the way through the bottom for caulking from the outside. A bedding compound that stays soft and tacky is desirable. Some have reported good results with ordinary asphalt roofing paste or compound. As an additional precaution against possible leaks, ⅜ inch pine stopwaters may be driven through each of the cross-plank bottom seams on either side of the centerboard slot. This will have to be done before the outer keel strip is put on.

The half-thwarts on either side of the forward end of the centerboard trunk are needed to brace the sidewise thrust of the big board. But they are made removable in case the boat is to be used for cruising with one or two persons sleeping on board. When these half-thwarts are removed, there is room for a sleeping bag on either side of the centerboard trunk. A tarp draped over the main boom, tied down securely, makes as snug a warm-weather shelter as anyone could want.

KEY TO CENTERBOARD DRAWING

1. Five 9/16" holes 2" apart through the centerboard trunk for hanging the centerboard and adjusting its location.

2. Tackle for raising and lowering the centerboard. Leads aft and is cleated within easy

COMPOSITE CENTERBOARD DETAIL — 20' SHARPIE

reach of the helmsman. Adapted from H. Willyams; redrawn by W. Garden.

3. Post, centerboard trunk—oak, Douglas fir, 3″ x 1½″. Mortised through the cross-planked bottom and fore-and-aft bottom stringer.

4. Aft post centerboard trunk—oak, Douglas fir construction lumber, 3″ x 1½″.

5. Fore-and-aft outside stringer or keel strip—oak, Douglas fir, 8″ x 1″. Tapers to 6″ wide at bow end.

6. Bed logs, centerboard trunk—Douglas fir, 3½″ x 1½″, glued to the sides of the centerboard trunk, which rests on the planked bottom. Bolted from side to side through the trunk end posts.

7. Bed logs bolted through the bottom and bottom stringer with 6½″ x ⅜″ galvanized carriage bolts spaced 6″ apart. Trunk scribed and fitted to the bottom curve, and set in non-drying bedding compound.

8. Removable thwarts—spruce or fir, 1″ x 9″ brace the centerboard trunk. Notch over side frame and fit into socketed cleat fastened to the side of the trunk.

9. Socketed cleat—fir, 1½″ thick.

10. Cap, centerboard trunk. Slotted forward end for centerboard lever arm.

11. Reinforcing strips—fir, 1″ x 4½″, extend the length of the trunk and under after thwart. Forward ends bored for centerboard pivot bolt. After ends support thwart and serve as partners for the mizzenmast.

12. Mizzenmast.

13. Mast step—fir or yellow pine, 1½″ thick.

14. Thwart—fir, 12″ x 1″.

15. Lead, approximately 20 pounds. Slab ½″ thick recessed into the interior of the centerboard before it is glued together.

THE RUDDER

It was well, I think, not to attempt any alteration in either the size or shape of the rudder for the 20-footer, at least not at first. If and when any problem should arise in this connection, there will be time enough to take care of it then.

The rudder shaft that came with the 18-foot boat was iron and seemingly hand-forged by a blacksmith, according to Storrow, with the lower end forked and curved to attach to the wooden blade of the rudder and at the same time to brace and reinforce it. It must have been quite old, and may have been salvaged from a former boat. Blacksmiths capable of such work are a rarity today. We had best consider some alternative.

The rudder, like the centerboard, can very well be made up of two thicknesses of ⅝-inch plywood glued together, streamlined somewhat by planing and sanding, and covered with fabric-reinforced plastic. For the rudder shaft, a short piece of brass or bronze rod approximately ⅞ inch in diameter will be just about right, if such can be had. Frequently, remnants or secondhand pieces of bronze propeller shafting long enough to serve can be found in boatyard scrap piles. With a hacksaw and a flat file, slot one end of this rod for a distance equal to about half the width of the rudder blade, and into this slot insert a rectangular piece of flat brass ¼-inch thick. This need not extend beyond the shaft more than 2 inches on either side. The two can be brazed together or through-riveted. Next, this assembly is recessed into the interior of the rudder blade before the two pieces of plywood which form it are glued together.

After the glue has cured, holes are bored through the wood and brass on either side of the shaft, for rivets, which are put in and drawn up tight. If the shaft is installed in this manner, it can never loosen as long as the blade of the rudder holds together.

The shaft turns in a length of pipe which is threaded tightly into a block of wood glued to the inside of the bottom. The upper end of the pipe is likewise threaded into a block glued to the underside of the deck. The rudder assembly hangs from two lock nuts and a washer. Should it be necessary to unship the rudder, the lock nuts are easily loosened. One of them could be bored for a cotter pin, if it were considered necessary. The wooden tiller is bolted to a short metal arm keyed to the head of the rudder shaft and held down with lock nuts and a washer.

In summary, this simple 20-foot boat has real possibilities for modest cruising for those who don't mind roughing it a bit. She is easily beached, and, with her shoal draft, it is possible to explore out-of-the-way places along the shore that the ordinary yacht never sees or dreams exist. For two teenagers who can sail and swim, but who have never before been strictly on their own, a boat like this can be a major part of growing up and a grand adventure.

1 6

The Peapod

......................●......................

Years ago as a boy down Quoddy way, I first heard a story about two lobstermen riding out a gale in a peapod, far from land. Nearby was a schooner, reefed down and pitching hard, which offered to take the men aboard. The men declined. They preferred to ride out the heavy seas in the safety of their pod. In other versions of this tale, the lobstermen became Indian porpoise hunters and their boat a canoe. No matter how the yarn went there must have been some truth in it, because the peapods, like the sea-going canoes they resemble, are wonderfully able boats.

Some say that peapods originated in the lower waters of the Penobscot Bay in the neighborhood of North Haven about 1870, but there were small double-ended boats on the Maine coast long before then. Chances are that some of them had a canoe shape, even if the peapod name didn't come until later.

Captain Ethan Allen Eliot of Calais had a small, cedar double-ender built in the 1840s when he stayed home several years from the West Indies trade to pilot on the St. Croix. His boat was very light, so if need be he could carry it over the mud flats on his back. When the tide favored he would put off down river to pick up incoming vessels—square-riggers to load with ton-timber for England. Outward-bound craft, once they got clear, would set him over the side in his little boat, and he would make his way back up river in all weather and at all hours. He carried a small sail to help.

Now and then he must have run across Passamaquoddy Indians in their sea-going canoes bound for Grand Manan or Pleasant Point. They, too, would be sailing sometimes, perhaps with a bunch of thick spruce brush high in the bow if they didn't have canvas.

Was the peapod copied from the canoe? Not deliberately, I would say. But everyone on the Coast was familiar with sea-going canoes. The first settlers borrowed the Indian canoe for use in their early fisheries. Long familiarity with the canoe and its good qualities had stamped the image in the minds of the fishermen so that later on when the special needs of the lobster fishery called for husky, easy-rowing boats, some of these would naturally turn out to resemble the canoe.

There were all manner of peapods. And it would be difficult to draw an exact line between pods and other small double-enders. Some deep, sailing pods were closer to double-enders like the Nomans Land boat than to the canoe. In others, resemblances could be found to such early double-enders as the whale boat, the Merrimac River wherry, and the York boat. But the typical pod is closer to the canoe. Fifteen feet is the average length; both ends are exactly alike.

There are good reasons why the peapods had caught on in the Maine lobster fisheries before 1880. Lobsters were getting thinned out. Prices were low. Fishermen had to scratch to make a day's pay. In the lower Penobscot Bay where the pod was very popular, lobster fishing had begun in a serious way about 1848 or 1850.

At first lobsters were astonishingly abundant. In 1864, Captain S. S. Davis was running a lobster smack from the Muscle Ridges. He loaded 5,000 lobsters and averaged a trip every seven to nine days. Three men, tending from 40 to 50 pots each, caught all the count lobsters Davis could carry. But by 1879 the cream had been skimmed in that locality, and it took fifteen men instead of three to supply Captain Davis, and even then he was sometimes obliged to buy from still others to make up a load. As lobsters got scarcer, the fishermen had to tend more and more pots. For a few years in the late 1860s trawls were widely used, but after 1870 the use of trawls decreased as fishermen found they did better by scattering their pots over a wide area, which meant more and more rowing, and that is where the peapods came in.

Small sailing craft were also widely used— the Muscongus boat, Matinicus boats, and others. Unlike the large sailing pods, which usually carried spritsails, these boats were sloop rigged. But the wind has to be right for sailing, and it is not easy for one man to sail and tend pots at the same time, though some did it with the tiller rigged with a knife and comb arrangement that could be set to swing the boat in a wide circle while a pot was being hauled. Such maneuvers require plenty of room and call for gybing. Not a few men were lost from a clip on the head by a flying boom.

The peapods were not the only rowing workboats used by the Maine lobstermen before the gas engine gave oars the back seat. There were wherries, Whitehalls, Reach boats, dories, and others, named and nameless. But the favorite seems to have been the pod, and there must have been a lot of them in use, judging from the extent of the lobster fishery at that time.

Government figures for 1880 record close to 1,200 fishermen supplying 23 lobster canneries on the coast of Maine with 9,494,284

pounds of lobsters valued at $94,943 to the fishermen—one cent per pound. And this is only part of the story. There were 58 Maine-owned lobster smacks, 16 of which ran to Portland, where 1,900,000 pounds of lobsters were handled the same year. These figures represent a lot of rowing, in all kinds of weather. With one-cent lobsters, a man could not afford to lay up ashore much, even in those days.

Few peapods were identical, and some differed widely. There were lapstreak pods as well as those built smooth-seam or "set-works," an old-time New England boatbuilding term. Variation in the amount of deadrise and rocker was considerable. A few had a bottom plank instead of the usual keel projecting below the rabbet line. In some of the sailing pods that were kept in the water all the time, there were false keels as deep as six inches. Certain of the pods had a plumb stem like the Whitehall boats. Others had the forefoot cut well back, so the stem was quite raking. Some had slack bilges, and in others the bilges were very hard.

Pods were as different as the men who used them and built them. Maine fishermen, more often than not, are also competent boatbuilders. Many of the fishermen designed and built their own pods; in contrast, the dories of the Massachusetts lobstermen were standardized and mass produced by a few professional builders. Building their own boats, individual fishermen could experiment and adapt them to their own special preferences and requirements. In the long run this would mean improvement of the model.

COMPARING SOME PEAPODS

Comparison of some pods will give an idea of the range of the model and some of its possibilities. There isn't a better general example of the peapod type than the boat whose lines are reproduced from Howard I. Chapelle's book, *Boatbuilding* (W. W. Norton, 1941). This is the same pod Chapelle had as a tender for his pinky, *Glad Tidings*, and naturally he had ample opportunity to test its qualities. He has this to say about the boat: "It was a typical lobsterman's

15 FOOT PEAPOD
After Lines by H. I. CHAPELLE
Feet and Inches

16 FOOT ROWING PEAPOD
FEET AND INCHES

rowing pod and though very heavy she was wonderfully stiff and rowed very well into a wind and sea. For open-water work where the boat does not have to be lifted out, I would prefer a pod to any other small skiff I have ever seen." This is high praise, and coming from someone like Chapelle who really knew small boats as few others do, it means something. The construction details are on the heavy side, but that is the way the fishermen built them to stand the gaff of lobstering day in and day out.

The 16-foot rowing pod is my own idea for use on the St. Croix River. She is intended to be a much lighter boat, built lapstrake from three-eighths-inch cedar with a bottom plank, instead of the more usual keel, to make her easier to drag over the flats and also to facilitate the installation of a centerboard. To help her rowing

16 FOOT ROWING PEAPOD
Lines, MCF August, 1951 — Midsection Detail.
Gunwale 1⅛" × ⅝" × ⅝" Oak, Riveted through Timber Heads, Thwart Knees, Sheer Plank.
Faired Knees Sided ¾" Apple-Hack Riveted to Thwart and Notched and Screwed to Laps.
Chamfer
Lap Fastening – Riveted Copper Cut Nails through Timbers and on 2" Centers between. Garboard, 1st and 2nd Broads fastened with No. 8 Bronze Screws to Bottom Plank and Fitted Floors.
Sheer Plank ⅝" Hard Wood-Oak, Ash, Elm.
Planking ⅜" Maine White Cedar ¾" Laps - 10 Strakes.
Bent Frames ⅞" × ⅝" Spaced 6" on Centers White Oak Select Second Growth Butts Heavy Wide Grain.
End, Floor
Floors Fitted to Laps-Sided ⅞" Spaced 12" - Natural Crooks. Apple, Oak, Hack.
Limber
Bottom Plank ⅝" Oak, Pine
Removable Shoe ½" Pine.

15 FOOT SAILING PEAPOD

FEET and INCHES

qualities, there is extra length, easy bilges, and considerable rocker. These features would make her an easy boat to plank. The forefoot is cut away for quick response in choppy water, as in some of the sea-going canoes of the Passamaquoddy Indians.

A very different pod is the fifteen-foot sailing model, whose rowing qualities have been reduced in favor of exceptional stiffness. Hard bilges and a five-foot beam would enable this boat to carry a lot of canvas for her length. Typically her rig would be a large spritsail furled by unstepping the mast. The sharp, deep forefoot and the deep, false keel would hold well against slippage to leeward. Such pods often had permanent rudders rigged with a yoke and tiller lines. Of the three, this boat would be the most difficult to build. Her planks would be crooked with lots of sny and bend.

A peapod of note is the one built in the winter of 1950 by Captain Charles F. Norton of Birch Harbor. The order called for a light but sturdy boat. Captain Norton furnished the following measurements and specifications for the design worked out by himself and his partner: 14 feet, 6 inches long; 4 feet, 4 inches beam; 18 inches depth amidships, with 8 inches sheer; very little deadrise—approximately 2 inches—and about the same amount of rocker. This pod was built on a bottom board instead of a keel, and planked smooth with eight strakes finished one-half inch thick. She has timbers one-half by one inch, seven inches on centers. She is built of Maine cedar on white oak.

Captain Norton can qualify as an old-timer who knows a thing or two about pods. His model is pretty true to the type as described more than 75 years ago in the U. S. Fish Commission reports, when the pod was the leading workboat of Maine lobstermen. These old pods were commonly built with a bottom board, like Captain Norton's, but more were planked lapstrake than smooth. Average measurements were 15½ feet long, 4½ feet beam, and 1½ feet depth. Although the Fish Commission reports place the origin of the pod at North Haven, Captain Norton writes that to his knowledge the first were built at Milbridge, Maine, with Steuben and Addison taking up their building soon after.

The Chapelle pod, described previously,

came from Jonesport, and it is the same general model as the Norton boat, although it is built with a keel and is of much heavier construction: length, 15 feet; beam, 4 feet, 2 inches; depth, 19 inches.

A pod owned by John W. Twitchell of Barrington, Rhode Island, is of average beam, being 4 feet, 2 inches wide, but the length is only 13 feet and 2 inches. He states that the stem is nearly plumb, which would shorten the overall length somewhat. Her hard bilges are those of the sailing pods of the lower Penobscot Bay.

In 1941, Twitchell had two of these boats built by the late Nate S. Eaton of Mountainville, Deer Isle. He has the highest praise for them, saying that they are very fast both rowing and sailing. The pod has a centerboard, rudder, and a good-sized leg-of-mutton sail, unlike the older sailing pods which generally had deep, false keels

and spritsails. The breasthooks and thwart knees, which Twitchell mentions with particular satisfaction, are characteristic of the better old-time construction, which utilized timber grown to shape for maximum strength and bracing.

The Van Ness pod, which was built by Bendix in Prospect Harbor 75 years ago, differs from the models so far considered. The bilge is slacker, and there is more deadrise and rocker. Indeed, there is an almost extreme amount of rocker rounding up into a forefoot that is cut away more than is usual. The waterlines show no reverse curve at the ends in contrast to the hollow entrance of most pods. Both Van Ness, who took off the lines, and Arnold Paine, who owned the boat at one time, agree that she was exceptionally able and easy to row and handle. She performed best with a load, they state, being somewhat tender when light. This is obvious from her slack bilges and exceptional

STATIONS SPACED 1'3" - AT ENDS 1'4".

CONSTRUCTIONAL HALF SECTION

A MAINE PEAPOD
LINES TAKEN OFF BY C. W. VAN NESS
FAIRED BY WILLIAM ATKIN
BUILT AT PROSPECT HARBOR BY BENDIX ABOUT 1900.
REARRANGED FOR THE MCF BY J. GARDNER

SAIL
HOIST - 6'½
LEACH - 9'
HEAD - 5'
FOOT - 7½

rocker, which would give her short bearing on the water without ballast to pull her down.

All the boats so far mentioned are smooth planked, but before 1900, lapstrake pods were in the majority, like the Jonesport model of 1883 in the National Watercraft Collection of the Smithsonian Institution. This boat is a keel pod that measures 15 feet, by 4½ feet, by 1½ feet. She has only seven strakes and her timbers are about two feet apart. This means heavy scantlings. The timbers would probably be sawn frames of hackmatack because of their large size and because that wood is plentiful in Washington County and good oak is not.

Only seven strakes on a boat of this depth and beam mean wide planks and thick ones—over half an inch. Such planks are stiff and must be put on as they bend naturally, without forcing. This will influence the shape of the hull, making for easy bilges, rising floors, no hollows or reverses in the waterlines, and no abrupt changes in line anywhere. Such construction is strong and rugged and not difficult to build, but makes a heavy boat—one too heavy to be pulled in and out of the water.

Alfred Brooks, writing in the *American Neptune* about the boats of Ash Point, Maine, of about 1900, describes several double-enders that I would consider peapods, although he does not use that name. These boats are exactly alike at both ends, a characteristic that sets pods off from some other double-enders, for example the small double-ended Reach boat built with a straight sternpost. What Brooks calls the best of these Ash Point boats shows lines much like those of my 16-foot rowing pod shown in this chapter. The similarity was accidental. What I did borrow from to some extent and used for checking and comparison was the fore half of the Herreshoff Columbia Lifeboat. There is also a similarity to the Van Ness pod.

My 16-foot peapod is planked lapstrake, for which this model is well adapted with its moderate bilge, ample rocker, and gradual waterlines. The indicated construction is light but strong—that of the standard yacht tender. Special emphasis is put on the use of natural crooks and woods that cannot be bought in ordinary lumberyards. Along the Maine coast, especially for those who own a farm or woodlot, it is possible to pick out choice logs and natural crooks of hackmatack, oak, elm, apple, and so forth, and have them sawed at a local mill, putting them away to season for future use. I recall sawing cut knees of apple and hackmatack by hand—it is surprising how much can be accomplished along this line with elbow grease and a sharp handsaw.

The stems for this boat would be made from single crooks without splicing, so that there is solid, unbroken grain running from breasthook to bottom board. Breasthooks from knees of suitable grain should be worked into both ends and securely riveted to the stem and gunwales. In combination with a hardwood top strake and well-fitted thwart knees, this will make a boat that will never sag or hog. As a primitive substitute for such bracing, the Indians would sometimes lash a strong log lengthwise in their canoes when obliged to cross a wide stretch of rough water.

The fitted floors are most essential. They give support to the garboard and the lower boards, which when unprotected rent and crack easily and are one of the weakest spots in an improperly constructed lapstrake boat. The floors also provide good fastening for the floor boards, which besides forming a surface to step on are also strengthening members. Many of the older pods had bent half-timbers across the keel besides their full-length frames. When this construction is used, the lower laps should be backed up by fitted wedges in the spaces between them and the frames to give solid bearing.

Great pains should be taken to get wide-grained white oak from the butts of fast-growing second-growth trees for the bent timbers. The heavier the wood the better, and it should be air-dried, and not too dry at that. Brittle, fine-grained, lightweight red oak is nearly worthless for bending stock. Elm would be a better choice, and if used the timbers should be a little larger. Copper cut nails are preferable to wire nails for rivet fastening. Bronze screws—an excellent fastening that they did not have in the old days—can be used to advantage in many places.

Brass screws are worthless. While galvanized fastenings are not suitable for light lapstrake construction, still, they can be used for heavier boats with larger members like the Jonesport model.

Today, carvel or smooth planking is generally preferred. Why, I don't know, because for my money lapstrake planking has the edge. I have built both kinds of boats, and I don't think that lapstrake is harder, as some claim; that is, once you get the tune in your head. Smooth planking requires more lumber—one-half inch being the minimum finished thickness for a smooth-seam peapod, and nine-sixteenths nearer the average. This means that planks must be backed out to fit the turn of the bilge, and this will require stock three-quarters of an inch thick and upwards. Lapstrake planks require no backing out, so that a one-inch board will give you a pair of three-eighths planks—one for each side of the boat, split apart after the board has been lined out and cut to shape.

In addition to backing out, smooth-seam plank require beveling, and a boat so planked must be planed smooth and fair after the plank are all on. Lapstrake plank have only to be beveled, and they can be smoothed and rough sanded on the bench. Of course there is some extra fastening with a lapstrake job, but no holes have to be bunged or puttied. Smooth-seam work is easier repaired, but replacing lapstrake planks is not too difficult. With a smooth-seam boat more depends upon the timbers, for that is all that holds it together. There is no question that a well-built lapstrake job will be lighter and stronger, and to my eyes it will look more like a boat.

Anyone thinking of building a pod will do well to give it a lot of thought and study. The flexibility of design holds great possibilities, and some pitfalls.

REFERENCES:

Chapelle, Howard I., *American Small Sailing Craft*, Norton, 1951, pages 217-222.

Chapelle, Howard I., *Boatbuilding*, Norton, 1941, page 402. Plans 15-foot pod.

Brooks, Alfred A., "The Boats of Ash Point, Maine," *The American Neptune*, October, 1942.

Van Ness, C. W., "A Maine Peapod," *Yachting*, February, 1932.

Mitman, Carl W., *Catalogue of the Watercraft Collection in the U. S. National Museum*, 1923, page 187. Description of Jonesport model.

Goode, George Brown, *The Fisheries and Fishery Industries of the United States*, Government Printing Office, 1887, Sec. V. Vol. 2, page 671. Description of Maine peapod.

BUILDING A 14-FOOT POD

To exemplify carvel construction in a course in recreational boatbuilding given at Mystic Seaport, we chose to build a peapod as our second boat. We picked the peapod as a distinctive New England workboat type—useful, aesthetically pleasing and attractive, not too large, too expensive to build, too fancy, or too difficult for construction by most learners, provided they have guidance.

We started from the beginning, going about it much the same as a fisherman would do, or used to do. That is, we looked over a number of pods, made some basic measurements—length, beam, rise of sheer, depth amidships, and the like—took a few rough templates, and proceeded to work out our own design. After sketching the basic shape on paper, we roughed out preliminary lines from which we made cardboard templates of the profile, sheer half breadth, and body sections. With these we began to shape a lift half-model of pine.

As this model took shape under plane and spokeshave, we could see exactly what alterations and refinements were required to give a fair hull with the characteristics we had previously decided upon. Shaping a three-dimensional half-model permits a much surer control over hull form than working in two dimensions on the drawing board. Besides this, the planking shapes, later on, can be lined out on the scaled half-model, a procedure which helps greatly when planking an unfamiliar hull for the first time.

Because this pod, like most pods, is a true double-ender, that is of identical shape on either side of the midsection, only one-half of a half-model was required—in actuality, a quarter-model. This permitted using a larger-than-usual scale, 3 inches to one foot, in fact, or one-quarter size, and this large scale in turn made possible more accurate measurement of lines and dimensions from the model.

As for the full-size laydown of this 14-foot boat, there is ample room for it on one standard 4 x 8 sheet of plywood, considering that only one-quarter of the hull need be drawn. This is an important consideration in setting up class instruction where a number of separate but identical laydowns are required in order to allow everyone in the group to participate in this basic boatbuilding operation—six separate laydowns in the present instance at Mystic Seaport in addition to the first, or master, laydown.

From the master laydown have been taken the lines, offsets, and stem dimensions reproduced here. The lines are laid out exactly as they would be drawn on a 4-foot by 8-foot sheet of

OFFSETS-14' PEAPOD measured to inside planking.		STEM	STA. 1	STA. 1½	STA. 2	STA. 3	STA. 4	STA. 5	STA. 6	STA. 7
HEIGHTHS	SHEER	2-4-0	2-2-1+	2-1-1	2-0-1+	1-10-5	1-9-5	1-8-7+	1-8-5	1-8-4+
	BUTT. 1	—	1-8-2+	1-0-1+	0-9-3+	0-6-2	0-4-5	0-3-7	0-3-5	0-3-4+
	BUTT. 2	—	—	—	1-7-4	0-9-5+	0-6-7	0-5-3	0-4-6	0-4-5
	BEARDING	—	0-8-2+	0-5-6+	0-4-3+	0-3-2	0-3-0	0-3-0	0-3-0	0-3-0
	RABBET	—	0-7-0	0-4-5+	0-3-4	0-2-5	0-2-4	0-2-4	0-2-4	0-2-4
	KEEL	—	0-5-4	0-3-3+	0-2-3+	0-1-5	0-1-4	0-1-4	0-1-4	0-1-4
HALF-BREADTHS	SHEER	0-1-0	0-6-4	0-9-4+	1-0-4+	1-5-3+	1-9-1+	1-11-6+	2-1-3+	2-1-7
	W.L. 18"	0-1-0	0-5-4	0-8-6	0-11-6	1-4-7+	1-9-0	1-11-7+	2-1-4+	2-2-0
	W.L. 15"	0-1-0	0-4-4+	0-7-4+	0-10-5+	1-3-7+	1-8-2	1-10-2	2-1-1	2-1-5+
	W.L. 12"	0-1-0	0-2-7+	0-5-6	0-8-6+	1-2-2	1-6-6+	1-10-2	2-0-1+	2-0-5+
	W.L. 9"	0-1-0	0-1-3-	0-3-1-	0-5-3+	0-10-6+	1-3-6+	1-7-6	1-10-1	1-10-4+
	W.L. 6"	0-1-0	—	0-1-0+	0-2-1+	0-5-4	0-10-0	1-2-4+	1-5-3+	1-6-0
	DIAGONAL 1	0-1-5	0-5-7-	—	0-10-3	1-1-3	1-3-4	1-4-5+	1-5-1	1-5-2-
	DIAGONAL 2	0-1-2	0-7-3	—	1-1-6	1-6-4	1-10-1+	2-0-6+	2-2-4	2-2-6

DIAGONAL 1: OUT 1-2-0 ON BASELINE, UP 1-6-0 ABOVE BASE LINE.

DIAGONAL 2: OUT 2-0-0 ON W.L.6, UP 2-0-0 ABOVE BASE LINE.

DIMENSIONS GIVEN IN FEET, INCHES, & EIGHTHS PLUS OR MINUS ONE-SIXTEENTH.
J.G.'71

plywood. The overlap of lines so produced, while not usual on the drawing board, is common practice on the mold loft floor and is really not as confusing, given a little study, as might appear to some at first glance.

A brief word as to the characteristics of the pod laid out here. Its 14 feet overall of length is about average for working pods, and so is its ample maximum beam of 52 inches inside planking, 53 inches outside. An inside depth of

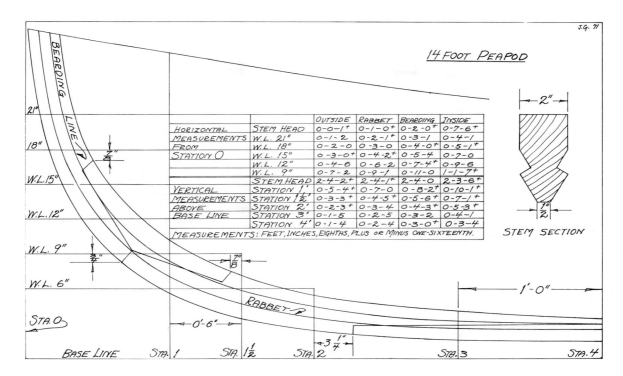

		OUTSIDE	RABBET	BEARDING	INSIDE
HORIZONTAL MEASUREMENTS FROM STATION 0	STEM HEAD	0-0-1+	0-1-0+	0-2-0+	0-7-6+
	W.L. 21"	0-1-2	0-2-1+	0-3-1	0-4-1
	W.L. 18"	0-2-0	0-3-0	0-4-0+	0-5-1+
	W.L. 15"	0-3-0+	0-4-2+	0-5-4	0-7-0
	W.L. 12"	0-4-6	0-6-2	0-7-4+	0-9-6
	W.L. 9"	0-7-2	0-9-1	0-11-0	1-1-7+
VERTICAL MEASUREMENTS ABOVE BASE LINE	STEM HEAD	2-4-2+	2-4-1+	2-4-0	2-3-6+
	STATION 1'	0-5-4+	0-7-0	0-8-2+	0-10-1+
	STATION 1½'	0-3-3+	0-4-5+	0-5-6+	0-7-1+
	STATION 2'	0-2-3+	0-3-4	0-4-3+	0-5-3+
	STATION 3'	0-1-5	0-2-5	0-3-2	0-4-1
	STATION 4'	0-1-4	0-2-4	0-3-0+	0-3-4

MEASUREMENTS: FEET, INCHES, EIGHTHS, PLUS OR MINUS ONE-SIXTEENTH.

STEM SECTION

14 FOOT PEAPOD

approximately 17½ inches amidships should give plenty of capacity and freeboard.

This boat shows rather more sheer than some, a rise of 8 inches from amidships to the extreme ends. She also has more deadrise than some of the flat-floored working pods; her underwater lines are hollow and gradual at the ends and fairly sharp for a boat as short yet as beamy as this one. These features in combination should make her fairly easy to row.

This hull, with its gradual bilges and rounded forefoot, should not prove difficult to plank with half-inch cedar. Unlike flat-floored pods, this boat has sufficient deadrise for an oak keel batten ½ inch by 3¾ inches, overlaying the keel sided 2 inches and molded 1½ inches. The keel batten provides a back rabbet for the garboards and for limbers alongside the keel.

Timbers are to be steam-bent white oak continuous from gunwale to gunwale where possible. Spaced 6 inches on centers, these timbers are to be ⅞ inch wide with a molded thickness of ⅝ inch. This permits fastening the half-inch planking with one-inch no. 8 silicon bronze screws, set slightly below the surface of the finished plank for puttying.

The building setup should be for right-side-up building, with the molds spaced 2 feet apart except at the ends, where extra molds are placed as needed to retain the designed shape. Ribbands are fastened to the molds with screws and washers, and spaced close enough to form and to support the timbers when they are bent in hot between the molds. By spacing the timbers on 6-inch centers and the molds 2 feet apart (one foot at the ends), all timbers can be bent in in one operation before the molds are removed.

The first plank to go on is the so-called "binder," that is the plank next below the sheer plank. The second is the garboard. Planking proceeds from the bottom up and from the topsides down with the last strake, or the "shutter," going in just above the turn of the bilge. Plank butts may be glue-spliced on the boat, so that butt blocks may be avoided if desired.

BUILDING A 14-FOOT LAPSTRAKE PEAPOD

In developing the design for this 14-foot rowing peapod, I kept the following objectives in mind:

OFFSETS 14-FOOT ROWING PEAPOD		STEM	STA. 1	STA. 2	STA. 3	STA. 4	STA. 6
HEIGHTS	SHEER	2-4-0	2-2-5	2-1-1	1-11-6	1-10-6	1-9-6
	BEARDING	—	0-7-6	0-3-3	0-2-7	0-2-5	0-2-4
	RABBET	—	0-6-1	0-2-7	0-2-3	0-2-2	0-2-1
	KEEL	—	0-4-2	0-1-2	0-0-7	0-0-6	0-0-4
	BUTTOCK 1	—	1-6-6	0-9-2	0-5-6	0-4-2	0-3-2
	BUTTOCK 2	—	—	1-6-3	0-10-1	0-6-7	0-4-6
HALF-BREADTHS	W.L. 6	0-0-7	—	0-2-7	0-6-2	0-9-7	1-3-6
	W.L. 9	0-0-7	0-1-3	0-5-5	0-10-5	1-3-2	1-8-2
	W.L. 12	0-0-7	0-2-7	0-8-4	1-1-6	1-6-0	1-10-6
	W.L. 15	0-0-7	0-4-2	0-10-3	1-3-5	1-7-3	1-11-7
	W.L. 18	0-0-7	0-5-4	0-11-6	1-4-6	1-8-3	2-0-3
	SHEER	0-0-7	0-7-7	1-1-6	1-6-3	1-9-4	2-1-0
DIAGONAL B		0-1-4	0-5-5	0-10-2	1-1-4	1-3-2	1-5-0
DIAGONAL A		0-1-2	0-7-6	1-1-4	1-6-2	1-9-5	2-1-3

DIAGONAL A 2' ABOVE BASE LINE   OUT 1'-8" ON W.L. 9
DIAGONAL B 1'-6" ABOVE B.L. OUT 1'-2" ON BASE LINE.
OFFSETS MEASURED IN FEET, INCHES & EIGHTHS
TO THE INSIDE OF THE PLANKING.   J.G.

1. The boat should be as safe and seaworthy as it is reasonable to expect in an open 14-foot rowboat.

2. It should not be too much for one person to handle and should row easily. Although it is not intended for racing, it should be capable of a fair turn of speed.

3. It should not be too difficult to build in the ordinary home workshop by an amateur with modest woodworking skills, even though round-hull construction in general is not the easiest way to build a boat.

As mentioned previously in this book, in the past there were many variations of peapods depending upon where they were used, under what conditions they were used, and who used them. Some peapods were sailed, where long distances were covered, but more were rowed. Those that were sailed—for example, those developed for open-water sailing around Matinicus Island—were larger and more powerful than the ordinary rowing kind, and were fitted with plank-on-edge keels, which in some cases extended 5 inches or 6 inches below the bottom of the boat. Other sailing pods were fitted with centerboards, such as some that were built on Deer Isle.

For hauling lobster pots set among the rocks and ledges close to the shore, rowing pods were required. These were often quite flat in the floors, which in a round hull produced a wide, rather flat bottom with a sharp, quick turn at the bilge as it rounded up into the topsides. Such a hull had plenty of initial stability to support a heavy waterlogged lobster pot when it was hauled up and over the side. But boats like this were not the easiest kind to row, and, besides, that hard bilge with its quick, sharp turn was difficult to build, either carvel or clinker.

Examination of the mid-section shape at stations 4 and 6 in the accompanying lines of our new peapod will reveal how a hard, difficult bilge has been avoided by giving the bottom a moderate amount of deadrise (upward slope), and the topsides some outward rake or slant. The result is a relatively slow, easy turn at the bilge, which will help greatly in planking. A hull so shaped will heel quicker than one with a harder bilge such as is generally found in sailing models where stiffness, that is, resistance to heeling, is desirable.

But we are not offering a sailing model here, and the more moderate bilge curve as shown not only makes for easier planking, but for an easier rowing model as well. A harder bilge curve in these central body sections would necessarily produce more of a mid-section bulge in the waterline curves, resulting in increased resistance to hull movement through the water.

The buttock curves, as they appear in the profile view in the lines, show a relatively flat, easy run, which carries well into the ends of the boat. The entrance is relatively sharp as is shown by the hollow or reverse in the ends of the waterline curves. All these factors contribute to make this a low-resistance, easy-rowing hull.

The boat is a true double-ender with both ends exactly alike. This simplifies construction greatly, and there are no disadvantages for a rowing model. In a sailing model it is usually desirable to make the stern fuller to provide more bearing aft.

The stems are moderately raking and cut away at the forefoot. This obviates a tendency to yaw when towed, as generally occurs with boats with plumb stems when they are towed behind a larger vessel. This peapod could very well serve as a tender for a large yacht. Also, the shape to which the stems are laid out is an easy and economical one to build. As the detailed drawing shows, these stems can be made up of pieces got out of an ordinary oak plank. Steam bending is not required, nor is lumber with grown-in curves.

The keel can be cut to shape from a 12-foot oak plank 4½ inches wide and 1¾ inches thick.

The hull can be planked either carvel or lapstrake, but I recommend the latter, for a lapstrake hull is both lighter and stronger. Lapstrake planking can be got out and finished at the bench, including sanding, so that when the planks are fastened on the boat no additional surfacing and smoothing is required, as is necessary with carvel planking. Nor is any "backing," that is, hollowing the inside of the plank to fit the curve of the ribs, required either.

Beginners are frequently afraid of the beveling that has to be done in fitting the laps of clinker planking. It is far less difficult than it might appear to be, and planking for this hull has been laid out to make beveling as easy as possible.

Nineteen inches of depth amidships insures a generous amount of freeboard. The extra couple of inches of topside height will not increase windage appreciably, but it will add to the carrying capacity and the rough water capability of this boat. Three or even four adults can be carried easily; even more could be accommodated should the boat be used as a tender over short distances in relatively calm water.

The boat is designed to be built with nine strakes to the side of northern white cedar planking ⅜ inch thick. A few knots are no great matter. They can be replaced with tapered plugs (a little larger on the outside) of dry white pine or cedar. Better glue them in.

DISTANCES FROM STATION NO.2-FEET, INCHES, EIGHTHS							
MEASURED ON WATER LINES	W.L. 6	W.L. 9	W.L. 12	W.L. 15	W.L. 18	W.L. 24	SHEER
RABBET	0-11-5	1-3-2	1-5-5	1-7-3	1-8-6	1-10-5	1-11-2
BEARDING L.	0-9-2	1-1-5	1-4-2	1-6-2	1-7-6	1-9-7	1-10-4
INNER FACE	0-2-4	0-9-2	1-2-4	1-5-0	1-6-5	1-8-6	1-9-4

The stem and keel are oak, as is the keel batten. The keel requires a 12-foot piece at least 4½ inches wide and 1¾ inches thickness finished. A shorter piece the same thickness will make the stems and stem knees. If at all possible, this oak should be seasoned and dry, and the keel plank should be straight and true, without kinks or twists. A dense piece of red oak, yellow bark oak, or the equivalent, will do nicely and would probably be better here than a piece of white oak, which tends to twist and pull as the moisture content changes. With scantlings of this small size, there is little danger of red oak rotting if it is sound and solid to begin with.

Lay out the stem pieces, the stem knees, and the keel from the full-size laydown, presumably already made cut to the exact shape, and fit together accurately. All the necessary dimensions are contained in the offsets and the drawing of the stem detail.

Figure 1 shows how the stem and keel assembly is bolted together. The direction in which the bolts run is important. They should be located as shown. This way they tend to pull the joint together when they are taken up tight. If they were slanted the other way, that is away from the middle joint, tightening them would act the other way, tending to open the joint.

Some builders would glue up this stem and keel assembly before bolting it, putting the screws in the ends of the stem knee to help hold it from slipping until the glue sets. Of course, the assembly must be well clamped and care must be taken to see that it does not slip out of true. After the glue has hardened, it is easier to bore for the bolts and put them in.

When the stem and keel are bolted together, but before the rabbet is cut, half-inch white pine stopwaters are put in as shown. These are tightly driven plugs or dowels of dry pine for tight swelling when the water strikes them. They are located in the joint just inside the rabbet line, and go through from side to side. Plank ends will cover them, and caulking will be driven in tightly against them later to stop any possible seepage of water through these joints at the base of the stem.

Before the boat can be set up for planking, molds must be made. Their shape will be taken from the body plan in the full-size laydown. When the set-up is made, the molds will be positioned 2 feet apart on stations 6, 4, and 2. As the ends of this pod are exactly alike, two molds for each of these three stations are all that are required. No. 2 common one-inch

pine boards, actual thickness ¾ inch, will do nicely.

The mold shown in Figure 5 is for station 6, which comes at the widest part of the boat and is made up of four pieces cleated together. The No. 2 molds can be made of only two pieces each.

It will be seen that the mold shown in Figure 5 extends beyond the sheer to the ladder frame line. This is drawn in the full-size laydown 2 feet 4 inches above the baseline and parallel with it. All the molds are extended to this line. Thus, when they are set up on the ladder frame foundation, they will all stand at the right height in relation to one another. The centerline is clearly marked on the molds, which are notched to receive the keel batten, as shown in the full-size body plan.

This boat can be planked either right-side-up or bottom-up as shown in Figure 5. If he chooses to plank right-side-up, the builder can rivet the laps without assistance as he goes along, but everything else is harder: fairing the set-up, cutting the garboard rabbet, laying out the planks, fitting the laps, and so forth. Consequently, I recommend planking bottom-up on the ladder frame. A method has been worked out, as presently will be explained, for getting around the need to rivet the laps as the planks are put on.

For a thorough explanation of the ladder frame method of setting up a boat of this sort, see Chapter 2.

The stem rabbets are best cut with the stem and keel assembly lying flat before the keel batten is added and this assembly is laid over the molds in position on the ladder frame. Cutting a rabbet for the first time can be tricky. Figure 2 shows how it is done. The bearding line and the rabbet line are laid out from the offsets and the stem detail. Using the block as shown in Figure 2, points locating the *apex line* are obtained, and the apex line is drawn.

In cutting the rabbet, an apex line is carried straight down with the chisel, at the same time paring toward it with the chisel from either side, until the block fits, as shown.

FIG. 2

Without the apex line to go by, it is easy to go astray and to cut too much or in the wrong place. It is best to cut short sections of rabbet at intervals, and then clean out the intervening sections that remain.

The keel batten is oak, ⅝ inch thick and 3¼ inches wide, and it is screwed every 6 inches or thereabouts to the keel. Epoxy glue is also recommended. Beveling the keel batten to receive the garboards is best done on the set-up where the correct amount of bevel can be directly obtained from the station molds at 2-foot intervals.

Except at the ends of the boat, the keel batten bevel does not change much between stations, and what little there is can be easily worked fair with a rabbet plane. But toward the ends in the vicinity of Station 3 there is more bevel and it changes faster. Getting it right may not bother the experienced professional, but it can mean trouble for someone attempting this operation for the first time.

However, a sliding jig, as shown in Figure 3, takes out the guesswork. To set it up, a temporary batten the same thickness as the planking stock and 3 inches or 4 inches wide is bent around the forms in approximately the

PLANKING WIDTHS – APPROXIMATE CHECK WITH BATTENS TO LINE OUT LAPS				
STATIONS	6	4	3	2	1
GARBOARD	$4\frac{1}{8}$	$3\frac{5}{8}$	$3\frac{3}{8}$	$3\frac{1}{4}$	$\frac{3}{4}$
1	$4\frac{1}{4}$	$3\frac{7}{8}$	$3\frac{3}{8}$	$2\frac{3}{4}$	$2\frac{3}{8}$
2	$4\frac{1}{4}$	4	$3\frac{5}{8}$	3	$2\frac{1}{2}$
3	$4\frac{1}{8}$	$3\frac{5}{8}$	$3\frac{3}{8}$	3	$2\frac{1}{2}$
4	$3\frac{1}{4}$	$3\frac{1}{8}$	$2\frac{7}{8}$	$2\frac{5}{8}$	$2\frac{1}{8}$
5	$3\frac{3}{8}$	3	$2\frac{5}{8}$	$2\frac{1}{2}$	$2\frac{1}{4}$
6	$3\frac{1}{4}$	3	$2\frac{3}{4}$	$2\frac{3}{8}$	$2\frac{1}{4}$
7	$3\frac{3}{8}$	3	$2\frac{3}{4}$	$2\frac{1}{2}$	$2\frac{3}{8}$
SHEER	$4\frac{1}{2}$	$4\frac{1}{4}$	$4\frac{1}{8}$	$3\frac{7}{8}$	$3\frac{3}{8}$

same position that the plank above the garboard will later occupy, and is temporarily tacked in place with small nails. A sliding jig like the one shown in Figure 3 moved along this batten will give the correct bevel at any place that it is applied, and the cut can't help being right.

Much of the success of a clinker planking job depends on the number of plank, their widths, and how they line out. Nine strakes should be about right for this boat, and the widths given were carefully worked out on a scale half model. While they are not exact, they are close. Adjustment will need to be made, but in most cases this adjustment will not be more than ⅛ inch either way.

It is desirable to lay out all the plank on one side at the same time so that they can be viewed as a unit. Only in this way is it possible to harmonize all the adjustments, to equalize the widths, and to make sure that all is right, for boats are judged for appearance as completed units, and not separate plank by separate plank.

To lay out the plank, eight battens the length of the boat will be required, each ⅞ inch wide, the width of the planking laps, and ⅜ inch thick, the thickness of the plank. These will represent the planking laps and are temporarily tacked to the molds where the laps will later come, in accordance with the planking widths given.

After all of these battens are on, they are adjusted as necessary to give fair, pleasing, and uniform lines, their positions are marked on the molds and the stems, and these marks are carefully transferred to the other side of the boat.

Before attempting to plank this boat, the beginner is advised to read the sections that apply in the Appendix of this book.

The planking for this boat has been laid out as already noted for a ⅞-inch lap. In greater part, the upper edge of the planks, that is, the edge toward the sheer, will be thinned to 3/16 inch in planing the bevels. Exceptions, of which there are a very few, can be seen in the lay-out of the lap bevels shown in Figure 4. Number 1 shows that at Station 6 the upper edge of the sixth plank from the bottom has been thinned slightly less than 3/16 inch because the curvature of the side at that point requires this in order for the lap surfaces to close. This plank can be prepared and put on with the normal amount of lap bevel throughout, and the removal of a thin shaving or two with a small plane when the plank is in place on the boat will be all that is needed before the next plank goes on.

Number 3 of Figure 4 shows the top edge of the third plank from the bottom at Station 6 with less than the normal amount of bevel. This is because of the width of the plank above. If it were narrower, the angle with the mold, that is to say with the section curve, would change, permitting a normal amount of bevel. In this case the full amount of normal lap bevel is not planed off in preparing the plank at the bench. It will be observed that the more curvature there is in the sectional shape, the narrower the planks must be for the laps to close, but where the sectional shape

FIG. 4

STA. 6 - PLANKS
5, 6 & 7

STA. 2

STA. 3

GARBOARD

GARBOARD

GARBOARD

STA. 6

1. MORE THAN NORMAL BEVEL
2. NORMAL BEVEL $\frac{3''}{16}$
3. LESS THAN NORMAL BEVEL

is straight or flat, width does not matter.

It is worth mentioning that an old fashioned spokeshave with a wood stock makes an excellent tool for roughing off the laps, to be finished with a small, sharp block plane.

For those unaccustomed to clinker planking, it will help to draw full-size sections of the planking at the various stations. To be useful, however, this must be done with precision and accuracy. When this is done, the builder can see ahead of time exactly what lap bevels will be required.

Actually this is not a hard boat to plank. For the most part the beveling is straightaway and uniform. I believe, nevertheless, that if I were laying out the planking for this boat a second time, I would make the garboard and the next two planks above slightly wider,

which would allow the planks on the turn above to be slightly narrower. For one thing, this would normalize the lap bevel at Number 3, Figure 4, as already considered.

It is necessary to shape the ends of the planking, the hood ends so called, so that they will mate together and lie flat and level when fastened in the stem rabbet. The standard way to do this is detailed in Figure 6. An easy way of cutting the tapering recess into which the shouldered edge of the overlapping plank fits is to make a shallow kerf with a fine-tooth dovetail saw guided against a thin strip of straight batten tacked on the lap line. The necessary amount of wood can then be removed from the gain, so called, with a sharp chisel and finished with a small rabbet plane.

To hold the laps together and the planking

FIG. 5

FIG. 6

in place until the planking is finished and the boat can be turned over and riveted, the planks, as they are put on, are nailed through the laps into the molds. For this purpose, standard long, thin, coated nails are used with leather washers about ⅝ inch in diameter, dinked out of stiff, heavy leather with a hollow punch. These washers are then pierced with an ice pick to make a hole for the nail. This nail and washer arrangement holds well when driven through the lap, applying pressure

to the lap, and is easily drawn out later with carpenter's tongs. When the time comes to timber out the boat after planking is completed, ribs will go in where the molds come out. Rivets through the laps and these ribs will occupy the same holes previously made by the nails.

Ribs or frames will be spaced 8 inches apart on centers, that is two ribs in each 2-foot space between stations, where there will also be the ribs that have replaced the molds. Thus, the rib spacing throughout the boat will be on 8-inch centers with rivets through the ribs, and with two rivets through the laps, equally spaced between each pair of ribs. Altogether, fastenings through the laps will be spaced approximately 2⅝ inches apart.

Ideally, ribs should be the best white oak from butts of young, fast-growing trees, steam bent and continuous from rail to rail. A thickness of 9/16 inch and a width of ⅞ inch would be sufficient. If it should be necessary to butt the ribs on the center of the keel batten, half ribs of the same size, continuous across the keel and extending from seat riser to seat riser, should double every other frame.

1 7

A Spurling Rowboat

As recently as 50 or 60 years ago—say before 1920—in most of the towns along Maine's more than a thousand miles of coastline, you could have found at least one man locally renowned as a boatbuilder. Not that boatbuilding had to be his sole, or chief, occupation. Often it wasn't and perhaps he didn't average a boat a year. But at a time when almost anyone could whack together something that would float, at least, this man was looked up to and respected as a master and his boats were sought after and imitated. Not infrequently his reputation and his boats lived long after he had passed away.

Boatbuilding in those days was more than a mechanical trade, it was esteemed as an art. Those who excelled set high standards for themselves and practiced building for pleasure as well as for profit, with the latter often the lesser consideration.

A glimpse of what it was like in those days is afforded by the account by Alfred Brooks, mentioned in the last chapter, of the boats of Ash Point, Maine. Today, Ash Point is only a few minutes' drive from Rockland, but back at the turn of the century the trip back and forth by horse and wagon, including shopping and other business, used up the better part of the day and was not too frequently made. People stayed home more in those days, and the people of the small fishing community of Ash Point were self-sufficient to an extent that is hard to

realize now, producing much of what the simple needs of the time required. Of course, they built their own boats, of which four types, according to Brooks, were then in use: dories, wherries, double-enders, and small sloops.

Boatbuilding was a winter job. According to Brooks, many of the men built boats for their own use if they felt like it. However, Freeman Ratcliff and his son Paris built boats for others. "The ownership of a Ratcliff boat was like owning a Rolls-Royce car today," that is to say, in 1942, when Brooks wrote his article.

Another view of boatbuilding as it was practiced along the Maine coast several generations ago is to be found in the chapter on Isle au Haut fishermen in Wasson and Colcord's *Sailing Days on the Penobscot*. The construction of small boats, specifically peapods and wherries "flourished to an astonishing extent" in the Penobscot Bay area. Boatbuilding came naturally to these people, it seemed; nearly everyone had attempted a boat at one time or another.

Finished boats came out of the strangest places: attics, cellars, henhouses, and ramshackle waterfront sheds. Nearly everyone had a wood-lot, and it was a general practice to cut logs for boat lumber in the wintertime along with the firewood. However, the roots of cedar and hackmatack for frames, stems, knees, and the like had to be dug when the ground was soft in the spring or fall.

A full bow and a fine run mark the Spurling skiff. This is the first boat Arthur Spurling built.

The would-be builder might have taken several years to accumulate the required lumber. How satisfying it must have been finally to complete a boat of lumber whose every piece had been selected, cut, and carefully stored away against the day of building. How different from the boat whose materials come from the store in a can! It may be that the latter sort of boat serves just as well for transportation, but a lot of the fun and satisfaction have been lost, notwithstanding.

Unlike furniture, small boats in the past were rarely stored under roofs. They were built to be replaced, and, when they wore out, they were abandoned to the weather and soon rotted away. So many fine examples of the boat-builder's art have perished utterly. So many superlative craftsmen have been all but forgotten in the short space of a couple of generations; their boats, shops, patterns, tools—everything—gone, reduced to names that only a few old-timers remember.

Nevertheless, more remains than often we might suppose. The question is for how long. It is my guess—may I say, educated guess—that if a thorough, coordinated search could be made from one end of the Maine coast to the other, and the Canadian Maritime provinces should be included as well, an immense amount of historic material, including actual boats, would still be found as surviving and recoverable. The institutional resources to undertake this job in a systematic fashion do not exist at this time, al-though marine museums and others are doing what they have the means for. Already, interested amateurs are beginning to make a significant contribution. One of the first things needing to be done is to search out and locate what still exists that is worth recording and preserving. Here the camera helps greatly. Photographs are only a part of the complete record, but an indispensable part.

The photographs taken in the summer of 1971 by Robert Sutter from White Plains, N. Y., of "set-works" (carvel) tenders built by Arthur M. Spurling of Islesford, Little Cranberry Isle, Maine, are a case in point. Spurling, now in his 90s, has not built a boat for more than 20 years, yet a number of his tenders are still in use and highly prized by their owners. In fact, the first one he ever built many years ago is still tight and seaworthy.

The photographs taken by Sutter tell a great deal, but need, of course, to be supplemented by detailed measurements and a list of specifications. The molds used by Spurling have disappeared, so that lines need to be taken off one or more of the boats. All Sutter was able to obtain in the way of patterns were several transom shapes laid out on building paper, yet even these by themselves are useful and more than worthy of preservation.

The photographs show a craft which was once much used along the coast of northern New England, both as a tender for larger boats and a general purpose rowboat. Twelve feet is

(Above) Detail photographs of the Spurling 12-foot tender. Note that the high stern knee prevents the use of an outboard motor.   (Left) Arthur M. Spurling of Isleford, Maine, who was 94 when this photograph was taken in 1972.

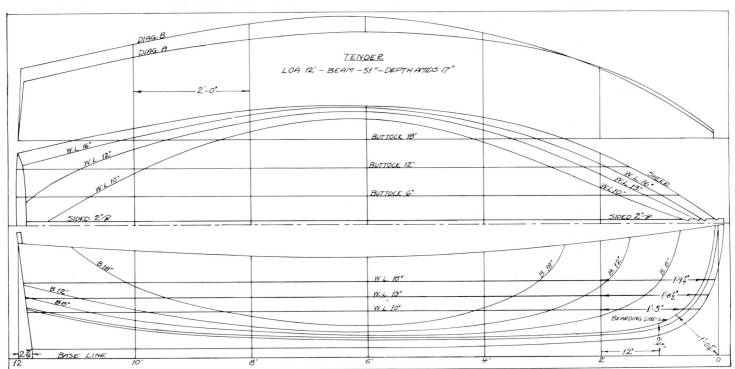

The lines above are for a 12-foot skiff similar to the Spurling model.
The offsets for this boat are on the next page.

OFFSETS INSIDE OF PLANKING - FEET, INCHES, EIGHTHS. 12-FOOT SKIFF, NATIONAL FISHERMAN, SEPTEMBER 1972								
	STATIONS	STEM	2'	4'	6'	8'	10'	TRAN.
HEIGHTS ABOVE B.L.	SHEER	2-3-4	2-0-2	1-10-2	1-9-2	1-9-4	1-10-6	2-0-3
	KEEL BOTTOM	—	0-3-1	0-2-2	0-2-0	0-2-0	0-2-0	0-2-0
	PARTING LINE	—	0-4-6	0-4-1	0-4-1	0-4-6	0-6-5	0-10-7
	BUTTOCK 6"	—	0-8-5	0-5-1	0-4-5	0-5-5	0-8-1	1-1-2
	" 12"	—	1-3-0	0-6-7	0-5-3	0-6-6	0-10-2	1-3-5
	" 18"	—	—	0-10-4	0-6-5	0-8-7	1-3-2	—
HALF-BREADTHS	SHEER	—	1-3-2	1-10-6	2-1-1	2-0-5	1-8-6	1-3-4
	W.L. 16"	—	1-0-6	1-9-2	2-0-7	1-11-3	1-6-6	1-0-4
	W.L. 13"	—	0-10-4	1-7-6	2-0-0	1-9-7	1-4-0	0-4-6
	W.L. 10"	—	0-7-5	1-5-2	1-10-3	1-7-5	0-11-4	—
	KEEL	—	0-0-6	0-0-6	0-0-6	0-0-6	0-0-6	0-0-6
	DIAG. A.	—	1-3-4	1-9-0	1-11-0	1-9-2	1-5-7	1-0-6
	DIAG. B.	—	1-3-0	1-10-6	2-2-3	2-0-5	1-8-2	1-3-3

the most usual length, although some were built as small as 10 feet. Four feet or slightly more was the normal beam for a 12-foot boat. They were built both lapstrake and set works, but more often the latter. The set works boats were best planked of cedar, finished a plump ½-inch thick. Oak frames were often steam bent ahead of time on forms, beveled after cooling, and finally set in place to receive the planking. The frames would be joined across the keel and keel batten with a natural crook floor sawn out of apple, hackmatack, or more rarely an oak limb crook. Sometimes the frames were bent in continuous from gunwale to gunwale.

Such boats were for utility, not for show. Generally fastened with galvanized iron boat nails, and painted, the boats were heavier and more serviceable than the ultra-light, varnished yacht tenders which often resembled them in shape.

The lines reproduced herewith are not for the Spurling boat but are drawn from notes that I took some years ago from a boat closely like it. (The plans for her stem are reproduced in the Appendix, where cutting a stem rabbet is discussed.) The boat I measured also had a reputation for good capacity and easy rowing, and was a fine sea boat. I was told that the boat was built in Maine, in the Penobscot Bay region the owner thought, but he could not recall just where, or who the builder was.

One or more of the Spurling boats should be measured and recorded before they disappear. Aside from the historic record, this is a sturdy, useful type that would appeal to amateur builders if plans for it were available.

1 8

The St. Lawrence River Skiff

Sailing without a rudder! A boat that handles smartly on all points of sailing with nothing resembling a rudder or substituting for it—no steering oar, no fin, no appendage of any sort extending overboard into the water. Most modern-day, salt water sailors are incredulous. Such a craft is outside their experience, and it is hard to imagine how it operates. On first consideration it seems impossible to sail without a rudder.

Yet it is possible, and is done, as it has been done for over a century, although it may develop that this sailing technique is older than now appears.

To maneuver without a rudder requires a particular type of boat, as shall be explained in detail later on. As far as we know the only craft so sailed is the St. Lawrence River skiff, a distinctive, lightly built, clinker double-ender, running up to 22 to 23 feet long for sailing models, a type which seems to have originated on the St. Lawrence River in the vicinity of the Thousand Islands, possibly at Clayton in Jefferson County, N. Y., in the late 1860s.

Directly in line between Clayton and the Canadian town of Gananoque in the Province of Ontario, midway in the St. Lawrence at a point where the river is several miles wide, lies Grindstone Island. Here, beginning in 1884, the American Canoe Association held its annual meets with hundreds of enthusiastic devotees of

the canoeing sport, both with paddle and sail, in attendance. Here in 1886 an American canoeist won the international trophy cup in competition with visitors from England's Royal Canoe Club.

For a brief few years, the canoe, and particularly the sailing canoe, dominated the American sporting scene. Thus, in its Midsummer Holiday Number for August, 1885, *The Century Magazine*, the leading American magazine of that day, featured a long article by Henry Eckford titled "Camp Grindstone." While this was in the main an account of the exciting and fashionable goings-on of the ACA canoeing set at Grindstone Island, the author went out of his way to extol the admirable qualities of the St. Lawrence River skiff, as well as to describe the singular manner in which it was sailed. Apparently Eckford's was the first account of the skiff to appear in print.

Here is what he had to say about the skiff itself: "At the Thousand Islands there is an indigenous boat for fishing and rowing, remarkable for the methods by which it is managed under sail. Visitors call it a skiff, natives a skift. Holding five or six persons easily, it is of strong, yet light build, and in its lines probably the most beautiful rowboat afloat. Birchbark, Peterboro, Rob Roy, Shadow, Nautilus, Pearl, the hulls of all these must yield in gracefulness to the skiff."

This is high praise, indeed, for the names listed are those of the most popular and highly-

The Thousand Islands area around Clayton, New York, the center of St. Lawrence skiff development.

thought-of sporting canoes of that day.

Local tradition has it that the St. Lawrence River skiff was first built in all essentials the same as it has remained to this day in about 1868 by Xavier Colon in Clayton, N. Y. Whether research now in progress will confirm this, or whether some similar prior craft from which it may have developed will yet be revealed, remains to be seen.

However, it is clear that the skiff developed as a guide's workboat used primarily to take fishing parties to and from the fishing grounds in Thousand Islands waters. The Thousand Islands, so called, in reality number something like 1,800 islands and occupy a 50-mile stretch of river which is 12 miles wide at its upper end where it leaves Lake Ontario, and is still more than a mile wide at its lower end before the rapids begin. Here is some of the best, if not *the* best, muskellunge fishing in North America. Here also are to be found in abundance pike, pickerel, bass, perch, as well as numerous lesser species.

After the Civil War, the "summer visitor" came into increasing prominence in nineteenth century America. Farm boys, who had left the country in their youth to find fortune in the burgeoning cities of the Northeast, had in the decades following the Civil War accumulated the means permitting them to return with their families to vacation among the scenic beauties of unspoiled nature. They flocked to the seashore, to the mountains, and to inland rivers and lakes.

In New York the Adirondack woods and the Thousand Islands were greatly favored by vacationers. This was the era of vast, often palatial, summer hotels. While those of sedentary inclination relaxed on cool, spacious verandas, the more active took up canoeing or went fishing, especially the latter, for in those halcyon days the "big ones" had not all been caught, and pollution had not yet sullied the purity of aboriginal waters.

In the Thousand Islands region, because of the extent of fishing grounds and the distances

(Above) St. Lawrence skiffs in front of the Thousand Island House. The guides and sports are ready for a day of fishing. (Right) A fishing guide, one of many in a trade that provided motive power as well as fishing brains before the advent of the outboard motor.

needing to be traveled to reach them, a special sort of boat was required. This was before the day of motors. There were only two ways of moving a boat—by oars or by sail. Besides, it could get rough on the wide, open waters of the St. Lawrence, for example the windy stretch of water off Gananoque, called the Forty Acre Shoals, a favorite lurking place for muskellunge.

A boat for the Thousand Islands had to row as easily as possible when it was calm, yet be able to hoist canvas and sail when a breeze sprang up. Guiding fishermen was highly competitive. The guide who could get back and forth to the favorite fishing grounds in the least possible time with the least possible trouble naturally got the cream of the business.

An account in *Forest and Stream* in 1889 states that St. Lawrence River skiffs "are used everywhere about the Thousand Islands for fishing, rowing, and sailing, to the exclusion of all other small boats. They are handled by professional boatmen who show the greatest skill in their handling. . . . The chief peculiarity of the boat is the absence of a rudder, even in sailing,

and steering being done by trimming the sheet and changing the balance of the boat. The boatsman brings her up into the wind by moving into the bow, and causes her to fall off by moving aft, handling her as perfectly as could be done by a rudder."

A longtime resident of Rochester, N. Y., a former summer visitor to the Thousand Islands whose experience with St. Lawrence River skiffs goes back to the 1890s, states in a letter written some 18 years ago that these skiffs were used by all fishing guides in the Thousand Islands region before the appearance of the small gas engine. Such skiffs, he explained, were very fast off the wind and were raced by the guides to and from the best fishing grounds. His father, who went on his honeymoon in such a skiff about 1880, had a St. Lawrence River skiff when he lived in

Stability test of a St. Lawrence skiff was shown in the Illustrated Catalogue *of D.A. Bain, Clayton, New York, about 1884. The guide rowed from the forward seat; the passengers relaxed in the comfortable after positions.*

Toronto, in which he used to sail to the Thousand Islands, camping on the shore at night, often in the company of friends also traveling in skiffs. When our informant and his brother were 10 years old, their father bought them skiffs.

"We used them on Lake Ontario," he related, "and almost every year sailed to the Thousand Islands in them, where we often brought them back by steamer because of prevailing westerly winds. Given fair weather and a southwesterly wind we could sail from Rochester to the Thousand Islands, a distance of about 150 miles, in about three days, camping on the shore at night."

Farther along in the letter, our correspondent goes on to say that "the St. Lawrence River guides in the Thousand Islands used to hold annual regattas. There was great rivalry between the guides of Gananoque, Ontario, and those belonging at Clayton, New York. The St. Lawrence skiffs were normally sailed without rudders by 'ballast.' To come about one moved his weight forward keeling the skiff to leeward. My father had rudders put on our boats for use

on Lake Ontario where high waves frequently interfered with the ballast method of steering."

Rudders were also used on the so-called "batwing" boats, a special, over-rigged type of skiff developed prior to 1910 exclusively for racing. The name derives from the over-size sail which was heavily battened and of a shape somewhat similar to the wing of the nocturnal creature which it recalled.

Here is Henry Eckford's summary of how to sail a skiff from the August, 1885, issue of *The Century Magazine:*

It sailed, with the aid of a small centerboard, by means of a large spritsail, the mast being stepped well forward when in use. The main peculiarity of the skiff under sail is that neither rudder nor oar nor paddle is needed to guide it. Some persons help themselves to come about on a fresh tack with the oars, but this is not at all necessary, and is held in great scorn by a good sailor. The latter walks unconcernedly up and down his boat, pays her off the wind, or brings her up close hauled as if by magic. The secret lies in distributing the weight of the sailor forward or backward. In order to bring the boat into the wind with the needed swiftness, he moves suddenly forward quite to the mast. This buries the bow of the boat, and the stern shaped like the bow, rises up and is swung around by the wind. As soon

A race among St. Lawrence skiffs.

as the sail shakes well in the wind, the skiff-man runs aft, thus raising the bow, which is helped about by the wind, and depressing at the same time the stern. All this without steering-oar or rudder, or the help of oars in the rowlocks.

It is curious to see how sensitive such a boat is to the weight of a man. Running free, he sits nearly aft. Should it be necessary to run directly before the wind, he gets as far astern as possible; while to come up into the wind the reverse movement is made. First lessons in this unique boat deal severely with the shins of the novice and with the paint inside the boat, but a little practice gives mastery. In the skiff it is considered dangerous to make the main-sheet fast to the gunwale, because the boat is so long, narrow, and shallow that it might be easily caught in one of the squalls that come with little warning down from the islands. Many will not use the running-block, caught to the gunwale with a snap-spring, which keeps the sail flat and holds it well. The simple rope is preferred and held in the hand ready to be loosed at once. The block and tackle might be hampered in an emergency and the boat turn over. Of course the skiff is not the best sailer to windward in the world, and a good regatta canoe under full sail can generally beat her, especially if the wind be light.

Another view of the sailing skiff is to be found in a short account of skiff sailing at Grindstone Island recently supplied by James C. White, M.D., of Boston. Dr. White, who has sailed skiffs for many years, is still an avid sailor. It is mighty fine sport as he describes it:

In the 1800's and '90's, before the days of motorboats, the Morgan and Leavitt families who summered at the head of Grindstone Island were entirely dependent on the combination rowing and sailing St. Lawrence skiffs, not only for their fishing, but for marketing as well. Indeed, our grandparents thought nothing of taking a guest with baggage the four miles from Clayton to the head of the island, or of sailing this distance to church and back on Sundays or to get a cake of ice to cool their drinks on other days of the week. Fishing, which in the old days was a frequent pastime, was done with the larger skiffs sailed or rowed by the boatmen.

After the advent of motorboats their offspring have used these superbly designed skiffs for many years. Races were usually held in a stiff southwesterly breeze over a figure-eight course which we called the "corkscrew." The first leg was around Papoose Island, then a reach with the wind abeam through the lee of Whiskey Island. After rounding it in the reverse direction by beating to windward the course was dead before the wind between Whiskey and Papoose where the puffs blew hardest.

The tricks to win were to get through the lees of the two islands with the minimal loss of headway, to tack the boat about smartly, and finally to jibe to cross the finish line at the Rum Point dock. In order to jibe you have to pull up the centerboard, sit on the extreme stern of the boat and haul in the sheet, hoping that you can pay it out smoothly enough not to capsize or get thrown overboard as the sail suddenly catches the wind on the other side and tilts the boat down to the gunwale. Some of the world's best yachtsmen, including Mike Vanderbilt, who skippered *America*'s Cup defenders, came to grief in this way.

A skiff race underway on the St. Lawrence in the old days.

To illustrate how maneuverable these little skiffs are when well handled, we used to play a game of tag within our small circle of islands. Each boat had a two-man crew, a tennis ball, and fish landing-net. The purpose was for the boat which was "it" to avoid being tagged by the tennis ball thrown by one of the crew of four or five pursuing boats. If the ball missed the dodging boat or its sail, it had to be retrieved with the fish-net. Collisions were rare and no skiffs were ever seriously injured.

The children of the oldtimers, who are now in their seventies, are too stiff and off balance to carry out the rapid, well-timed maneuvers required for this type of competition, but still enjoy sailing in quieter waters as much as ever. Unfortunately our boats are too old and valuable as antiques to let the grandchildren take over the old exciting games for which they were used for over a half a century.

As you can see, old-timers, and some not so old, who were reared on the upper reaches of the St. Lawrence, invariably praise the St. Lawrence River skiff in the highest of terms.

Admittedly the boat is good, but is it that good? This is a question that some are bound to ask, suspecting that local loyalties and long and fond associations might have colored such partisan views. But we do not have to rely on the word of the local advocate, nor trust his unsupported judgment, for there are others, both qualified to speak and unbiased by local ties, who are equally lavish in their praise.

One such fan of the skiff was the late Dwight S. Simpson of Boston, the eminent naval architect and international authority on wooden construction, who at the time of his death headed one of this country's leading firms specializing in the design of large commercial fishing vessels. Simpson did not mince words:

"The true St. Lawrence skiff," he said, "is about the best small boat ever developed for more or less open water."

This judgment is expressed in a piece Simpson once wrote for *Forest and Stream*, not to be confused with *Field & Stream*, currently published. *Forest and Stream*, going back to the second half of the nineteenth century, the first, and for a long period the leading, boating journal in this country, suspended publication some years ago, but complete files are to be found in some of the larger libraries, for example the New York Public Library, and specialized libraries like that of the Adirondack Museum at Blue Mountain Lake, New York. Simpson's article on the skiff is in Volume 93, beginning on page 248. It contains a set of lines, dimensioned details for the identical stems, and a table of offsets. Those desiring to build a skiff would do well to obtain a copy. However, they should insist on a photostat or even a photographic enlargement of the offsets, which were printed in reduced size.

Simpson's lines were based on extensive research. He consulted old catalogs, of which there were a considerable number, and visited and consulted builders of skiffs along the river.

"I was surprised to find in my research," he wrote, "that the skiffs of most (though not all) of the old builders, while sharp at both ends,

SAIL PLAN OF ST. LAWRENCE SKIFF.

were not really 'double enders,' the after body being decidedly finer than the fore body. The line of the sheer and keel and stem profile is the same for both ends, otherwise there is real difference in the modeling. . . . Owing to this difference the boat obtains the best possible trim—down slightly by the stern . . . without thought on the part of the casual user, whether loaded with one, two, three, or four passengers. This makes her row easily, and the high, full blow makes her dry and buoyant in a head sea."

Simpson treated the skiff solely as a pulling boat, not mentioning until his final paragraph, and more or less as an afterthought, it seems, that skiffs were sailed as well as rowed. "Skiffs were at first fitted with a single gaff-rigged sail, but later were rigged canoe fashion, and this boat will carry comfortably about 80 sq. ft. in the main and 25 in the mizzen. Usually sailed without a rudder, the steering being done by

trim of the sails and shifting the weight of the crew forward or aft. A centerboard or other lateral plane should be fitted of about 2¼ sq. ft. in area."

The rigging observations, it must be said, are not entirely correct. Normally and originally these skiffs were sprit-rigged, not gaff-rigged. A few in time may have been canoe-ketch-rigged similar to the partly decked-over sailing canoes of the late nineteenth century, but these would have been exceptional and comparatively few. These canoe-ketch-rigged skiffs must have steered with rudders, as the mizzen would have interfered with the free movement of the crew essential for balance steering.

The standard sprit rig, which was early adopted and never improved upon for ordinary sailing, is shown in the sail plan published in *Forest and Stream* for April 25, 1889, and reproduced here. Offsets, scantling dimensions, and lines superbly drawn were also given in the 1889 issue of *Forest and Stream* and reproduced here. These details were furnished by Dr. A. Bain of Clayton, New York, who was the proprietor at that time of the St. Lawrence River Skiff, Canoe, and Steam Launch Company of the same town, having bought out Xavier Colon's original skiff-building business. Nevertheless, the skiff shown is Colon's model, which appears to have reached its final perfected form. I very much doubt if any basic improvement in skiff lines has since been made. Final proof of this waits, however, until lines of other and more recent builders have been drawn for comparison.

This 1889 Colon boat, like the skiffs Simpson observed much later, is not a true double-ender. While in profile the ends are alike, the after sections, as in the Simpson skiff, are molded leaner and sharper. Likewise, the Colon skiff, being fuller forward, will normally trim slightly down by the stern.

To sail these boats, agility, quick reflexes and a bit of daring are required. Yet they are safe enough for those who know how to manage them, and learning how is not so difficult, if one has instruction. The skiff is a remarkably stable craft for its size, and it is true that a 150-pound man can stand on the gunwale of a skiff of intermediate length in smooth water without putting it under. The 20 and 22-foot boats, more commonly used for sailing, are even more stable due to their greater length.

While it is possible for the tyro to capsize any small sailboat, an important part of sailing skill is knowing how to avoid a capsize, as well as what to do should it happen. On rare occasions in jibing the skiff in a strong wind, it might be necessary to go overboard momentarily to hold her upright, and then to clamber quickly back again over the end. That this is an advanced maneuver hardly needs saying; it is one that requires split-second timing, yet it is one which can be executed with safety, albeit with wet pants, by the experienced sailor.

Of course, the wise beginner does not attempt to jibe his skiff in a hard blow.

Experienced and avid skiff sailors claim

ST. LAWRENCE RIVER SKIFF

there is nothing quite like sailing the St. Lawrence River skiff. The exhilaration, the keen sense of movement and speed, and the lively action on the water add up to something that is close akin to flying, they say. Under the urging of a skillful sailor, his skiff comes alive—it responds almost like a part of his own body, becoming in a measure an extension of himself, and yielding sensations and experience not otherwise attainable.

Harold Herrick Jr., one of the most active promoters of the present skiff revival, has sailed skiffs from boyhood, and is still sailing skiffs with undiminished zest and enthusiasm. He learned to sail the hard way—by himself. Since then he has taught others, including his own children and the children of summer neighbors in the vicinity of Grindstone Island, and has found that the basic skills can be imparted by organized instruction in reasonable time and with a minimum of frustration, although only determined and continued practice makes perfect. From the beginning he has promoted the idea of an organized program of sailing instruction, finally initiated at Clayton. The following account sketching in part what is involved was written by Herrick at my request:

Lying four miles up river from the town of Clayton, New York, birthplace of the classic St. Lawrence River skiff, is the head of Grindstone Island commanding an unexcelled view of the river—18 miles west across open water to Kingston, Ontario, and extending north and south for a width of five miles from Gananoque, Ontario, to the American shore. Splitting this large body of water rise two majestic islands named Wolfe and Howe for British generals of historic renown.

It was here one summer as a youth that I first stepped into one of these unique double-ended boats with folding centerboard, 8-square sprit-rigged sail, and

	20ft. boat.	15ft. boat.
Length over all	20ft.	15ft.
L. W. L.	19ft. 1 in.	14ft. 3 in.
Beam, extreme	3ft. 6 in.	2ft. 7 in.
Draft	8 in.	6 in.
Least freeboard	8 in.	5 in.
Sheer { Bow	10 in.	8 in.
Sheer { Stern	10 in.	8 in.
Fore side of stem to mast tube	2ft. 9 in.	2ft. 0 in.
Coaming { Fore end	3ft. 11in.	2ft. 2 in.
Coaming { After end	17ft.	12ft. 9 in.
Rowlocks	8ft. 9 in.	6ft. 7 in.
Slot { Fore end	6ft. 10in.	5ft. 1 in.
Slot { After end	9ft. 5 in.	7ft. 0 in.
Mast, deck to truck	8ft. 7 in.	6ft. 5 in.
Diameter { Deck	2 in.	2 in.
Diameter { Truck	1 in.	0 in.
Boom, length	12ft. 2 in.	9ft. 1 in.
diameter	1 in.	1 in.
Sprit, length	10ft. 6 in.	7ft. 11in.
diameter	1 in.	0 in.
Sail, foot	11ft. 10in.	9ft. 10 in.
luff	7ft. 1 in.	5ft. 4 in.
head	5ft. 6 in.	4ft. 1 in.
leech	12ft. 9 in.	9ft. 7 in.
tack to peak	12ft.	9ft.
clew to throat	12ft. 8 in.	9ft. 6 in.
area	76sq. ft.	43sq. ft.

TABLE OF OFFSETS, 20FT. BOAT.

Stations	HEIGHTS Deck	HEIGHTS Rabbet	HALF-BREADTHS Deck	No. 5	No. 4	No. 3	No. 2	No. 1	Rabbet
0	2 2		0¹						0⁴
2	1 10²	2²	8⁷	8¹	7¹	1 5⁴	3⁴	1	0⁴
4	1 7²	0²	1 3²	1 2⁷	1 2³	1 1	10	5	1³
6	1 5²	0¹	1 7¹	1 6⁷	1 6⁶	1 5⁶	1 2⁷	8⁴	1⁷
8	1 4		1 8⁷	1 8⁴	1 8⁴	1 7⁷	1 5⁴	10⁵	2
10	1 3⁶		1 9	1 8⁹	1 8⁷	1 8⁴	1 6	11¹	2
12	1 4		1 8³	1 8³	1 8²	1 7⁴	1 5¹	10⁴	2
14	1 5	0¹	1 6⁴	1 6²	1 6	1 4⁴	1 2³	8²	1⁷
16	1 7¹	0⁴	1 2³	1 1⁷	1 1²	11⁴	9¹	4⁷	1³
18	1 10²	2²	8	7³	6⁴	5¹	3⁴	1⁴	0⁴
20	2 2⁴		0¹						0⁴

TABLE OF OFFSETS, 15FT. BOAT.

Stations	HEIGHTS Deck	HEIGHTS Rabbet	HALF-BREADTHS Deck	No. 5	No. 4	No. 3	No. 2	No. 1	Rabbet
0	1 8		0⁷						0³
2	1 4⁶	1⁶	6⁶	6¹	5²	4¹	2⁶	0⁴	0⁴
4	1 3²	0⁴	11⁴	11²	10⁶	9⁶	7³	3⁶	1¹
6	1 0⁶	0¹	1 2²	1 2²	1 1⁶	1 1²	11³	6⁶	1⁶
8	11⁷		1 3⁶	1 3⁶	1 3²	1 2⁷	1 1	7⁷	1⁴
10	11²		1 3⁶	1 3⁶	1 3⁶	1 3²	1 1⁴	8²	1⁴
12	11⁷		1 3²	1 3²	1 3	1 2⁶	1 0⁶	7⁷	1⁴
14	1 0⁶	0¹	1 1⁶	1 1³	1 1³	1 0⁴	10⁶	6²	1⁶
16	1 2⁶	0⁴	10⁴	10²	9⁷	8⁷	6⁶	3⁶	
18	1 4⁶	1⁶	8	5⁴	4⁴	3⁷	2⁶	1	
20	1 8		0¹						0⁶

Harold Herrick, Jr., self-taught yet now-expert skiff sailor, hauls the sail taut as he prepares to come about.

Start of tack shows sail drawing well. The sprit is too short; it's a substitute for the proper one, which was broken.

Body weight is brought forward to depress the bow and lift the stern, which is at the point of swinging about.

On the new tack, the boat slides easily through the water, leaving only a slight wake behind her sleek run.

Showing her power, a St. Lawrence skiff barrels across the finish line in a race.

unstayed mast. In a stiff breeze from the southwest I took off on a tack which was the beginning of many years of sailing pleasure on the river. Needless to say, I had to use oars at first to come about, and was forced to capsize the skiff to stop forward motion when coming in for a dock landing.

Through trial and error the technique of coming about without oars was mastered, and then began attempts to maneuver the jibe, resulting in a seemingly endless number of overturns. These are my early memories of wet pants and the challenge of the rudderless skiff.

Today this sailing craft still provides the same challenge and satisfaction and thrills of split-second timing. But with years of "hacking around" and racing, one's reflexes and habit patterns tend to become automatic like the trained field-trial retriever.

Anyone who can even in a small way acquire the knack of coordinating body movement with sail handling will have taken the first big step in attaining the alertness and sensitivity required for managing this rudderless sailing craft. Positioning body weight forward or aft as needed and to leeward with the sail is the basic

secret of getting her going. This is something which must be learned by doing. Besides, I know of no reference books on skiff sailing.

In a heavy wind, one's movements are slow and deliberate, while in a light breeze the faster the better, especially in coming about. The sail is nipped in taut, centerboard jerked up, and with your rush to the bow the stern spins around. As the sail fills on the new tack, speed in moving aft and at the same time shoving down the centerboard is most critical for keeping full headway.

Many skiff races have been won or lost on the precision of this maneuver. In a heavy breeze, fast movement forward when coming about will result in taking water over the bow and leeward rail, and could end in "operation swamping."

In tacking one must also adjust weight position in the skiff with the sail. With practice the sailor gets the feel. How well is proven by his wake line. Here again, I have seen inexperienced racing sailors with their weight too far forward and the sail too closely hauled. Result: the skiff is only crawling along.

The skiff's leeward angle is also important. In a

heavy breeze it is not unusual to lash a spare sprit fore and aft across the thwarts to get toe purchase for hiking out, otherwise the sail cannot be hauled flat in order to obtain maximum speed without taking water to leeward.

Now we come to the most critical maneuver for a St. Lawrence skiff in a stiff breeze, the jibe. Body weight is concentrated in the extreme stern of the skiff as one sails down wind. The secret is to whip in the sail tight to swing the bow. If your weight concentration aft is not sufficient, you will not be able to jibe, as the bow will not swing around, being offset by the wind velocity on the sail. Should this be the case, one resorts to coming about.

However, when the bow has swung sufficiently to pick up the wind, shift your weight to windward and clear the sheet instantly as the boom swings around. The centerboard has been pulled up and the slightest mistake means "the drink." In a gale wind, with no downhaul, I have had the boom lift up in a jibe so that it swung completely around in front of the mast. Should this happen, drop the sheet, throw your body overboard to windward, and hold on! I have experienced this but once, a memorable occasion, in a 30-mile wind, and I should prefer not to have my reflexes tested again in this way.

Skill in the use of the four-bladed, folding metal centerboard, with a handle for working it up or down, can influence the performance of the skiff. A little centerboard is most necessary to substitute for a rudder in keeping a straight run down wind in the 19-foot Miller racing skiff.

And so finally to those seasoned sailors from both fresh and salt water who have never before taken on St. Lawrence River skiff sailing, I say: "Good luck, good swimming, and remember to take a long-handled pot for a bailer."

THE ST. LAWRENCE SKIFF COMPARED TO THE MAINE PEAPOD

Whether the St. Lawrence River skiff, developed for fresh water, is equally suited for use on the ocean is something to be considered. A few St. Lawrence River skiffs made their way to the ocean in times past, but what their performance was in comparison with saltwater craft appears not to be on record.

It is a well-known fact that waves build up very quickly, and to towering heights, on large freshwater lakes, and the Great Lakes in particular are notorious for rough water during storms. Yet at one time it was not uncommon for trips to be made in these skiffs, using both oars and sail, from one end of Lake Ontario to the other, with the voyagers camping out on the shore when night overtook them. Such trips occurred in summer, and presumably in good weather; yet even so, winds of moderate force must have been encountered, nor could the water always have been flat calm.

Nor was the water always calm in the vicinity of the Thousand Islands where the St. Lawrence leaves Lake Ontario. Between Clayton, New York, the birthplace of the skiff and Gananoque, Ontario, on the Canadian shore, lie several miles of open water. Bertha Fry Hall, daughter of Lucien Fry of Fry and Denny, famed builders of skiffs at Clayton in the late 1890s and early 1900s, recalling her girlhood, wrote me in a letter: "As you doubtless know, there is nothing more seaworthy than a good St. Lawrence skiff. I have rowed across the river in a gale when all the freighters were anchored or tied up."

Then she went on to make a most interesting and significant observation: "We were in Norway a number of years ago and visited the museums housing the Viking ships. They are mounted on supports; and as I stood at the bow looking aft, the lines were identical with those I had seen so often in my father's boat factory."

Apparently this refers in particular to the museum in Oslo where the large Gokstad burial ship is preserved together with the three smaller king's boats found in it, ranging from about 19 to 30 feet. These three double-enders are exhibited on inconspicuous supports at good height above the floor for viewing, and it is true that the lines of these king's boats are strikingly similar to those of the skiff. Also, these ancient Norse craft were superlative sea boats whose lines have not been improved upon in more than a thousand years.

This, then, provides support for the assumption that the skiff would also give a good account of itself at sea. It would make an interesting experiment to test the skiff on salt water in comparison with the performance of standard saltwater types.

The Maine peapod, in particular, comes to mind in this connection. In some of their features, the skiff and the pod, two nineteenth-century double-enders, are quite dissimilar. In other respects they have considerable features in common. The one makes a good foil for the other.

To begin with, the origins of both the skiff and the peapod, presumably dating from the early nineteenth century, are obscure. Both began as workboats, and while the peapod always remained such—a plain, functional craft without frills—some of the later skiffs attained the ultimate in finish, varnish inside and out, trimmings of walnut and mahogany, inlaid decks, and generally exquisite workmanship.

It has been theorized in the case of both craft that they developed from the Indian birch canoe. While it is clear that they both replaced aboriginal canoes, in a sense, and that they resemble canoes to the extent of being double-ended, there are nevertheless abundant double-ended craft of European origin that might have served as prototypes, including the Viking boats already mentioned.

The Indian birch was plying the St. Lawrence when the whites arrived and remained in use down to fairly recent times even after the bateau had superceded it to a large extent as a freight carrier. Certainly those who devised the forerunners of the perfected skiff were thoroughly familiar with the lines of the birch canoe.

An unsigned article on the skiff in *Forest and Stream* for April 25, 1889, states: "The exact origin of the boat is not quite clear: it is practically but a large canoe, and so it might be considered an enlargement of the ordinary open canoe so common on the St. Lawrence; but as the drawings show, it resembles much more closely the decked canoe of the States in model and construction."

The foregoing is not quite so. Let it be noted that while the lines of the skiff above the water do resemble the canoe, there is a marked and important difference below the water. The lines of the skiff show a rather considerable angle of straight deadrise, which the Indian birch does not have and cannot have on account of its manner of construction. And this amount of deadrise, which allows good bearing in

combination with fairly deep displacement, is a critical factor in the skiff's superior performance, as it is in the Whitehall boat and other planked boats with similar underwater lines.

Indeed, the construction of the skiff is nothing like that of the canoe; the skiff could not possibly have borrowed anything essential from the canoe. "The decked canoe of the States" in its construction owed nothing to the Indian canoe, but was wholly in the wooden boatbuilding tradition of Europe.

The skiff built by Xavier Colon at Clayton, New York, in the early 1870s, or possibly a few years earlier, set the basic form. There was no subsequent evolution to speak of. Alterations or modifications by the numerous builders who followed Colon were never more than minor or superficial changes, limited mainly to finish. The pattern established by Colon was never improved upon.

Yet it is certain that Colon did not devise his perfected skiff all at once and all of a piece, without prototypes or precursors of some sort. The boats previously used on the river have not survived, and no plans, models, or detailed accounts of their construction can be found. But tradition has it that the early guides built their own boats in the wintertime, and even took part in skiff-building bees, helping each other.

For the fishing guide on the river before the day of motors, a good boat was all important. It was his livelihood, no less. The guides with the best boats got the cream of the business. To row 20 miles a day and often more, an easy pulling boat was desirable. That the boats were able is attested to by the lack of a single record of a guide's skiff ever having been involved in a fatal accident.

We do have one hint of what the earlier skiffs were like from an account of the Hon. Thomas G. Alvord's fishing experiences as published by Haddock in his *Souvenir of the St. Lawrence River*. Alvord, a Syracuse attorney and an inveterate fisherman, put out from Alexandria Bay one September morning in 1852 to wet a line for the first time in the famed waters of this river. As he explains in a letter written in 1895, "At that time Alexandria Bay was the Mecca of fishermen and Clayton the headquarters of square-timber cutting [shipbuilding], and no boatman or fisher-folk hailed from there until some years thereafter."

The fishing guide's boat at that time was not a canoe, yet apparently its only resemblance to the Colon skiff of 20 years later was its double-ended shape:

The boats of that day were but the crude prototypes of the present exquisite ones, which have no superiors on the globe in form, finish or perfect adaptability, with their well-matched oars, centerboards, cushioned chairs, and other requisites, superior in all respects for the uses to which they are put.... I embarked on my first fishing excursion in a boat made of pine (not piano finished), sharp at each end, not more than 14 feet long, low-sided, with naked wooden boards, without back-rests, for seats. Loaded down almost invariably on the return from a day's fishing with their human cargo and catch of fish, the gunwales would be perilously near the level of the water of the river.

The early beginnings of the Maine peapods are even more obscure than those of the St. Lawrence skiff. The notion that they may have originated from birch canoes will not stand examination, either, although bark canoes were still used by Indians on the Maine coast until the late nineteenth century. It must be admitted that the large, low-ended bark canoes employed by the Passamaquoddy Tribe for shooting porpoise in the rough waters around Grand Manan Island were not unlike peapods in shape. In construction, however, there was nothing in common between the fisherman's pod and these sea-going canoes.

Fishermen commonly built their own pods, as guides appear to have built their own skiffs at one time. Occasionally, local boatshops and some builders became known for their excellent pods. But peapods were never produced in large commercial factories as skiffs were beginning in the 1880s, when the business established by Xavier Colon was taken over in 1887 by Dr. A. Bain of Clayton, who with the backing of New York City capital put up a factory measuring 50 feet by 100 feet and three stories high. Nor was there ever developed one standardized pea-

pod model, as in the case of the Colon skiff. On the contrary, and within rather loose limits of size and form, a nearly infinite variety of pods was produced, nearly every one different according to the special requirements, or even whims, of individual fishermen and builders. Pods were built both clinker and carvel, with keels and with flat bottom boards, with abundant sheer and bottom rocker, as well as straight on the bottom and flat on the top.

In some, stems were plumb, in others, raking. Some showed slack bilges and a marked angle of deadrise, while others were broad of beam with very flat floors, the latter being favored by lobstermen willing to sacrifice rowing ease to gain initial stability for hauling their pots.

As far as I know, no mention of a peapod was ever included in a printed catalog, while at least a dozen different nineteenth century boatbuilding concerns issued catalogs in which St. Lawrence River skiffs are listed.

The first peapod lines to appear in print that I have seen accompanied a piece in *Yachting* for February, 1932, by C. W. Van Ness. (See Chapter 16.) Built by Bendix in Prospect Harbor, Maine, this pod used for lobstering had been put together in the local blacksmith shop and was framed with "natural bend hackmatack from the woods nearby." This pod showed an unusual amount of sheer and bottom rocker, which rounded up in raking stems very sloping and cut back in the forefoot. In a light condition a boat of this shape was bound to be lively and tender, but put a load in such a pod and she would settle down, yet continuing to pull easy. It is said that this pod was used in January for tending traps set nine miles offshore, and on more than one occasion got caught out in storms but always managed to make it home.

In 1969 Gordon Bennett of Clayton found a set of skiff molds in the old Colon house in that town. Presumably these were molds belonging to Xavier Colon, if not his original set. From outline tracings of these molds supplied me by Bennett, I worked up a set of skiff lines which turned out to be typical in all respects, and are shown herewith. The lines of the 16-foot rowing pod are also shown printed approximately to the same scale to facilitate comparison. The similarities between these two sets of lines are rather marked in several respects. Of course, as already stated, some pods would show entirely different lines.

19

The Rangeley Boat

The Rangeley boat is a distinctive American sporting boat that has been in use on the Rangeley Lakes of Maine for something like 100 years and was well known to past generations of fishermen for its numerous excellent characteristics. It was not limited to the Rangeleys, for by 1900 it was in common use by fishermen on the Belgrade Lakes, on Sebago Lake, and on other large lakes in western and southern Maine.

Pictures of Rangeley boats have been published in abundance, but mostly in stories about fishing, where the attention was focused on the fishing and not on the boats. The boats were there as part of the Rangeley background—essential, but taken for granted. No one thought to pay the slightest attention as to how they were formed or constructed.

At one time there were at least three different boatshops at Rangeley actively engaged in building and repairing these boats. Now there are none. Local boatbuilders can make more money putting up camps and houses, and working on large government construction jobs. Mass-produced, factory-made boats have been brought in from the outside, decadent and inferior in design, yet capable of supporting an outboard motor.

There is still a limited demand for the old boats. There are still fishermen who like to row; as one expressed it in a letter to me: "Per-

sonally, I do not like to use a motor as I enjoy the response I get from a boat in rowing, and of course it is good exercise." Nor is the last such a minor consideration. There is no doubt that if there were more rowing and other similar regular wholesome exercise, there would be fewer heart attacks and other kinds of degenerative physical breakdown.

Unfortunately today's limited demand for Rangeley pulling boats is not enough to support professional builders. The old boats are fast falling into disrepair or wearing out completely, and there are no replacements.

On the other hand, there is amateur interest, and the model is a particularly good one for the amateur builder. By this, I do not mean the tyro without woodworking experience, but rather someone who has already built a boat or two, who has the feel of tools and materials, and who wants his next attempt to be at least a cut or two above a plywood boat or the ordinary kit boat.

The Rangeley boat's handsome shape and superior performance put it at least on a par with any boat in the same class and length range, yet its construction is fairly simple. This is because professional builders over the years simplified and standardized the construction in order to cut building costs. Besides, it was built for utility, not for show, and hence was painted, not varnished, and consequently does not require

A Rangeley boat at Belgrade Lakes, Maine, about 1900.

the fussy, time-consuming attention to finish that varnished construction exacts. If one has a good set of molds, in turn based upon a fair set of lines, and has practiced a little at fitting lapped, or clinker planking, the rest should be "duck soup," as the saying goes.

To appreciate fully the Rangeley boat, one needs to have experienced it in its native haunts. The Rangeley Lake region is unlike any other part of Maine—big lakes, wide expanses, mountains, sparkling, clear air, and deep woods close at hand. The fishing has always been superb. Our grandfathers and great-grandfathers sought refuge in such a place from the large city crowds— and once there, spent time in boats, boats very similar to the one whose lines are reproduced here, although not quite the same, for the one shown is a latter-day example, with a modified transom stern intended to support an outboard motor, but still not widened so much as to spoil the boat for rowing.

It appears that the first planked boats in the Rangeley Lakes region, following the Indian birch canoe, were built on a model brought from the New York lakes following the Civil War. And it further appears, although it is not definitely certain, that these early boats had small, high-tucked, transom sterns, as well as abundant sheer curves. Toward the end of the nineteenth century, however, the well-known double-ended model had established itself as the standard Rangeley type. The double ends persisted until some time after World War I, when increasing use of outboard motors forced a reversion to the transom stern.

Some double-enders were converted simply by sawing off one of the ends and nailing in a vertical bulkhead of heavy plank to support the motor. In the attempt to prevent such conversions from settling too much at the stern when underway, projecting flat, fin-like contrivances called "squat boards" were sometimes installed. Such improvised conversions of the double-ender were far from satisfactory. Instead, builders began experimentation with transom-stern models in which the after sections were widened and flattened to provide more support for the motor. Carried beyond a certain point,

Square-stern Rangeley boats at Quimby Pond, Rangeley, Maine, about 1900.

Fishing on the Belgrade Lakes about 1900. These two Rangeleys appear to be somewhat smaller in size than the standard model.

such modification in form can spoil the good rowing qualities of the model, and this is precisely what happened in too many cases.

As can be seen from the lines of the Ellis model, however, the boat remains essentially a double-ender below the waterline, although a transom for a motor was added and the after sections were filled out somewhat above the load line to prevent the stern from settling too far with the motor in place and running.

The transom is not large enough, however, to support large, high-powered motors, and for that reason this model is not to be considered a speedboat. It is axiomatic that speedboats are poor or useless as rowboats, and vice versa. This is a dual purpose craft—still a good rowboat, yet

This Rangeley is slightly smaller than the usual. She is 16 feet, 6 inches overall with a 45-inch beam. Her top two strakes are clinker, with carvel strakes below. This photo was taken at the Red Spot Fishing Club on Lake Umbagog, Upton, Maine, in 1967.

RANGELEY BOAT - TRANSOM STERN FOR OUTBOARD.
BUILDER, H. N. ELLIS, RANGELEY, MAINE - 1930'S.
TAKEN OFF 1967 - RED SPOT FISHING CLUB, LAKE UMBAGOG, ME.
17' L.O.A.   BEAM INSIDE AMIDSHIPS · 4'.   DEPTH AMIDSHIPS · 15".
SHEER AT BOW · 11½" - AT STERN · 5".   LINES TO INSIDE PLANK.
JOHN GARDNER   DEC. 1967.

FEET and INCHES

one that can be driven efficiently at moderate speeds with light, low-horsepower outboard motors.

It might be mentioned in passing that the bow half of this Ellis boat is practically identical to that of the classic double-ender. Thus from these lines it would be easy to derive lines for a double-ender, simply by reversing the bow half and making it serve for the stern as well. In fact it would not be necessary even to redraw the lines. A double set of molds for the bow half would make the whole boat.

THE ELLIS RANGELEY BOAT

The boat from which our lines were taken was built some time in the 1930s for the Red Spot Fishing Camp on Lake Umbagog, the most southerly and westerly of the Rangeley chain. H. N. Ellis built the boat at his shop in Rangeley, Maine, and B. R. Burdsall, now president of the club, well remembers transporting the new boat from Rangeley to Upton on top of his Buick, although he is not sure of the precise year. This boat has been in service every summer

since at the Red Spot Fishing Club and is tight and sound still. It was through the cooperation of the Red Spot Fishing Club that I was able to measure and record the details of this boat.

Lake Umbagog is quite shallow in places and lies open along its greatest length to prevailing winds, so that it can, and does, become extremely rough on short notice. It is known as a treacherous lake, and its summer storms are often sudden and violent. A boat that has given reliable service without any mishaps for a fishing camp on such a lake for over 30 years must be a

OFFSETS – 17 FOOT RANGELEY BOAT										
STATIONS	STEM	2'	4'	6'	8'	10'	12'	14'	15'-2"	TRAN.
HEIGHTS SHEER	2-5-1	2-0-2	1-8-7	1-6-7	1-6-0	1-6-0	1-6-6	1-8-1	1-9-2	1-1-1
KEEL	—	0-5-0	0-4-3	0-4-0	0-4-0	0-4-1	0-4-3	0-4-6	0-5-0	0-5-3
3" BUTTOCK	—	0-8-3	0-5-5	0-4-3	0-4-3	0-4-4	0-4-7	0-5-6	0-7-0	0-10-7
6" "	—	1-1-0	0-7-1	0-4-7	0-4-6	0-5-0	0-5-3	0-7-0	0-9-1	1-1-6
9" "	—	1-6-2	0-8-4	0-5-3	0-5-0	0-5-1	0-5-6	0-8-0	0-10-7	1-4-1
12" "	—	—	0-10-0	0-5-7	0-5-1	0-5-3	0-6-3	0-9-3	1-0-6	1-11-0
15" "	—	—	1-0-3	0-7-0	0-5-6	0-6-0	0-7-4	0-11-1	1-3-3	—
18" "	—	—	1-5-1	0-8-5	0-7-0	0-7-2	1-2-1	2-2-1	—	—
HALF-BREADTHS SHEER	0-0-4	0-11-5	1-6-6	1-10-5	2-0-0	2-0-0	1-10-5	1-7-7	1-5-3	1-0-0
KEEL	"	0-1-0	0-1-1	0-1-2	0-1-2	0-1-2	0-1-2	0-1-0	0-0-7	0-0-6
9" WATER LINE	"	0-3-3	0-10-1	1-6-4	1-8-4	1-8-0	1-5-7	0-11-3	0-5-7	0-2-0
12" " "	"	0-5-3	1-2-6	1-9-1	1-10-5	1-10-3	1-8-4	1-4-2	0-11-1	0-4-1
15" " "	"	0-7-1	1-5-1	1-10-1	1-11-5	1-11-4	1-9-7	1-6-5	1-2-5	0-7-6
DIAG-OVALS DIAGONAL A	—	0-4-6	0-6-5	0-9-0	0-9-1	0-8-7	0-8-4	0-7-2	0-5-7	0-3-4
" B	—	0-7-5	1-0-6	1-4-6	1-5-4	1-5-3	1-4-1	1-1-2	0-10-6	0-6-6
" C	—	0-10-5	1-6-5	1-11-3	2-0-7	2-0-4	1-11-0	1-7-4	1-4-3	0-11-5
" D	—	1-0-5	1-9-6	2-4-4	2-4-0	2-3-6	2-2-1	1-11-1	1-8-1	1-2-1
MEASURED IN FEET, INCHES & EIGHTHS TO INSIDE OF PLANKING										
LINES: NAT. FISHERMAN, JAN. 1968 & "BUILDING SMALL BOATS FOR OAR AND SAIL."										

BASE LINE
3" 6" 9" 12" 15" 18"

No. 1. Inner stem.

No. 2. Outer stem.

No. 3. Brass stem band, ⅜″ wide.

No. 4. Planking, 5 16″ thick.

No. 5. Sheer plank.

No. 6. Garboard plank.

No. 7. Bottom board, of "keel batten," ½″ thick.

No. 8. Outer keel strip, ¾″ thick.

No. 9. Ribs 11 16″ x ⅞″. Upper corners rounded off.

No. 10. Gunwale.

pretty good boat. Besides, the members of Red Spot Fishing Club are fishermen of the old school who row and like to row. They wouldn't have put up with a boat that long that didn't handle well.

The Red Spot Fishing Club was founded in 1908 by a small group of Boston and New York businessmen who liked to fish and who had previously summered in the Belgrades. The same families still hold and enjoy the club's 40 acres of unspoiled wilderness on the secluded shores of this beautiful mountain lake. One of the present members, first brought here as a small boy by his parents, has spent at least part of every summer here since the club opened in 1908.

As you must have guessed, "Red Spot" refers to the red spots found on the square-tailed trout (brook trout) that are caught in this lake. Such trout weighing as much as eight pounds have been caught here, as well as larger numbers of a somewhat smaller, but still respectable, size. Mounted specimens of the best hang on the walls of the dining hall in the main lodge to confound the doubting Thomases.

A few general words about the construction of the Ellis boat before we get specific:

No rabbeting is necessary although the effect achieved is that of rabbeted construction. The inner bottom board, or "keel batten," if you prefer, needs only slight beveling with a plane, and the outer keel strip covers the edges of the garboard exactly like a chiseled rabbet. In like manner, the inner stem piece is beveled with the plane as needed for the plank to lie fair, and after the planking is fastened on, its ends are covered by an outer stem piece, which is put on last.

The thin, narrow strakes of plank bend easily and conform without any difficulty or need for steaming to the rounded curves of this hull. Yet one thing that is somewhat tricky but not especially difficult is lining out the shape and widths of the plank. There are 11 of these on each side as the stem detail shows.

The laps originally were fastened with small

A party at the Red Spot Fishing Camp, about 1920. The guide is standing in a boat whose model is assumed to be the same as or similar to the first planked boats in the Rangeley lakes region. Note the small, high-tucked transom stern and the unusual amount of sheer curve. The boat at the left is a classic Rangeley double-ender.

nails or tacks of blued Swedish iron, which lasts sufficiently well in fresh water. They were merely bent over and clinched into the wood. Copper nails were not used, as experience proved they were softer than the iron nails and would not hold if merely clinched. To fasten with copper rivets would require a great deal more work, but rivets would be required if the boat were to be used in salt water, and are best in any case.

Ribs are not put in until planking is complete. The planking is done on several removable molds set up on the bottom board. These are removed as the ribs are bent in.

The reverse curve in the lower ends of the floors next to the keel assembly is not accidental. This brings the top, or inner surface of the bottom board in line with the top edges of the garboards and the planks above, so that there is no kink in the portion of the ribs extending across the bottom of the boat. The ribs are small; a kink here would tend to break them.

The ribs were fastened through the planking laps from the outside with nails that were clinched on the inside of the rib. Nails were left out of the laps where the ribs lie, until the ribs were bent in after planking was finished.

In building this boat the main things are good molds, a good planking job and careful

An Ellis-built transom-stern Rangeley at the Red Spot Fishing Club. This boat has a high, shapely bow that resembles that of the Adirondack guideboat.

fastening. If one is not familiar with clinker planking, some practicing should be done until one gets the hang of it. Basically, it is not difficult. The same holds for the fastening; practice at the bench a while before starting the actual job.

SETTING UP

The offsets for this boat are measured to the inside of the plank, which is the proper way

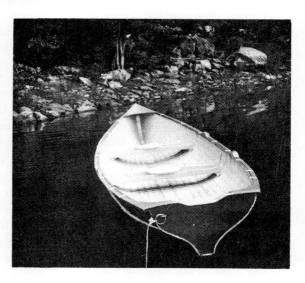

Details of the Ellis square-stern Rangeley boat. (Above left) The midship thwart with a stool-top seat and tray for fishing gear. Note the stretcher across the walkway as a brace for the rower's feet. (Above right) The bow seat and inner stem. The walkway has been removed to show the bottom board or keel batten. (Right) The stern view shows the boat to be virtually a double-ender below the waterline. The transom has been outlined in white to make it stand out against the dark water.

for a small boat, allowing the molds to be made directly to the dimensions given without deductions. The planking thickness for this boat is 5⁄16 inch. This is one boat whose lines, without fail, should be laid down full size and carefully faired before starting the building.

As mentioned previously, the Rangeley's two-piece stem is an ingenious simplification giving in effect a rabbeted stem without the difficulty of cutting the rabbet. The planking is fastened to the inner part and made leakproof. The outer part, which covers the ends of the planking, is not put on until after the planking operation has been completed. This permits the

plank ends to be dressed off with a sharp block plane, an easy way of getting a good fit.

The outer stem, which is hardly more than a finishing piece and a cutwater, is fastened, as shown, by screws through the inner member. Thus it would be easy to renew, and can be tapered until it is nearly sharp at its outer edge, which is then covered by a very narrow half-round brass stem band.

The inner stem is probably best made of oak, although it could be spruce (treated with preservative), Douglas fir, or mahogany. It is got out of 1¾-inch stock to the dimensions and molded shape shown. When beveled, its outer edge will be a uniform one inch in width its whole length. Adding two thicknesses of 5/16-inch plank gives a total end width of 1⅝ inches for the outer stem to cover. Hence the outer stem cut to its molded shape is got out of stock of this thickness.

Instead of keeping the thickness of the stem uniform its entire length, it could be tapered somewhat from top to bottom, retaining the top siding of 1¾ inches but thinning it, let us say, to 1¼ inches at the bottom. There would still be enough landing or "back rabbet" for the planking, but to taper it thus would not lighten the boat by much, while adding considerably to the labor and difficulty of making the stem.

It should be noted that the makeup of the keel is similar to that of the stem; that is, there is an inner and an outer part, with the outer part serving to strengthen and to protect the bottom, but not needed to make the boat watertight. However, unlike the composite stem, the two members of the keel assembly are beveled and fastened together when the boat is first set up and before planking starts. The two should not be glued together, but merely dressed internally with a non-hardening bedding compound, so that if the outer keel piece should ever become badly worn on the rocks, it could be taken out and replaced by a new one.

As this is a lapstrake boat, it must be built right-side up. This is to give the planker easy access to both the outside and the inside of the laps, as the planking proceeds, which in lap-

STEM DETAIL RANGELEY BOAT

strake boats must start from the keel with the garboard and proceed upwards to the sheer, to allow each succeeding plank to lap over the one below it. When the boat is built upright in this way, the planker can reach over the top of each strake as it goes on to rivet or clinch the lap fastening from the inside, while with his left hand he can press the backing iron or "hold-on" against the head of the rivet or nail on the outside. In this manner one man by himself can manage the lap fastenings easily.

Should it be attempted to build the boat bottom-up, as works best with carvel planking, two men would be required to fasten the laps if rivets were used. One would have to crawl under the boat to rivet from the inside, while his partner held the backing iron on the outside. This requires double labor, and besides, riveting in the cramped quarters under the boat is awkward and inconvenient, at best.

To set up for building, the "backbone," consisting of the inner stem, the inner and outer keel strips, the stern transom, and the transom knee, are first assembled, fastened together, and set upright on posts, horses, or some other device. This set-up should be high enough to bring the boat up to a convenient height for working, but not so high as to make it difficult to rivet the topsides.

At 2-foot stations set up molds of pine (ordinary one-inch pine boards will serve nicely) made from the full-size laydown of the lines, which for a round hull of the Rangeley's shapeliness is absolutely essential. There are seven molds in all. Ordinarily there will be no mold at station 8, as this section was merely put in to aid in fairing the lines. These molds must be painstakingly plumbed, leveled, and squared with the centerline of the boat, so that they sit precisely on their individual section lines. Check each mold carefully athwartships with the level on the sheer line and the load waterline, both of which must be marked on the molds when they were assembled on the full-size laydown of lines on the floor. Once in position, the molds must be solidly secured with shores, braces, and temporary longitudinal battens, as needed; all will be removed as the planking proceeds.

The molds might have to be faired slightly if the temporary battens, or "ribbands," when bent on in more or less the same line that the plank will follow, do not lie exactly fair on all the molds, do not quite touch the molds in a few places, or in other places show "high" spots. The fairing process will require shimming up the low spots and planing off the high spots to bring everything perfectly into line. Unless this preliminary fairing is faithfully and accurately carried out ahead of time, it will be next to impossible to do a respectable job of planking.

There is another reason, as well, for getting the molds exactly where they belong on their respective section lines. This is so the exact location of the ribs can be measured from them and laid out as the planking is carried up the side. The ribs are bent in after planking is completed, and fastened through each lap. Obviously, the places where the rib fastenings will eventually go must be left vacant while planking is going on. Yet the lap fastenings between the ribs must be put in from the beginning to keep the planks in place and to hold the hull together until the ribs are fastened in.

The planks as they are bent on, or "hung," are temporarily fastened to the molds with screws, one at each station. These are later removed and plugged when the molds are taken out after planking is completed. It is a good plan to use small washers under the heads of these screws to keep them from hauling into the plank. Furthermore, such screws should be put in only at such points where the plank bears directly on the edge of the mold, for if there is not a wood-to-wood contact, pressure applied to the screw will almost invariably split the plank.

After the backbone is set up, before planking can start, the hull surface has to be divided up and lined out. (For a complete discussion of this process, see the Appendix.)

PLANKING

The Rangeley is planked lapstrake, or clinker as it is also called. Because beginners do not understand this method of planking, or know what is required, they tend to approach lapstrake planking as a fearsome bugaboo, when actually in such a type as the Rangeley, it is quite simple and easy, provided one knows how to go about it. Rather than presenting difficulties, this method of planking offers a number of advantages.

First, lapstrake plank do not need to be hollowed, or "backed out," on the inside surface to conform to the curve of the hull sections or ribs, which in the Rangeley show a marked amount of round. "Backing out" requires specially curved or rounded planes, and is a relatively skilled operation.

Furthermore, carvel planking, or "set-works" in old-time New England boatbuilding parlance, must be smoothed and made fair on the outside after it is on and fastened to the ribs, by planing, scraping, and sanding. This also is a skilled operation requiring experience and judgment to do properly. On large wooden vessels in the old days it was a trade by itself known as "outboard joinering," performed by a specialist who was called an "outboard joiner."

With lapstrake planking both backing out and outboard joinering are bypassed entirely. In fact lapstrake planking may be given its final smoothing on the bench before it is "hung" in place on the boat. For this, a modern power belt-sander gives excellent results and is a real time-saver.

Second, the lapstrake planking of the Rangeley bends easily into place without steaming, as would not be the case with some carvel plank that is thicker. This is partly because the Rangeley's clinker plank are narrow—there are 11 strakes to the side—and partly because they are quite thin—in fact only $5/16$ inch thick. Lapstrake planking can be made thinner than carvel planking, and generally is, because doubling at the laps adds stiffness and strength, and because thickness for depth of seam is not needed to hold the caulking, which carvel plank requires to be made tight. Obviously, the Rangeley does not require caulking. Having so many strakes to a side means more work and more fastening, but the advantages more than make up for it.

There is much less danger of splitting or

"renting" with narrow plank like these. As individual plank are quite narrow, cumulative changes in width from shrinking and swelling are reduced. Thus strain on fastenings is reduced, there is less tendency for the seams to open when the boat dries out, as well as less chance of the plank buckling when the boat remains in the water and becomes thoroughly soaked. Narrow plank are also easier bent, and when they are only $5/16$ inch in thickness, like these, none of them will need to be steamed.

Third, the narrow clinker strakes of the Rangeley are easy to splice, which can be done on the boat as the planking operation proceeds, because the laps hold the splice scarphs. Scarphs are made with long matching bevels, in length eight to twelve times the thickness of the planking, and planed to a feather edge at each of the scarph ends. The mating surfaces of the scarph are lapped together with epoxy adhesive between, which, when set, makes a glue joint stronger than the original wood itself. (For a more detailed discussion of scarphing, see the Appendix.)

The ease with which plank can be spliced on this boat, together with the fact that the hull structure is not weakened in the least by numerous splices, and further that no heavy or clumsy butt blocks are required, adds up altogether to a very great advantage. It means that comparatively short lengths of planking stock can be used and that the grain can be kept straight for maximum strength. Knots and sapwood can be avoided, which provides both quality in planking lumber and its economical use.

The manner in which these planks are lapped gives maximum strength and tightness. First the lap bevels are of generous width, $13/16$ inch on the average, but in actual practice probably ranging from ¾ inch to ⅞ inch. This is more than twice the thickness of the plank. Yet the laps are not beveled excessively, so that ample wood remains for strength. In fact, as can be seen on the drawing, the four lower plank are hardly beveled at all—just enough wood is removed to bring the lap surfaces in contact. This means that the inner surfaces of these plank will bear on the molds, and later on the ribs, only at one spot that is directly in back of the lap itself, which is all that is required, for that is where the fastening, or more precisely, the rivet goes through.

The rest of the plank coming above the four or five nearest to the keel are more or less uniformly beveled on their upper edges so that about ⅛-inch thickness at the edge remains. The inner lap of the plank next above, which comes down over and mates with the under bevel, is planed to fit.

As can be seen on the drawing, very little wood is removed to make a fit, due to the curved side of the hull. While the under bevel of these upper laps will be more or less uniform throughout, the outer bevel that matches or mates with it will change from station to station,

and these changes in bevel will have to be picked up from the boat, and each plank fitted individually.

Changes in bevels are easily determined and measured with short sections of planking stock the same width as the plank being worked at the bench. Such pieces are held against the mold and lapped on the beveled edge of the plank already in place, exactly where the next plank is going, and by inspection are beveled to fit. This is done on separate short pieces at each mold station. These pieces are then taken to the bench where the bevels are transferred to the plank in preparation. The width of the lap bevel has already been scribed on with a pencil gauge of some sort. At each mold station as marked on the plank, the correct bevel is transferred from the block already fitted at that station. Thus, with a sharp block plane or spokeshave, the wood between these stations is carefully shaved down to get a fair, continuous beveled surface between each station.

Examination of the drawing of the planking laps will show that the inner bevels on the lower edges of the upper planks are extremely shallow. Only a shaving or two has to be removed to attain a snug fit against the beveled edge of the plank below. Thus a strong, heavy lap remains.

In fitting the laps of this boat, one general principle applies: lay out the lap bevels so as to take off just as little wood as possible.

Beveling the laps is an operation which often panics the beginner. If he will keep his cool, go slowly, practice a little at the bench, be content even if he spoils a plank or two at the beginning, he will make out all right and will find before he reaches the end of the job that he can often tell by "eye" how much bevel is required, and will be at a loss to understand what it was about this operation that scared him so much at the outset.

An experienced planker will make perfectly fitted laps so that once they are drawn up by rivets they need nothing between them and are perfectly tight as they are. For laps that do not fit that snugly, some kind of flexible sealer between is not a bad idea. Sometimes all that is needed is to turn the boat upside down so that paint will run into the laps. But if the right sort of adhesive sealer is put on the inside surfaces of the laps during planking, not only will water-tightness be insured, but also the adhesion will strengthen the hull over and beyond the regular metal lap fastenings. Whatever is used should be flexible enough to allow the laps to give in order to work with the boat, both when the planks swell or shrink and when the boat moves in a seaway.

As the finished planking on this boat is only 5/16 inch thick, it is often possible to get out planks for both sides at once from one-inch thick planking stock, to be split in two with a thin circular saw or bandsaw after being sawed and planed to shape. Often this method can be used to save both time and lumber, as well as to insure identical plank on both sides of the boat.

TIMBERING AND FASTENING

As originally built at Rangeley, these boats were fastened with a small clinch nail of pure Swedish iron, which, without any galvanizing, lasted well enough in fresh water. Copper nails had been tried, but they were not strong enough and consequently loosened. Copper rivets had not been used because of the additional work which they required.

Today, the old type of iron nails are not available, so far as I know, and if there were any chance that the boat would be used in salt water, they would not be suitable. I do not hesitate to recommend copper rivets—they are somewhat more work, perhaps, but well worth it. (See the Appendix for riveting instructions.)

Usually when timbers are bent into a boat after it has been planked, the laps are pre-bored for the nails and the nails inserted in the holes ready for driving through the timber once it is bent down into place. Nails put in in this way pull the timber tightly against the planking all the way around for a snug fit. But the timber must be hot so as not to split, and the timbers for this boat are so small that they would be bound to cool quickly, so quickly that it might not be safe to try to nail through them without boring.

For rivets for this boat, I suggest copper nails about 1½ inches long. Cut copper nails are preferred, but wire copper nails will do quite well. Over 2,000 will be needed. That's a lot of riveting, it's true, but not too excessive, once the builder has the hang of it. And it will make a wonderfully tight, strong job.

After the boat is planked and riveted, a light sponging with hot water will swell out the dents made by the riveting hammer, and after a light finish-sanding the boat is ready for paint.

FINISHING OFF

The interior arrangement of the Rangeley is simplicity itself, yet the location of the two rowing thwarts is critical for rowing trim and balance. As for the stern sheets, the builder can put them in to suit himself, or leave them out entirely. A small stowage compartment or locker could be built underneath if one wanted to. This is purely a matter of personal preference, as any normal construction here would not affect the performance of the boat.

The rowing thwarts are unusual, if not unique. The raised round seat in the center, like the top of a stool, is comfortable to sit on, in part because it is hollowed out somewhat. It can be fitted with a thin cushion for the fisherman who spends long hours out on the lake.

On either side is a handy shelf with sides on it so that things put into this recess cannot fall out into the bottom of the boat—a most con-venient feature for the fisherman. The bottom of these thwarts is made of ⅜-inch plywood, which is glued and screwed to the stiffening supports on either side. These stiffeners should be of spruce or Douglas fir, preferably, although almost anything, even pine, will do.

The thwarts are braced on either side with metal angle braces made of ⅜-inch rod with the ends flattened, as shown on the drawing, and bored with ¼-inch holes for bolts and round head screws. Ordinary iron rod is generally used for boats kept in fresh water. In working bronze rod, care must be taken not to heat the metal too hot, as it will crumble. Brass should not be used as it is worthless for this purpose.

The removable floorboard is made in two pieces that fit together endwise under the middle thwart. One bolt projecting from the bottom with a wing nut is sufficient to hold these in place. The ends are secured by metal hooks, as shown in the drawing.

The rowlocks now commonly used in these boats are of the ring type, sometimes called "round socket rowlocks." They remain on the oar permanently and have a pin which slips into a socket in the gunwale. Such oarlocks permit the oars to trail in the water when playing a fish, providing, of course, that the oars have leathers with shoulders which prevent the oars from sliding out of the oarlocks.

Stretchers to brace the feet against when rowing are shown screwed to the bottom board. Modern rowboats do not always have stretchers, but it is difficult to row properly without good bracing for the feet, and these should not be overlooked or omitted.

2 0

The Wherry

········•········

The old working wherries once extensively employed by New England fishermen have all but disappeared. Except for the meager sketches by Alfred A. Brooks illustrating his account of "The Boats of Ash Point, Maine" in the *American Neptune* for October, 1942, and the lines of the boats reprinted herein from the pages of the *National Fisherman*, no representation of lines for the New England wherry can be found in print.

The so-called "wherries" formerly built for the U. S. Navy seem to have been quite a different kind of boat, and it would be interesting to learn how they happened to get their name. Sheet 2 of the U. S. Navy Standard Plan No. 226, being lines and offsets for a 14-foot wherry, dated July 24, 1912, has been reproduced in much reduced size by Bill Durham in his privately printed *Standard Boats of the United States Navy, 1900-1915.* This boat, very much the same as standard dinghies of Whitehall derivation, does not have a bottom board, but has rather the conventional rabbeted keel of uniform siding throughout, in a word what H. I. Chapelle called a "scantling" keel.

If there is one single characteristic above all others which is distinctive of the old working wherry, it is its plank keel, which provides its flat bottom. The wherry's bottom is not as wide as the bottom of the Banks dory, but rather like that of the Swampscott dory; it is quite wide

enough for the boat to ground out firmly in an upright position, and to serve as a shoe for dragging the boat up and down the beach. Indeed, there is a close resemblance between the New England wherry and the Swampscott dory, and because the former appears to have been the older boat, the latter may well have been derived from it.

Before dories were built at Swampscott, Massachusetts, the fishermen of that town imported their boats from Salisbury Point on the Merrimack River above Newburyport where the Lowell family had been building boats since pre-Revolutionary times. These boats, according to investigations by Andrew L. Harris, reported in John Albree's historical sketch, "The Swampscott Beaches" published in 1905 in the *Register* of the Lynn, Massachusetts, Historical Society, were called "wherries" and were hauled over the road on wagons for delivery at Swampscott. This would have been prior to 1840, for this is the approximate date when boatbuilding as a business was started on the Lynn and Swampscott beaches.

Perhaps the "wherries" observed by Rev. William Bentley, Salem diarist, at Halibut Point off the extreme tip of Cape Ann in May of 1799, had also been built by the Lowells at Salisbury Point. As Bentley recounts: "We then put out into the bay among the wherries, which are small flatbottom boats and are as numerous

U.S. Navy wherry from Standard Boats of the United States Navy, 1900-1915, *by Bill Durham.*

as Jebacco Boats and which in good weather make two fares a day & sometimes take as many as five hundred Cod & Haddock. They are rowed cross handed by one man & even by boys of 10 & 12 years."

In another entry in his diary made from Gloucester 18 years later, Bentley noted "40 wherries within the piers near Straightsmouth."

Nor was the resemblance of the Swampscott dory to the wherry overlooked by Brooks in his *American Neptune* article already cited, although his opinion of this dory is not high, stating he "never could see any justification for the round-sided or Swampscott dory, they are as hard to build as a wherry and neither as fast or as seaworthy under sail or oars."

Colonial wherries were built without benefit of designers' lines, and mostly by amateurs. By "amateurs" I mean those not regularly working at boatbuilding as their main occupation. The working tradesman regularly employed the year round for wages in the commercial boatshop does not appear on the American scene until quite late, for the most part. In fact there were almost no commercial boatshops in early times that limited their production to small craft.

On the other hand, the shipyard for the construction of large vessels was an ancient establishment that required numerous specialized tradesmen regularly employed for wages. Building vessels of any size was an enterprise of magnitude for which were needed large amounts of capital and equipment and many trained "hands"—shipwrights, caulkers, riggers, shipsmiths, and others.

This view of Newbury-port, Massachusetts, in the nineteenth century shows a variety of ships and small craft, including what appears to be a wherry, center, also seen in the enlarged detail at the right.

There were men in eighteenth-century ship-yards who swung the broad-axe all their lives and did nothing else, and others who bored holes for treenails until old age overtook them. Only with a specialized labor force regularly employed was it possible to build large wooden vessels with any dispatch in a day when every-thing had to be done by hand. The ship car-penter could not very well be self-employed. To find work at his trade he had to hire out at some shipyard.

Building a small boat was quite a different proposition. The nails and lumber for a skiff or a wherry were easily come by, and farmers and fishermen could, and did, build themselves boats in their barns and dooryards at odd times when they didn't have anything else to do.

Although the larger shipyards had skilled

LOA — 16'
BEAM 4'-5"
DEPTH AMIDS. 1'-8"

MAINE WHERRY
ASH POINT AFTER BROOKS

specialists who turned out yawl boats, gigs, and other small craft with which to equip their new vessels, such comprised only a minor fraction of the small boats in use in colonial New England, when nearly everyone lived within sight of the water, when travel was generally easier by water than by land, and when the small boat occupied much the same place in the economic and social life of that time as the auto does today.

Life could not have gone on in pre-Revolutionary New England without its multitude of small boats, yet these were so common and so taken for granted that they scarcely ever got into the historical record except as an occasional bare name. Those who wrote, wrote about politics and religion but not about such lowly subjects as small boats or household furniture. Much of the latter has come down to us intact in the interiors of old buildings. Eighteenth century tables, chairs, and chests have survived mainly because the wood of which they were constructed was protected from the weather. But the small boats of that period, subjected to hard use and exposed to the elements, sooner or later wore out and rotted away.

These small boats were not entirely lost, for some small pockets of eighteenth-century culture continued to exist in isolated areas on the coast of Maine well into the nineteenth century, retaining folkways and artifacts that elsewhere had long since disappeared. Some of the peapods and wherries built in Penobscot Bay until quite recently were definitely colonial survivors.

There are two sorts of Maine peapods. The more recent is a typical late-nineteenth-century boat, carvel or smooth planked, with a keel and steam-bent oak ribs. In addition it is a true double-ender, being identical at the bow and the stern. The old type was quite different. It was a heavier boat, clinker planked with a bottom board and natural-crook sawn frames. While sharp at either end, the older pods were often fuller and higher at the bow.

In construction the older pods and the Maine wherries were identical or nearly so. In hull form the chief difference was the wherry's small, high-tucked transom stern. However, at the load waterline the wherry was virtually a double-ender which launched as well stern-first into the surf as any peapod.

In short, the older pods and the wherries were much the same kind of boat as appears from descriptions by George Wasson, in *Sailing Days on the Penobscot*, and Alfred Brooks, in *"The Boats of Ash Point, Maine,"* both of whom were well acquainted with the boats about which they wrote. Wasson had much to say about pods, but strangely he did not mention wherries, although he must have seen them. Brooks had much to say about both wherries and "double-enders," although he never referred to the latter as "peapods." Of the Ash Point double-enders and wherries, Brooks stated that they both had a flat bottom board 6 inches to 12 inches wide, and both had much the same shaped hull in its lower part.

In *Sailing Days On The Penobscot*, George Wasson, born in 1855, wrote in delightful detail of Isle au Haut as it once was. Even as late as the period of Wasson's own personal recollection, life on this isolated Penobscot Bay island still moved in much the same way as it had a century earlier. For instance he noted the absence of horses and wheeled carts and told how supplies were hauled across the island on sleds by oxen.

As previously mentioned in this book, on this island, as well as throughout the bay region, small-boat building burgeoned. Every sailor and fisherman, it seemed, was an occasional boatbuilder as well. Nearly everyone had built, was building, or planned to build a boat. From out of barns, sheds, cellars, one-time henhouses, and dooryards the new boats kept coming. Boatbuilding was in the blood and the breed. It was something to do in between times, something to dream about, something to plan for, something to talk about around the stove at the store. It was economic gain, recreation, and an art form all in one.

The favorite type, according to Wasson, was the peapod, clinker-built with planks got out of "live-edge" cedar boards, and ribbed with natural-crook hackmatack frames. A "wide, heavy bottom board" allowed the boat to be run aground and to be dragged over rough beaches with impunity. The flat bottom board both in the wherry and the old-time pod is extremely convenient for beach work, especially where tides run strong on rocky shores. Some of the wherries were built so that the bottom board, when worn, could be easily removed and replaced. Some were made with the bottom board in two layers so that the outer one, or "false bottom," as it was called, could be renewed with a minimum of difficulty.

Besides allowing the boat to sit upright on the beach, run easily on rollers, and withstand dragging, the flat bottom board on its inner side afforded a convenient and solid landing for the feet of the natural-crook side frames. A heavy bottom board of hardwood, as they were often made in both the wherries and the older pods, is not a disadvantage as some might suppose. Some weight in the lower part of a pulling craft used in rough water helps to keep it moving ahead steadily between strokes of the oars once headway has been attained, especially when the boat is laboring in a seaway.

THE BUILDING PROCEDURE

Brooks observed that the Ash Point wherries and double-enders were not built with benefit of drawn lines or lofting. The same was true for Isle au Haut peapods and Lincolnville salmon wherries. The building procedure for all of these old clinker types must have been essentially the same. First off, the bottom board, stem, and transom were got out, sometimes from patterns, borrowed, inherited, or saved from earlier ventures, and sometimes by "eye." These were then assembled and set upright on horses or stocks of some sort at a convenient height for working. Bevels and rabbets as necessary were cut. The bottom board was shored down to the required camber or "rocker." A center mold or "shadow," as it was called, was inserted amidship. After a final check with level and plumb, and when everything had been securely shored and braced, preparations for planking were complete.

Planking proceeded by "eye" from the bottom up, starting at the garboard and getting out the plank in identical pairs, so that both sides could be carried up together. As the planks went on, the laps were riveted.

Today's first-time builders may require additional molds. The old builders of lapstrake boats seemed generally to have managed well enough with the single center mold or "shadow." They did not try to force the strakes, permitting the natural bend of the lumber to influence the shape of the boat. Lapstrake planks, especially the thicker sort, cannot be forced, bent, and twisted to anywhere near the extent that steamed carvel planks can.

The old way was not to fit the ribs or frames until the planking was complete. Brooks stated that in his day the Ash Point builders used strips of white oak soaked in water but not steamed. Wasson related that, on Isle au Haut, peapods were ribbed with natural crooks of hackmatack carefully notched to fit the jogs of the laps. This is the method still employed in England, and possibly was commonly used in this country in colonial times, although rarely seen now.

The frames of the salmon wherry examined by Smithsonian experts in 1959 were cut from natural crooks obtained from white cedar stumps or roots. They were not notched to fit the laps. Furthermore, they are fairly light, so as to be almost frail in appearance, yet, having en-

dured more than 60 years of hard use without serious breaks, they cannot be considered inadequate. Obviously, these frames were fitted and installed after the planking was done, especially the first set of frames in the fore end of the boat. These are true cant frames set out of square with the centerline of the hull. This permits them to lie flat against the curve of the planking without beveling. This also gives them a forward slant as they run up the side of the boat.

Cant frames such as these were formerly employed to frame full-ended vessels in order to avoid excessive beveling of the frames. Such frames are not difficult to scribe into place after the planking is on, but they are extremely difficult to lay out accurately ahead of time on the mold loft floor.

The planking of the Robie Ames salmon wherry whose lines are shown here is native

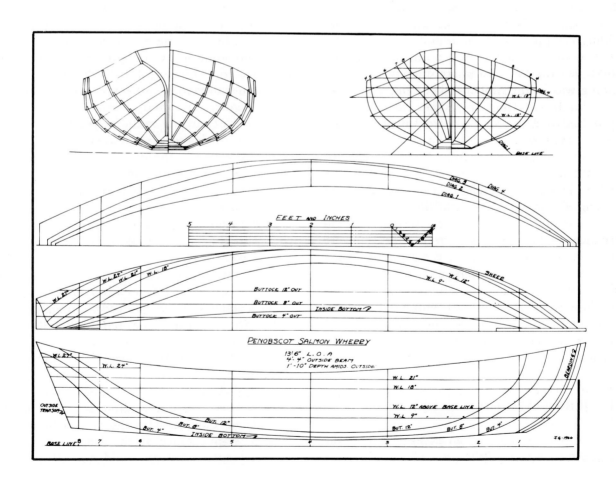

PENOBSCOT SALMON WHERRY

13'6" L.O.A
4'-4" OUTSIDE BEAM
1'-10" DEPTH AMIDS. OUTSIDE

Maine white cedar ½ inch thick and lapped 1⅛ inches. There is very little beveling of the laps. Half-inch planking for a clinker boat of this size is fairly heavy, and this with the stout laps gives the hull extra strength. Besides, Maine white cedar, with sound knots and twisted grain, while harder to work, is tougher and more resistant to splitting than the clear straight-grained species such as most Virginia white cedar.

The lapped planking and the native cedar in combination produced an exceptionally strong, flexible, lasting hull; otherwise it would never have stood up so well under continuous severe use for longer than a man's ordinary working lifetime. The principle strength of this remarkable boat resides in its clinker plank.

In summing up the foregoing, two points may be made. The first is that the rugged strength and endurance of this archaic type of lapstrake hull came from its Maine white cedar and copper-riveted laps. The second is that this kind of lapstrake construction was widely used, very successfully, by farmers and fishermen who were not professional boatbuilders, although they had a good eye for boats. Only the simplest hand tools were available to them, they had never studied drafting or design, and not one in a hundred had the slightest notion of lofting a set of lines.

I do not say that some clunkers were not built. There are vast individual differences among men in mechanical aptitude, as well as in patience and in perseverance. Still, on the whole, craft that did meet the test of use and endurance—and sometimes even beauty—were produced by those who were essentially home builders and amateurs. Craft at least as good can still be built of the old materials according to the old designs and methods with hand tools by amateurs of ordinary ability and skill, provided they are willing to take the time and care required.

THE MERRIMACK RIVER WHERRY

One wherry that was an exceptionally good boat, according to Ephraim C. S. Clark, who drew its lines as he recollected them in 1961, was the Merrimack River wherry *Axa*. This boat was Clark's first boat when he was a boy growing up on the Newburyport waterfront. The *Axa* was the tender for a sailing scow of the same name, belonging to his grandfather, Otis Dwinells, who used it 60 years ago and earlier to freight coal up the Merrimack to Groveland. Ordinarily, when not in use, the tender hung athwartships against the transom of the scow, above the water, parbuckled close, sheer in and bottom out.

The wherry *Axa*, as Clark remembers, had six frames sawn from hackmatack knees, and six strakes of lapped cedar planking. The ends of the garboards were wider than the other strakes, like those of a dory, running up on the stem and stern post to straighten the top edge of the plank and the planking lines above.

Axa's stem construction was the same as in a dory; that is, instead of a single rabbeted stem, the stem was made in two pieces, the principal inner part beveled sharp to receive the planking, and the outer part, or "false stem," as it is sometimes called, bent in place to cover the plank ends and fastened by nailing through into the inner member. This method avoids the difficulty and labor of cutting rabbets, yet the result in small craft of this sort is just as strong, tight, and lasting. The line in the drawing representing the stem shows the location and profile shape of the inner part before the outer, or "false," stem is bent in place.

The stern of the *Axa*, although typically wherry in shape, was made in an unusual way. Clark recalls that the entire stern, comprising a 12-inch transom, curved stern post, and stern knee joining the bottom board, had been hewed out in a single piece from a cedar stump. A large stump would have been required and much patient and skillful axe work must have gone into the job. At the Adirondack Museum there is a primitive guideboat with its transom stern sculptured from a spruce stump in the same manner. This is an old method. It harks back to the ancient dugout. The specialized boatshop, making its appearance on the American scene in the nineteenth century, could not afford such

MERRIMACK RIVER WHERRY, "AXA"
NEWBURYPORT, MASS. ABOUT 1880

SCALE

LINES BY EPHRAIM C. S. CLARK, 1961
TRACED BY J. GARDNER, 1966

DIAG 1
DIAG. 2

18" W.L.
15" W.L.
12" W.L.
9" W.L.
6" W.L.
3" W.L.
24" W.L.
SHEER

LINES—
INSIDE, PLANKING & BOTTOM.
OUTSIDE, STEM & STERN.

L.O.A. 12'—0"
BEAM 4'—6"

BOW

24" W.L.
18" W.L.
15" W.L.
12" W.L.
9" W.L.
6" W.L.
3" W.L.

SHEER

DISPL. APPROX. 750 LBS.

BOTTOM
BASE LINE

HALF-BREADTH BOTTOM

11   10   9   8   7   6   5   4   3   2   1

work. It did not suit mass production or "hurry-up" methods. This is the sort of thing a man would do for himself when time was not too pressing.

As in older construction, natural grown crooks or knees figured extensively in the *Axa*'s build. The two thwarts were kneed in, as was the transom at the sheer on either side. Another natural crook formed the breast hook.

The *Axa* was rowed with oar straps instead of thole pins. A hole for a small mast went through the forward thwart.

All in all there was nothing too unusual about *Axa*'s build, except it might have been slightly old-fashioned even in 1880. What is unusual about the *Axa* is her shape, particularly her snubbed ends and the reverse rocker of her bottom. Clark called attention to these two unique features, and I would add another—her unusual amount of deadrise, which gives her

almost a V bottom, even though her bottom board amidships is 9 inches wide.

Clark thinks the wherry might have had snubbed ends so they wouldn't project past the transom of the scow. As for the "reverse rocker" in the bottom board, which makes it appear hogged, this was supposed to have some connection with the boat's excellent qualities in sea and surf, but just how is not too clear. Perhaps the boat was accidentally hogged without any adverse effect on her original good performance, or perhaps the hog was purposely put in by the builder in accordance with some theory of his own. I am sure such "reverse rocker" in the bottom was never typical or common in wherries, and indeed the *Axa* is the only one with this peculiarity I have come across so far.

The angle of *Axa*'s deadrise is quite extreme and it is possible that Clark's recollection has exaggerated it slightly. In a light condition this boat would balance delicately and would heel so sharply that it could pitch the unwary occupant overboard, although she could only roll down so far. With a load, however, the *Axa* must have been exceptionally steady and stable, for in that condition her unusual hull form would have combined both broad bearing and deep draft. For 12 feet of length, the *Axa* is exceptionally burdensome. She is deep and has body, unlike some craft which seem to be all ends with no middle.

Loaded to her 12-inch waterline (12 inches above the baseline) the *Axa*, as represented by Clark's lines, would displace approximately 750 pounds, ample for at least three ordinary occupants plus the weight of the boat. Freeboard amidships would then be 12 inches, while draft would be approximately the same (depth to inside of bottom, 10½ inches). The amidships bearing on the water at the 12-inch loadline is 43 inches, as much as the total beam for many ordinary 12-foot rowboats. However, the sides of the *Axa* from this level upward round out rapidly, permitting several hundred pounds of additional weight to be added without diminishing the freeboard to any hazardous or uncomfortable extent, while increasing steadiness and stability.

The *Axa* is not a racing shell but a working tender, burdensome and stable (when loaded) and good both in sea and surf. Her lines deserve to be known and might be well worth study and experimentation where ordinary types do not fill the bill or leave something to be desired.

THE LINCOLNVILLE SALMON WHERRY

Let's look at a downeast wherry. Reproduced here are the lines and details of a salmon wherry surviving from the now defunct salmon fishery formerly carried on off the beach at Lincolnville, Maine. Through the kindness of the owner, Osborne Wade of Lincolnville, we had the boat on loan at Mystic Seaport a few years ago, where we were able to photograph it and measure it accurately. As far as I have been able to determine, only three of the salmon wherries once used in the fishery at Lincolnville yet remain, this one and another belonging to Wade, and the

Robie Ames wherry formerly at the Adirondack Museum and now in the small craft collection at Mystic Seaport.

The New England wherry, it seems, came about as close to extinction and oblivion as is possible without disappearing completely. The Ash Point wherries have long since gone. The Cape Roseway wherry (could this have been the Cape Rosier wherry?) was described briefly by George Brown Goode in his *Fisheries and Fishery Industries of the United States*, 1887, Sec. V, Vol. II, p. 672.

According to Chapelle, this type may be considered extinct as no model has been found. Described by Goode, "The Cape Roseway wherry employed in the lobster and inshore fisheries of Penobscot Bay, Maine, especially in the vicinity of Castine, is a lap-streak boat with a sharp bow, round bilge, narrow, flat bottom, and very narrow, heart-shaped stern. It ranges from 12 to 18 feet, is entirely open, and seldom provided with sails."

The sharp bow of the Cape Roseway model differs from the round bow of the specialized salmon wherry, and besides, wherries were commonly sailed as well as rowed both at Lincolnville and Ash Point. Otherwise the Goode description applies quite accurately to these other Penobscot Bay wherries.

If such boats were once found quite widely

distributed in Penobscot Bay and possibly to the eastward of it, might there not still be survivors hidden away which have gone unnoticed to date? The prospect is an intriguing one. Some painstaking detective work might yet pay off.

Although the Wade wherry was built for the Lincolnville fishery, and was so used for many years, it differs somewhat in two respects from most of the other salmon wherries. The bow of the Wade wherry, while fairly full, is not as round as most of the other boats, and its stern with its wider transom is not quite as high as was generally the case.

The salmon fisherman knelt in the bow of his boat directly abaft the stem to overhaul his nets and bring the fish aboard. Some of these salmon were big and scrappy, and, if the fisherman was a heavy man, as well, more than ordinary fullness and displacement was required at the bow. The photograph of a wherry with centerboard and spritsail taken at Lincolnville Beach about 30 years ago by John Leavitt shows a full-bowed, lean-sterned boat more typical of the general run of the salmon wherries than the Wade boat.

The lean, high-tucked stern with its small transom was functional, for it facilitated launching stern-first into the surf, as was frequently required in getting these boats off the beach. In the Robie Ames wherry, the stern stands higher than the bow, a feature found in some fishing dories, and for the same reason.

Although the stern of the Wade wherry is not as high as some of the other salmon wherries, it is still relatively high, making the boat a virtual double-ender on its waterline even when loaded. Its additional bearing aft carried through to the relatively wide transom adds greatly to steadiness aft.

It is worth noting that the shape of the stern, deep and sharp below, yet flattening out directly above the tuck, is not unlike that of the Staten Island oyster skiff or the New Jersey beach skiff. All three are flat-bottom, clinker-built craft with sufficient likenesses to suggest derivation from a common ancestral type, possibly a prototype Colonial wherry now completely forgotten.

Osborne Wade and the wherry he loaned to Mystic Seaport at the left, foreground. The smaller wherry at the right has an inwale and what appears to be slightly more delicate lines. (Photo by John Kochiss)

The Wade salmon wherry in profile shows her full lines. (Photo by Lester D. Olin)

Less highly specialized than the usual run of salmon wherries, that is, neither so full in the bow nor so lean at the stern, the Wade wherry is undoubtedly better suited for general use, and indeed it is an excellent small sea boat either for oars or for sail with the addition of a centerboard. This boat will handle easily, show fair speed under either oars or sail, carry a load, stand some weather, and take a lot of punishment. The build is quite rugged.

The false bottom can be seen here. The removable pieces served to absorb punishment on rocky beaches and could be replaced when worn out. (Photo by Lester D. Olin)

The Wade wherry's double flat bottom with replaceable outer layer is made to take the wear of rough beaches and enables the boat to sit firmly upright when hauled out. One man can pull it on or off the beach and take it in or out through moderate surf.

There is nothing fancy about this boat, nor is it actually too hard or too fussy for the handy amateur to build. In fact, the construction is fairly simple, and, for a tough, reliable little ship to knock about the shore in, no other boat of its size comes to mind that would serve any better.

Planking is Maine cedar a half-inch thick. Any northern white cedar is first choice for planking, but Virginia cedar is not recommended, as this southern cedar is too brittle and splits too easily. Small knots won't do any harm, if they are sound. The planks are really tougher and stronger because of them, and if a few are loose, these are easily plugged. As the boat is painted, knots will not show when the job is finished. The shape of the Wade wherry is such that I believe it could be planked without steam provided the cedar is not too dry. However, steam for some of the planks would make things easier. For planking the replica of the Robie Ames salmon wherry built at Mystic Seaport a few years ago, steam was required because of the full, round bow.

Width of lap is normally 1⅛ inches, although where the side curve is greatest, the lap width may have to be slightly reduced to obtain wood-to-wood closure of the laps. In fitting the

Interior view of the Wade wherry shows the broad bottom plank, the mark of the type. (Photo by Lester D. Olin)

With the seat removed, one can see how the garboard and second planks are faired into the stern-post, making the wherry a virtual double-ender.

laps, just as little wood is removed as is possible to get a snug fit. For some of the laps no wood at all has to be planed off. This gives a strong hull which depends on its lap fastenings to hold

(Left) This salmon wherry fitted for sailing with a spritsail and center-board was photographed in Lincolnville, Maine, in the early 1940s by John Leavitt. (Right) Salmon wherry on display at the Adirondack Museum. The low platform that should cover the base of the stem is hanging from the framing in the stern. It was used by the kneeling net tender. Because of the camera angle, the bow does not appear as full as it actually is. (Photo courtesy of the Adirondack Museum)

it together and tight, at least as much as internal framing.

The lines are drawn to the inside of the planking, and the points that determine these lines lie in the upper inside edges of the inner bottom and the eight strakes of plank. By working from these points located at the intersection of the sections with the inner lines of the planking, the laps may be laid out as I have done for the two sections in the accompanying drawing. In this way, if laid out full size, the precise amount of beveling required for each plank is easily determined.

Lap fastenings are copper nails spaced approximately 2½ inches apart and riveted over burrs. The inner bottom, ⅞ inch thick, was usually made in Lincolnville wherries of old-growth yellow birch. Oak would do as well, or even good quality mahogany could serve as a substitute.

The ribs or frames in the Lincolnville wherries are most unusual, being got out of white cedar roots selected and dug to give the shape required. The siding and molding is approximately one inch, but rather more than this than less, particularly the molding toward the foot, and at the stern where the frames take a reverse curve, and are scribed to fit the jogs of the lower planks.

Note that there is no inwale, and that the gunwale on the outside is in section about one inch square, tapered to ¾ inch at the ends. The breasthook and likewise the stern quarter knees are exceptionally large, and got out of natural-crook cedar roots like the frames.

The rabbeted stem, sided 2 inches and molded approximately 3 inches, is likewise cut from a cedar knee, as is the inner stern knee or stern post. These members do not have to be cedar crooks, which in the past were easily obtainable at Lincolnville, but could just as well be hackmatack or any other suitable boatbuilding timber. Nor is it necessary to use natural crooks. The frames could be laminations glued to shape on a form.

It is not necessary to follow these lines exactly, although it would be wise not to depart too far from them and only for well considered reasons. No two wherries, I believe, were ever built exactly alike. The wherries sketched by Brooks in the *American Neptune* show some marked variations both in size and hull shape, yet all are easily recognizable as wherries. A wherry intended mainly for sailing would conceivably differ considerably from one built for rowing. One of the great attractions of a type like the New England wherry for the amateur designer and builder is the scope it gives for variation and individuality.

2 1

The Origin of the Whitehall

......................•......................

All sail set, a ship rounds Race Point off the tip of Cape Cod bound for Boston. Racing out to meet her, oars flashing, their leg-o-mutton sails drawing, are several small, open boats. Each is provided with a long, slender pole with a hook at the end to which is lashed a length of nine-thread line. Someone in the foremost boat dexterously hooks the rapidly moving vessel at her fore lee chains, pays out to a safe distance, then warps alongside, and one of the occupants springs nimbly aboard. He is a runner from some "deepwater boarding house," or from one of the competing outfitting establishments located on Boston's Hanover and North streets in the 1870s and the 1880s. He is out to line up trade before Jack Tar makes port, and a sly half-pint discreetly slipped here and there to the crew when the officers are looking the other way can work wonders in getting prospective customers into a receptive frame of mind.

The slim, tidy craft that brought the successful runner all the way out across Massachusetts Bay was a Whitehall boat, in length not more than 20 feet, perhaps only 18 feet, and not a great deal over 4 feet in beam. Thwarts, stern bench, and the top strake would probably have been finished bright, as would have been the varnished backrest with the boat's name in gold leaf.

The authority for this description is the late Captain Charleton L. Smith of Marblehead, Massachusetts, from whose recollections of Boston Whitehalls in *The Rudder* for August, 1943, the above brief account is paraphrased. Captain Smith, who was born in 1869, grew up on the Boston waterfront.

The port of Boston in those days teemed with enterprise. The harbor was white with incoming and outgoing sail. A flood-tide of commerce surged across the wharves. Vessels large and small from far and near discharged and took on cargo in a kaleidoscope of activity, color, sounds, and smells, and Smith as a lad was there and took it all in and never forgot. Once, as he recalled, he counted 18 Whitehalls in the "Cow Pen," as the enclosure at the forked end of Lewis's wharf was then called. When Whitehalls were at their peak in Boston, it has been estimated that there were 75 in service in the harbor.

For all their fancy trimmings, these runners' Whitehalls were workboats as hardy and as business-like as the men who owned them. One of these owners, according to Captain Smith, was a saltwater boarding house owner by the name of Sorensen, Captain Alfred Sorensen, who had a case full of rowing prizes and life-saving medals for sailors he had pulled out of the briny deep. As one story goes, Sorensen once far outran the Whitehall fleet. It was in the winter-time and, broad off the tip of Cape Cod, the wind freshened to a "howling gale." Did Alfred panic? Not a bit. Stowing mast and sail, he payed out his warp for a sea anchor and lay head

These two Whitehalls of classic design were built recently to meet their owners' wish for fine pulling boats aboard their sailing vessels. The elaborately finished yawl boat above was built for the replica schooner America *by R.D. Culler and the Concordia Boat Company of South Dartmouth, Massachusetts. Below is one of the sleek ship's boats built by Dick Shew of South Bristol, Maine, for the topsail schooner* Shenandoah.

into the storm for some 36 hours, until he picked up an inbound ship and came home.

The beginnings of the Boston Whitehall are vague, just as the beginnings of the Whitehall type in general, in spite of its popularity and renown, are also vague and shadowy. Some even question that it originated on this side of the Atlantic, holding that the boat was introduced from England and that its name was taken from Whitehall in London.

However, there is also a Whitehall Street in New York City where Howard I. Chapelle and others have written these boats were first built. Chapelle cites the opinion of W. P. Stephens, who thought that the type came into existence sometime in the 1820s in New York City, having first been built by former Navy Yard apprentices who had derived their model to some extent from the old naval gig.

Of course the Whitehall had antecedents, if only we knew how to unravel that tangled skein of history, as all distinctive boat types have antecedents and are a combination of old and new elements, with much more of the former than the latter. The pronounced conservatism of sailors and seafaring men, often noted, and their predilection for sticking with the tried and the tested, have always worked to insure a high degree of continuity in the development of hull design, both for small craft and for larger vessels.

If the Whitehall did first appear as a distinct and recognizable type in New York City in the 1820s, it was quickly and widely adopted in use. Chapelle thought that Whitehalls were in mass production in New York boatshops by 1840. The water taxi service carried on by "Battery boatmen" recalled the celebrated ferrying service of the Thames watermen, part of the pageant of London since the sixteenth century.

The Whitehall was not a ship's boat but a vehicle of harbor and coastwise transportation. Intended primarily to be rowed, but capable of a good showing under sail as well, it was fast, seaworthy, and trim. Whitehalls were in great demand in the days of sail on the waterfront of a busy commercial port such as was New York City in the early nineteenth century. Not only were these boats the choice of crimps and boarding house runners, but of nearly everyone else as well who required reliable and expeditious transportation about the waterfront or from one part of the harbor to another—ship chandlers, brokers, newspaper reporters, insurance agents, doctors, pilots, ships officers, port officials, and many others.

Gentlemen of that day, seeking a pleasure boat, frequently adopted modifications of the Whitehall workboat. Naturally, Whitehalls were raced. Perhaps it was the influence of the Whitehall as much as anything else that made rowing the principal American competitive sport on the Eastern seaboard at the midpoint of the nineteenth century. The rise and decline of rowing as a major competitive sport in this country, from the eighteenth century to nearly the end of the nineteenth, will some day make a fascinating book. At least one section of that book will be devoted to the Whitehall.

Once the Whitehall was established in both Boston and New York, inter-city competition

began. Captain Smith, from Boston, relates that an early challenge from New York resulted in a match race for $1,000 (a large sum in those days) rowed between a New York Whitehall and a Boston Whitehall on neutral water at Springfield, Massachusetts. The Boston Whitehall, the *Gookin Brothers*, a fast runner's boat built by Partelow, won in a morning race. To satisfy the disgruntled challengers, a second race for a wager of $500 was rowed on the afternoon of the same day with the same result, clearly establishing the superiority of the Boston boat and its crew.

When and how the Whitehall first arrived in Boston is not clear, but if it was brought from New York, it must have been quite soon after its inception. No evidence for an independent derivation for the Boston Whitehall has yet appeared, although the Boston Whitehall has some distinct differences in construction from the New York Whitehall, at least as far as we can tell, considering that no authentic specimens of early New York Whitehalls, with one possible exception, are to be found. Two examples of the Boston Whitehall, however, exhibiting its distinctive construction, have survived and are now to be seen in the small craft collection at Mystic Seaport.

Captain Smith was of the opinion that the first Boston Whitehalls were produced about 1870 by Charles M. Partelow in his shop on Commercial Street. It is true that C. M. Partelow was an early builder of the Boston Whitehall, but it is doubtful if he was the first, or if he originated its distinctive features of construction. There were several Whitehall builders contemporary with Partelow, two of the best known being Dick Sullivan and Cragin & Sheldon. However, as we shall see, the boatbuilding firm later organized and managed by C. M. Partelow's second oldest son, H. V. Partelow, did eventually initiate a new method of framing and planking which cheapened Whitehall construction and changed it radically.

The most distinctive feature of the classic Boston Whitehall as built approximately 100 years ago was the special manner in which it was framed and planked. There seem also to have been less readily discernible characteristics of the shape or hull form which in combined effect produced a unique boat in contrast with the New York Whitehall. Yet this is difficult to determine or analyze concretely, for as far as I know, no contemporary New York Whitehalls have survived for direct comparison. H. I. Chapelle, on page 197 of his *American Small Sailing Craft*, gives the lines and some construction details for a boat built at the Brooklyn Navy Yard in 1890, and claimed to be representative of the standard New York Whitehall of the period between 1860 and 1895. While similar to the Boston boats, its proportions are not quite the same. For one thing it is a slightly beamier boat with shallower deadrise. Also, it is built with a flat plank keel 6½ inches wide amidships.

Neither of the two Boston Whitehalls which survive at Mystic Seaport are standard runner's workboats of the 1870s. According to Captain Smith, such boats in order to be eligible for rowing competition had to conform to certain restrictions laid down by the Boston boat clubs of the time to prevent the appearance of racing freaks. The rules read that boats must be between 17 and 20 feet in length, not less than 4 feet in beam or 19 inches in depth amidships, and must be rowed on the gunwales.

The standard runner's boat brought to near perfection in racing competition set the norm for the type. Two such, mentioned by Captain Smith as "very fast boats on the Charles at that time," and both built by Partelow, were the *P. F. Gilmore* and the *Joseph Edwards*. But if such runner's boats established the norm, there were numerous variations within the norm— Whitehalls built in different lengths and sizes, for different purposes, yet all recognizable as Whitehalls. The smallest seem to have been the 12-foot rowboats once to be seen on the pond in the Public Gardens. In boats any shorter than this the superior characteristics of the type would mostly disappear, though the construction would not differ from full-size boats. Few, if any, were ever built longer than the 21-foot runner's boat in which, according to Captain Smith, August Motto won all the cups and first-

place money in the final days of the sport, before the motorboat put an end to it.

In their annual catalog for 1891, H. V. Partelow & Co. listed six grades of "fancy Whitehall row and pleasure boats" ranging in price from $6 per foot for Grade A, down to $3.75 per foot for the cheapest galvanized fastened grade, the length of the boat to be specified by the customer to suit his individual requirements.

A 17-FOOT WHITEHALL

The longer of the two Boston Whitehalls at Mystic Seaport is a fancy pleasure Whitehall apparently built at Boston, Massachusetts, in 1879: length 16 feet 9 inches, beam to outside of planking, 3 feet 7 inches, inside depth amidships to top of keel, 15½ inches. This boat was intended to be sailed as well as rowed, for it is fitted with a box for a metal daggerboard, 9 inches wide by ¼ inch thick. There are two separate sockets for a 2½-inch diameter mast, one considerably aft of the other, apparently so that the position of the mast could be changed to suit different rigs. A sliding seat for the oarsman on runners extending over the top of the daggerboard case is a refinement not to be found in the runner's workboat. Yet in essentials the boat conforms to standard Boston Whitehall construction, although its scantlings are reduced to an absolute minimum, and its hull lines are drawn extra lean and fine.

Edwin M. Bailey of Amesbury, Massachusetts, the donor of this boat, has this to say about it:

The boat belonged to my father, E. Wm. Bailey, who was born in 1863 in East Pittston, Maine. He went to high school in Charlestown, Mass., graduating in 1881. He had the boat when he was in high school, and I am fairly sure that he bought it second hand. So I would guess it was built in the late 1870's.

In 1882 he moved to Amesbury, and sailed the boat around Cape Ann to the Merrimack River and up the river six miles to Amesbury. I do not think it was built in Amesbury, in fact, I am sure it was not.

The boat lay upside down in my grandfather's cellar for over 40 years. Before my father died in 1940, he told me to take the boat out of the cellar, and if it was in good condition, to use her, if not, to burn her. After he

(Above, right, and opposite page) A fancy 17-foot Whitehall on display in the North Boat Shed of Mystic Seaport. She is obviously a pleasure boat, not a working boat, yet the construction is practically identical, though lighter with smaller scantlings. Note the sliding seat, the spoon oars, and the very unusual circular oarlocks with a moving inner ring attached to the oar, producing the effect of a universal joint. The boat is fitted for sail with two mast steps and a metal daggerboard. (Photos by Russel A. Fowler)

died, my brother and I pulled her out of the cellar and found her to be in good condition. We found the spoon oars, the machined, fitted oarlocks, the boom and gaff, the hand-sewn sail and jib, and the rudder. We never found the backrest for the stern sheets. I made a dagger board out of sheet steel, and sailed her in the Merrimack River for two seasons. Then a leak developed around the dagger board box and I did not launch her again. . . .

It was a very easy rowing boat, as you no doubt know, and I could sail her sometimes for half an hour without touching the tiller ropes, by moving my weight backwards and forward. This was with the wind two points forward of the beam to two points abaft the beam. Closehauled or running free, she required the rudder.

The peerless workmanship found in this boat, its exquisite lines, and delicate yet sturdy construction which has lasted so well after so many years, bespeak the hand of a master craftsman. Although we do not know the name of the builder, there is good reason to conclude that this boat came out of one of the leading Boston boatshops of the era, when the boatbuilding craft was practiced on a level which we do not begin to approach in this country today.

One characteristic of this Boston Whitehall

mentioned by the former owner deserves comment. On certain points of sailing she steered without touching the rudder merely by shifting weight forward or aft, that is by slight changes in the fore-and-aft balance of the boat. This is precisely the way St. Lawrence River skiffs are sailed, as explained in a previous chapter. Both these types are long and lean of hull and lightly built, with rigs basically much the same.

A 13-FOOT WHITEHALL

The shorter of the two Whitehalls at Mystic Seaport donated to the museum's small craft collection by William F. Peach of Marblehead is 13½ feet in length, 4 feet amidships inside the planking, and 19 inches deep inside from the sheerline amidships to the top of the keel. Its precise origin and date of construction are uncertain. Apparently the boat was built in Maine in the 1920s, yet we have it on the authority of a master boatbuilder who as a

13-FOOT BOSTON WHITEHALL - MYSTIC SEAPORT - 1969.

FEET AND INCHES

The 13-foot Whitehall as she appeared when donated to Mystic Seaport by William F. Peach.

young man worked for the Partelow firm in Boston building Whitehalls and other small craft, and who subsequently built Whitehalls elsewhere, that this particular boat is an authentic Boston Whitehall in its general details, and that in the main it can be considered representative of the nineteenth-century Boston boats. Admittedly it is only galvanized-nailed instead of being copper-fastened and burred, and it does not have the fine hardwoods, the finish, or the varnish and gold leaf of the fancier boats, yet in its proportions and basic construction it is essentially true to the type.

The man who made this identification was Charles A. Lawton, a native of St. John, New Brunswick, born in 1858, who came to Boston as a young man, going to work as a boatbuilder for H. V. Partelow & Co. at their Auburndale plant on the Charles River in 1882. H. V. Partelow's chief claim to our remembrance today is that he was the one who built the famous

Boston swan boats still plying the pond in the Public Gardens.

Charles M. Partelow had four sons. The second oldest, H. V. Partelow, had in Charlie Lawton's words, "a head for business." He took over the management of his father's boatshop, and, by the early 1880s, expanded it to include a canoe factory at Auburndale, a thriving boat livery at Riverside Station on the Charles across from the shop and livery of J. R. Robertson, a rival builder, a large showroom occupying two storefronts on Atlantic Avenue in Boston, and a marine railway, a yacht yard, and a boat and steam launch factory at Marblehead. In the 1891 issue of their annual catalog of boats, canoes, engines, marine hardware, and miscellaneous fittings and equipment, running to 59 pages, H. V. Partelow & Co., after claiming 50 years of experience in the boat manufacturing business, stated that they were confident that they produced the finest and largest variety of boats and canoes in the United States.

According to Lawton, the Partelow concern revolutionized the construction of Whitehall boats about this time when they started planking them over molds, and bending in steamed ribs after planking was completed. This new method of construction, subsequently adopted almost universally for the production of yacht tenders and similar craft, did not produce a superior Whitehall, but it did substantially reduce building time and cost. For a time thereafter, as Lawton recalled, the Partelows did a "whale" of a business.

Yet, not so long after revolutionizing Whitehall construction, the firm failed, started up again, and then within a few years, failed again, both times for large amounts, and, after a third abortive attempt at continuing in business in Charlestown, finally closed down for good. It seems to have been the canvas canoe, as much as anything else, that finished the company off.

Quite suddenly about the turn of the century, hundreds, if not thousands, of canvas canoes appeared on the Charles River, displacing the more expensive Adirondacks, St. Lawrence River skiffs, pleasure Whitehalls, and varnished, all-wood canoes which had been the mainstay of

the Partelow business. Boatbuilding within Boston's city limits went into permanent decline, which no doubt was the reason Lawton left around 1900 to go to work for E. Gerry Emmons in Swampscott. In 1908 Lawton removed to Marblehead to work for James E. Graves, where, well along in his 80s, he was still building fine yacht tenders when I made his acquaintance in the early 1940s.

Charles Lawton was a superb craftsman. His pre-eminence as a boatbuilder was unquestioned in Marblehead. His reputation was prodigious. His last boat, completed in his 90th year, was a fine, varnished 12-foot yacht tender which showed the Whitehall influence, although it was not a Whitehall. Few builders in the prime of life and professional career could have equaled it.

My acquaintance with Charlie Lawton soon ripened into friendship. Naturally, I admired his skill as a boatbuilder, and was much impressed with reports of his past achievements, for even then Charlie Lawton was well on the way to becoming a legend in Marblehead. Whenever the opportunity presented itself, I encouraged him to talk of his early experiences. He thought highly of Whitehall boats, and often spoke of them, recalling the early years in Boston when he was building Whitehalls for the Partelows. That concern was frequently hard put to meet its payroll, it seems, and the crew was never quite sure, according to Charlie, whether or not they would get paid at the end of the week.

There were other noted builders of Whitehalls, Dick Sullivan, for one, whose Commercial Street shop had for a sign a three-foot replica of a Whitehall hanging over its entrance. Sullivan also had come to Boston from St. John, where he had once worked for a time for Charlie's father and uncle. Charlie's great-grandfather, John Lawton, a Philadelphia boatbuilder born in 1758, and a Loyalist at the time of the American Revolution, had emigrated in the 1780s to St. John.

Somehow in talking with Charlie, I became enamored of the Whitehall. Charlie explained classic Whitehall construction to me in detail,

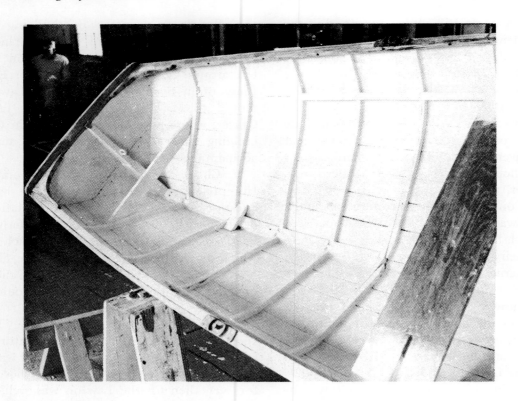

The simple construction of the after end of the 13-foot Whitehall is revealed here. Note the hogging piece over the keel and the boxed frame ends. (Mystic Seaport photo by Louis S. Martel)

and let me copy a draft of Whitehall lines he had made, as well as trace the outlines of molds for Whitehall stem and stern transom assemblies retained from his Boston days, molds which he later gave to me and which I still have. It was he who called my attention to the smaller of the two Whitehalls now at Mystic Seaport. At that time, in the early 1940s, this boat was in use in Marblehead during the summer as a yacht tender, and was stored in the winter at Graves's Front Street yard.

After Charlie recommended this boat as a good example of Whitehall construction, I studied it closely from all angles, took measurements, and went back occasionally for another look, and thus got its details stamped indelibly into memory. Then I left Marblehead, and with the passing years lost trace of the boat completely. A couple of times I made inquiries as to its whereabouts, but with no success. Finally I reluctantly assumed that it had disappeared without leaving a trace.

Then one summer, Captain Jerry Smith, son of Captain Charleton Smith, notified me that his neighbor Bill Peach on Stony Brook Road, Marblehead, had a boat in his backyard that I might want to take the lines from. The first look told me that it was the same Boston Whitehall that I had given up for lost, although in the intervening years its color had changed from white to black, long storage away from the water had opened gaping seams, and along the way it had acquired an ugly rope bumper around its sheer after the manner of a yacht tender. Otherwise it was in fine condition, little changed from the way I remembered it nearly 25 years earlier.

In the acquisition of this boat, Mystic Seaport made a significant addition to its small craft collection. As H. I. Chapelle observed, the Whitehall is "perhaps the most noted of American rowing workboats." The Boston Whitehall was a principal sub-type of the basic Whitehall. This boat is the only reliably documented example of this sub-type so far found and available for study. It complements beautifully Mystic's other Whitehall, the 16-foot 9-inch boat presumably built at Boston in the 1870's, also a very rare

survival, and substantiates much of the detail found in Captain Charleton Smith's account of the Boston Whitehall published in *The Rudder* in August, 1943.

AN UNUSUAL ONE-PIECE STEM

When the 13-foot Boston Whitehall was prepared for exhibit at Mystic Seaport, it was found necessary to remove the floorboards and bow and stern sheets in order to strip and repaint the inside of the boat. This allowed an unobstructed view of the interior and the framing, so that details of construction ordinarily hidden could be seen. These details are of particular interest to prospective builders, and, because they are permanently out of sight when the boat is in use, which is the condition in which it was to be exhibited, we had the photographs taken of the stripped interior, which are reproduced here. These will repay close study. While it has often been said that a picture is worth a thousand words, there are many things in boatbuilding that must be seen, touched, or otherwise directly experienced through the five senses, that no amount of explanatory verbiage can convey.

The construction of the stem was puzzling at first, and it would have been impossible to determine how it was made without the removal of the bow sheets and the cleat on the inner face of the stem which supported it. Getting this out of the way not only allowed the inner to be viewed and photographed, but, more important, permitted the making of a template of the inside of the stem.

By relating this template to a corresponding template taken from the curve of the stem rabbet on the outside of the boat, it was possible to determine the molded width of the stem, which could not have been done otherwise except by removing the planking or drilling holes through the stem.

The result was surprising. When these two templates, one for the inner curve of the stem, and the other for the outer, were correctly positioned with relation to each other, we found

Exterior view of the bow shows how the keel is scarphed to the stem. With the paint removed, the irregular grain of the stem is revealed. The stem actually runs aft all the way to the left of the photo. (Mystic Seaport photo by Louis S. Martel)

that the greatest molded width, occurring at the turn of the forefoot, was no less than 4¾". This is more than had appeared and more than we had expected.

True, it was obvious from the first that this stem was out of the ordinary. The usual construction method is to build up the stem from a three-piece assembly: first, the stem, proper, which can be got out of an ordinary plank, if need be, although some curve in the grain of the lower end is desirable; second, a knee of curved natural-crook grain, if possible, which fits against, and reinforces, the inner side of the forefoot extending a short distance along the top of the straight keel where it meets the stem, tying the two together; and, third, an apron piece of greater width of siding than the outer and principal stem piece, fitting against its inner side and running from the upper end of the forefoot knee to the stemhead. The apron provides backing (back rabbet) and fastening for the hood ends of the planking.

As it was clear from the first glance that the

stem of this boat was not fabricated in this manner, the possibility was considered that it might have been steam-bent, and that perhaps it was made up of two or more steam-bent pieces joined together. For instance, if of two parts, the inner and outer parts could have been joined lengthwise, with the joint hidden by the rabbet. However, examination of the stemhead revealed no such separation or joint. Nor were there any breaks or joints to be found either on the inside or the outside of the stem, except where the straight keel was scarphed in at the end of the stem. It then became clear that the stem was one piece throughout.

Could the stem have been steam-bent as a single piece? This seemed unlikely when we determined the amount of molded width. While it is possible, of course, to steam-bend oak of this width to curves as sharp as this, it is not easy, and special equipment not found in the ordinary boatshop would be required. Besides, inspection of the grain of the wood in this stem showed it to be irregular rather than straight,

(Above and below) Interior views show the framing and the one-piece stem, which ends at a natural-crook floor timber. Note the lapped sheer strake and the bead on the wide plank below it. (Mystic Seaport photos by Louis S. Martel)

and running slashwise in places rather than parallel to the lengthwise run of the stick. In selecting lumber for a bend as difficult as this, it would be strange not to choose wood with a straight, regular grain.

Taking all these things into consideration, we can only conclude that this stem was gotten out of a natural-grown crook of some sort. Although limb crooks of oak of the required curvature are sometimes found, stump crooks or knees of the requisite shape occur more commonly. In either case, natural crooks make the best possible stems, and, while oak was used for this boat throughout, hackmatack also makes a perfectly adequate stem for boats of this size.

Using natural crooks means problems for most amateur builders. Unless the builder can go into the woods and dig a suitable knee, or find a limb crook of the right curve, he will have to settle for something else. It hardly needs saying that timber of this sort is not to be found in lumberyards.

However, there are two perfectly acceptable alternatives; one, the ordinary three-piece stem assembly already mentioned, and the other, a glued, laminated stem. Epoxy glue for this latter

purpose has now been thoroughly proved, and the technique is simplicity itself: A rough form is used to give the shape, and a few clamps are used to pull the strips together and hold them until the resin has hardened.

There are two methods of lamination to choose from. One uses strips thin enough to bend without steaming, and gluing takes place immediately. The other calls for fewer but heavier and thicker strips, which must be steamed to bend. These are then allowed to dry out before gluing and reclamping. Those who still can't bring themselves to trust glue completely and who would feel better using some reinforcement can add a number of long, thin, bronze screws put in from the inside, but they are really not needed.

There is one thing about the one-piece stem which should be mentioned, for it might escape notice even though it is shown in the drawing. The siding of the stem on its after side inside the planking is 1⅝ inches, while at the rabbet line it is only 1⅜ inches. This means that the outer portion or edge of the stem must be thinned by ¼ inch (⅛ inch on each side) before the rabbet is recessed. There is special reason for this. It is done so that the stem will not appear to be too thick and clumsy from the outside of the boat, while at the same time providing sufficient wood inside to afford good backing for the hood ends of the planking. As already pointed out, with the standard three-piece stem assembly, the apron, which is molded heavier than the main stem piece, provides this required extra width of backing, or "back rabbet," for the plank ends.

Rabbeting the one-piece stem is undoubtedly the fussiest and most difficult operation in building a Whitehall, and the beginner is advised to go slowly and to be sure he understands what he is doing, otherwise he may find himself in trouble. The standard composite stem is considerably easier to rabbet.

As to how close the tolerances are in rabbeting the single-piece stem, note that in the diagram of the rabbeted stemhead of this 13-foot Whitehall, the ends of the planking are not shown square, but are cut back about ⅛ inch on the inside. This leaves a little additional thickness of undisturbed wood between the two rabbet cut-outs. There is nothing extra to spare than this.

The internal structure at the stern is simplicity itself. The strip that is fastened on top of the deadwood to afford back rabbet for the garboards where they rise toward the stern is oak sided 1¾ inches, which is ⅛ inch more than the siding of the inside after edge of the stem, and ⅜ inch thicker than the sternpost, keel, and deadwood. This member, added to the top of the deadwood and after end of the keel, is neither a knee nor a keel batten, but possibly might be called a "hogging" piece by the British. It can be sawn out of an ordinary oak plank, as it has no curve to mention, and is fastened down with screws. The lower ends of the after frames are boxed into it, which is a neat way of securing them, besides adding to the structural strength of the after bottom.

Hidden from sight in the photographs, but critically essential nonetheless, are the two stopwaters, one in the rabbet at either end of the deadwood to close the joints and prevent leakage at these two points into the bottom of the boat.

THE IMPORTANCE OF A FLOOR KNEE

Among the W. P. Stephens papers in the manuscript collection of the G. W. Blunt White Library at the Mystic Seaport is an outline tracing bearing the following penciled notation printed across its length: "Floor Knee From Meredith's Shop, Presumably Deadrise Of Whitehall Boat. W. P. S."

This is more important for the history of the Whitehall boat, I am inclined to believe, than might first appear. To my satisfaction at least, this simple outline furnishes the needed clue to a number of perplexing questions concerning the form and construction of the Whitehall and bearing upon the origin and use of the original New York working boats. In a real sense this floor knee outline constitutes a "missing link." To my knowledge, about the only tangible bit remaining of the New York working boats, at least that we can put our hands on, is this outline of a floor knee.

If this one molded shape can be accepted as authentic, as I believe it can, and as I shall presently attempt to show, we shall have more to work from than might at first be supposed. Quite a lot can be told from it, both as to what the Whitehall was and what it was not. Besides, this molded shape does constitute a link to some Boston Whitehalls which have survived, for instance the two that are now preserved in the small craft collection at Mystic Seaport.

Just as the paleontologist from an ancient, fragmentary, fossilized bone can often determine to a considerable extent the characteristics of the prehistoric animal of which it once formed a part, so the small craft historian from the shape of this floor knee should be able to reconstruct and establish some significant features of the working Whitehall boats of New York. By great good fortune it happens that preserved in the simple molded shape of this floor knee is one of the principal determining elements of the boat's shape. If we had had a choice, we could hardly have picked for examination a more significant single member of the craft's structure.

First, however, it is necessary to establish

the authenticity of the molded shape of this floor knee, and to place it within the historical context in which it acquires significance. To do this we must consider the source from whence it comes. How did it happen to be found among W. P. Stephens's papers?

No man could have been better qualified by experience, interest, and specialized knowledge to rescue the Whitehall from oblivion than W. P. Stephens. Yet time was against him, and the job was never finished. Born in 1854 in a day when rowing was the foremost American competitive sport, Stephens took up sculling early and came into intimate contact with some of the best oarsmen of the time, both American and British. After graduation as a civil engineer from Rutgers, he began building boats, and in 1880, at the age of 26, he was operating his own boatshop in Rahway, N. J. That same year he participated in founding the American Canoe Association, becoming one of its 23 charter members. At the first meet held at Lake George, N. Y., in August of 1880, Stephens won the first race in one of his own "Jersey Blue" sailing and paddling canoes.

The following year Stephens moved operations to West New Brighton, Staten Island, renting a boatshop formerly occupied by a builder of working Whitehalls, William Meredith by name, but known about the waterfront as "Billy English." Billy English, was supposed to have built a fast boat to satisfy the requirements of his clientele, reputed to have been mainly harbor thieves and junkmen.

Stephens was a frequent and popular contributor, under the pen name of "Jersey Blue," to *Forest and Stream*, the foremost boating publication of the period. He was not long in becoming its canoeing editor at the time the sailing canoe, derived from the British Rob Roy, was at the height of its popularity in the Northeast. In 1884, *Forest and Stream* brought out the first edition of Stephens's *Canoe and Boat Building for Amateurs* with 24 plates. Within the next 25 years this book was to pass through more than a dozen editions with an increase in the number of plates of drawings to 30 and finally to 50. This book was probably the most widely read and influential work on small craft construction ever published.

With the decline of the sailing canoe and its permanent eclipse before the end of the century, Stephens turned to yachting. There seems to have been a period when writing and editorial work did not suffice for a living, for in a letter to Captain Charleton L. Smith, written when Stephens was 82, Stephens mentioned that he was sailing his little ketch, *Snikersnee*, probably for the last season, attempting to make up for the years of duty on tugboats and steam yachts when he missed all personal sailing. Incidentally, it proved not to be the last season for *Snikersnee*, for in May, three years later, he explained to a correspondent that he was about to go down to the yacht club to beach and pump out his little yacht, which was leaking badly.

Duty at sea did not seem to have interfered either with Stephens's writing or yacht designing. His ability as a designer was demonstrated in one notable instance by his 15-foot waterline *Ethelwynn*, first winner of the Seawanhaka Cup, defeating the challenger, the English half-rater, *Spruce IV*, in 1895, as well as boats by Herreshoff and other eminent American designers. As a writer he continued to publish, in time winning distinction as the foremost reporter of international yacht racing.

With the inception of *Lloyds Register of American Yachts*, Stephens became its editor, a position he continued to hold until he was past 80. In addition to Stephens's early *Canoe and Boat Building for Amateurs* were *American Yachting*, 1904; *Traditions And Memories of American Yachting*, 1942, reprinted from *Motor Boating*; and *The Seawanhaka Corinthian Yacht Club, Origins And Early History, 1871-1896*, published posthumously in 1963. This last book and related investigations into yachting history took much of his time and effort toward the end of his life, preventing the completion of his investigation of the Whitehall. Stephens died in 1946 at the age of 92.

What a pity Stephens could not have carried his Whitehall research to its conclusion! His qualifications for the job were perfect: his skill as a working boatbuilder, his background in competitive rowing and sailing both as a sailor and a designer, his knowledge of yachting and his experience as a yachtsman, his achievements as writer, reporter, and historian, and in addition his personal recollection of the New York harbor scene when working Whitehalls were still in use—these taken altogether are pre-eminent qualifications. And for these same reasons, what he did do deserves our particular consideration, even though some of his work is incomplete.

At the outset of the 1930s a stir of interest in the Whitehall boat and early days on the New York waterfront found expression in letters published in the local newspapers. Stephens took a leading part in this exchange. The "race boats" of the early nineteenth century came in for particular attention. The New York *Sun* on March 9, 1934, published a letter by Eugene L. Baptiste of Montclair, N. J., claiming that the race boat, *Knickerbocker*, built by his ancestor, John Baptiste, in 1811, was the first Whitehall rowboat. After winning a notable race by a quarter of a mile against an "English" challenger (apparently a New York boat, but produced by a builder of English extraction), the letter continued, the *Knickerbocker*, painted white with a green gunwale and a gold stripe, was hung for public view in Scudder's Museum from which it was later transferred to the American Museum at Broadway and Ann Street. Also known as Barnum's Museum, the building with all its contents was destroyed by fire in 1865. Incidentally, Stephens as a small boy had visited this museum, but failed to recall seeing this boat.

Other winning race boats by John Baptiste (sometimes Baptis) were the *New York* in 1818 and the *General Lafayette* in 1824, which beat a rival race boat, the *Mapes*, in an historic race.

John Baptiste was succeeded by his son Edward who later sold the business and boatshop at 660 Water Street to a famous builder of metal lifeboats by the name of Raymond. According to claims put forward by the descendants of John Baptiste, his race boats were never beaten in an important race, yet ironically it was the race boat *American Star*, built by Baptiste's arch rival and oft-defeated compet-itor, the "Englishman" Chambers, that the Whitehallers of New York presented to General Lafayette in 1825 during his visit to America, and that Lafayette took back with him to France on his return.

Because the professional boatmen who early in the nineteenth century frequented Whitehall slip at the foot of Whitehall Street and were known as Whitehallers took a prominent part in race boat competition, some have concluded that the working Whitehall used in harbor service was derived from the race boat. Stephens believed that this was not the case. As to which came first, service boats or race boats, Stephens felt certain it was the former, a point on which he proceeded to correct his admirer and collaborator, Captain Charleton L. Smith of Marblehead, who had assumed priority for the race boats in an early piece on Whitehalls published in a Boston newspaper.

To support his view that the service boats came first, Stephens cites evidence for a more or less continuous ferry service between lower Manhattan and the New Jersey shore from at least 1661, and most probably carried on to a large extent, especially in the beginning, in rowboats. While none of the actual boats so used come into clear view earlier than the beginning of the nineteenth century, Stephens assumed that there must have been a gradual evolution from heavy ships' boats. As the city grew, need arose for larger craft capable of transporting horses and horsedrawn vehicles, and for this purpose periaugers came to be used, described by Stephens as large flat boats fitted with two masts and sails.

The first Commodore Vanderbilt, Stephens observed, began life as a skipper of a periauger plying between Staten Island and the Battery. The *Boston Weekly News Letter* of March 18, 1756, has it that one of the Staten Island ferryboats, presumably a periauger, with 13 passengers and three horses, sank between Bedlows and Oyster Island with 11 drowned.

Apparently not all of the early periaugers or pettiaugers were large flat craft fitted with sails. Derived from log dugouts or pirogues, some of these pettiaugers must have been sharp craft and fast, or relatively so, under oars. From the *Boston Weekly News Letter* of May 6, 1756, we learn that a Cape Cod whaleboat with a crew of six on the way to Albany stopped off at Manhattan to race one of the local pettiaugers for a wager of $20, winning with "greatest ease."

These early boats, pettiaugers and the like, have receded into the depths of time, leaving hardly more than their names. Only with the race boats after 1811 or thereabouts and the working harbor-service craft of the Whitehallers and the Battery boatmen from about the same time or a little later do actual boats appear. Certainly by the time we are able to distinguish the race boats and the working boats, they are distinctly different types. The former were clinker planked, the latter carvel. The race boat was nearly flat of sheer, lean, long and narrow in proportion to its over-all length. Thus the *Mapes*, beaten by John Baptiste's *General Lafayette*, was 25 feet over-all, while the *American Star* was slightly less than 27½ feet. The race boat was crewed by a coxswain and four men, each pulling a single oar.

The largest of the working Whitehalls of 19 feet were pulled ordinarily by two pair of 9-foot sculls, although the smaller 17-foot boats used for running lines to the piers were operated at times with only one pair. There were other differences as well.

These two types were not the only pulling boats to be found in New York harbor prior to the Civil War. In a large painting depicting the arrival of the *Great Western* in New York in 1839, Stephens distinguished, besides race boats and working Whitehalls, a pleasure barge with ladies in the stern sheets. In commenting on the annual spring race of the working Whitehalls around Robbins Reef Buoy, the only race in which these boats engaged, Stephens explained that most of the racing about New York at that time was done in shells, gigs, barges, and the "New York working boat," which was between a shell and "a half-outrigged gig."

In a letter written in 1934 to a correspondent who suggested the Whitehall might have originally been a lake boat from Whitehall, N. Y., Stephens is quite definite in rejecting this hypothesis. He explained: "I have seen a great many light rowing boats built on South Street years ago, but those which might be called pleasure boats were distinctly different from the Whitehalls. While the pleasure boats were all lapstrake, the working boats were carvel built; but there was a still greater difference in model. I would attribute the origin of the Whitehall boat to ships boats and similar small craft in use about New York City and not to a model from an inland lake."

Again in 1936 he wrote: "We had in New York fifty years ago many fine light rowing boats similar to the Whitehall boat, but lighter in build and more elaborate in finish—a distinct type."

Elsewhere he explained: "Great numbers of these were sent throughout the country from the New York boatshops, the Whitehall name accompanying them."

Today, almost any small pulling boat with a nearly plumb stem, rounded bilge, and "wine glass" stern is called a "Whitehall," and this is not likely to change. Yet while form is part of it, and an essential part, the main thing is the unique way in which the true Whitehall was framed and put together. No true Whitehall can have the following: clinker planking, an open gunwale, or strip ribs bent in hot after planking is complete. In these respects the working Whitehalls of both New York and Boston seem to have been nearly identical.

The exchange in the newspapers concerning race boats and Whitehalls set Stephens in motion, and he undertook to see if he could locate any of the old boats or anyone who had rowed, or who had built them.

On May 7, 1934, Stephens talked with Ernie Akers, then foreman of the Nevins yard at City Island, who told him that in 1888, when he was 18 years old, he had worked for Tom Blackwell, a boatbuilder in Astoria, building Whitehall boats for junkmen. Some of the boats were sold to Staten Island.

These boats, Akers recalled, were about 19 feet in length, carvel planked of ½" white cedar on frames approximately ¾ inch by ⅞ inch, spaced 9 inches. A top strake of white oak was beveled on its lower edge to lap over a matching beveled edge on the plank below, and was ornamented with a small bead which came just above the lap fastenings. The inside was finished with a foresheets, two rowing thwarts, and a horseshoe bench aft. Flat thole pins about 2½ inches by ⅝ inch were mortised through the gunwale to socket in a steadying cleat below.

Just a year later on May 8, 1935, Stephens spoke with Captain Bill Quigley, last of the Battery boatmen, whom he found on the Battery Wall. Quigley, 73 and retired from the water, had been born at No. 6 State Street and had rowed in the harbor for 55 years. According to his recollection, the large service boats, the same for the Battery boatmen and the Whitehallers, were 19 feet long, confirming Akers. In beam they were 4½ feet and in depth 20 inches. After the large boats went out, the 17-foot boats continued to be used to run lines to the piers. In his recollection of interior detail, including the flat thole pins, Quigley did not differ materially from Akers. Quigley was able to furnish a lead to a surviving boat, but upon investigation this boat was found to be heavily and crudely constructed and hence unrepresentative. The following year Stephens talked with Quigley again, but it seems without learning anything further of any importance.

Toward the end of 1935, after H. I. Chapelle had apparently informed Stephens that Captain Charleton L. Smith of Marblehead was an authority on Whitehalls, Stephens wrote him. Smith lost no time in replying. He greatly admired and respected Stephens and the subject of Whitehalls was dear to him. Besides, he and Stephens had much in common, for Smith was also a fine boatbuilder, a deepwater sailor and a yachtsman, and an author as well: he had published two books of juvenile fiction about adventures at sea and was a frequent contributor on nautical subjects to Boston newspapers. An exchange of letters and information followed, extending over a period of nine months, during which there was some slight give and take, yet remarkable agreement on essentials throughout. It seems clear that working, rowed-on-the-gunwales Whitehalls both at Boston and New

York during the 1870s, the 1880s, and the 1890s were practically identical.

Captain Smith accepted Stephens's correction on the origin of the service Whitehall, that is to say that the working boat had not developed from an earlier race boat, and in consequence Smith left this out of his final article on the Whitehall, the previously mentioned one published in *Rudder* in August, 1943, shortly before his death.

Stephens for his part stated that Smith's account of the method and procedure of Whitehall construction had refreshed his recollection, and he gracefully accepted Smith's correction of timber dimensions previously obtained from Akers.

The method of timbering a Whitehall is worth going into in some detail, for it is unique to the Whitehall, as far as I know, and is one of its most distinctive features. Timbers are set up square with the centerline of the boat in matched pairs, one futtock to a side, before planking starts, so that the carvel strakes can be fitted and fastened to the timbers ahead of time over the same mold or "timber block" shaped to a somewhat greater curvature than that of the sides of the boat. In preparing a pair of timbers to go into the boat, they are straightened out as much as necessary to fit against the ribbands at the station they are to occupy, and they must also be beveled at the bench to fit the fore-and-aft curvature of the sides, for, as previously mentioned, they are always set square with the centerline of the boat. Timbers are also tapered lengthwise. The molded depth of the timber at the head where it jogs into the underside of the gunwale is considerably less than the molded depth at the bottom end or the heel.

Captain Smith, in correcting the uniform ⅞-inch molding dimension which Stephens obtained from Akers, stated that a correctly proportioned timber of standard ¾-inch siding would be molded ¾ inch at the head, but at the heel it would be molded 1⅜ inches. This last dimension I consider to be excessive, except, perhaps, for a very heavily built 20-foot boat.

In the 13-foot Whitehall now at Mystic Seaport, the timbers, which are sided ¾ inch, are molded ⅞ inch at the heel, tapering to a molding of ½ inch under the gunwale, and this is not a lightly built boat by any means, in spite of the fact that it is only 13 feet long.

As Captain Smith explained in his letter of January 3, 1936, to Stephens: "Yes, it was the custom to bend a great many timbers at one steaming, and force them under window sills, work benches or other convenient places, where they wouldn't straighten out. When ready to timber a boat, they shaped one pair of these frames to suit the eye and placed them amidships. Next they straightened out a pair by eye to go half way from the bow. Then the same thing was done half way to the transom. A few ribbands were bent around these few frames, and they shaped the timbers to the ribbands until the boat was all timbered out. Invariably they had a beveled frame with taper from heel to head."

What is not mentioned is that each pair of timbers was riveted through the heels to a natural-crook floor knee, which passed across the top of the keel and was fastened to it. This made an exceptionally strong and neat arrangement. This floor knee, cut out to the deadrise

angle of the boat, extended out 10 or 12 inches on either side of the keel in the midsection of the boat. Thus, in a boat of 4 to 4½ feet in beam, the floor knee extended across half the width of the boat, the center half. This conforms closely to the old standard rule for deadrise in small boats, a rule handed down from the eighteenth century or possibly earlier, namely that the deadrise of the bottom (rise from the dead flat) should be half the beam of the boat.

The very term "deadrise" means a straight rise of bottom or floor extended out from the side of the keel at whatever angle of rise a particular design calls for. In a slack-bilged boat like the working Whitehall, the angle of deadrise is relatively steep. Thus, in the 13-foot Whitehall at Mystic Seaport, the angle of deadrise amidships is 15 degrees, which turns out to be identical with the angle of deadrise for the floorknee pattern found among Stephens's papers. Captain Smith in one of his letters, in commenting on a Whitehall model which seemed to him to have a rather flat sheer, observed, "I never considered a Whitehall very flat; rather they were easy shaped in every way, with a sharp floor, next to no bilge, and a very S-like stern." This is indeed the Whitehall shape, and given the width of beam, the depth amidships, and a floor pattern with the angle of deadrise, the shape of the midsection is predetermined within rather close limits. The curvature from bilge to sheer cannot vary much one way or the other. The boatbuilder's experienced eye can find the happy medium without recourse to thwartship molds.

When Stephens took over the Meredith shop in West New Brighton in 1881, he found, according to his letter to C. G. Davis, March 8, "a timber block for bending the frames, molds for the stem, forward rabbet, transom and after deadwood, and odd parts," but no thwartship, or section, molds. Assuming that there had been thwartship molds originally, he concluded that Meredith's son-in-law must have taken them. But why only these without the rest of the molds?

All through the intervening years Stephens had retained the Billy English molds, as he explained in writing to Captain Smith on August 9, 1936. "I have . . . the stem mould, rabbet mould, after deadwood and timber block for the 19 foot boat; also a complete stem ready for the apron, and other moulds for the 17 foot boat. I have no thwartship moulds. If there were any, there were probably three. What I lack to plot from these are three or four breadths at the gunwale and the rise of the dead flat; of course the timber block shows over bending."

The foregoing is from his last letter to Smith, at least the last that we have. Three years later in replying to an inquiry from the West Coast asking about progress in his investigation of the Whitehall, he explained that there is much in this connection that he would like to do, but that so far he had been unable to go farther. His study of yachting history was taking most of his time. Stephens was then 85.

My surmise is that Stephens never quite gave up the idea of sometime completing his work of Whitehall restoration. I would guess that subsequently in going over the Meredith molds, and in particular the "odd pieces" mentioned in his letter to Davis, he discovered the floor knee, or at least came fully to realize its significance, as he had not previously.

With the angle of deadrise obtained from this knee, together with the approximate beam, which he had, and the depth amidships, a thwartships mold was hardly necessary. Being aware of the importance of this piece for a future reconstruction of the working Whitehall, Stephens traced its shape, marked it for identification, and placed the pattern among his papers.

BOATS SIMILAR TO THE WHITEHALL

There are so many small boats, similar in some respects and different in others, which have been called Whitehalls, that in discussing them complete confusion reigns unless there is some established and recognized norm to which they can be related and compared. While it is common and convenient to use the term, Whitehall, when describing a boat, it is often inaccurate and misleading to do so, for many variations of the type have appeared at different times and in different places.

Since boats bearing the Whitehall name first came into view, there has been considerable evolutionary change. This development presents us with the problem of determining or deciding what constitutes the true Whitehall, the Whitehall norm, so to speak.

Shall it be the early Whitehall as built in New York, or the later model developed in Boston, or a composite of the two, with possibly the inclusion of features from other sources as well? And if we should decide on working out a composite norm, by what standard or procedure should we attempt to do this? We know definitely, and precisely, and in detail what the Boston Whitehall was like, since two authentic models are available for study at Mystic Seaport. For me the Whitehall type attained the summit of its development in the classic Boston boat, which justifies taking it as the "norm" for comparing and classifying other boats with Whitehall characteristics to a greater or lesser degree.

In my judgment the ultimate Whitehall is exemplified by the fancy 16-foot 9-inch Boston

This large, heavily built boat, photographed in Falmouth Foreside, Maine, in 1952, shows a Whitehall influence. Neither the cast bronze thwart knees nor the small half-round finishing off the bottom edge of the top strake are typical of the classic Whitehall.

An excellent pulling boat similar to a Whitehall. Unlike the classic Whitehall, she has a clinker build, flat, closely spaced bent ribs, and a transom without a wine-glass reverse curve. This boat is also beamier than the true Whitehall and is flatter in her floors.

Star of Noank, *which is a replica of* Favorite, *a 11'9" strip-built boat of Whitehall lines built somewhere east of Boston about 1900.* Favorite *is now in the small craft collection at Mystic Seaport.*

Whitehall formerly belonging to E. Wm. Bailey of Amesbury, and now at Mystic Seaport. It is to be understood, then, that henceforth when I use the term "Whitehall," it is the Boston Whitehall which I have in mind, and to which I make reference.

One small pulling boat often taken to be a Whitehall is the *Favorite*, which first came to Mystic Seaport on loan more than a quarter of a century ago. In 1951 when her owner, Captain Elwell B. Thomas of Stonington, Connecticut, finally donated her to the Museum, he stated he believed she had been built somewhere east of Boston "about 50 years ago," bringing her within the period of Whitehall dominance. Quite small for a Whitehall, in fact only 11 feet 9 inches overall, *Favorite*'s lines are basically Whitehall; her construction is different, however, for she is strip-built. This is most unusual, both in consideration of her lines and from the standpoint of her size.

In 1966, Robert Bruce Small, crew coach at South Kent School, South Kent, Connecticut, secured lines and construction details from Mystic Seaport and had a replica of this boat built for his personal use, except that the new boat was strip-built entirely of mahogany, which finished bright inside gives an unusually handsome appearance. *Star of Noank*, as she was named, has proved to be a most satisfactory and "pleasurable" craft, according to her owner.

Let him explain in his own words:

She handles quite well. In flat water she will carry at one stroke per minute, and she will cruise a mile in twenty minutes (with moderate effort). For a boat of her size, she has good cruising range, a maximum of five miles in Fishers Island Sound from Groton Long Point. She has some shortcomings (but what boat doesn't?). Mainly she is quite quick in her motion as one moves about aboard her. I suspect that this quickness of motion could be smoothed out by the addition of 50 to 75 pounds of ballast. Surprisingly enough, she tows quite well at moderate speeds and is a pretty good boat in a sea. . . . Although *Favorite* is not a true Whitehall, I think she would provide a good basis for a 14' pulling boat. I would retain her tumble home aft—it is a handsome line—and I would retain her unique keel/skeg arrangement with slight modification. However, I think she would be improved by having slightly less deadrise amidships, a slightly sharper entry, and more flare forward to increase her stability. Finally, I think I would want a slightly deeper forefoot to keep her on course in

A 15½-footer belonging to Bob Rose of Lake Linden, Michigan. She is not a true Whitehall but resembles one in certain respects, such as her narrow beam of 44 inches. It appears that the boat does not have the solid deadwood aft of a true Whitehall; rather it is planked down to the bottom of the keel, producing "hollow garboards," an excellent method of building but not Whitehall construction. The boat may have been built around 1900.

This pretty 12-foot yacht tender, though not a Whitehall, shows a definite Whitehall influence. She was built by by Charles Lawton in his 90th year (1948) and is an example of the fine craftmanship of the old-time builders.

quartering head wind. I know these ideas would complicate building problems and increase costs; but, I believe, the end result would be worth it.

For individual enjoyment of rowing and the beneficial effects of this wholesome exercise (at least the equal of jogging) several of the traditional workboat pulling types are particularly well suited, namely dories, wherries, peapods, guideboats, Rangeley boats, a wide selection of skiffs, and, of course, the Whitehall. It is this latter type of rowing involving adaptations of our traditional small pulling workboats which especially needs to be encouraged, but first off suitable boats must be more easily available than they now are. So on to the construction of a 17-foot Whitehall.

22

A Whitehall Pulling Boat

······•······

Whitehalls were built from 12 to 20 feet long. Some of the larger ones intended for sailing were quite beamy and were fitted with centerboards. But the best of the Whitehalls and the most typical were 17 to 18 feet long. If built shorter than this, they tended to lose their good qualities, so that the very short ones of 12 and 13 feet were somewhat degenerate. It is often forgotten, now, what an important factor length is for the best performance of small craft to be driven at moderate speeds. The longer boat moves easier through the water and is more seaworthy than the shorter one.

Most yacht tenders are too short to row really well or to take much weather. Francis Herreshoff has stated that prior to 1890 his father modeled his yacht tenders on the Whitehall, as was the common practice in that period. This boat, he recalls, rowed easily when loaded, but towed poorly and rated only fair as a sea boat. Later N. G. Herreshoff discarded this Whitehall-derived model for improved tender models he worked out himself. The Lawley tender, it should be noted, though of superb construction, remained close to its Whitehall ancestry, and is generally acknowledged by those who have used both kinds to have been inferior in performance to the later Herreshoff models.

Now this might seem a poor recommendation for the Whitehall boat, but the point is that

the model suffers greatly when shortened to yacht-tender length, and should not be judged in this abbreviated length. But 70 or 80 years ago, the reputation of the larger Whitehalls was so pre-eminent and good boatbuilders were so thoroughly steeped in the habits of Whitehall construction, that when they built yacht tenders, these naturally took shape as miniature Whitehalls. And, as has been noted, even the 12-foot and 13-foot Whitehalls did pull very easily, far easier than most of the scurvy tubs that pass for rowboats today. This was due in large measure to the fine entrance and clean delivery of these boats, and because the length of the load waterline was stretched to the absolute limit by making the stem plumb and the forefoot deep and sharp. The plumb stem is the main reason why they did not tow well. The deep forefoot would bite into the seas, causing the boat to yaw.

As for the larger Whitehall, the true exemplars of the type, these are by no means obsolete, and their suitability for modern use will bear investigation. For those who want a boat of dual utility, that will give superior performance for both rowing and sailing, the Whitehall is as good as there is. For lake fishing, the 17- or 18-foot Whitehall powered with a small air-cooled inboard engine should prove a natural. The model drives easily and quietly. Moving at a good turn of speed or throttled

SEVENTEEN FOOT WHITEHALL
MOULDED BEAM 53½ INCHES.
INSIDE DEPTH AMIDSHIPS 19½".
INNER TUCK UP 9¾".

John GARDNER, 1953.

down to a crawl, this hull should be comfortable, stable, and completely seaworthy.

Every good boat is a compromise—or more accurately, many compromises. Desired qualities often clash. A tender broad as a sawed-off molasses puncheon would be very buoyant and steady to step in and out of, but try to row it. On the other hand, the slack-bilged splinter that slips along without a ripple may need its oars in the water to keep it right-side up. Length in a small boat is always a prime virtue, and it is a great harmonizer of conflicting elements. In the 17-foot or 18-foot Whitehall there is an excellent reconciliation of the diverse qualities needed to make a good boat. Its long waterlines combine a fine, sharp entrance and a clean, tapering delivery. There is no drag aft, even when the boat is deeply loaded. The upper works forward have sufficient fullness and flare to keep her head above the seas and to turn these outboard.

A moderate amount of deadrise eases the bilge but does not permit the boat to drop so deep as to preclude passage and landing in shallow water. Without bunching, the after quarters are buoyant enough to give steady bearing and a firm seat on the water. The small, high, heart-shaped transom affords ample room in the stern sheets, while allowing a stern shape nearly equal in weatherly qualities to the double-ended boat of comparable capacity, and permitting a saving, over the double-ended boat, of at least a couple of feet in overall length.

THE LINES

The lines of the 17-foot model shown here embody a lot of research and comparison of data from several sources. I think that the resulting lines are fairly typical of the larger Whitehalls, somewhat an average of the type as built in Boston and the vicinity. Of course with any boat built as extensively as the Whitehalls, there was bound to be a lot of variation. No doubt if we had the data, the step-by-step evolution of

SEVENTEEN FOOT WHITEHALL BOAT

	STATIONS	Bow	1	2	3	4	5	6	7	8	9	TRANS
HEIGHTS ABOVE BASE	SHEER	2-4-4	2-3-3	2-0-5	1-10-4	1-9-3	1-8-7	1-9-1	1-9-7	1-11-2	2-0-1	2-1-3
	BUT. 18"	~	~	~	0-10-1	0-7-1	0-6-4	0-7-0	0-9-5	1-3-5	~	~
	BUT. 12"	~	~	0-10-6	0-5-6	0-4-6	0-4-4	0-4-7	0-6-6	0-11-4	1-3-2	1-7-3
	BUT. 6"	~	1-8-3	0-4-5	0-3-3	0-3-0	0-3-0	0-3-1	0-4-1	0-7-3	0-11-0	1-3-6
	INNER RAB	~	0-2-0	0-1-6	0-1-6	0-1-6	0-1-6	0-1-6	0-1-6	0-3-0	0-5-5	0-9-6
HALF BREADTHS	SHEER	0-0-7	0-7-4	1-5-7	1-11-4	2-2-0	2-2-6	2-2-1	2-0-0	1-7-7	1-5-1	1-2-0
	W.L. 18" UP	0-0-7	0-5-5	1-3-4	1-10-2	2-1-3	2-2-5	2-2-1	1-11-7	1-7-3	1-3-5	0-9-5
	W.L. 15" UP	0-0-7	0-4-7	1-2-3	1-9-1	2-0-5	2-2-1	2-1-5	1-11-1	1-5-3	0-11-5	0-4-7
	W.L. 12" UP	0-0-7	0-4-1	1-0-7	1-7-4	1-11-2	2-0-7	2-0-4	1-9-3	1-0-7	0-7-1	0-2-0
	W.L. 9" UP	0-0-7	0-3-2	0-10-5	1-4-7	1-8-5	1-10-3	1-9-7	1-5-0	0-8-2	0-3-7	0-0-7
	W.L. 6" UP	0-0-7	0-2-3	0-7-4	1-0-4	1-3-6	1-4-7	1-3-6	0-10-3	0-4-2	0-1-2	0-0-7
	INNER RAB.	0-0-7	0-0-7	0-0-7	0-0-7	0-0-7	0-0-7	0-0-7	0-0-7	0-0-7	0-0-7	0-0-7
DIAGS	DIAG. A	~	0-6-6	1-4-5	1-10-6	2-2-4	2-3-5	2-3-2	2-0-6	1-8-1	1-4-5	1-0-4
	DIAG. B	~	0-5-5	1-2-1	1-7-3	1-10-0	1-11-1	1-10-4	1-7-4	1-2-0	0-10-2	0-6-0
	DIAG. C	~	0-4-0	0-10-2	1-1-2	1-2-4	1-2-6	1-2-1	1-0-0	0-7-7	0-5-0	0-1-5

STATION 1 TO INNER RAB STEM	6" W.L.	9" W.L.	12" W.L	15" W.L.	18" W.L.	SHEER
	0-7-3	0-8-6	0-9-1	0-9-3	0-9-5	0-10-0

STERN RAKE 0-1-5 MEASURED ON BASE LINE FR'D OF STA. 10.
STATIONS 1 TO 8 SPACED 2'. STATIONS 8 TO 10 SPACED 1 FT.
WATER LINES SPACED 3". BUTTOCKS SPACED 6".
BASE LINE BOTTOM OF KEEL. LINES TO INSIDE OF PLANK.
DIAGONAL "A" UP 2', OUT 2'6" ON 12" W.L. DIAGONAL "B"
UP 18", OUT 18" ON 9" W.L. DIAGONAL "C" UP 12", OUT
1'9" ON BASE LINE. OFFSETS IN FEET, INCHES & EIGHTHS.

the type could be traced. There would be superior Whitehalls, and some not so good, but in the long run the model would strike a general average—a run-of-the-mill Whitehall that some scores of ordinarily competent journeymen boatbuilders by long practice could build with their eyes closed, if need be.

The design for this 17-foot Whitehall is based on the data and molds, previously mentioned, given me by Charles Lawton before he died. The molds included a mold for his Whitehall transom and the rabbet mold for the deadwood and tuck. He also gave me a sketch of the lines that he drew about 1940 for a 13-foot "fancy Whitehall." This sketch was never faired thoroughly and shows the influence of his many years of building yacht tenders.

For the 17-foot Whitehall I have taken the transom shape and size, also the height of the tuck and sweep of the after rabbet, almost exactly from Lawton's molds. Checking, I have found that this transom is very close, in fact surprisingly so, to the transom shown by Chapelle in his drawing of the lines of a 16-foot

Boston Whitehall as taken off by Albert Green in 1876. The rise of the after rabbet to the tuck, following Lawton's mold, is flatter and more gradual than the curve shown in Greens' lines, which in my judgment is rather too quick to plank easily.

For over-all depth and beam, I have worked within the limits established by the old Boston Boat Clubs for racing Whitehall workboats. These were given by the late Captain Charleton L. Smith in his article on the Whitehall boat in *Rudder* for August, 1943—overall length between 17 and 20 feet, beam not less than 4 feet, depth not less than 19 inches, rowed on the gunwale, and weighing not less than 265 pounds. I have followed the midsection shape shown by Captain Smith in his specimen lines, which seems a good average for the Whitehall type.

While it is true that Lawton's lines for his fancy Whitehall do not show the deadrise as being straight, still he often told me that the old rule for the Whitehall was a straight deadrise amidships for half the width of the boat, and that is the way I have made it in my lines.

Another feature mentioned as characteristic by Lawton was considerable flare of the topsides forward, sometimes giving a slight reverse curve to the shape of the first set of frames. But most Whitehall lines I have examined get ample flare forward without such reverse. I have avoided this reverse as it tends to put a difficult twist in the top planks.

Whitehall construction, now nearly unknown and lost to this generation of boatbuilders, combined strength and lightness with numerous shortcuts that developed during the years that the Whitehall was mass-produced by the hundreds if not the thousands. The amateur builder will do well to adopt, at times, certain of the Whitehall methods, especially that of shaping and beveling the timbers in pairs after they have previously been steam-bent and have cooled, using these timbers as secondary molds, and planking on them directly.

THE FOUNDATION

Whitehall construction was a method worked out by scores of smart builders over many years under exacting competition. It was simplified and highly standardized. There was very little that was not thought of or tried out. All legitimate shortcuts were adopted but without sacrifice of quality. Framed with white oak, planked with northern white cedar, and copper fastened throughout, the Whitehall was tops.

Although occasional laydowns must have been made, the practiced builder did not generally bother with offsets. He had the tune in his head, so to speak. In ordering a new boat, it was sufficient to specify a few key dimensions—the LOA, beam, depth amidship, height of tuck, and possibly width of transom and amount of sheer. (The tuck is the point where the garboard, transom, and sternpost come together.)

From standard molds of thin pine, the stem, transom, deadwood, and other curved members would be marked out and cut to shape. For example, a single transom mold, cut to the contour of one of the symmetrical halves of a standard transom would suffice to lay out a Whitehall transom of any desired size, the mold being adjusted on the rough stock according to the required depth and width. The stem rabbet and also the curve of the rabbet aft along the deadwood were marked out from standard rabbet molds that were moved a little this way or that to suit the builder's eye and the dimensions of the particular boat under construction. It should be noted in this connection that even a considerable difference in length did not change the sectional dimensions much, so that a couple of additional feet in length overall might not mean more than an extra inch of depth and two or three extra inches of beam.

The backbone of the boat, sometimes called the "foundation" was all of the best white or "yankee" oak. The members that comprise it— including the apron and forefoot, the keel, deadwood, stern post, and transom—were fastened together and secured right-side up on a stout horse made of a wide, straight, two-inch plank set on edge. The keel of the Whitehall is perfectly straight and was laid level about two feet off the floor to bring the boat to a convenient height for working. The stem and sternpost were plumbed and the transom was horned to a perfect right angle with the longitudinal centerline. Staylathes tacked to the walls of the shop and to the rafters secured these members in position.

The Boston Whitehalls had a "scantling" keel, that is, a straight strip uniform in section varying from 1½ inches to 1¾ inches square. Aft, the sternpost and deadwood stood on top of it, and forward, the keel met the stem and was reinforced by an extension of the forefoot which ran back on top of the keel for 2 feet and sometimes more.

Between the forefoot and deadwood there was no keel batten or anything to form a back rabbet for the garboards, so that the cross floors connecting the butts of the ribs rested directly on top of the keel and were fastened to it. In this midsection the top corners of the keel were beveled so the square edge of the garboard would fit perfectly snug with only a slight caulking seam on the outside.

Of course the stem, forefoot, and deadwood were rabbeted in the conventional way. Most of this was cut out at the bench, except that some wood was frequently left in the stem rabbet to enable adjustment there after the frames were raised and faired as insurance for getting a perfect fit for the garboards and hood ends. Rabbets were simple as pie for the practiced professional. But the amateur and occasional builder will do well to go slowly and carefully here, and take the greatest pains, even laying out in pencil numerous full-sized sections of the rabbet to cut from.

The old builders commonly used only one section mold, called a "shadow." This was made to the inside shape of the midsection. The shadow method, by the way, is still employed occasionally by older builders, as I observed in 1952 in the Whalen Brothers shop in Calais, Maine. It requires special skill, however, and is not recommended for beginners, who should make separate molds for each section in their laydown.

The shadow was set in place and carefully plumbed and horned, and then secured. Around it were sprung fairing battens, the same thickness as the plank (½-inch pine). These battens were put on symmetrically in pairs, running from the stem rabbet to the transom. Their lay determined the shape of the boat, and judgement and a sure eye were required to spring them properly. It was a quick method, but the amateur need not despair. With multiple molds made from a carefully faired lay-down, he can achieve the same results, but with a much greater expenditure of time.

After the battens are on comes timbering. The ribs are put in cold in fitted pairs, shaped and beveled identically so that both sides of the boat will be the same. Timbers are of white oak, preferably selected from the butts of young, fast-growing trees that yield heavy wood and wide grain. The timber blanks are steam-bent to

Diagram labels:

SHEER PLANK ⅝" OAK LAPPED 1" ON BINDER STRAKE.

TRANSOM ⅞" OAK.

CEDAR PLANK BACKED OUT TO CURVES. ½" FINISHED THICKNESS.

DEADWOOD LET INTO STERNPOST.
STERN POST LET INTO KEEL.

BASE LINE

STERN POST

LIMBER

#16 - 2½" BRONZE W. SCREW

FLUSH RIVETS

STOP WATER

5/16 BRONZE DRIFTS

BASE LINE

STATION 9

INCHES AND EIGHTHS

TRANSOM AND DEADWOOD 17 FOOT WHITEHALL BOAT

¾" OAK TIMBERS MOULDED WIDER AT BUTT.

FLOORS TO TIMBERS 10D COPPER WIRE NAILS STAGGERED AND RIVETED OVER BURRS.

1¾" OAK STERNPOST, DEADWOOD, AND KEEL TAPERED.

STA 9

5/16 BRONZE BOLTS

FLOORS TO DEADWOOD #12 - 2½" BR. WOOD SCREWS.

KEEL TO DEADWOOD #16 BR. W. SCREWS BETWEEN BOLTS.

STA 8

9" WATER LINE

FLOORS ⅞" OAK

3" SQUARES

OUTER RABBET   INNER RABBET

DEADWOOD

KEEL

STOPWATER

BASE LINE

STA 7

STA 8

shape around forms and allowed to dry out for several days or weeks. They are given a little more bend than is required, for they can always be straightened out a trifle, if necessary, while it is impossible to give them more bend once they are cool and set. The shape from station to station does not change radically, making it possible to get along with only a few different bending forms for the entire boat. One of the tricks is to leave the timber blanks quite a bit longer at either end than will be needed. When cool and set, the bends can be adjusted lengthwise to get just the right curve.

The blanks should be about 1¾ inches wide, so a pair of timbers of ¾-inch siding can be split out of them on the circular saw, after the bend is in. Also, allowance in thickness should be made for a heavier butt, which is sometimes molded 1⅛ inches where it is riveted to the floor. Extra wood must also be allowed for bevels, which are put on at the bench with plane and spokeshave as the frame is tried in place against the ribbands, from time to time, until it lies flat and true.

The inside of the timbers should be beveled parallel to the outside, giving a diamond-shaped cross-section for the frames toward the ends of

the boat. Each pair of timbers is joined together at the butts by an oak floor, which is screwed to the keel. The ribs are riveted to the floor with ten-penny copper nails. Amidships, the floors will extend on either side of the keel 10 to 12 inches, conforming to the pitch of the deadrise, which is straight in the Whitehall for about half the width of the boat. Thus, these floors will have something of a flattened vee shape, so that it is best for strength to get them out of crooked live-edge boards with a run of grain conforming somewhat to this shape.

In some of the shorter, lighter Whitehalls, the floors were omitted on top of the forefoot and deadwood, and the frames that ended here were notched rather deeply into these members and nailed securely. While this is a neat, easy method, cross floors are stronger, and I have indicated these for the 17-foot model except for the two forward sets of frames.

The floors, which are sided ⅞ inch, are to be fastened to the keel with two screws far enough apart to allow a ⅜-inch limber to be cut between them out of the bottom of the floor. Fore and aft where the lower ends of the ribs come against the siding of the forefoot and the deadwood, respectively, their tips are snipped off to provide limbers. Limbers are most important so that the boat can drain the entire length of its bottom.

When the ribs and floors are all beveled and in and fastened securely, the boat is ready for planking. But before going on to that stage, it is necessary to revert to some details that need more explanation.

When possible, a knee from hackmatack or white oak should be used for the stem; such natural knees were much used in the best of the old boats. Lacking a knee, there is an excellent substitute construction in which parts of a pieced stem are cut out of oak plank. Of course, a curved plank with a swirling grain should be selected, especially for the end of the forefoot that fastens on to the bottom of the fore part of the stem. This method of framing a stem, as shown in the detail drawing, was widely used in Boston shops in the late nineteenth century for plumb-stemmed small craft, including St. Lawrence River skiffs and the double-ended Adirondack, popular for rowing on the Charles in the 1890s and sometimes mistaken, today, for a variety of peapod. The extra siding of the tapered apron is to give more bearing in the rabbet for the hood ends, as the topsides get fuller at the bow. The apron is let in as far as the apex line of the rabbet for convenience in cutting the rabbet. The forefoot is made to run back on top of the keel for reinforcement and to provide a back-rabbet for the forward ends of the garboards.

In the past, the stem assembly was fastened with bolts or riveted drifts. It can just as well be fastened with heavy bronze screws—No. 16s or No. 18s—and with several advantages. Properly put in, screws pull up very tightly. They do not stick out like bolts and do not require boring through and plugging the outer edge of the stem, which is thinned down to ⅜ inch. Waterproof glue can also be used to advantage on the stem joints, but it must genuinely waterproof and not merely "water resistant." It may be advantageous to bolt the keel to the forefoot. Five-sixteenths inch diameter bronze carriage bolts are suitable.

Wherever the rabbet crosses a joint, as

between the keel and forefoot, or deadwood and sternpost, a stopwater must be put in to prevent leakage. These round, pine plugs that run at right angles through the joint from side to side, must fit tightly, and the holes for them should be bored just inside the outer line of the rabbet so that the caulking in the garboard seam bears firmly on them. The most common mistake is to bore the hole too far inside the rabbet, where the caulking cannot reach the stopwater, allowing the water to seep in between. Four ⅜-inch stopwaters are called for, as indicated.

Five-sixteenth-inch diameter bronze bolts are proposed for the deadwood, and bronze drifts of the same diameter should be used to secure the lower end of the stern post. It is important that the members that join the stern-post be let in to one another as shown in the detail. Waterproof glue is also desirable here. True, the old builders had neither waterproof glue nor bronze screws, but as good mechanics who in their day prided themselves on being up-and-coming and up-to-date, they would certainly have adopted both screws and glue had they been available.

It might seem that there is not enough fastening in the stern assembly, so it may be pointed out that the after end will become amply strong and rigid when the boat is complete, that is, when the plank are screwed to the transom, the gunwales and their connecting knees riveted to the transom, and the stern bench is in place and secured to the sternpost and to the after frames. The stern bench is not merely a place to sit. It is also a bracing member that ties the entire stern together, imparting great rigidity to the end of the boat when properly fastened in.

There is a chance that the after end of the keel could split where it is bored for the drifts that pass up into the sternpost. For reinforcement, three flush rivets are shown. A better, but more expensive device would be a bronze casting let in flush to cover the end of the keel and to run partway up the sternpost. In case a rudder were to be shipped, a socket might be provided in this casting for the bottom pintle.

To secure the floors to the keel, I settled on

No. 12 bronze screws, but not without some misgivings. Bronze screws, even Everdur, do not last too well in damp oak. Nor is a large screw desirable, as boring for it could unduly weaken the narrow floors. Copper nails would loosen. Through rivets would be very long, indeed. Perhaps 2½ or 2¾-inch hot-dipped galvanized blunt-point boat nails would be the strongest and most lasting fastenings here—two to a floor and toed in to pull against each other.

Comparing the scantlings of this 17-footer with that of an original 13-foot Whitehall, differences will be found that might seem to anyone other than a boatbuilder too slight to notice. Yet I have had to argue with myself to justify each of these increases, and it may be that this boat is slightly on the heavy side. This is not such a bad fault in a 17-foot boat that can stand a little extra weight; it is not intended to be tossed around like a light tender.

Compared to a 13-footer, the siding of the stem, keel, deadwood, and sternpost has been increased from 1½ to 1¾ inches. The keel is molded ¼ inch deeper. The transom thickness has been increased from ¾ inch to ⅞ inch. The timbers are spaced on 9-inch centers instead of 9½-inch, and, while their siding of ¾ inch has not been changed, they are molded heavier at the butt and ⅛ inch heavier at the gunwale. The floors have been increased from ¾ inch by 1 inch to ⅞ inch by 1¼ inches. The cedar planking is ½ inch finished, and the oak sheer strake ⁹⁄₁₆ inch. The gunwales will be about ⅛ wider and thicker all around, with corresponding increases in the breasthook and interior knees. While ship carpenters might not have needed divisions less than 8ths marked on their rules, as old Tom Hines used to say, your builder of small boats was a different breed of cat who was very fussy over 16th and even 32nds.

PLANKING

Whitehall planking shows a few special features, otherwise standard planking methods are used. It might prove helpful to run through the main planking operations as used by pro-

fessionals for the Whitehall. These operations, which apply to smooth-seam boats, even upwards of 40 feet, are as follows:

1. *Lining*, which is dividing up the hull surface and lining out fair, uniform plank shapes of desirable width and taper.

2. *Spiling*, which is picking up the plank shapes from the curved surface of the hull and laying them out flat on the planking stock.

3. *Getting Out*, which is sawing out the plank to shape, planing the edges true and to the line, and beveling them, and backing out, that is, planing the back of the plank hollow to fit the curve of the ribs.

4. *Hanging*, which is bending, setting down, and fastening the plank in place.

After these four steps, the planked hull is planed smooth, caulked, scraped, and sanded.

And now, a few special features of Whitehall planking:

When the ribbands are spaced and bent on prior to timbering, the position of the binding plank is determined and a space is left for it so it can be put on without disturbing any ribbands. The binding plank, or "binder," which is the plank below the sheer plank, is the first to go on. This is required because the sheer plank laps over it exactly as if the boat were clinker built. The sheer plank in this boat is ⁹⁄₁₆-inch oak, lapped 1¼ inches and chamfered to ¼ inch on the lap edge, which is finished in all true Boston Whitehalls with a shallow ¼-inch bead for appearance. Riveted up solid, this heavy, lapped sheer plank is the staunchest of construction.

Next, after the binder and the sheer planks are on, the two planks directly below them are hung and fastened. At this point in Whitehall construction, planking is interrupted, and the builder proceeds to install gunwales, breast hook, risers, thwarts, bench, knees, and all interior work. The boat, being right-side-up, is in a convenient position for this work—chips and shavings can fall through the unplanked bottom—and the boat is made rigid by this interior work, so that when it is turned over to get at the bottom, it does not go out of shape.

This interior work completed, the boat is removed from its "landing," that is, the heavy

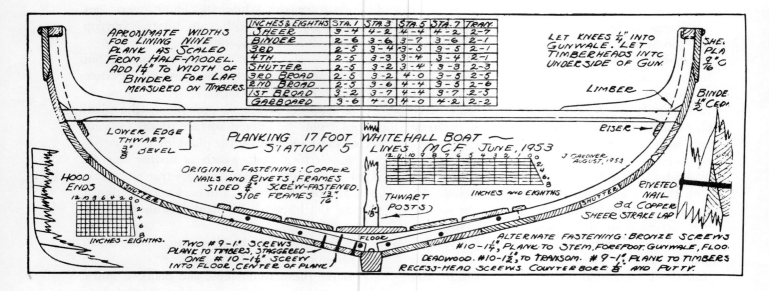

INCHES & EIGHTHS	STA. 1	STA. 3	STA. 5	STA. 7	TRAN.
SHEER	3-4	4-2	4-4	4-2	2-7
BINDER	2-6	3-6	3-7	3-6	2-1
3RD	2-5	3-4	3-5	3-5	2-1
4TH	2-5	3-3	3-4	3-4	2-1
SHUTTER	2-5	3-2	3-4	3-3	2-3
3RD BROAD	2-5	3-2	4-0	3-5	2-5
2ND BROAD	2-5	3-6	4-4	3-5	2-6
1ST BROAD	3-2	3-7	4-4	3-7	2-5
GARBOARD	3-6	4-0	4-0	4-2	2-2

plank set edgewise under the keel, and is turned bottom up on two horses of convenient height. Planking is resumed, starting with the garboards. In this particular boat, three broads will follow them, and finally the shutter at the turn of the bilge will finish the job. Of course plank is always hung and fastened in symmetrical strakes, so that one side is never more than one plank ahead of the other.

Originally, copper nails and rivets were used in plank fastening, but I believe that bronze screws properly selected for size and correctly put in would be just as strong and lasting, would pull tighter, and are certainly easier and quicker to use. In this type of construction it is essential to calculate the size of the fastenings very precisely, for the best of woodwork is to no avail when a boat gets "nailsick." In case screws are used, it might be on the safe side to make the timbers slightly heavier, say $13/16$ inch instead of $3/4$ inch.

Even if screws are to be used, it is perhaps best to rivet the sheer strake lap with 8-penny nails, heads set flush as I have shown. This is strong and looks neat with the top strake bright, as is proper for the Whitehall. Opinion may differ as to the size of screws, but for plank to timbers I would choose No. 9, 1 inch long. These would be set below the finished surface $1/8$ inch and puttied, which means they would ex-

tend $5/8$ inch into the white oak timbers.

The holes should be bored exactly the right size, as experimentally determined, to give the threads maximum grip, but not to strain the screw when driving or split the timbers. Lubricate the screws with soap. I prefer putty instead of bungs, because bungs would have to be $3/8$ inch in diameter, which requires going too deeply into $1/2$-inch plank to make the bung secure. As the boat is to be painted, the appearance of putty or wood bungs is all the same.

For planking to stem, forefoot, gunwales, thwart knees, floors, deadwood, and all other places where there is plenty of wood in the backing member, a slightly larger screw is desirable, that is a No. 10 in lengths of $1\frac{1}{8}$ inches and $1\frac{1}{4}$ inches. For the plank ends on the transom, a No. 10, $1\frac{1}{2}$ inches should be used, because the screw will be going into end-grain wood. Bronze is the only acceptable kind of screw. Brass is too weak, and galvanized screws do not hold well in small sizes because of their inferior threads. The recessed-head screw is far superior to any other kind, both for driving and for appearance.

Nine plank to a side are best for this boat. Eight plank would do, but with 10 plank the hood ends would be too narrow. Plank should be lined in fair, sweeping curves, as straight as possible. For this a lining batten is required. This is a straight, uniform strip of wood, longer than the boat, that will take a fair curve when bent edgewise. White pine is the best wood for such a batten, which for this boat would be ⅜ inch thick by about 1¾ inches wide.

For lining, consider the hull shape of a boat like the Whitehall in two sections—the first section is the topsides down to a fair sweep running along the turn of the bilge, which is obtained by tacking the lining batten on the timbers in an easy, natural position, and the second section is the bottom. Divide up the topsides so the plank will line out to be as straight and uniform as possible, except that the sheer plank is made somewhat wider both for strength and appearance. For the bottom, the planks can be wider than those in the topside, as the term "broads" indicates.

Try to manage the lining of the broads so as to avoid excessive curves; being out of sight, the shape does not matter so much as in the topsides. In this boat run both ends of the garboard up as high as possible without "fishtailing" the plank—a fishtailed plank is one wider at the ends than in the center. Keeping up the ends of the garboard will tend to straighten out the broads. Besides, upsweeping plank ends, so long as they are not overdone, are desirable for appearance. When the hood ends sag, especially in a full-ended boat, an ugly, drooping condition results. This is known as "moose shoulders" down Nova Scotia way. (For more details on battens and spiling, see the Appendix.)

Now on to getting out the plank: After the planks are roughed out to shape by saw, their edges are jointed with the plane exactly to the lines. Some put on the edge bevels next, and back out last to fit the curve of the ribs. For plank as thin as ½ inch, and for a boat of the size and curvature of this 17-foot Whitehall, the old builders often backed out the plank before beveling, hollowing them exactly to templates of thin wood marked against the ribs. For hollowing, a couple of backing-out planes are needed, that is, wooden smoothing planes with slightly convex soles and irons ground to suit. Too much curve in the bottoms of the planes makes it difficult to do an exact job.

After the planks were backed out, the edges are beveled. To get the correct bevel, which increases, a small planker's square with a tongue about 1 inch long (see drawing) is used. This is held against the inside of the hollow, the angle of the blade of the square indicating the amount to be planed off the side edge of the plank. In this way the bevel is divided between the two abutting planks, which is neater construction and better for caulking than leaving one plank edge square and putting all the bevel on the other.

On a boat like this, the planks should form a perfectly tight seam on the inside, and should open just enough on the outside to permit a very thin thread of wicking to be rolled in. Some open the seam slightly after the boat is planked by plowing it with a thin, sharp, flat fid of lignum vitae. Another way is to burnish or compress the outer edges of the plank, before the plank is hung, by rubbing them firmly lengthwise with the hammer handle. After the wicking has been rolled into such seams and primed with thin paint, they may be sponged with hot water, and they will close tightly around the cotton.

This boat is a slack-bilged model that will take plank easily. It may be necessary to soften a couple of feet on the fore ends of the garboard and broads to get them to twist into place, but steaming is not necessary. To make the hood ends pliable, a teakettle of boiling water is sufficient. Wrap the end of the plank in some old woolen rags to hold the heat and soak with hot water, letting the rag-wrapped plank set a while to soften.

Start hanging the plank by clamping the hood end securely into the stem rabbet. Wrap the plank around the timbers firmly and carefully. Don't jump it. Use plenty of clamps, sets, wedges, and whatever else is necessary to get the plank down snugly and tightly throughout. A way positively guaranteed to split a plank is to try to pull it into place with its fastenings. In thin planks like these, planks and timbers must be wood-to-wood before any fastening is attempted. If a seam does not close up properly, by all means take the plank off and fix it. As has

Though classic Whitehalls were carvel planked, lapstrake versions have been built. The photographs above and right show Golden Wings, *built to the lines of the 17-foot Whitehall by Bob Coe of Waldron Island, Washington. The hull is finished bright.*

been explained, great pains should be taken with the fastening, especially in light construction like this where there is no margin for error. Drills need to be exactly the right size. Counterboring should be neither too deep nor too shallow.

If the shutter is spiled with care, it should give no trouble. A snug fit is desirable, but not so snug that hard pounding is required to force the shutter down into place. Half-inch cedar is too soft to hammer much. Don't be afraid to take the plank out several times to plane off a fine shaving where required.

After the boat is planked, very little outboard planing should be necessary. In fact, the backed-out plank should be gauged ½ inch at the bench and the outside rounded off nearly to thickness on a convex curve corresponding to the hollow of the inside. If this is done accurately, only a few shavings will need to be planed off after planking, and the wicking may be rolled directly into the seams after the plank are on. Planing should be done first in a fore-and-aft direction, then all over lightly at an angle of 45 degrees. This last is called "traversing," and is required for a smooth job. In scraping and sanding, the hull should also be traversed as well as gone over in a fore-and-aft direction.

Of course the hood ends of the plank in the stem rabbet, and the garboard seam next to the keel and deadwood, will need to be caulked with a thin iron and the mallet. In these parts the cotton must be driven firmly, but not so hard as to strain the plank or fastenings, or to go through where there is no back-rabbet. The boat is puttied and painted in the conventional way, except that usually the top-strake, transom, gunwale, thwarts, bench, and interior knees were finished bright in the original Whitehalls.

STATION 5

6"

PLANK KEEL 1¼" OAK
ALTERNATE CONSTRUCTION
FOR CENTERBOARD

17' WHITEHALL
SPRIT SAIL RIG
BOSTON, 1870.

DEEP-WATER
KEEL

JG.

THE SAILING RIG

Whitehalls were tuned for an ash breeze, but like most small boats in the pre-gasoline era, they were generally rigged for canvas, too. When special provision for sailing was desired, builders increased the beam and often installed a centerboard.

The 17-foot model described here for building is of generous beam for a Whitehall, without being too wide to row. If a centerboard is wanted, it must be located so that the rig can be balanced. Also it should not take up any more space than is absolutely necessary or obstruct rowing. Furthermore it must be tight, and constructed so as not to weaken the boat. It is best, if a centerboard is to be installed, to use a plank keel about 6 inches wide amidships where the

board goes through, tapering to the siding of the stem and sternpost at the ends. If there is any question about scantling, err on the heavy side, for a box that works or leaks is good for nothing.

The suggested rig is modest. Certainly the hull would carry more sail, but this is safe and practical to start with. Anyone who intended to sail this boat a lot would undoubtedly want to work out his own rig by experiment, to suit his own needs and preferences. The spritsail was typical and very widely used by contemporary small sailing craft, although the leg-of-mutton sail was also seen. Sometimes a small jib was used.

As shown, the sail can be furled in an instant by wrapping it around the mast, which is light spruce and unstayed. The mast can then be

THWARTSHIPS SUPPORT UNDER BENCH, STATION 8.

FEET and INCHES

THWART KNEE

BACK REST

STRETCHER CLEAT

SEVENTEEN-FOOT WHITEHALL
MCF JUNE, 1953
J.G.

quickly unstepped, lifted through the thwart, and stowed along the thwarts when the boat is under oars, or while waiting for a breeze. The sail is shown with a club. Sometimes spritsails had full-length booms, but more frequently they were loose-footed.

FINISHING OUT

The interior construction of the Whitehall is simple, light, and strong. Essentially it is the same construction more recently used for fine yacht tenders such as those that Lawley built at Neponset, Massachusetts, except that these later boats had the modern open gunwale bent in on the inside of the timbers instead of forming a tight cap over the timberheads.

As was previously explained, the Whitehall interior, with the exception of the floorboards, was put in before the bottom was planked while the boat was still upright on its landing. The gunwales are ⅞-inch oak 1⅛ inches wide on the flat and tapering at the extreme ends to ⅞ inch. They are installed in one continuous piece running from the transom to a snug fit against the apron, and are beveled slightly so they pitch outboard to conform, for appearance, to a moderate thwartships camber.

The gunwale rests on top of the timberheads, which are let into its under side about ⅛

inch, enough to lock them securely. The bow is tied together with a breasthook, preferably made from a natural crook of apple or white oak. This is rivet-fastened with 10-penny copper wire nails through the gunwales and top strakes. The stem, apron and breasthook are drawn together by a through-length of ¼-inch copper rod riveted up tightly. At the stern the knees are also riveted to the sheer and transom.

The seat risers are screwed to the timbers eight to 8½ inches below the top of the gunwales. These risers should be ½ inch by 2 inches, tapering to 1¾ inches at the ends. This will bring the upper surface of the thwarts 7 to 7½ inches below the top of the gunwales, which is the standard distance.

The thwarts are 8 inches wide, ⅞ inch thick, run to the skin, and are notched snugly around the frames. Originally the best workmanship called for two knees on either end of the thwarts. Ralph Davidson of New Castle, New Hampshire, used this construction 50 years ago. I have seen such boats on the St. Croix built at that time or earlier with double sets of knees all around. As a boy I knew a retired boatbuilder from Portsmouth, New Hampshire, who told me he went into his father's shop in that city some years before the Civil War as a young lad of 13. His first job, he recalled, was pushing a hand saw 10 hours a day roughing out applewood knees. Lots of them were used in those days.

While suitable crooks for thwart knees are not to be found in modern lumberyards—even hackmatack knees are almost unheard of today—there are still plenty of apple trees, and, if a person has in mind to build a boat, he can keep a lookout for suitable timber and store it away against the day of building.

There is a good substitute for natural-grown knees—laminated knees. These are glued up from ⅛-inch strips of ash or mahogany. Oak is harder to glue properly because of an acid in that wood.

The strips for laminated knees should be got out about 2 inches wide on the circular saw. A lamination this wide can be split into a pair of matched knees. The prepared strips should be bent around a form of suitable shape and drawn up with plenty of clamps until the glue has set. If the strips are got out on a sharp, well-filed saw, they will be smooth enough as they come from the saw to glue.

The thwarts and thwart-knees join the gunwales and upper planks, and, with their supporting posts, form important bracing members—they are trusses as well as seats. The thwarts need to be strong. Ash or mahogany are good timber for them, but oak is too heavy. In spacing them in a boat of this size, seating capacity has to be taken into account, but above all it is necessary to provide for good rowing trim, either for one or two oarsmen. Where the mast hole goes through the second thwart, a heavy oak cleat for reinforcement is required on the underside.

The bench that occupies the stern sheets braces and stiffens the entire after end of the boat. Of course the bench is laid out especially for sailing. When the boat is being rowed, one or two may sit in the stern, and for their comfort a backrest is indicated, as was customary in such boats. The backrest fits into shallow notches in the gunwales and a ⅜-inch pin in the bottom of the rest slips into a hole in a small plate set flush into the surface of the bench. The bench is made of the same stuff as the thwarts and is notched to fit tightly around the sternpost and timbers. It is screwed down to cleats on the transom and to the seat risers. At station No. 8, the bench rests on a bridging cross-member, the ends of which halve on to the pair of timbers closest to that station, forming a partial bulkhead. The forward ends of the bench are joined to the after thwart and are securely cleated underneath.

The longitudinal floorboards are sometimes fitted snugly and are sometimes spaced slightly apart. They will be ½ inch thick, except the center one, which is thicker so that it can be shaped on the underside to fit the top of the cross floors. Under the last thwart, which is the low point of the boat, the center strip has a 4-inch hole for sponging out the bottom. For proper drainage it is well to have a light brass chain threaded through the limbers, for these are small and easily plugged with loose dirt. Also, they are out of reach, for the floor strips form a partial ceiling and are screwed down tightly to the cross-floors, not the frames. This ties the bottom together and strengthens and stiffens it a great deal. Pulling the chain back and forth clears the limbers.

Chocks are indicated for stretchers for the oarsmen to brace against. Obviously these should be as low as possible, with corners well rounded off. Three sets of rowlocks are shown. The standard location is to center them 11 inches aft of the aft edge of the rowing thwart. The rowlock socket is set into an oak pad ⅝ inch by 1¾ inches by 11 inches, and beveled as shown. This is a reinforcing piece that fastens into the sheer strake and gunwale.

For ornamentation, the old Whitehalls had a shallow ¼-inch bead run on the following members: lower edge of the gunwale, both edges of the seat risers, both edges of the floor ceiling and both upper edges of the thwarts. The under edges of the thwarts were chamfered ⅜ inch to give them a slimmer appearance.

1	BOOM JAWS WHITE OAK, LOCUST, NATURAL CROOKS THRU RIVETED.	MAST 10'-6" DIA. 3" TAPERED NEAR HEAD TO 1¾. BOOM LESS JAWS 9'-6" DIA. AT JAW 1⅝.
2	ROLLING HITCH, SNOTTER TO SPRIT.	DIA. MIDDLE 2¼. DIA. END 1⅜. SPRIT 12'-9". DIA. LOWER END 1½ DIA.
3	LEAD BLOCKS EITHER SIDE FOR 2-PART JIB SHEET.	MIDDLE 1¾. DIA. TOP 1¼. SHOULDERED TO ¾" TO FIT PEAK GROMMET.
4	2 METAL PLATES BRONZE, BRASS, STAINLESS EITHER SIDE BLADE. SWING-UP RUDDER & THRU RIVETED.	FOUR LENGTHS OF BOAT BUILT FROM THESE MOLDS. 14-FT. BOAT AS SHOWN. 15-FOOT BOAT
5	BOTTOM RUDDER SUPPORT RIVETED THRU DEADWOOD WITH RUDDER-PIVOT ROD FIXED IN IT.	SPACING OF 4 CENTER MOLD STATIONS INCREASED 3". FRAME SPACING 9". ENDS UNCHANGED. 16-FT. BOAT OPEN AT STA. 5.
6	RUDDER PIVOT ROD 5/16" DIA.	ADDING ANOTHER 2-FT. MOLD STATION. FRAME SPACING 8". ENDS OF BOAT UNCHANGED
7	SLOTTED RUDDER HINGE SLIPS ON PIVOT ROD WHEN RUDDER IS TILTED SIDEWAYS.	17'-3" BOAT. SPACING OF 5 CENTER MOLDS INCREASED 3". FR. SPACING 9". ENDS
8	UPPER RUDDER HINGE SLIPS OVER TOP OF PIVOT ROD. TURNS ON UPPER SUPPORT.	UNCHANGED. NOTE: PLANK WIDTHS, SHEET ONLY APPROXIMATE. FAIR P. LINES ON SET-UP.

14-FOOT SAILING WHITEHALL

FEET AND INCHES

Plans for a 14-foot sailing Whitehall. The sail plan above and the plans on the next two pages provide sufficient detail for the amateur to build a good multi-purpose Whitehall. The planking widths, the first ever shown for a Whitehall, were taken off a 2"=1' scale model of the boat. A description of the building process for this boat appeared in the February and March, 1977, issues of the National Fisherman.

1	KEEL 1½" x 1½" OAK. ALSO DEADWOOD, STERN POST AND STEM.	20	THWART KNEES ⅞" OAK, HACKMATACK, APPLE.
2	PLANKING ½" FINISHED TH'K, NORTHERN WHITE PINE, CEDAR, CYPRESS, D. FIR.	21	MAST STEP OAK 2½" x 5" x 13" RIBS AT STATION 3 LET IN AND RIVETED
3	SHEER STRAKE ⁹⁄₁₆" OAK, CLINKER.	22	BEDLOGS C.B. CASE 1¼" OAK.
4	RIBS OAK, SIDED ¾" MOLDED 1" AT FOOT ¾" HEAD, CAN BE GLUE LAMINATED.	23	CLEATS NOTCHED FOR THE RIB ENDS BOTH SIDES C.B. CASE OAK SIDED 1¼"
5	FLOORS OAK SIDED ⅞".	24	HEADLEDGES C.B. CASE OAK SIDED 1¼" MOLDED 2½"
6	FLOORS ENDS C.B. CASE SIDED 1¼".	25	SIDES C.B. CASE ¾" W. PINE, D. FIR
7	STERN POST SIDED 1½".	26	CAP C.B. CASE ⅞" W. PINE, FIR, OAK.
8	TRANSOM ⅞" TH'K OAK, MAHOGANY	27	CENTER BOARD ¹³⁄₁₆" OAK.
9	INWALE OAK 1" x 1¼" ENDS TAPERED	28	DEADWOOD 1¼" OAK.
10	OARLOCK PADS OAK 9" x 1¾" x ¾"	29	BUILDING MOLD AT STATION 5 CUT
11	RISER ⅝" PINE 3" WIDE, 2½" AT ENDS		OUT TO FIT OVER BED LOG
12	SHEER TRIM 1" H. ROUND ¾" AT ENDS.		ASSEMBLY / BEDLOGS, RIB CLEATS
13	BREAST HOOK ⅞" OAK, APPLE, LOCUST		AND HEADLEDGES. THIS IS FASTENED
14	STERN QUARTER KNEES ⅞" OAK, HACK.		TO THE FOUNDATION ASSEMBLY /
15	STERN SHEETS BENCH ⅞" W. PINE, FIR.		STEM, KEEL, DEADWOOD, STERN POST.
16	CLEAT BENCH TO THWART ⅞" OAK, PINE		AFTER SETTING UP ON STOCKS, TRANSOM
17	MIDDLE THWART ⅞" SPRUCE, FIR, PINE		IS ADDED & MOLDS PLACED AT STA'S 1, 3,
18	FORWARD THWART HOLED FOR TWO MAST POSITIONS ⅞" SPRUCE, FIR, PINE.		4, 5, 6, 7 WITH RIBBANDS. RIBS ARE
19	MAST PARTNER CLEAT ⅞" OAK GRAIN RUNS FORE AND AFT GLUED AND SCREWED TO THWART.		STEAM BENT OVER FORMS, BEVELED & TAPERED AT THE BENCH & CLAMPED IN PLACE TO THE RIBBANDS WHILE STILL SOFT.

(Above) A 15-foot Whitehall built at Mystic Seaport. (Below) The White-hall Donoughue, *restored by Bob Baker. (Courtesy of Mystic Seaport)*

23

The Sea Bright Skiff

........................•........................

Before the gasoline engine, the shore fisheries in various locations along our northeast coast developed several closely related small boats for getting off and on the beach, often through moderate surf. These were of clinker build, virtually double-enders on their load lines and below, with relatively narrow, flat bottoms and round bilges. Of particular note are the wherries of colonial New England, of which a few surviving examples are still to be found on the Maine coast, the round-sided Swampscott dory, and the Sea Bright skiff of the New Jersey beaches. While their flat bottoms allowed these boats to sit upright on the beach, their sharp, high sterns permitted launching stern-first into the surf, as well as riding back on the surf bow-first when coming in to land on the beach.

The renown of the sea skiff of the New Jersey beaches, or the Sea Bright skiff, its more distinctive name, as a sea boat—able in surf, seakindly and safe in capable hands beyond most small craft of its size—has spread far beyond the exposed beaches of northern New Jersey. That the Sea Bright skiff originated as a special and possibly a unique development of those beaches alone, as is sometimes claimed, is a highly doubtful hypothesis, for there are several other American small craft types as old, if not older, which so closely resemble it and each other in all important respects that it is most unlikely they originated independently of each other.

The Maine salmon wherry of the Penobscot Bay region, the Saint John River salmon boat, the Staten Island skiff (also known as the "Yankee skiff" in the Chesapeake where it was once extensively used in the oyster fishery), and to some lesser extent the round-sided Swampscott fishing dory—all of these have so much in common with the early New Jersey sea or beach skiffs, before their gradual transformation brought about by their adaptation for the gasoline engine, that there is good reason for surmising all these craft to be the offspring of a common ancestor—the military bateaus of the French and Indian Wars of the mid-eighteenth century.

Peter Guthorn in his important book, *The Sea Bright Skiff and Other Jersey Shore Boats* (Rutgers University Press, Brunswick, N. J.), makes no attempt to go back to the eighteenth century, but starts with the boat adopted by fishermen operating off the beaches of northern Monmouth County near what is now Sea Bright, beginning about 1845. At that time a rising influx into New York City of large numbers of immigrants accustomed to fish in their diet made a profitable venture of fishing off the beaches south of Sandy Hook, which were close enough to market for the catch to arrive there in a fresh condition. According to Guthorn, in 1850 in the Long Beach area, fishing engaged 63 proprietors, each with two to four employees, as well as boats, seines, and other equipment.

No boat, accurate drawing, picture, or half-model has survived from this earliest period. Nevertheless, Guthorn's research has produced a considerable body of information as to what these early boats were like. This information is by no means complete, in fact it contains serious gaps, yet there is enough to enable us to make a start in the rescue from oblivion of this worthy craft. By bringing together, comparing, and collating bits and pieces of data from many diverse sources, by extrapolating from similar but later craft to supply missing details, by calling upon a boatbuilder's judgment and intuition, by utilizing acquaintance with trade practices and the characteristics of the building materials used, we may be able to recover and organize sufficient detail to enable present-day builders to construct reproductions of the early beach skiff worthy of its prototype and not inferior to it in performance.

At the beginning of his book, Guthorn lists some of the dimensions and other characteristics of the earliest beach skiffs. They were about 15 feet long, he tells us, with 5 feet of beam, increasing in length after 1880 to 17 feet. The flat, slightly rockered bottom was tapered toward the ends from a maximum width amidships of approximately one-third the beam; this varied somewhat with different builders. At the stern, a transom, which he describes as U-shaped, raked about 30 degrees from the vertical. The bilge was round or rounded. Planking was lapstrake of white cedar. Single garboards twisted or rolled as they extended aft from amidships to fasten vertically on the stern-post, producing a planked-up skeg and a reverse chine at the after end where the garboard and the plank above (the "tuck" plank) came together.

This is scarcely enough information to draw a set of lines from, but enough to set some definite boundaries within which to work. Although the Jersey beach skiff reaches back to the 1840s and even somewhat earlier, it seems safe to assume that it did not change much for several decades, that is, comparatively little before 1880 when Guthorn states that the length of the fishing skiffs was generally increased to 17 feet. Thus we can accept with some confidence as typical of the early skiffs the three tintype photographs of the *Lizzie*, a beach skiff built by Isaac or William Seaman before 1872, presumably about 15 or 16 feet in length. The Seamans of Jersey were early and leading builders of sea skiffs who figured prominently in the development of this craft. In fact the term "sea skiff" first appears in print in an advertisement by William Seaman in 1885. The importance of these early photos of the *Lizzie*, then, as primary sources of information, can hardly be over-stressed.

From the photo giving a clear view of the stern from almost directly aft, the relative length of the skeg in comparison with the vertical length of the transom is readily determined. The *Lizzie*'s transom is not U-shaped, but quite definitely forms a broad V, five planks high with the top strake standing plumb or approximately so. Not until a later period, after the sea skiff had become a much larger and chunkier power

Two boat types with a planked-up skeg and reverse chine construction similar to the Sea Bright skiff. On the left is a St. John River Salmon boat from New Brunswick (Photo by Russell A. Fowler) and below is a Lincolnville Salmon wherry from Maine (Photo by Lester D. Olin)

(Above) Beach skiff Lizzie *being launched into the surf in 1892. (Left)* Lizzie *under oars with mast and sail stowed aft. (Below) Half-model of a typical rowing-sailing beach skiff of about 1900 as built in 15- and 17-foot lengths by Neill Campbell of Belmar, N.J. The model shows a skeg modified to take a stern bearing for a gas engine. (Photos from* The Sea Bright Skiff and Other Jersey Shore Boats *by Peter J. Guthorn; Rutgers University Press)*

craft, did the transom assume a U-shape. From this photograph the general shape and proportions of the transom and skeg are easily sketched, although we shall not be able until later to assign precise dimensions to them as parts of the craft we are undertaking to reconstruct.

An enlargement of the second photo of the *Lizzie*, a broadside view of the boat under oars, provides an outline of the boat in profile, allowing an estimate of the amount of stern rake, which appears to be 36 degrees rather than 30. Taken together, these three photos of the *Lizzie* reveal a great deal to the boatbuilder's eye, a great deal more in fact than is easily set down in print. They are of prime assistance in laying out the boat for one thing, in lining out the plank, of which there are six strakes, not to mention giving the location of the mast, the shape and approximate size of the sails, and the position of the rowing thwarts.

What is principally lacking up to this point is a profile outline from which, assuming the length to be 16 feet, we can pick off with proportional dividers the least depth amidships and the heights of the bow and stern, from which in turn the amount and curve of the sheer, as well as the bottom rocker, can be drawn. We also lack enough of a halfbreadth view, assuming a width amidships of 5 feet, to give the width of the stern as well as proportional dimensions for laying out the half-breadth shape. Also, we lack a midsection outline for comparison, and as a check. All three of these desiderata—profile, halfbreadth, and midsection—are to be found in Guthorn's book. An adequate profile view for scaling with the proportional dividers is obtained from enlargements of two broadside views of the same Campbell half-model, which the author states is typical of the 15- to 17-foot rowing and sailing beach skiffs of about 1900. The general proportions of this half-model correspond rather closely with what can be observed in the three tintype photos of the *Lizzie.*

However, it should not be overlooked that on the model the lower part of the planked-up skeg projects somewhat and stands vertical, an innovation found in conversions to power of the rowing and sailing skiff to provide a seat for bolting on an outside stern bearing and stuffing box. This is clearly to be seen in a photo of skiffs on the beach at Sea Bright about 1907. Otherwise the 1907 skiffs are definitely of the rowing and sailing model with abundant sheer, a well-raked V transom, and six planks to a side.

The use of the profile view of the Campbell half-model requires judgment and some discretion. The stern rake seems excessive and· is found to be something like 40 degrees. At the bow the stem also appears to rake more than is shown by photos of the older boats. Such differences may be discrepancies due to camera distortion, which must be taken into account in scaling all photographs of boats, or they may be special Campbell characteristics, for according to the author, each of the builders had his own characteristic model, which differed in certain respects from those built by the others.

A number of halfbreadth views of the beach skiffs are included in Guthorn's book, but they are all for larger and newer boats, yet neither so large or so new as to be significantly altered in their basic proportions. Witness to a long established halfbreadth shape is obtained by comparing the beam to the transom width in a number of representative skiffs dating from about 1870 to 1940.

A 25-foot surf boat on skiff lines drawn some time between 1870 and 1880 by William A. Seaman of Branchport for the U. S. Life Saving Service has a transom width that is 65 percent of its greatest beam, as scaled with proportional dividers. A comparison of section widths of pound boats built by Seaman and L. B. Newman, as recorded in a boatbuilder's notebook and reproduced by Guthorn, yields transom-to-beam ratios of 65 and 68 percent. For a typical 21-foot Seaman skiff built in 1919, the transom width is 66 percent of the beam. A 21-foot regulation sea skiff advertised by Seaman about 1935 shows a transom width that is 67 percent of the beam. A 26-foot open-type sea skiff advertised by the Keyport Boat Works in 1925 has a transom width that is 69 percent of the beam. For the Seaman pound boat model as built from 1918 to 1940, the transom width was 66 percent of the beam.

Thus in all these boats examined, the greatest difference in transom-to-beam ratios amounts only to four percent—from 65 to 69 percent. Taking these ratios into consideration, we settled on a transom width for our reconstructed model of 68 percent of the given beam of 5 feet, amounting to a transom width at the sheer line of 3 feet 4¾ inches.

By working from the profile proportions developed from the Campbell half-model, we established a height for the transom. By scaling the enlarged photo of the stern of the *Lizzie,* we not only derived the vertical measurement of the transom scaled along the rake of the stern, but also a measurement for the planked-up skeg, and, in addition, transom widths at measured intervals. We could not accept the 40 degrees of transom rake as taken from the Campbell model of 1895, particularly as another photo of what appears to be the same model seems to show a rake of 38 degrees, strongly suggesting the possibility of camera distortion. Neither could we accept a rake of only 30 degrees, feeling this was not enough, and was closer to the later power skiffs, rather than to the earlier boats for oars and sail.

In checking, we found the Seaman surf boat of 1870-80 to have a stern rake of 33 degrees.

The stern rake of the *Lizzie*, as far as can be determined from the broadside photo, is 36 degrees. The typical 21-foot Seaman power skiff of 1919 shows a stern rake of only 16 degrees, for, as the development of the power skiff proceeded, the angle of stern rake became progressively less. Judging 40 degrees to be too much and 30 degrees too little, we kept close to the angle measured for the *Lizzie* by adopting an angle of stern rake of 35 degrees.

For purposes of comparison we were able to scale off with proportional dividers the midsection shape of the Seaman surf boat of 1870-80 from her lines published in Guthorn's book. As we have the beam, height, and bottom for the midsection of our reconstruction, it is principally for a comparison of deadrise and bilge curves that the midsection shape of the surf boat was obtained. The surf boat shows more topside flare than we have estimated to be representative of the early beach boats, and we have been guided here to a large extent by the photos of the *Lizzie*, the 17-foot by 6-foot

Joralemon utility skiff of 1905, and the fishing skiffs on the beach at Sea Bright in 1907 and 1908, all appearing in Guthorn's book.

After deriving lines, drawn to a scale of 1½ inches equals 1 foot, principally from the sources reviewed, these were translated into wood, that is to say a working half-model, which was made as fair as possible and yet as close to the shape of the *Lizzie* as could be determined from her photos. Likewise, six strakes of plank, the same as the *Lizzie*'s, were carefully laid out on the half-model, using thin pine battens and dressmakers' pins, lining the strakes as nearly as we could to conform to those on the *Lizzie*.

The lines were then taken off the half-model and laid out on the drawing board as they are reproduced here. They are drawn to the inside of the planking, and are laid out much the same as dory lines, as these beach skiffs, also called beach dories, are closely similar to dories both in shape and construction. The principal construction differences for the beach skiff are a rabbeted stem, a thick bottom board rabbeted

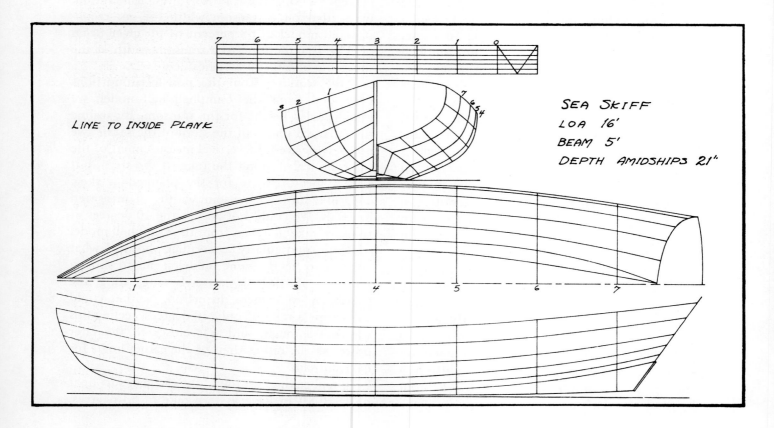

LINE TO INSIDE PLANK

SEA SKIFF
LOA 16'
BEAM 5'
DEPTH AMIDSHIPS 21"

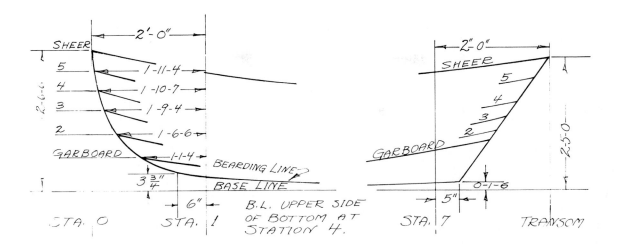

for the garboard, and the combination of planked-up skeg and reverse chine. The reverse chine—not a very good term, but the best we have for this particular feature of construction—is also found in the Maine salmon wherry, the Saint John River salmon boat, and the Staten Island skiff. It is their most distinctive feature, and is indicative of a common origin.

SETTING UP

The lines represent the upper inside edges of the six strakes of this clinker hull. The upper inside edge of the flat bottom board is also shown. Because we are working from the inside of the planking, measurements for the bearding line on the stem, rather than for the rabbet line, are given in the offsets. How the latter is derived is shown in one of the drawings and will be explained in detail later.

While this skiff is planked much the same as a Swampscott dory, it has a rabbeted stem and bottom board, and, in this particular case, a rabbeted stern post, which the dory does not have. These features increase the difficulty of construction considerably, and there is some question whether they are worth the extra effort. A well-built Swampscott dory will last as long and take as much abuse and pounding on beaches and in the surf as a Jersey sea skiff, as

	SIXTEEN FOOT SEA SKIFF	STEM	1	2	3	4	5	6	7	TRAN.
HEIGHTS	SHEER	2-6-6	2-1-5	1-10-5	1-8-7	1-8-3	1-9-2	1-11-2	2-1-7	2-5-0
	5	2-2-1	1-8-7	1-5-4	1-3-7	1-3-2	1-4-1	1-5-7	1-8-7	2-0-2
	4	1-10-0	1-4-0	1-0-1	0-10-3	0-9-5	0-10-7	1-0-6	1-4-0	1-7-2
	3	1-5-6	1-0-0	0-8-0	0-6-1	0-5-4	0-6-6	0-9-1	1-0-5	1-4-0
	2	1-0-6	0-8-3	0-5-2	0-3-0	0-3-0	0-4-0	0-6-3	0-10-2	1-1-1
	GARBOARD	0-7-0	0-5-3	0-3-0	0-1-5	0-1-1	0-2-0	0-4-5	0-8-6	0-10-7
	BOTTOM	—	0-2-6	0-1-3	0-0-2	0-0-0	0-0-1	0-0-7	0-1-5	0-1-6
HALF-BREADTHS	SHEER	0-1-0	1-2-1	1-10-7	2-4-0	2-5-7	2-5-4	2-3-5	2-0-6	1-8-7
	5	0-1-0	1-1-6	1-10-3	2-3-5	2-5-4	2-5-2	2-2-6	1-11-5	1-8-1
	4	0-1-0	1-0-1	1-8-4	2-1-4	2-3-2	2-2-5	2-0-3	1-8-5	1-5-5
	3	0-1-0	0-10-0	1-4-7	1-9-4	1-10-5	1-10-0	1-7-5	1-3-7	1-1-1
	2	0-1-0	0-7-3	1-1-1	1-5-2	1-6-1	1-5-2	1-2-2	0-9-6	0-7-1
	GARBOARD	0-1-0	0-4-2	0-9-2	1-0-5	1-1-3	1-0-5	0-9-6	0-4-2	0-0-4
	BOTTOM	—	0-1-0	0-5-4	0-8-4	0-10-1	0-9-2	0-6-2	0-2-2	

OFFSETS IN FEET, INCHES, AND EIGHTHS.
TAKEN TO INSIDE OF PLANKING, INSIDE OF BOTTOM,
TO BEARDING LINE ON RABBETED STEM, AND OUTSIDE
OF TRANSOM. STATIONS SPACED 2 FEET APART.

the double-ended surf dories built by William Chamberlain of Marblehead for lifesaving boats for the Boston Metropolitan Commission have amply demonstrated. Likewise these same 19-foot surf dories later built in Swampscott by George Chaisson proved themselves in service along the whole length of our eastern seaboard.

The necessity for cutting a stem rabbet is avoided by the dory's two-piece stem construction. The inner stem is beveled to take the hood ends of the plank, which extend to the stem's outer edge. These are fastened and planed off square to conform to the curve of the stem profile. The outer, or "false," stem is then bent on to cover the plank ends and is securely fastened into the inner stem. The result is for all practical purposes the same as a rabbeted stem but is much simpler and more easily attained.

It would be quite easy to substitute a dory-type stem for the rabbeted stem shown here for the Sea Bright skiff. In that case, the inner stem could be laminated to the shape of the stem profile, and the outer stem could be a piece of steam-bent oak. This assembly adequately through-fastened would make a good, strong job. Alternately, the inner stem could be steam bent, although this would be a somewhat more difficult bending job than required for the lighter outer stem.

Guthorn, in his book, lists scantling dimensions for a typical 16-foot general service skiff. The stem as given there is steam-bent white oak, sided 1⅛ inches with a 4-inch molded dimension. Bending 4-inch oak requires special equipment, easy enough for the commercial boatshop but beyond the reach of most amateur, one-time builders. For that reason I show a pieced-stem

easily put together from ordinary straight-grained 2-inch thick oak plank. Of course, if one could get a natural crook of oak or hackmatack of the right shape for the stem, that would be my first choice and, in my estimation, the best stem of all, but such timber is so unusual and difficult to obtain today that it hardly need be considered.

As previously mentioned, in laying out the stem rabbet for this skiff we work from the bearding line, the measurements for which are given in the offsets. Although this skiff is clinker planked with strakes finished ½ inch thick, I have laid out the stem rabbet for ¾-inch thick planking. After the rabbet is cut, it is easy to mark the rabbet for half-inch plank using a small section of ½-inch thick block for a gauge, which is slipped around in the rabbet to mark against. On the forward face or edge of the stem a ½-

inch–wide strip is marked in the center for the stem band, either half-round or half-oval brass. The excess wood is next cut away between the line marked inside the rabbet and the line marking the outside edge of the stem band. By this method, instead of merely laying out and cutting a ½-inch rabbet to begin with, two advantages are secured. More back rabbet surface is obtained for landing the hood ends of the planking on and for fastening them, while the outer part of the stem, forward of the planking, is made thinner both for improved looks and for a sharper, easier entrance.

Even though I have increased the stem siding of 1⅞ inches given by Guthorn to 2 inches, there will be less wood in the finished stem because of the amount cut away in trimming down the ¾-inch rabbet, yet the greater stem siding gives more back rabbet surface for landing the plank.

The flat bottom, or plank keel, as this is sometimes called, is pine, 1⅞ inches thick. A dory bottom in a boat this size might be one inch thick, more likely ⅞ inch, but the dory would have an outer bottom of ½ inch or ⅝

inch, or at least part of an outer bottom along the outside covering the bottom edges of the garboard strakes. This double-bottom construction is like the two-piece stem, in that it is easier to construct than the single, thick, rabbeted bottom. Also, the outer part is easily renewed, should it become battered or worn on the beach.

I have shown a rabbeted bottom for this boat because this construction was usual for beach skiffs, although it seems that the double bottom was occasionally used for beach skiffs and favored by a few builders. I think I would probably use a double bottom myself. While the Maine salmon wherry has what amounts to a double bottom, this is only at the ends and along the sides, with the inner, middle portion uncovered. It is important that the side pieces should be straight on the inside edges and parallel to the centerline of the boat. If the side strips are curved more or less to conform to the sides of the boat, their inner edges will drag.

The stern construction as shown for this boat may appear to some to be heavier than needed. Yet the after end of the bottom takes a lot of pounding on landing and in getting off the beach. If the after end of the bottom board is brought to a shim point and is not covered or protected in some way, trouble can result.

In this skiff both the end of the bottom board and the ends of the garboard are recessed into a solid sternpost with plenty of bearing, with good fastening, and well forward of possible impact damage. A rabbeted sternpost such as this is more work but worth it, I think. The 4-inch siding of the post in the heel makes it possible to bore a shaft hole in case it is desired to install a small inboard engine. In that case the fastenings holding the two-part sternpost assembly together could be placed on either side of the center to permit a small shaft hole to be bored on the centerline between them. Enough wood should be left on the bottom of the sternpost aft of the rabbet to allow bolting on the outside stuffing box and bearing. In case this boat should be considered for power, it would be quite easy to make it 18 feet long instead of 16 feet by adding 2 feet in the middle, with almost no other changes.

The two-piece sternpost shown is readily got out of ordinary 4-inch stock. No wide widths are required. Oak is not necessary, but good quality hard, or longleaf, pine will do nicely. In fact the whole stern, including the transom, can very well be made of hard pine. Guthorn's specifications call for 1¼-inch white cedar for the transom. I would rather have hard pine, but not over 1⅛ inches thick.

As I previously indicated in connection with the stem, a natural grown knee of the right shape for the sternpost would be ideal. In that case the siding could be 3 inches or even narrower, this depending in part on whether or not it is to be bored for a shaft. A capable builder can shape such a natural knee so that its siding tapers from, say 4 inches where the end of the bottom jogs into it, to less than an inch at its extreme after edge.

In the Maine salmon wherry, the natural crook sternpost got out of a large white cedar root is tapered to a sharp edge under the transom and the after ends of the garboard, and one or two of the strakes above are run back and sawn off square and flush with this after edge

after they are in place and fastened. These plank ends are covered with a beveled strip of oak similar to the dory's false stem and through-fastened into the sternpost on the inside. This strip extends partway up the width of the transom and is fastened into it and through into the upper part of the sternpost, which reinforces the inside of the transom. This is a solid way of finishing off the stern, although a bit clumsy in appearance. The bottom end, which otherwise would be exposed, is covered by the wherry's false bottom.

This same construction could be used for the sea skiff. In fact it would be both possible and easy to build this skiff with a two-part dory stem, a double bottom without rabbeting, and a wherry stern, also without rabbeting. In such a boat no rabbeting in any part would be required, with a considerable saving in labor, especially for the inexperienced builder.

FRAMING AND PLANKING

Guthorn's specifications call for planking of ½-inch or ⅝-inch thick white cedar, but ⅝ inch seems pretty heavy for a 16-foot boat and for that reason I have drawn up this boat for ½-inch planking. For myself, I'd rather have good quality northern white pine than cedar for planking, or Maine, rather than Virginia, cedar. With small, sound knots, the Maine cedar is ever so much tougher than some of the wide, clear southern cedar that looks beautiful in the board but splits so easily.

White oak frames ⅝ inch by 1⅛ inches, spaced 8 inches on centers, are called for. The oak should be the best obtainable, from butt logs, if possible, newly cut, and sawn to follow the grain. There is a great difference in oak, and some of the light, open-grain red oak is quite worthless.

The planking laps, 1⅛ inches in width, should be copper riveted, between the frames as well as through them. At stations 6 and 7, I have shown floors in the hollow trough between the garboards with their upper edges curved and the frames bent in on top of them and running continuously from gunwale to gunwale. Aft of station 6 such floors will not be in the way and they add greatly to the strength of the boat where it is especially needed.

This boat could be framed with natural crook timbers, which was the old way and the method of framing still to be seen in survivals of the Maine salmon wherries and the St. John River salmon boats. Also laminated frames, epoxy/Versamid-glued, could be made up to simulate natural crooks, if one wished to do so. It is only fair to say that more work is required for laminations than most realize who haven't done this previously.

According to Guthorn, skiff bottoms were made of spruce or cedar. I like neither for this purpose. Spruce rots too easily and cedar is quite soft. For my part I would choose pine, either northern white or southern yellow, or good quality Douglas fir.

FINISHING OFF

Brass screws are mentioned on an equal footing with bronze, but I want no part of the former. Brass screws are too weak and do not last especially well either. I would want bronze bolts also. The price difference between poor and superior fastenings for a boat of this size amounts to so little that it is hardly worth considering.

Inwales and gunwales, I believe these are what Guthorn calls clamps and rub strakes, are best made of oak. Dimensions for clamps are given as ⅝ inch by 1⅜ inches and rub strakes as ⅞ inch by 1¼ inches. Clamps or inwales are to be fastened through the timberheads and sheer strake with 8d copper nails riveted over burrs, while the gunwales or rub rails can be screwed on.

Thwart knees, breasthook, and quarter knees are best made out of natural crooks, limb or root, of apple, hackmatack, oak, or other, if you can get them. In a pinch, laminated substitutes can be glued up. Thwarts can be made of spruce, for the wood is stiff, strong, and light, and there is little chance of rot developing here.

THE SAILING RIG

Primary propulsion for the original beach-launched working craft of the northeast coast was supplied by ever-reliable oars, but many of the early boats were also rigged to sail. Small spritsails predominated, except for the Swampscott's leg-o-mutton sail and small jib. Eventually many of these boats rigged to sail were equipped with centerboards, but just when centerboards were first put into such craft is uncertain.

In Swampscott, Massachusetts, in the old days, the summer dory fishermen in good weather used to leave the beach under oars at dawn, usually in a dead calm. By late afternoon, when it was time to start home, a brisk on-shore breeze would have sprung up, so sails were raised and the loaded boats would come riding in before it. No centerboard was required and an oar sufficed to steer. As time went on, sailing rigs were enlarged and improved, and modified sailing versions of such craft were developed with centerboards and rudders.

Alfred A. Brooks, in his account of the boats of Ash Point, Maine, in the early decades of this century, as published in the October, 1942, issue of the *American Neptune*, shows the lines and rig for two large sailing wherries; one, a capacious 16-footer built by Luther Hurd about 1870, and the other, Elmer Witham's 18-foot *Siroc*. Of something like 1,500 pounds displacement, *Siroc* was partly decked and carvel planked, although built on wherry lines. Neither of these Ash Point sailing wherries was equipped with a centerboard, and consequently, while fast and seaworthy off the wind, they did not do so well to windward. Both carried a sprit main and a small jib, a rig very similar in fact to that of the Jersey beach skiff *Lizzie*, which we have attempted to reconstruct here.

Of these various beach craft which we have been considering, the Swampscott dory was carried farthest in its development as a sailboat. From about 1900 to 1920 and even somewhat later, dories were the most numerous and popular small sailing craft in this country. Still remembered are such dories as the Beachcomber

The Lizzie, *set up on the beach in 1892 to have her picture taken. (From* The Sea Bright Skiff and Other Jersey Shore Boats *by Peter J. Guthorn; Rutgers University Press)*

and Alpha, the Clipper dory, the X-dory, the Riverside dory, followed by larger and more powerful craft like the Yankee dory, the Massachusetts Bay Indian, and the Marblehead Town Class, which has recently taken a new lease on life in fiberglass.

The Jersey sea skiff, to the contrary, developed in the direction of power rather than sail. Peter Guthorn's book does not include details of a single example of these boats rigged to sail within the past 100 years. However, the photograph he shows of fishing skiffs on the beach at Sea Bright in 1908 gives evidence that some of these boats still carried small sails at that time. In at least three boats out of more than the score shown on the beach, spars lying flat with the sails rolled up on them can be seen, and one of the boats has mast and sail raised. Another photo of working skiffs at Sea Bright the previous year does not have a single spar or sail showing. This was taken at the very beginning of the transition to power, as is indicated by a boat in the photograph with its primitive installation of a small inboard engine.

It appears that the Sea Bright skiff was never popular as a small sailboat either for racing or for other pleasure sailing. The reason is not at all clear, considering the great popularity achieved by the sailing dories. There is no intrinsic reason why the sea skiff could not have been developed as an outstanding small sailboat. Only it wasn't. Nevertheless, for those today who want a boat that can be both rowed and sailed, one that is a fine sea boat, that handles easily on and off the beach, the early Jersey beach skiff, exemplified by the *Lizzie*, is certainly to be considered.

When it comes to picking a sail plan, there are a number of different rigs which would be suitable. But we have chosen to follow, as closely as careful scaling with dividers allows, the old tintype photo of the *Lizzie* under sail, which Guthorn reproduces in his book. Basing our scale on the assumption that the *Lizzie*'s length was 16 feet, although it just as likely was a foot shorter, we get a sail area of 70 square feet for the main, and 15 square feet for the jib, or 85 square feet combined sail area, which is not excessive for a boat of this size. The boat could probably carry more, but general utility and ease of handling is the object here rather than ultimate speed.

The rig could hardly be simpler, with the sprit main lashed to the short, unstayed mast

(Above) Suggested sail plan for the Sea Bright skiff. (Left) Robert Crockett's 16-foot Sea Bright skiff has a similar sail plan, though the jib club is not balanced. This boat was built by the Rose Bay Boat Shop in Lunenburg, Nova Scotia.

but not to the boom. In the photograph the end of the boom seems to extend by the mast somewhat like a sprit, but this is not clear, and it might have had crude boom jaws, although there was definitely no gooseneck fitting. To douse the rig one merely has to unsnap the jib club from the stemhead, lift the boom, wrap the sprit and sails around the mast, and lift the whole rig out of the step and mast thwart. The spars are short enough so that the resulting compact bundle is easily stowed within the boat.

The mast should be spruce, 3 inches in diameter at the bury through the thwart, tapering to 2 inches at the head. The main boom tapering toward either end should not be over 2 inches at its thickest part, the sprit and jib club likewise not over 1½ inches. Sitka spruce for the spars is excellent, of course, but expensive and often difficult to obtain. Many lumberyards

today carry rough Canadian spruce ledger boards, which come 16 feet long. Selected boards stripped up on the circular saw to avoid knots, and glued up with epoxy, can be shaped into spars of the finest kind. Or if one lives Down East, it is possible in some areas to find suitable spars growing on the stump in spruce thickets. After cutting, these should be protected from weather and worms until they have seasoned before being worked down to size with drawknife and plane.

In the photographs of the *Lizzie* the thwart that serves for mast partners seems to be at gunwale height. This is not necessary, and as putting this thwart at gunwale height tends to fill up the boat, I have drawn it in the reconstructed plan at the same height as the rowing thwarts. This is the way it was generally found in dories and wherries. In the latter, there were sometimes two mast positions for different rigs and sail areas.

It is extremely difficult to achieve a well-balanced rig by calculating sail areas and mast positions ahead of time on the drawing board. There are so many variables, and the values for these are so easily changed in a small boat by changing conditions of trim, heel, and loading, that generally one must try a new rig, experiment with it, and make various changes and adjustments before it is satisfactory. In the case of different rigs and different sail areas for different weather conditions, having more than one mast position is desirable if not essential. Likewise the design and positioning of the center-

board is an important element in achieving a balanced rig.

None of the photographs that we have of the *Lizzie* shows a centerboard or centerboard trunk. In assuming that there was a centerboard, and in including one in my reconstruction, I have consequently had a free hand. The heavy, wide pine bottom of this skiff is ideal for the installation of a centerboard trunk and is strengthened rather than weakened by the addition of such centerboard construction as is shown here. In addition to centering it approximately under the combined centers of effort of the two sails, which brings the forward end up close to the mast as in sailing dories, I have made the board quite long, yet narrow enough to fit under the rowing thwarts. The extra length makes up in area what the board lacks in width, although 14 inches is not excessively narrow. When a long board is raised and lowered, the center of lateral resistance shifts considerably in the fore-and-aft direction. This affords flexibility in achieving balance of rig. Besides, keeping the board below the thwarts does not interfere in any way with the use of the boat for rowing, and at the same time the thwarts brace and secure the centerboard trunk.

The bed logs for the trunk are not oak, but pine, a full 2½ inches thick and bolted through the 1⅝-inch thick pine bottom with ⅜-inch galvanized iron carriage bolts on 6-inch centers. This generous fastening with the wide bearing surface of pine bed logs coated with a non-hardening bedding compound should give a solid, perfectly tight box. End posts are oak 2 inches wide and extending through the bottom slot for caulking from the outside.

The bolts through the bottom should be set so that their heads come just under the surface, to be covered with bottom compound rather than bunged. It may be desirable to tighten the nuts slightly several times at intervals after the installation of the trunk, and each time this is done, the heads will tend to draw up a little deeper into the bottom, so it is wise not to set them too deep to begin with.

The board, made of two pieces of oak

finished ⅞ inch thick, is pinned together with 5/16-inch diameter drifts spaced 6 inches on centers as shown and precisely marked and bored. The upper section 5 inches in width is bored halfway through from either edge. The holes can be bored to meet exactly in the center if the drill is sighted both ways (by the operator of the drill and an assistant) as drilling proceeds and the drill is made to follow exactly the line of the hole as marked across the surface of the board.

A piece of lead is set into the board as shown to add weight to it in addition to the weight of the oak and the drift pins. The lead can either be run in hot, or a block of lead of the right thickness and shape can be set in cold and swelled around the edges with a hammer and punch so that it grips the wood solidly and cannot move or fall out.

A short rope pennant spliced into the strap eye on the upper side of the board serves to raise or lower the weighted board to the desired height and is made fast to a cleat on the outside of the box. For a pivot a piece of ½-inch brass rod will do nicely and needs only to be driven through tightly fitting holes bored through the trunk logs and cut to come flush on either side.

No rudder is shown, although one might easily be added. The main reason for this is that it seems that the *Lizzie*, like early Swampscott dories, did not have a rudder, but was steered with an oar.

24

The Barnegat Sneakbox

················•················

One of the old small-boat favorites is the famous Barnegat sneakbox. Tradition has it that the first sneakbox was built on Barnegat Bay in 1836. Its flat, spoon-shaped hull draws little water and is easily dragged over mud or sand. Sitting very low in the water, the sneakbox is easily disguised as a shooting blind. Originally, this type of hunting skiff was built of a size small enough to be easily handled by a single hunter, that is, about 12 feet by 4 feet, and was rigged with a small spritsail.

According to W. P. Stephens, most of the early Barnegat boats were fitted with a dagger-board inserted through a small trunk from which it could be removed entirely. H. I. Chapelle explained that at first these daggerboards were "scimitar-shaped" and were hung to one side well off-center. This was to permit the hunter to stretch out full length beside the board in a 12-foot boat. Later when the type was developed and enlarged for recreational sailing and for cruising, the location of the board was shifted to a more "normal" position on the centerline of the hull, and the removable dagger-board was replaced by a pivoting centerboard, sometimes of galvanized iron boiler plate.

Soon after the inception of the sneakbox, someone, no doubt shocked by its novelty, dubbed it a "devil's coffin." Its low, flat, "melon-seed" hull might have looked precarious and unsafe, but actually it is not so at all. Used

as intended and not overloaded with canvas, the sneakbox is to be trusted fully. She is not an oceangoing packet, it is true, but when used in sheltered and semi-sheltered waters, she is a comfortable, secure, and surprisingly able little craft.

Indeed, the good qualities of the sneakbox and its inherent potential beyond a limited specialization as a shooting boat were soon recognized by boating enthusiasts. Following the Civil War came a flowering of recreational boating in this country. The widespread and intense activity involving small craft, and sailing canoes in particular, during the 1870s and 1880s is often lost sight of today. One has only to dig back in the files of *Forest & Stream* for these decades to discover how highly the sneakbox was then regarded among sportsmen and small craft amateurs and sailors.

Some of this material on sneakboxes is to be found in *Canoe and Boat Building—A Complete Manual For Amateurs*, by W. P. Stephens. The drawings of the Barnegat Cruiser that are reproduced with this article are adapted from Plate No. 39, which accompanied the Stephens book. Plate No. 38 shows a large 16-foot shooting box.

I might add that Stephens's plates were printed separately on individual sheets and folded in a packet which went with the book. Over the years many of these separate plates have been mislaid or destroyed, so that few complete sets remain, with popular items like the sneakbox particularly hard to find. Persons interested in the sneakbox should not fail to get Stephens's book from the library to read the relevant sections in the text, which provides dimensions, a sail plan, and much miscellaneous data of importance.

A much easier source to obtain, and one fully as important in its way as Stephens, is Chapelle's *American Small Sailing Craft*, published by W. W. Norton in 1951. Both of the sneakbox drawings included by Chapelle, a hunter's box built in 1880 and a more modern "arc-bottom" modification, were made from take-offs of the actual boats by the author. They are complete to the minutest detail, and include offsets and sail plans. In contrast, Stephens's drawings omit some minor details, such that any knowledgeable boatbuilder, either amateur or professional, might be expected to supply himself without difficulty. Neither Stephens nor Chapelle provides complete step-by-step building directions, although Stephens gives more of such information than Chapelle, whose book is a technical and historical treatise and not a building manual.

The modified sneakbox or Barnegat Cruiser shown by Stephens is the culmination of a great deal of special study and experimentation with sailing and cruising sneakboxes by N. H. Bishop of Toms River, N. J. At the time Stephens was writing his book, Bishop had under his supervision a number of such Barnegat Cruisers building at Toms River for members of the American Single-handed Cruising Club. The lines were taken from Seneca's boat previously described in *Forest & Stream*. "Seneca" was the pen name of a popular contributor to *Forest & Stream* who wrote extensively on sneakboxes. As Bishop was the man who took a sneakbox from Pittsburgh to the Gulf of Mexico down the Ohio and the Mississippi, later recounting his experiences in a book, *Four Months In a Sneak Box*, the Barnegat Cruiser comes to us with the highest of recommendations.

Stephens's paragraph of introduction to the Barnegat Cruiser is worth reproducing:

The sail plan for W.P. Stephens's sneakbox featured a balanced lug rig.

The prominence given to cruising of late years by the increased growth and importance of canoeing has brought many into the ranks who do not care for so small a boat as the canoe, but who wish a strong, roomy and serviceable boat, either for cruising or for general sailing, alone or with one or two friends. The canoe is really a boat for one person, and must be capable of being paddled, sailed, and handled on shore by one; but where these conditions do not prevail a different type of boat may often be used to advantage. In places where the boat must lie afloat and a fine canoe would be damaged; in open waters where there is no occasion to haul up the boat, and where transit by rail is not an object; in shooting trips and other cruises where several persons, and perhaps a dog, must be carried, the boat shown in Plate XXXIX will answer admirably.

Dimensions furnished by Stephens for the Barnegat Cruiser are as follows: Length 14 feet 0 inches. Beam 4 feet 6 inches. Depth at gunwale 1 foot 1 inch. Sheer, bow 8½ inches. Sheer, stern 4 inches. Draft, loaded 6 inches. Freeboard 7 inches. Crown of deck 8 inches. Fore side of stem to mast tube 2 feet 9½ inches; to trunk, fore end 3 feet 1 inch; to trunk, aft end 6 feet 3 inches; to well, fore end 11 feet; to rowlocks 9 feet 1 inch; to bulkhead 12 feet. Diameter of

HEIGHTS		HALF-BR'S	DIAGONALS	
SHEER	BOTTOM	SHEER	A	B
0	1-9-6	1-9-6	0-0-0		
1	1-8-1	1-3-2	0-11-5	1-2-4	1-2-6
2	1-6-6	0-10-0	1-4-4	1-7-4	1-7-6
3	1-5-4	0-6-0	1-8-5	1-11-7	2-0-3
4	1-4-2	0-3-0	1-11-7	2-3-1	2-3-6
5	1-3-3	0-1-0	2-2-2	2-5-1	2-6-3
6	1-2-6	0-0-2	2-4-1	2-6-5	2-8-1
7	1-2-3	0-0-1	2-5-2	2-7-2	2-9-0
8	1-2-2	0-0-0	2-6-0	2-7-4	2-9-6
9	1-2-1	0-0-2	2-6-1	2-7-1	2-9-5
10	1-2-2	0-1-0	2-5-7	2-6-3	2-8-6
11	1-2-5	0-2-2	2-4-6	2-4-6	2-7-2
12	1-3-1	0-4-3	2-3-1	2-2-6	2-5-0
13	1-3-5	0-7-4	2-1-1	1-11-6	2-2-1
T	1-4-1	0-10-5	1-10-6	1-9-0	1-11-3

Sneakbox after W.P. Stephens — 14' × 5' × 1'-2"

mast tube 3 inches. The rig is a balance lug of 118 square feet in area.

ORIGINAL CONSTRUCTION

The directions for the construction of the hull furnished by Stephens, which follow verbatim below, are worth close study, for the same general order of building procedure applies in composite construction:

In shape the new cruiser resembles the old sneakboxes, but is deeper than most of the latter. The board is of steel plate ¼" thick, pivoted at the fore end in place of the daggerboards once common in these craft. The construction is quite peculiar. Both keel and planking are of white cedar ⅝" thick. The keel is flat, in one piece. . . . There is no stem piece, but the keel is bent up, forming the stem. The garboards . . . end along the gunwale, instead of in a rabbet in the stem, as in most boats.

In building, after the keel is fastened to the stocks, with the proper curve, the stern and moulds are put in place. Then two [harping] pieces are sawn out of 1" the shape being taken from the deck line on the floor. These pieces are screwed in place, at the height of the lower side of the deck, and remain permanently in the boat. The ribs are now bent and fitted in place, nailed to the keel, and the upper ends of the forward ones are nailed to [the harping] pieces. The correct breadths of each plank may be taken from the body plan on every frame. The frames are of sawn cedar 1⅛"–1⅙" and spaced 10". The trunk is of pine, deck and ceiling ½" cedar. . . .

MODERNIZED CONSTRUCTION

For a number of reasons, as will appear, the sneakbox hull is particularly suited to a construction utilizing glued splices and laminations, plywood and synthetic reinforced thermoplastic (SRP) covering. While such construction is neither particularly simple nor easy, the amateur may find it easier than older methods, especially the planking with ⅝-inch cedar, which would certainly require steaming, as well as careful lining, backing out and rounding, beveling, fitting, and caulking.

One should not get the idea that the new materials are particularly cheap; to the contrary they are relatively expensive. The expense is worth it, however. A covering of SRP greatly strengthens a hull without adding much weight, renders it completely and permanently watertight, and prevents water soaking, something that invariably happens to cedar planking when left for long periods in the water.

Composite wood-plastic construction requiring gluing procedures and the applications of plastic reinforcement tends to be time consuming and often goes very slowly in building new and unfamiliar designs. This may be a serious disadvantage for the commercial boatshop, which must figure its labor costs today closely. The amateur should not mind spending extra time if it produces superior results. Any amateur considering boat construction should think twice before undertaking a project, if he must be niggardly with his time. It is no good to rush, particularly with adhesives and plastic.

In adapting Stephens's Barnegat Cruiser for building with modern materials, I have made some changes to improve the sneakbox for present-day use and home construction. The principal change is an increase of 6 inches in the beam, so that this 14-foot boat is now 5 feet at its widest point. This amount of beam would be excessive for most craft of the same length, but not for this shallow, spoon-shaped hull with its rounded, overhanging sides. The additional beam adds appreciably to sailing stability without undesirable effects, such as a significant increase in weight, and it also provides a greater displacement without an increase in draft. With two occupants and a considerable amount of equipment and camping gear, this widened version can still slide across water too shallow for any other craft except the lightest canoes.

The most remarkable thing about these lines is that all hull cross-sections in the body plan are, in outline, parts of the same master curve. The practical import of this is that, as the boat is built with laminated frames, only one gluing form is required for all the frames in the boat. This means a considerable saving in labor.

FRAMING

The frames, spaced on one-foot centers, are laminated spruce glued with epoxy adhesive. For both frames and deck beams, laminations of spruce glued with epoxy adhesive are recommended. An inexpensive source of excellent lumber for laminated frames is widely available in rough, air-dried spruce ledger boards of good quality, selected and stripped up with the circular saw to avoid large and unsound knots. A few small, sound knots well distributed throughout the lamination does not detract from its strength. Strips $\frac{1}{8}$ inch to $\frac{3}{16}$ inch thick and roughly 2 inches wide are got out on the circular saw, which gives a slightly rough surface ideal for epoxy gluing. Enough of these strips are bent around the form to give 1¼ inches of molded width when the rib is finished. Two half ribs of $\frac{7}{8}$-inch finished siding can be got out of each glued assembly of 2-inch wide strips. As a glance at the drawings will discover, each complete frame is made up of two half ribs. The construction sections show the half-ribs butted on the bottom centerline and joined by an oak floor molded 2 inches and sided $\frac{7}{8}$ inch, and fastened with ¼-inch through bolts. Another way would be to let the ends of the half-ribs extend by one another across the bottom.

Forms for gluing both frame and deck beam laminations are easily made from a flat piece of heavy plywood to which are bolted pieces of 2 by 4 sawn to conform to a desired curve as previously marked out on the plywood. A light brushing of hot paraffin is all that is needed as a release to prevent the glue from sticking to the form. Curved mating blocks and plenty of C-clamps pull the strips firmly into position against the form until the glue sets.

While laminated frames and deck beams may be made up in advance of their use, assembly starts with the formation of the laminated curved keel or keel batten, the forward extremity of which also serves for the stem. The strips or layers of ¼-inch marine plywood, which comprise the inner keel, are bent to shape and glued on stocks cut to the required profile curve of the bottom. The skeg of tapered 1¼-inch oak forms the after portion of the stocks, and the keel batten is fastened to it permanently. Forward, a plank on edge sawn to the profile curve is set up, plumbed, and secured, and the keel strips coated with glue internally are bent into its hollow and temporarily fastened.

Next, the frames are put in place and are beveled and secured for planking. The frames themselves act as molds, but a few battens serving as ribbands will facilitate setting the frames, especially the forward ones, which require considerable beveling. Also a couple of battens temporarily fastened on either side will help to hold the faired shape secure until planking has started, for which the boat must be turned over.

Forward where the keel sharpens slightly in a widened V-section, frame ends and floor will rest on top of the inside of the keel strip or batten. Aft, where the bottom is nearly flat, it will be necessary to recess the floor and frame feet slightly so as to drop them enough to give a flat bearing for the garboards. This is shown in the accompanying construction sketch. Note also the provision for limbers, for it is of critical importance for the bottom to drain completely to its lowest point about amidships.

As part of the framing-out operation, the sheer harpings at the bow are cut out to the half-breadth shape of the deck, are notched to receive the timberheads of the first three frames, and are fitted in place and fastened to the head of the inner keel or keel batten where it rounds up in place of a stem. Aft of the harpings, two ⅜-inch by 1½-inch battens with glue between are fastened to the inside of the timberheads along the deck or sheer line. This is more easily done with two battens because of the twist. Outward of this laminated clamp, the spaces between the timber heads are filled in solid with pieces the width of the laminated clamp and glued to it. This makes a solid landing at the deck line the whole length of the boat for fastening the plank ends, which, because of the spoon shape of the hull, round up and terminate along the sheer.

Of course, the outer surfaces of the sheer harping at the bow, as well as the filler blocks between the timberheads, must be carefully beveled to conform to the rake of the side flare, but this is done, or finished, after the framed-out hull is turned over for planking. The keel batten is also beveled and faired at this juncture.

Considerable beveling of the inner keel is required toward the bow where some sharpness or V-section develops. Hardly any beveling is required aft. Because of this the inner keel is made three layers thick at the bow and back nearly to station 7, while aft of this it drops off to two layers, so continuing to the stern.

PLANKING

The distinctive and unusual shape of this hull—more specifically its relatively great beam, its shallowness, together with the open round of its extreme side flare—constitutes a special planking problem. Instead of the bow ends of the planking (the "hood" ends in older terminology) landing in a stem rabbet in the usual way, they run up to the sheer on the curved bow to meet the deck and fasten into the solid harping piece ingeniously provided for just this purpose. Who first devised this manner of securing the plank ends is not known, but Stephens showed it in the 1880s, and presumably this planking practice originated long before Stephens reported it. It is possibly unique to the sneakbox.

Offhand, I cannot recall just this same method of lining plank and handling plank ends as used for any other hull. The nearest thing to it is the Scandinavian pram with the hood ends of its planks landing on a small, steeply raked bow transom. Actually there is some resemblance between the two types, except that the sneakbox is relatively much wider and shallower and more flaring than the pram.

For his 16 feet by 4 feet 11 inches by 1 foot sailing sneakbox, W. P. Stephens specifies carvel plank finished ⁹⁄₁₆ inch thick. Although the lining of the plank is not shown, Stephens, in the construction section for his Barnegat Cruiser, does indicate representative planking widths ranging from 4 inches to 6 inches. This would mean that some hollowing or "backing out" of the inner sides of the planks would be required, even though the wide and gradually

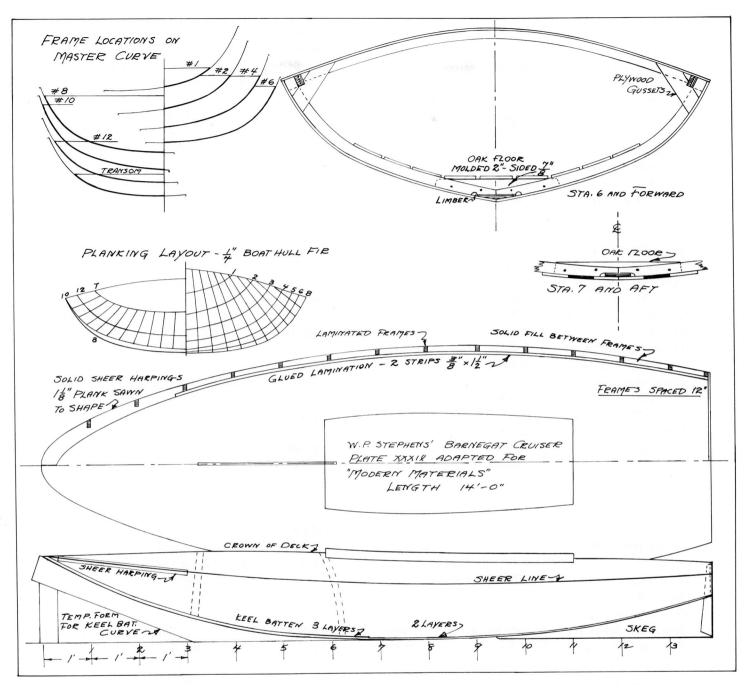

FRAME LOCATIONS ON MASTER CURVE

#1 #2 #4 #6

#8
#10

#12

TRANSOM

PLYWOOD GUSSETS

OAK FLOOR
MOLDED 2"- SIDED 7/8"

LIMBER

STA. 6 AND FORWARD

OAK FLOOR

STA. 7 AND AFT

PLANKING LAYOUT - 1/4" BOAT HULL FIR

10 12 7   1 2 3 4 5 6 8

8

LAMINATED FRAMES

SOLID FILL BETWEEN FRAMES

GLUED LAMINATION - 2 STRIPS 3/8" × 1 1/2"

SOLID SHEER HARPINGS
1 1/8" PLANK SAWN
TO SHAPE

FRAMES SPACED 12"

W. P. STEPHENS' BARNEGAT CRUISER
PLATE XXXIX ADAPTED FOR
"MODERN MATERIALS"
LENGTH   14'-0"

CROWN OF DECK

SHEER HARPING

SHEER LINE

TEMP. FORM
FOR KEEL BAT.
CURVE

KEEL BATTEN 3 LAYERS

2 LAYERS

SKEG

1' 1' 2 1' 3 4 5 6 7 8 9 10 11 12 13

flaring sides of the sneakbox do not show any abrupt curves or sharp turns. Because of this, that is, because the side curves of the sneakbox hull are so flat and gradual, even though it is a round-sided boat, it is possible to plank it with perfectly flat strips, provided these are kept fairly narrow. This makes it possible to plank

with strips of thin plywood without hollowing or backing out, and yet to achieve a satisfactorily round hull surface with only light sanding.

For the 14-foot by 5-foot by 1-foot 2-inch composite hull for which the lines and offsets are given here, 11 to 12 strakes of 1/4-inch marine fir plywood on either side are recommended. Where the hull curves are practically flat, the planking can be as wide as 4 inches. Where there is more curve and at the ends, planks will narrow to 2 inches and even less.

Planks will be put on in continuous strips, in one piece from bow to stern, spliced before installation from standard 8-foot by 4-foot panels. The length of the scarph tapers should be 12 times the thickness of the planking stock, or 3-inches for ¼-inch plywood. The scarphs should be epoxy glued and sanded smooth on both sides after the glue has set. Well-made scarphs after sanding should be nearly invisible and are just as strong as the rest of the plywood. Plank splices must be systematically staggered on the boat.

Narrow plywood strakes pulled tightly against the frames with No. 6 1-inch bronze screws or No. 8 1-inch brass screws (the increase in size is to make up for the weaker metal) should give a hull surface very close to round when completed. Any slight tendency to show knuckled seams can be removed by sanding before the outer covering of SRP is applied. As bronze screws are extremely expensive, some economy may be achieved by using 1¼-inch Anchorfast nails in the less critical areas of the hull surface.

FINISHING OUT

After the boat is planked it is turned back on its bottom so that access may be gained to the interior, and narrow fiberglass or polypropylene tapes set in a stiff epoxy mix are laid over all inside planking seams, carefully cutting for length to fit between the frames. After the tape reinforcements have set up hard, the boat is turned back again bottom up.

In most cases a single layer of 4-ounce Vectra or Versatex polypropylene fabric set in epoxy resin will suffice, plus an overlay of Dynel (for its greater resistance to abrasion) to cover the bottom. As the sneakbox is a shallow-water craft that will be frequently grounded on sand and gravel, this overlay of Dynel, also epoxy-bonded, should not be omitted.

Inside the hull, the plywood before painting should be thoroughly soaked with a good oil-based wood preservative like Wood-Life or Cuprinol. In addition, an application of heated linseed oil diluted to help penetration would be all to the good. This should not be applied until after all epoxy adhesives and surfacing resin on the outside have hardened.

Next the deck beams and deck are installed. Each frame is topped by a deck beam of laminated spruce. The deck beams and frames are joined at the ends with plywood gussets glued and screwed in place and notched slightly to fit against the underside of the sheer clamp, previously put in. Some of the deck beams could have been put in previously, serving in place of cross spalls to hold the shape of the hull during planking, but not so many as to prevent convenient access to the interior before the tape reinforcements are put on the planking seams. Of course, the centerboard trunk must be installed before the deck is in place. Some builders might prefer to attend to the trunk before the boat is planked. This is a boatbuilder's option and depends in part upon the style of trunk and board selected.

The deck should be of ¼-inch marine fir plywood covered with SRP. This makes a deck both stronger and tighter than the ½-inch pine originally specified by Stephens.

We cannot give here completed details and directions for constructing a sneakbox throughout. For such further details, and for building directions to some extent, you should refer to previously published sources, especially W. P. Stephens and H. I. Chapelle. All we have attempted to do here is to show how the traditional sneakbox hull may be adapted to composite wood-plastic construction. By such construction it is possible to get, I believe, a hull of superior strength and lightness, to be made from materials more easily and widely obtainable today than is suitable natural sawn cedar for planking, for instance, as well as a hull easier for home builders to frame and plank than if they used the older methods.

Appendix

Notes on Boatbuilding Methods

......................•......................

ASSEMBLING AND RABBETING STEMS

Assembling and rabbeting a stem seems to be a difficult operation, though it is not. Because procedures for putting together, shaping and rabbeting stem assemblies are often treated perfunctorily in boatbuilding manuals, it will be worthwhile, I think, to examine these operations in detail. As an example, I include on pages 256 and 257 the details of the stem for the 12-foot round-bottom skiff shown in Chapter 18.

The term stem derives from the older word, stam, which the English Oxford Dictionary defines as a "stem or stalk, a trunk or stump of a tree," citing a seventeenth-century agricultural work, which mentions stamwood as "the roots of trees grubbed up." The original material for boat stems was stamwood, whence the name, and there is nothing better to this day for a boat stem than stamwood, providing you can get it.

In the past, builders of fine varnished yacht tenders got their stems, as a rule, out of hackmatack knees. Hackmatack, also known as tamarack, is a species of eastern larch whose principal roots grow out approximately at right angles from the stumps, and close to, or on, the surface of the ground. Root wood is the toughest part of the tree, and usually it was possible to select knees whose curved grain conformed closely, if not exactly, to the designed shape of the stem. Thus it was possible

to get out the stem in one piece without cutting across the grain, achieving maximum strength without excessive bulk of timber. Hackmatack made a handsome stem in which toughness was combined with light weight.

Still lighter stems for the Adirondack guideboats were cut from red spruce root crooks obtained from stumps left by the lumbermen. White oak knees are the finest kind, but were used to a lesser extent for boat stems, possibly due to the difficulty of digging them. Even root crooks of northern white cedar served for the stems of Maine salmon wherries.

Of course, you won't find stump knees or root crooks for sale in today's lumberyards. There are plenty still growing in the woods, but unless the modern boatbuilder undertakes to dig his own, he will have to be content with substitutes. There are a number of ways of piecing together several short, relatively straight, sections of lumber to get the desired curvature. Also, it is possible to steam-bend straight pieces to the designed shape, and, in addition, the same result can be attained by laminating a number of strips thin enough to bend easily. (See the next section of this Appendix.)

A composite three-piece stem is recommended for the boat under consideration. In this case the continuous curved section will be on the outside, backed up by an apron piece, so called, at the top, joined below by another inner

253

backing piece, which extends aft on top of the keel some 8 inches and is securely fastened to it. We do not have any specific name for this lower backing piece that I know of, although, according to Eric McKee, it would be called a "dead wood" piece in the south of England.

The curved outer piece, continuous from stemhead to where it splices into the keel, could either be glue-laminated from oak strips or a single piece steam bent. I recommend the former for a number of reasons. For one, good bending stock, and the means for steaming a piece of the required size are not always readily available, while lamination offers no special problems—

except the clamps needed, possibly, but with some ingenuity effective substitutes can be improvised.

I want especially to direct attention to the way in which a stem assembly like this should be put together, and why it is made up as it is. Essentially it is made up of two layers: an outside layer of laminated or steam-bent wood in one continuous length and an inner layer in two sections placed end to end. These two layers are laid out so that they come together on the apex line of the planking rabbet, which I also refer to as the parting line precisely because the stem assembly is intended to separate along this line

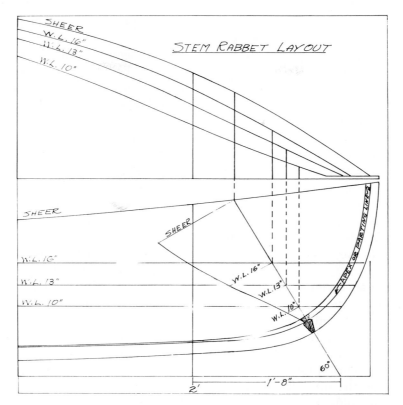

STEM RABBET LAYOUT

in order to facilitate cutting the planking rabbet.

Otherwise, the different "sidings" (thwart-ship thicknesses) of the inner and outer stem-pieces would have made the planking rabbet extremely difficult to lay out accurately. The different sidings or thicknesses of the parts that make up this composite stem range from $1\frac{3}{8}$ inches to $2\frac{3}{4}$ inches, which greatly complicates lofting and layout if the stem assembly is treated as a unit rather than as separate pieces to be joined together after the planking rabbet has been cut, the method we have adopted here.

The simplest sort of stem is the one-piece stem with the same siding throughout, which is another way of saying that its port and star-board side surfaces are flat and parallel to each other. Lofting of the planking rabbet lines is quite simple and their transfer to the stem piece equally easy.

The procedure for cutting the planking rabbet under these circumstances is illustrated in the accompanying diagrams labeled Figure 1 and Figure 2. Figure 1 shows a short section of a stem of uniform siding with the planking rabbet

FIGURE 2

FIGURE 1

marked out on one side but not cut. Number 1 is the rabbet line; number 2, the apex line; number 3, the bearding line. Numbers 1 and 3 are given in the original lines and are marked on the stem pattern when that is lifted from the full-size laydown.

After numbers 1 and 3 have been transferred to the stem piece, number 2, or the apex line, is derived as follows: A series of construction lines, numbers 4 and 6, as well as others like them, are drawn. These cross lines are laid out square with the rabbet and bearding lines when these are straight, and where they are curved the cross lines are drawn "normal" to the curve, which is to say they take the shortest distance across.

Number 5 is a small rectangular block of the planking stock to be used, which has been accurately squared at either end. This is applied edgewise. One corner is placed directly over the intersection of the cross line with the rabbet line, and the line of the opposite surface or face is made to pass through the intersection of the cross line with the bearding line. If the two edges lying over the space between the rabbet line and the bearding line are marked, the outline will appear as a right triangle when the block is removed, as is seen at number 7. The hypotenuse of this triangle extends between the rabbet and the bearding lines and its two legs intersect in the apex line. After a series of these points have been established along the length of the stem piece, a batten is run through them and the apex line marked, preliminary to cutting the planking rabbet.

It should be noted that if any one of these triangles so marked could be made to rotate on its hypotenuse as an axis, the path it would describe in passing through the wood of the stem would correspond exactly to the shape of the planking recess or rabbet when it is correctly cut.

It should be added that in cutting a stem rabbet of this kind, a perpendicular cut with a sharp chisel is made along the apex line first. Then the wood is carefully pared away with a sharp chisel, working toward the apex line from both the rabbet line and the bearding line, until

the sample block of planking stock fits perfectly.

In Figure 2, the plank rabbet was first laid out for planking ¾ inch thick. This was done on the lines laydown. The stem pattern was marked accordingly, and the stem was so laid out. When the planking rabbet was cut, a block ¾ inch thick was used. Figure 2 shows a ½-inch thick block being used to mark the excess wood to be removed when ½-inch thick planking is used for this boat. The reason for doing this is to provide additional back rabbet surface for supporting and fastening the hood ends of the planking.

Compare the difference in the width of the back rabbet surface in Figure 1 and Figure 2. As the angle at which the hood ends of the planking meet the stem grows larger and becomes more obtuse, the width of back rabbet surface decreases. In some full-ended boats, an ordinary parallel-sided stem with uniform siding throughout would not provide enough back rabbet surface to afford secure fastening for the hood ends of the top-side planking. The method generally used to correct this is to back up the upper part of the stem on the inside with a thicker piece called an apron. A convenient way of doing this is to fit the apron to the outer stem at the apex line. This is what we show here for both the upper and lower backing members of this composite stem.

The outer section of this stem is of a uniform 1⅜-inch siding throughout. This is quite sufficient for the exposed portion of the stem for this boat, affording a sharp entrance and a neat, trim appearance. However, if this narrow siding were extended to the whole stem, there wouldn't be sufficient width of back rabbet to land the ends of the upper planks securely, or the forward end of the garboard. For this reason the inner portions of the stem were given an increased siding ranging up to 2¾ inches.

The three parts of the stem assembly are first got out to their molded shape and accurately fitted together and temporarily fastened with large screws from the inside. These screws are next removed, and the pieces taken apart and beveled. The back rabbet bevels are cut on the inner pieces, as are the bevels to receive the ends of the planking on the outer portion of the stem. This is done according to full-size sectional outlines laid out at regular intervals along the stem as shown in the drawing at an approximate 8-inch spacing.

A separate diagram shows one method for laying out these sections from the lines plan. Actually all that is needed for laying out a section is the angle at which the planking meets the center plane of the boat, except that this angle must be taken normal to the curve of the stem, or "square" with it, in boatbuilders' parlance, at the point where the section is laid out.

The angles used to lay out the stem sections are easily taken from a half model should one prefer to work directly from a model rather than lines, and, even if lines are used, a half model can be a great help and is well worth making. Such a half model should be shaped to the inside of the planking, and its stem profile should represent the apex line of the hull rather than the rabbet line.

After the stem pieces have been beveled according to the sectional diagrams laid out as explained, they are reassembled using an application of epoxy glue and drawing up tightly on the screws. When the glue has set, this composite stem should be as strong, or stronger, than if it had been got out of a single piece.

THE TWO-PIECE DORY STEM

As can be seen in the various plans for boats in this book, stems can be rabbetted or made up of two parts—an inner main stem and an outer false stem. For the latter type of construction, let's take a look at the stems for a Lawton dory skiff and the Chamberlain skiff shown in Chapter 5. The dimensioned layouts of both boats' stems are shown here.

Note that these layouts are for the shape of the inner or main stem. The outer false stem, which covers the plank ends, is, in standard dory construction, a strip of oak, put on last, steamed, bent into place, and fastened while it is still hot. After it has cooled, it is planed to

shape. It should be faired off nicely in conformance with the lines of the bow, to give as easy an entrance as possible.

The main stem can be made solid or laminated. Here we will consider a laminated one.

The best way to make a gluing form for a laminated main stem is first to lay out the shape on a piece of plywood, ½ inch thick or thicker. Generally a scrap, or secondhand, piece can be obtained for this, to save the expense of new wood. Next, solid backing blocks for clamping against are fitted to the line of the stem and screwed on through the plywood from underneath. As the stem will finish to a 1½-inch siding

13 Foot Dory Skiff
C. A. Lawton, 1947

Stem 14 Foot
Chamberlain Skiff

and will be glued up from strips slightly wider to compensate for any slight irregularities that might result from slippage during gluing, the backing blocks can be bandsawed out of short pieces of 2 x 4s. The blocks should be fastened on with plenty of 2-inch No. 12 or No. 14 screws; to glue them on as well would be an excellent idea, for this form must be absolutely rigid and adequately strong to withstand powerful clamping pressures, especially if a resorcinol resin glue is used.

I prefer to place my clamping blocks on the concave side of the stem curve, so that the clamps pull the laminations into a cavity, so to speak. Whether this is the better way, I cannot say for sure, but it seems to work better for me.

The form should be well waxed with several coats of Simonize or an equivalent wax to prevent the glue from sticking to it. The surfaces of the laminating strips should be rough, just as are usually left by the ordinary circular saw, for this helps to hold a film of glue in the joint, which is essential for a strong bond when gluing with epoxy. The laminations, after preliminary clamping, are tapped down with a block and hammer to rest snugly against the plywood base throughout. This evens them up edgewise and at the same time seals the bottom of the stem lamination so that the epoxy adhesive does not settle by its own weight and leak out before it has hardened. The epoxy adhesive should be applied liberally. It is far better to have too much glue rather than too little, as the excess is easily planed off after it has hardened.

Once laminated, the stem could be beveled at the bench to receive the planking before it is attached to the bottom. The bevels are quite easily obtained from the laydown. However, this is unnecessary, and I do not especially recommend it. For the amateur, it is probably easier to bevel the stem after the frames have been set up and are being faired for planking. A long strip of plywood serving as a fairing batten and extended across the frames in a fore-and-aft direction to overlap the stem will show exactly how much must be planed off in order to receive the ends of the planking. A centerline is marked on the outside surface of the stem, and the bevel

is cut to about ⅛ inch of this line on either side of it.

Those who laminate the main stem may decide to laminate the false stem also. This can be done on the same form used for gluing the inner stem, with some slight adaptations, or it can be done directly on the boat itself, provided the epoxy glue used is thick enough not to run out of the joints before it hardens. It can be thickened by the addition of Cab-O-Sil, a thixotropic agent, which is a very fluffy, finely divided, powdered silica manufactured by the Cabot Company of Boston, and obtainable from most plastic supply firms.

The recommended technique for laminating the false stem directly on the boat is to tack each layer as it is applied with just enough fine brads to hold it in place. After the required number have been bent on, several temporary pressure blocks are screwed in place to hold the laminations in firm contact until the glue has hardened. These temporary pressure blocks can be sawn out of any convenient scrap stock, and are cut to fit the curve of the stem. They are fastened with long, slim screws, which go through the laminations into the main stem beneath.

Screw holes must be bored to prevent splitting the thin layers, especially if these are oak. After the glue has set, the pressure blocks, which need not be especially thick, by the way, are removed and discarded, and the screws which held them, if slim enough and not too long, may be set in and bunged, to remain as the permanent fastening of the outer stem.

It might be mentioned also that the strips forming the laminations of the outer stem are put on somewhat wider than this member will be when finished, and are later planed off and faired after the glue has hardened.

If a resorcinol glue should be used by someone sensitive to epoxy, the laminated outer stem should be glued on a form so that the requisite pressure can be secured by the use of clamps. Resorcinol resin glue requires ample pressure for satisfactory joints, which in this case means at least six or eight strong C-clamps as well as solid, fitted pressure blocks to transmit the clamping pressure evenly throughout the gluing surfaces. I should caution you, however, that some of the resorcinol resin glues are not always reliable with certain species of oak, in particular some of the white oaks.

PLANKING

Most of the boats in this book—the Rangeley for instance—are relatively easy to plank, although some who do not know might think otherwise. To say that a boat is easy to plank does not mean that it will plank up quickly. The contrary is more apt to be true. But to the amateur builder, the amount of time required is not too important, for his labor comes for free. Aside from the cost of materials, the amateur's main concern is whether the job falls within the range of his capability. He will be well advised not to venture into undertakings too exacting and advanced for his limited experience and skill.

Planking is not too difficult for the amateur, provided he is not in a hurry, can follow directions, and is able to use hand woodworking tools with fair proficiency. It must be set down at the outset, although it might seem too elementary to need saying, that no one should even think of building a planked boat unless he can measure accurately with rule and square, sharpen and set a plane, saw to a line, and otherwise employ carpenters' tools with moderate facility. There was a time when American boys in growing up acquired such basic woodworking skills as a matter of course. No more. In this button-pushing age, one can no longer take such fundamentals for granted.

This said, we may further explain that the Rangeley and other classic craft described here are better adapted to amateur construction than some other models, because over the years the professionals who built these boats to sell simplified and rationalized their construction. They did this to save labor and to keep the cost down so they might compete favorably in the market with other small-craft types, yet still retain the boats' superior characteristics and fine performance.

While all operations in building small craft are important and require care and competence, still the planking of a boat must be accounted the principal operation, and it is a good planking job above all else that makes a superior, or even an acceptable, boat. Planking is the boatbuilding skill par excellence. A good finish house carpenter can step into a boatshop and lay deck or cabin sole, scribe in bulkheads, build lockers and berths, or do a number of similar things first off as well, or nearly as well, as the experienced boatbuilder, but put him at planking without preliminary instruction or practice, and he is sure to botch it. This is because planking is a highly specialized operation, with methods, procedures, "tricks of the trade," if you will, that are not needed or used elsewhere.

In all the books on boatbuilding written in the last hundred years or so since books on boatbuilding (not shipbuilding) began to be written, there is no adequate treatment of planking that I know of, and the aggregate of planking information in all of them put together does not get into the subject in depth. This is mainly because those who so far have written the books are not the actual builders of boats with tools in hand, but rather persons somewhat removed from the building operation, that is to say architects, designers, engineers, and draftsmen. These people know all there is to know about hull lines, mathematical computations, and theory in general, but none, as far as I know, has as yet paid much attention to the practical problems involved in covering the hull surface with suitably proportioned strakes of wooden planking. To this day this essential operation has been left to the working boatbuilder. He has not written it down for various reasons, but mainly because he is usually not a writer, and thus much of traditional planking methods and procedures have remained virtual "trade secrets" in a day when there are not many trade secrets left.

For the foregoing reasons, the planking operation is prone to give the amateur trouble, and because he cannot find the instruction he needs in books, he goes haltingly and tends to exaggerate the difficulties that confront him.

LINING PLANK

In lining out plank, the builder tries to get shapes that will run as straight as possible when laid out in the flat on the planking stock. Excessively curved or crooked planks not only waste lumber, but are weaker than straight planks, because their curved sweeps cut across the natural grain of the board. The builder also tries to get shapes that look well on the boat, and this is especially important in clinker boats like the Rangeley where the lap lines stand out prominently. Not infrequently these two desiderata conflict, requiring artful compromise. Nevertheless, with certain hull shapes some crooked strakes are unavoidable.

With some such crooked strakes it would be difficult, if not impossible, to find boards wide enough to get them out full-length in one piece. Crooked strakes are usually made up of two or more shorter lengths, to save lumber and to give a straighter grain in the component pieces. One common example of the use of the spliced strake to permit the use of narrower boards, and to give a straighter, stronger grain, is the sheer plank of the knuckle-sided Swampscott dory, which is commonly made in two parts joined somewhat aft of the center of the boat. The strakes of the Adirondack guideboat were made up of two and three pieces each, primarily to get as straight a grain as possible for maximum strength. The narrow, clinker strakes of the Rangeley are also easily spliced. One thing that must be remembered is that splices in planks must be well separated from plank to plank. A judicious use of scarphed splices well distributed throughout the planking fabric makes planking easier and saves lumber, but under no condition should such splices be bunched up or allowed too close together in adjoining strakes.

The hull surfaces of different small craft types vary greatly in shape and proportion, each presenting its own special problems to the planker. Those experienced with one type often have trouble when they attempt to line out the planking for another type with which they are not familiar. In this connection, let me repeat a suggestion that has proved helpful in the past.

Anyone planning to plank an unfamiliar hull shape should first make a scale half-model, and on this practice laying out the planking with light strips of pine for battens held in place with thumbtacks or large pins. By trial and error in this manner, he can work out pleasing and uniformly proportioned planking lines, the spacings between which are then scaled off and transferred full size to the molds of the actual boat.

It may be helpful to the non-professional to cite a few common problems met with in spacing off and lining out plank. First, consider the dory garboard, the top edge of which is lined out on the boat (that is to say, on the frames serving as molds and the stem and stern transom) to show a pronounced curve or sweep with the ends running up quite high on the stem, and usually almost as high at the stern. Judging from the lining batten as it is thus tacked in place on the side of the boat, it appears that this plank has a great amount of hollow curve in its upper edge. However, when the shape of the plank is spiled off and laid out on the planking stock in the flat, it will be found that the top edge of this plank is actually nearly straight. Had it been lined out to look flatter or straighter on the boat, the top edge of this plank, when laid out flat, would have taken a convex curve, necessitating a corresponding concavity or hollow curve in the bottom edge of the plank next above, causing this next plank to be quite crooked. By running the ends of the dory garboard up high on the stem and at the stern, the lower planks of the dory are made nearly straight, which saves planking material and produces stronger planks because of their straighter grain.

Because of the dory's high sheer, enough uncovered stem surface still remains above the upswept garboard to provide ample landing width for the hood ends of the remaining plank. This would not be the case if the dory had a straight sheer like the standard round-sided yacht tender, made to lie as flat and low as possible when turned bottom up on deck. Such a tender will be relatively big-bellied to carry a load, yet the stem will be short because of the flat sheer. Nine or ten strakes will be required to fill out the girth amidships. Yet, should the garboard be carried up high on the stem as in a dory, sufficient length of stem rabbet would not remain to allow sufficient width for the hood ends of the eight or nine plank remaining. To get them all on, these ends would have to be made too narrow and pointed to look good or to fasten properly.

I have seen many poorly lined planking jobs and they were most unsightly as well as structurally inferior. Some years ago a boatshop in Amesbury, Massachusetts, which had formerly built dories exclusively, added a round-hull stock sailboat to its line. Built like dories by dory builders, obviously, these boats the first year showed extremely ugly plank shapes, a wide, high-swept garboard, and wedge-shaped upper plank with narrow pointed hood ends. Later this was rectified after the plankers learned how to line this round hull.

When properly lined, the upper edge of the garboard of the standard round yacht tender will look, when the boat is viewed in profile and square off from the side, straight or nearly so. But lay this plank out in the flat and you will see that the fore end is narrow and that it hooks down somewhat. This is due to the twist, and the pinched-in shape of the entrance below the load waterline, as well as the necessity of keeping the end of the garboard low. This ugly hook in the end of the plank disappears when the plank is bent and twisted into place on the hull. Sometimes, due to a bad job of lining, such a hook can still be seen in the fore ends of planks after they are in place on the boat. Such drooping ends, aptly called "moose shoulders," offend the eye and are avoided by the professional planker.

The Rangeley is not a hard boat to line for plank; this is particularly true for the 17-foot H. N. Ellis boat described in Chapter 20. While its 4-foot beam gives considerable center girth, the stem is high enough, because of the ample sheer, to provide ample landing room for 10 planks above the garboard. The ends of these can be kept wide enough to look and fasten well.

But let's get specific: lining the shape of the plank does not take place until after the boat has been set up and faired for planking. This means that the backbone—stem, keel, and transom—is set in place with section molds at indicated stations. For example, in the Rangeley boat (Chapter 20), the molds are spaced 2 feet apart, making seven molds in all. Ordinarily there would be no mold at the No. 8 station shown on the drawing as this section was put in merely to aid in fairing the lines.

In the case of a new boat being built for the first time from scratch, it is necessary to decide on the number of planks and their approximate widths, and to space them off on the stem, transom, and at the center of the boat. In very few boat plans are the number and the widths of the planks given.

In dividing up the sides of the hull into equal plank spacings at various selected locations, a simple but convenient device called a "diminishing batten" is easily prepared and used (see next page). Of course, the same results can be obtained with a rule and arithmetic, but the diminishing batten is quicker and avoids figuring. It is not needed as much on small craft as on larger vessels where planing widths have frequently to be adjusted and where there are many more stations to measure. It is important to realize that a separate diminishing batten must be marked out for each different number of plank.

After the line representing the upper edge of a strake of plank has been tentatively and approximately located and marked at the bow, stern, and midsection, and possibly at other locations in between, a fair lining batten is run through these spots and temporarily tacked in place with small nails only partly driven in so that they may be easily pulled with the claw hammer. Usually it is best to start nailing at the center of the boat and work either way to the ends. Directions for making up a lining batten follow this section.

After the batten is in place, it is sighted carefully from various heights, stances, and angles. In this way, unfair places, if any, are discovered, and are corrected by raising the batten slightly here or depressing it slightly there. When

THE DIMINISHING BATTEN ~ A CONVENIENCE FOR SPACING OFF EVEN WIDTHS OF PLANK ON THE SIDE OF A BOAT. LAY OFF A NUMBER OF EQUAL SPACES, EACH ONE AS MANY INCHES LONG AS THE NUMBER OF PLANK REQUIRED. THE 2ND SPACE DIVIDED INTO EIGHTHS REPRESENTS EIGHTHS OF AN INCH, AS EACH FULL SPACE ON THE BATTEN REPRESENTS ONE INCH OF PLANK WIDTH.

THIN, FLEXIBLE STRIP OF WOOD

FIVE PLANK

$2\frac{3}{8}"$ WIDE $3\frac{3}{16}"$ WIDE $3\frac{9}{16}"$ WIDE $3\frac{1}{2}"$ WIDE $3\frac{1}{16}"$ WIDE

J.G.

the plank line is finally true and fair throughout, it is clearly marked on the molds at each station.

The inherent tendency of a properly made lining batten is naturally to assume a fair curve or sweep when bent without being forced at any point. Often when a place shows unfairness, it is necessary only to pull a single nail for the batten to spring into place and thus to correct its line more or less automatically. Thus, in lining plank, a good batten supplements the boatbuilder's eye, and one serves as a check on the other. The boatbuilder's eye is educated by sighting the batten, and by the judicious and painstaking use of the batten, the novice can usually do an acceptable job of lining, which otherwise would be impossible for him. The lining batten is an indispensable planking tool that must be kept in good condition, so that it does not become twisted, warped, split, or scarred along its edges.

Some builders line all the planks at the start. Others work piecemeal. Often as planking proceeds, and in clinker planking especially, slight cumulative errors creep in after a few strakes are on, requiring adjustment in lines laid out previously if the planking is to come out right. Thus, as the planking goes up the side of

the boat, it may be necessary to reline some of the upper strakes. Here the diminishing batten may be used to advantage to check plank widths and spacings. However, it is always the lining batten that has the last word as to what the widths and shape of the strakes will be.

To keep the planking on both sides of the boat running the same is not quite as easy as it sounds. Frequently, inexperienced plankers fail to keep port and starboard hood ends on the stem of equal height and width. The two ends on either side of the stem rabbet should match exactly. Slight discrepancies from side to side in the mid-part of the hull, where the eye cannot easily detect them, are not particularly serious, that is, as long as they remain small, but a close watch should be kept for them nevertheless, and immediate adjustments made to minimize them as quickly as possible when found.

THE LINING BATTEN

As already discussed, lining out a boat hull for planking requires a lining batten, which the builder must make for himself. Such a batten is a uniform strip of wood with parallel sides, a flat, rectangular cross section, and a length somewhat greater than the boat to be planked. For example, the Rangeley boat (Chapter 20), requires a suitable lining batten that would be something like 1¾ inches to 2 inches in width, 5⁄16 inch to ⅜ inch in thickness, and 19 feet to 20 feet long. Clear, soft, straight-grained northern white pine is probably the best material for a batten, since it is a wood that is close grained, springy and uniform in bend, and soft enough to take nails without splitting.

The edges of a lining batten must be perfectly regular and true, so that in whatever way it is bent, a fair curve or sweep is produced. "Fair" is a trade term meaning a continuous, uniform sweep without lumps, holes, or irregularities of line of any sort. The ultimate test of fairness is what boatbuilders call a "good eye," which a few seem to come by naturally, but which most must acquire through practice and experience. As the old boatbuilder would say, "If it looks right, it is right." But it depends, of course, on who is looking. Fortunately for the novice, there is an aid to the unpracticed eye. The fair line is inherent in straight-grain wood itself, that is to say the long uniform cell fibers of straight-grain wood naturally assume fair curves or sweeps when they are bent.

In picking out pine for a lining batten, considerable pains should be taken in selecting the wood, for the quality of individual planks or boards can vary considerably. Try to get a section of plank that is straight, free from knots, and quite soft. Occasionally pine planks will be found that are harder than is normal for the species and some will be found with a pronounced grain that is not characteristic of pine. "Brashy" is the old Maine word for such lumber, which is strictly to be avoided. Brashy lumber comes from deformed, misgrown trees that are sometimes found on rocky, exposed hillsides. The wood has ingrown stresses and is prone to warp and split. Far better for our purpose is the softer wood from lush pines that grew fast, straight, and tall in rich bottom land.

Soft, straight-grained spruce can be used for lining battens but is more likely to warp than northern white pine. Port Orford cedar is quite good, and less apt to warp than our native northern white cedar. A select grade of soft Philippine mahogany will serve, as will cypress possibly, although it splits easily. By and large, a soft wood with as little grain as possible is to be preferred.

The hardwood species are of no use whatsoever for lining battens. A warped or twisted batten is useless, and any that get into this condition should be discarded. Obviously, battens when not in use should be stored in such a manner as to minimize the possibility of warping and twisting. Preferably they should lie flat and straight on a long rack where the air can reach all sides equally.

Long boats require long battens. For instance, as previously mentioned, the Rangeley boat will require a lining batten some 19 to 20 feet long for best results. Pine lumber of suitable quality in such lengths is not easily come by today. Fortunately, however, long battens can be spliced up from shorter lengths of stock, and, if this is properly done, the result is just as good as the unspliced batten from full-length lumber. It may even be possible to produce a better batten in this way, for the same quality of wood may be had throughout from the same high-grade section of plank.

If the finished width of the batten is to be 2 inches wide, the strips from which it is to be spliced up should be at least 3 inches wide to start with in order to provide ample extra wood for edging and sizing. The number of scarphs will depend on the length of the stock available. Three or four in a 20-foot batten are not too many. The length of the scarph bevel should be at least 12 times the thickness of the stock, and this should be left thicker when spliced than the finished thickness of the batten to permit straightening and sizing.

The scarph bevels must be accurately planed to a feather edge at the ends in order to secure perfectly fitting joints. Strong glue and careful procedure are required to obtain a perfect glue joint. As the batten will be kept dry and under cover, a completely waterproof glue is not required. If epoxy adhesive is used, the meeting surfaces of the scarph should be slightly and evenly roughened with a fine wood rasp or coarse sandpaper, for it is necessary that a thin film of resin be retained in the joint.

For a simple but excellent gluing jig or press, two pieces of smooth board slightly wider and longer than the scarph are required. One side of each is thoroughly waxed. On the waxed surface of one block the scarph to which glue has been applied is assembled and tacked in place with several fine brads to prevent slippage. The other block is laid on top, with the waxed surface over the scarph, and firm pressure is applied with two or three C-clamps. The wax prevents the glue, which is squeezed from the scarph, from sticking to the pressure blocks. When the glue has thoroughly hardened, the clamps and blocks are removed and the brads pulled out.

After the batten is glued, it is laid on the bench, or on a long plank serving as a bench. One side is planed smooth and true with a sharp jack plane. Next it is turned on edge, and the upper edge is planed as true as possible with the longest plane available, a long joiner if possible.

The batten is now ready for the circular saw, which should be sharp and smooth cutting; a planer-tooth blade is best. The edge already planed is run against the fence, which is set wide enough so that the saw blade barely brushes the other edge of the batten when it is run through. The fence is then set in an eighth of an inch or so, and the batten, turned over to reverse the edges, is run through again. This process is repeated several times, trimming one edge and then the other, until the width has been cut down to the desired 2 inches. By then, the two edges should be perfectly even and true, and parallel throughout. The fence is then set ⅜ inch from the blade, or according to whatever thickness is desired for the batten, which is run by the saw on edge with the previously planed surface against the fence. The batten is now trued and sized and ready for use.

Any extra care or labor expended in making a good lining batten will be repaid many times over before the boat is finished. To the experienced boatbuilder, all this may seem so obvious and simple as not to be worthwhile considering in detail. For the novice, however, it should serve to smooth over some otherwise rough going.

CLINKER OR LAPSTRAKE PLANKING

Clinker or lapstrake planking deserves to be more widely used. It has a number of advantages over carvel planking, and for some hull forms is the easier method. But inexperienced builders tend to shy away from it. This is because they do not understand how it is done, and because it has never been explained to them.

To the best of my knowledge no fully adequate explanation of clinker planking techniques has yet found its way into print. Some of the books hardly mention it. Others go only part of the way, skipping over, or leaving out entirely, essential steps and procedures.

Books at best, with their drawings and printed explanations, are only partly effective and a poor substitute for actual planking experience under the tutelage of a skilled craftsman. Still it is possible to convey enough with words and sketches to put the beginner on the right track, and to give him some directions to go by, enough to insure a reasonable chance of success, provided he keeps his wits about him. There are in fact a number of books that take up lapstrake planking which are worth looking into, and they are quite good as far as they go, but none is complete in all details, and all of them, at least all that I have seen, leave out things here and there that I consider important or even essential.

High on the list of books to be considered is H. I. Chapelle's *Boatbuilding* (W. W. Norton, N.Y.), for 35 years a standard work in its field. A much less extensive treatment of clinker planking is to be found in Robert M. Steward's more recent *Boatbuilding Manual* (International Marine Publishing Company, Camden, Maine), but one that will bear looking over, nonetheless.

Quite recently there have been two books

by British authors devoted entirely to this method of boatbuilding. Eric McKee's *Clenched Lap or Clinker* (National Maritime Museum, Greenwich, England), although only 30 pages long, contains considerable which is new to print, and John Leather's *Clinker Boatbuilding* (International Marine Publishing Company, Camden, Maine), a full-length book, includes much supplementary information. Both McKee and Leather treat the subject according to British methods, which frequently differ from American building practices. But the contrast between British ways and American ways can be instructive.

It is important to understand some of the advantages as well as the disadvantages of lapstrake construction. Although it is not suitable for some hull types and should not be considered for them, for others it is the natural and proper method and superior to any other that might be used.

While I have done my part to bring modern materials to the attention of amateur builders, and do not regret having done so, I must say I am sometimes disturbed when I find someone using glued-strip construction for a classic type that is better and easier built clinker. Generally this happens because the builder does not understand the advantages of clinker construction, or is afraid to try it, having never done it, but having heard somewhere that clinker is too difficult except for highly skilled professionals. Actually this is not so at all.

What are the advantages? Clinker boats tend to be light and strong, but flexible, making them faster and easier in a seaway, a characteristic of lapstrake craft since the time of the Viking longships. Clinker planks can be finished and sanded smooth at the bench before they are bent in place on the boat. This means substantial saving in labor over carvel planking, for the latter method requires that planks be hollowed on the inside, that is "backed out," to fit the curve of the frames, and after the hull is planked, the outside must be planed fair and sanded smooth. In addition the planking seams on a carvel hull must be caulked, while clinker hulls do not require caulking.

In order to hold caulking, carvel planking is rarely made thinner than ½ inch finished thickness, and to allow for the backing required for round-sided hulls the planking stock to start with will need to be from ⅛ inch to ¼ inch thicker than this, requiring a total thickness of ⅝ inch to ¾ inch or more. For clinker-planked boats of approximately the same size, the planking ordinarily will not be more than ⅜ inch thick and possibly only 5⁄16 inch. This means that for some of the classic clinker types such as the Rangeley boats, St. Lawrence skiffs, light yacht tenders, dinghies, and similar craft, the strakes for both sides can be laid out in single thickness on one-inch rough lumber to be split in two edgewise with a fine rip saw or band saw after being cut to shape. This can result in a substantial saving in lumber, not to be taken lightly considering current prices of planking stock.

One disadvantage of clinker boats is that it is not easy to replace damaged planks. However, with the epoxy glues and related materials now available, split planks can often be repaired on the boat without removing them.

Not every hull shape is suitable for clinker planking. Carvel planking is more versatile in this respect. By hollowing, bending, and twisting, carvel plank can be forced into all sorts of difficult shapes, as clinker plank cannot. The novice will be well advised to stick with classic clinker types, at least to start with, and be content to copy proven craft, adhering closely to them in such things as lap width, plank thickness, number and widths of planks, and especially to the way the hull surface is laid out or "lined" for planking.

What seems most to worry many beginners is fitting the laps, for of course a tight wood-to-wood fit of the lap surfaces must be secured throughout if the boat is not to leak. It is possible to secure a tight, leak-proof boat by using a flexible polysulphide compound in the laps, even in badly fitting ones, although applying this material is likely to be a messy procedure.

Laps should never be glued, as this prevents the normal slight movement back and forth of the lap surfaces occasioned by swelling and shrinking as the boat absorbs moisture or dries out. Splits in the plank or the laps will almost inevitably occur if the laps are rigidly glued.

Swelling and shrinking of the plank can be minimized and the wood stabilized to a great extent by soaking the planking with hot linseed oil (heated in a double boiler and diluted about 20 per cent with paint thinner or turps). Several applications until the wood is saturated, applied before painting, are required for best results. Clinker plank so treated will remain permanently tight under most conditions, provided they are well fitted to start with. In painting, after the oil has dried, the paint should be thoroughly worked into the laps.

But to return to fitting the laps. Where the sides of the boat are straight or only slightly curved, there is no problem. All that is required here is careful planing to get a tight fit. But where the frames show more curve, and particularly amidships on the turn of the bilge on hard-bilged boats, it may not be so easy to close the laps, unless the operation is carefully laid out in advance.

Four factors need to be taken into consideration: (1) the curvature of the hull, (2) the width of the plank, (3) the thickness of the plank, and (4) the width of the lap.

If the curvature of the hull is too abrupt, or the width of the plank too great, or the plank too thin, or the lap too wide, it will be difficult, and perhaps impossible, to close the lap. Of the four, plank width is most readily adjusted. Once a model is selected, the curvature of the sides can hardly be altered without basic alteration of the design. The plank thickness is generally established at the outset, and likewise is not open to adjustment as construction proceeds.

While lap width may not be reduced below the minimum required for secure fastening, there is still some slight margin for adjustment. But plank widths can generally be made as wide or as narrow as required, without adverse effect on the structure or appearance of the boat, if the planks are lined out properly. How to go about this will be explained shortly.

On Sheet 1 are shown planking layouts for the midsections of four clinker workboats ranging in length from 14 feet to 15 feet 5 inches. In all four the sheer planks and the bottom planks are wider than those on the round of the bilge. The first boat, left to right, is a wide, heavy working skiff 14 feet 5 inches long with 5 feet of beam. This is closely like a working skiff built in Rhode Island a hundred years ago, and in active use there until quite recently. The half-inch-thick planking is unusually heavy for a clinker boat of this size and the 1⅛ inches laps are extra wide. This hull shows a good amount of deadrise and some flare at the sheer, hence the turn at the bilge is moderate.

By making the sheer plank, the garboard, and the broad quite wide, it is possible to plank this boat with only seven strakes. However, the planks on the turn are only about half the width of the garboard and the sheer planks, yet even so, the laps for planks 5 and 6 do not quite close at the bottom. This does no harm, and is done to give ample wood for the lap fastenings. Besides this slight gap will fill with paint, and will not show when the boat is in use. The same thing occurs with the lap of the fifth plank of the wherry.

In all four boats the plank widths are laid out so that those planks on the turn of the bilge, where the greatest curvature is, are considerably narrower than the bottom and sheer planks where the side, or sectional, shape is straighter. As these narrower planks—that is, narrower amidships—carry forward to the stem and aft to the stern, they will hold their widths to a greater extent than will the top and bottom planks, that is, they will not "diminish" as much, to use the trade term. Or to put it another way, these middle planks will line out more nearly parallel sided. In most cases it is desirable for the ends of all the plank landing on the middle and upper stem, with the exception of the sheer, to show approximately the same width. Generally the sheer plank should be wider.

The lining or layout operation that established the planking lines, that is the planking widths, shapes, and relative locations on the hull, is a highly critical part of clinker construction, much more so than for carvel planking. Not only is this important, as we have seen, to get laps that will close easily, or even close at all, but the planking lines stand out so distinctly on a clinker hull that, unless they are right, the appearance is spoiled.

In building a first boat, it is highly desirable to have access to one already built to go by. With such a model it will be easy to copy the planking layout, number of planks, their widths, lining, lap widths and bevels, and so forth. With a little care, even the most inexperienced builder should be able to avoid serious mistakes.

If one undertakes to build from a drawing without having an example of the craft at hand to consult, chances are that some details will be missing. In fact most building plans now available for small craft do not go into planking at all, leaving this up to the builder. If it is his first boat, or even his first clinker boat, it will not be strange if he makes a mess of it, unless he has something more to go on.

How to proceed under such circumstances? As soon as the lines have been laid down, the body section with the greatest amount of curvature (usually the midsection) should be reproduced full size on the drawing board so that a layout of the plank sections can be worked out for it. This will consist mainly of adjusting the widths of the given number of strakes to get good closure of the laps without making some of the strakes excessively wide and others too narrow. Extremes should be avoided. Plank thickness, lap width, and number of planks are usually given or established at the outset, but conceivably any one, or all, of these might have to be adjusted to get a satisfactory planking arrangement. In some cases, additional sectional layouts of the planking at other hull locations might be desirable for comparison.

The results obtained from the sectional layout provide the basis for the lining operation; that is, the lengthwise layout from stern to stem of planking width and shapes. I cannot recommend too strongly that the inexperienced builder start by making an accurate scale half-model of the hull of convenient size, say, on the order of 1½ inches equals 1 foot for a 16-foot boat. A trial layout of the planking is made on this half model, lining out the planks with miniature white pine battens representing the planking laps (made to scale, of course) and held in place with dressmaking pins. This procedure allows the builder to see the planking layout as a unit, and permits such adjustments as are required to correct any unfairness and to insure a pleasing and harmonious planking arrangement throughout. The corrected batten or lap locations are marked on the half model before the battens are removed.

Some experienced builders may feel that they can skip the half model, but I recommend that they use battens to lay out the lap locations on the building molds as soon as they are set up and secured in position. These lap-width battens should be stiff enough to bend fair between the molds, and battens for all of the planking laps should be put on the molds at the same time so that the planking arrangement can be viewed as a unit.

Plank locations previously worked out on the half-model are transferred to the full-size setup. Adjustments, and more than a few, will nearly always have to be made, until all of the battens run fair and the whole arrangement looks pleasing and right as a unit. This will take sighting and resighting from every angle, and this fairing process should not be hurried. In fact it is best to go away and come back several times before the fairing operation is completed.

Finally, the adjusted lap locations are marked top and bottom on the molds, and transferred to the other side of the boat so that both sides are identical, and the planking

as it proceeds should be held strictly to these lap locations. In this way it is easy to maintain fair planking lines and to come out right at the end, something not easy for the inexperienced builder to do otherwise.

Beveling the laps can be a real bugaboo for the inexperienced. It takes care, and it takes knowing how, and what complicates things is there are several different ways of going about it, each applying to some particular boat or type with its own special requirements.

Some of the St. Lawrence skiffs, for example, have their laps brought to a feather edge and are planed so they are quite smooth outside, almost like a carvel hull. Some boats like the heavy working skiff on Sheet 1 have a minimum amount of wood removed in fitting the laps, so that some of the lap joints are not planed at all, in this case the lap between the garboard and the next plank above. British boats are more apt to be built this way with only the least possible amount of wood removed in fitting the laps, what the British call "hemming," according to Eric McKee. Leaving as much wood as possible in fitting the laps makes for a strong lap joint, but it tends to produce a heavy, not to say clumsy, look which can be avoided by thinning the lap somewhat, but not to the extent of weakening it unduly.

Where the model permits it, and this is governed by the amount of curve in the sectional shapes, a uniform amount of bevel can be planed off the underside of the lower edge of the overlapping plank, and the lap bevel on the underside of the plank below can be planed to fit.

An example of this is shown by Lap Diagram No. 1 on Sheet 2, where a uniform bevel of ⅛ inch by ¾ inch is planed off the lower inside edge of the planks when they are prepared at the bench. Lap Diagram No. 2 shows how a thicker, heavier lap joint would result if the overlapping edge were not beveled.

The method that I am suggesting here, and it is not the only method by any means, for fitting and "hemming" the laps consists of planing whatever is required for a fit off the bevel on the top edge of the under plank and doing this on the boat. This amount is not uniform or constant, but varies from thicker to thinner as the curvature of the side varies.

Generally, the professional will first cut the correct lap bevel at each mold station using a gauge of some sort representing a cross section of the upper, or overlapping, plank at that station in order to get the correct amount of bevel. When this is done for all the stations, he will next proceed to bevel the sections between the stations, depending more or less on his eye and acquired skill to get the lap sections true and fair from station to station. This is not easy for beginners who are apt to take off too much or too little wood, producing a lumpy lap surface which will not close tight.

However, if the beginner will adapt the method detailed on Sheet 2, he can, by taking care, plane a perfect lap. A small, sharp plane set fine is needed. One small enough to fit in the palm of the hand is best for this.

A batten as long as or longer than the boat, and stiff enough to bend true and fair, is temporarily tacked to the section molds so that its lower edge (it is understood, of course, that the boat is being built right-side-up) coincides with the marks on the molds representing the extreme upper edge of the plank in the process of being hung. A gauge for testing the lap bevel, such as is shown on Sheet 2, can then be applied at any place along the side of the boat to indicate the exact amount of lap bevel required on the under plank. There is absolutely no guesswork. With ordinary care a perfect fit can be achieved throughout.

There are various ways of reducing the thickness of the laps at the ends so that the ends of the planks will fit together to lie flush in the stem rabbet and on the transom, what McKee calls "chasing." These methods have been pretty well explained already in the books previously mentioned.

There is one more thing I should mention about lapstrake planking. For a one-off job, and especially for a first boat, I would recommend building it right-side-up, but set up high enough to work under comfortably. If this should require a plank a foot or so off the floor to stand on while working on the top side, that would be quite all right. Building right-side-up permits the builder to rivet the laps as he goes along without the assistance of a helper. In the production shop, boats are often built upside-down on a special form with all the riveting being done at one time after the planking is completed and the boat has been removed from the form and turned right-side-up. But I do not recommend this for the beginner and his first lapstrake boat.

SPILING

Spiling is the technique that enables a boatbuilder to take off the shape and dimensions of any structural part of the hull, and to transfer that shape to a flat plank, timber, sheet of plywood, or whatever, so that when it is cut to the line, and bent, twisted, or otherwise forced into place on the boat, it will fit perfectly.

A boat is all curves and bevels. Because many of its component parts assume different shapes when they are incorporated into the hull fabric than what they had laid out flat (planking in particular), the methods of the house builder, utilizing mainly the square and the plumb line, do not suffice for the boatbuilder.

The shapes that boatbuilders have to deal with are so complex that without a special technique with which to determine them, and to duplicate them, boatbuilding would be a slow, tedious process, and one extremely wasteful of materials. Boats probably could be built by hit-or-miss methods of cutting and trying, and cutting and trying again until a fit was achieved with methods that miss far more often than they hit, methods sometimes resorted to by the inexperienced and the unskilled, although there is a better and an easier one at hand.

There is nothing difficult or mysterious about spiling, although it might seem so at times. Quite the contrary, spiling procedures are simple and straightforward, yet few of the numerous boatbuilding books and manuals now in print treat this subject competently and adequately. More often their directions are defective and misleading.

One recent, widely touted work, purportedly on "simplified boatbuilding" for amateurs and home boatbuilders, fails to include spiling in the index, although it allots a full half-page of text and three sketchy diagrams to its consideration. All three of the diagrams are defective, with one seriously in error. This last is a diagram of the "reference line" method of spiling, in which reference lines fail to appear on the spiling batten shown transferred to the planking stock, which is where reference lines are required, and the only reason for having them. In redrawing this diagram, the author apparently saw fit to dispense with reference lines in the precise place where they are indispensible.

This may seem an extreme example, but another comes to mind almost as horrible. About 30 years ago, a Massachusetts man got into the public eye by building a vessel in his backyard intended for a voyage around the world. In the process he became a boatbuilding expert, and one spin-off was an article in a national yachting magazine presenting a spiling gadget of his own devising, which, in addition to everything else, mounted a spirit level. Nothing could have been more unnecessary, useless, or ludicrous to a professional boatbuilder.

While the principles underlying spiling procedures are quite simple, their application, depending on the circumstances, can take many different forms and variations. Much of this is difficult to put into words. In boatbuilding as a whole, as well as in the other manual trades, much is involved that words—and especially printed words—do not cover very well. Yet, in spite of this, it is possible to set down some useful notes and directions for spiling.

As previously pointed out, spiling is a method developed by boatbuilders for transferring shapes. In order to transfer shapes, they must first be recorded in some way. In spiling, this is most commonly done by marking thin strips of wood, called "spiling battens," as are used in the planking operations. Spilings are also marked on templates of approximate shape, as in fitting plywood bulkheads in the interior of a vessel.

If the correct procedure is followed, and the required steps of the spiling operation are accurately performed, the shape of any part of the hull can be marked for duplication—quickly, easily, and accurately enough for any practical need. Considering the geometry of some of the complex curves involved in planking a round-sided boat, it will be seen that a great deal of intricate mathematics is bypassed by this simple manual procedure.

In marking spiling battens or templates, three different methods are most commonly used, and these we shall consider here without going into others of more limited applications, such as the use of a chalk line to take the shape of the planking of large wooden vessels, such as nineteenth century Gloucester fishing schooners.

The three different methods for marking spiling to be considered here are shown in the diagrams on page 275: (1) reference lines, (2) intersecting arcs, and (3) the spiling block. Some boatbuilders prefer one, some another, but generally make use of all three at one time or another, for each works best in certain situations or places, as usually becomes evident in actual practice.

Spiling is commonly thought of in connection with planking, although, as we have seen, it can be employed for taking the shape of any part of the vessel. Spiling battens used in planking are wooden strips of varying lengths, or widths, roughly approximately the same as the planking, and of pine, fir, cedar, or other soft wood that planes and nails easily. Battens are used over and over again, with the pencil marking planed off each time, so that they tend to become quite thin. To begin with, they are usually under a half-inch thick.

Thin battens in long lengths tend to be flimsy, and in long lengths they are apt to sag edgewise when they are being temporarily tacked in place on the side of the boat unless precautions are taken. In tacking a batten on the side of a boat, be it long or short, it is best to start at the center of the batten and work out toward the ends. In the case of a long batten, if there is an assistant handy to hold up the ends until the nails are in, so much the better.

Edge-set—edgewise springing or sagging of the batten—must be prevented when using a spiling batten. Should it get into the batten when it is put on the boat, or afterwards when it is tacked on the planking stock, the identical amount of distortion will be automatically transferred to the plank, which will then have to be sprung (edge-set) back into place to make it fit when it is hung on the boat. This can present serious difficulties, especially with clinker planking.

For holding spiling battens on the side of the boat, for cleating them together (unless small screws are used), and for tacking them to the planking material so they won't slip out of position while the marks are being transferred, small common nails 1 inch to 1¼ inches in length are used. These are not driven all the way in—enough of each nail is left out for the claw hammer to catch. These tacking nails hold better in cleating together two short lengths of spiling batten if they are driven in at an angle, first in one direction then in another. It is better to put in a few extra, rather than too few, for if the cleat should slip, the spiling operation must be done over.

When a spiling is to be taken for a long, curved plank, it is best to use two or three short pieces tacked on the boat end to end to make up the required length. The spiling is marked, and then the ends of the short battens are well cleated together before disturbing them, so that they can be removed from the boat in one continuous length and placed on the planking stock (board) without any change in their relative positions one to the others. When the spiling batten is put on the boat, it could be cleated together before it is marked, but then some of the marks would come on the cleats, with more chance for inaccuracy.

After the batten is placed on the wood, the marks are checked to see if they all come on the wood, and that defects like sap and bad knots are avoided. When the optimum position for the batten is found, each of the component pieces of the batten are temporarily tacked in place with two or more small nails so that they cannot accidentally slip or be moved, after which the cleats holding them together are removed so that the spiling marks beneath them can be reached for transfer.

Although edge-set should be avoided as a rule, there are times when it cannot be helped or is even deliberately put in. Some planking species, including white cedar, retain grown-in stresses, especially in flitch-sawn, or live-edge, boards, so that when planks are sawn out of such boards, their shape as marked tends to change. If the change is slight, the plank can generally be sprung into place, otherwise it may have to be discarded.

Now and again, it will be found that the board intended for a plank is not quite wide enough to get the plank out as spiled. However, it may be possible to get wood enough for the batten by springing (edge-setting) it slightly in and tacking it on. If this is done gradually, with care to get a uniform change of curve throughout, the board can often be saved. The resulting plank, although slightly straightened, will have the requisite width and a fair edge so that it can usually be sprung into place to give a tight fit

The longer a plank is and the thicker it is in relation to its width, the easier it is to bend edgewise; consequently, with large vessels, edge-setting planks was frequently resorted to

by design to save lumber and to expedite the planking process. On small craft, however, it is not recommended, as a rule, and especially not in the case of clinker planking.

Clinker planking is usually both thinner and wider than carvel planking for the same size craft. The laps of clinker plank that are edge-set tend to gape open and are hard to get tight. In addition, the frames in lapstrake boats are usually not put in until after the boat is planked, consequently there are no frames to fasten into as planking proceeds to hold the plank in place, as in a carvel-built boat. Thus, edge-setting the planks of a clinker boat is very apt to lift the planks off the molds, altering the intended shape of the hull.

In spiling for clinker plank, special precautions are advised for the best results. If the plank is at all long and/or crooked, the spiling batten should be made up, as previously described, of two or three short pieces cleated together, and in light construction small screws, say No. 4s or No. 5s, are to be preferred over nails for fastening the cleats.

The width of the spiling batten should be about the same as the plank, and it is best put on like a plank so that it overlaps the edge of the plank from which the spiling is taken, and it would be advantageous to under-bevel the overlapping edge of the batten somewhat, very much as if it actually were a plank.

All this may seem over fussy and tedious to some, but believe me, it is worth doing and will pay off, especially for the novice and the occasional builder. There is an old saying that applies here: "The long way around is the shortest way home."

Each of the three methods for marking the spiling batten and the plank in turn, which have already been mentioned and are illustrated in the accompanying diagrams, require some additional explanation.

1. *Reference lines*: This may be the oldest method, and it seems to be the most commonly used in Great Britain. After the batten is tacked in place on the side of the boat, lines—at intervals ranging from a few inches apart to a foot or more—are drawn across the

PLANKING

SPILING
BLOCK

SPILING BATTEN

TIMBER

BATTEN CLEAT

SPILING
BATTEN

THREE METHODS OF SPILING

TRANSFER OF PLANK LINE
FROM SPILING BATTEN
TO PLANKING STOCK

REFERENCE
LINES

R R R

PLANKING STOCK

INTERSECTING ARCS

ADJUSTABLE SPILING BLOCK

PLANK LINE

batten and carried on to the edge of the plank, from which the spiling is to be taken. These lines run more or less square with the edge of the plank, or normal with its curve, and are commonly drawn by the professional using a pencil marking along the edge of his folded two-foot pocket rule.

Next, dividers are set to a convenient distance that will reach from the edge of the plank on to the batten all along its length. When this setting has been referenced on the batten so that it could be recovered if it were accidentally lost, it is stepped off from the edge of the plank along each line, and plainly marked on the reference lines on the batten. After the batten has been lifted from the boat and located and tacked in place on the planking stock, the reference lines are extended on to the board using the straight edge of the rule and the pencil.

Next, the original setting of the dividers is checked on the batten to make sure it has not changed, is stepped off along each reference line from the point on the batten to give a point on the extension of the line on the board, being the original spiling procedure exactly in reverse. This gives a row of points on the board through which a fair batten is run or "lined," which, when marked, produces a line exactly the same as the line of the edge of the plank on the boat—that is, if the spiling has been accurately done.

Basically, it is all a matter of measuring along the reference lines. How best to lay out these lines—the fine points, that is—will vary somewhat from job to job, and calls for experience and judgment, yet the method is very nearly foolproof if care is taken and the procedure is carried out accurately. It is best to make a reference mark, or "sir mark," so-called, at whichever end of the plank goes on the boat first, usually the bow end, so that the plank can be hung exactly where it belongs on the first try by matching the mark on the plank with the mark on the boat. This is especially necessary for garboards. Also, for the bow end of garboards, where they turn up sharply in an abrupt curve, best results are often obtained by making an exact template for a short distance and cleating it to the end of the spiling batten when the latter is tacked in place and before the spiling is taken. The dividers should be applied uniformly with all measurements taken from the top of the plank or from its bottom edge, as may be decided for a particular job, but never haphazardly from both top and bottom.

2. *Intersecting arcs*: This is probably the method most used in this country in recent years. Spiling by intersecting arcs is quick and accurate, and generally applicable to any situation in boatbuilding. Pencil dividers are opened to a convenient setting, which is marked on the batten for reference in case the dividers are dropped or some other mishap occurs to alter the setting. With the pointed end of the pivot leg placed exactly on the edge of the plank being spiled, an arc is swung marking the spiling batten. If the position of the legs of the dividers is now reversed so that the point of the pivot leg is placed anywhere on the arc marking the batten, an arc now swung will pass through the original point on the edge of the plank and the intersection of any two secondary arcs swung from points separately located anywhere on the original arc will establish the location of the original point. In this manner, points for the plank line on the planking stock are established from arcs on the spiling batten. This may sound involved, but it isn't. A glance at the diagram on page 275 should make it all perfectly clear.

Accuracy will be increased if the points for the intersecting secondary arcs are taken a good distance apart on the original arc rather than close together, and for that reason, the arcs on the spiling batten should be as long, within reason, as is convenient to make them. Here again, experience and judgment enter in, and sometimes arcs must be quite short due to special circumstances.

Aside from the manner in which points are established, as just explained, the method of spiling with intersecting arcs is governed by the same considerations as already explained for reference lines.

3. *The spiling block*: In using the spiling block, the batten is handled exactly the same as for the other two methods. When the spiling block is used, it is of particular importance for the batten cleat to be put on after the batten is marked, for obvious reasons.

The block is placed on the batten with one edge coinciding with the line to be transferred, and a pencil is drawn along the opposite edge of the block marking the batten. In some cases, a continuous line is drawn on the batten; that is, the line is transferred in its entirety, but more often it is not. A series of short lines suffice, which, when they are transferred to the planking stock, are connected with the lining batten exactly as if they were a row of points.

The diagrams on page 275 show two types of blocks—one that is flat, and another which is adjustable. It is plain that when the flat block is used to transfer lines from the batten to the planking stock, the edge of the block will be raised above the planking stock the thickness of the batten, and unless the pencil point is held exactly plumb and directly under the edge of the block, the mark will not be accurate. To insure against error from this source, an adjustable block is sometimes used, but through practice the professional generally learns to get accurate results with the flat block, not bothering with the adjustable one.

Flat blocks so used are generally rectangular in shape, 1½ inches by 2¼ inches. Both the long way and the short way can be used, depending on the width of the gap to be spanned in order to get a mark on the template, but when the long way of the block is used, the line on the batten so obtained should be clearly and immediately marked for identification as such, otherwise confusion and errors are bound to occur.

Best results for taking complicated templates for interior bulkheads of plywood and the like are obtained by using the spiling block. It is best adapted for short lines and intricate shapes. With care and some practice, the most intricate shapes can be fitted perfectly using templates and the spiling block.

Of course, with all spiling methods allowance must be made for bevels. In addition there are numerous other fine points that will become apparent as you proceed. As with everything else, facility and accuracy come with experience and practice.

SCARPHING

Since so many of the boats described for building in this book call for scarphed planking, some general directions for making epoxy-glued splices, both of plywood and ordinary boards of sawn lumber, will be useful. First of all, scarphs to be joined should be neatly made, of course, so they fit well when brought together. Yet the meeting surfaces should be slightly roughened with a rasp or sandpaper, for epoxy is strongest when a slight film of glue (a few thousandths of an inch thick) remains on the joint.

Epoxy does not require high clamping pressures (like the resorcinol glues for example). Often when clamps are not available, or in places where ordinary clamps won't reach or fit, glue joints can be drawn together by nailing. Sometimes the nails can be left in; other times they are removed after the glue has set. In the latter case, they are generally driven through pads or strips of plywood or other material, so they will exert pressure, yet permitting access to their heads so they may be easily removed later on.

Using epoxy glue, it is possible—and not difficult—to splice plywood of any width. The width of a scarph should be not less than eight times the thickness of the plywood, but 12 times the thickness is better. The scarph bevels of the joining ends are cut on a fair uniform taper and are brought nearly to a feather edge, but not quite. The excess is sanded off after the glue has set. When this has been done, a well-made splice can hardly be found.

If much plywood splicing is to be done, a simple but adequate jig can be set up for use with a power router. For a boat that requires only a few splices, a sharp, low-angle block plane is all that is required. The plane's blade or iron should be set at an angle of 10 to 12 degrees. Low-angle planes are made for smoothing end grain, and plywood is approximately half end grain.

One other important tip in planing scarphs for splicing plywood: the thin end should be supported during the planing. Usually the end of the bench will do nicely for this. If the bench is uneven, another piece of plywood or a wide board can be placed underneath the end and just even with it to give the necessary support when scarphing.

Before gluing a plywood scarph, it is prudent to check the alignment of the splice by clamping the pieces in place on the boat. Also, it is best not to cut the panels to exact size and shape until after the splices have been glued. Some extra wood left on the edges of the panels will permit a final adjustment before the piece is fastened, should this be required.

One simple method of gluing up a splice in plywood as wide as the sides of a boat is to apply glue to both surfaces, fit them together, and rest them on a large, heavy plank. A couple of small nails into the plank will keep the surfaces from slipping out of alignment. Then a strip of board is laid across the top, roughly the width of the scarph and directly over it. A line of 10d nails driven through the scarph into the plank beneath at intervals of 3 to 4 inches will apply enough pressure to pull the joining surfaces together. Of course, the surfaces of the plank and the board must be either waxed or covered with paper to keep glue squeezed out of the splice from sticking to them.

For pulling together glue joints and holding them until the glue has set, double-headed, or "staging" nails, so called, are useful. They can be driven in tightly enough to exert considerable pressure, yet the protruding outer head makes them easy to draw later with a claw hammer or bar. In gluing softwood planks with epoxy glue, staging nails can be used in place of clamps to a considerable extent.

After the glue is set, the nails can be pulled, their holes plugged, and the splice sanded on both sides. Properly done, the splice will hardly show, not at all if painted, and the result will be as strong as the rest of the panel.

Besides plywood, ordinary boards of sawn lumber can be spliced. For instance, I suggested that scarphing the clinker planking of the Rangeley (Chapter 20) offers two distinct advantages: (1) butt blocks, as are required for joining lengths of carvel plank, are avoided, and (2) short lengths of planking lumber can be used. This means substantial saving in the cost of planking material, for some of the strakes for the Rangeley in full length take pronounced curves, which to get out in one piece would require premium-priced wide boards, difficult to obtain nowadays, at best. Even lumber with some knots may be used, for in getting out shorter lengths of plank, it is often possible to lay out the cuts in such a way as to avoid the knots.

Furthermore, in full-length strakes of marked curvature, some cross-grained wood cannot be avoided, resulting in a loss of strength. But with spliced strakes of several shorter lengths, the grain can be kept straight throughout, so that spliced strakes make a stronger boat, provided the scarphs are well distributed or "staggered," as boatbuilders say, in addition to being properly made and glued.

Splices in sawn boards should be bevel scarphed to a feather edge on each side; the length of the bevel should be eight to twelve times the thickness of the plank. The scarph surfaces should be glued with epoxy adhesive on or off the boat. If the scarph is glued on the boat, it should be clamped with the simple clamping jig shown in the accompanying sketch. This jig is merely two blocks of wood (hardwood is best) well waxed on the inner surface to prevent sticking, and drawn tight with one 1¾-inch No. 12 wood screw, which passes through the splice and hauls it tightly between the two blocks. When the glue has set up hard, the jig is removed by loosening the screw, and the hole is plugged. This jig fits between the laps, so as not to interfere with planking, and thus planking can proceed from strake to strake without waiting for splices to harden, or the removal of the clamping jigs.

If you prefer, splices can be glued off the boat. One way is identical to the plywood scarph method already described: Assemble the splice on a plank with a short piece of board on top covering the splice, and drive a few nails through this "sandwich" to hold the surfaces of the splice in place and in contact until the glue is set. Afterwards, the nails can be pulled and plugged. The bottom plank and covering board may either be waxed or covered with paper to prevent the excess glue from sticking.

Scarph laps in sawn boards are easily planed with a sharp block plane, although in commercial boatshops, such as those operated at Rangeley, a planing jig was used. The plank end to be scarphed was inserted in the jig, a handle was pushed back and forth a few times, and the sharp cutter attached to it and set on an angle produced a perfect scarph bevel more or less automatically. Such a device is a great time-saver and more or less a necessity in a commercial shop. It is not difficult to contrive, and, even though planking scarphs are easily made with a block plane, some amateur builders might want to devise a scarphing jig. This could easily be done today with a high-speed router, which many amateur woodworkers have and are familiar with. With the plank end clamped in position in the jig, and with a few passes of the router, the scarph bevel would be perfectly cut in the proverbial "jig time."

RIVETING AND TIMBERING

The planking laps of classic lapstrake boats can be fastened with rivets or clinched fastenings. Copper rivets are used to fasten the planking laps of many of the boats discussed in this book, both through the timbers and between them, instead of clinched fastenings. Although rivets may mean a little more work, I believe they pull up tighter and are not as apt to work loose as clinched fastenings, when properly put in. J. Henry Rushton of Canton, New York, the famous nineteenth century builder of light boats and canoes, thought otherwise and used clinched fastenings. In one of his catalogs he explained why: "When we try to rivet-fasten the ribs of a cedar boat, the result is seldom satisfactory . . . with the clinch fastening the slender end of the nail will curve back into the wood before the shank will upset. The annealed copper is not weakened by such a clinch, and it is our experience that such a fastening will last as long in the wood."

Rushton's implication here is that, unless properly done, rivet fastening is inferior. When riveting is incorrectly done, that is, when too big a hammer is used and the blows struck are too heavy, when the rivets are not clipped short enough, when the burrs used are sloppy and don't hold firmly when forced down with the burr set—especially when all of these conditions obtain together—the rivets will buckle and cripple within the wood, without drawing tight, even to the point of sometimes splitting the lap. When this happens it is not the fault of the rivet, but rather the fault of the riveter.

By the same token, if nails are not properly clinched so that the points turn neatly back into the wood, they will not draw tight and will also sometimes split the lap. Furthermore, for a proper clinch job, nails must be exactly the right length, neither too long nor too short, and they must be a particular type of cut, clinch nail. Wire nails won't do at all for clinching, but they can be used for riveting, although they are not as good for driving through hot timbers as cut nails.

I believe it takes more skill to clinch lap fastenings, and to do it right, than to put in rivet fastenings, although the former is certainly the faster method of the two for the skilled professional who has acquired the knack through long practice. W. P. Stephens, Rushton's contemporary and competition, held for rivets.

Riveted laps were standard for clinker yacht tenders and other fine small craft built along the coast, and indeed, before small screws were available, rivet fastening was used for the best carvel construction as well, which almost invariably was built with soft cedar planking.

The Rangeley boat was clinch fastened, but the nails used were of imported pure Swedish iron, which lasts quite well in fresh water, as ordinary steel nails do not. However, I was informed that copper nails had been tried previously for clinch fastening Rangeley boats but had been given up because the clinched copper nails were too soft and thus "worked" in use, thus allowing the laps to loosen in time. Whether Rushton's soft copper nails ever loosened, I do not know. Perhaps bronze nails would work if those of suitable shape for clinching could be had, with metal hard enough to hold firmly. Yet bronze nails might be too stiff, with a tendency to split delicate laps when clinched.

All things considered, perhaps it is best to confine ourselves to rivets and learn to do riveting correctly. First, the right kind of a nail is needed. Copper wire nails can be used, but copper cut nails are far superior. The copper cut nail is desirable because its square (really rectangular) point can be driven through hot timbers with less chance of splitting them than a round wire nail. Furthermore, the right size is important. A nail that is too large or too heavy will strain or split delicate laps, as large nails require too much hammering to head up. Bronze nails or other "hard" nails should not be used because they are too hard to head over. Only soft copper nails head over easily.

Second, the burr, or rove, as this is sometimes called, must not be sloppy, that is, too large. Rather, its hole should be tight enough so that, when the burr is driven over the point of the nail and forced down firmly against the wood on the inside of the lap, it will hang tightly until the rivet has been headed over.

Third, the excess length of rivet protruding beyond the burr must be clipped off just right—enough for a good head and not a bit more, for any extra length left on for heading will tend to make the shank of the rivet buckle or "cripple" in the wood. This is extremely important. Exactly the right amount of length must be left for heading, no more or no less.

Fourth, a proper riveting hammer must be used. For small-boat work the hammer should be under half a pound in weight, including the handle. The latter should be of hickory, shaved down close to the head to the diameter of a lead pencil, to give the handle flexibility. For some reason, not wholly clear, a hammer with a long, narrow head works better and balances better than one that is short headed (assuming, of course, that the two hammers are of equal weight).

More than likely, a suitable riveting hammer will not be found for purchase, although some light upholsterer's hammers could possibly be adapted and give good results. However, a perfectly serviceable hammer can be made from

BURR SET

RIVETING HAMMER

GLUING JIG FOR PLANK SPLICE

hole lengthwise into one end about 1½ inches.

In addition to the hammer and the burr set, you will also have to have a "hold-on." Here, weight (as much as you can conveniently hold in one hand) is an advantage. It should fit the left hand (if you are right-handed) comfortably, with the surface that is applied against the wood smooth and slightly convex. There should be no sharp edges or corners to dig into the plank inadvertently.

When riveting, that is, when forming a head over the burr on the inside of the lap, with many light, quick blows of the hammer, the hold-on must be pressed tightly and firmly against the head of the nail on the outside of the lap, else a bent or crippled rivet or even a split lap will result.

Nails should not be driven through the laps without drilling for them first; the holes should be slightly smaller than the shank of the nail to insure a tight fit. Those who are new to riveting should practice at the bench on laps identical to those on the boat until they get the hang of it. Not until they can head over rivets perfectly should they attempt it on the boat. Those who leave their practicing for the boat will surely regret it. Riveting small copper fastenings is best done with very light but rapid blows. These upset a head without bending or crushing the rivet itself. With a heavy hammer and a few heavy blows, the rivet is likely to bend and split the wood, and it never draws tight. With many rapid tapping blows, a nice head forms, the burr draws up tightly, and the rivet itself is not mashed, deformed, or crippled into the wood.

For a specific example of riveting and timbering, let's take the pram in Chapter 2. When all the locations of the fastenings are marked, the molds are removed from the planked-up shell, and holes are bored through the laps where the timber rivets are to come. Next, nails are driven in from the outside so that their points are just flush with the inside of the skin. In this condition the hull resembles a huge pincushion. In the meantime the timbers have been prepared and are steaming. After an hour of hot, wet steam, timbers of this size, if of good quality white oak and not fully seasoned to

a piece of steel drill rod ⅝ inch in diameter and 3¾ inches long. One end is squared off and given a very slight convex round, the other should be rounded like the ball end of a ball peen hammer. The middle of this head is drilled at right angles to take a hickory handle. No hardening is needed, as the copper to be pounded is much softer than the steel. The hole for the handle should be elongated so as to give enough room for the handle without weakening the head unduly. This is an easy way to make a good hammer, which, I doubt, you could find to buy today.

For a burr set, a piece of the same ⅝-inch drill rod 4 inches long will do. Drill a ³⁄₁₆ inch begin with, will be soft and limber enough to "tie into knots."

The hot timber is quickly forced down into the interior of the boat along the lines previously marked for it. Clamped to the sheer at either side, the timberheads projecting above the sheer may be tapped with a nail hammer to drive the hot timber down against the laps. Generally it is tacked into the keel batten with a small nail to keep it from slipping out of place.

Quickly, then, the boatbuilder, starting on the outside from the bottom or garboard with his nailing hammer, drives the nails already entered in the laps, driving each in turn as he goes up the side to the sheer, while he backs up on the inside with a heavy hold-on, applied against the timber as close as he can get to the nail he is driving without preventing its going through. The inertia of the heavy hold-on forces the hot timber tightly against the inside surface of the lap, and twists the timber, as may be required, making it lie flat against the inside of the planking. Once the timber is down in place, the nails will hold it until the timber cools, which quickly occurs, and then nothing will move until the riveting can be done. This is usually done later and in one operation.

When laid out and organized in this manner, timbering is quickly and simply accomplished. Otherwise, all sorts of difficulties might be met with. Unless the position and location of the timbers are marked in advance, they could never be got in evenly. Unless the holes are bored through the laps and the nails inserted ahead of time, timbers could neither be fastened before they cooled, nor drawn tightly to the inside of the boat while still hot and flexible. The nails used should be blunt-ended cut nails. Sharp-pointed nails are likely to split the timbers. To be on the safe side, the nails should be bored for.

FRAMING WOOD

As far as I am concerned, the only wood to use for steam-bent timbers for the boats in this book is the best genuine white oak that can be obtained. It should not be over dry. Long seasoning tends to make wood brittle, oak especially. In fact, wood for steam-bent timbers can come directly off the stump, for steaming drives out the sap and seasons the wood, so that small timbers, although growing the day before they go into the boat, will be as hard as a piece of horn after they have been steamed and then dried out for a couple of weeks.

The best wood for white oak timbers comes from the butts of young, healthy trees that have grown fast. The wider the grain and the heavier the wood the better. Wood from the upper parts of the tree is always softer and weaker. Some of the red oaks are worthless for timbers, especially the weak, brittle, fine-grained wood from old, large, slow-growing trees of the species appropriately known in the boatshops as "piss" oak.

Rushton specified red elm for timbers, but I have never used it and do not know enough about it to recommend it for this purpose. Many of the Rangeley boats also used elm timbers. White ash bends beautifully, and some selected white ash from the butts of young trees is nearly as hard and strong as good oak. But unfortunately ash rots easily when exposed to weather. Perhaps it could be treated with preservative of some sort, but I don't recommend risking it until some experimentation has been done.

LAMINATING FRAMES

An alternative to steam-bent frames is glued, laminated frames, bent in and fastened while the glue is still soft. This becomes especially feasible with an epoxy/Thiokol adhesive, which will not run out of the joints, especially those which are vertical, before it sets up. Epoxy resin is a fairly heavy material, and some adhesive formulations, especially the slow-setting ones, like some of the Versamid mixes, have a bad tendency of leaking or creeping out of joints when there is any chance for the still-liquid glue to run downhill. The "buttery" consistency of the epoxy/Thiokol obviates this.

For a laminated frame of ⅝ inch thickness or molding, five strips of ⅛ inch thickness will be required. Such strips are got out carefully to their exact size on the circular saw and are made long enough to bend in from gunwale to gunwale, with a little extra to extend above the gunwale on either side, for ease of handling. (The example given here is for continuous frames; the method is applicable to single frames as well.)

In putting in a frame, five strips are first selected, adhesive is applied to their meeting surfaces, and the strips are stacked one on top of the other as they are to go on the boat. The bundle is then tightly wrapped at intervals with several turns of masking tape to hold the lifts together, although they can still slip against one another in a lengthwise direction. The bundle is then bent into place in the boat in accordance with the line of the frame already marked. Forced down approximately into position, the two ends of the frame are clamped to the sheer on either side so that they can be tapped down to make contact with each side plank and the bottom, by pounding the ends with a hammer.

The frame is now ready to fasten in place. The fastenings, either screws or rivets, if properly put in, will draw the frame layers tightly together and hold them in position until the glue hardens. The turns of masking tape should hold the laminae pretty nearly where they belong as the frame is fastened, but to insure perfect alignment, several small hand screws will be useful and convenient. Such hand screws have wooden jaws and threaded steel spindles. A small size is best for these hand screws—those with a 4-inch jaw and a 2-inch opening. A couple will suffice. In fact, one is all that is absolutely necessary, to be used wherever a fastening is about to be put in to force the laminae into perfect sidewise alignment, and to hold them there until the fastening takes over. The hand screw is then shifted to the location for the next fastening and so on. However, several hand screws at various places along the frame are a great convenience.

If this procedure is followed, ordinary care taken, and the excess glue is wiped off with a cloth after the fastening of the frame is completed, it will be hard to tell after the job is done whether the frame is laminated or solid—at least to the cursory glance.

PLYWOOD FOR DORY CONSTRUCTION

Dory construction was perfected before plywood or waterproof glues were developed. Your oldtime dory builder managed quite adequately without these materials, yet that is no reason for our not using them. In fact, plywood and glue can be employed to advantage for dories, as well as for the construction of many of the other older types of small boats. Thus the design of the 19-foot surf-dory (Chapter 13) and many other boats in this book call for both.

The theory has been advanced that the dory developed from an abundance of wide pine boards. Given the wide lumber from the primeval pine forests of New England, and the need for strong and inexpensive boats for the fisheries, the various dories naturally took shape as the most economical way of putting together wide boards into boats of the desired characteristics. But the big pines are gone, and it is far from easy today to get white pine boards sixteen to eighteen inches wide as are required for the garboards of a surf-dory. If plywood can be made to do, here is a plentiful supply of wide lumber the use of which will permit the retention of the advantages of wide-board design. However, in using plywood for garboards, the right sort of plywood must be selected, and several minor departures from standard dory construction will have to be made in applying it to the boat.

For the 19-foot surf-dory in Chapter 13, the plywood selected was marine grade, ⅜ inch thick, 5-ply Douglas fir. This was for the garboards, for gussets for splicing the frame futtocks and the two-piece stems, and for the bulkheads of the two end-compartments enclosing the styrofoam flotation. As the garboards of the surf-dory are approximately 19 feet long, they are spliced in the center, which is their narrowest part, and as the boat is identical at both ends, one pattern can be used for marking out the four pieces needed for making up the two garboards. Thus it is possible, by taking care, to lay out the garboard pieces on a 4-foot by 10-foot sheet and to have enough left over to make the frame and stem gussets, as well as the end bulkheads. This procedure requires laying out a garboard pattern before the frames are assembled and the boat is set up. Such a pattern may be obtained with sufficient accuracy from a scale half-model of the boat, most conveniently made 1½ inches to the foot.

Douglas fir plywood was chosen for the good and sufficient reason that that was the only kind of marine grade available at that time. Apparently for such reasons as the abundance and the large size of Douglas fir timber, the good gluing qualities of that wood, and its high strength-weight ratio, Douglas fir dominates the plywood field. Other woods or combinations of woods, however, can now be found in marine plywood.

Superior grades of exterior (waterproof) plywood are manufactured especially for boatbuilding purposes. Different manufacturers designate this special grade with various names, for instance "Armorbond," "Marine," and "Boathull." No matter the designation used, the inner plies of marine plywood with respect to core gaps, solid veneer, and the like are better than those of industrial exterior-type plywood. However, there is no difference in glue, as all exterior grades have the same waterproof glueline.

Anyone who intends to use plywood for small boat construction will do well to inform himself thoroughly about plywood specifications, select his wood with care, and demand a product that conforms to standards. (A good place to get such information is the Douglas Fir Plywood Association, 1119 A Street, Tacoma, Washington.) The requirements for small boat construction are fairly critical, especially as dimensions must be kept down to save weight, but without sacrifice of strength.

There is an important reason why 5-ply plywood is to be preferred over that of 3 plies for planking and other boat parts subject to immersion and soaking. That is because in the 5-ply product there is less wood in the thinner veneers to swell and shrink as the moisture content varies, hence less strain on the glueline. In 5-ply plywood, a greater proportion of the

wood is glue impregnated, reducing swelling and shrinking stresses still more. Plywood is made with the grain of its composite veneers crossing at right angles, and recurrent stresses are set up by the expansion and contraction of these veneers. Thus the wood as it gets wet, and dries out, is always pulling at the glueline. Modern waterproof glues have tremendous holding power, but good boatbuilding practice calls for all possible measures to mitigate the strains to which the glueline of plywood will be subjected. One of these is to coat the surface of the wood with paint and special sealers to prevent it from soaking up water too fast or drying out too quickly. It is the powerful stress set up by abrupt change in moisture content that does the worst damage.

As the edges of the plywood, by their exposure of end-grain wood, take up or give off moisture most rapidly, they are the most vulnerable part of the plywood and need special protection. On the edges, the veneers first separate or are split apart by accidental blows, abrasion, or other mechanical injury. In the surfdory the lower edges of the garboards are not only coated with applications of sealer and paint, but also the ½ inch outer bottom of oak is extended to cover the garboard edges, with a liberal coating of bedding compound placed between. The upper edges of the garboards, beveled 1⅛ inches to lap under the broad strake, are coated with three applications of No. 900 rubber sealer before the lap is riveted together. At both ends of the boat the garboards are sealed and bedded before being covered by the steam-bent false or outer stem. Thus all edges of the garboards are protected by sealing and covering with other members of solid wood. It may be positively stated that good building practice requires that plywood edges always be covered, and when plywood is adapted to traditional boat types, design and construction should be modified to permit such covering.

In the past the garboards of a standard 19-foot dory would have been of pine ⅝ inch thick; for light construction, ⁹⁄₁₆ inch thick. Chamberlain built his gunning dories with planking of ½-inch cedar. In substituting plywood for the garboards, that of ⅜ inch thickness is the best choice. Plywood ¼ inch thick, available only in 3-ply construction, is not solid enough for a boat of this size, nor is it stiff enough to bend fairly in the garboard width around frame-molds spaced 32 inches apart. On the other hand ½-inch plywood would be unnecessarily heavy and stiff. Possibly ⁵⁄₁₆-inch 5-ply Mexican or African mahogany plywood would be the best choice of all for garboards for a 19-foot dory, if such a plywood could be found.

In the dry condition, ⅜-inch plywood garboards will be a little lighter in weight than garboards of ⅝-inch pine, in spite of the added weight of the glue in the plywood. In a water-soaked condition, the thicker pine planking would certainly be considerably heavier, especially as a portion of the plywood is made impervious to water by its four layers of glue.

BORING FOR CENTERBOARDS AND RUDDERS

When assembling large, flat pieces, such as centerboards and rudders, some amateur boat-builders have difficulty boring for the fastenings. Care must be taken to bore a hole that is straight and true. The following instructions should help simplify the job:

For both rudders and centerboards, cut out the component pieces and fit them, temporarily assembling them on a flat surface like a level bench top. These pieces will all be of the same thickness of stock, for any tapering and thinning is left until the assembly is solidly pinned together.

Clamp this preliminary assembly so it can't move, and exactly mark on the exposed upper surface the location of each pin with a firm straight line the length of the pin. This line represents the center of the pin. Separate the parts and square the pin lines down across the edges of the piece. Next, with a combination square or some other gauge, set to half the thickness of the boards, mark through the lines already squared across the edges, gauging always from the upper, marked side of the boards.

Now the exact locations for boring the holes for the pins have been found and are marked on all edges by the intersection of the squared-down pin line with the gauge line. At these intersections holes of the right size for the pins may be precisely centered and started with a sharp-spurred bit in a hand brace.

If a pin is to pass entirely through a board, the hole is started on both edges and is bored halfway through from either side to halve possible error. If the two holes do not meet precisely, they usually come close enough so that the drill bit will lead through from side to side, so that, after reaming, a pin can be driven through. The important thing is that by this method the correct location of the holes on the edges of joining pieces is maintained. An attempt, starting at one edge, to bore a long hole edgewise through two or more thin boards will generally result in having the drill break out through one side or the other before the hole is complete.

A better way, when several thin pieces or boards are to be pinned together edgewise, is to bore each piece separately. If preassembled and properly marked to begin with, and provided the marks are followed, the holes will line up perfectly when the parts are reassembled, and the pins can be driven without trouble.

A spurred bit is not suitable for boring long holes, for such bits have a tendency to "run off." Either a "bare-foot" ship's auger or a long twist drill is better. (A short twist drill may be lengthened by brazing on an extension of drill rod.) It is assumed that an electric machine will be used.

When drilling the builder will need assistance for sighting. The piece to be drilled is clamped flat on the bench. A straight, narrow strip of board is laid with one edge exactly on the marked line of the hole to be drilled, and it should extend somewhat beyond the piece toward the drill. By sighting along the edge of this stick, the man with the drill can line his hole one way. The hole is lined the other way, that is up and down, by an assistant standing off some distance at right angles. He calls out to the drill operator to move up or down to keep the shank of the drill parallel to the run or line of the sighting stick.

By using this method and exercising care, holes 8 inches or 10 inches, or longer, of nearly perfect alignment, can be bored edgewise through thin, flat stock.

ASHCROFT CONSTRUCTION

Many classic craft are adaptable to the Ashcroft method of construction, which uses planking made up of two layers of narrow, thin strips, laid diagonally with the boat's centerline and glued together. To describe this method, let's look at the Rangeley boat, which has an ideal form for the task.

Construction by the Ashcroft method lies well within the capability of the amateur with modest woodworking skill, and it will not be overly expensive, as prices run today. In fact, one of my guiding considerations in including this material was to help keep down costs. Low-cost, easily obtainable lumber is specified, and the use of expensive metal fastenings has been kept to a minimum. The amount and kind of adhesives required should not run the price up excessively. The number of tools required is small—in addition to a few standard hand tools, a staple gun will be needed, as well as the use of a circular saw to rip out the planking strips.

This method of planking was first devised and successfully used in the early years of this century by an Englishman, Herbert J. Ashcroft. Ashcroft planking, as it came to be called, achieved considerable popularity for a time, especially in Australia, and Ashcroft's book, *Boatbuilding Simplified*, was published in several editions—the third revised edition, and the last, as far as I know, appearing in London about 1920.

What Ashcroft lacked was waterproof glue, which did not become available to the boatbuilding trade until the 1940s, during World War II. Although Ashcroft built successful boats without modern adhesives, special care had to be taken to get a leak-proof hull without them. Given a reliable waterproof glue, the effective-ness of Ashcroft construction is immensely enhanced. The revival of up-dated Ashcroft building methods, using modern glues, is over-due, offering special inducements to the un-skilled builder.

As its originator claimed, Ashcroft is a simplified method, avoiding the principal difficulties of both clinker and carvel planking—there is no need to line out and diminish planks, spile their shapes, back them out to fit the round of the ribs, or bevel clinker laps. Mainly what is required in the way of planking is a quantity of thin, narrow strips got out to uniform width and thickness on a circular saw, and ordinary care in applying them to the building form.

For planking strips, almost any wood will do that is not too hard, that takes glue well, and that bends fairly easily. Naturally, woods which rot easily should be avoided. For the boat we are considering, I suggest spruce, northern white pine (but not Ponderosa), and Douglas fir. These can be had in comparatively inexpensive construction grades and are commonly carried by local retail lumber dealers. There are several kinds of cedar, both eastern and western, and particularly northern white cedar, which would be excellent, but cedar is apt to be more expensive and is not as widely stocked as the other types.

Because the strips required for this boat are less than 3 feet long and not more than 2 inches wide, they may be got out of the cheaper grades with knots and other defects by cutting up the material so as to avoid the blemished parts. Thus, rough spruce staging boards, No. 2 common white pine, or Douglas fir framing lumber can be made to serve quite adequately. Considerable wastage occurs in stripping up this material on the saw, which makes a thin, sharp blade desirable. The strips need not be smoothed or planed. In fact, they glue better with epoxy just as they come from the saw.

Bob Sheffields, of Binghamton, N. Y., who built a 16-foot Adirondack guideboat using the Ashcroft method, found that 1/8 inch thick spruce was quite adequate. Because white pine is neither as stiff nor as strong as spruce, probably

14' RANGELEY BOAT
ADAPTED FOR ASHCROFT CONSTRUCTION
FROM LINES AND OFFSETS IN THE
MYSTIC SEAPORT PLAN COLLECTION

a thickness of ³⁄₁₆ inch would be better if pine is used, which I am suggesting for this boat. For Douglas fir, ⅛-inch or ⁵⁄₃₂-inch strips will suffice.

Even though the strips are thin enough to be relatively flexible, best results will be obtained if they are softened by steaming before they are bent on the form. Boiling them will serve just as well, and in some cases, boiling will be easier to accomplish. Various devices can be improvised for doing this. One is easily made from a section of large-diameter copper tubing slightly longer than the strips to be boiled. Secured in an upright position, with its lower end capped or plugged, the tube is filled with water

and the flame from an ordinary small soldering torch is applied to the side of the tube. The water will soon boil. A few minutes in the tube will render strips pliable enough to bend easily, and as heated strips are removed to go on the boat, fresh ones are inserted to keep the planking operation proceeding continuously.

If a suitable length of large tubing is not to be had, a narrow, tight wooden box can be substituted. Through its closed lower end there should protrude a foot or so of smaller-diameter copper tubing, its bottom end capped or plugged. A torch applied here will soon bring the water in the box to a boil. This box can be

The Ashcroft method. (Top) Setting up the first form. (Center) The ribbands and stringers in place. (Bottom) The beginning of planking. In the original method, both layers of strips were put on together. (From Ashcroft's Boatbuilding Simplified)

nailed up almost anywhere and, with care, is quite safe. Such a box is easily made out of four

pine boards well nailed together, with the seams caulked with a strand of cotton wicking set in heavy paint or mastic of some sort.

Before the strips are bent in place on the boat, a proper form must be constructed to receive them. Such a form set bottom up can be seen in the accompanying illustration reproduced from the third edition of Ashcroft's book. Molds are made in the usual way from the faired lines of the body sections, from which the thickness of the longitudinal ribbands or stringers has been deducted.

Building is done bottom-up, and the best way of setting up the building form is by the ladder-frame method, which is fully explained for the light 10-foot Herreshoff pram described in Chapter 2. Incidentally, this pram has an ideal shape for Ashcroft construction.

As the final shape of the boat can be no fairer than the form on which it is planked, no pains should be spared in getting it right. If the boat is to have fair lines, the ribbands or stringers must run fair and true, and there must be enough of them to support the planking strips in fair curves when these are bent into place. If the supporting stringers are placed too far apart, unsightly knuckles could develop in the skin of the finished hull. At the turn of the bilge, where the curve is quickest, the stringers will need to be closer together than on the flat of the bottom or high on the topsides. As shown in one of the illustrations in Ashcroft's book, the stringers appear to be rather far apart.

In the original Ashcroft method, planking strips were nailed to the longitudinal stringers, which remained in the finished hull as an integral part of the structure. But because of the added strength derived by gluing together the two layers of planking strips, we should not need to retain all of our form ribbands as permanent hull stringers. Perhaps four on each side so retained would be sufficient, with the hull lighter and its interior less cluttered as a consequence.

For permanent stringers for the boat under consideration, I suggest one at the turn of the bilge, one on the flat of the bottom about midway between the turn and the keel batten, another above the turn to serve as a seat-riser, and the fourth along the sheer line to become the inwale. Additional ribbands would be necessary to get a fair shape, but these would be fastened to the molds and would remain with the form when the finished hull is lifted off. The stringers that are to become part of the completed hull may be tied to the molds with thin but strong cord to hold them in place preliminary to planking. If they were nailed or screwed to the molds, there would be no way of removing these fastenings after the hull was planked. Fine, strong wire twisted to draw tight could also be used to hold the permanent stringers in place, to be clipped and pulled out of the finished hull afterwards.

Stringers for this boat might well be made ¾ inch thick by 1 inch wide. Those which are to remain in the hull should be smoothed and sanded with the inside corners nicely rounded. Spruce or Douglas fir would be suitable material, or some other wood which holds nails at least moderately well. White pine and white cedar are too soft.

The Rangeley boat is perfectly straight along the bottom, which makes it easy to set up. The inner keel or keel batten, either oak or selected Douglas fir, is a strip ¾ inch thick, 4 inches wide and tapered at the ends. This taper and the amount of beveling required is shown in the accompanying drawings. Likewise are shown the filler pieces at each end and how they are shaped and beveled also.

As this boat is exactly alike at either end, two identical inner stem pieces are worked out of 2-inch thick stock, either oak or Douglas fir, according to the shape and dimensions given. In fastening these to either end of the keel batten, two triangular knees of the same 2-inch thick stem stock are required, thinned and tapered to the thickness of the inner stem and the end of the keel batten.

The inner stem pieces, stem knees, and keel batten are nailed and glued together before being placed on the molds already set up and secured on the ladder frame. After the keel batten assembly is in place, its bottom is beveled, and the bottom filler strips are glued and fitted at either end.

The ends of the longitudinal ribbands or

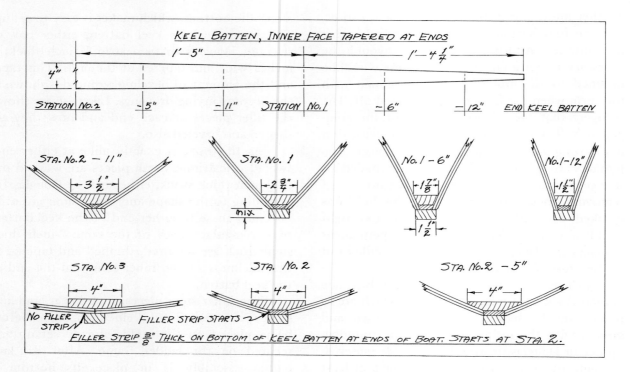

stringers must land precisely against the back of the inner stem pieces, and also must line up exactly with the fayed or beveled surfaces of these inner stems. Perhaps some planing will be required here to achieve a fair backing surface for the planking strips. Stringers that are to remain in the hull must be fitted neatly where they come together and fasten behind the inner stem.

When all underlying surfaces are fair and smooth, the planking strips are put on. According to the original Ashcroft method, both layers were put on together, the under layer one strip in advance of the upper, with the seams in the top layer falling midway on the strips in the under layer. Of course, both layers had to run at the same angle and in the same direction. In this way there were no openings to leak, that is if the two layers were pulled snugly together, with paint or flexible bedding of some sort between. The strips were nailed through and clinched, both to the permanent stringers and to themselves as the planking proceeded. Steaming the strips to make them soft for easy bending did not interfere with this process, as it would have if glue had been used between the two layers. It

is doubtful if reliable results could be obtained by applying glue directly to steamed or boiled wood before it has cooled or dried.

When glue is used, an alternate method may be adopted. The strips softened by steaming or boiling are bent on at an angle of approximately 45 degrees from the centerline, starting at the middle of the boat and working toward the ends. They are laid as close together as possible, and are held down in place with staples put in wherever needed. The entire hull surface is covered in one operation and left to dry. When sufficiently dry, the strips, starting at the middle of the boat, are removed one at a time, edge-trimmed with a sharp block plane to lie snugly against the adjoining strip, and fastened permanently in place, both with glue and nails to the keel batten and the permanent stringers. Small annular nails of bronze or Monel, ¾ inch long, are best for tacking down this inner layer.

The first layer of strips should fit together as tightly as possible, so that when the outer layer is glued on, the adhesive does not leak through. It is well, in any case, to wax the ribbands that remain on the mold, so that if glue does work through, it will not stick to them. In any case, for best results, a thick epoxy paste should be used between the two layers, either a proprietary formulation or ordinary liquid epoxy well thickened by the addition of Cabot's Cab-O-Sil.

After the first layer is permanently nailed in place and the glue has set, the surface can be rough sanded to prepare for the application of the second layer, which is done like the first. Before the bending operation starts, however, the position of the underlying ribbands and the permanent stringers should be clearly lined out and marked on the surface of the under layer to guide nailing. Instead of laying the second layer in the same direction as the first, as Ashcroft did, a stronger hull will result if we put on the top layer at right angles to the one underneath. With glue between the two layers, there is no chance of leaks where the strips cross.

The procedure for the outer layer is the same as for the under layer. The softened strips are bent on and temporarily stapled in place. After they have dried, the staples are removed, and the strips are fitted and put back permanently with glue and nails. For the latter, annular nails 1 inch long can be used. The heads are set slightly below the surface, and the indentations filled with hard facing compound, which also is used to fill any slight openings between the strips. When this has hardened, the outer surface is sanded true and painted.

The completed hull is next removed from the mold, and its inner surface is treated in the same manner as the outer. It is then ready for the addition of seats, floorboards, flotation, gunwales, rowlock pads and sockets, and the two outer stem pieces. The latter are carefully fitted to the outer surface of the inner stems. A thick coating of epoxy paste is applied, and the outer stem piece is drawn up tightly with large screws through the inner stem from the inside.

The last piece to go on is the outer keel strip, for which screws and glue are also used. Finally, if desired, half-inch-wide, half-oval brass stembands, extending down over the ends of the outer keel strip, may be added, both for reinforcement and to dress up the appearance of the boat.

BOATBUILDING GLUES

Glues are now used so extensively in wooden boatbuilding as to be practically indispensable. With quality boat lumber in diminishing supply and constantly rising in price, boatbuilders are being forced to consider glued construction. The regular use of glues in the boatshop is a fairly recent development; it began about thirty years ago or so during World War II when adhesives embodying various synthetic thermoplastic resins first began to be used by boatbuilders. Prior to this, casein glue was used since early in the century for gluing hollow spars. Casein glue is an organic compound, the basis of which is milk. Water resistant but not waterproof, it still proved satisfactory for gluing spars provided the joints were protected by varnish. In the 1930's, phenol-formaldehyde resins requiring heat and high pressure during the curing cycle were developed by the plywood industry to obtain a waterproof, chemically inert, high-strength bond, but these resins were too critical and exacting in their application for ordinary boatshop use.

In the 1940's, wartime demands upon the boating industry stimulated the introduction of new methods and new materials, including thermoplastic adhesives. First to appear were urea-formaldehyde, or plastic resin, glues, then resorcinal resin glues, followed closely by the epoxies. Since then a number of other plastic adhesives have been introduced, but because of their limited and specialized application, we shall not consider them here.

Urea-formaldehyde glues. There are two distinctly different types of urea-formaldehyde glues. The best known and the most widely used is the one-part type exemplified by Weldwood plastic resin glue distributed as a dry brown powder that is dissolved in water before applying. The other is a two-part system developed by the CIBA Co., Ltd., sold as Aerolite 306. It consists of a white powdered resin made liquid by adding water before it is applied to one surface of the joint. The other joint surface is moistened with a separate liquid hardener, and the two surfaces are brought into contact to effect the cure.

Weldwood plastic resin is relatively cheap and easily obtained because of its wide retail distribution. In accurately made, closely fitted joints, it cures stronger than the wood, but loses strength rapidly where there is a build-up of thickness in the glue line of an ill-fitting joint. Directions for its use specify a temperature of 70° F or higher for a proper cure, and enough clamping pressure is required to force the glue out of the joint.

CIBA's dual-system urea-formaldehyde glue, namely Aerolite, was developed in Britain during World War II for the manufacture of Mosquito bombers. Joints made with it are stronger than the wood, completely waterproof, mold-proof, insect-proof, and do not deteriorate with age or from exposure to the elements. It is gap filling without loss of strength up to a glue-line thickness of 1/16 inch. Only enough clamping pressure on joints to bring the meeting surfaces into firm contact is required. Although it will be retarded, cure will take place at temperatures as low as 50° F. Cost is moderate. It is easy and clean to use, and economical because there is no wastage in applying it. It does not stain, and the glue line in well-made joints is nearly invisible. For splicing planking and plywood, for gluing up spars, for laminating deck beams and curved ribs, and for other similar uses, Aerolite is not likely to be excelled.

Resorcinol Glue. As a boatbuilding glue, resorcinol has served well, and some boatbuilders still swear by it. Yet there can be little doubt that everything that resorcinol can do, epoxy can do better. Close, accurately fitted joints glued with resorcinol are waterproof, lasting, and stronger than the wood, but resorcinol is not gap filling at full strength, and for best results, according to the U.S. Plywood Corp., the glue line should not be thicker than 0.005 inch. High pressure clamping is required. The curing temperature should not fall below 70° F, and resorcinol should not be used when the moisture content of the wood is above 15 per cent. Furthermore, resorcinol stains wood badly, and for that reason is not desirable for gluing wood that is to be varnished. On the plus side, it is reasonably priced and readily available in retail quantities almost everywhere.

Epoxies. Epoxy's versatility and superior adhesive qualities may be judged from the literally hundreds of different epoxy formulations now in use throughout industry for gluing wood, metal, and plastic. In short, it is used for practically every gluing need. Most of the large manufacturers of chemicals, such as Shell, Dow, Union Carbide, and General Mills, produce extensive lines of epoxy resins as well as their own lines of hardening agents and copolymers. By selection and combination, chemists can formulate tailor-made epoxy adhesives with almost any desired combination of characteristics—slow cure, rapid cure, resilient or rigid bond, resistance to chemicals, adhesion to damp wood, and so forth. Because wooden boatbuilding on a commercial scale has come close to dying out in recent years, there has not been the same incentive as elsewhere in industry to develop epoxy formulations especially adapted to boatbuilding needs. Nevertheless, epoxy is available to boatbuilders in a number of formulations with characteristics no other adhesive products can match.

If the boatbuilder has some elementary knowledge of chemistry and the inclination to experiment with various standard epoxy resins, copolymers, hardeners, activators, and the like (obtainable from dealers in thermoplastic supplies), he may be able to formulate his own adhesive combinations that will work well for him. When epoxy adhesives for boat work were something of a novelty and had not been as widely adopted as they are today (1990), that was definitely a way to go, and one that I considered in detail in the first edition of this book.

Since that time, however, in response to greatly increased demand, numerous proprietary formulations of adhesive epoxy have come on the market and are now widely distributed, and when not obtainable over the counter they may by ordered by mail. The best of these have been thoroughly tested and proven in use. For occasional use and for the one-off boatbuilder, such superior proprietary formulations remove any reason to attempt to mix one's own, saving time and expense and insuring successful gluing results.

Three brands that I have used with first-rate results are Chem-Tech, Inc., 4669 Lander Road, Chagrin Falls, OH 44022; Fibre-Glass Evercoat Co., 6600 Cornell Rd., Cincinnati, OH 45242; and System Three Resins, Inc. 5965 Fourth Ave. S., Seattle, WA 98108. The epoxy adhesives put out under these three brand names have a number of desirable if not essential characteristics. In all likelihood there are others that share these same characteristics and are equally good, but I have used the three named and can vouch for them from experience. Their superior qualities are as follows:

1. Under ordinary conditions and when used with reasonable precautions, they are nonsensitizing and nonhazardous for all but a very few individuals who are naturally allergic to epoxy and should not attempt its use under any circumstances.

2. They are comparatively slow-setting, which is desirable for the nonprofessional builder, who often finds that a gluing operation takes longer than planned. Ample time for unforeseen adjustments can make the difference between a proper job and a botched one.

3. They are easy to mix in either one-part or two-part proportions that are not highly critical as to exact amounts. This makes for convenient and economical use of materials.

4. It is highly desirable for the glue mix to stay where it is put—not to run freely and not to leak out of critical joints. This is the case with Fibre-Glass Evercoat. Small amounts of a thickening agent like Cab-o-Sil, for one, added to Chem-Tech or System Three will bring them to the optimum consistency. A liquid, runny mix is difficult to handle, messes up the work, and is all but impossible to keep off hands and clothing, increasing the chance of becoming sensitized.

5. They have some resilience after hardening, and joints glued with them are capable of absorbing a moderate impact without shattering, which is not the case with some glue mixes that cure glass-hard.

Both Chem-Tech and System Three issue brochures with directions for using their products as well as epoxy adhesives in general. And of course there is much additional material in print that would be helpful to the inexperienced.

Preface
More Building Classic Small Craft

·······················•·······················

The selection of small boats in this book includes a diversity of types for markedly different needs and uses. They are good boats and will be appreciated, I hope, even by those who have no immediate plans to build. But it is primarily for the prospective builder—itching to get to work on a boat in his garage, shed, cellar, or backyard—that this book is intended.

The dories, tenders, skiffs, peapod, duckboat, pilot gig, modified Herreshoff 17-foot rowboat, and other boats in these pages are all tried and proven models that have passed the test of use and are not forbiddingly difficult for nonprofessionals to tackle. Indeed, the directions for building and the explanations of boatbuilding procedures given here have been worked out first and foremost for inexperienced nonprofessionals. Through writing how-to-build articles for amateur boatbuilders for the past 33 years and instructing upwards of a thousand of them in my

classes in recreational boatbuilding at Mystic Seaport Museum over the past 14 years, I have come to understand and respect their needs.

With one exception, all of the boats were subjects of articles written by me for the *National Fisherman* within the past 10 years. The exception is the article on the McInnis "bateau," which appeared originally in *WoodenBoat* magazine. Those articles have been revised, expanded, and in a couple of cases completely rewritten for inclusion here.

The most notable feature of this book is its large number of detailed construction drawings, 125 such drawings in all, representing on the order of a thousand hours or more of exacting work bent over the drawing board. How many weekends were spent in this way I hesitate to say and am reluctant to recall, sometimes working into the wee hours of Monday morning when there were deadlines to meet for the *National*

Fisherman. Had it not been that the bulk of this work had already been done, this book would probably never have been written. To have produced this bulk of drawings from scratch and all of a piece would have been impossible.

In addition to their specific application to the boats in this book, these drawings taken together also constitute something of a reference manual of wooden boatbuilding practices and procedures, a manual of wide general application. Considerable is to be learned from it even though none of the boats included are built.

Finally, it should be understood that this book, unlike so many books offering boats to build, contains *all the information* needed for the building procedures. There are no additional plans to buy. There are no blueprints. None are needed. Everything required in the way of directions and information is between these covers, although sometimes some careful study may be necessary to dig it out. It is the same with blueprints. As long as drawings are legible, it is a waste of time and paper to blow them up to blueprint size. A tip to builders: Xerox the pages that you will be referring to frequently, and use them in place of the book. It will save wear and tear on your book and keep it clean.

"Classic small craft," "vintage boats," "heritage boats," "traditional small craft"—these expressions are not-entirely-satisfactory attempts to name and characterize a special kind of small boat that has made a spectacular comeback in the last 25 or 30 years and is now enjoying well-deserved popularity and acclaim.

The 19th century in America was an era of rapid material progress and unprecedented technical innovation. When the century drew to a close, our native small craft had attained a diversity of form and an elegance of design combined with functional utility that was previously unknown and is unexcelled to this day. These developments carried over into the early decades of the present century, but by 1940, for reasons too involved to go into here, the tide had turned sharply and had ebbed far out. The old boats had slipped out of use and out of sight, and were almost forgotten. Few if any Whitehalls, Swampscott dories, wherries, peapods, Adirondack guide-boats, St. Lawrence River skiffs, Rangeley boats, or others like them continued to be built and used. Rowing had become a thing of the past. Wood as a boatbuilding material seemed well on the way out.

That is how it appeared on the surface. Underneath a ferment was working. Following the lead of Howard Chapelle and Francis Herreshoff, more and more small craft enthusiasts, from 1950 on, turned their efforts to the revival of our small craft heritage. This revival built up steam during the 1960s and swept the country in the 1970s. Classic small craft have now come into their own again and are here to stay.

It is always possible to go to extremes. There are some who make a fetish out of wood, and others make a fetish out of what is old, simply because it is old. Some antique boats were better left undisturbed on the rubbish heap of the past. And while I cherish and value wood as much as anyone and prefer it above all other boatbuilding materials, I cannot deny that thermoplastics are worthy materials for some boatbuilding applications when properly used. Epoxy glue and similar thermoplastic adhesives are a boon to boatbuilders, and had they come along earlier they would most certainly have been adopted by 19th century boatbuilders, who were realists and not blind to a good thing. But good things can be abused, and I have to take a dim view of the current fad for slobbering messy, expensive, ineffectual plastic all over wooden construction that would be perfectly adequate without it. Very much on the plus side, however, are the better grades of marine plywood, which has proved itself a superior material for lapstrake planking even though some purists still tend to look down their noses at it.

Nothing is more central to the American boatbuilding tradition than a readiness to try new things and to accept worthy innovations when they appear. From time immemorial boatbuilders have been looking for shortcuts and improvements. The best way and the easiest way. It is the sailors who are more apt to be the conservatives, being understandably reluctant to go to sea in untried experiments that could drown them. Boatbuilders who are true to their trade are conservatives in the best sense of that word, holding steadfastly to the ways of the past when they are good ways, and prefering the old ways, perhaps, but displaying realism enough to adopt the new when it proves better. *The best of the old with the best of the new.* That is the motto and the spirit of this book.

Occasionally I am asked why anyone would go to all the bother of building a boat—especially a classic boat using wood and hand tools—when there are any number of boats you can buy. Why, indeed! To ask the question is to miss the point, and all the fun.

People build all sorts of boats for all sorts of reasons.

I doubt if they always could tell you why. Maybe in part it is because they like the feel of sharp tools cutting into wood. Wasn't it Francis Herreshoff who said there was nothing nicer than the tangy smell of cedar shavings fresh from the plane, and their springy feel underfoot? Building a boat is a grand way to relax, let down, and get away from it all, as in the case of one overworked physician in a mid-American city who revealed that in off hours he would escape to the attic of his house, where he had a trimaran under construction. Building a boat is a challenge for some, an opportunity to prove themselves; others find a way to realize their individuality, and still others find a temporary retreat to earlier, simpler ways from a time when machines seem to be closing in on us. And there is the end product, the completed boat itself, unique and resplendent, the apple of the builder's eye.

John Gardner
Mystic, Connecticut

1

Herreshoff Rowboat and Modified McInnis Bateau

...................•.....................

HERRESHOFF ROWBOAT

In October 1947, the lines of a rowboat were offered to the readers of *Rudder* magazine by its most illustrious contributor, L. Francis Herreshoff. In those days *The Rudder* was riding the crest of a wave of unprecedented popularity and interest on the part of the boating public, the like of which has not been seen since.

Every month brought new articles by Herreshoff. Some issues contained as many as three separate contributions, which a widening circle of readers awaited with the keenest anticipation and received as inspired doctrine.

The wave set in motion then was the wave of the future, and its force is still felt. Much that has taken place on the boating scene since, and is taken for granted today, dates back to Herreshoff's writing of a

generation ago and to the views and ideas he expressed then. The immense and instant response of his readers leaves no doubt that many people had only been waiting for someone to express publicly with force, logic, and authority the substance of their own inner feelings and convictions, yearnings and intuitions.

In that time, rowing for recreation was almost unknown in this country. With the exception of a highly specialized form engaged in as a competitive sport by an elite of college athletes, rowing in the United States had all but disappeared. Why should anyone row when motors were so cheap and so readily available?

Herreshoff thought otherwise, and when he announced that what America needed, among other things, was a good rowboat, he spoke a radical doctrine. Today it is not necessary to make a case for recreational rowing, or to recapitulate the arguments

A modified Herreshoff rowboat built by Myron Young, of Laurel, New York, from plans and construction details in this chapter. "There have been no problems with the construction," Young reported. "Herreshoff's lines and your changes and construction methods worked very well."

put forth in Herreshoff's classic book *The Common Sense of Yacht Design*. But the rowboat he advocated is worth some consideration, falling as it does, somewhere between the fragile racing scull and what Herreshoff characterized as the "heavy, ill-shaped rowboat of several hundred pounds."

What Herreshoff had in mind was "a good seaboat," very easy to row and not difficult to plank. The lines of such a boat he presented to us in Figure 357 of *Common Sense*. Like so many others back in the 1940s, I subscribed to *The Rudder* to make sure I saw Herreshoff's latest contribution as soon as it appeared in print and to have all his articles on file for frequent rereading. Entranced by the rowboat lines in the October 1947 issue, I immediately scaled off an enlargement as best I could, from which I made a scale half-model, the one now tacked over the entrance to the small-boat shop at Mystic Seaport. Ever since I first saw its lines, it has been high on my list of boats to build some day. In the summer of 1979 I received a request for offsets, and soon after I received a second request. I finally had the incentive to work out the details for building this boat, or at least one very much like it.

The First Model Worked Up from Herreshoff's Lines

Although Herreshoff did not provide offsets, construction details, or anything in the way of scantling dimensions or other specifications, he certainly intended that the lines should be built from, or at least that they should provide basic proportions and design characteristics for boats subsequently to be built. The only hint given for construction is that the 17-foot boat with its 42-inch beam should be light—under 100 pounds. The boat I worked up in 1979 and presented in the February 1980 issue of *National Fisherman* would be a bit heavier, but still it would not weigh much more than 100 pounds.

The alterations I made in the lines were minor and would not affect the performance perceptibly. I made them solely to simplify the building of the round hull shape by an inexperienced amateur.

First, I made my version of this boat a true double-ender. Her stems are exactly the same, so that duplicate molds can be used at corresponding stations forward and aft of the midsection. The differences between the bow and stern ends of a boat built exactly

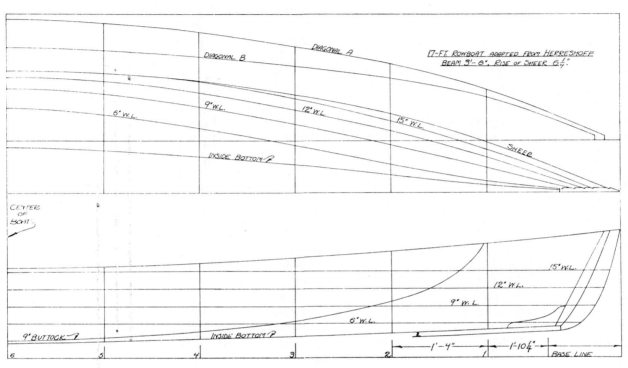

		STEM	1	2	3	4	5	6
HEIGHTS	SHEER	1-9-7	1-7-7	1-6-4	1-5-3	1-4-4	1-3-7	1-3-5
	INSIDE BOTTOM	0-5-3	0-4-7	0-4-2	0-3-6	0-3-2	0-2-7	0-2-5
	9" BUTTOCK	SHEER 1-7-7	—	0-9-6	0-6-3	0-4-6	0-3-6	0-3-1
HALF-BREADTHS	BOTTOM	0-0-3	0-1-3	0-3-1	0-5-0	0-6-3	0-7-4	0-8-0
	6" W.L.	0-0-3	0-2-0	0-5-0	0-8-4	0-11-2	1-1-5	1-2-6
	9" W.L.	0-0-3	0-4-3	0-8-3	0-11-7	1-3-0	1-5-1	1-6-1
	12" W.L.	0-0-3	0-6-1	0-10-6	1-2-3	1-5-3	1-7-2	1-7-7
	15" W.L.	0-0-3	0-7-5	1-0-3	1-4-1	1-6-7	1-8-4	1-9-0
	SHEER	0-0-3	0-8-7	1-1-6	1-5-0	1-7-2	1-8-5	1-9-1
	DIAGONAL A	0-0-7	0-8-7	1-1-2	1-4-1	1-6-5	1-8-2	1-8-7
	DIAGONAL B	0-1-1	0-7-4	0-10-5	1-0-7	1-2-3	1-3-4	1-4-1

17-FT. DOUBLE-ENDED ROWBOAT ADAPTED FROM HERRESHOFF. OFFSETS TO INSIDE OF PLANKING AND BOTTOM. FEET, INCHES, EIGHTHS.

DIAGONAL A UP 1-7-6 ABOVE B.L. AND OUT 1-9-0 ON 6" W.L.

DIAGONAL B UP 1-3-4 ABOVE B.L. AND OUT 9" ON 6" W.L.

to the lines Herreshoff drew would be so slight as to have no discernible effect on performance, but those differences would add work in building.

The evolution of the Adirondack guideboat took the same course. The first double-enders were slightly asymmetrical fore and aft, but when the guideboat attained the peak of its development, bow and stern were built exactly alike. Performance was not altered, but a substantial saving in building labor was gained.

The basic hull shapes of the Adirondack guideboat and the Herreshoff rowboat have much in common. Both boats have flat, plank bottoms. In short, the guideboat and the Herreshoff rowboat have much the same sectional shapes. The boat Herreshoff drew is a foot longer than the standard full-size Adirondack guideboat of 16 feet. In maximum beam the difference is greater—42 inches for the rowboat against 38 inches for the guideboat.

Bottom widths differ even more. For the rowboat, inside width amidships of the flat bottom is 16 inches; for most 16-foot guideboats the corresponding bottom width is normally between 8 and 9 inches. This extra width should make the rowboat less tippy than the guideboat, although the latter was adequately stable and entirely safe when handled correctly. Nevertheless, in comparison with flat-floored utility rowboats and wide, outboard craft, the Herreshoff rowboat might appear to be somewhat tiddly. After all, it was intended to be an easy, fast-moving rowboat, not a working skiff the side of which one can sit on with impunity.

Inside depth amidships scales 12 inches in the Herreshoff lines compared with 11½ inches in a 16-foot Grant guideboat. In my initial model (as well as in my second and final model) I increased the sheer height uniformly throughout by 1 inch, making the inside depth amidships 13 inches. I counted on this increase to improve seakeeping qualities without increasing windage significantly.

One major difference between the Herreshoff rowboat and the Adirondack guideboat is the amount of bottom rocker, or fore-and-aft camber. In the former it is 2¾ inches, as I drew it, while in the latter it is barely more than 1 inch for a 16-foot boat.

As mentioned above, my biggest departure from the original Herreshoff lines was in the shape and construction of the stems. I drew the same shape and dimensions at either end, although I suggested that builders could lower the height at the stern by an inch or so if they thought this would improve the appearance.

Herreshoff did not indicate a stem construction, but the curved shape he drew suggests a conventionally rabbeted stem and a rabbeted sternpost. Further, the amount of stem curve might require curved timber or a steam-bent stempiece.

Instead, I chose a stem very similar to that found in the Rangeley Lakes boat, although the one I used is even simpler (see the drawing on page 10). Consisting of two pieces, it can be sawn to shape from ordinary straight-grain plank and requires no rabbeting. The inner piece is easily beveled in place after the boat has been set up for planking. The outer piece may be shaped and beveled at the bench, then attached to the inner part after planking has been completed. This is the most easily constructed stem that I know, yet it is wholly adequate and pleasing in appearance, at least to my eye.

I worked up the boat to be clinker-planked with eight strakes got out of standard 4-by-8-foot panels of ¼-inch marine plywood, spliced as required. Laps and splices would be glued with a flexible adhesive and fastened between frames with clinched copper tacks. Strakes would be fastened to the frames with screws or copper rivets. Glued laps can add much strength and make the boat completely and permanently tight whether left in or taken out of the water, a most desirable feature in any boat that is to be hauled about on a trailer. More complete building instructions applicable to both this and my second model begin on page 9.

The Second Model

My first article about the Herreshoff rowboat, in *National Fisherman*, February 1980, brought a highly encouraging response. Buzz Nichols of Beach Haven Gardens, New Jersey, was one of those dropping a favorable word:

> I enjoyed reading your article about the Herreshoff boat. . . .In May of 1978 I was living in Long Beach, California, and had the impulsive desire to buy a rowing dory for recreation. By a stroke of good fortune I came across a fellow named Ellis E. St. Rose, in Venice, California. He built such a boat as you describe in your article. It was after that design by Herreshoff, and the only difference from what you

describe that I can detect is that the laps of the clinker planking were fastened with brass screws, not copper rivets.

While in California, I made a number of cross-channel trips from Catalina Island to Long Beach, a distance of 28 miles. In one crossing, August 1978, I made the trip rowing single in 5 hours 47 minutes. The boat is excellent in the open ocean, and does very well trolling while running offshore.

Certainly this was a highly favorable report. One that was just as favorable but much more detailed can be found in an article by Allan H. Vaitses in *Rudder*, January 1955. Somehow I overlooked this article until Bill Davis of Virginia Beach, Virginia, kindly sent me a copy. Davis, who works for the Farrell Steamship Lines in Norfolk, was one of those who initially suggested a how-to series for the construction of this boat. Anyone interested in the Herreshoff rowboat would be well rewarded to find Vaitses's very interesting account. Some of the salient points follow.

On "every decent work day" of a 32-month span — to avoid a lengthy roundabout trip around the harbor — Vaitses rowed one of the Herreshoff boats back and forth across the mile-wide harbor between his home on Mattapoisett Neck and the Burr Brothers' Boat Yard on Neds Point. Vaitses figures this amounted to 1,200 miles under oars, and at the end the boat was in good shape and none the worse for nearly three years of continual use. Before settling on the Herreshoff rowboat, Vaitses tried or considered various craft, but for one reason or another none proved suitable. Round-bottomed yacht tenders drew too much water. Semidories weighed too much. A flat-bottomed skiff was too slow, very wet, and "a bear in a crosswind."

The boat had to be light because the beach at Mattapoisett was rocky and shoal, not over 3 inches deep for a distance of 200 feet offshore. Planked semidory fashion with ⅜-inch cedar, this 17-foot boat weighed no more than 125 pounds soaking wet.

According to Vaitses, this boat was at least twice as fast as an ordinary rowboat and would outdistance anything under oars except racing shells. In a moderate breeze most ordinary small sailboats were no faster. Frequent timing of trips across the harbor indicated a top average speed of 6 m.p.h. with ordinary 7½-foot oars and a stationary thwart. A speed of 4 to 5 m.p.h. could be kept up indefinitely, and short bursts of 7 m.p.h. were possible. With spoon oars and a sliding seat she would undoubtedly do better.

Vaitses pointed out certain limitations in the type. When the boat is pulled straight on into a steep chop, her sharp bow tends to knife into solid water, and without decking at her ends she will fill unless slowed down. Second, she lacks initial stability to some extent, though not as dramatically as an Adirondack guideboat or a canoe. Her apparent tenderness may bother some not used to such boats, but it is no problem if one keeps in the middle. Certainly it would be possible to tip her over through carelessness on the part of the occupants, but blame should not be attached to the boat.

Vaitses thought that because of her low sides, 500 pounds was about the limit of his boat's load capacity, but he feared that making her more high sided would increase her windage unduly. I considered this also, but I decided the boat would benefit from the inch of freeboard I had added, while the increase in windage would be too small to matter.

After reading Vaitses's article, I made a second and final revision of the lines drawn by Herreshoff. The new section lines and the accompanying table of offsets that appear herewith represent quite a lot of work and thoughtful study. These 12 sectional outlines, numbered .5 to 6, represent all of the required frame shapes. This body plan of sectional shapes and their measurements recorded in the table of offsets was taken from a full-size laydown of lines that was thoroughly worked over and faired. This work hardly needs to be done again. Laying out the sectional shapes full size from the offsets as given should suffice, and the shapes should be accurate enough to build from.

Note that the offsets are measured in sixteenths rather than the usual eighths of inches, and that in some cases pluses are used when a measurement runs a bit over. When the sections are laid out, the diagonals rather than the waterline measurements should govern if significant discrepancies between the two arise. I don't anticipate any such discrepancies.

The principal difference between the first lines that I drew up for this boat and the revised lines presented herewith is a considerable increase in the sheer beam, particularly forward. This has meant filling out the topsides significantly. This has been accomplished, however, without the slightest alteration in the underbody shape. Thus, below the load waterline the

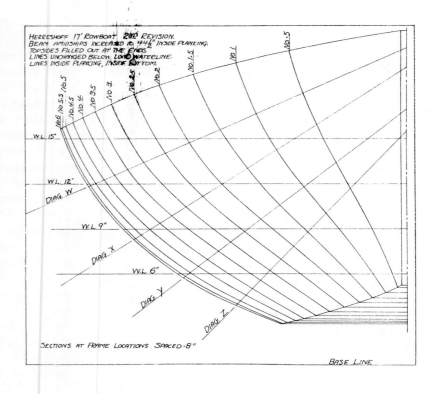

HERRESHOFF 17' ROWBOAT. 2ND REVISION.
BEAM AMIDSHIPS INCREASED TO 44½" INSIDE PLANKING.
TOPSIDES FILLED OUT AT THE ENDS.
LINES UNCHANGED BELOW LOAD WATERLINE.
LINES INSIDE PLANKING, INSIDE BOTTOM.

SECTIONS AT FRAME LOCATIONS SPACED 8"

BASE LINE

HERRESHOFF 17' ROWBOAT. 2ND REVISION. FRAME STATIONS SPACED 8" APART. BOTH ENDS OF BOAT ALIKE.

	STATIONS	STEM	No..5	No.1	No.1.5	No.2	No.2.5	No.3	No.3.5	No.4	No.4.5	No.5	No.5.5	No.6
HEIGHTS	SHEER	1-10-2	1-8-13	1-8-0	1-7-4+	1-6-8+	1-5-15	1-5-5	1-4-13	1-4-7	1-4-2	1-3-14	1-3-11+	1-3-10
	INSIDE BOTTOM	0-5-5	0-5-2	0-4-12	0-4-7	0-4-2	0-3-13	0-3-8	0-3-4+	0-3-0+	0-2-14+	0-2-12+	0-2-11+	0-2-11+
HALF-BREADTHS	INSIDE BOTTOM	0-0-6	0-0-10	0-1-6	0-2-4	0-3-2	0-4-0+	0-5-0	0-5-14	0-6-10	0-7-2	0-7-10	0-7-15	0-8-1
	6" W.L.	0-0-6	0-0-15+	0-2-3+	0-3-11	0-5-2+	0-6-13	0-8-8	0-10-0	0-11-7	1-0-10	1-1-12	1-2-7	1-2-11+
	9" W.L.	0-0-6	0-2-4	0-4-6	0-6-9	0-8-9+	0-10-10	1-0-6	1-2-0	1-3-6	1-4-8	1-5-6+	1-6-0	1-6-2
	12" W.L.	0-0-6	0-3-12	0-6-12+	0-9-6	0-11-13+	1-1-15	1-3-10	1-5-2+	1-6-5	1-7-3	1-7-14	1-8-5	1-8-7+
	15" W.L.	0-0-6	0-5-4+	0-8-12+	0-11-9	1-2-1	1-4-0	1-5-12	1-7-0+	1-8-1	1-8-14+	1-9-7+	1-9-12	1-9-14
	SHEER	0-0-6	0-7-8	0-10-15	1-1-10+	1-3-13+	1-5-7	1-6-14	1-7-15	1-8-12	1-9-6	1-9-13	1-10-0	1-10-2
DIAGONALS	DIAG. W	0-0-8	0-7-4+	0-10-9+	1-1-2	1-3-4+	1-5-0	1-6-7+	1-7-10	1-8-9	1-9-5+	1-9-14	1-10-3+	1-10-5+
	DIAG. X	0-0-8	0-6-14	0-9-14+	1-0-3+	1-2-3	1-3-11	1-4-15	1-6-0+	1-6-15	1-7-11	1-8-5+	1-8-13	1-8-15
	DIAG. Y	0-0-8	0-5-12	0-8-6	0-10-6	0-11-14+	1-1-4	1-2-6	1-3-6	1-4-4+	1-5-0+	1-5-11	1-6-1+	1-6-3+
	DIAG. Z	0-0-9	0-5-4	0-7-9	0-9-4+	0-10-9	0-11-12	1-0-13	1-1-10+	1-2-7	1-3-1	1-3-9	1-3-13	1-3-15

DIAGONAL W UP 21", OUT 20" ON 12" W.L. DIAGONAL X UP 19¾", OUT 21" ON 6" W.L. DIAGONAL Y UP 17" OUT 14" ON 6" W.L.
DIAGONAL Z UP 15½", OUT 9" ON 6" W.L. MEASUREMENTS IN FEET, INCHES, AND SIXTEENTHS.

boat remains exactly the same as before, whereas above the load waterline the topsides are substantially fuller. The profile is unchanged.

In my first set of lines, when I raised the sheer by one inch, I nevertheless maintained Herreshoff's original beam, which pulled in the side flare. In the revision, I have let the side flare out, and as it runs forward from amidships I have progressively increased it, so that at station 1, which is only 22¼ inches aft of the forward edge of the stem, the sheer beam has been increased from 17¾ inches to 21⅛ inches, a net increase of 4⅛

inches. This is a lot! And the reason for it is to give more buoyancy and lift to the ends.

Allan Vaitses stressed the tendency of his boat with its sharp bow to knife into waves and take water when running into a head sea. He cautioned that in such circumstances it was necessary to hold back on the oars and slow down; otherwise the boat would fill.

This boat, as originally designed, did not have much buoyancy in its ends. What I have attempted to do here is to add buoyancy and lift but without slowing down the boat by spoiling Herreshoff's fine entrance at the

HALF-BREADTHS	STEM	1	2	3	4	5	6
INSIDE BOTTOM	0-0-6	0-1-5	0-4-0	0-6-7	0-8-6	0-10-2	0-11-0
+6" W.L.	0-0-6	0-2-2	0-5-7	0-10-3	1-1-5	1-4-3	1-5-6
+9" W.L.	0-0-6	0-4-5	0-9-2	1-1-6	1-5-3	1-7-7	1-9-1
+12" W.L.	0-0-6	0-6-3	0-11-5	1-4-2	1-7-6	1-9-0	1-10-7
+15" W.L.	0-0-6	0-7-7	1-1-2	1-6-0	1-9-2	1-11-2	2-0-0
SHEER	0-0-6	0-9-1	1-2-5	1-6-7	1-9-5	1-11-3	2-0-1

D.S. CONNELLY'S WIDENED VERSION HERRESHOFF/GARDNER ROWBOAT

4-FOOT BEAM. HEIGHTS AS ORIGINALLY SHOWN. DIAGONALS TO BE DEVELOPED.

load line. I do not say that the boat as now revised will not take water in a head sea, but I believe it will take considerably less, and with the addition of light end decks, or even temporary canvas coverings of some sort, this should be a much drier and safer boat. In my own boat, now in the planning stage, I am seriously considering installing very light end decks of ⅛-inch plywood with a small but adequate amount of foam flotation tucked away underneath.

Another reason for increasing the sheer beam was to give more purchase for the oars. The beam amidships to the inside of the planking is now 44½ inches. Add the thickness of the planking and that of outside gunwales, and you have between 46 and 47 inches. If the oarlock sockets are installed on the outside of the gunwales, as is the standard practice in the Adirondack guideboat, the rowing beam amidships will be not less than 46 inches, which in my estimation is ample for 8-foot sculls; for rough-water work I believe I would go with 7½-footers. For those who might want greater rowing span, folding outrigger oarlocks are now available. These would increase the effective rowing beam by several inches.

Of course, the rowing thwarts must be properly located, and this will be treated in detail below. Let me say now, however, that there should not be more than two rowing thwarts for this boat, and that they should be positioned in the center of the boat with only good arm reach between them—enough so that the oarsman on the forward thwart will have ample reach when two are rowing. If the two thwarts are properly located, the rowing span need not be less than 45 inches for either.

I consider this to be adequate, although Daniel S. Connelly of Cleveland Heights, Ohio, a knowledgeable connoisseur of small craft whose opinions I value

and respect, feels that a 48-inch rowing span is better. Accordingly, he offers a widened version of this design, which opens up to 48 inches. I have copied his proposed table of half-breadths and submit it here for consideration.

It should be noted that Connelly's overall increase in beam derives basically from his increase of bottom width amidships from 16 to 22 inches. This will produce a somewhat slower boat, in my opinion, but one with increased initial stability. For those who desire a somewhat steadier boat and would not mind a slight loss of rowing speed, the Connelly boat might prove more satisfactory. Connelly's letter explaining his reasons and commenting on the design follows:

I am sure the Gardner/Herreshoff design is a winner, partly in view of your determination to keep weight on the low side.

I remembered Vaitses' article on commuting under oars, but had forgotten details including the boat used. I immediately reread it. His mild criticism of the boat regarding load-carrying capacity and initial stability emboldened me to forward a little experiment of my own.

Based on my feeling that a gunwale beam of 4 feet is about the minimum for a rowing boat, I simply expanded your design to reach this goal. As the method of achieving this with the least violence to your nice lines I simply expanded half-breadths of the flat bottom to increase maximum width of flat from 16 inches to 22 inches, and used your topsides as drawn for Stations 2 through 6. Stem siding was increased, and the added width at Station 1 was cut to one-half the geometric increase. I believe this would give fair lines within ⅛ inch when laid down full size on the scrieve board, depending on the quality of the batten used. For your file I attach the resulting half-breadths.

I have not had time to try these on the drafting board.

Regarding Vaitses' comment about the problem of water coming aboard in head seas—it ought to be possible to make a very lightweight, quickly detachable bow deck which would keep out 90 percent of the water without impeding maintenance.

Connelly had previously written to call my attention to the Reelfoot boat, which was developed on Reelfoot Lake in northwestern Tennessee and described in detail by George Laycock in the 1957 edition of *Sports Afield Boatbuilding Annual*. Laycock's article included a drawing by Edson I. Schock detailing lines and construction. Laycock claimed that the Reelfoot boats, which were built for many years by the Calhoun family of Tiptonville, Tennessee, numbered nearly 3,000 on Reelfoot Lake at the time he wrote the article, and had been exported all over the United States. This seems an awful lot of boats on a single lake, but I am not questioning that figure since I know nothing of that lake or the boats in question, except from the *Sports Afield* account.

Connelly forwarded a copy of the article to me, along with the following comments:

The striking similarity between your design and the Reelfoot Lake boat fascinates me. I am sure that the Reelfoot boat antedates October 1947 (date of the original Herreshoff article) by an appreciable interval, and the text of the enclosure tends to support this. It therefore appears to me that these are two designs of completely independent origin.

	Reelfoot	*Gardner*
LOA	15'10"	17'1"
Beam, inside	42¾"	42¼"
Depth, inside	12½"	13"
Max. width flat bottom	24"	16"
Bottom rocker	2⅞"	2¾"
Rise of sheer	5⅞"	6¼"

You will note that the Reelfoot drawings were prepared by Edson I. Schock—and thus, I presume, are properly faired. They are based on measurements by George Laycock in 1956. The photograph of one of these boats under bow-facing oars shows a rough job, but this may be a much abused livery boat. The photo of the completed boat shows what seems to be very acceptable workmanship. Apparently construction is carried out with hammer, saw and drawknife. Note the construction time quoted!

The article claimed that "two Reelfoot boatbuilders could build the entire boat in one day." I assume this meant they could assemble a boat in one day from pieces precut from patterns. Even then it would have been a long day, with a lot of hustle and not many smoke breaks.

The construction shown in the photos looked heavy—too heavy to produce a total weight for the boat of only 150 pounds, as claimed. And when the cypress with which many of them were planked soaked up, the weight was certainly more than 150 pounds. Apparently Reelfoot Lake is shallow, and so the bottoms of these boats were originally sheathed with a sheet of "tin"—presumably thin galvanized iron. Later, fiberglass was used. Because of the many stumps rising above the surface of the lake, hinged oars were used, permitting the oarsman to row facing forward.

Connelly's letter concluded with the following comments:

I am particularly pleased to see this latest of your designs. I feel that some of the builders of traditional rowing craft are not making realistic choices if rowing for recreation is their aim. Some of the boats are strictly working craft, intended to provide a working platform with load carrying capacity in fairly adverse weather conditions, with ease of propulsion important, but of secondary consideration.

I am also pleased to see you recommend plywood for planking. I have a 15-foot Lyman outboard, built in 1953, lapstrake-ply planked, and apparently as sound as the day it was completed, in spite of having been used by previous owners with a 40 h.p. engine.

This last comment, confirming my choice of marine plywood for planking, was most welcome inasmuch as there is still considerable unfounded prejudice against its use.

Before I go on to construction details, I'll excerpt one other letter that was sent soon after the appearance of the first of my articles on the Herreshoff rowboat. Bill Cannell, a boatbuilder in Camden, Maine, liked the Herreshoff rowboat so much he built one for his own use. How this came about and what came of it is related in Cannell's letter:

After you have looked at the accompanying...photograph you will understand that it was with no little interest that I read your article in the February *National Fisherman*.

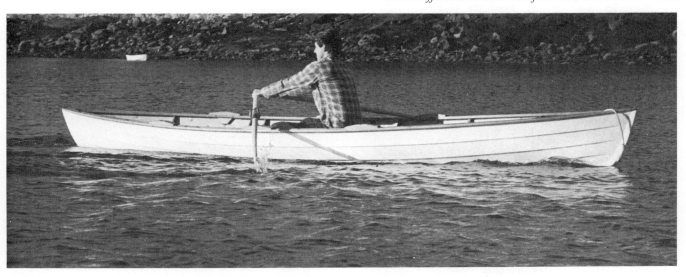

Another close relative of the Herreshoff rowboat, this one built by Bill Cannell of Camden, Maine. The oarlock sockets for the after rowing position are very far aft. (Courtesy Bill Cannell)

The boat in Figure 357 of Mr. Herreshoff's *Common Sense of Yacht Design* has intrigued me for a long time, and two summers ago, having a slack period in building, I decided to do something about it. I called Muriel Vaughn and asked her to send up what she had on the boat, which was only that one drawing. She also mentioned that Allan Vaitses had built a boat to these lines and promised to send an article he had written on the boat for *Rudder*.

After waiting for the lines to arrive in the mail a couple of days, my enthusiasm gained such momentum that I said the hell with it and went ahead and began my own drawing of a very similar boat. I wanted to preserve the same basic proportions, but if possible further simplify her.

First of all, like you, I opted for waterlines symmetrical fore and aft to cut down the time of lofting and pattern making for the sawn frames. The sheer, however, is not symmetrical.

I made my design slightly wider on both the bottom and the sheer and gave the sections a bit more curve in the topsides. I also decided to eliminate the vertical keel that appears in Mr. Herreshoff's drawing for the sake of simplicity. For the same reason I ran the stem and bottomboards together in a sharp forefoot.

One design change I would make now is the arrangement of the rowing stations. Hoping to preserve perfect trim with either one or two oarsmen, I drew and built her with three rowing stations. When I went out for a spin with Maynard Bray to try her out for the first time for any distance with two rowing, it became apparent that the oarlocks at the after rowing station lacked sufficient spread, and made rowing there very tiring. Two thwarts would have been better.

Mr. Herreshoff's description of Figure 357, "a good sea boat, very easy to row, and not difficult to plank up," is a good goal in the recreational rowing boat of today, and fortunately this boat seems to fulfill these requirements. There should be more boats of this type because they are so easy to row and are fast, and they are relatively simple to build, an advantage to the amateur builder and professional alike in terms of time and cost. As for seaworthiness, a boat of this type can handle any conditions which would be either fun or rational for the recreational oarsman to go out in.

Construction Details

As I stated earlier in the chapter, one of my primary considerations was to simplify construction as much as possible in the interest of the nonprofessional backyard builder while preserving the essential integrity of Herreshoff's design. Since Herreshoff provided no construction details, I felt justified in incorporating features from the Adirondack guideboat and the Rangeley Lakes boat. Both are craft of outstanding merit and ability proved through generations of use. Hundreds of each have been built and have given good service.

Note: The stem bevels and related measurements in this drawing apply with precision only to the author's first revision of the Herreshoff boat. The author's second model, with flared topsides, requires somewhat greater stem bevels. In its general detail the drawing applies to either model. To get exact stem bevels for the second model, finish the bevels during the planking process.

The stem construction adapted from the Rangeley boat could hardly be simpler or easier to make. There is no rabbet to lay out and cut, and no curved timber—either natural crook knees or steam-bent pieces—is required. Instead, the stem assembly is made up of three pieces cut out of ordinary straight-grain plank 1¼ inches thick. These are the forefoot, the inner stem, and the outer stem. Although the accompanying

drawings show the stem construction in complete detail, it may be helpful to mention the order of construction and call attention to several details.

The forefoot and inner stempiece are fastened together, and this assembly is then fastened to the bottom board prior to making the setup for planking. In planking, no special care need be taken that the hood ends of the planks conform exactly to the shape of the

1	BOTTOM BOARD NORTHERN WHITE PINE 13/16" THICK
2	INNER STEM SIDED 1 1/4" BEFORE BEVELS OAK, MAHOGANY, RIFT GRAIN DOUGLAS FIR.
3	OUTER STEM SIDED 1 1/4" BEFORE BEVELS OAK, MAHOGANY, DOUGLAS FIR
4	FOREFOOT SIDED 1 1/4" OAK, MAHOGANY, DOUGLAS FIR.
5	PLANKING, MARINE GRADE AA FIR PLYWOOD 1/4" THICK.
6	SCREW TOGETHER AS SHOWN. EPOXY GLUE ALL JOINTS. PRECAUTION AGAINST SLIPPAGE, ASSEMBLE DRY. REMOVE SCREWS. DISASSEMBLE. APPLY GLUE. ASSEMBLE AND REPLACE SCREWS.

MODIFIED HERRESHOFF ROWBOAT

SHEER

outer edge of the inner stempiece. Provided the planks are not too short, this fit can be achieved after planking is completed by trimming the ends with a sharp block plane. The outer stempiece is then fastened on with screws from inside, as the drawing shows. It should be noted that in beveling the inner stempiece to receive the ends of the planking, its outer edge is held to a uniform width of ¾ inch throughout.

Although it is possible to determine the precise amount of bevel required for the ends of the planking from the laydown of lines, I suggest that inexperienced builders wait until after the setup for planking has been made before completing this bevel. By laying a batten across the frames to simulate planking, one can easily determine the exact amount of stem bevel, obviating any danger of cutting off too much.

It will add greatly to hull strength if the three members of the stem assembly are glued as well as screwed together. To prevent slippage, fasten the members together dry at first, then remove the screws, apply the glue, and finally, reseat the screws. Glue is slippery, and it is extremely difficult to keep joints properly aligned if glue is applied before fastening holes are bored.

This boat could be set up with the use of molds and planked in the ordinary way. It could be set up either right side up or upside down. Each of these two methods has advantages and disadvantages. With the boat right side up, it is easier for one person working alone to rivet the laps as planking proceeds. Most builders find it easier to fit the garboard and the laps with the boat upside down.

The boat might be planked bottom up on a ladder-frame setup with molds on 16-inch centers to correspond to an 8-inch frame spacing. As the planks were put on, they could be temporarily secured to the molds with long, slim, resin-coated nails through the laps. The nail heads are padded with round washers of thick leather slightly smaller than a dime. These press firmly on the lap without marring the wood, permitting the nails to be easily pulled with nippers when planking is completed and the molds are removed for timbering. This method, developed for the construction of the four-oared gig *General Lafayette* at Mystic Seaport, worked out very well for that boat. Frames could consist of steamed white oak bent in and riveted after the boat had been planked and turned right side up. In locations where suitable oak bending stock is not available, laminated ribs would be another way to go, and could be easier, lighter, and just as strong as steam-bent oak. Glued laminations of thin strips of spruce would be suitable.

Here, however, we shall consider quite a different approach to setting up and planking the Herreshoff rowboat. The method I have in mind was developed for building the Adirondack guideboat. With this method, no molds are required. The timbers or ribs, got out to shape ahead of time and fastened to the bottom board, serve as molds, and the planking is applied directly to them and permanently fastened in place as planking proceeds.

The 66 ribs or frames that are required for the standard guideboat are cut out of natural crooks obtained from large spruce stumps. They are so stiff and hold their shape so well that when they are set up and fastened to the bottom board all that is required is a spacer batten sprung around the sheer to equalize their fore and aft spacing at their upper ends. No internal cross bracing is needed.

The Herreshoff rowboat can be built in exactly the same way. Its foundation is a bottom board, like the guideboat's but wider. Although I am not suggesting that the frames for this boat be got out of large spruce stumps, I have found that stiff, preshaped frames or ribs can be laminated from thin spruce strips. At first, I assumed that it would be necessary to steam-bend these strips, which would have complicated the process. But I then found that strips ⅛ inch thick or slightly less and 1½ inches wide could be bent dry and glued on forms, and that once the glue had set they were completely rigid and stiff, with no springback whatever. The frames must be clamped to the forms until the glue has set.

With frames set 8 inches apart on centers, 48 of them are required for this 17-foot boat. Because the boat is the same at either end, and because both sides are the same, only 12 different shapes are required, and because the shape changes so slightly from frame to frame, only two or three short pieces of heavy plank will be required for the gluing forms, sawn to shape and altered as the shape changes. If 1½-inch strips are used, a matching pair of ⅝-inch by ⅝-inch frames is produced with each gluing. Making the frames for this boat turns out to be a relatively simple job. The material required can be rough spruce staging planks, obtainable almost anywhere, whereas good bending oak is not.

Bevels for the frames can be taken from the diagonals relative to the frame spacing of 8 inches. Only toward the ends of the boat will the frame bevels be great enough to matter. One way to make accurate plank forms on which to glue up the laminated frames is to lay out the sectional shapes, which is to say the body plan, on heavy paper (a good grade of detail paper would do nicely) and then with carbon paper trace the frame shapes on thin wood in order to make molds for each frame section. From these, the plank forms for gluing the laminated frames can be marked and cut to shape.

The method for gluing up laminated frames. In the foreground is a frame in the gluing form. In the background are three frames nearing completion. This method is also used for the modified McInnis bateau described later in this chapter. (Mary Anne Stets photo, Mystic Seaport)

All the frames for this boat can be made up piecemeal ahead of time and put aside until it is convenient to set up for planking. This is a schedule that lends itself to the home workshop, where circumstances often force the construction of a boat to be an intermittent and drawn-out process. Being able to build this boat without molds will cut not only the time required but the expense as well.

Although some may want to stick with the time-tested method of construction with molds, I intend to build this boat with preformed, laminated frames, and am already gluing them a few at a time when I can find the time to do so.

The boat should not be difficult to build, although it will not plank quite as easily as the original Herreshoff design. Its greater fullness in the topsides at the ends results in more bend and sny in the plank ends. In its construction, this boat resembles both the dory and the Adirondack guideboat, which, despite differences in shape, are closely related types. Both are planked on preshaped frames attached to flat bottom boards.

Before setting out to build this boat, the prospective builder would be well advised to review dory construction and, if possible, to read Kenneth and Helen Durant's *Adirondack Guide-Boat* (Camden, Maine: International Marine Publishing Co., 1980).

Dories are built both right side up and upside down, just as this boat can be. Advantages and disadvantages of the two methods have already been touched on. When the bottom-up method is followed, it is easier to fit the garboard to the bottom—and a good joint is essential if the boat is to be tight. Yet if rivets are used through the frames when the boat is bottom up, riveting becomes more difficult, generally requiring a helper to hold on. When the boat is built right side up, one person can do the riveting quite nicely.

If you should decide to build bottom up, the laps could be fastened to the frames with ¾-inch number 6 bronze flathead wood screws. This would be easier and faster than rivets, but considerably more expensive. On the other hand, if the holes through the frames for the rivets were bored snug, the nails might hold sufficiently well without burrs and peening until planking was completed and the boat turned over. Then one person could conceivably handle the heading over of the rivets. Even so, the services of a helper to hold on would be eminently desirable.

As I stated above, I am planning to build my boat with lapstrake planking of ¼-inch fir marine plywood. The plank laps will be glued with epoxy and pulled tight between the frames with copper tacks just long enough to clinch over about ⅛ inch on the inside and spaced 1¼ to 2 inches. Holes for the tacks will be made with an awl so that the soft copper will drive through the plywood without crippling. This is similar to the method used for fastening guideboat laps, except that the latter require two rows of tacks, one driven from either side.

It is easy to clinch over the ends against a smooth iron hold-on of some sort by reaching under and behind, even when the boat is being built bottom up. A boat constructed in this way, with plywood planking and glued laps, will remain perfectly tight both in the water and out. For keeping water absorption to a minimum, I cannot recommend too strongly that you saturate the planking inside and out with repeated applications of linseed oil, thinned about 20 percent with mineral spirits and applied boiling hot. The mixture should be heated in a double boiler in order to keep it below its flash point, and every sensible precaution should be employed. This ought not to be done until the glue has thoroughly cured, and the oil in such a saturation job will require several weeks to solidify and cure before the boat can be painted.

The accompanying construction drawings should be carefully studied. Most of the important points are indicated by the 24 numbered references, each of which is addressed in turn:

1, 19. The bottom, like those of the dory and the Adirondack guideboat, should be northern white pine, if possible, finished ¾ inch thick. Douglas fir, juniper, Port Orford cedar, or cypress could be substituted. The required width amidships is 16 inches, and since boards this wide are not easily obtained, two 3-inch strips may be glued with epoxy to the edges of a 10-inch board. There should be no difficulty in bending the planks to the very moderate rocker in the bottom.

2 – 4. The stem assembly, consisting of the inner and outer stems and the stem knee, is fully diagramed on pages 10 and 11. These pieces could be made of oak, but a lighter wood would save some weight. Good-quality rift or quarter-sawn Douglas fir would be excellent. Guideboat stems were spruce, and mahogany is another possibility.

This three-piece assembly should be made up and fastened together before it is incorporated in the boat. The inner stempiece and the stem knee are permanently glued and screwed together, but the outer stempiece is merely screwed on so that it can be taken off when the boat is set up for planking. After the boat is planked, the outer stempiece is refastened.

Because the screw holes have already been bored, it will go back exactly where it is supposed to go and line up perfectly. One caution: Inexperienced builders had best not attempt to bevel the inner stem completely before planking, and should leave a little wood for a final fairing as planking proceeds.

5, 18. The seat risers and seat-riser doublers may be of pine, fir, or Port Orford cedar, sized ½ by 2½ inches. Besides supporting the thwarts, these are important structural members that greatly stiffen the hull. Risers are fastened to the frames with 1-inch number 8 bronze screws. Doublers span three frames and are glued and screwed to the risers. They support the ends of the thwarts and provide ample wood to receive three 2-inch number 12 screws put in through the ends of the thwarts.

6. Thwarts or seats are spruce, for stiffness with lightness. They are 8 inches wide and ⅞ inch thick. The under edges should be beveled for appearance.

7. Type and placement of the oarlock sockets are similar to those in the Adirondack guideboat. By locating the oarlock sockets on the outside of the outwale, a 4-foot spread is obtained for the forward rowlocks and a 45½-inch spread for the after rowing position.

8. The outwale is fir, spruce, or mahogany, 1¾ inches deep by 1¼ inches amidships. It is beveled to meet the flare of the sides, so that when fastened in place, the outer side stands plumb. The outwale tapers

from 1¾ inches amidships to about 1 inch at the ends. It can be riveted through the timberheads or screw-fastened from the inside. It should be glued to the top strake of the planking as well as screwed or nailed with small anchor-fast annular nails driven through the planking from the inside.

9. End decks are plywood, ⅛ inch thick for lightness, although ¼-inch stock like the planking can be used without much of an increase in weight.

10. The coaming or *deck circles* (guideboat terminology) can be strips of oak ⅜ inch thick and 3 inches wide, steam-bent, and cut to shape to conform to the crown of the deck. Alternatively the coaming can be glue-laminated over a form with the use of thin strips of mahogany, ash, or other wood in the manner in which the frames are laminated. The coaming stands 1 inch above the deck. The radius for the deck circle is 28 inches from a center located 6 inches aft of station 3.

11. Deck beams are spruce, molded 1½ inches and sided ½ inch. There is 1 inch of crown in approximately 3 feet of length.

12. Backing for the coaming or deck circles is in two halves—sawn, bent, or laminated to shape. These two halves butt on the afterdeck beam to which they fasten and extend to the sides of the boat. They are curved both to correspond to the curvature of the deck and to fit the round of the deck circles, which are screwed to them.

13. Filler pieces are fitted between the frames and glued to the inner side of the top strake. These are pine,

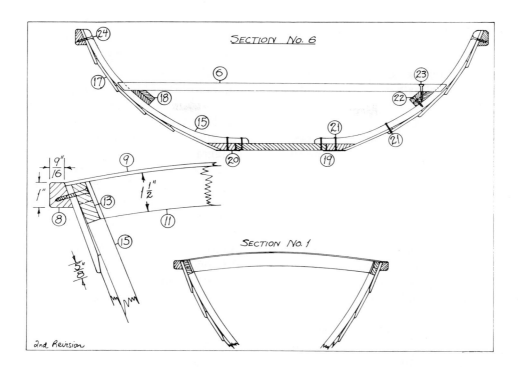

SECTION No. 6

SECTION No. 1

2nd Revision

1½ inches wide and ½ inch thick. Together with the ends of the frames, these filler pieces form a continuous shelf that is set below the sheerline by the thickness of the deck. The shelf supports the sides of the deck and is the structural member to which the edges of the deck are fastened. The filler pieces are also notched to receive the ends of the deck beams. The sheer plank is cut down by the thickness of the deck, which permits the outer edge of the deck to come flush with the outside of the planking. This edge is then covered and hidden by the outwale.

14. A breast cleat, hardly large enough to be dignified with the term breasthook, supports the outboard end of the deck and is fastened to the inner stem.

15. The method of laminating the frames in this boat has been explained above. The frames in the ends of the boat require considerable beveling and should be glued up ¾ inch thick to allow for this.

In gluing my frames I use 1½-inch-wide strips of seasoned, quarter-sawn Douglas fir, from which I can get out a matching pair of half-frames for either side of the boat. Since the boat is double-ended and there are 12 frame stations (or rather 11 on either side of the middle frame station), a total of 46 half-frames of 12 different shapes will be required. This will necessitate 12 differently shaped gluing forms.

Because the shapes change so gradually, however, slight alterations in the forms from station to station

can be made, so that actually only about three separate pieces of 2-inch plank will be required for the gluing forms. Although I am using Douglar fir for my frames, spruce, which was used for the guideboat frames, would be excellent.

Some mahogany might do for gluing up frames. Oak does not glue very well as a rule, and it is heavy. Pine is too weak, as are cedar and juniper.

16. Bottom cleats are located as shown. They are of oak, laid on the flat, ⅝ inch by ⅞ inch, and screwed or riveted in place, the latter being stronger. Note the way the frames and bottom cleats are located: No limbers are required to drain the bottom, for water runs around the ends.

17. As stated above, planks are ¼-inch marine plywood, either fir or mahogany. One 10-foot sheet and one 8-foot sheet will be ample. Planks are put on in two and three pieces, glue-scarfed together. Splices should be located so as to break joints as much as possible. The 8-foot and 10-foot sheets are convenient for this.

18. The seat-riser doubler has been treated under 5.

19. The glued bottom joint has been dealt with in 1.

20. The edge of the garboard plank and the joint it makes with the bottom may be covered with a strip of fiberglass or Vectra tape put on with the same epoxy used for gluing the laps. This is needed to protect the

raw edge of the plywood garboard; a wood strip of any thickness would drag somewhat and slow down the boat. The Adirondack guideboats used a strip of thin iron put on with small screws, but the fiberglass is simpler, easier, and probably better.

21. It is recommended that the frames be copper-riveted through the bottom on both sides of the two glued joints in the bottom plank.

22. One-and-a-half-inch number 10 screws go through the seat-riser doubler into the seat riser and the frames.

23. Two-inch number 12 screws go through the ends of the thwarts into the seat-riser doubler and the seat riser. There are three screws in each end.

24. Frames are fastened to the outwales with 1¼-inch number 8 screws or through-rivets.

For glue I am using Chem-Tech T-88. Although I can no more guarantee it from a health standpoint than I can any epoxy glue, I have had no bad reports from those using it, and I find it the least caustic and irritating of any of the epoxies that I have tried.

Sequel

After concluding the series on the modified Herreshoff rowboat that I wrote for the *National Fisherman* in the spring of 1980, I started building one of the boats, intending to complete it for the Mystic Seaport Museum's Annual Small Craft Workshop, held the first weekend in June. There wasn't much time, and to ensure that the boat would be finished I decided to eliminate the end decks as originally diagramed and replace them with simple semicircular laminated breasthooks at either end. These I glued on a form, using thin strips of white ash and epoxy, as shown in the diagram. White ash was used not only because it is strong and glues well, but because the Douglas fir strips used for the laminated frames would not take the greater amount of bend required for the circular breasthook.

This alternate construction worked out very well, as it did for boats built by Myron Young on Long Island and David Scarbrough at the Rock Hall Boat Shop, Burgess, Virginia.

As it turned out, there was ample bracing at the ends even without the decks, and because of the added fullness of the ends they proved to be sufficiently dry under reasonable conditions of use. Further, the elimination of the end decks resulted in appreciable savings in materials, labor, and weight.

To make a more versatile seating arrangement, the thwarts were relocated, and the two parts hinged as diagramed, so that they could accommodate long-legged rowers. The boat can now be correctly trimmed and rowed in either direction with one, two, or three occupants and with one or two oarsmen.

A recent builder, Allan Esenlohr of Newton, New Jersey, and Fishers Island, New York, has rigged his modified Herreshoff boat to sail. "Sailing is a good and pleasant change when one is tired of rowing," he

Components of the modified Herreshoff rowboat. In the background is a breasthook being laminated over a form, and above it are three frames taking shape. The stem molds are also shown. (Mary Anne Stets photo, Mystic Seaport)

Views of Myron Young's modified Herreshoff rowboat. (Courtesy Myron Young)

MODIFIED HERRESHOFF - PLANK WIDTHS - INCHES AND EIGHTHS						
STATIONS	1	2	3	4	5	6
GARBOARD	5-4	5-4	5-3	4-7	4-4	4-2
NO. 2	3-4	4-1	4-3	4-4	4-6	4-6
NO. 3	2-6	3-1	3-3	3-5	3-4	3-5
NO. 4	2-7	3-1	3-3	3-4	3-4	3-5
SHEER	2-6	3-2	3-3	3-4	3-5	3-5
ADD BOTTOM THICKNESS TO GARBOARD WIDTHS.						
ADD LAP WIDTH TO NOS. 2, 3, 4 AND SHEER.						
WIDTHS TO BE ADJUSTED FAIR TO SUIT EACH						
INDIVIDUAL BOAT WITH FAIR LINING BATTEN.						

reports, "but this boat is a 'rower's' boat." And so it is. Sailing this boat is not particularly recommended.

Planking widths taken off my boat are given in the accompanying table. Such widths must be adjusted in the fairing process to suit each individual boat. Nevertheless, this table can save the builder a good deal of trouble. In building lapstrake, it is always desirable to have proven planking lines to work from, either taken from a good example of the boat already built or worked out on a scale half-model. The omission of planking lines from working plans for clinker-built boats is a grave defect. Even so, most plans now available for lapstrake boats fail to include them.

MODIFIED McINNIS BATEAU

This 12-foot 8-inch cartop boat, building directions for which follow, is intended to meet the needs of a broad segment of the boating public. Well adapted for hunting and fishing, it is equally well suited to a wide range of recreational uses. It is not a particularly difficult boat to build, nor will the materials required be hard to obtain or excessively expensive.

Both the hull design and the method of construction recommended here have been tried, tested, and found superior. The two are compatible, and their combination gives every indication of producing a craft of merit.

The hull shape has been adapted with only slight modifications from a multichine plywood design that Walter J. McInnis worked out in 1940 for Mumford Brothers, commercial builders in Amesbury, Massa-

chusetts. McInnis called the boat a "voyageur's bateau," and clearly intended it primarily for hunting and fishing, and as a replacement for the ordinary canvas canoe. Construction was ultralight—especially for 1940, before the advent of thermoplastic adhesives. The three wide planks of the multichine sides were backed by ash seam battens, and ¼-inch Weldwood was used for its slightly rockered flat bottom. Weight of the completed boat is said to have been on the order of 63 pounds. After the company that was building them got into financial difficulties and shut down production, their stock of unsold boats was picked up by the Vermont fish and game wardens, which says something for the quality and characteristics of the boat!

Best known as one of this country's leading designers of large power craft, Walter McInnis is equally adept as a designer of small craft for the sportsman. An avid fly fisherman, McInnis is a longtime member of a famous Megantic sporting club in the Rangeley Lakes region. In the winter of 1949–50 Earle R. Rumery, then manager of the Marblehead Boat Yard Company in Biddeford, Maine, built one of these boats. He retained the shape but modified the construction considerably. Rounding the slightly knuckled shape of the sides, he framed them with flat ribs, covering the outside with canvas, canoe fashion. Weight was increased to about 75 pounds, but displacement, righting arm, stability, and other hull characteristics remained essentially unchanged.

McInnis commented on Rumery's boat in a letter published in *Outdoor Maine* in April 1960. He had this to say about its capacity and stability: "Three of us totaling in weight close to 600 pounds have fished from it, been able to stand up in it, fly cast or spin, all at the same time, using the alternate firing method, *without* danger of capsizing. She is a remarkable little boat." Responding to editorial comment on this letter, Rumery forwarded two photos of his boat, which were printed in *Outdoor Maine*'s June issue. "The first picture with the stern of the boat in the water," Rumery wrote, "was snapped on a trip taken by my son and me when we were carrying about 300 pounds of duffle across the lake. In the other picture we were just returning from a hunting trip, on which we had gotten a black bear and a large buck and doe, which we had carried across the lake in the boat." Perhaps in two trips, as all of this seems rather a lot for a single trip. In any case, an impressive performance for the little boat.

More than two decades later, Rumery wrote in response to my inquiry:

I am glad to report that the boat is still in service at my wilderness camp in northern Maine. My son recanvased it this past year. . . .It has proved to be an ideal boat for fishing and hunting. Its stability is excellent, and—not that I recommend this for the general public—I have stood up in it a great many times, casting and fly fishing, while another person was rowing. The location of our camp makes it necessary for us to portage across the lake, since there are no roads to it. We have crossed the lake when it has been blowing hard, when in fact a larger boat, but of poor design, would have capsized. Our boat rows very easy and paddles very well.

So much for the boat's capacity, and for its handling and seakeeping characteristics.

The method of construction offered here, selected as the easiest and most suitable, is an adaptation of the building method developed over many years for the Adirondack guideboat. This adaptation of standard guideboat construction was first applied by me when I built the modified Herreshoff rowboat discussed earlier in this chapter. Apart from requiring some care and precision, this construction method is not difficult; it is well within reach of amateurs having basic woodworking experience and a minimum knowledge of lofting, spiling, and lapstrake planking. Though in no sense a boat to be stitched together in an afternoon or a weekend, it would go together more easily and quickly, I am convinced, than a Lawley yacht tender, a Delaware ducker, or a Rushton Wee Lassie, to cite several well-known classics that have been built successfully by amateurs.

No steam bending is required, no rabbeted keel or stems, no beveled chine strips, and no setup using molds, since planking is applied directly to the preshaped laminated frames. For this reason, the frames must be accurately shaped, and this requires an accurate full-size laydown of the frame sections, from which thin plywood patterns of the individual frame shapes are taken.

The materials required are readily obtainable almost anywhere. They consist of $3/16$-inch marine plywood for the planking and $3/8$-inch plywood for the bottom; spruce for the laminated frames, stems, and breasthooks and for the internal across-bottom intermediates, the outside fore-and-aft bottom runners, the thwarts, and the risers; mahogany, cherry, or other hardwood for the gunwales; small bronze screws, ring nails, rivets, and copper tacks for fastenings; epoxy adhesive; and a few yards of narrow fiberglass tape.

Spruce, the standard timber for framing Adirondack guideboats, is recommended for laminated frames and stems because it is stiff and strong yet light in weight, and because it glues well. Since it will be used in short pieces and thin strips, these can be cut to advantage, if one avoids knots, from rough eastern red spruce lumber, the kind widely sold for staging planks and ledger boards. Neither white pine nor white cedar is strong enough for this use. Clear, rift-sawn, old-growth Douglas fir makes a good substitute, but not the unseasoned, sappy, slash-sawn fir commonly supplied as construction lumber. The best marine-grade plywood that can be bought is none too good. Sapele ply is recommended as being strong and hard and having good abrasion resistance. Okoume plywood is lighter but softer, and has less impact strength. A good grade of marine fir would be quite adequate.

For the best results, one should observe the following order of construction. First comes the laydown of lines. An accurate full-size laydown is absolutely essential for obtaining the shapes of the bottom, the two stems, and the frames. Because the two ends of the boat are exactly alike, only one stem pattern is required, and only 10 different frame patterns, one for each station. From each of these 10 patterns four identical laminated frames will be made, one for each of the four identical quarters of the hull.

The gluing form and the procedure for laminating the stems are fully diagramed. Spruce strips $1/8$ inch thick, previously stripped on the circular saw, are coated with epoxy glue and clamped tightly into the curve of the gluing form, which will have been well

	STEM	½	1	2	3	4	5	6	7	7½	STERN
GUNWALE	1-11-2	1-7-6	1-5-5+	1-3-3	1-2-1+	1-1-6	1-2-0	1-2-7	1-4-7	1-6-6	1-9-5
A	1-5-0+	1-1-5+	0-11-2	0-8-4+	0-7-3	0-7-0	0-7-2+	0-8-3	0-10-6+	1-0-6+	1-4-1
B	0-11-1	0-7-7	0-5-3+	0-2-6	0-1-6	0-1-3	0-1-6	0-2-6+	0-5-2+	0-7-3	0-10-2+
C			0-0-6+	0-0-3	0-0-1	0-0-0	0-0-1	0-0-3	0-0-6		
PROFILE		0-1-6	0-0-6+	0-0-3	0-0-1	0-0-0	0-0-1	0-0-3	0-0-6+	0-1-5	
GUNWALE	0-0-4	0-7-4	1-0-5	1-7-0+	1-10-6+	1-11-0	1-10-2	1-7-1	1-0-7	0-8-2	0-2-4+
A	0-0-4	0-6-2	0-10-7	1-5-3	1-8-5	1-9-6	1-8-7	1-5-5+	0-11-4	0-6-7+	0-1-6
B	0-0-4	0-4-1	0-7-6	1-1-4	1-4-6+	1-5-7	1-4-7	1-1-6	0-8-2+	0-4-5	0-0-7
C	0-0-4		0-2-6	0-7-1+	0-10-0	0-11-0	0-10-2	0-7-4	0-2-7		
½ FALSE KEEL	0-0-4	0-0-4	←———————————— STRAIGHT ————————————→							0-0-4	

waxed beforehand to prevent sticking. Later, a small block is glued to the stem blank and then trimmed so that it fills out the necessary sharp angle at the bottom of the stem. Dimensions are given for obtaining the bearding line, which governs the beveling of the stem. Prudence suggests not cutting back this bevel fully, but rather leaving a little wood to be trimmed later when the planking is fitted. This is glued and nailed in place. All that is needed to cover the ends of the 3⁄16-inch planking is a strip of 5⁄8-inch bronze half oval.

The frames, which will finish 9⁄16 inch sided and 11⁄16 inch molded, are laminated in the same way. Gluing forms need not be as heavy as the one required for the stems, and if the frame laminations are made up in order, the form will need only slight recutting in changing from one frame to the next. If the strips are sawn from 1½-inch-thick stock, there will be plenty of wood for the glued-up frame blanks to be split on the saw and dressed to make two frames to go opposite each other in the boat. To fill out the sharp angle at the

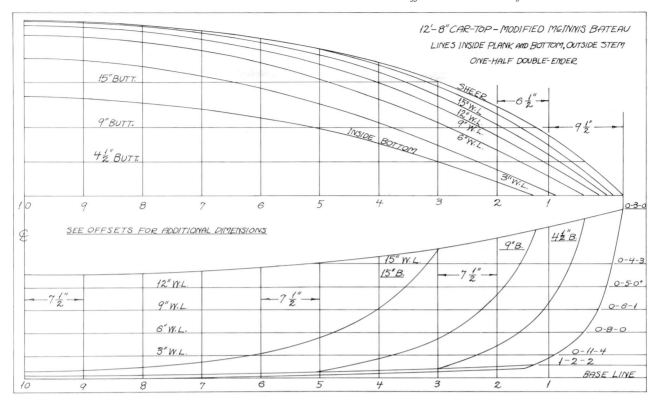

12'-8" CAR-TOP - MODIFIED McINNIS BATEAU
LINES INSIDE PLANK AND BOTTOM, OUTSIDE STEM
ONE-HALF DOUBLE-ENDER

SEE OFFSETS FOR ADDITIONAL DIMENSIONS

chine, small blocks are glued on and then trimmed to fill out the curve, as was done with the stems. This is done, of course, before the glued-up frame blank is split in two lengthwise. Bevels for the frames are obtained in the usual way from the laydown of section lines. Because of the considerable angle of bevel on the frames at stations 1, 2, 3, 4, and 5, the molded width of the blanks for these frames might well be increased by an additional ⅛-inch strip to allow for the wood that will be planed away in beveling.

Assuming the bottom is to be made up from standard 4-by-8 panels of ⅜-inch plywood, it will have to be spliced at one end. Scarf widths should be 12 times the thickness of the material, or 4½ inches here. Scarf surfaces should be accurately planed *almost* to a feather edge; a scant ¹⁄₃₂ inch of edge thickness should be left. Epoxy glue is applied to the two surfaces, and these are brought precisely together, tacked to prevent slippage, placed between two well-waxed boards wider than the scarf, and nailed through the scarf from one side to the other with enough large nails to bring everything tightly together. When the glue has fully cured, the nails are pulled, the boards removed, the nail holes through the scarf joint plugged, and the edges of the scarf sanded smooth.

12'-8" CAR-TOP. MODIFIED McINNIS BATEAU
SECTION LINES INSIDE PLANKING
AND BOTTOM

12'-8" CAR-TOP — MODIFIED McINNIS BATEAU											
STATIONS	STEM	1	2	3	4	5	6	7	8	9	10
HEIGHTS — SHEER	1-10-1	1-7-6	1-6-3	1-5-0+	1-4-0	1-3-1+	1-2-5	1-2-1+	1-1-7	1-1-6	1-1-6
BOTTOM	0-1-5	0-2-4	0-1-4	0-1-1	0-0-7+	0-0-6	0-0-5	0-0-4	0-0-3+	0-0-3	0-0-3
BUTT. 4½"	—	0-9-7	0-4-2	0-1-1	—	—	—	—	—	—	—
BUTT. 9"	—	—	0-11-0	0-5-1	0-2-4	0-0-6+	—	—	—	—	—
BUTT. 15	—	—	—	1-4-7	0-9-2	0-5-2+	0-3-2	0-2-1	0-1-4	0-1-1	0-0-7
HALF-BREADTHS — SHEER	0-0-0	0-7-7+	0-11-5+	1-3-0	1-5-4+	1-7-3	1-8-5+	1-9-5+	1-10-3	1-10-7	1-11-0
W.L. 15"	0-0-0+	0-6-4+	0-10-6	1-2-3	1-5-2						
W.L. 12"	0-0-0+	0-5-2+	0-9-3	1-1-1+	1-4-2	1-6-4	1-8-1+	1-9-3	1-10-2	1-10-6	1-10-7
W.L. 9"	0-0-0	0-4-0	0-7-7	0-11-5+	1-2-7	1-5-2+	1-7-1+	1-8-4+	1-9-5	1-10-1+	1-10-3
W.L. 6"	0-0-0+	0-2-3+	0-6-0	0-9-5+	1-0-6	1-3-2+	1-5-4	1-7-1	1-8-1+	1-8-7	1-9-1
W.L. 3"	0-0-0	0-0-3	0-3-2+	0-6-5	0-9-5	1-0-1	1-2-1+	1-3-6	1-5-0	1-5-6+	1-6-1
BOTTOM	—	0-0-0+	0-1-6	0-4-3+	0-6-7	0-8-6+	0-10-2	0-11-3	1-0-2	1-0-7	1-1-1
DIAGONAL 1	0-0-0+	0-6-3	0-10-0	1-1-1+	1-3-5	1-5-3+	1-6-6+	1-7-6	1-8-3	1-8-7	1-9-0
DIAGONAL 2	0-0-0+	0-6-1	0-9-7	1-1-2+	1-4-1	1-6-2	1-8-0+	1-9-3+	1-10-3	1-11-0	1-11-1

DIAGONAL 1 15" UP. OUT 15" ON 3" W.L. DIAG. 2 15" UP. OUT 18" ON 9" W.L.

OFFSET MEASUREMENTS, FEET, INCHES, EIGHTHS. INSIDE PLANK AND BOTTOM, O.S. STEM

Finally, in preparation for assembly, the bottom is cut out exactly to its faired *inside* shape. The locations of the frames and the across-bottom intermediates are lined across the inside surface of the bottom, and the stems are fastened on at the ends with glue and screws from the outside. Special care should be taken so that the two stems line up exactly with the centerline of the bottom. The bottom is not beveled until the setup on the ladder frame for planking has been made and the frames have been fastened in place. Beveling the bottom is part of the final fairing operation before planking.

The ladder frame and horses for the setup are made as diagramed. Required are several lengths of standard 2-by-6 floor joists and 1-inch spruce ledger board or the equivalent, to be nailed together. It is essential to pick out joists that are straight, and they should be seasoned and dry; otherwise they are likely to twist out of true. The uprights that support the bottom of the boat must vary in height, of course, so that they will conform to the designed fore-and-aft rocker of the bottom. The bottom is easily sprung down to rest on them and is secured with screws, which are fastened through the bottom with large washers under their heads. After the planked-up hull is removed from the form, the screw holes through the bottom are easily plugged.

When the bottom has been leveled athwartships, the stems are accurately plumbed and aligned before being secured in place. After this has been done, the frames and the cross-bottom intermediates are fastened in place at their respective locations, as previously marked on the inside of the bottom, with screws through the bottom. The frames are beveled before they are fastened to the bottom, and are placed so their heel bevels coincide with the curve of the bottom. This is also the time to fasten the bottom runners with screws (1½-inch number 8 wood screws) into the frames and intermediates inside. Not until all of this has been done is the bottom beveled to conform to the rake of the side frames—the object being a garboard that fits tightly when it is sprung in place along the chine knuckle and fastened.

The recommended approximate shape for the garboard, taken from a scale half-model of the hull, is shown. The dimensions given here will be close, but they should be relined on the boat with a fair batten just the same. If the bottom and ends of the plank stand a little proud when the plank is on, they are easily trimmed flush with a sharp block plane—the proper tool for trimming plywood.

Before planking starts, a fairly stiff batten is bent around the timberheads at the sheerline and attached at its ends to the stems. The frames are then correctly

12'-8" CAR-TOP
MODIFIED McINNIS BATEAU

FEET AND INCHES

spaced along this batten and temporarily attached to it. Twists of soft wire serve well for this. This is essentially the same procedure that is followed in planking an Adirondack guideboat. The laminated frames are stiff enough so that cross spalls or spreaders will probably not be necessary.

After the garboard is fastened in place, a stiff batten or ribband should be bent around the frames just above the turn of the bilge on either side and temporarily fastened to the stems at both ends. By this means the frames can be equalized. Any that bulge however slightly will be pushed back. Any that are slack can be pulled flush and wired. After the second and third plank from the bottom are on and fastened, this ribband will no longer be needed and can be removed. The reason that such a ribband may be needed is that ³/₁₆-inch plywood planking is not stiff enough by itself to pull the frames into line.

All of the planks, if gotten out of standard 4-by-8 panels, will have one splice. This can be done as the planking is put on the boat. Splices should be staggered as much as possible, starting with the garboard, which can be spliced amidships. All splices should be planned so that they land on frames, to which they should be fastened. Scarf length for ³/₁₆-inch plank is 2¼ inches. Splices are glued with epoxy. They will need to be clamped together until the glue sets, and this can be done with two small waxed blocks, one inside and one out, through-bolted with a small machine bolt. After the blocks and the bolt are removed, the hole through the splice is easily plugged.

The garboard shape with its wide ends is indicated by the shape of this particular hull with its ample sheer and the considerable width of its flat bottom. The wide end uses up space, tending to straighten out the run of the planks above and allowing them to diminish

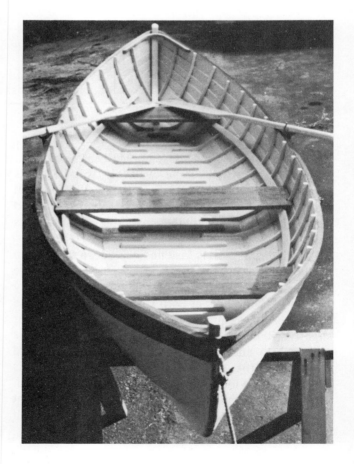

A modified McInnis bateau built in Kansas by Robert McElroy, M.D., and his nephew, from the instructions presented in this chapter. "The boat required about three months of part-time work to construct," McElroy wrote. "It was a very good experience for both of us who had never built something of lapstrake construction."

slightly in width from amidships to the ends, which contributes to a pleasing appearance. The average width of the five planks above the garboard will be about 2⅞ inches amidships, diminishing to about 2½ inches at the ends, plus a ½-inch lap. A ½-inch lap is ample for a plank thickness of ³⁄₁₆ inch.

Laps are glued with an epoxy adhesive, thickened with Cab-O-Sil or something similar that will prevent running. Planks are nailed through the laps into the frames with ¾-inch bronze or stainless ring nails, except for the bottom edge of the garboard, where the molded width of the frame at the chine knuckle swells enough to take a 1-inch number 6 or number 7 screw. Between the frames the laps are pulled together, so the glue will have a chance to set, with ⅜-inch copper tacks spaced about 2 inches and clinched on the inside. A very fine, sharp awl, such as those used for guideboat tacks, would be just the thing to pierce the hard plywood and prevent the soft copper tacks from crippling. The ends of the planks are both glued and well nailed to the stems.

Where the bottom bevel is sufficiently wide to take tacks, they are put in the lower edge of the garboard between frames, just as they are in the laps. Otherwise, the screws into the bottoms of the frames should pull tight enough to ensure a tight glued joint along the chine edge between the frames. In any case, this joint is finally made permanently tight by being covered with a narrow strip of fiberglass tape set in epoxy.

The outside of the hull, even to a priming coat of paint, can be completed before it is removed from the form and set right side up. Some, however, might want to put the gunwale on after the hull is turned over, in order better to resight the sheerline and possibly to give it a final fairing.

There is nothing special about installing the risers and the thwarts. Information for locating them is given in the diagram. The thwarts have been located to accommodate either one or two occupants and to permit rowing or paddling. Oarlocks are the type standard for guideboats.

Laminated breasthooks are shown at the two ends. They are glued up on a form, which—to secure a good fit—should not be made until the gunwales are on. Because of the tight bend, the strips for laminating will have to be thinner than those for the frames. If white ash is available it can be used here, since it bends more easily than spruce and is stronger and heavier. These laminated breasthooks should be fastened with copper rivets through the gunwales.

No floorboards are required, and the bottom will drain easily around the ends of the intermediate cross cleats. Although the flat bottom is quite wide, it is more than adequately stiffened and reinforced by the outside bottom runners fastened through into the frame feet and the intermediates. Frames, intermediates, and runners are glued as well as screwed in place.

Weight should fall somewhere between 85 and 90 pounds. It could be made lighter if scantlings were shaved, but I like some safety factor.

Key to the numbered diagram:

1. *Plywood bottom:* ⅜ inch thick.
2. *Laminated spruce frames:* Sided ⁹⁄₁₆ inch, molded 1¹⁄₁₆ inch.
3. *Six plywood planks:* ³⁄₁₆ inch thick.
4. *Across-bottom intermediates:* Spruce, 1⅛ inches wide, 1¹⁄₁₆ inch thick.
5. *Bronze wood screws:* 1½-inch number 8.
6. *Bottom runners:* Spruce, 1⅛ inches wide, ¾ inch deep.
7. *Thwarts:* Spruce, 9 inches by ¾ inch.
8. *Post:* 1½ inches by ¾ inch.
9. *Riser:* Spruce, 1¾ inches by ¾ inch, tapering to 1 inch by ¾ inch at the ends.
10. *Gunwales:* Mahogany, cherry, or other hardwood, 1½ inches by ⅞ inch amidships, tapering to 1 inch by ¾ inch at the ends.
11. *Copper rivets:* Gunwale through frame heads, also gunwale through breasthooks.
12. *Lap fastenings into frames:* ¾-inch bronze or stainless ring nails.
13. *Copper tacks:* ⅜ inch, through laps between frames. Spaced about 2 inches.
14. *Fiberglass tape:* Two inches wide, set in epoxy.
15. *Bronze screws:* One-inch, number 6 or number 7, through bottom edge of garboard into frames.

Recommended epoxy glue: Chem-Tech T-88 thickened with Cab-O-Sil when necessary.

Suggested references: For a detailed explanation of guideboat construction, see *The Adirondack Guide-Boat* by Kenneth and Helen Durant. My book *Building Classic Small Craft* (this book's predecessor) offers guidance for lapstrake planking and spiling. The complete references are given in the Bibliography.

2

Pilot Gig

························•························

Late on Friday the 13th of December 1907, the seven-masted steel schooner *Thomas W. Lawson,* having lost her bearings in the fog, found herself in Broad Sound within the Western Rocks at the Isles of Scilly off England's Cornish coast.

The largest schooner ever built—over 400 feet long with her topmast head 155 feet above the deck—the *Lawson* had encountered two severe gales while crossing the Atlantic, which had blown out all but six of her sails and carried away all her lifeboats. And now on that fateful night she found herself in a perilous position close to a lee shore and in the direct sweep of a rising gale.

Pilot boats put out from Saint Marys and Saint Agnes islands, and the Saint Agnes boat got close enough to set William Cook Hicks, a Trinity House pilot, on board, but they could do nothing more in the

raging storm as darkness closed down. At about 1:15 in the morning of the 14th the 150-ton port anchor chain parted, and directly the starboard anchor gave way as well. As the helpless vessel was blown toward Annet the crew took to the rigging, and in less than 15 minutes she struck Shag Rock, rolling over and breaking in two between the number 4 and 5 holds. All hands were thrown into the sea except the pilot Hicks, who had lashed himself to the rigging and was carried down with the ship.

When day broke no sign of the *Lawson* was to be seen except a welter of wreckage floating off Saint Agnes and Annet. Although the gale still raged and seas were running mountain-high, the six-oared pilot gig *Slippen* put out with double-banked oars and a crew of 12. Of these, five were named Hicks. All morning they searched, finding only corpses, and

The pilot gig Treffry, *built in 1843, has survived generations of hard use despite her light build. (F.E. Gibson photo, Scilly Isles)*

finally one seriously injured crewman with his side badly mangled.

In the afternoon the search was continued. This time the *Slippen* apparently held a crew of six, and pulling as far as the Hellweather Ledges they spotted two survivors clinging to some rocks. Frederick Cook Hicks, eldest son of the drowned pilot, undaunted by the surf, swam a line to the exhausted men and brought both away safely. One was the captain, George W. Dow of Hancock, Maine, whose wrist was broken, and the other, Edward Rowe of Boston, the engineer. In recognition of his heroism that day, Fred Hicks was presented with gold watches by the U.S. government and the owners of the *Lawson*, and the members of the *Slippen*'s crew received gold medals.

This rescue is remembered because of the *Lawson* as well as the tragic involvement of the Hicks family. Yet it was but one of many gallant rescues carried out in Cornish pilot gigs. These superb seaboats, developed on the coast of Cornwall nearly 200 years ago, best demonstrated their unique qualities in the treacherous waters surrounding the Isles of Scilly.

In the bygone days of sail they competed as pilot boats, provided local transportation between the islands and the mainland, participated in rescue and salvage work, and were favored by smugglers when smuggling was rife along this stretch of coast. It has been said that at one time more rum and brandy were smuggled into Cornwall and Devon than lawfully entered the Port of London.

Situated 28 miles off Land's End at the convergence of two major sea-lanes—the English Channel and the Bristol Channel—the Scillies consist of some 145 low-lying islands and rocks. Many of the outer reefs and ledges are submerged at high tide, and the water around them is commonly 20 fathoms or more. Thus, vessels that strike them are likely to sink without leaving a trace.

The Western Rocks beyond Saint Agnes comprise 10 square miles of hidden perils. In fog, mist, and darkness this extended barrier of lethal rocks often went unperceived, because of its low silhouette, until the vessel struck. From the time of the Romans the Scillies were dreaded by mariners, yet because of their location merchantmen were forced near them.

In bygone centuries the Scillies were a favored haunt of pirates, buccaneers, and wreckers. It is said that at one time wrecking was a chief means of livelihood for the inhabitants. It is hard to realize that these islands, so peaceful today and bright with flowers grown for British florists, were once overrun with freebooters and cutthroats of many nationalities.

Smuggling lasted longer, well into the 19th century,

in fact. With the Channel Islands only 170 miles away and the coast of Brittany even closer, smuggling expeditions bringing back French lace, silks, brandy, and other contraband were well within the capability of these slim but seakindly six-oared gigs.

Richard Gillis of the Newquay Rowing Club, who has done so much to rescue and perpetuate these extraordinary boats, wrote in the journal *Country Life* that John Nance, a famous Scilly pilot born around 1800, made in his lifetime 25 smuggling trips to Roscoff on the French coast. The round trip aggregated about 250 miles of open sea, something of a feat for open boats averaging not more than 30 feet in length and about 5 feet in beam.

Some of these trips by Nance could have been made in *Bonnet*, built before 1833 and still sound and racing today after being restored in the 1950s. *Bonnet* was the boat used by John Nance's son, James, also a well-known Scilly pilot, born in 1831.

According to Gillis, on one of their smuggling trips John Nance and his crew kept at the oars for 30 hours straight, holding their gig head-on in seas when caught in an unexpected blow. These gigs were very fast and in a chase could usually outdistance Customs sail by hauling directly to windward. To discourage smuggling, England at one time prohibited the construction of eight-oared gigs.

Gillis believes that *Bonnet* was built by the Peters family who originated these pilot gigs. John Peters is credited with building the first one in 1790 or 1791 in the village of Saint Mawes, close by Falmouth on the Cornish coast. Three generations of Peters were responsible for the lion's share of boats built in the pilot gig's heyday, and the Polvarth yard whence they came belongs today to Frank Peters, a direct descendant, who is still building boats.

Gillis relates a tale about *Bonnet* that is too good to pass by. As the story goes, this gig took its name from an old lady who had a reputation for witchcraft. When the gigs pulled away for a job of pilotage, the old lady would run to the top of the hill and wave her bonnet to send the gig so named out ahead of the rest. After her death her son would carry the Old Lady's bonnet to the hilltop, place it on a bush, and say, "Now, Mother, do your best."

And for years after, apparently for reasons of superstition, the name *Bonnet* was never mentioned by the crew, who instead took care to refer to their boat as "the old hat."

In the days of sail these slim, sinewy, ultrafast gigs were active in pilotage and salvage along much of the Cornish coast, from Falmouth to Newquay and Padstow. At Newquay, Edgar March tells us, it was not unusual for competing gigs to race offshore as far as Lundy Island, some 50 miles and more, with expectation of picking up an inbound vessel.

But it is on their exploits in Scilly waters that their chief fame rests. At this dangerous crossroads of the sea-lanes the need in former times for pilots was continual and urgent. During prolonged spells of easterly weather, for instance, upward of 100 sail frequently would be found lying at anchor off the Roads, waiting to proceed.

For their skill and daring the local pilots were renowned among mariners everywhere. Their knowledge of the surrounding waters and the adjoining coast was minute. No risk daunted them, no weather was too bad to hold them ashore when their services were required.

The Bryher gig *Golden Eagle*, faster then either *Albion* or *March*, which she was built to supersede, carried out some notable rescue and salvage work. When the steamship *Sussex* was wrecked in December 1885, *Golden Eagle* rescued part of the crew and shared in the salvage of 200 bullocks and other cargo, including flour, lard, tinned beef, frozen geese, and turkeys.

A list of her exploits given by March includes saving the crew of the steamship *Brinkburn*, bound for Le Havre with cotton, in 1898; coming to the assistance of the French barque *Paranee*, stranded with a cargo of coconuts, a year later; and on the same night standing by the ship *Eric Rickmers* from Bangkok, loaded with rice.

When in April 1910 the Atlantic transport liner *Minnehaha* stranded on a hidden ledge in thick fog, *Golden Eagle* was on hand to assist in the rescue of passengers and crew. *Czar,* another Bryher gig, built to beat *Golden Eagle,* also participated in the salvage work on *Minnehaha,* which went on for three weeks and included the swimming ashore of 234 head of cattle.

Cattle were roped by the horns so their heads would be held above water, and towed to shore. When the Liverpool steamer *Castleford* was lost in June 1887, two pounds a head were paid for each steer landed on Annet. At that time *Gipsy,* a Scilly-built gig, was holed in the port side by the horn of a fractious bullock. The hole was still there, covered by a patch, when the Padstow Rowing Club refitted *Gipsy* in 1955.

O&M (after Obadiah and Mary, the names of her owners), another Scilly gig participating in that

The pilot gigs were sometimes rigged for sailing. The Nornour, *one of the surviving gigs, is shown with her lug rig off the Cornish coast. (F.E. Gibson photo, Scilly Isles)*

salvage operation, was not so lucky. Her whole bow was stove when a bullock fell on her from the deck. Mishaps of this sort were not uncommon. On one occasion, a bale of cotton being rolled into a gig slipped and crashed through the bilges of ¼-inch-thick elm plank.

In the estimation of March, who should know, no finer rescue effort is to be found in the annals of Scilly gigs than the one that saved two lives when the steamship *Delaware* went down off Fearing Ledge in December 1871. With engines stopped and sails blown out in the violent northwest gale, *Delaware* swung broadside on a mighty sea, then another close behind swept over her and she was gone. Sometime after, watchers from South Hill on Bryher spotted two men on half a boat, two on a spar, and one on some wreckage.

The gig *Albion*, 30 feet long with 5½ feet of beam and weighing close to half a ton, was picked as the best boat to go. Six oars were lashed crosswise to the thwarts, and this enabled 12 men to lift her up and carry her half a mile overland to Rushy Bay, where they launched her stern first into a following sea and wind. Running before the towering combers and gaining a little between each sea, they finally made the

lee of the North Hill on Samson, whence they could see that the two men previously seen on the half boat had managed to land. To reach them it was necessary for the nearly spent crew to carry the gig overland once again, some 200 yards across an isthmus of scrub and slippery rocks. Up a steep bank and down the other side they went, opposed by the full force of the December gale and in constant danger of dropping the boat and smashing her frail plank on the rocks.

But they managed to make it safely, and this time the launch went straight into the screaming blast, the huge waves standing the trembling gig nearly on end. Finally they reached White Island, picked up the two half-naked survivors, and returned to Samson. This time the exhausted crew did not attempt to carry their gig back over the high ground. With the two survivors they made their way to the East Par, where they huddled together for warmth and rest in the shelter of a rock to await the gig *March*, whose assistance had been signaled from the top of North Hill. Upon the arrival of *March*, the crew of *Albion* transferred to that boat and fought their way back to Bryher with the two survivors, who received hot drinks and were put to bed.

The crew that remained on Samson spent a cold

December night in the open, and in the morning had the task of manhandling *Albion* back across the isthmus. Regretfully we must add that those who carried out this heroic exploit received neither acknowledgment nor reward beyond the gratitude of the rescued men.

No account of these gigs should fail to mention that they were sometimes sailed, and that they were both fast and handy under canvas. March describes an urgent trip under sail from Bryher to Saint Marys and back to fetch a doctor on a wild night in rain and a hard sou'wester. The crew hugged the bottom of the boat—its mizzen set, its fore lug double-reefed, and several hundredweight of stone ballast aboard—bailing as the waves slopped over the rail. On one occasion, he relates, a mighty wave picked up the gig so that her rudder hung completely free, the boat spinning around with the lee gunwale buried and the crew bailing for their lives. The *Sussex* made the three-mile run in 15 minutes.

With the passing of merchant sail and ensuing changes in shipping and the development of improved aids for navigation, the heroic age of the pilot gig was brought to an end. Many came ashore for keeps and perished through neglect. The ignoble fate of one, it is said, was to become the roof of a chicken run. Others continued to find limited employment at the islands, such as transporting wedding parties—the last in 1929—and carrying loads of cut flowers and potatoes to the mainland.

In more recent years, going back to the 1950s, rowing clubs both on the Cornish mainland and on the Scillies have brought about a flourishing revival of gig racing. Not a few of the famous old gigs have been restored and are now racing. Prominent on this list are such names as *Bonnet, Shah, Dolly Varden, Nornour, Slippen, Czar, Golden Eagle, Dove, Newquay,* and *Treffry*. The Scilly gigs race regularly during the summer, with interisland and ladies' races once each week.

At Saint Marys, Tom Chudleigh has built several new gigs, including two completed in 1974, *Active* and *Good Intent*. *Active* is on the lines of *Treffry,* built by Peters in 1843. This was the longest pilot gig built until *Active,* and is generally considered the finest.

From Harold Kimber, who assisted Chudleigh in the construction of *Active*, I received the lines of *Treffry* and some of the construction details for *Active*. The process that led to this was set in motion when I read Edgar March's *Inshore Craft of Britain in the Days of Sail and Oar*.

Although I had been vaguely aware for a long time of the gigs variously employed for piloting, salvage, smuggling, and lifesaving along the English coast, it was not until I read the chapter on pilot gigs in March's book that I got a close-up look at these boats as they had been developed and used in Cornwall and particularly at the Isles of Scilly. These Cornish pilot gigs are all but incredible. If their capabilities and performance had not been fully and incontrovertibly attested, one would be obliged to reject as fanciful some of the feats attributed to them.

How well and how long they lasted in spite of the rough usage to which they were subjected is not the least remarkable thing about these remarkable boats. *Newquay,* built in 1812, is still afloat and racing albeit having undergone extensive repairs. And *Treffry,* also still alive, the gig whose lines are given here, was built in 1832.

Nor are these alone. At least 10 still in commission have lasted well over a century. As far as I know, no other class of boats anywhere can boast such a record of sheer endurance.

March's detailed account of these Cornish gigs was something of a revelation, yet my interest was further whetted by the realization that these gigs showed a number of similarities to early American Whitehall boats. *American Star,* the famous race boat given by the Whitehall boatmen of New York to General Lafayette on his last visit to the United States in 1826 and still preserved on the Lafayette estate in France, is a four-oared gig of 27 feet whose lines are surprisingly like those of the Cornish pilot gigs. Although she was built in Brooklyn, her builders were two brothers who had learned their trade in England.

To follow up this lead and see whether a closer and more definite connection could be made between American Whitehalls and British pilot gigs, I wrote to Harold Kimber in England, one who could likely provide additional information about these boats and perhaps even a set of lines. It was a shot in the dark, but as things turned out, it went straight to the mark.

Kimber, a master boatbuilder with over 50 years of the trade under his belt, had come out of retirement temporarily in 1972 when he was commissioned by the British National Maritime Museum to build a replica of a 26-foot 9th-century Viking *faeringen* (four-oared boat), one of the three king's boats found inside the Gokstad burial ship dug up near Oslo, Norway.

I visited Harold when he was engaged in this project at Cory's Bargeworks in Charlton, a London suburb,

The four-oared gig General Lafayette *skims over the Mystic River. Built by the author in the winter of 1974-75, she is a replica of the early American Whitehall boat* American Star, *which was presented to General Lafayette in 1826. The similarity to the Cornish gigs is remarkable. (Kenneth E. Mahler photo, Mystic Seaport)*

and was greatly impressed both by the difficulties of his undertaking and by the quality of his workmanship. Upon completing the faeringen, Harold went back to his home afloat, *Brue Gull,* a Griffiths-designed 28-foot centerboard cutter, which he had built in 1966 for his retirement.

His cruises up and down the English coast occasionally took him to the Isles of Scilly. Here, it seemed, was the place to go for lines, and Harold wrote, "I will try to get lines of the Scilly gigs, but am not at all sure that any exist. The Peters family who built most of them seem to have used one set of molds which were spaced a little differently, or padded out a bit or vice versa, in order to alter lines, as it appeared to be required. I know that this is what Tom Chudleigh does."

Imagine my surprise, not to mention elation, when in December 1973, after a long hiatus, word came from Harold that he had engaged to help his friend Tom Chudleigh and had sailed to Scilly, laid up *Brue Gull,* and was presently building a 32-foot gig—a reproduction of one built at Saint Mawes on the Cornish mainland in 1842.

His letter continued:

This brings me to the reason for writing so promptly [?]. I am enclosing herewith a very incomplete and crude lines plan and offset table of this boat. Both time and facilities to do better were just not available. In fact I made up molds in the actual boat, and the new one is now about one-third planked (clinker 5/16-inch elm), lovely, long, easy lines, but a bit of a headache using unstable wet wood. Can you possibly get the enclosed knocked into shape properly, and produce two sets of lines for me?

I laid out a preliminary draft of the boat and sent it to Harold with queries about a number of things that I questioned or did not understand. These he answered, besides making notes and additions on the drawing he returned. In particular I had suggested that section 1 seemed a bit too full, likewise section 8, and I had indicated with dotted lines the amount of easement I judged to be indicated.

Harold agreed: "This boat [*Treffry*] has been repaired and obviously forced outwards near Station 1. After setting up our molds we had to ease quite a bit off number 1 to fair it in. Numbers 1 and 8 as you show them dotted are probably correct." Further, he went on to say that "the deadrise [of the sections] is curved as shown—your sections are okay. Most of the gigs have camber on the keel. *Treffry* has more than others." As the drawing shows, the keel line is not

OFFSETS: FEET, INCHES, EIGHTHS TO INSIDE OF PLANK											
		STATIONS	1	2	3	4	5	6	7	8	9	TRAN.
HEIGHTS ABOVE BASE LINE	SHEER	3-9-0	3-5-1	3-2-2	3-1-2	3-1-0	3-1-6	3-4-0	3-8-0	3-9-7	4-0-0
	RABBET	1-1-2	1-0-7	1-0-7	1-1-0	1-1-4	1-2-1	1-3-1	1-3-7	1-4-4	1-4-6
	BOTTOM KEEL	0-10-0	0-9-5	0-9-5	0-9-6	0-10-2	0-10-7	0-11-5	1-0-5	1-1-1	1-1-4
	9" BUTTOCK	3-0-4	1-6-7	1-3-2	1-2-7	1-2-7	1-0-4	1-7-0	2-3-4	3-2-1	—
	18" BUTTOCK	—	2-6-5	1-7-7	1-5-5	1-4-7	1-7-0	2-2-0	—	—	—
HALF-BREADTHS	SHEER	0-9-6	1-7-7	2-1-5	2-4-0	2-4-1	2-3-0	1-11-0	1-3-2	0-11-4	0-7-4
	32" W.L.	0-8-1	1-6-3	2-0-7	2-3-2	2-3-5	2-2-0	1-9-2	0-11-5	0-6-1	0-0-5
	LOAD W.L.	0-5-1	1-2-2	1-9-4	2-1-0	2-1-3	1-10-5	1-4-3	0-6-2	0-2-7	0-0-5
	KEEL	0-0-7	0-0-7	0-0-7	0-0-7	0-0-7	0-0-7	0-0-7	0-0-7	0-0-7	0-0-5
DIAG-ONALS	DIAGONAL A	1-0-3	2-0-4	2-7-5	2-10-5	2-10-7	2-8-5	2-3-5	1-5-7	1-0-4	0-7-0
	DIAGONAL B	0-10-0	1-6-6	2-0-3	2-2-4	2-2-6	2-0-5	1-7-7	0-11-7	0-6-7	0-0-5
DIAG. A 4' ABOVE BASE LINE, OUT 2'-3" ON L.W.L. DIAG. B 3' ABOVE B.L. OUT 1'-2" ON L.W.L.											

straight, as is usual in most other types, but rises considerably in a gradual curve as it moves aft.

Additional correspondence followed. In February 1974 Harold had the following comments:

With regard to your queries on *Treffry,* the ends of the thwarts fit the skin snugly, as do the hanging and the lodging knees. The undersides of the lodging knees are not notched to seat on the risings. At each end of each thwart there are two hanging knees which we call "thwart" knees. The planks lap three-quarters of an inch, and only the top edges are beveled. There are no solid floors, only bent frames and half frames. Stretchers ship into notches attached to margin planks screwed to the timbers. These also support the movable ceiling or bottom boards. *Treffry* has been retimbered at some time, and the replacements are not "joggled" over the plank lands as originally done, and as we are doing in the reproduction. Frank Gibson produced the enclosed photos yesterday. Will get some of the new boat on completion.

TYPICAL PILOT GIG DETAILS FROM NOTES BY HAROLD KIMBER AND PHOTOGRAPHS.

1. THWARTS, ELM ¾" THICK. BOWED SLIGHTLY UPWARD BY POST.
2. HANGING OR THWART KNEES NATURAL CROOKS. 2 TO A THWART.
3. LODGING KNEES AGAINST INSIDE OF PLANK ON TOP OF RISER AND FASTENED TO IT.
4. RISER 9" BELOW SHEER GENERALLY, 11½" STATION 1. 9½" AFTER THWART.
5. GUNWALE MOLDED 1⅝" SLIGHT TAPER AT ENDS. ⅞" THICK.
6. STRETCHERS LET INTO CLEATS FASTENED TO THE MARGIN STRIPS.
7. MARGIN STRIPS SCREWED TO THE TIMBERS.
8. THOLE PIN PADS BORED WITH TWO 1-INCH HOLES 4½" ON CENTERS.
9. KEEL SIDED 1¼" MOLDED 3½".
10. TIMBERS ⅝" x ⅝" TAPERED TO ⅝" x ½" AT HEAD. FITTED OVER LANDS. 6" ON CENTERS.
11. ALTERNATE TIMBERS END JUST BELOW RISINGS.
12. CROSS BRACE HOLED TO TAKE END OF BOOMKIN FOR SAILING RIG.
13. PLANKING 12 STRAKES CORNISH NARROW-LEAF ELM ⁵⁄₁₆" THICK.
14. FILLER PIECE BETWEEN THWART KNEES.
15. 1" DIA. HOLES 4½" ON CENTERS FOR THOLE PINS.
16. REMOVABLE POST FORCED UNDER THWART TO GIVE SLIGHT UPWARD BOW.

Tom Chudleigh had engaged to build not one but two gigs. Harold, however, was unable to remain in Scilly to see their completion. After he left there was difficulty in obtaining suitable materials, and so *Good Intent* was not finished until late in 1974. *Active*, however, did remarkably well in the interisland racing in the summer of 1974. "Nothing could come near her most of last season," Harold wrote at the time, "as her light weight and extra length stood her in good stead against the old shorter and heavier boats."

The lines given here are quite reliable, I believe. Of course, as mentioned, *Treffry* has changed shape somewhat, though only slightly, over the past 140 years. Besides, the boatbuilder's "eye" has the final say, and no two boats are ever built exacty alike, even on the same molds.

The drawing of the construction details that accompanies the lines attempts to be accurate as far as it goes, which, it must be said, is not very far. Note the heading "Typical Pilot Gig Details From Notes by Harold Kimber and Photographs." Only dimensions given by Harold are specified. This drawing is not intended to be scaled, and no scale is provided.

For instance, as to the laying out of plank, their number and thickness were given, as were the specifications that they were beveled on the top edge only and that the width of the lands or laps was ¾ inch. In addition, the length of the side to be covered was obtained from the lines. In the laying out of the plank widths, these were varied according to the amount of curvature.

Since the garboard and the sheer planks lie nearly flat, they were made 4½ inches, including the laps, whereas on the turn of the bilge, where there is maximum curvature, plank widths were reduced to 3½ inches. Whether the actual planking was lined in this manner I had no way of knowing, but this seemed logical and right. Generally the spacing and proportions of the planking are left to the boatbuilders and almost never appear in an architect's plans.

In March's book, plans but no offsets are given for the Newquay gig of the same name, but these are so small and badly reproduced as to be partly illegible and largely useless from a builder's standpoint. Furthermore, the source is not given, and we are not told whether full-size prints of the original drawings are available.

There appears to be a need to measure and record the details of these extraordinary boats much more accurately and fully than has so far been done. It is

Above: *Tom Chudleigh's shop in the Scilly Isles. On the right is the pilot gig* Treffry. *On the left is her replica,* Active, *under construction.* Right: *One of the two gigs built by Tom Chudleigh in 1974.* (F.E. Gibson photos, Scilly Isles)

hoped that this will not be put off until it is too late.

Although all of these gigs were built on the general model originated by the Peters family, there had to have been considerable minor variation from boat to boat. *Newquay*'s keel in the plan reproduced by March is shown to be quite straight, yet the keel for *Treffry,* as measured by Harold Kimber, has 4 inches of fore-and-aft camber or rocker.

As March explains, gigs from different islands or locations on the mainland raced for jobs, and when a gig was frequently beaten, the company that owned it would have another built in hopes of getting a faster boat. Thus *March* was built to beat *Albion, Golden Eagle* to beat *March,* and *Czar* to beat *Golden Eagle.*

March gives a list of scantlings, but does not say from what gig or gigs these measurements were taken.

This list is by no means complete, and varies somewhat from the dimensions provided by Kimber.

The keel, according to March, is molded 3½ inches and sided 2 inches; Kimber has it molded 3½ inches and sided 1¾ inches. March makes the planking ¼ inch thick, Kimber, ⁵⁄₁₆ inch.

Timbers, according to March, are ½ inch wide, ½ inch at their thickest, and ¼ inch at their thinnest section. In the two reproductions of *Treffry—Active* and *Good Intent*—timbers are ⅝ inch by ⅝ inch tapered to ½ inch molded at the head. It is not clear if the ⅝-inch-molded dimension applies before or after the timbers are notched or joggled to fit the lands.

March states that "notched timbers only were used. The men knew just where to cut each before steaming and when placed in position it exactly fitted every overlap." I must say this runs counter to my best judgment. My experience is that timbers so cut before steaming would almost certainly break at the notches when bent, no matter how well they were steamed and how superior the bending stock. The only feasible way, it seems to me, is first to bend the timbers to shape and then to notch them after they have cooled and dried to some extent.

How much the exceptional qualities of these gigs depended on the superiority of the planking material remains to be determined. The Peters clan who built most of the famous old gigs got their own lumber, selecting choice logs from young trees of narrow-leaf Cornish elm. These were buried in creek mud and left to season slowly for five years, after which they were removed, sawn, and stacked under cover for another year before they were used. As for the exceptional strength and flexibility of this elm planking, when *Slippen,* built about 1830, was repaired in 1953, a 4-foot strip of bilge planking had to be removed. Bent into a complete circle, this 120-year-old strip would spring back into shape when released, without the slightest distortion or damage. I doubt if any other planking material could meet this test. I have never seen any that could. Can it be that the signal superiority of these gigs derives ultimately from their unique planking timber?

This discussion of pilot gig construction could go on and on in spite of the relative paucity of exact data available to us at present. Much of March's lengthy chapter is given over to this subject, but without answering a fraction of the questions it raises. What is known for certain and recorded about these boats is only a small part of what remains to be determined.

A 1977 reproduction of the Treffry *on her sea trials. She was built from the plans in this chapter by Paul Schweiss (standing, with the tiller lines) of the Clinker Boat Works, Tacoma, Washington, for the Eureka Rowing Club, Eureka, California. There is growing interest in these gigs among amateur and professional boatbuilders. (Keith Bauer photo)*

3

Merrymeeting Bay Duckboat

If any class of traditional American small boats can lay claim to a native origin, certainly it is our duckboats, of which there is such a diversity. Duck hunting, first for market and subsistence and later for sport, has utilized over the years a variety of specialized craft. The earliest of record are the dugout log canoes obtained from the Indians and employed by the first settlers at Salem, Massachusetts, more than three and a half centuries ago. According to William Wood's *New England Prospect,* published in London in 1634, these were "made of whole pine trees, being about two foot & a half over and 20 foote long; in these likewise they go a fowling, sometimes two leagues to sea."

Three hundred years later the descendants of the settlers were still hunting ducks at sea—that is to say, from the islands in outer Marblehead Harbor—but they had given up log dugouts for light, double-ended gunning dories.

One of the more highly specialized gunning boats, one that has not been taken over for any use other than duck hunting, is the Merrymeeting Bay sneak float. The name comes from the large body of water formed by the confluence in a common estuary of Maine's Androscoggin and Kennebec rivers. This wide expanse of open water, long esteemed by duck hunters, requires a safe and seakindly craft that is also capable of stealthy approach to swimming ducks. The superior qualities of the Merrymeeting Bay sneak float as a gunning boat are widely known among duck hunters, yet as far as I can determine, its lines and construction details have never before been published.

The boat from which I have taken the lines and details presented here is probably as genuine a specimen of the type as has survived. It belongs to George Stadel, the Stamford, Connecticut, naval architect who had it built some 20 years ago. Stadel and his two sons have hunted extensively with this float in the area of Long Island Sound adjacent to Stamford, and attest to its superior qualities.

15' MERRYMEETING BAY SNEAK FLOAT

STEM DETAIL

TO APEX LINE
A 2'-2 1/8"
B 2'-2 3/4"
C 2'-2 7/8"
D 2'-2 1/2"
E 2'-0 3/4"

OFFSETS - FEET-INCHES-EIGHTHS, MEASURED INSIDE 5/8" PLANKING, OUTSIDE TRANSOM.

HALF-BREADTHS		STEM	14'	13'	12'	10'	8'	6'	4'	2'	TRAN.
	APEX-INNER RAB.										DIAGONAL A
	SHEER	0-11-6	0-2-5	0-2-3	0-2-6	0-1-6	0-1-4	0-1-4	0-1-6	0-2-6	DIAGONAL B
	BUTTOCK 6"			0-11-2	0-11-6	0-10-6	0-10-3	0-10-4	0-10-1	0-10-7	1-0-0
	BUTTOCK 12"					0-5-2	0-3-5	0-1-4	0-1-6	0-2-1	DIAGONAL C 0-2-7
	BUTTOCK 16"							0-8-1	0-2-7	0-1-7	0-1-6 0-3-7	DIAGONAL D
HEIGHTS	SHEER	0-0-3	0-5-0	0-9-2	1-1-2	1-7-2	1-9-2	1-10-2	1-11-5	1-11-7	1-8-4
	W.L. 7 3/4"	0-0-3	0-3-6	0-8-0	1-1-6	1-6-0	1-9-3	1-10-6	1-9-3	1-6-2	
	W.L. 5 3/4"	0-0-3	0-2-3	0-6-0	0-7-6	1-4-4	1-8-0	1-9-3	1-8-6	1-4-0	
	W.L. 3 3/4"	0-0-3	0-1-1	0-3-1	0-6-2	1-2-0	1-5-5	1-7-2	1-6-4	1-3-5	1-1-2
	HALF SIDING KEEL 7/8. BASE LINE BOTTOM OF KEEL.										

		STEM	14'	13'	12'	10'	8'	6'	4'	2'	TRAN.
	DIAGONAL A	0-1-0	0-5-0	0-9-3	1-0-6	1-6-2	1-9-1	1-10-1	1-9-6	1-6-0	
	DIAGONAL B	0-1-0	0-5-1	0-9-3	1-0-3	1-5-1	1-7-5	1-8-4	1-6-4	1-4-5	
	DIAGONAL C	0-2-0	0-5-4	0-9-5	1-0-4	1-3-0	1-2-3	1-8-0	1-2-0	1-6-7	
	DIAGONAL D	0-2-0	0-6-0	0-9-5	0-10-4	0-11-6	1-0-7	1-0-6	1-0-5	0-10-7	

BASE LINE

SHEER
APEX LINE
STEM LINE
KEEL
RABBET LINE

BUTTOCK 16"
BUTTOCK 12"
BUTT. 12"
W.L. 5 3/4"
W.L. 3 3/4"
BUTT. 6"
SHEER

BASE LINE

The builder was Will Rittal, who lived at the head of Merrymeeting Bay. Rittal, well known in those parts as a builder of sneak floats, was in his nineties when he built this one, his last, on molds acquired as a young apprentice, and the molds, according to Stadel, were old even then.

The hull is shapely, the carvel planking expertly lined. Though the construction is not fancy, the workmanship is neat and shows the hand of the experienced professional builder. The scantlings are quite heavy and the construction substantial, presumably to enable the boat to withstand rough-water use and to last.

Lines are drawn to the inside of the plank, and consequently the rabbeted stem is laid out from the apex line or inner rabbet line. The keel is not rabbeted, and the garboards butt against it so that the inner side of the garboard plank comes flush with the top of the keel; there is no covering keel batten or "hog."

In order to reproduce this boat in plank as it was traditionally built, it is essential to use the same number of planks of approximately the same widths, and the same lengthwise shapes, or *lining,* to use the boatbuilder's term.

Up to now, the art of lining plank—and it is something of an art—has been left to hands-on boatbuilders. It can't be worked out on the drawing board, and the naval architects do not go into it. How to go about this essential procedure is not explained in any of the boatbuilding manuals that I am acquainted with.

I cannot emphasize too strongly that for all classic small-craft types, and for round-hulled types particularly, the plank lining—including the number of planks, their widths taken at regular stations, and their lengthwise shapes—is something that has been worked out and perfected through generations of trade practice. There will be variations in the lining among different examples of the same class or type, some better and more skillfully done than others, but in general they must all conform rather closely to the same standard pattern in order to get acceptable results. Ease and efficiency of construction, hull strength and watertightness, economy in the use of planking material, and—no less essential—a pleasing appearance of the finished hull all depend on a correct and skillful lining job.

How is the inexperienced builder to line out his boat properly? There is one cop-out that is sometimes resorted to: He can engage a professional builder to do this part of the job for him, although qualified professionals are not so easy to find today. The way that I recommend, however, is essentially the one that I have followed here for this particular sneak float.

1. Locate one or more (preferably more) good examples of the type. Measure and record the plank widths at regular measured stations the whole length of the hull. In addition, examine and study the layout of the planking carefully and take notes.

2. Make an accurate scale half-model of the boat to be planked. Dry pine, white or sugar, is the best wood for this. The larger the model, within reasonable limits, the better. For this 15-foot sneak float a scale of 2 inches to 1 foot works well, and produces a model 30 inches long.

3. Making use of the number and width of the planks previously recorded, and at the same time taking into account the general layout of the planking of the type, as previously observed, line out the planking on the scale half-model. To do this, lay off the planking widths at their respective stations along the length of the hull, one plank at a time, and run a lining batten through these points to connect them and to fair the line so made. Small strips of white pine are best for these lining battens. For lining the plank shapes on the sneak-float model, I found that strips $7/32$ inch by $3/32$ inch in section worked well for battens.

To hold the batten in place, I used a number of miniature awls made from darning needles, the eye end of each being inserted into one end of a small stick about the size of an ordinary lead pencil. The needle points go through the batten without splitting it, are easy to insert and withdraw, hold well, and do not leave big holes.

When the location of the lining batten has been adjusted to suit, mark its line lightly with a sharp soft-lead pencil. This makes it easy to erase the line if you desire to change it, as you may have to do several times before all the lines are adjusted to suit.

In this way the entire side of the boat (model) can be lined out so that the layout of the planking can be seen in its entirety. This is the best and surest way that I know to get a uniform and pleasing layout throughout. Various considerations, which I can't go into in detail here, enter into a skillful lining job, such as using the diminishing batten, which I have explained in the first volume of *Building Classic Small Craft* (page 264), increasing the width of the planks where the hull

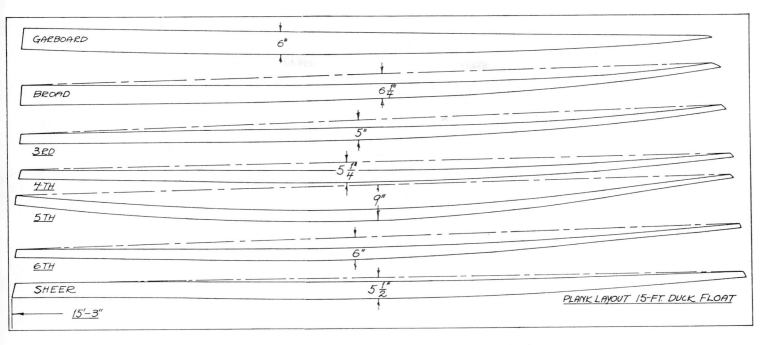

PLANK LAYOUT 15-FT. DUCK FLOAT

APPROXIMATE PLANK WIDTHS								
	TRANSOM	2'	4'	6'	8'	10'	12'	13'	14'
GARBOARD	5-7	5-12	5-12	5-10	5-3	4-10	3-14	2-6	1-4
2 ND	5-3	4-14	4-10	4-3	3-11	2-15	2-4	1-14	1-9
3 RD	2-9	2-14	3-0	3-6	3-1	2-9	2-1	1-10	1-7
4 TH	2-4	2-10	3-0	3-4	3-0	2-9	2-1	1-11	1-6
5 TH	2-4	2-10	2-15	3-0	2-14	2-10	1-14	1-9	1-2
6 TH	2-4	2-8	2-14	3-2	2-14	2-8	1-12	1-7	1-5
SHEER	3-12	4-1	4-6	4-6	4-5	4-0	3-4	2-10	2-2

15' MERRYMEETING BAY DUCK FLOAT. WIDTHS IN INCHES & SIXTEENTHS. STATIONS MEASURED FROM AFTER PERP.

surface flattens out next to the keel, and decreasing the width where there is an increase in curvature, as at the turn of the bilge. Experience, experimentation, or both will help to avoid planking shapes that produce excessive sny (edgewise curvature) when laid out flat on the planking stock.

4. Once the scale half-model has been lined to suit, the planking shapes can be spiled from it and laid out flat, in miniature, on the drawing board, exactly as they would be laid out full size in planking the boat. Not only is it possible to tell in this way if adjustment in lining would be desirable, but you can also determine quite closely the widths of the boards required—no small consideration these days with the price of planking material as high as it is.

This is the procedure I have followed for the sneak float. Reproduced here is a layout of the planking showing the width of the boards required. As can be seen, all the planks are quite straight and call for boards not wider than 6 inches, except for number 5, which also could be got out of narrow boards if it were glue-spliced from two pieces.

In addition, a table of planking widths has been made up, from which the planking shapes can easily be lined out full size on the boat. A fair lining batten will be required for this, preferably one of white pine, say 1¼ or 1⅜ inches by ⅜ inch in section, tacked in place with small (number 2 common) nails.

Note that the planking widths given are specified *approximate*. This is because in lining out, some slight

OUTSIDE TRANSOM

STATION 12' FROM STERN

STATION 4' FROM STERN

adjustments are always required in order to satisfy the discerning eye. The builder's eye is the final arbiter for fairness.

This layout of plank shapes with its accompanying table of plank widths is a new departure for how-to boat plans. Given the approximate width, shape, and lining of the strakes, the inexperienced builder need not hesitate to undertake carvel planking even for such a hull shape as this. It is my contention that building plans for planked boats cannot be considered complete unless they include plank widths and planking layout. A general study of planking widths and layout for traditional wooden small craft remains to be done and is much needed.

Because the boat is wide, flat, and low-sided, I would use a ladder-frame setup and plank the hull upside down. Resting the ladder frame on a couple of ordinary sawhorses would bring it to a convenient height for working. Conventional planking procedure is recommended. Molds from which the combined thickness of ribbands, steam-bent frames, and planking has been deducted are set up on two-foot stations, as laid off on the lines plan. The ribbands are fastened in place fore and aft, and close enough to keep the steam-bent frames from kinking. Next, the frames are

Left: *An interior view of George Stadel's sneak float shows the high position of the rowing thwart with storage box beneath, the flat run of the coaming, and the arrangement for the oarlocks. Less clearly visible are the lapping frames and the short floors.* **Below:** *Will Rittal was in his nineties when he built Stadel's float at the head of Merrymeeting Bay, Maine. The carvel planking is expertly lined. (John Gardner photos)*

bent in on 9-inch centers. Frames may be either continuous from one side to the other, or in two sections lapped across the keel, as shown. This done, the keel with the stem and the stern transom attached is laid in place and secured, and planking may proceed.

It appears that some of the later floats were strip-planked, perhaps by builders who lacked the confidence or skill for carvel planking. Because of the shape of the hull, which tapers toward the bow, strip planking would present some problems as well. I should want to reserve judgment on strip-built floats until I had a chance to inspect them. Nevertheless, to me strip planking suggests decadence.

The hull lines are well adapted to composite construction, such as the Gougeon Brothers' WEST System, which would result in a much lighter boat, and one that would remain tight when taken from the water for a considerable length of time. This might be worth considering by someone intending to haul the boat from place to place on a trailer.

The construction drawings reproduced herewith, while not showing everything, contain sufficient information, I am sure, to build from authentically. Careful study of the drawings is recommended.

The following are numbered in the drawings for easy reference:

1. *Keel, stem, and sternpost or stern knee:* Oak, sided 1¾ inches and molded as shown in the lines plan. Stem can be got out of a width of oak plank, with some curved grain if possible. Lay out so that the cross grain comes at the stemhead end.

2. *Timbers:* Oak, steam-bent ¾ inch by ⅞ inch, laid on the flat. Spacing, approximately 9-inch centers. Ends lap over the keel and are nailed.

3. *Timbers:* Oak, steam-bent ¾ inch by ⅞ inch, laid on the flat. Five in all. Spaced as shown.

4. *Planking:* White pine finished ⅝ inch thick.

5. *Decking:* White pine ⅝ inch thick and canvas-covered.

6. *Coamings:* White pine ⁹⁄₁₆ inch by 5½ inches. Top lines straight when installed in boat. Coamings sit plumb.

7. *Deck beams:* Oak, sided ¾ inch, molded 1⅜ inches. Ends let into sheer plank ⅛ inch.

8. *Two deck supports:* ¾-inch pine, shaped as shown and fastened through the hull.

9. *Half-round trim:* Covers edges of deck canvas. One inch by ¾ inch, tapered slightly at bow end for appearance.

10. *Removable backrest and thwart:* Fits tightly against the inside of the coaming, resting on cleats fastened to the coaming. The forward side slopes at a convenient angle to serve as a backrest for a bow occupant seated in the bottom of the boat. Under the top, which forms a rowing thwart, there is a shelf and a shallow compartment that opens aft. Is lifted out easily.

11. *Supports for rowlocks:* Braced as shown and bolted on either side with ⁵⁄₁₆-inch carriage bolts through the deck.

12. Davis rowlocks number 3.

13. Cleats either side at the stern for removable seat or thwart.

14. *Hole for sculling oar:* Located as shown. Lined with leather. Diameter after lining, 1¾ inches.

15. Dotted line indicates deck camber. One beam mold will suffice for side decks.

Not shown are the gratings or platform in the bottom for occupants to sit on. They are located well above any seepage in the bottom.

4

15-Foot Flattie Skiff

......................•......................

At the late-winter small-craft gathering at Mystic Seaport in 1980, a teenager asked me to recommend a boat for quahogging. What he had in mind apparently was something simple and sturdy that would be easy and inexpensive to build, a utility workboat that he could knock around the shore in or take across the bay when the weather permitted.

He mentioned a length of 16 feet, but since then I have concluded that a foot or two less would probably be adequate, easier to handle, and somewhat cheaper to build. The boat that I am offering here will be only an inch or two under 15 feet overall, although it could easily be stretched out a foot longer—no longer, if it is to be planked with 16-foot boards. Also, it could be made a foot or so shorter without any difficulty.

What we have here is a variation on one of the most common and widespread small utility boats ever built, one that is found the entire length of the New England coast. Such flats belong to a very ancient type used widely in Europe centuries before fishermen brought them to the New World. In Maine it would be a large flatiron skiff; on the south shore of Connecticut, a small sharpie rowboat. Its wide, cross-planked bottom makes a steady working platform having great initial stability.

Admittedly, the flat bottoms of these boats do pound when driven into a chop, but this characteristic will be minimized in the design shown here, which has been made quite narrow and sharp forward for this reason. Some length is essential in order to achieve this narrow entrance. This is why such skiffs built as short as 12 feet or less almost invariably turn out to be overfull and stubby forward, tending to bang unmercifully when it gets the least mite lumpy.

Although these flats have great initial stability, they lack the seakindly characteristics of round-hull craft, and are not suited to go outside where the big ones roll. Under such conditions they could roll, or be thrown, completely over. Although the round hull might roll down, it would hang on and then roll back. As long as this limitation is recognized and respected, and as long as these flats stay in sheltered or semisheltered waters and are used with ordinary common sense, they are perfectly safe, as their continued use by the thousands over the years makes clear.

Because of its wood construction and large scantlings, the flat detailed here would float upright and quite high in the water should it ever fill. You could climb aboard over either the side or the stern if you ever fell overboard. Although I do not advise walking around inside a small boat, you could walk around inside this one without danger of tipping over. I am confident that this boat will pass Coast Guard level-flotation and stability requirements with flying colors.

The skiff detailed here is strictly for rowing, but it could easily be converted for sailing and would sail handily. To install a centerboard trunk and centerboard would be no great job, and this hull, rigged as a small sharpie, is capable of some speed.

I have gone to special pains to make this skiff as simple and inexpensive to build as possible in this time of inflated costs, and still have it hold together and last for a reasonable length of service. And how long is that? This is definitely not a Herreshoff yacht built to last a century, but I am certain that it will give good service for 10 years and even longer. And in 10 years of knocking around, this simple skiff will pay back its initial cost several times over. In this day of early obsolescence for nearly everything we use, 10 years is longer than the life of most cars and household appliances, and in 10 years the original owner will probably have graduated from quahogging and gone on to larger and more expensive vessels.

In any case, it is partly because of such considerations that I have specified fastening this skiff not with bronze screws that cost a king's ransom, or with old-type boat nails now almost impossible to find, but with ordinary hot-dipped galvanized common nails, available at almost any good lumberyard or hardware store. However, they must be hot-dipped galvanized nails, not the electroplated kind, which are worthless. Hot-dipped galvanized common nails in a wooden rowboat that is kept puttied and painted are certainly good for at least 10 years.

Because of the difficulty of finding sources of supply for special boat lumber, as well as its high cost, I call

for this skiff to be constructed almost entirely from number 2 common 1-inch white-pine boards. These are distributed throughout the country and available at most retail lumberyards. The only other lumber required is a 12-foot length of 2-inch-by-6-inch Douglas fir. So-called 1-inch boards of number 2 common white pine come planed and smooth on both sides and ¾ inch thick. They are used principally for interior finish, shelving, and simple furniture. They will have some knots. If these are sound and solid, not too large or too numerous, a board will be just as strong or even stronger for having them. In the cross-planked bottom, boards will be tougher with sound knots and will wear better.

Such boards require no surface planing. Sides, bottom, transom, keelson, thwarts, and various smaller members are all ¾ inch thick, and have only to be cut out to their molded shapes. In some places, for greater strength and more secure nailing, two ¾-inch thicknesses are doubled up to make 1½ inches. For joining these mating pieces solidly, epoxy glue is specified; I have also specified 1¾-inch copper clinch nails for pulling the two thicknesses together and reinforcing the glue joint. Only a relatively small quantity of these clinch nails is needed, and probably not more than a pint of epoxy glue. If care is taken to minimize skin contact, the short-term use of this small amount of glue will present no health hazard of any consequence.

The high cost of tools and the present scarcity of good ones are factors to be reckoned with. Unless you have machinery and a well-filled tool chest, some of the small-craft designs offered to inexperienced amateurs are simply out of the question. For this boat, no power tools whatsoever are necessary.

As for hand tools, the following minimum list will suffice: plane (smoothing or jack), handsaw, hammer, 1-inch chisel, rule, square, cheap plastic protractor, one or two 4-inch or 6-inch C-clamps, caulking iron of some sort (can be improvised), putty knife, and paintbrush. If you have a ripsaw in addition to a crosscut, this will make the job quite a bit easier. Of course the saws, plane, and chisel should be sharp and kept sharp, if at all possible. It hardly needs to be said that sharp tools make a tremendous difference.

Building should be started upside down on a flat floor or even the ground, which will give level support athwartships for the legs of the two molds. The surface need not be level fore and aft, although this would be desirable. In preparation for setting up, the stem is cut out and the stem cheeks glued and nailed on either side. This assembly is beveled to receive the plank ends, and the keelson-to-stem block is nailed on as shown.

The bottom edges of the two garboards are marked out and cut to the line. Their forward ends are cut to match the rake of the stem, and the lap gains are cut at bow and stern. The transom is cut to shape and the bottom and side cleats are glued and nailed on the inside. The sides and bottom of the transom are beveled, and the recess that receives the after end of the keelson is cut in the bottom cleat.

Initially, in setting up, the forward ends of the garboards are nailed to the stem assembly with 2½-inch staging nails. These are double-headed nails whose inside heads hold while the outer heads stand out far enough from the board for easy pulling. Later, after the preliminary setup is completed, necessary adjustments for fairness have been made, and everything is correct, the temporary staging nails are pulled and replaced with the permanent fastenings. If you lack staging nails, ordinary common nails with thick leather washers under the heads make good substitutes.

Once the garboards are nailed to the stem, they are bent in place around the two molds and secured to them with staging nails. This done, the after ends of the two planks are pulled in and nailed to the transom assembly, which has been set at its proper rake and braced to the floor or the ground with temporary legs nailed with staging nails. At this stage in the construction the shape is established. The stem must be carefully plumbed and the molds leveled from side to side. Any appearance of twist or sag, any difference in

SECTION MIDDLE BOTTOM TRANSOM

HORIZONTAL SECTION SIDE OF TRANSOM

OUTSIDE FACE TRANSOM

⑦

⑤

3½" 118° ⑫

25 13 22

SIDE PLANK

CLEAT

GLUE

¾"

72½" TRANSOM

OUTSIDE FACE TRANSOM

⑦

¾" 3½"

28° 7/0 118°

BOTTOM

3" CLEAT

BEVEL

CLEAT

OUTSIDE TRANSOM INSIDE CLEAT

BEVEL 3½"

3'-7"

2"

1'-1½" 9¾"

2'-6½"

TRANSOM INSIDE DIMENSIONS

15' FLATIRON/SHARPIE SKIFF

2" 21 17 16

⑮ FRAMES 4'-8'-12' ⑪

3" POST 24

⑫ 14 5½" 2"

CHINE PIECE CUT-OUT

3" KEELSON

PAD OUT SHEER PLANK

FLOOR SHEER

MOLD 4' FROM BOW

SET-UP BASE LINE FLOOR OR GROUND

4'-4½" SHEER

1'-10" 108° 1'-4⅜"

3'-6"

MOLD 8'-4" FROM BOW

SHEER

1'-6" 11⁷/₄

LAP GAINS AT PLANK ENDS

1"

3'-1¼"

1'-6" 101° 1'-10"

2'-6½"

MOLD 4' FROM BOW

11¼" 7⅝" 7⅝" 7⅝" 7¾" 1" LAP 8" 8½" 9" 9⅞" 10⅞"

16' 14'-9 14'-7 14' 12' 10' 8' 6' 4' 2' 2⅜" 0

SHEER PLANK

16' 14'-4½ 14'-1⅛ 13' 12' 10' 8' 6' 4' 2' 3" 0

11¼" 8⅝" 9¾" 10⅜" 10⅞" 11⅛" 10¾" 1" LAP 10¾" 10⅞" 10⅞"

GARBOARD

J.G 4/80

the sides, or any other unfairness must be corrected now.

When this has been done, the keelson is fitted at the bow and nailed to its block on the stem. Staging nails secure it for the time being in the notches cut for it in the two molds, and its after end is cut off so that it fits in the recess previously cut in the bottom cleat of the transom, where it is securely nailed.

The setup will now be solid and secure, and the chine pieces may be fitted against the inside bottom edges of the garboard planks. These chine pieces may be in two or even three lengths, which will make them easier to install. Their function is not to add longitudinal reinforcement, but to provide sufficient thickness for securely nailing the cross-planked bottom. Because of this, they must be glued to the inside of the garboards and have the additional reinforcement of copper clinch nails. A C-clamp or two will be useful here for pulling the chine pieces tight against the garboard as nailing proceeds. The nails hold the chine pieces in position until the glue sets.

Time—a day or more—should be allowed for the glue to set before the cross-planked bottom is fitted and nailed. Before this is done the meeting edges of the garboards and the chine pieces must be planed fair to receive the ends of the bottom cross planks, which, in order to be tight, must lie perfectly flat and touching throughout. Cross planks should be no less than 4 inches wide and no more than 6 inches. Planks wider than this will cup, and their seams tend to open too wide when the boat dries out.

For nailing the ends of the cross planking, 3-inch nails are used, with 1¾-inch copper clinch nails through the keelson at the center. Nails are driven through the plank ends into the chine pieces exactly as shown in the drawing. This keeps them a good distance away from the ends and minimizes the chance of splitting the chine pieces.

In some working skiffs of this type, there are no chine pieces and the garboard is made a full 1 inch thick on the bottom edge to receive the bottom nailing and is planed so that it tapers to a thickness of ¾ inch at the top edge. This is done most easily with a power surface planer, and requires stock a full inch or more thick, neither of which can be counted on here. Because the chine pieces must be depended upon to hold the bottom nailing, I can hardly overstress the importance of bonding them securely to the garboards with epoxy glue liberally reinforced with copper clinch nails.

Bottom cross planks should fit tightly together on the inside, and are beveled as diagramed to give ⅛ inch of open caulking seam on the outside. After several cross planks have been nailed on, a space the width of one plank and slightly narrower at one end than the other is skipped and several more planks are nailed on, and so on until the bottom is covered. After this is done, planks tapered to fit but longer than necessary are driven into the vacant spaces lengthwise, in the manner of long wedges. These planks produce an extra tight fit and wedge the planks tight on either side.

Further, to ensure tightness under the cross-plank ends, one may set them in a flexible bedding compound. Some, including the late Pete Culler, have used asphalt roofing and flashing cement for this. Because the first bottom plank at the bow narrows almost to a point, it would be advisable (in order to prevent splitting) to put it on with the grain running fore and aft and set it in epoxy glue in addition to nailing it. Before the bottom is put on, a caulking seam should be planed on the outside bottom edges of the garboards.

After the bottom is nailed, the heads of the nails should be set slightly below the surface for puttying and the ends of the cross planks planed flush with the rake of the sides. The bottom seams and the seam along the edge of the garboards are caulked with cotton set in tight with iron and mallet (or hammer), but not so hard as to break through into the inside. Seams should be filled with cotton to about ³⁄₁₆ inch from the top. Seams so caulked are thoroughly soaked with thin oil paint, not latex. Red lead is best for this. When the seams have dried, they are filled to the surface with flexible bottom-seam compound.

The skeg and bottom rub strips can now be put on as diagramed. To minimize drag, bottom strips must be put on to run fore and aft and parallel with the centerline. Rub strips that are bent around the outside of the bottom drag water behind their curve and are unacceptable. The skeg, cut out of 2-inch-by-6-inch fir, is taper-planed from a thickness of 1½ inches where it fits against the bottom to ⅝ inch at the lower outside. This is to minimize drag.

The bottom can be finished even to final painting before the boat is turned right side up and the sheer planks bent on. To ensure a tight boat, the builder cannot be too painstaking in planking, caulking, and finishing the bottom.

The top edge of the garboard is perfectly straight, and the lower edge of the sheer plank will also be

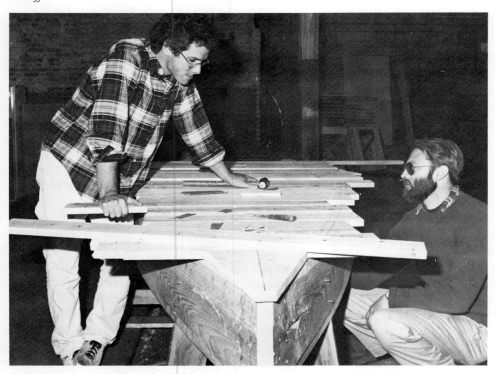

A flattie under construction at Mystic Seaport as a maritime-skills project supplemental to a marine-educational program for college undergraduates. After several cross planks have been nailed on, a slightly wedge-shaped gap the width of one plank is incorporated. Then several more planks are nailed on, followed by another gap, and so on. Tapered planks are later driven lengthwise into the gaps to tighten the edge-to-edge fit of the planks. (Mary Anne Stets photos, Mystic Seaport)

straight if the molds under it are padded out with ¾-inch-thick strips as diagramed. There are no lap bevels, only the lap gains cut in at the ends so that the ends of the two planks will lie flush on the stem and transom. The 1-inch-wide laps are fastened with copper clinch nails spaced 2 inches to 2½ inches apart. After the sheer planks are on, their top edges, previously rough-cut to the diagramed widths, are carefully sighted and planed so that they give a fair sheerline throughout.

In the keyed references that follow, *pine* signifies number 2 common 1-inch white-pine boards, ¾-inch exact thickness. *Fir* is 2-inch-by-6-inch Douglas fir, select quality, rift-grain fir if possible, no sap. One 12-foot length of fir should be sufficient for the job.

1. *Stem:* Fir.
2. *Stem cheeks:* Pine.
3. *Keelson-to-stem block:* Fir.
4. *False stem:* Pine.
5. *Transom:* Pine.
6. *Transom side cleats:* Pine.
7. *Transom bottom cleat:* Pine.
8. *Garboard planks:* Two 16-foot, 12-inch-wide pine boards; exact dimensions: 11¼ inches wide and ¾ inch thick.
9. *Sheer planks:* Same as garboards.
10. *Chine pieces:* Pine.
11. *Side frames:* Fir.
12. *Keelson:* Pine.
13. *Bottom cross planks:* Pine.
14. *Bottom rub strips:* Pine.
15. *Thwarts:* Pine.
16. *Thwart cleats:* Pine.
17. *Outwales:* Pine.
18. *Skeg:* Fir.
19. *Quarter knees:* Fir.
20. *Breasthook:* Fir.
21. *Oarlock pads:* Fir.
22. *Copper clinch nails:* 9-penny, 1¾ inch.
23. 2-inch hot-dipped galvanized common nails.
24. 2½-inch galvanized nails.
25. 3-inch galvanized nails.

Sequel

A flattie skiff shortened to 14 feet was selected in 1981 for construction as a supplementary learning project in a special undergraduate program for college students. The choice proved to be a good one. The two skiffs built each semester are sold to cover the cost of materials, and there is a waiting list of would-be purchasers. From all reports received so far, the owners are well satisfied with them.

This solidly built skiff makes an excellent utility workboat, is unusually stiff and stable under conditions of ordinary use, and has unusual loading capacity. But it is too heavy to be easily handled and transported out of the water, and hence is unsuited for trailering. On the other hand, under a press of sail the boat would stand up well and would not prove to be a laggard.

Scaling the boat down from 15 to 14 feet was done simply by taking a foot out of the midsection while leaving the ends completely alone. That meant changing the location of the two thwarts in order to maintain sufficient rowing room between them, and making sure that the oarsman on the forward thwart would not be cramped for stretch, especially if he should have long arms.

If the skiff is built in a shop with a wood floor that can be nailed into, the setup for building will be easy. If there is a cement floor or no floor at all, it is recommended that the setup be made on two long planks—the heavier the better—laid parallel and flat, and far enough apart for the mold extensions, or "legs," to stand on them. The two planks are cleated together solidly with several lengths of board as cross members, the boards at the ends being positioned so as to support extensions from the stemhead and the transom stern. Such a building platform is easily leveled, provides secure nailing for the setup, and is easily taken apart and the lumber salvaged when the building job is completed.

It was previously suggested that because the first piece of bottom planking at the bow is narrow and triangular, it should be put on with its grain running fore and aft to reduce the danger of splitting when it is nailed. A good way to do this is to make up the piece from two identical triangular lengthwise pieces, with the grain in each running parallel to the hypotenuse (that is, the outer edge). The pieces are glued together so that the glue line follows the centerline of the boat. In this way the short grain in the two pieces will come on the inside, on the glue line, and the grain on the outside will run parallel with the chine of the boat.

The inner chine strips must be well bonded to the inside of the garboards so that the thickness at the bottom edge will be doubled and secure nailing for the bottom cross planking will be ensured. The importance of securing a perfectly solid bonding here cannot

College students provide the ash breeze for a 14-foot version of the 15-foot flattie described in this chapter. Power could also come from a dory sailing rig or a small outboard. For the latter, 10 h.p. would be plenty; much more than that would tend to make the stern squat and the boat pound in any sort of chop. (Mary Anne Stets photo, Mystic Seaport)

be overstated. Epoxy glue thick enough not to leak out of the joint is applied to the meeting surfaces of the chine strips and the garboards, which are pulled tightly together with C-clamps for fastening either with clinch nails or screws put in from the outside. If the latter are used, number 12 1¼-inch screws are recommended, with the heads set slightly below the surface for puttying. The garboard is bored for them, but not the inside pine chine strip, so that they will draw well.

When the bottom cross planking is nailed in place, holes slightly smaller than the nails should be bored through the ends of the cross planks, but not into the chine strips below, for maximum holding power. A slight bevel should be planed off the outside of the bottom edge of the garboard to provide a caulking seam not greater than 1/16 inch, in order that a strand of cotton may be driven between the lower edge of the garboard and the cross-planked bottom.

The directions given above for building this 14- or 15-foot flattie skiff are generally applicable to most cross-planked, flat-bottom skiffs, of which there are many variations.

If the builder finds he wants to adapt the flattie for sailing, the sailing rig with centerboard detailed for the 16-foot Swampscott dory (see Chapter 14) will do nicely. He will probably want to change the shape of the rudder, however, making it shorter and wider, the better to conform to the dimensions of the flattie's stern, while moderately increasing the area of its wetted surface. He need not be restricted to a spritsail, and could just as well employ a leg-o'-mutton or a sliding gunter. Also, the sail area could stand a modest increase, for this rather heavily built boat with its wide, flat bottom will stand up well and needs a fair amount of canvas to get her moving. But there must definitely be provision for reefing down, and anyone intending to sail this boat should not be averse to hiking out when conditions require it.

5

Two 8-Foot Prams

......................•........................

Ultrashort boats are not my cup of tea, and I should never think of designing a boat as short as 8 feet unless there was a demand for it. But over the years I have received a number of inquiries about building plans for dinghies, tenders, prams, and similar tabloid rowing craft of 8 feet and even less in length.

There is no substitute for length. Longer boats row and handle more easily, carry farther, and are better seaboats. They tend to be heavier, however, and they take up more room. For the owner of a small yacht these can be deciding factors in choosing a tender.

I do not recommend scaling down a 10-foot dory skiff to 8 feet because I think it would still be too heavy to cartop, but also because it is a sharp-ended model. In reducing the length of a sharp-ended boat to this extent, it would be unwise to decrease the beam in the same ratio, since to do so would likely result in too great a reduction both in stability and in carrying capacity. In order to ensure acceptable performance, it is generally necessary to leave the beam more or less alone or to reduce it only slightly. A relatively broader hull shape results, one that requires considerably more bend in the side planks to get them to land on the stem. This can greatly increase the difficulty of construction.

For a tender or dinghy as short as 8 feet the pram shape will produce a better boat with respect to capacity, stability, and seakindliness, and the properly designed pram will be easier to build than sharp-ended models. Whether such a pram will be pleasing to the eye is another matter, and depends to a large exent on whose eye is looking.

Yet the pram, even in short lengths, is far from being a box. Its heavily rockered bottom and slanting bow transom enable it to make headway with surprising ease, and for this reason prams generally tow well, a prime consideration, of course, if the boat is to be used as a yacht tender.

AN L. FRANCIS HERRESHOFF–INSPIRED PRAM

The little boat offered here is very close in shape to the pram that L. Francis Herreshoff designed as a tender for the *Nereia,* lines and construction details for which are to be found on pages 170–72 of his *Sensible Cruising Designs.* My attention was called to this design recently by a person who approached me with questions about building it.

Herreshoff recommended a type of dory construction that would have produced a nice solid boat, but a heavy one. His larger pram of similar construction, designed for *Marco Polo,* is extremely heavy. Further-

more, I don't believe it would be possible to plank the bottom of the *Nereia* pram with ¾-inch pine boards without steaming them, because of the amount of rocker, and my guess is that even with steam you might have a tussle with that bottom curve.

Herreshoff said the *Nereia* pram would be heavy, and suggested that it could be built lighter with "laminated wood." Herreshoff had a thing against plywood, and seems not to have been able to bring himself to use the despised term.

Nevertheless, thousands of excellent small craft have been built out of plywood, and if it is used properly and is of good quality to start with, there is nothing the matter with using plywood for small boats. I have laid out the boat shown here to be built with plywood, which should produce a yacht tender light enough to be taken on deck without excessive straining.

Note that two standard 4-by-8-foot panels are ample for the sides, bottom, and ends. The thickness is ¼ inch. Marine grade is recommended because good-quality exterior fir is increasingly difficult to find.

The boat shown here is a couple of inches shorter

than the *Nereia* pram so that the sides can be gotten out of standard 8-foot panels. It is also slightly wider and slightly deeper, and the curve of the bottom toward the bow has been eased just a bit to give an easier bend, but not enough to hurt performance appreciably.

I have not given lines and offsets, but instead have provided actual dimensions for the bow and stern transoms and the three molds that remain in the boat as frames. This simplifies and shortens the building process a lot. The boat is set up for building on a ladder frame dimensioned to give the precise locations of the mold-frame assemblies, which are centered, plumbed, stayed in place, and then beveled for planking.

Materials in addition to the plywood include boards of ¾-inch finished thickness, epoxy glue, nails 1 inch, 1¼ inches, and 1½ inches long, and a few screws of assorted lengths. Small screws—say ¾-inch number 6 bronze wood screws for fastening the plywood to the chine strips and the seam battens—are optional.

The main dependence is upon glue, however, and small nails should be quite sufficient to hold the plywood in position until the glue has set. Annular

nails—also known as ring nails—are recommended. Where there is danger of going through, as with 1-inch nails through ¼-inch ply into the seam batten, these nails should be driven on somewhat of a slant, which also makes them hold better.

Epoxy glue is the only kind recommended. Those unacquainted with this adhesive would be well advised to familiarize themselves with its use before starting to build.

The frames, chines, seam battens, seats, skeg, bottom strip, and so forth are all dimensioned to be gotten out of ¾-inch thick lumber. Northern white pine, spruce, Douglas fir, mahogany, or Alaskan cedar may be used. White cedar and redwood are too soft. Ponderosa pine and sugar pine rot too easily. Oak might be used, although it is heavy.

For those who are not experienced boatbuilders, it will be helpful to outline an order of work. To start, the ladder frame, the frames for the bow and stern transoms, and the three molds that become frames and remain in the boat are made up in advance, as dimensioned.

BEVELS		Bow Tran.	Stern Tran.	Sta. No.1	Sta. No.2	Sta. No.3
	SIDE ABOVE KNUCKLE	68°	82°	77°	82°	86°
	SIDE BELOW KNUCKLE	56°	76°	74°	82°	84°
	BOTTOM	36°	70°	76°	85°	84°

STATION No. 2

When the ladder frame has been secured at a convenient height for working on horses or otherwise, the molds and the transom frames are set in place, after which they are beveled and faired for planking. The amount of wood to be taken off in beveling and fairing is determined by long battens, which, laid lengthwise of the boat, must sight fair from bow to stern and at the same time touch the edges of the frame molds throughout.

This done, the chine strips and seam battens are cut in, fastened with screws and glue, and faired and beveled as necessary to conform to the rest of the framing. The chine strips and seam battens will bend in more easily if they are a few feet longer than the boat. The resulting overhang at either end need not be cut off until after the side planking is on and it is time to cover the bow and stern with plywood.

The side planks require spiling and are put on first. Next comes the bottom, but before this is put on it will be necessary to plane the chine strips fair, so that the bottom ply will lie with a fair and touching fit throughout. The bottom ply is glued on and nailed with 1½-inch nails into the chine strips and the bottom crosspieces throughout. The ends receive their plywood covering last.

Before the boat is turned right side up, a reinforcing strip is run down the center of the bottom the length of the boat and a small skeg is fastened to it at the stern end. This strip is bedded with glue and fastened into the inside bottom cross members with 2-inch number 12 screws, bronze or galvanized. Later, after the boat is turned over, fastenings will be put through the bottom ply from the inside into this outside keel strip. Strips 1½ inches wide, ⅜ inch thick, and chamfered on the upper edge are put on the lower edge of the plywood bottom with glue and 1¼-inch nails.

Before the boat is turned over, the outside gunwale strips are glued on and screwed into the frames. If this is done just before the boat is turned over, then as soon as the boat is right side up it will be easy to nail through the plywood from the inside before the glue sets. In any case, the glue should be tight throughout.

About all the woodwork that remains on the inside is the installation of the seats. These are important bracing members. The after thwart is supported by, and well fastened into, the center framing strip of the stern transom. On the inside of the bottom, several thin strips, ⅜ inch or ½ inch thick, may be extended fore and aft on top of the bottom crosspieces and fastened into them to serve as a walkway.

Although the final beveling and fairing of the frames, including the inside framing of the bow and stern transoms, will need to be tested and very likely adjusted after the frames have been set up (in order to fair them for planking), preliminary beveling of frames and transom framing should be done at the bench when the frames are assembled. The bevels provided for this were taken from a scale half-model, and will be found to be fairly accurate, if not exact.

When rowlocks are located, the center of the

oarlock-pin socket should measure 10½ inches aft of the after edge of the center thwart.

For extra strength it might be well to make the frames, transom framing, chine strips, and seam battens of oak, although it is heavier than the other woods listed. The additional weight would probably not amount to more than 3 or 4 pounds in any case.

It is recommended that the boat be well saturated inside and out with hot linseed oil thinned with about 30-percent paint thinner or turps before painting. Heat the oil in a double boiler to keep it below the flash point. Several applications should be made, until the wood will not absorb any more. Allow the wood to dry thoroughly before painting it. Such treatment prevents rot and minimizes water absorption.

The comments that follow are keyed to numbers in the accompanying diagrams.

1. *Two 2 x 4s:* These should be dry and *must be straight.*

2. *Cross cleats:* One-inch pine or spruce. These are located so as to place the frame molds in the right location for beveling. Their locations must not be changed.

3. These two uprights, inclined at an angle of 58 degrees, support the bow transom frame in the correct position. If necessary, they should have additional bracing so that they hold firm.

4. Uprights for supporting the stern transom frame.

5. *The forward frame mold of three frame molds:* These are made from ¾-inch thick lumber. They are made long enough to reach the baseline occupied by the ladder frame. After the boat is planked and turned over they are cut off at the sheer and rounded.

6. *Plywood gussets either side of the frames for connecting the sides of the frames with the bottom cross members:* Glued and nailed; ¼-inch plywood scrap.

7. *Cross spall of 1-inch (¾ inch net) lumber for securing the ends of the frame molds:* Notch the ends for the frames to fit into them and nail, allowing the frame to come up flush against the cross cleat *(2).*

8. *Bow transom frame:* Made from ¾-inch lumber as diagramed. The pieces that make up the frame are halved together and glued. The outline in the diagram is made to the inside face of the frame, so that beveling will not change the shape. The frame pieces should be positioned as dimensioned on the diagram and temporarily fastened into the uprights *(3)* with screws until ready to be covered with plywood.

9. *Stern transom frame:* Same as *8.*

10. *Bow knee:* Put in before the bottom is put on in order to afford fastening for the outside keel strip *(20).*

11. *Stern knee:* Same as *10.*

12. *Seam battens:* 2¼ inches by ¾ inch.

A pram built in 1976 from the plans presented here. This was Ralph Carlsen's first boatbuilding project, and the boat has received much favorable comment over the years. The photograph was taken in the pram's sixth summer of hard use as a tender in New York and New Jersey waters.

13. *Outside gunwale strip:* 1¾ inches by ¾ inch, tapered slightly toward the ends. Glued to plywood topsides and screwed into frames.

14. *Center thwart:* Nine inches by ¾ inch. Notched around middle frame and glued and screwed to seam batten. Sufficient Styrofoam for flotation can be located under this thwart.

15. *Stern thwart:* Eight inches by ¾ inch. Important bracing member. Ends fastened to sides of the boat, after edge to the middle cleat and the inner face of the transom.

16. Short riser glued to sides of boat for supporting low bow seat.

17. *Quarter-inch-thick plywood bottom:* Fastened with glue and 1½-inch nails to chine strips and bottom cross members after the plywood sides are on.

18. *Quarter-inch plywood covering bow transom:* Glued and nailed to transom frame. Put on after sides and bottom.

19. *Plywood covering stern transom:* Same as *18.*

20. *Outside keel strip:* Two inches by ¾ inch. Glued to bottom. Nailed or screwed to inside bottom cross members and bow and stern knees.

21. *Skeg:* ¾-inch thick lumber. Securely fastened

at appropriate locations with long screws from inside and outside.

22. *Bottom cross member:* 1⅛ inches by ¾ inch, located between frames: Two of these are shown. Two more could be added for extra reinforcement at bow and stern.

23. *Frame cross member:* 1⅛ inches by ¾ inch. Fastened to side members with ¼-inch plywood gussets (see *6*).

24. *Triangular filler piece between plywood side gussets:* Glued in place.

25. *Center strip bow transom frame:* Two inches by ¾ inch. Halved into top and bottom strips and glued.

26. *Bottom strip:* Both bow and stern transom frames; made 2½ inches wide to provide extra wood for beveling.

27. *Chine strips:* 1½ inches wide, ¾ inch thick. Beveled to take the bottom plywood sheet after the sides are on. Made 2 feet longer than the boat, or even longer, to facilitate bending into position. Screwed and glued into frame notches.

28. Short cleats of the same material as the seam battens *(12)* are glued and screwed or nailed to them to give extra support to the ends of the center thwart.

29. *Outside chine strips:* 1½ inches by ⅜ inch. Cover the exposed edges of the plywood bottom and are put on with glue and 1¼-inch nails.

30. *Sole flooring or walkway strips:* ½ inch thick and 6 to 7 inches wide amidships, tapering fore and aft to correspond to the shape of the boat.

31. *Limbers:* ½ inch by 1 inch, cut through all the frames and bottom cross members.

A PRAM OF SURPRISING ABILITY

This pram is functional and plain, perhaps, but not ugly. It is not intended to vie in looks with classic varnished yacht tenders by Lawley, Herreshoff, or Nevins, but I do believe it will hold its own in performance with any 8-foot version of such 10-foot and 12-foot round-hulled classics, and at the same time will be much easier and less expensive to build.

In the early 1960s I designed and built a pram for my own use. The family auto was a Falcon, which at that time was a small car, and I wanted a boat that could be loaded on top of it without a struggle, yet one

PRAM 8'-0" × 4'-3½"
J. GARDNER, JAN. 1979

OFFSETS – FEET, INCHES, EIGHTHS						
STATIONS	S.T.	ST. 4	ST. 3	ST. 2	ST. 1	B.T.
HEIGHTS — SHEER	1-8-3	1-8-2	1-8-3	1-9-1	1-10-6	2-0-7
HEIGHTS — CHINE	0-9-6	0-8-7	0-7-3	0-8-1	0-10-4	1-0-0
HEIGHTS — BOTTOM	0-5-1	0-4-2	0-2-5	0-3-4	0-6-7	0-7-6
HALF BREADTHS — SHEER	1-10-4	1-11-7	2-1-4	2-0-2	1-8-0	1-2-0
HALF BREADTHS — CHINE	1-6-7	1-7-4	1-8-1	1-6-0	1-1-2	0-11-0

LINES INSIDE PLANKING, STERN AND BOW TRANSOMS

that would take three persons in safety under reasonable conditions and without crowding.

The performance of this pram far surpassed my expectations. It rowed more easily, carried more, and proved a better seaboat than I had hoped for, yet it was light enough for me to load and off-load without assistance—that is, after I had worked out a procedure for doing it.

What is the explanation for this pram's exceptional carrying capacity, its stability, its restrained motion in a seaway, and the ease with which the boat rowed in spite of its abbreviated length of 9 feet 5 inches overall? After some consideration, I concluded that the pram's superior performance was due principally to two main characteristics of the hull shape: first, its deeply Veed bottom combined with extra wide beam, and second, the pronounced longitudinal curve of its bottom rocker. The deep V made for deep displacement, which steadied the boat, giving it a firm "hold" on the water that shallow, flat-bottomed craft sliding and bouncing around on the surface do not have. The exceptional amount of fore-and-aft bottom curve, continued in the upward slant of the raking bow transom, resulted in easy, unimpeded slippage through

the water, the boat tending to slip up and over rather than dig in and drag.

Because I was pleased with the pram's performance and found it relatively inexpensive and simple to build—lacking difficult planking bends due to its pram shape—I thought it an ideal craft for the amateur builder. The upshot was that I published lines, offsets, and building directions in the *National Fisherman* in 1963.

Since then many of the prams have been built, all with satisfactory results as far as I know. One reader who has an island in a large lake in Maine built two to transport supplies in. An upstate New York doctor who had never constructed a boat before was immensely pleased with one he built for his grandchildren. Several have been rigged to sail and apparently sail quite well, although the pram was designed for rowing.

More recently, those articles from the *National Fisherman* were reprinted as Chapter 3 in the first volume of *Building Classic Small Craft*. Although the materials from which this pram is built can hardly be called classic, the pram shape definitely is.

It was precisely from this book that the impetus

came for working out the design and details for the 8-foot pram we are now considering. In October 1978 I received the following letter from a man in Yarmouth, Maine:

> In your book, *Building Classic Small Craft,* page 36, your plans to build a plywood pram are exactly what I would like, except I'd like to get plans to make one from a standard piece of exterior plywood 4 feet by 8 feet, so the finished boat would be under 8 feet. I'd be using it as a means to get out to a larger boat. Please advise if you have these plans or know where I could get them.

I didn't have such plans at the time, but the request set me thinking. In the 9-foot-5-inch pram, section 4 is 18 inches aft of section 3, which is located slightly aft of amidships, and these two sections are almost exactly the same shape. To cut out that 18-inch section of hull between them and thereby bring them together could be done without disturbing the rest of the boat, and without changing the lines in any significant way except to shorten them, and the resulting length would be just under 8 feet. The proportions of the hull would be altered, it is true, and this would make the beam considerably greater in proportion to the length, but otherwise the lines would remain practically the same.

This is more or less what I have done. In addition to reducing the overall length to just under 8 feet, however, I have reduced the maximum beam from 55 inches to 51 inches, which would still seem ample for an 8-foot boat.

In general, the construction will be much the same as that described for the longer boat in *Building Classic Small Craft,* except that I have worked out a number of minor alterations that should make the boat easier to build, and lighter, but without any loss of strength or durability. These will be fully explained below. The ladder-frame setup is retained, and the building molds, or what serve as building molds, at stations 1, 2, 3, and 4 become part of the permanent hull structure and remain in the boat as frames.

The bow and stern transoms consist of internal framework covered with plywood, which is not put on until the boat is set up and ready for planking with keelson, chine, and full-length longitudinal risers fastened in place. This procedure makes for easy installation of these longitudinals, which previously were tricky to fit, cut, and bend in place after the finished transoms were on. Now the ends of these longitudinals can extend as they will through notches cut for them in the inner framing of the transoms. After they have been bent in place and fastened, the projecting ends are cut off flush with the surface of the transom framing, and the outer covering of plywood is applied. The side panels go on next, and finally the two bottom panels.

The accompanying diagram shows how these panels are laid out and cut from two 4-by-8-foot sheets of plywood. There will be some plywood to spare, almost all of it needed in finishing the interior. Plywood thickness is ¼ inch or a slightly thinner 5 millimeters. I cannot recommend too strongly marine-grade plywood—the best. The ordinary exterior grade presently available is too poor in quality to be considered.

The patterns for these plywood panels were taken from a solid quarter-size half-model, carefully made to a scale of 3 inches to 1 foot. If the boat conforms to the offsets given here, these panels should fit. In any case, prudence suggests that some checking of the boat be done before the plywood is cut.

Also, as I have noted, the bottom panels should be cut at least 1 inch oversize to allow for adjustment and ample covering of the bottom edges of the side panels. Should the side panels turn out to be slightly scant, only an insignificant reduction of the freeboard would result, but if the bottom panels should be undersize, that would be real trouble.

Spruce is recommended for longitudinals, frames and framing, thwarts, floors, and so forth. Spruce is strong and light, and it holds fastenings quite well. It also glues well, and glue is specified for use throughout, wherever wood meets wood. This is the strongest kind of construction, requiring a minimum of metal fastenings, particularly bronze wood screws, which are now priced all out of reason.

The keelson and the chines can be laminated from two or three thinner strips. Gluing is done when they are installed. They will be easier to bend that way, but stiffer and stronger when the glue sets than if put in solid.

The stern thwart will attach to the stern transom, serving to brace it and the whole stern. Likewise, a low seat will brace the bow.

These are some of the principal details and changes. Full details follow.

The pram is set up for building on a ladder frame, for which two 9-foot lengths of 2-inch-by-6-inch construction lumber will do nicely. Make sure they are

8' PRAM FEB. 1979

true, straight, and relatively dry. The ladder-frame setup is supported on horses at a convenient height for working, and is far and away the simplest and easiest method for building a boat of this size. Pay particular attention to the location of the cross cleats when locating the building molds (as dimensioned on the accompanying drawing), since the correct positioning of the molds depends on this.

The only kinds of lumber needed are ¼-inch marine plywood, either fir or mahogany, and spruce boards planed ¾ inch thick. One inexpensive source of spruce is the rough 1-inch spruce lumber now widely distributed and sold as spruce ledger boards. Frequently they are available relatively free of knots, so that in stripping them up on the saw to obtain the narrow widths required, it will be possible to obtain relatively clear stock.

For metal fastenings, screws, which would ordinar-

ily be used, can be largely replaced by bronze ring nails, sizes 12 and 14, which are much less expensive and entirely adequate in combination with glue. One advantage of spruce is that it takes and holds nails quite well for a softwood.

Although metal fastenings will play a part in holding this boat together, the main reliance will be on glue, and for that I especially recommend either of two formulations of epoxy: Chem-Tech T-88 or Cold-Cure. Cold-Cure will set at temperatures as low as 35° F. and will adhere to wet wood. Chem-Tech T-88 also cures at low temperatures and bonds damp wood. This property is important if lumber is not as dry as it should be, as sometimes happens. Both Chem-Tech T-88 and Cold-Cure are gap-filling to a reasonable extent, giving some tolerance in fitting joints.

If epoxy cannot be used, an adequate nonsensitizing substitute is Aerolite 306, which may be obtained

INSIDE or FORWARD FACE OF BOW TRANSOM FRAME

SECTION B-B

BEVEL TRANSOM SIDES 125°
BEVEL TRANSOM BOTTOM 146°

SECTION A-A

GLUE
1" # 12 BR. RING NAILS
1/4" PLYWOOD

BOW TRANSOM FRAMED WITH 3/4" SPRUCE TO
BE COVERED WITH 2 PIECES OF 1/4" PLYWOOD
VIEW FROM OUTSIDE LOOKING FORWARD.

REMOVABLE MOLD STATION 1

REMOVABLE MOLD STATION 3

from Woodcraft Supply Corp., 313 Montvale Ave., Woburn, MA 01801. Cold-Cure epoxy is made by Industrial Formulators of Canada, 3824 William St., Burnaby, B.C. V5C 3H9, Canada. Chem-Tech T-88 is distributed by Chem-Tech, 4669 Lander Rd., Chagrin Falls, Ohio 44022. Also on the market are a number of other epoxy glues that would do quite adequately, but the builder is advised to do some testing before choosing one for the boat.

Every place where wood comes together in this boat should be glued as a way of compensating for the scaled-down dimensions of the scantlings. The keelson is a laminated member formed of two ½-inch thick strips of spruce glued together when they are bent into

place on the molds. The two strips will bend more easily than one 1-inch strip, but when the glue sets, the laminated member will be stiffer and stronger than if it were a solid, 1-inch thick piece.

Another place glue provides light but strong construction is in the covering of the bow and stern transom framing with ¼-inch plywood. Glue is used where the pieces constituting the transom frames are halved together and where these halved joints are reinforced on the inside with plywood gussets.

Before the boat can be set up on the ladder frame for planking, the internal framing for the bow and stern transoms must be assembled and glued and section molds made for stations 1, 2, and 3. Molds for stations 1 and 3 are temporary and are removed when the planked hull is lifted off the planking form.

The mold at station 2 remains in the boat and is the location of the rowing thwart. The thwart itself is removable, as is a dory thwart. The space beneath it is covered with plywood, which glues to the side frames to form a bulkhead that completely fills the area, supporting the thwart and bracing the sides and the bottom of the boat at this point.

The internal fore-and-aft stringers—namely the keelson, the two chine strips, and the two risers—are well after the stern transom is set up in place, it is not shown in the drawing. Also, it rakes so little that there is no need to go to the trouble of developing it.

Both the stern sheets and the seat in the bow are important structural members, bracing their respective ends of the boat and tying the sides to the end in one rigid unit. They are glued (1) to the risers that are glued to the sides of the boat and (2) to the cleats, which are in turn glued to the plywood covering of the transoms. The importance of these reinforcing assemblies and their careful installation cannot be overemphasized.

I suggest to prospective builders, especially if this happens to be their first venture at boatbuilding, that they spend some time studying the drawings. Time so spent will not be wasted. It is not possible to take in everything at a glance, and all too easy to miss important details the first time around.

The drawings have been numbered for easy reference. Every item should be considered in turn and located on the drawings. There should be an effort to visualize how each member is made, how it will fit into the finished structure of the boat, and how it will relate to adjoining members when it enters the building sequence. In a word, an effort should be made to build the boat in one's head as fully and completely as possible before picking up the tools.

As previously mentioned, this 8-foot pram is closely similar both in design and construction to my 9½-foot pram featured in the early 1960s in *National Fisherman* and since then widely and successfully built. It would help, I am sure, to review the *National Fisherman* articles for the plans, the building directions, and especially the photographs of the 9½-foot pram. These have since been reprinted in my *Building Small Boats for Oar and Sail* (now out of print) and in the first volume of *Building Classic Small Craft*.

1. *Side planking:* Quarter-inch or 5-mm first-quality marine plywood, fir or mahogany. After the ladder-frame setup has been made and the molds have been faired, and the risers, the chines, the inner keel or keelson, and the transom framing are in place, the side panels go on.

They go on first—that is, before the bottom panels—and are glued and nailed to the risers, chines, and transom framing. When applied, the side panels should be slightly larger, by ⅛ inch or so, than their finished size, so they can be planed to conform to the chines and the ends of the transoms after they are in place and fastened to the boat. As previously stated, the sides must be well glued to the chines and the risers.

made longer than their neat length in the boat so that they can extend through notches in the framing of the transoms cut to receive them. This makes their installation much simpler than the usual procedure.

After the stringers are in place and fastened, their ends are trimmed off flush with the outside of the transom framing, which is then covered with plywood, well glued and nailed. Next the side planks go on, and last, the bottom. All are well glued.

Because of the extreme rake of the bow transom as well as the considerable in-curving of the sides to meet it, there is a lot of beveling on both the sides and the bottom. The accompanying diagrams show both the inside and the outside and the amount of beveling required.

The recommended way is to lay out the shape of the inside face on a flat surface—a piece of heavy plywood will do—and make up the frame to fit these lines. After the halved joints have been glued and reinforced with plywood gussets according to the drawing, the beveling is done. The notches for the fore-and-aft stringers need not be cut until the transom frames are in place on the ladder frame, and so are not shown in the drawings.

The stern transom, unlike the bow transom, requires very little beveling, and since this can be done just as

STATION No. 3

8 FOOT PRAM

The nails or screws that hold them in place until the glue cures are supplementary. Screws are not necessary, but if they are used, they should be ¾-inch number 8 bronze. One-inch number 12 bronze ring nails would be more than adequate. If their points break through the inside of the chine and riser strips, these are easily filed off. Longer nails might be used at the ends for fastening to the framing of the bow and stern transoms.

2. *Bottom planking:* These two panels are likewise ¼-inch or 5-mm first-quality marine plywood. They are brought to a tight edge-to-edge fit along the inner keel strip or keelson (see *3*), but should be slightly oversize so as to extend beyond the ends and sides about ⅛ inch, to be planed off flush with the outside after the glue has set. Fastenings are nails or screws, the same as those for the sides. It should be kept in mind that the outer plywood covering of the bow and stern transoms is put on with glue and screws or nails, like the sides, before the bottom panels go on.

3. *Internal keel or keelson:* This is made up from two strips of clear spruce, 2 inches wide and ½ inch thick, sprung in place over the molds with glue between the strips and held together until the glue has cured with clamps and a few temporary nails. The two strips bend more easily than a single strip of the combined thickness and hold their curved shape after the glue has set.

The recess cut into the molds for holding this member should be just deep enough so that when the keelson is planed to match the V of the bottom only the least possible amount of wood is removed in fairing. This is important. As much of the keel strip as possible should remain after planing, for strength and secure nailing of the bottom panels.

The keel strip will be made up longer than the boat so that its ends will project through the notches cut in the framing of the bow and stern transoms to receive it. After it has been bent in place, glued, and fastened with 2-inch number 10 screws, the ends are cut off flush with the transom framing, to be covered later with the outer facing of plywood, like the sides.

4. *Chine strips:* These are ¾-inch clear spruce and are 2 inches wide before being beveled to conform to the V of the bottom, after they have been bent into place around the forms. When they are so installed, they are fastened to the permanent frame that serves as a mold at station 2, and at either end to the bow and stern transoms. (The chine strips are notched, or let in, flush to these three members.) Fasten with 2-inch number 10 screws or the equivalent, and set in glue.

5. *Risers:* These full-length longitudinals are likewise clear spruce, ¾ inch thick and 1½ inches wide before beveling. The top edges are beveled so they will be level and horizontal athwartships. This is because

8 FOOT PRAM

FEET AND INCHES

the middle thwart and the end seats rest on the risers, and the end seats want to be glued to them. Like the chine strips, the risers are let in flush to both the sides of the permanent frame at station 2 and the transom framing at either end of the boat. The risers are likewise longer than the boat when installed, and are fastened, glued, cut off flush, and covered when the outer facing of plywood goes on.

6. *Outer keel strip:* This longitudinal is clear spruce, ¾ inch thick or deep by 1 inch wide. It is installed after the bottom plywood is on. Just enough is planed off the joint where the bottom panels come together on the keelson to seat the outer keel strip. It is bedded in glue and fastened with 1½-inch number 10 screws or with 1½-inch or 1¾-inch ring nails, after which the ends are cut off flush with the outside of the transoms.

If desired, it can be cut shorter to allow splicing in a small skeg tapering from ¾ inch deep at the splice to about 2½ inches at the stern. Such a skeg could improve directional stability for rowing. It should be fastened from the inside as well as from the outside. Inside fastenings, 2-inch or 2½-inch number 12 screws or the equivalent, are put in through the keelson. Such a skeg can be tapered and thinned to ⅝ inch on its bottom edge.

7. *Outside bottom stringers:* Full-length stringers of clear spruce, ¾ inch by 1 inch put on flat. It is

important that they run parallel with the outer keel strip. These are important structural members that help directional stability and also serve as rubbing strips that protect the plywood bottom. These are put on with glue and fastened through the bottom into the six internal floors and the frame at station 2 with 1½-inch number 10 screws or number 12 ring nails of the same length.

These bottom stringers cannot be put on, of course, until the boat has been planked and turned over and the internal floors installed. Extra fastenings between the floors, put in from the inside through the plywood bottom into the bottom stringers before the glue sets, would add stiffness and ensure a good fit for the glue. These fastenings could be either ¾-inch number 8 screws or 1-inch number 13 ring nails.

8. *Outwales:* The outwales are glued up from two full-length strips of clear spruce, ½ inch thick and 1¾ inches wide. The bottom edge of the outer strip is beveled as shown in the drawing. The outwales are put on after the boat has been planked and turned over. They are glued to the sides of the boat and are nailed through the plywood sides from the interior of the boat with two rows of 1-inch number 12 ring nails spaced about 6 inches apart. They are also fastened from the outside into the frame at station 2, and at the ends to the corner knees *(23)*.

9. *Floors:* There are six internal floors made of ¾-

inch spruce, dimensioned as shown in the drawing, spaced 9 inches on centers, and located as shown. The width of the floors narrows toward the forward end of the boat. The one shown in the drawing is located at station 3, at the greatest width of the boat. The floors are fitted and glued to the bottom and fastened through from the outside with 1-inch number 12 ring nails. They are notched to fit over the keelson, but the bottom points are trimmed off high enough to provide adequate limbers for through passage of bilge water.

10. *Grating cleats:* There are seven grating cleats similar in shape and material to the floors, but not notched over the keelson or fastened to it or to the bottom. They provide support and fastening for the grating slats.

11. *Grating slats:* These are ½-inch spruce or white pine dimensioned and uniformly tapered as shown, and spaced ½ inch apart. They are fastened to the grating cleats with 1-inch number 12 ring nails as shown.

12. *Removable rowing thwart:* ¾-inch spruce or white pine, 9 inches wide and located as shown in the drawings. This thwart is not fastened in but is removable, being merely notched to fit over the sides of the frame at station 2, as in a Banks dory. It also rests on the risers and on the stiffener *(22)* fastened to the top of the plywood bulkhead *(21)*. This thwart is left loose for ready removal so that the boat may be lightened when it is taken out of the water.

13. *Frame at station 2:* This substantial bracing member located approximately amidships is reinforced by the plywood bulkhead *(21)* extending from side to side below the thwart *(12)* and stiffened by a spruce strip (see *22*) ¾ inch thick and 1½ inches wide.

14. *Bow seat:* Spruce or white pine, a foot in width and long enough for a snug fit across the bow end. This is glued and nailed to the risers and to the cleats across the inside face of the bow transom. In addition to serving as a seat, this member braces the bow end of the boat and strengthens it immensely.

15. *Cleats, bow seat to transom:* ¾-inch spruce, 2 inches wide and beveled on the top edge to match the under side of the bow seat. Glued to the inside of the plywood facing of the transom and nailed from the outside with 1-inch number 12 ring nails.

16. *Stern seat:* ¾-inch spruce or white pine 11 inches wide, fitted to the after end and glued to the risers and to the cleats across the inside face of the after transom. Like the bow seat, the stern seat doubles as a bracing member reinforcing the stern. Fastened in the same manner as the bow seat.

17. *Cleats, stern seat to transom:* ¾-inch-by-2-inch spruce, fastened in the same manner as the cleats at the bow *(15)*.

18. *After floor grating:* Assembled from *10* and *11*. Nailed as shown with 1-inch number 12 ring nails. Made readily removable so that the boat may be lightened when it is taken out of the water for cartopping or stowage aboard a yacht.

19. *Forward floor grating:* Same construction as *18,* and likewise removable from the boat.

20. *Cleats for mounting oarlock sockets:* ¾-inch spruce 2½ inches wide and 9 inches long, glued to the inside of the boat and through-fastened into the outwale with 1½-inch or 1¾-inch number 10 screws.

21. *Plywood bulkhead:* Quarter-inch plywood, scribed and fitted to the bottom and sides of the boat at station 2, coming to the height of the seat risers, and glued and nailed with 1-inch number 12 ring nails to the after face of the permanent frame *(13)*.

22. *Stiffener:* Glued to the after face of the plywood bulkhead at the same height as the risers, and nailed with 1-inch number 12 ring nails.

23. *Corner knee braces:* ¾-inch mahogany or oak, laid out with the grain running parallel to the hypotenuse of their triangular shape. Each of their two sides is fastened with two screws, one through the end from the inside into the wale, the other from the outside through the outwale into the knee, close to its corner.

6

Four Canoes

Recreational small craft have never been more popular or numerous than they are now on both our East and West coasts. Their increase in the past 10 years, which has been nothing less than phenomenal, is almost certain to continue, for very good reasons. In an era of mounting costs and restricted budgets, many are finding that it is not necessary to own a large and expensive vessel in order to experience much of the pleasure and excitement of yachting. Indeed, affordable smaller craft open up additional areas of boating pleasure.

This applies in particular to canoes and kayaks, whether they are used for white water, wilderness cruising, sailing, racing, or lazy relaxation on summer afternoons. And those who build and maintain their own canoes and kayaks, as increasing numbers are doing, find additional fulfillment in working with tools and materials, in using their hands and their brains, in building something that is both useful and beautiful.

The growing popularity of canoes is reminiscent of a similar involvement with canoes for sport and recreation in this country a century ago, but with at least one important difference. Few of the earlier canoes were built by the owners; construction then was left largely to professionals. Part of the difference today is the availability of modern plastic glues and fabric reinforcements. When these new materials are used in combination with strips and veneers of wood, acceptable and even superior canoes and kayaks can be produced in home workshops.

Construction methods may have changed radically, but canoe design—that is, hull shape—has been little improved if at all in the last hundred years, except in the case of a few highly specialized racing canoes. We have not been able to improve on the shapes that were once built at Peterborough (Ontario), or by J. Henry Rushton, W. P. Stephens, R. J. Douglas, E. M. White, H.N. Morris, and other late-19th-century builders whose names are less well known.

Unfortunately, builders who would like to reproduce these older models today are more often than not unable to find lines and offsets. The usual practice in the past was to build from molds, most of which have long since disappeared. Because lines and offsets were not used, they were not recorded, and in the rare instances when they were, they were hardly ever published.

Included in this chapter are lines and offsets for four of these earlier canoes, which are not to be found elsewhere, I believe. Two are typical early sailing canoes, both from obscure sources. The third is a Peterborough plank canoe built by the Canadian Canoe Company. It is primarily a paddling canoe, but it has been adapted successfully for sailing. The fourth is Rushton's Arkansaw Traveler, which by Rushton's own account was developed on Canadian (Peterborough) lines.

A PETERBOROUGH PLANK CANOE

The Indian birchbark canoe, whose form the Peterborough builders reproduced in planks and strips of wood with very little change, was developed and perfected as a workboat for transportation and the hunt, and so it remained and was built for unnumbered generations. It was not until shortly after 1850 at Peterborough, on the Otonabee River, that the Indian canoe was first adapted and successfully built for use as a pleasure craft.

According to Donald Cameron, in a paper read at the Peterborough Historical Society in 1975, it was sometime between 1850 and 1860 that John Stephenson of Ashburnham and Tom Gordon of Lakefield "led off in the building of plank-and-rib canoes." Stephenson's son Alfred told Cameron that his father, born in 1830, built the first canoe to replace the birchbark and the dugout and that it was a board canoe. The Gordon descendants agree that this may well have been the case, but claim that Tom Gordon "designed and manufactured for sale the first plank canoes."

These two builders may have been the first, but William English of Peterborough, who started building in 1861, and Daniel Herald of Gore's Landing, Rice Lake, were not far behind. That all four of these Peterborough-area builders seem to have gotten started more or less simultaneously is an indication that the plank canoes must have been a success from the outset, and that they were in considerable demand almost as soon as they appeared.

They were, in fact, a radical departure in construction, the first ones requiring only three planks to fill out the side. Later, when wide boards of cedar and basswood became harder to get, the number of side planks was increased to four.

John Stephenson had previously run a planing mill. This would have been no later than the 1850s, and at that time such woodworking machinery was quite new. Without a means of producing a plentiful supply of cheap, wide boards of a uniform ¼-inch thickness, Peterborough plank canoes would have been out of the question. In casting about for new uses and an expanded market for the quantities of smooth planed lumber that his mill could produce, it was natural that Stephenson should come up with the idea of building wide-board canoes. The time was certainly right for replacements for the heavy log dugouts then in use and the Indian birch canoes that were in short supply.

The wide-board plank canoe is uniquely a Peterborough product, a boat that was never built commercially outside the area. Although these canoes were not copied—at least in their construction—they greatly influenced and may even have initiated the production of all-wood canoes, which flourished in the United States from roughly 1870 to shortly after 1900.

The construction of the wide-board all-wood canoe is relatively simple and straightforward, although how it was possible to cup the ¼-inch boards sufficiently to conform to the hard turns at the bilges without splitting the planks is a mystery to me. Some have claimed that the boards were softened and made pliable by sponging with hot water, but I have not yet tried it to see how this was done. In any case, the planks were clinch-nailed to bent ribs spaced 6 inches apart on centers. This was the rib spacing found on the remains of an old William English canoe.

Between the ribs, the plank seams are covered with sections of batten stock, which were also used for ribs in the William English canoe. There the ribs and battens are half-rounds of Canadian rock elm measuring a scant ¾ inch wide and ⅜ inch thick. This apparently was a uniformly produced mill product gotten out in quantity on a shaper. Clinch fastenings are slim, cut nails of bronze or hardened copper, ¾ inch long and stiff enough to drive through the hard rock elm without crippling.

As a boy, Albert English, Donald Cameron's informant, assisted his father in building plank canoes. This was perhaps around 1915 or slightly before. (Albert was born when his father was 69.) He vividly recalls his difficulties in bending the boards and pulling them into place in order to get them to conform to the curves of the sides so that they could be nailed.

It was probably due to such difficulties, as well as to the increasing shortage of clear, wide lumber, that wide-board construction was eventually replaced to a great extent by other methods, mostly variations of strip construction. Strip construction has much to recommend to amateur builders now.

There must have been a rapid evolution from the first wide-board plank canoes, but that evolution was never recorded and is now lost. Certainly the first models must have been much heavier and more crudely lined than the highly perfected hulls that have survived and come down to us as Peterborough canoes.

Whether the builders ever made use of lines is doubtful. From the canoes that still exist, and from what is to be seen in builders' catalogs and in photographs, it appears that there were no more than a few closely similar standard shapes. Apparently builders at the time had concluded that the optimum canoe shape for general recreational use had been attained.

Jack Hazzard of Washington, D.C., in his nineties and still active as a canoeist, purchased a new 16-foot William English all-wood canoe in 1920. In 1980, using this canoe as a plug, he glued up a paper replica that has since seen considerable use and proved quite successful. The paper replica is laid up with strips of a strong, brown kraft paper bonded together with a

Jack Hazzard sailing his William English Model 21 canoe, the same model shown in this engraving from an early catalog of the William English firm. Hazzard describes the rig on his 16-foot by 30-inch Blue Bonnet *as a "patched-up" affair of 60 square feet that sailed well but not too fast. The photo was taken in 1930.*

On the Potomac River, Jack Hazzard tries out the paper canoe he built in 1980 using his 1920 William English boat as a plug.

waterproof plastic adhesive. The result is both strong and very light. Sufficient rigidity is attained by internal bracing with wood strips. When an old canoe that has not lost its shape is available to serve as a plug, such construction would seem to have real possibilities for the home workshop.

Paper combines exceptional strength and toughness with exceptional light weight. At one time paper boats seemed to offer great promise in this country. For a brief period slightly more than a hundred years ago, paper racing shells by Waters, Balch and Company of Troy, New York, won most of the important races in college rowing. What was lacking then, and for a long time thereafter, was a reliable waterproof adhesive. Now that we have plastic resin glues that are completely and permanently waterproof, there is no reason why paper should not come into its own as a boatbuilding and canoe-building material.

A more conventional method of canoe construction, and the one principally used by Peterborough builders, is to start with a building form over which steamed ribs are bent. At first the Peterborough builders covered the ribs with wide strakes of planking—three, and then four, boards to the side. Wide boards were followed by longitudinal strips with ship-lap edges, although one of the Peterborough builders briefly tried a tongue-and-grooved strip, and another backed the seams between his wood strips with long strips of thin brass with edges that turned and clinched into the wood. In all cases the wood strips were nailed to the ribs with small nails, the points of which barely came through and were turned back into the rib.

Quite recently a new form of strip construction for canoes has developed. Ribs are omitted, strips are edge-glued together, and this shell-built hull is covered inside and out with a thin overlay of fiberglass. An extremely lightweight, handsome boat results. Practitioners of this method claim the boat is adequately strong, but I have yet to be convinced that ribs can be omitted with impunity. Although I have no knowledge of failure by any glued-strip canoe, I do know of a small sailboat so built that developed lengthwise splits in the sides when dropped a short distance into the water in launching.

The lines and offsets appearing here were taken from a canoe formerly owned by William B. Coolidge of Washington, D.C. Several years ago he donated the boat to the Mystic Seaport Museum, Mystic, Connecticut, and it is now in the small-craft collection there.

Small metal plates that serve as reinforcements on the outside of the sheer strakes, backing up the ends of the two thwarts, are stamped with the name of the Canadian Canoe Company, the builder. According to a booklet on sailing canoes published by the American Canoe Association in 1935, the most popular and fastest open canoes then available in stock models for adaptation to sailing were Model 16, built by the Canadian Canoe Company, Peterborough, Ontario, and Model 64, built by the Peterborough Canoe Company, Peterborough. "The two model numbers designate cedar canoes of rib-and-batten construction," the booklet explains, "but these manufacturers also furnish an identical model both in basswood rib and batten and in longitudinal cedar strip construction. Lengths of all models are 16 feet, beam 31 inches, depth amidships 12 inches and weight approximately 75 pounds." The dimensions cited correspond exactly

	STATIONS	STEM	1'-0"	2'-0"	3'-0"	4'-6"	6'-0"	8'-0"
HEIGHTS ABOVE BASE LINE	SHEER	1-11-5	1-7-3	1-4-7	1-3-7	1-2-7	1-2-4	1-2-0
	RABBET	—	0-3-5	0-2-3	0-2-0	0-1-7	0-1-5	0-1-5
	BUTT. 2½"	—	1-7-3	0-5-6	0-3-6	0-2-4	0-2-0	0-1-7
	BUTT. 5"	—	—	1-1-2	0-5-6	0-3-2	0-2-3	0-2-0
	BUTT. 7½"	—	—	—	0-10-3	0-4-3	0-2-6	0-2-2
	BUTT. 10"	—	—	—	—	0-6-0	0-3-4	0-2-5
HALF-BREADTHS	SHEER	0-0-3†	0-2-4	0-5-2	0-7-7	0-11-2	1-1-3	1-2-5
	W.L. 11½"	0-0-3†	0-1-7	0-4-6	0-7-5	0-11-5	1-2-0	1-3-2
	W.L. 9"	0-0-3†	0-1-5	0-4-1	0-7-1	0-11-3	1-2-1	1-3-4
	W.L. 6½"	0-0-3†	0-1-1	0-3-0	0-5-6	0-10-3	1-1-5	1-3-1
	KEEL RAB.	0-0-3†	0-0-3†	0-0-3	0-0-3	0-0-3	0-0-3	0-0-3
	DIAGONAL	0-0-4	0-2-5	0-6-0	0-9-2	1-1-3	1-4-0	1-5-2

Left: *Measurements are given to the outside of the ¼-inch thick planking. The diagonal, which is shown in the lines drawing, is 15 inches above the baseline and 19 inches out on the baseline.* **Below:** *The Canadian Canoe Company boat donated to Mystic Seaport by William Coolidge. The lines and offsets presented here were taken off this canoe. (Mystic Seaport photo by Mary Anne Stets)*

with those of the Coolidge canoe, which is also of cedar rib-and-batten construction, and this combination of evidence would seem definitely to establish it as a Canadian Canoe Company Model 16.

According to Walter Schalle of the American Canoe Association, it was for one of these Model 16 Canadian canoes with a modified length of 17 feet that the rig shown here was designed and built by Adam Wahl, an ACA member. Schalle believes it to be the fastest lateen rig ever raced in the ACA. (After 1913 the ACA established a "special" racing class of decked canoes that permitted lengths up to 17 feet.) During the early 1920s Wahl won 20 of 21 consecutive races; he finished second in the other, due to a broken mainsheet.

Wahl's Canadian Canoe Company 17-foot special had long decks, no seats, two thwarts, a cut-down keel, and an extra-wide gunwale. The advantages of its rig—in particular the simplicity and ease of handling—are obvious.

The outfit is so well balanced that the boat could at times be sailed without the steering paddle, directional control being maintained simply by moving the leeboard. Nevertheless, due to the location of the mast, the rig was not easy to install.

Sail plans for rigging these canoes have been published in various places. The American Canoe Association booklet "Sailing Canoes" (June 1, 1935) contains several with full details and specifications. Jack Hazzard, already mentioned as the owner of a William English Peterborough, wrote several articles in the 1930s for *Popular Science Monthly* and other publications, for canoeing enthusiasts interested in converting their stock-model paddling canoes for sailing. Others as well published such material about that time.

Most of the canoes converted to sail were the so-called rag canoes—the canvas-covered stock models built for paddling. But no lines of stock canoes were published for the would-be builder. There were various reasons for this.

First, the canoe companies had a proprietary interest in their models, and inasmuch as they were in the business of building canoes to sell, they were not about to provide lines for the use of home builders. Second, it would not have been ethical for anyone else to have taken off the lines of such canoes and circulated them while they were still being built commercially, even if this could have been done legally at the time. Finally, the work of taking off such lines, fairing them, and drawing them so that they could be used is considerable, and ordinarily it would not have paid anyone to do it. It was principally for these reasons that no hull lines or measured offsets for the cedar and basswood three- and four-plank Peterborough stock canoes of the 1920s and 1930s were published, as far as I have been able to discover.

But since then the companies that produced these canoes have gone out of business and disappeared, and after a half century or so their designs have passed into the public domain. There is no longer any reason why these designs should not be freely available to anyone wishing, and able, to use them.

J. HENRY RUSHTON'S ARKANSAW TRAVELER

No one of the old-time builders has fared better in the current revival of classic American small craft than J. Henry Rushton, whose first lightly built boat for wilderness travel was assembled in a Canton, New York, barn in 1873. Before his death in 1906, several thousand lightweight canoes and rowboats bearing the Rushton name were produced. The recognition now accorded Rushton by canoeists and frequenters of our lakes and inland waterways is fast reaching the degree of adulation paid by yachtsmen to the Herreshoffs of Bristol.

With the publication of Atwood Manley's *J. Henry Rushton and His Times in American Canoeing* in 1968 the Rushton revival was well on its way. Amateur builders have taken to reproducing his designs—for one, the diminutive clinker canoe Wee Lassie. Since the appearance of Manley's book, scores of Rushton canoes and boats have turned up, and others are coming to light all the time, from the most unlikely places. That many of the canoes require only minimal restoration before they are ready to go back in the water speaks well for Rushton's construction methods and the quality of his materials.

It was not enough to be a first-rate builder in the face of the intense competition that characterized the boatbuilding business in this country in the first quarter of the 19th century. To survive and prosper, one had to be an able businessman as well. Rushton was not lacking in this respect. In addition to facing the same American competition that forced into bankruptcy such concerns as the R.J. Douglas Company of Waukegan, Illinois, and H.V. Partelow and Company of Boston, Rushton had to compete with the builders in Peterborough, which was not far from the Rushton factory in Canton, New York. Tom Gordon, Herald and Hutchinson, William English, and James Z. Rogers (who operated the Ontario Canoe Company) were producing superior canoes and exporting them in increasing numbers to the United States.

In the 1880s Rushton moved to meet his Canadian competition head on by adding to his line a 15-foot-by-30-inch "Canadian-model" canoe obviously adapted from those built at Peterborough. There must have been a favorable response, for in his 1891 catalog he announced his "Canadian-model" canoes would now be available in five lengths, from 12 to 16 feet. His explanation to his customers reads as follows: "Believing our Canadian model a superior one for an open canoe for cruising and hunting, we have decided to build it in several lengths. The beam will be nearly the same in all. The construction will be *smooth skin* by our regular methods. Decks and seats as shown..., bent oak stems, ribs spaced 2 inches apart."

The crew of J. Henry Rushton's Canton, New York canoe factory sometime before 1893. Rushton is seated in the front row with papers in his hand. Nelson Brown, his foreman, stands at left in the second row. The Rushton factory was one of the best known in this period when canoeing was the rage.

Will Kip, an associate foreman in Rushton's canoe factory, stands in either a Ugo model or Arkansaw Traveler canoe (it is difficult to tell one from the other at this angle) while boating in company with Old Joe Ellsworth, Rushton's mentor. Old Joe is in a Rushton Princess. They are on the Little River near Canton, New York, about the late 1890s or earlier.

Although the construction of Rushton's Canadian-model canoes differed somewhat from their Peterborough counterparts, they were identical in shape, or nearly so, judging from lines published in Rushton's 1891 catalog. Although these lines are not dimensioned and not large enough to build from easily and accurately, they were skillfully drawn. They may have been the work of the Racine, Wisconsin, naval architect Fred W. Martin, mentioned by Rushton in his so-called *Book of Knowledge* as having drawn lines for him. Whoever the draftsman was, he must have been familiar with Peterborough canoes.

It could not have been long after the appearance of the 1891 catalog that Rushton gave Benjamin Kip, who was working for him at the time as a draftsman, directions for drawing lines for an especially fine canoe. This boat was to be part of the Rushton exhibit at the forthcoming Columbian Exposition, which was scheduled to open in Chicago in 1892 but was delayed until 1893 because of the financial panic of that year. This panic all but ruined Rushton, for he had badly overextended himself financially in preparing an exhibit that would outshine his competitors, both American and Canadian.

After the canoe was built it was discovered that the keel was slightly warped. Rushton rejected it, selling it

to Kip for $10. This was Rushton's first Arkansaw Traveler. When the Kip estate was settled some years ago, the canoe was sold to the Wells family of Massena, New York. Following damage sustained in the second Rushton Memorial Canoe Race at Canton in 1963, Nathaniel Wells restored the canoe completely, and the family now use it and maintain it in tip-top shape. In commenting on this canoe to Atwood Manley, Nat Wells characterized it as "an extremely tippy number, like all Arkansaw Travelers."

How many Arkansaw Travelers were built, and what the demand was for them and for the other Canadian-model paddling canoes—the Ontario, the Igo, and the Ugo—in the difficult period following the Columbian Exposition, when the Canton business was barely able to keep its head above water, is not known. In the 1895 Rushton catalog the Arkansaw Traveler, listed under "Canadian Model Light Paddling Canoes," gets a full page. It was offered in four lengths, from 14 to 17 feet; in one grade, "A"; and four different styles of decking. Illustrations consisted of a profile view of a finished canoe and greatly reduced hull lines. It was described as follows:

These canoes are uniformly 18 inches deep bow and stern, and 10 inches amidships. The planking is ¼ inch

This Arkansaw Traveler, photographed in the Rushton shop prior to 1916, had the "Style C" decking—that is, 3 inches of deck all around, with a slight coaming. (Courtesy the Canton Library)

thick and ribs are spaced about 2½ inches center to center. Gunwales are of the usual width, and the material and workmanship throughout are of the best.

The canoe is a modification of the well known Canadian canoe. It combines to a marked degree, fine lines, ease under paddle, safety, and stiffness. It is somewhat lighter than the Ugo canoe. It rivals the birch bark in weight and speed, and is more staunch, seaworthy and durable.

This is a canoe that requires some care in handling except from expert canoeists. It is not built like a racing shell, but at the same time is fast enough to be in a class with them.

This canoe is ordinarily finished with two thwarts instead of seats, as is shown. Average weights with

Style A decks are from 51 pounds to 65 pounds according to length.

In both the 1903 and 1904 catalogs the four Canadian-model paddling canoes are virtually unchanged, except that the weight of the Arkansaw Traveler is reduced to "40 pounds and upwards, according to size and style of decking," in 1903, and to "45 pounds and upwards" in 1904. In keeping with the changed format of these two catalogs, the hull lines of the Arkansaw Traveler are twice the size of previous representations, making them large enough, but just barely, to scale up to a workable size. This I have done, and the results are presented here. Of course, to

A drawing of the Arkansaw Traveler taken from the 1904 Rushton catalog.

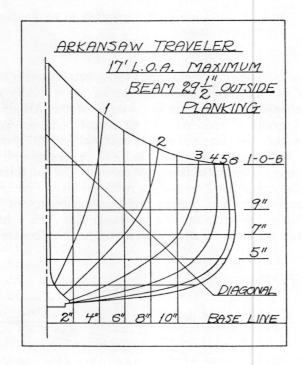

ARKANSAW TRAVELER
17' L.O.A. MAXIMUM
BEAM 29½" OUTSIDE
PLANKING

Scantling dimensions and construction details have been obtained from *Iola,* a Rushton canoe in Mystic Seaport Museum's small-craft collection. *Iola* has been identified as an Arkansaw Traveler, and is so listed in Bray's *Catalogue of Mystic Seaport Museum's Watercraft Collection,* although it was built without thwarts, and its dimensions differ slightly from those of the Arkansaw Traveler in the Rushton catalogs.

Iola is planked lapstrake but finished smooth, as the catalogs specify—a method by which Rushton achieved a superior result. The laps are planed to a feather edge, bedded with thick varnish, and fastened with very small tacks, Adirondack-guideboat fashion. Today, gluing might be easier and even more effective.

At a glance, Rushton's construction is deceptively simple. But a canoe like the Arkansaw Traveler is not put together as easily and as quickly as might appear. A cautious approach and accurate work is indicated on the part of the inexperienced. Rushton's production methods were exactingly contrived for turning out a high-quality product by the quickest and most economical means possible. No allowance was made for false moves, and every shaving counted.

For those who would follow in Rushton's footsteps there are two important sources of information. One is the numerous catalogs he published over nearly a quarter of a century. Unfortunately, very few have survived except for those in the library at the Adirondack Museum and those in the public library at

bring the lines of a 17-foot boat up to working size from a total overall length of 6½ inches is an exacting job involving plenty of opportunity for distortion. But I must say the lines faired out well in enlargement, which indicates they must have been accurately drawn in reduction.

	STATIONS	STEM	1	2	3	4	5	6
HALF-BREADTHS	SHEER	0-0-2	0-4-3	0-8-5	0-11-6	1-0-7	1-1-5	1-2-1
	W.L. 1-0-6	0-0-2	0-3-7	0-8-4	0-11-6	1-0-7	1-1-5	1-2-1
	W.L. 9"	0-0-2	0-3-0	0-7-2	0-11-0	1-1-1	1-2-1	1-2-4
	W.L. 7"	0-0-2	0-2-3	0-6-0	0-10-1	1-0-5	1-2-1	1-2-4
	W.L. 5"	0-0-2	0-1-4	0-4-1	0-8-0	0-11-3	1-1-3	1-1-7
	INSIDE KEEL	—	0-0-4	0-1-2	0-1-5	0-1-6	0-1-6	0-1-6
HEIGHTS ABOVE BASE LINE	SHEER	1-8-6	1-4-5	1-2-0	1-1-0	1-0-6	1-0-5	1-0-5
	INSIDE KEEL	—	0-3-0	0-2-2	0-2-0	0-2-0	0-2-0	0-2-0
	BEARDING AT KEEL	—	0-3-0	0-2-2	0-1-6	0-1-4	0-1-4	0-1-4
	2" BUTTOCK	SHEER 1-6-6	0-6-1	0-2-7	0-1-7	0-1-5	0-1-5	0-1-5
	4" BUTTOCK	SHEER 1-5-0	1-1-3	0-4-7	0-2-6	0-2-1	0-1-7	0-1-6
	6" BUTTOCK	SHEER 1-3-4	—	0-7-0	0-3-6	0-2-5	0-2-1	0-1-7
	8" BUTTOCK	SHEER 1-2-2	—	0-10-7	0-5-0	0-3-1	0-2-4	0-2-2
	10" BUTTOCK	SHEER 1-1-3	—	—	0-6-7	0-4-0	0-3-0	0-2-4
	DIAGONAL	0-0-5	0-5-1	0-9-5	1-0-7	1-3-1	1-4-3	1-4-6

DIAGONAL UP 1'-3" ON CENTER LINE. OUT 6" ON 9" W.L. AND 10" ON 5" W.L. KEEL PLANK ¾" THICK OAK. MEASUREMENTS IN FEET, INCHES, AND EIGHTHS. MEASUREMENTS INSIDE PLANKING. STEM SIDED 1". BOTH ENDS THE SAME. STATIONS 1'-5" APART.

STEM DIMENSIONS 17' ARKANSAW TRAVELER MEASURED TO RABBET. STEAM BENT OAK. MOLDED 1½" SIDED 1" TOP – 1⅛" BOTTOM.

Canton, New York. In 1983, however, William Crowley's *Rushton's Rowboats and Canoes*—a facsimile reprint of the 1903 catalog, supplemented by some fine photographs and related material—was published for the Adirondack Museum by International Marine Publishing Company. The other source is, of course, Manley's *Rushton and His Times in American Canoeing.*

These are the printed sources. I should point out, however, that the surviving Rushton boats themselves are a basic primary source not to be overlooked. Much is to be learned about their construction from direct examination, but much more could be learned if they could be taken apart piece by piece. Until the day when a wrecked survivor turns up, a boat too far gone for restoration and thus a candidate for dissection, we cannot be entirely sure just how some things were done. We don't know, for example, exactly how the Rushton keel rabbet was cut.

The construction process developed in the Rushton shop is taken up in detail in the appendixes of Manley's book. Not everything is explained here, but the great deal that is stands up remarkably well when checked against actual boats and the known building procedures of Rushton's contemporaries.

RABBETED KEEL 17-FOOT ARKANSAW TRAVELER
DISTANCES MEASURED FROM THE FORWARD PERPENDICULAR.
PLANKING ONE-QUARTER INCH THICK. BEVELED 45 DEGREES.

Manley tells us that Rushton's son, J.H. (Harry) Rushton, was still alive when Manley was writing his book. Harry had worked in his father's shop and had carried on the business for a time after the elder Rushton's death. He was thoroughly familiar with the details of the construction process and had a good memory. His account, included in Manley's book, is surprisingly complete and precise after a lapse of some years, although there are several things that should have a fuller explanation. I cannot recommend too strongly a thorough study of Harry Rushton's account, together with an attempt to visualize each step in the building procedure he describes.

Boats like the Arkansaw Traveler—in fact, all of Rushton's lightly planked cedar boats—were planked *bottom up.* The various sectional molds, made from a full-size laydown in the usual way, were attached at the proper heights and distances to what is called a *bed piece.* As far as I can determine from photos and from reading between the lines, this is what we now generally call a *building form,* which consists of a number of pieces instead of a single one.

Apparently this arrangement stood on the floor and supported the molds at a convenient height for working. Another way of supporting the molds during the planking process would be to use a ladder frame, directions for which are to be found in several places elsewhere in this book.

DETAILS—17-FOOT ARKANSAW TRAVELER

FIRST RIB

5/16" COPPER TACKS - 3/16" HEAD

7/8"

5/8" No. 4 W. SCREWS

7/8"

GARBOARD SHOULDERED AGAINST OUTER STEM

17' ARKANSAW TRAVELER
DETAILS FOREFOOT AND END DECKS

INWALE

1/2" No. 4 RD. HD. B.W.S.

STATION 1
17" FROM FR'D PERP.

BAND 1/8" TH'K. ENDS 11/16" WIDER AT
CENTER. FINISH 3/16" ABOVE DECK

DECK CROWNED 1/2" IN ONE FOOT

3/8" BRASS HALF OVAL

5 1/2" R

How many molds were used, how far apart they were set, and just how they were positioned is not stated. For this particular Arkansaw Traveler, the molds could probably be set on the stations given in the lines plan, where they are shown to be 17 inches apart. However, it might be found expedient to change this mold spacing slightly so that the molds come exactly where ribs will be placed.

In that case, as planking proceeds an occasional long, thin, resin-coated nail with a large leather washer under the head can be driven through the planking lap into the mold. A few of these here and there will keep the planking tight against the molds as the planking operation proceeds. Later these nails are pulled, as they have to be when the planked-up "shell" is removed from the building form and turned right side up for ribbing. If the molds are positioned correctly, the holes left by these nails can be covered by the ribs and the holes themselves may be reused for rib fastenings.

This may seem like a lot of trouble, but when clinker planking is laid up over molds, it frequently tends to pull away as the strakes are put on. Unless there is some way to hold the planking tight against the molds until the "shell" is complete, the designed shape will be lost.

What Rushton did to prevent this is not explained. This method of using long, thin nails with large leather washers for easy pulling worked well for me when I built the 27-foot four-oared racing gig *General Lafayette,* which was clinker-planked with ¼-inch white cedar. I recommend the procedure highly.

Most, if not all, of Rushton's rowboats and planked cedar canoes had flat plank keels of ¾-inch thick red oak, and I believe I know why. It was not that white oak was not available. Rather, it was that white oak tends to twist and turn in small sections and to pull out of true. Well-seasoned red oak of good quality is much more stable and dependable in this respect.

I recall old-time boatbuilders referring to white oak as "too strong" for light keels and the like—the fastenings couldn't hold it. As just mentioned, Rushton rejected the first Arkansaw Traveler his firm built because a slight twist developed in the keel. Could it have been made of white oak?

As for lasting, it appears that select, well-cared-for red oak in small sections lasts adequately well, as attested by a good number of surviving Rushton boats. Their red oak keels are still sound after 70, 80, and even 90 years of use.

One thing not explained by Harry Rushton is just how the Rushton plank keel is rabbeted to receive the garboard plank. The tightness of the boat depends upon a good job here, and it is a tricky operation because the plank angle, or deadrise, changes continuously from nearly flat amidships to almost vertical at the ends of the boat.

The Adirondack guideboat avoids a keel rabbet entirely, its bottom being beveled like that of a dory. This allows the garboard to run down by, and its lower edge is planed off flat in line with the rest of the bottom surface. To protect this edge, one adds a thin, narrow, metal shoe.

This construction is feasible for the guideboat with its rather steep angle of deadrise amidships, but not for a boat like the Arkansaw Traveler, which has a flatter bottom and only about 5 degrees of deadrise amidships. The Rangeley Lakes boat has a similar problem. Here a plank keel is rabbeted centrally, but the rabbet dies out toward the ends, and the edge of the garboard is carried down by to be planed off flush with the bottom surface. In this case, however, a shoe is added that covers the bottom and the exposed edges of the garboard.

The Arkansaw Traveler has no shoe and shows a close seam the whole length between the bottom and the garboard plank. How this was done is not shown anywhere. It has been necessary to work out a method, and the one detailed in the accompanying drawing will result in construction that is tight and strong.

The procedure should not be too difficult, although it is admittedly a fussy operation to cut. Whether this is the way Rushton did it remains to be seen. The answer, as mentioned, will have to wait until we can take apart an old Rushton boat.

When the boat is set up for planking, the flat keel is fitted into the recesses cut in the molds to receive it. The keel is then forced down and secured one way or another so that it takes the slight fore-and-aft "rocker," or camber, that is required.

The inner stempieces, beveled to receive the ends of the planking, were first secured to the ends of the keel plank. The outer stempiece covers the ends of the planking, thus making a stem rabbet—or rather the cutting of a stem rabbet—unnecessary. This simplification saves both time and labor.

The same method is used in building the Rangeley Lakes boats and may have been borrowed from Rushton. Although it appears that the Rangeley Lakes boat was derived from New York State prototypes, this did not occur until after Rushton had begun to build using this method.

Harry Rushton states that the stems were steam-bent to shape over a form, two 1-inch strips at a time. One of these served as the inner stem, the other, the outer stem. The Arkansaw Traveler in the collection at Mystic Seaport Museum shows inner and outer stempieces molded ¾ inch rather than 1 inch (although they are sided 1 inch), and these are the dimensions I have given the stempieces for the 17-foot Arkansaw Traveler considered here.

Whether there would be any problem from so-called springback—a slight loss of shape when the bent pieces are removed from the mold—I do not know. If there were, what allowances Rushton might have made remain uncertain, but this is something that has to be taken into consideration.

Now that we have reliable waterproof glues, laminated stems are quite feasible for this boat. Where facilities for steam bending are not readily available, laminated stems might be the way to go. Certainly there would be no problem of springback with laminated stems.

The outer stem is fastened through the inner stem with several flathead wood screws. In this case 1¼-inch number 12 bronze screws would be about right. The addition of glue would greatly strengthen the joint and is recommended.

One of the most difficult operations in building this boat—more difficult than rabbeting the keel plank—is "backing out"—that is, hollowing the inside of the planking where needed so that it fits the sectional curves of the hull. These curves are fairly extreme at the turn of the bilge, in some cases requiring as much as $\frac{5}{16}$ inch of backing or hollowing.

Thus, the planking used here would have to be over ½ inch thick to start with. Furthermore, the hollowing—as well as the corresponding rounding on the outside—must be exact, and must be done prior to fastening the plank in place.

Once the fastenings are in (particularly the tacks through the laps, put in both from the inside and the outside of the boat), no wood can be removed, since the fastenings lie on the surface. If the boat is to be varnished, only light sanding and removal of dents by sponging with hot water may take place after fastening.

The problems faced here, and the order of skill and careful workmanship required, are much the same as for the Adirondack guideboat. For that reason, some might decide to apply cold-molded techniques—or some of the other current forms of glued construction—to this hull form.

As it was, according to Harry Rushton, his father

A sampling of other Rushton canoe models. **Top:** *The Huron paddling canoe, a huskier model than the Arkansaw Traveler.* (Courtesy Canton Library) **Middle:** *A sailing canoe owned by Nathaniel Wells of Massena, New York. S. Paul Rushton (standing) and his brother, Roy M., grandsons of the canoe builder, pose beside the boat at the American Canoe Association's Century Weekend Celebration in Clayton, New York, in 1980.* (Watertown Daily Times *photo*) **Bottom:** *A canvas-covered cedar canoe, the Indian Girl model. This lovely classic was owned in 1982 by Ray Jenkins of Tupper Lake, New York.*

used a thick varnish in the laps that hardened very much like glue. Consequently, the laps sometimes had to be chiseled apart in repairing a boat. Thus, for all intents and purposes this varnish was a glue, although a glue inferior to what is available now.

Getting metal fastenings identical to those used by Rushton is probably not possible now, unless you happen to discover an old stock hidden away in some 19th-century storehouse or attic. This also applies to the extra slim tacks and small sizes of cut copper nails available to Rushton. The nails were used for clinching through the ribs; the tiny tacks went through the edges of the laps when boats were built smooth, as was the Arkansaw Traveler.

The cut nails used for fastening the garboard to the bottom plank are no problem. Annular, or ring, nails of an appropriate size would do very well for this. Small bronze screws (number 4, ⅝-inch) are readily available for plank ends, and very small screws might be substituted for clinch nails in fastening through the laps into the ribs, just as they are in fastening the laps of Adirondack guideboats.

Although the extra slim tacks used through the edges of the laps are no longer produced, the somewhat stouter and readily available 5⁄16-inch copper tacks can be used instead if holes are made through the thin part of the lap to prevent splitting. Harry Rushton says that in the Rushton shop these fine tacks were driven through the white cedar laps without piercing for them beforehand.

For guideboats, however, holes through the thin lap edges were made with a very small pointed awl that was diamond-shaped and sharp on both edges. This was applied so as to cut *across* the fibers of the grain, thus avoiding any splitting. Eventually Lewis Grant replaced this awl with a small, high-speed drill.

When a drill is used, it should go no deeper than the thin side of the lap, leaving the thick side untouched for better holding. There is also no reason why ⅝-inch copper tacks could not be used through the laps into the ribs. This would leave ¹⁄₁₆ inch of the point for clinching. In this case the lap should be bored with a high-speed drill, as would be done in any case before ribbing started.

The ribbing process itself is explained by Harry Rushton. To what extent red, or rock, elm would be available for ribs, I cannot say. But as in the case of the stems, I believe good-quality white oak would be entirely adequate as a substitute.

AN R.J. DOUGLAS CRUISING CANOE

At a time when larger yachts are fast pricing themselves out of reach, the old-time sailing canoe has much to offer the adventurous sailor—as much, or more, in a small package than is to be found in many a larger and more costly yacht. It need not be expensive. It can be built and rigged in the home workshop, and there is an infinite variety, at least potentially, to meet every individual need or desire.

The thrills of racing competition have wide appeal, it is true, and the old sailing canoes are probably best remembered as racing canoes, but their potential for the more relaxed pleasures of cruising should be equally considered. Indeed, indications are that cruising canoes and canoes for afternoon sailing—in other words, canoes that are put to more relaxed and noncompetitive recreational uses—are showing the greater increase in popularity.

New building techniques and new building materials are making it possible for handy but relatively unskilled amateurs to construct designs that heretofore would have required a professional. And not a few, it should be said, find building their canoe as pleasurable and rewarding as sailing it.

The rise of the cedar sailing canoe in America in the final quarter of the 19th century was little short of meteoric, and its decline came with equal suddenness. As we look back across the years, it seems that the glorious days of varnished cedar and white sails had scarcely begun before they were finished.

Before the 1890s were over, the classic cedar canoe had toppled from its pinnacle and was swept aside by the surging competition of newly arrived bicycles, canvas canoes, gas marine engines, and larger yachts, followed by automobiles and a great deal more. But now, nearly 100 years later, interest appears to be turning again to the cedar-planked canoes, if only to a limited extent as yet. Whether a full-fledged revival will come remains to be seen, but here and there an occasional survivor from this bygone era is being restored, and scattered new ones are being built.

For the first 10 years or so after the introduction of canoe sailing into this country from England in about 1870, until the organization of the American Canoe Association and its first meet at Lake George in 1880, cruising canoes predominated. During the 1880s, largely because of ACA influence, canoe racing pushed to the fore. The result was highly specialized racing canoes that did not serve the broader recreational needs of the time. This shortcoming undoubtedly contributed to the decline of planked cedar and basswood canoes. Less costly and more adaptable means for satisfying those recreational needs appeared, notably canvas-covered canoes such as J. Henry Rushton's Indian Girl. It was the Indian Girl, more than anything else, that saved Rushton's business from near bankruptcy during the critical time following the financial panic of 1893.

Today the general-purpose cruising canoe has more appeal than the highly specialized racing canoe. In addition, it is not too difficult for amateur construction. Although opportunities for cruising with sail and paddle are considerably fewer than they were 100 years ago, there are still extensive waterways for the cruising canoe that are relatively uncrowded and uncontaminated. Puget Sound and much of the Great Lakes still offer spectacular opportunities for this type of boating.

In the fall of 1980 three men rowed a 17-foot Swampscott dory the more than 200 miles around Long Island. They took their time, stopping along the way to eat and sleep, and enjoyed themselves immensely—just the sort of cruise for which the right kind of sailing canoe is eminently suited. Such a canoe would also be suitable for an afternoon spin, an overnight trip, a weekend excursion, or perhaps even an extended voyage such as the one S. R. Stoddard completed in 1885 when he sailed his canoe, the *Atlantis,* from Glens Falls in upstate New York to the upper reaches of the Bay of Fundy. A news clipping that appeared while Stoddard was en route gives the flavor of this adventure:

AN ADVENTUROUS CRUISE—Mr. S.R. Stoddard of Glens Falls has begun his 2,000-mile trip in his canoe, the Atlantis. He left Glens Falls on

S.R. Stoddard's canoe, the Atlantis, *is shown at Delaney's Farm on Grindstone Island in the St. Lawrence River, circa 1884.*

LOTUS

AIR CHAMBER   WATER TIGHT STOWAGE   HATCH   HANDY STOWAGE   AIR CHAMBER

0 1 2 3 4 5 6 7 8 9 10 11 12 13 14

KITCHIN

0   5   10   15

Four cedar-planked canoes from the 1887 R.J. Douglas catalog. The Lotus, 14 feet by 28 inches, is a much lighter canoe than Our Cruiser and was designed more for a paddler than a sailer. Kitchin, 15 feet by 26 inches with a depth of 8 inches and a weight of 50 pounds, was designed for A.W. Kitchin of Chicago, who won many paddling races with her in 1886. The Georgia D. is 15 feet by 31½ inches, with a depth amidships of 10 inches and a weight of 70 pounds. She was the largest size stocked by the R.J. Douglas Company. Note the small centerboard just forward of the rudder.

Tuesday, the 7th inst., and arrived in New York—at the Knickerbocker Club boathouse—Friday evening last. He will sail along the north shore of Long Island Sound to New Bedford, across Buzzards Bay to Woods Hole, through the Vineyard and Nantucket sounds to Chatham Roads, around Cape Cod, across to Plymouth, along the coast to Boston and north to St. John, across the Bay of Fundy to Arcadia, up the basin and river of Minas to Truro, up the Gulf of St. Lawrence to Montreal, through Lake Champlain and thence home. The canoe was built under the instructions of Mr. Stoddard, himself. It is 18 feet long, 3 feet wide, 18 inches deep, draws 8 inches of water, and carries two sails of a pattern of the owner's invention. Mr. Stoddard, though having no fears of his safety, is alive to the fact that his course will encounter the dangers of Point Judith, the long stretch of coast at Cape Cod, with the sweep of the Atlantic, the Bay of Fundy fogs and high tides, and the Gulf of St. Lawrence. He will be accompanied by Professor Charles Oblenis, who joined him at Albany on the trip down.

GEORGIA D.

OUR CRUISER

Stoddard's *Atlantis* was somewhat larger than many of that period's canoes, as would be necessary to carry two travelers safely and with some degree of comfort on a long voyage across wide stretches of open ocean. The lines of Stoddard's canoe, built for him by Fletcher Joyner, former Adirondack guide and one of the leading canoe builders of his time, have not survived. This is unfortunately the case with many notable early canoes.

Nevertheless, considerable design data for these craft have survived, and await reclamation for use by today's builders. The best sources, of course, are the handful of sailing canoes from that period that still exist in museums and in the hands of private owners. As yet, however, the lines and details from most of these canoes have not been taken off, and to do so would present a lengthy, tedious, and exacting job at

best. Much work needs to be done to put this material in shape for builders to use.

There are a limited number of published plans, notably those by W.P. Stephens and the English designer Dixon Kemp. There is another source, which I have drawn upon here: the published lines and building information found in some of the catalogs of contemporary boatbuilding concerns.

The 14-foot cruising canoe presented here is one of four cedar-planked canoes offered in the 1887 catalog of R.J. Douglas and Company, Waukegan, Illinois. Three are sailing canoes; the fourth is a fast paddling canoe built for racing. Lines for the four canoes are reproduced in the catalog.

Although these lines are incomplete as given and much reduced in size, it is possible to supply what is missing and to enlarge them to a workable size, which

The sail plan for Our Cruiser shows a simple lateen ketch rig. The fanlike centerboard poses a challenge for anyone attempting to build her today.

is what I have done with the 14-footer, named Our Cruiser. According to the Douglas catalog, "This canoe is designed to meet the wants of those desiring a good staunch 'all around' canoe, and we think it is destined to become a very popular model." Consequently, I have selected this one as having the widest appeal for amateur construction.

At the time this catalog was issued, the Douglas Company was certainly one of the largest builders of boats and canoes in this country. It also built all manner of pleasure craft for sail and steam up to 40 feet or thereabouts. Its 1887 catalog, which runs nearly 70 pages, is replete with illustrations, and its abundant commentary makes interesting and informative reading.

In 1888 Merwin, Hulbert and Company of New York City, billing itself as "Manufacturers of Fire-Arms and Ammunition and dealers in a most complete line of High-Grade Sporting and Athletic Goods," brought out a large, 56-page catalog devoted in great part to boats manufactured by Douglas. The following statement appears on the inside cover:

To The Boat Loving Public: Being the General Eastern Agents of R.J. Douglas Co., Waukegan, Illinois (probably the largest boatbuilding concern in this country, and who, in all probability turn out twice

as many craft as any concern in the world, being fully equipped with the best machinery, staff of boatbuilders, experts and superintendents), we are able to make the prices found in the following pages....We carry, as far as our rooms will permit, a complete line of their goods. We have on sample at our salesrooms (26 West 23rd St.) a line of rowboats in the cheap, medium, and highest grades, canoes both sailing and paddling, shells and sail boats....We guarantee prompt delivery on rowboats and canoes; steam launches, sailboats, barges and shells are generally built to order.

Some idea of the amount of building carried on by R.J. Douglas and Company, as well as something of the firm's operating philosophy, may be gleaned from the remarks addressed "To The Boating Public" at the beginning of its 1887 catalog:

We are constantly securing the most expert men in the line of designers, draughtsmen, builders and finishers from all parts of the United States and Canada. We never "lay off" our builders in the fall, but pile up the stock, and at this writing have in stock 300 boats ranging from a 40 foot steam launch to a 10-pound canoe. We do not aim to make a cheap boat, i.e. without profit, nor put the price so low we have to

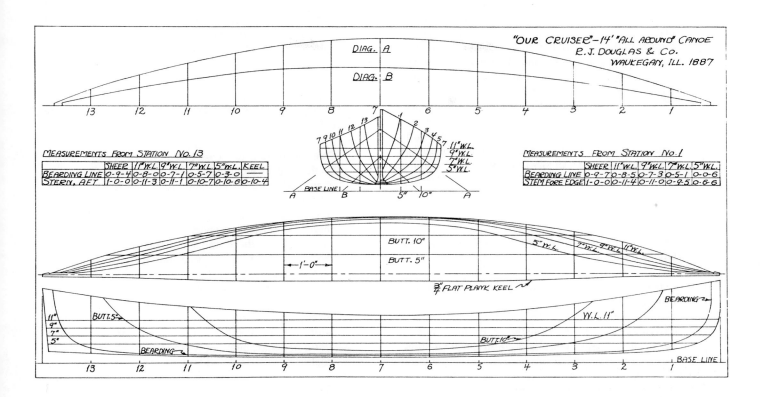

"OUR CRUISER" – 14' "ALL AROUND" CANOE
R.J. DOUGLAS & Co.
WAUKEGAN, ILL. 1887

DIAG. A
DIAG. B

MEASUREMENTS FROM STATION No. 13

	SHEER	11"W.L.	9"W.L.	7"W.L.	5"W.L.	KEEL
BEARDING LINE	0-9-4	0-8-0	0-7-1	0-5-7	0-3-0	—
STERN, AFT	1-0-0	0-11-3	0-11-1	0-10-7	0-10-6	0-10-4

MEASUREMENTS FROM STATION No. 1

	SHEER	11"W.L.	9"W.L.	7"W.L.	5"W.L.
BEARDING LINE	0-9-7	0-8-5	0-7-3	0-5-1	0-0-6
STEM FORE EDGE	1-0-0	0-11-4	0-11-0	0-9-5	0-6-6

BUTT. 10"
BUTT. 5"
3/4 FLAT PLANK KEEL
BASE LINE
BEARDING
W.L. 11"
BUTT. 10"
BUTT. 5"

"OUR CRUISER", 14' CEDAR CANOE. R.J. DOUGLAS & Co, WAUKEGAN, ILL. 1887

	STATIONS	STEM	1	2	3	4	5	7	9	10	11	12	13	STERN
HEIGHTS	SHEER	1-8-4	1-6-6	1-4-6	1-3-0	1-1-4	1-0-5	1-0-0	1-0-6	1-1-4	1-2-2	1-3-4	1-5-2	1-6-5
	BEARDING L.	—	0-4-4	0-2-6	0-2-4	0-2-1	0-2-0	0-1-6	0-1-6	0-1-7	0-2-0	0-2-3	0-4-0	—
	OUTER KEEL	—	0-3-1	0-2-3	0-2-1	0-1-6	0-1-5	0-1-3	0-1-3	0-1-4	0-1-5	0-2-0	0-2-4	0-3-0
	BUTT. 5"	—	—	0-8-6	0-5-1	0-3-4	0-2-4	0-2-0	0-2-1	0-2-5	0-4-4	0-8-4	—	—
	BUTT. 10"	—	—	—	1-0-0	0-6-3	0-4-1	0-3-0	0-3-6	0-6-1	—	—	—	—
HALF-BREADTHS	SHEER	0-0-4	0-4-7	0-8-1	0-11-0	1-0-6	1-2-0	1-2-6	1-1-4	1-0-0	0-10-0	0-7-2	0-4-0	0-0-4
	W.L. 11"	0-0-4	0-3-0	0-6-3	0-9-6	1-0-2	1-1-6	1-2-6	1-1-3	0-11-5	0-9-1	0-6-2	0-2-7	0-0-4
	W.L. 9"	0-0-4	0-2-2	0-5-1	0-8-6	0-11-4	1-1-4	1-2-5	1-1-0	0-11-1	0-8-3	0-5-3	0-2-3	0-0-4
	W.L. 7"	0-0-4	0-1-4	0-3-6	0-7-1	0-10-3	1-0-6	1-2-1	1-0-3	0-10-3	0-7-2	0-4-1	0-1-5	0-0-4
	W.L. 5"	0-0-4	0-0-6	0-2-2	0-4-6	0-8-1	0-11-1	1-1-1	0-11-3	0-8-7	0-5-3	0-2-7	0-1-0	0-0-4
	FLAT KEEL	0-0-4	0-0-4	0-0-7	0-1-2	0-1-5	0-1-6	0-1-6	0-1-6	0-1-5	0-1-2	0-0-7	0-0-4	0-0-4
	DIAGONAL A	0-0-5	0-4-3	0-8-0	0-11-1	1-1-5	1-3-6	1-5-1	1-3-3	1-1-3	0-10-6	0-7-7	0-4-2	0-0-5
	DIAGONAL B	0-0-5	0-2-0	0-4-2	0-6-1	0-7-5	0-8-6	0-9-5	0-9-3	0-8-3	0-6-4	0-4-5	0-2-3	0-0-5

MEASUREMENTS TO INSIDE OF PLANKING AT THE BEARDING OF STEM, STERN, POST & KEEL IN FEET, INCHES, EIGHTHS. DIAGONAL "A" 1'-4" ABOVE BASE LINE, OUT 1'-9½" ON BASE LINE. DIAGONAL "B" 9" ABOVE BASE LINE, OUT 9½" ON THE BASE LINE.

slight the work, but we do claim that building the number we do, and buying such quantities of materials, we can afford to do the same class of work for less money than others doing business. For instance, the cheap hunting boats; the men building them work on the same boats the year round, and material is gotten out in the mill in lots of 25 to 50 at a time. Again on "Lakeside," we build in lots of 25 to 50 before changing to other styles.

In canoes, while we do not illustrate a great variety of models, we do try to give a general idea of our most popular ones, and will say that for model, workmanship, and material, we challenge any builder in the world to produce finer.

More as to the extent and volume of Douglas's business:

Our nails and white lead are bought by the ton; our iron by the car. Our wood work, as far as it can be done, is gotten out by machinery. Our pattern work, designing of all kinds, draughting, casting, finishing, and iron and brass work is done in our own shop.... The fact that hundreds of our boats go to the Pacific Coast is alone evidence that we are building lower than others, quality considered, else they could not afford to pay freight for such a distance.

R.J. Douglas and Company used three planking methods for its various craft—clinker, carvel, and "ribband-carvel," the latter generally known today as batten-seam construction. Whereas some of the Canadian canoes built at Peterborough were planked ribband-carvel, Douglas canoes seem to have been planked clinker, like most canoes from the leading contemporary American builders such as Rushton, Joyner, and Ruggles. The clinker work carried out in the Douglas shop is described in part as follows:

We use machinery as far as it can be utilized, but this can only be done to a limited extent on clinker work, as all planks must be gotten out by hand, no two on a side being alike either in shape or bevel....Our hulls are all planked up to the wales before a rib is placed in them, and it is frequently the case that a boat is taken off the stocks in this shape (when some order comes in that is more urgent) and laid aside to be ribbed at our leisure. We merely mention this to show that a boat must be built to shape and not sprung, or it could not retain its shape. The consequence is, the planks have no strain on them, and the frame is put in only for strength, and can then therefore be much lighter than has been the

custom in years gone by....In this era of fine boats and good workmanship, no builder would have workmen in his employ who depend on the old way of springing planks into place, or of using white lead to make tight joints.

In the section of the catalog dealing with canoes is the following introductory statement:

We illustrate a few canoes herein, of styles that we shall keep in stock, and have aimed to combine as many "all around" good qualities in as few models as possible. On the other hand, we are prepared to build any and everything in the canoe line on short notice, and will furnish designs or build from drawings furnished by others, and we challenge comparison in workmanship with any other builder in America....

All of the material that goes into a canoe is of the finest quality, very carefully selected, and is as follows: i.e. Stems and sternpost, hackmatack or mahogany, ribs white oak, planking the finest of clear white cedar, all full length strakes, carlins of white wood or cedar, decks of Spanish cedar or mahogany, backrests, rudder and tiller, etc., of mahogany, coaming, partners, wales, etc., also of mahogany or Spanish cedar.

All of our canoes illustrated herein are fastened with copper nails and burrs and riveted, and right here let us say that all work as light as ¼ inch should be fastened in this manner, since when the planks are beveled the edges are very thin, and a clinched nail is driven back halfway through this thin edge, in order to draw it tight, and is thus very liable to draw through and make a short-lived boat, while, on the other hand, a burr on the inside, well riveted, makes a thin, light boat as little liable to spring apart as one much heavier fastened with clinched nails.

It takes much more time to fasten a boat in this manner, but it is the only perfect way on very light work and would invariably be adopted for this class of work were it not for the extra expense attending it.

In conclusion, we will refer our readers to the official account of the meet of the W.C.A. (Western Canoe Association) at Ballast Island last year (see "Forest and Stream," Aug. 12, 1886), and they can be the judges as to whether we got our share of the prizes....In a report of the meet published in the Cincinnati "Commercial Gazette," the writer says: "The best paddling canoes were 40 pounds weight and built by R.J. Douglas & Co., Waukegan, Illinois. They were beauties and glided through the water without a ripple. The best setting sails were a pair of sprits on R.P. McCune's "Pretzel" Tippecanoe, measuring together about 120 feet, the largest amount of sail carried by any canoe at the meet." The above-mentioned sails were also made by us, and the same maker makes all of our canoe sails now.

Beyond what has been quoted, there is no additional building information that might apply to the construction of Our Cruiser. I suggest, however, that a serviceable hull could be built to the lines set forth here by the same methods, and with the use of the same scantlings, that we described for the Arkansaw Traveler.

Although Douglas has insisted, with some justification, that riveted fastenings are superior, Rushton's clinched tacks and small, cut copper nails have stood the tests of use and time and would be quicker and easier. But because small, cut copper nails for clinching are not now available, necessity dictates rivets. Not so for the small tacks used by Rushton on thin laps, and in this case I would definitely follow his practice.

The stem and sternpost for Our Cruiser had best be natural knee bends of hackmatack, if available. If not, properly made glued laminations could be substituted. The stem might be steam-bent oak, like that of the Arkansaw Traveler, although the molded width required by Our Cruiser is much greater. Obviously, the sternpost could not be steam-bent.

The same oak bottom board or keel used in the Arkansaw Traveler, made to the same dimensions and rabbeted in the same way, may be used in Our Cruiser. One thing presents a bit of a problem: Radix centerboards are no longer manufactured, and such a canoe as this really requires a folding centerboard of some sort. I expect, however, that as demand builds up someone will start making them again. In the meantime, I am sure the resourceful builder will be able to improvise a substitute.

A 13-FOOT ENGLISH CRUISING CANOE OF 1883

The career of the classic wooden sailing canoes in this country was spectacular but brief. They dominated the American boating scene for barely 20 years before plummeting from view. This period began about 1870 with William L. Alden's *Violetta.* Modeled on the *Nautilus,* which was designed in England by Warrington Baden-Powell, vice-commodore of the Royal Canoe Club, it was built for cruising the coastal waters surrounding Long Island by Everson of Williamsburg, New York. The peak was reached at the International Meet at Grindstone Island in the Saint Lawrence in the summer of 1886, when American sailing canoes soundly trounced their British rivals in the racing events. And before 1900 it was all over.

But during this relatively brief period a great deal of experimentation with hull shapes and sailing rigs went on, knowledge of the results of which could prove of great assistance to present-day canoeists. The two outstanding published sources are W.P. Stephens's *Canoe and Boat Building for Amateurs,* with its 50 plates of working drawings of lines, construction, and rigs, and the voluminous works and numerous editions of the British naval architect and yacht designer Dixon Kemp. The amount of detail recorded by Kemp is prodigious. Another rich source that will repay some patient digging is the back files of *Forest and Stream.* All of these sources are long out of print and scarce, but are to be found in most large research libraries.

There are other contemporary sources, less well known, such as the British sporting publication *The Field.* In 1883 *The Field* printed an account by C. Penrose of a 13-foot cruising canoe built by R.J. Turk, professional builder of boats, punts, and canoes, in his shop on the upper Thames at Kingston, a London suburb. The cruising canoe was then at the peak of its popularity in Great Britain and North America.

The British had first made it popular when John MacGregor toured the waterways of Europe in 1865 in his first Rob Roy. This canoe served not only as his trusty conveyance but as his kitchen and bedroom as well, despite its diminutive dimensions—LOA 14 feet, beam 25 inches, and depth amidships 11 inches. His published account fired the popular imagination, and four more Rob Roys followed, along with cruises in the Baltic and the Holy Land. The Royal Canoe Club of London dates from 1866, and the New York Canoe Club, modeled on it, was founded in 1871.

Famous contemporary cruising canoes included Baden-Powell's *Nautilus* and W.P. Stephens's *Jersey Blue.* Rushton built his first Rob Roy in 1876, and continued to supply a widespread demand for them into the 1880s.

Later on, shortly before sailing canoes in general were to suffer a decline, canoe racing was to overshadow cruising. But in 1883 canoe cruising still

The "cruising and racing" sail plan of the Nautilus *as drawn by British naval architect Dixon Kemp for the 1886 edition of his* Manual of Yacht and Boat Sailing. *Her "travelling" sail plan featured a high-peaked, almost triangular mainsail that set on a short mast and could be stowed snugly and easily for paddling.*

held first place in popular interest and dominated boating sport.

The account in *The Field,* December 22, 1883, of the Kingston canoe launched and sailed in that year is reproduced here.

The following is a description of a cruising canoe which has been recently built by Mr. Turk of Kingston, for a member of the R.C.C., and is intended to combine, as far as possible, good cruising qualities with those demanded by the peculiar and somewhat unsatisfactory conditions of up-river sailing. She is the third canoe of an experimental series constructed in hopes of attaining these qualities; and it may be well, before proceeding to her description, to give some account of the objects aimed at.

The foremost requisite of a cruising canoe is that she should be capable of being carried easily by two men, without the necessity of dismantling, i.e., removal of gear, centerboards, etc. She should be capable of being carried to the water from the boathouse and launched at once without a lot of preparation. She must paddle fast and easily in a calm, sail well to windward and otherwise, and be dry and safe in broken water. She should have sufficient stability and size to render moving about on board, sleeping, and cooking &c., as safe, easy, and comfortable as possible, and finally, be well and simply fitted and rigged.

After a prolonged trial of several canoes built to the R.C.C. first class, these were condemned as insufficiently portable and generally too unhandy, and it was determined to experiment with a smaller and lighter craft.

With this view, a canoe was built in 1881 with a beam of 2 feet 6 inches and a length of 16 feet. The beam was thus limited, partly to assist in the reduction of weight, and partly to keep within the R.C.C. second class, in case any racing for that class should be instituted.

She was a great improvement on the first class boats in portability and in paddling, was fast under sail in anything like a true breeze, and remarkably dry and comfortable in rough water, very greatly surpassing the R.C.C. first class craft in this last respect. She was, however, hardly light enough for two men to portage. Weighing 120 pounds without her sails, or ballast, she could not sail her best at the weight of 150 pounds allowed by the R.C.C. second class; while the length which made her so good a sea boat also made her a trifle slow in the stays, which, though unimportant for below-bridge sailing, was found a fatal obstacle in the light, baffling airs of Kingston Reach.

In the following year a second canoe was built, in which the length was reduced to 14 feet and the beam to 2 feet 3 inches. She proved an entire success for paddling—so much so, that she was frequently launched for that purpose alone, and could be carried, with centerboard and gear complete, by two men, or even boys.

Her weight without centerboard, sails or gear, was 60 pounds. She performed very satisfactorily under sail, with the help of from 20 pounds to 40 pounds of ballast, when no luggage was carried; but her proportional length appeared to be too great for so light a boat to stay very rapidly or certainly without a steady breeze.

She was also inconveniently crank for cruising, as it required some steadiness to stand in her when light, and to move about on board.

The design (under consideration) has the beam of the first of these canoes, namely 2 feet 6 inches, which

13-FOOT CRUISING CANOE CIRCA 1883
P.T. TURK, KINGSTON, SURREY, ENGLAND
ADAPTED FOR COLD MOLDING. J.G. 1977

1 INNER STEM. BEVELED FOR PLANKING. 3/4" OUTER FACE. OAK, FIR, MAHOG'Y.
2 OUTER STEM COVERS PLANK ENDS AFTER PLANKING. 1/4" TAPERED.
3 FOUR #14-3" BR'N WOOD SCREWS. OUTER & INNER STEMS GLUED.
4 INSIDE BOTTOM STRIP 1/2 × 2 1/2 × 3/4 AT ENDS. OAK, FIR, MAHOGANY.
5 OUTSIDE BOTTOM STRIP 1/2 × 1 1/2 × 3/4 AT ENDS. OAK, FIR MAHOGANY.
6 BACKING PIECE EITHER END 18" × 3" × 1/2. BEVELED TO FIT.
7 PLANKING 2 LAYERS 1/8 CEDAR STRIPS. INNER LAYER RUNS THWARTSHIPS FROM INWALE TO INWALE. OUTER LAYER LENGTHWISE. GLUE BETWEEN.
8 DECK 1/8 AIRCRAFT BIRCH OR MAHOGANY PLYWOOD.
9 DECK BEAMS LAMINATED SPRUCE. SIDED 3/8, MOLDED 3/4".
10 INSIDE FORE-AND-AFT FULL-LENGTH STRINGERS 1/8 × 1/2 FIR MAHOGANY.
11 5/8 BRASS HALF-ROUND LEADING EDGE STEM & BACK 6" ON BOTTOM.

STATION 1
STA. 1
6 1/2" W.L.
2 1/4"
3' 6" 9"

OFFSETS—FEET, INCHES, EIGHTHS TO INSIDE OF PLANK & OUTER FACE INSIDE BOTTOM STRIP

DIAG. A 15" ABOVE BASE LINE. OUT 14 1/2 OR W.L. 6 1/2. DIAG. B UP 15, OUT 14" ON B.L. DIAG. C UP 12, OUT 9" ON BASE LINE.

DIAG. A
DIAG. B
DIAG. C

W.L. 3 1/2"
W.L. 1 1/2"
W.L. 6 1/2"
W.L. 9"
BOTTOM STRIP
B.L.

1' - 1"
3" 6" 9"

is found ample for comfort when cruising. Length is reduced to 13 feet, but as the stem and stern are upright, the reduction is more apparent than real. Her weight is 86 pounds, and as all the gear is the same as in the 2 foot 3 inches canoe, she is just 26 pounds heavier when complete. This weight was experimentally found to be light enough for portage by placing two 14 pound shot bags in the 60 pound canoe, which, with this addition, was still quite light enough to be carried with ease. Her remaining weights are as follows: centerboard, $\frac{3}{16}$ inch galvanized iron, 8 pounds; sails and paddle, 12 pounds; miscellaneous, 4 pounds; add weight of hull, 86 pounds—total 110 pounds. (The first-class canoes weigh about 170 pounds to 200 pounds; centerboard, 60 pounds; ballast, 70 pounds to 150 pounds.) With moderate-sized sails she will stand up very well with this weight; but when sailed without luggage, is all the better for 40 pounds of lead in shot bags, which bring up the total weight to 150 pounds, being the maximum allowed by the R.C.C. second class.

Only two canoes have hitherto been described in "The Field," and, as far as the writer is aware, only two have been built, in which the same objects have been aimed at; namely Mr. Baden-Powell's design for a cruising canoe...and the design of the American Jersey Blue from which a canoe has recently been built by Mr. Turk for a member of the R.C.C. Both of these canoes, though otherwise successful, have turned out rather heavy, and probably would have some difficulty in bringing themselves within the 150 pound limit for sailing. The present design differs from each of these, both in outline and fittings. It will be observed that the greatest possible amount of floor is given, extending in nearly a dead flat to three-fifths of the canoe's beam, and about the same proportion of her length. The depth is reduced to nearly 6 inches below the maximum which could be taken under the rule, in order to avoid being topheavy when lightly laden. This allows a great rounding of deck, which has accordingly been taken advantage of. The ends flare out well above water, and, together with the sheer, should help to keep her dry.

A somewhat unusual amount of rocker has been taken, which, with the short length of the craft, makes her stay with the quickness required for up-river sailing. Being rockered chiefly at the ends, and hardly at all in the middle 5 feet of her length, it does not greatly, if at all, detract from her speed. The lines are slightly fuller aft than forward, which is found to prevent any tendency in the bow to run under water.

Her construction originally was conventional, as noted in the *Field* account:

The planking is clinch-work [lapstrake], this having proved immensely stronger than the ribband carvel though not quite so pretty looking. Throughout the middle body, where the planks run nearly parallel with the keel, the "lands" [laps] are left full strength, as they offer little resistance to the boat's passage through the water, but greatly strengthen her, and perhaps add a trifle to initial stability, while at the ends they are fined down to nothing....The planking material is ¼ inch cedar with oak timbers; the keel is pine, the thickness required by the centerboard rendering a keel of this material sufficiently strong. Pine is also used for the deck carlines, on account of its lightness.

The timbers are ⅜ inch molded; ¾ inch sided, reduced at the head; spaced 13 inches with floor timbers between each throughout the middle of the boat. This gives sufficient strength to the boat to stand the strain of sleeping on board when hauled up, if ordinary care be taken to support the bilges. It is generally preferable, however, to let the boat lie afloat for sleeping, and she will be found to possess abundant stability for this purpose.

To build such a boat as this to the delicate scantlings of her original construction would tax the skill of many professionals, not to mention amateurs. Besides, the materials required are not easily found today.

On the other hand, the hull shape is well suited to cold-molding techniques. The materials required by these techniques are not hard to get, and the skills called for are not beyond the reach of the capable amateur possessing ordinary woodworking experience. And the well-built cold-molded hull will be just as strong and light as the original "clinch-work," if not more so.

If modern readers, indoctrinated perhaps by Coast Guard propaganda, should be inclined to doubt the capabilities of a canoe of these dimensions, let them consider this. In December of 1879 the London *Times* printed an account of a canoe built under the supervision of John MacGregor for a Tasmanian missionary. This canoe was 12 feet long with a 28-inch beam and a depth of 12 inches amidships; it weighed 79 pounds. "In addition to being fitted for a yacht at sea," the *Times* reported, "the canoe has been adapted to become a home on shore, locker, waterproof cabin, and patent cooking stove being provided." Thus contrived and outfitted, she carried her missionary owner "300 miles around the ironbound north and east coast of Tasmania," in safety, convenience, and some degree of comfort.

7

Down East Workboat

The 18-foot outboard-powered workboat offered here is similar to a well-known type developed and used in eastern Maine. Formerly, boats like this one were built of wood in local boatshops along the coast of Washington County from Jonesport to Eastport, and to a lesser extent by the local fishermen for their own use.

The hull shape derives from the so-called double-wedge model and is basically the same as that of early inboard-motor speedboats at the beginning of this century. The high bow and sharp entrance form something like a wedge turned up on edge, and the stern resembles another wedge rotated a quarter of a turn to lie flat.

Both the Canadian Cape Island lobsterboat and the early Jonesport lobsterboat have the double-wedge hull, which combines good seakeeping ability with speed. If this 18-foot boat were doubled in size without alteration of its lines or proportions, and if a solid deadwood, a sternpost, and a rudder were added, the result would be a classic Maine lobsterboat. There can be little doubt that the first outboard boats like this one were turned out by shops experienced in producing larger, wooden, inboard-powered lobsterboats. The resemblance is too close to be accidental.

In the summer of 1981 a Washington County reader of the *National Fisherman* asked if lines and details for building such outboard boats might be available somewhere. He had seen some of the older wooden boats of this type and liked them very much, but the local shops had stopped building them in favor of fiberglass. This reader wondered if the 18-footer's lines had ever been recorded, though he doubted that the local builders had worked from drawings.

I replied that although I did not have any such plans and did not know of any, I was not unfamiliar with the

Photographs and measurements of this old wooden craft were the basis of the plans presented in this chapter. Note her wedge-shaped bow, her foredeck, and the stout, well-braced transom cut down for an outboard motor. She is typical of the 18-foot workboats that originated in Washington County, Maine.

type. I also told him that if he could find a representative example to photograph and measure for some basic dimensions, and if he would send these measurements and a set of prints to me, I would work out lines and construction details. He complied, and so did I. The results are presented in this chapter.

Lines are given to the *inside* of the planking so that the molds can be made directly from them without having to deduct the plank thickness. Practically without exception, these boats were planked carvel, or smooth, yet there is no reason they couldn't be planked clinker, or lapstrake. In fact, this latter method has

certain constructional advantages that might commend it to some builders.

For a one-off carvel job, the boat should probably be set right side up. First, the "backbone" assembly of stem, keel, keel batten, and transom is positioned on the stocks, which are made high enough to give comfortable access to the bottom during planking. Next, the solid floors, correctly shaped from the full-size laydown of lines, are installed, and the molds are secured in place at their respective stations.

Ribbands are then run fore and aft on the outside of the molds from stem to transom on approximately the same lines that the planking will follow. These are temporarily fastened to molds with long wood screws and washers. The ribbands must be stout enough to support the steam-bent frames without giving when the frames are forced against them, and they should be spaced closely enough to allow the frames to take a fair bend, but no closer.

After this has been done, the boat is ready to plank. As the planking goes on, the ribbands are removed, one by one.

If many of these boats were to be built as stock items, it might be easier and faster to plank them upside down on a form—provided, of course, that there is a means for lifting the hull off the building form and righting it after planking is completed.

In building the planking form, the molds are cut down by an amount equal to the thickness of the ribbands plus the thickness of the frames. The ribbands are fastened to the molds, and the locations of the frames are marked on them. In framing out, as this is called, the hot frames taken from the steam box are bent around the *outside* of the ribbands and clamped to them until they have cooled and permanently taken the correct shape. The plank is fitted most efficiently while the hull is in a bottom-up position.

When it is time to lift the completed hull off the building form prior to turning it over, some provision must be made for collapsing the after molds sufficiently to clear the "tumblehome" at the stern. This generally can be done by making the after molds in two sections, which are held in place by easily removable screws.

Not only is it much easier to fit and fasten the plank when the hull is bottom up, but it is also easier to plane, smooth, and caulk the planked hull when it is in this position. But hulls that are at all large and heavy are not lifted and turned over easily and safely except with equipment and manpower not always available in small boatshops or one-man, backyard operations.

If this boat is to be planked clinker, the planks should be ½ inch thick instead of the ⅝ inch specified for the carvel hull. If one man is to do the job unassisted, it would be best to set the boat right side up. In this position he can, without help, rivet the lap fastenings as each strake goes on by holding on against the head of the rivet on the outside and peening it on the inside in one operation.

When a boat is built in this way, it is recommended that as the strakes go on they be temporarily secured to the molds. Ideal for this are long, thin, resin-coated nails that hold well in soft wood; thick leather washers

about ½ inch in diameter are placed under the heads. When these nails are driven in solidly, the washers apply firm pressure to the plank without marring it. When the time comes to draw the nails and remove the mold, the washers provide enough thickness to afford a good grip for the tongs or nail puller. The holes that are left can be used for fastening into the bent frames that replace the building molds.

When a clinker hull is planked bottom up, it is not necessary to rivet each lap separately as the planks are put on, provided the planks are accurately shaped and fitted and are temporarily nailed to the molds as just described. The lap nails are driven as planking proceeds, but no riveting need be done until all the planking is on and the boat has been turned over. Then one job can be made of it. This is the way planking is commonly done in the British Isles, and it certainly is the quickest and easiest way to accomplish what is at best a tedious operation. An assistant will be required to hold on against the heads of the nails on the outside of the hull.

A few words of warning: Nails or rivets driven through the laps should be bored for in advance. Holes must be exactly the right size, which can be determined beforehand by boring test holes in pieces of scrap wood at the bench. Lap nails should fit snugly.

Holes should be small enough so that the nail retains enough drawing power to pull the lap tight and hold it until it is riveted, but not so small as to run the slightest risk of splitting the lap. Holes may be drilled, or a brad awl of the right size may be used.

The end of the awl is beveled square across like a chisel and is applied *across* the run of the grain to sever its fibers. Meanwhile, the palm of the hand is used to apply pressure to the awl as it is briskly rotated from side to side. A quick, clean hole with no risk of splitting is the result. The knack is readily acquired, and for operations like this it is just as effective as drilling, if not more so.

The brad awl is one of those simple but truly effective, time-honored tools that for one reason or another have gone out of fashion. Unfortunately, those tools that have replaced them are generally more complicated and often less effective.

If riveting is to be delayed until the boat is turned over, it is of utmost importance that strakes be gotten out to the correct shape so that they do not have to be sprung edgewise for the laps to fit. Springing, or edge-setting, planks in this way is almost certain to cause

OUTBOARD WORKBOAT
18' LOA · 6'-4" BEAM · 2'-5" INSIDE DEPTH ADMIDSHIPS
EASTERN MAINE – PASSAMAQUODDY BAY

		STEM	STA. 1	STA. 2	STA. 3	STA. 4	STA. 5	STA. 6	STA. 7	TRAN.
HALF-BREADTHS	SHEER	0-0-4	0-11-7	2-2-0	2-9-6	3-1-2	3-0-6	2-9-2	2-4-6	2-1-6
	30" W.L.	0-0-4	0-8-4	1-11-7	2-8-6	3-1-1	3-0-7	2-9-5	2-5-1	2-1-7
	24" W.L.	0-0-4	0-6-7	1-10-0	2-7-1	3-0-3	3-0-6	2-10-2	2-6-2	2-3-2
	18" W.L.	0-0-4	0-5-1	1-7-5	2-4-5	2-10-4	2-11-6	2-9-6	2-7-0	2-4-2
	12" W.L.	0-0-4	0-2-7	1-3-0	1-11-5	2-5-4	2-8-5	2-7-6	2-5-7	2-4-4
HEIGHTS	SHEER	4-3-2	3-11-0	3-5-4	3-1-4	2-11-0	2-9-1	2-7-6	2-7-2	2-6-5
	BEARDING L.	——	0-7-6	0-0-6	0-0-6	0-0-6	0-0-6	0-0-6	0-0-6	0-0-6
	BUTT. 10"	——	3-1-4	0-8-7	0-7-0	0-6-3	0-6-1	0-6-1	0-6-0	0-6-0
	BUTT. 22"	——	——	2-0-0	0-11-0	0-8-2	0-7-2	0-6-6	0-6-5	0-6-4
	BUTT. 28"	——	——	——	1-5-0	0-11-1	0-9-0	0-8-3	0-9-2	0-10-7
DIAGONAL A		0-1-6	1-3-0	2-8-1	3-2-0	3-4-3	3-5-3	3-6-1	3-6-3	3-6-4
DIAGONAL B		0-1-1	0-6-6	1-8-3	2-4-2	2-9-0	2-11-2	2-10-2	2-8-1	2-6-2

18' OUTBOARD WORKBOAT

OFFSETS TO INSIDE 5/8" PLANKING. MEASURED FROM BASELINE IN FEET-INCHES-EIGHTHS.
DIAG. "A" UP 3'-6" ON CL-OUT 2'-4" ON BASELINE. DIAG. "B" UP 2' ON CL-OUT 3' ON 12" W.L.

them to gape at the laps. When this happens, the only way to ensure a tight boat is to complete the riveting as planking proceeds. Then it is still possible to get clamps on the laps to hold them together until they can be drawn tight and permanently secured by peening the rivets.

A tip for those with limited experience in getting out lapstrake planking: The closer the shape and width of the spiling batten to the plank to be spiled, the better. For greatest accuracy, the spiling batten should partially overlay the lap whose shape is to be taken.

Instead of copper rivets for the laps, nonferrous clinch nails can be used. They are quicker and perhaps easier to put in. However, in my experience, clinch nails do not hold as well as rivets for most jobs and are not as neat in appearance. Besides, the supply of suitable clinch nails is quite limited—more so at present than that of rivets.

Where there is sufficient thickness of wood for annular, or so-called ring, nails long enough to develop sufficient holding power, these can replace screws. Bronze wood screws have become so outrageously expensive that I refuse to recommend them. Hot-dipped galvanized wood screws, well coated with zinc (the only kind to consider), last fairly well but don't have much holding power in sizes under number 10 because of the buildup of zinc in the threads. Electroplated screws last little better than plain steel, and thus are quite worthless.

The relatively thin (⅜-inch) canoe-type frames originally used for this boat in eastern Maine and in the Canadian Maritimes now offer something of a fastening problem. The malleable old galvanized iron chisel-point clinch nails that were formerly used for this are no longer manufactured. Their wide, thin, sharp chisel points driven across the grain cut through the fibers much the same as a brad awl does and clinched over on the inside easily, neatly, and with good holding strength.

The 1½-inch copper clinch nail produced in Anacortes, Washington by Skookum Fastenings may be the best substitute fastening now available for the plank-to-frame fastenings in this boat, but I prefer rivets, even if they mean more work. The total plank-to-frame thickness of 1¼ inches is not enough for either annular nails or screws. For fastening the bottom planking to the 2½-inch oak floors, however, annular nails would be an excellent choice—say 1¾-inch or 2-inch number 11s. Likewise, number 10 or number 11 annular nails for the keel batten to keel and

number 9 or 10 for the floors through the keel batten into the keel are recommended.

These larger sizes should, of course, be bored for to prevent splitting. But care must be taken not to get the holes too large, especially in members that might be water-soaked at times, since the holding power of annular nails is greatly reduced in wet oak.

A word about mixing ferrous and nonferrous fastenings: I believe there is little danger of harmful galvanic action in this boat. Above the waterline any combination would be okay, but below the waterline, to forestall any possible trouble, the careful builder might want to avoid mixing.

Flat canoe frames are shown because that was the kind used in these boats, but there is no reason a builder could not substitute narrower, thicker frames if good bending stock were available. Probably the reason for these flat frames was the absence of such good bending species as white oak or Canadian rock elm in the region where the boats developed.

For carvel-planked boats, steam-bent frames might be sided 1 inch and molded ⅞ inch, although different builders might vary these dimensions somewhat. One advantage of these thicker frames, besides increased stiffness, would be that screws or annular nails could be used for plank fastenings. Eight-inch centers would be a normal frame spacing.

Of course, for clinker plank, frame sections would be smaller and spacing somewhat closer together. I should then want plank fastenings to be rivets, although clinched, plank-through-timber fastenings have sometimes proved quite adequate.

Much of the detail in the view at section 6 is self-explanatory and needs no comment. Note, however, the oak floors (3) that occur at each mold station. They provide a solid foundation for the wide, nearly flat bottom and good fastening for the bottom planking. These floors are cut back from the keel batten to provide 2-inch-wide limbers (6) on each side, allowing full-length drainage under the tightly planked bottom sole (9).

The middle plank (10) is removable to afford access for sponging out the bottom. The sides, inside, are sheathed tightly (11) as high as the risers (7), giving a large, tight, open working cockpit that extends as far forward as a watertight bulkhead under the after end of the bow deck. This bulkhead comes as high as the risers, leaving ample access between it and the deck to the underdeck stowage space.

The bow deck is copied from those shown in

1	PLANKING PINE OR CEDAR TO FINISH ⅝"	8	THWART PINE. SPRUCE. DOUGLAS FIR 10" × ⅞"
2	TIMBERS STEAM-BENT OAK ⅝" × 1¾"	9	FLOORING PINE ¾"
3	FLOORS OAK SIDED 1½" MOLDED 2½"	10	TRAP, REMOVABLE FLOOR BOARD
4	KEEL OAK SIDED 2" MOLDED 2½"	11	CEILING PINE OR CEDAR ⅝"
5	KEELSON OR KEEL BATTEN OAK ⅝" × 4"	12	INWALE OAK, PINE, FIR 2" × ⅞"
6	LIMBER 2" OPENING ALONGSIDE KEEL BATTEN	13	BUMPER GUARD OR RUBBING STRIP PINE 2" × ¾"
7	RISER PINE 3" × ⅞"		

STATION 6

photographs of typical down-east boats of this type. By comparative scaling we determined it to be approximately 5 feet 6 inches long and show it as such. These boats were often banging into heavy head seas, and such a deck, in combination with the high bow, kept a lot of loose water from coming aboard.

The photographs in my possession do not show any construction closing off the space under the deck, but I have included the watertight bulkhead because it seems to me that this would be a good storage area. A considerable amount of dry storage space for gear, clothing, and the like is thereby made available. Provision for locking it up ensures limited security for things left aboard while the owner is absent—including the motor.

It must be understood that anything more than limited security is impossible to guarantee. There is no way of turning a boat like this into Fort Knox. Determined thieves could even saw a hole in the side of the boat without too much difficulty, if the loot they were after seemed worth it. But this is an extreme scenario. What is important to guard against is the casual sneak thief who happens by when the owner isn't around. In this case, a padlock is ample deterrent.

A bulkhead located as specified also greatly braces and stiffens the hull to withstand the hard pounding

that boats like this must take when driven at high speed into a heavy chop.

The bulkhead is got out in identical halves from ½-inch plywood. It need not be marine grade. One-half-inch exterior fir, good on one side, will be quite adequate, since only the outside can be seen after it is in position. It fits tightly against the inside of the planking and the underside of the deck, and is scribed by using a template made up of thin pieces of wood; a spiling block takes off the exact shape. To seal it against leakage, it is well bedded all around—especially at the bottom—with an adhesive bedding compound such as Boatlife's Life Caulk or 3M's 5200, formulations that have good body and do not become brittle in curing. In addition, it should be well fastened to the heavy side frames, the deck beam, and the backing post. Number 11 or number 12 annular nails, galvanized wire nails, or galvanized boat nails, if any can be found, are all suitable for this. Number 12 hot-dipped galvanized wood screws could also be used.

The detailed drawing showing layout and construction of this bulkhead is keyed as follows:

14. *Plywood bulkhead:* Half-inch exterior fir, good on one side.

15. *Heavy backing timber:* Molded 1¼ inches but sided 1¾ inches, the same as the others. These are

SECTION A A

WATERTIGHT BULKHEAD

5'-6" AFT BOW

18' OUTBOARD WORKBOAT

molded twice as thick as the other timbers to provide solid backing for the plywood bulkhead and to ensure secure nailing. They can be steam-bent in one piece if good bending stock is available, or they can be laminated from two ⅜-inch strips glued and nailed together after they are bent in place.

16. *Deck beam:* Molded 2¼ inches, sided 1½ inches. Oak, or glue-laminated to the required curvature from thin strips of Douglas fir or spruce. Crown is 2½ inches in a span of 5 feet. Epoxy-glued, laminated deck beams like this are lighter than oak, yet adequately strong. Still, they take longer to make than solid beams sawn to shape from oak plank.

To frame out this short deck, five more beams will be required for a spacing of 11 inches on centers. The same beam mold can be used for all. The ends of the beams will land on a section of clamp fastened to the timberheads and running forward to the stem.

17. *Backing post:* 2½ inches wide by 1½ inches thick. Oak, Douglas fir, spruce, or hard pine. White pine might be used, but it is rather soft for good nailing.

18 and 19. *Horizontal and vertical framing for the opening through the bulkhead:* Same as *17.*

20. *Exterior plywood, good on one side:* With deck beams sided 1½ inches and spaced 11 inches on centers, leaving 9½ inches unsupported space between beams, ⅜-inch ply is probably thick enough. One-half-inch ply would make a very solid deck, but the extra weight is probably not warranted.

21. *Deck coaming:* Oak or white ash, ¾-inch finished thickness. Molded width is 6 inches, cut to the same camber as the deck. It extends 3 inches above the surface of the deck and reaches slightly below where the deck beam comes behind the face of the bulkhead. Whether or not the boat photographed originally had

STEM DETAIL
18' OUTBOARD WORKBOAT

HORIZONTAL MEASUREMENTS FROM FR'D PERP.					
ABOVE BASE LINE	51"	30"	24"	18"	12"
OUTSIDE STEM	0-0-1	0-4-5	0-6-1	0-7-6	0-10-4
RABBET LINE	0-2-6	0-7-2	0-8-6	0-10-4	1-1-4
BEARDING LINE	0-4-0	0-8-4	0-10-0	0-11-7	1-3-0
INSIDE STEM	0-5-5	0-10-5	1-0-2	1-1-5	1-6-5
INSIDE S. KNEE	—	—	—	—	1-11-4

VERTICAL MEASUREMENTS ABOVE BASE LINE				
FROM FORWARD PERP.	20"	31"	40"	50"
OUTSIDE STEM & KEEL	0-4-4	0-3-4	0-3-4	0-3-4
RABBET LINE	0-6-5	0-5-2	0-5-2	0-5-2
BEARDING LINE	0-7-6	0-6-1	0-6-0	0-6-0
INSIDE STEM & KEEL	0-10-4	0-6-0	0-8-0	0-6-0
INSIDE STEM KNEE	1-2-5	0-9-1	0-7-4	0-6-8

such a coaming is not certain since none is shown. Yet it is not unlikely, for one is needed to keep water from draining off the deck into the cockpit.

22. *Removable panel for closing the opening through the bulkhead:* Half-inch plywood.

23. *Backing piece:* 2½ inches wide by 1½ inches thick. Oak, Douglas fir, or spruce. This stiffens the panel and provides secure bolting for the hasp plate.

24. *Hasp plate:* Stainless-steel plate 3 inches by 5½ inches fastened by four ¼-inch bolts.

25. *Reinforcement plate:* Stainless-steel plate 2 feet long by 2½ inches wide, fastened through the coaming, bulkhead, and deck beam with seven ¼-inch-diameter bolts. This plate reinforces the coaming where the coaming covers the pocket into which the upper end of the removable panel fits when it is in place and the opening through the bulkhead is closed. Without this reinforcing plate the closure would be less secure, since the coaming could be split away more easily.

26. *Hasp staple:* This should be hardened if possible. Although shown through-bolted, it could be attached to a plate put on with screws, since the hasp plate is large enough to cover it completely.

27. *Half-oval trim:* 1½ inches by 2 inches by 1 inch. Oak. Although not shown in the photos, this should run the full length of the boat for appearance.

The primary consideration in the construction of the transom is sturdiness. Because the transom receives the full thrust of the motor, and because there is no telling how large a motor some might decide to use, the transom should be built extra strong, with a large safety factor.

My first choice would be oak, 1⅜ inches or 1½ inches thick. Hard pine or old-growth, rift-sawn, first-quality Douglas fir could also be used. Spruce is not suitable here because it rots too easily when exposed to the weather.

Two or three widths of plank will have to be joined together, since a single plank of the width required cannot be obtained. If it is made up of three planks, the strongest way to piece them together would be to drift them with ⅜-inch galvanized rod into the middle section from both the top and the bottom. It would not be necessary to drive the rods all the way through. A two-piece transom could be doweled together with short lengths of ⅜-inch galvanized rod.

Another way to make up the transom would be to use pine reinforced on the inner face with oak fashion pieces 3 inches wide and 1 inch thick, sawn to shape, epoxy-glued and screwed around the edge with number 12 or number 14 hot-dipped galvanized screws 2¼ inches long. The pine could also be fastened into the oak through the outside with number 10 or number 11 annular nails. To favor the grain, these fashion pieces should be got out in several short lengths, which are merely butted when they are fastened on. In nailing on the planking, it may be necessary to bore these fashion pieces so that they can take the plank fastenings.

Heavy quarter knees at the sheer are required, and these must be securely fastened through the inwale, timberheads, and sheer plank. Likewise, the stout central knee bracing to the keelson is needed. This knee should be bolted through keel and keelson.

One of the photos on page 92 shows the transom cut down, apparently for a motor with a 15-inch shaft. For rough-water use, a motor with a 20-inch shaft would be preferred by some. In that case, less of the transom would have to be cut away. In choosing an arrangement for mounting the outboard motor, it is recommended that the over-the-stern dry well specified by the Outboard Marine Corporation be considered. I show it in a diagram for the 20-foot garvey discussed in Chapter 12.

The stem and the stem knee should be laid out full size from the profile view, and templates of thin wood (¼ inch would be about right) should be made to fit the full-size lines exactly. The rabbet line and the bearding line are marked on the stem pattern, and holes about ³/₃₂ inch in diameter are bored about 2 inches to 3 inches apart through both the rabbet line and the bearding line for their full length. Prick marks can then be made through these holes on either side of the 2-inch-thick oak stempiece, and through these marks, using a narrow, flexible batten, both the bearding line and the rabbet line can be drawn. These lines are sufficient guide for cutting the stem rabbet; a small rectangular block of the ⅝-inch planking stock can be used for a gauge.

Whereas the stem can be sawn out from an ordinary straight piece of 2-inch-thick oak plank, the stem knee is best got out of 4-inch-thick stock, and if the grain is curved to correspond somewhat to the curve of the knee, so much the stronger and better. If only 2-inch stock is available, 1-inch-thick pieces can be glued on each side to give the 4-inch width needed at the after end for the back rabbet. In addition to gluing, these scabs should be well nailed.

Bolts are ⅜-inch galvanized, located as shown. It might be preferable to fasten the stem and stem knee together first, before bolting them onto the keel. If the stem and stem knee are first glued together and allowed to cure, it will be easier to bore for the bolts with less chance of slippage.

One ½-inch dry-pine stopwater, put in exactly as shown, will suffice. It should be cut off flush with the inside of the rabbet so that caulking can be driven tightly against it on either side.

Also shown is a method for getting the angles for cutting the stem rabbet, given the bearding line and a closely adjacent buttock line in the profile view. For accurate results the buttock-line plane should be fairly close to the center plane of the hull, especially if there is much curvature in the planking lines toward the bow. Here, the distance is 9 inches from the buttock to the face of the stem, 10 inches to the centerline of the hull.

8

Yacht Tenders

·····•·····

THE LAWLEY TENDER

When sailing yachts were at their zenith, which is to say during the couple of decades just prior to World War I and for a brief period afterward, two great building yards stood head and shoulders above all the rest in this country—Herreshoff's in Bristol, Rhode Island, and George Lawley and Son on the Neponset River just over the Boston line in Massachusetts. Both yards went out when the large yachts went out. The difference is that the Herreshoff yard is still green in our memory, largely because of the popular writings of L. Francis Herreshoff, whereas Lawley's, lacking a chronicler, is now largely forgotten.

Much of the Lawley story will never be told now, and a pity it is, for there was much worth telling. But most of those who were there are gone, and most of the fine yachts built there are gone as well.

Old-time yachtsmen still around will tell you that

Lawley yachts were unexcelled for finish in a day when finish was important and there was money to pay for it. And in no division or department of the Lawley yard were standards of finish and the quality of workmanship maintained more strictly than in the boatshop.

The man responsible for this was a canny, hard-bitten Scot who had learned his trade and learned it well on the banks of the Clyde. John Harvey was his name and he ran a tight ship. He held sway over the boatshop like a feudal lord over his fiefdom, and it has been said that even the management of the yard hesitated to venture across the threshold of John Harvey's shop without first asking his permission.

Woe to a new man who had the temerity to claim to be a first-class boatbuilder. John Harvey had to humble him and make him regret his brashness. Men who had worked for Harvey 10 and 15 years still had to come to him to have the shape of a thwart knee or

12 FT. LAWLEY YACHT TENDER
LINES RECONSTRUCTED FROM MOLD OUTLINES

FEET AND INCHES

		STEM-KEEL	STA. 1	STA. 2	STA. 3	STA. 4	TRAN.
HEIGHTS	SHEER	2-4-5	2-0-4	1-10-0	1-8-5	1-9-3	2-0-4
	BEARDING	2-4-4	0-1-4	0-1-4	0-1-4	0-1-4	0-7-3
	7" BUTT.	——	0-6-0	0-2-7	0-2-4	0-4-1	1-0-2
	14" BUTT.	——	1-8-7	0-5-1	0-4-1	0-6-6	1-4-0
HALF-BREADTHS	W.L. 3"	0-0-6	0-3-1	0-7-4	0-9-5	0-4-0	——
	W.L. 6"	0-0-6	0-7-1	1-3-5	1-6-7	1-0-0	——
	W.L. 9"	0-0-6	0-9-5	1-6-6	1-9-5	1-6-4	0-2-1
	W.L. 12"	0-0-6	0-11-3	1-8-0	1-10-6	1-8-7	0-6-5
	W.L. 15"	0-0-6	1-0-5	1-8-5	1-11-1	1-9-5	1-0-6
	W.L. 18"	0-0-6	1-1-5	1-9-2	1-11-3	1-9-5	1-3-2
	W.L. 21"	0-0-6	1-2-2	1-9-4	——	——	1-3-3
	SHEER	0-0-6	1-2-7	1-9-5	1-11-3	1-9-2	1-2-4
	DIAG. A.	0-0-7	1-2-5	1-10-0	2-0-1	1-10-1	1-3-7
	DIAG. B.	0-1-0	1-3-6	2-0-1	2-2-5	2-0-1	1-3-6
	DIAG. C.	0-1-3	1-3-7	1-8-3	1-9-1	1-6-5	0-11-0

OFFSETS 12' LAWLEY TENDER. FEET, INCHES, EIGHTHS
STATIONS

DIAG. A UP 21" ABOVE BASE LINE. OUT 14" ON B.L. DIAG. B UP 24½" ABOVE B.L. OUT 24" ON 6" W.L. DIAG C UP 24½" ABOVE B.L. OUT 26" ON 18" W.L. KEEL AND STERN POST SIDED 1⅜" breasthook marked out. When asked why he required this, and if experienced help were not competent to cope with such relatively simple operations, Harvey is said to have responded that if he permitted such matters to pass out of his hands, there soon wouldn't be any need for John Harvey.

In looking out for the boatshop he looked out for John Harvey as well. In his old age—the late 1930s, when the corporation had come upon hard times—contracts for launches and similar craft still included the stipulation that John Harvey would supervise, so great a reputation had he acquired.

In its heyday the Lawley boatshop sent forth a great variety of smaller craft, including power launches and some sailing yachts that would be considered of fair size today, although accounted small then. But of all the craft produced by the Lawley boatshop, none were more widely known or esteemed than Lawley yacht tenders.

In and around Boston and Marblehead in the days when Marblehead claimed with some justification to be the yachting capital of the United States, Lawley tenders were considered the ultimate, and the finest yachts carried them. Perhaps these tenders did not tow quite as well as those built to the celebrated Columbia lifeboat model by Herreshoff, but that is a matter of opinion. Besides, not many large yachts made a practice of towing their tenders.

Lawley tenders rowed well and carried well, and were fair and beautiful to look upon. Looks were not unimportant in a day when ostentation and conspicuous consumption were a not inconsiderable part of the yachting scene.

One of the hands who worked in the Lawley boatshop for many years, and who got along very well with John Harvey, no doubt in part because he posed no threat of any sort to Harvey's position, was Charles (Charlie) Chandler, a native of Barbados and a fine boatbuilder. During the long term of his employment in the boatshop at Lawley's, Charlie worked on and built many tenders, and at one time or another he went to the trouble of tracing the outlines of the molds for his own use. The construction of these tenders was standardized and embodied in a set of molds used and kept in the shop. You may be sure they were well guarded, and it is most unlikely that John Harvey would knowingly have permitted their removal in outline from the boatshop.

It is doubtful if the original molds still exist. Once a shop is shut down for good, molds and patterns are frequently thrown out, burned, or otherwise lost or destroyed. In this case, at least, Charlie's outlines of the tender molds have survived.

After Lawley's was permanently closed down, Charlie worked off and on for Fred Dion in Salem, Massachusetts, to whom he gave his copies of the tender molds, and when I worked for Fred he allowed me to copy the outlines for myself. After carefully tracing them with carbon paper on a large sheet of heavy brown paper, I rolled them up, put them away, and forgot about them. In 1977, while going through papers and plans that had been accumulating for years, I dug out the mold outlines and decided to record them and the information they contained in more permanent form. The results are the drawings and dimensions reproduced here.

The section shapes checked out with surprising closeness when I laid them out full size on the drafting table, and later on the drawing board. The tender considered here is the 12-foot length, the most popular and widely used size. Note, however, that the molds are marked so that they can be used, with different spacing and some slight adjustments, for tenders ranging in length from 10 to 14 feet.

The standard Lawley yacht tender was planked smooth or carvel, and the section molds were given to the inside of the planking. Consequently the same molds can be used for lapstrake planking, if desired. I cannot say for sure, but I assume that a few clinker tenders were probably built from time to time on special order at the Lawley shop.

In fact, there is a fine example of a varnished lapstrake mahogany and cedar tender of unknown origin in the small-craft collection at the Mystic Seaport Museum. It gives every indication of having been built from Lawley molds, now that I have compared it with the mold outlines shown here.

Note that the molds include those for the stem, the apron, the slightly curved forward end of the keel strip (which is otherwise perfectly straight and uniform in molded thickness and siding), the triangular section of deadwood, and the sternpost. No mold is required for the keel batten strip, which rests on top of the keel and provides back rabbet for the garboards. This backbone, together with the section molds and the transom, was all that was required for setting up the boat for planking. This was the Whitehall method previously developed for building the working Whitehalls, from which fancy American yacht tenders originated. I have a set of Whitehall molds, identical in all respects except the dimensions, that were used in the Partelow shop in Boston in the 1880s.

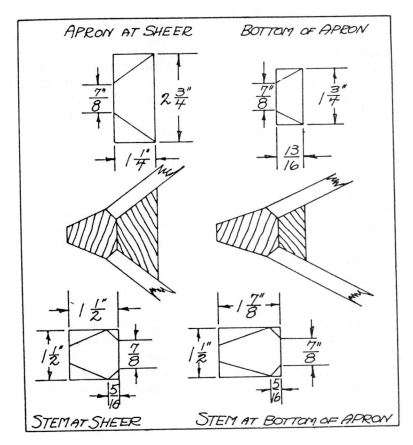

APRON AT SHEER   BOTTOM OF APRON

STEM AT SHEER   STEM AT BOTTOM OF APRON

The one-piece stem was generally got out of a hackmatack knee of suitable crook. Except for the mahogany transom, the rest of the frame would have been seasoned white oak.

The apron is fitted to the outer stem precisely on the inner rabbet or apex line, a method that considerably simplifies the rabbet-cutting operation. But mainly it was the width of the apron piece that supported fullness in the curve of the hood ends of the upper plank at the bow—a handsome characteristic of the Lawley tender. This shape was present to a slight extent in the Boston Whitehall, but was emphasized in the Lawley tender.

Lacking on Chandler's mold outlines are siding dimensions for the stem, keel, deadwood, and sternpost, as well as the thickness of the planking. Of course this was information that Charlie Chandler carried in his head; he had no call to write it down.

The following scantling dimensions have been obtained from a 12-foot carvel-planked Lawley yacht tender, hull 1710, supposedly built around 1920 and now in Mystic Seaport Museum's small-craft collection. Trimmed with teak instead of the usual mahogany and exhibiting the finest workmanship throughout, this tender was probably part of the matching outfit for some large Lawley-built luxury yacht. Bronze lifting rings fore and aft indicate that this tender was intended to be carried on board. The cast-bronze thwart knees, quarter knees, and breasthook are not found in early Lawley tenders, but became standard equipment after the Lawleys reached the pinnacle of their building career.

Overall length is 12 feet 2 inches and the beam, 4 feet 3 inches. The keel, stem, deadwood, and sternpost are oak, sided 1½ inches. The keel batten is oak, 2⅞ inches wide and ⅜ inch thick. Inwales are oak having a horizontal width of 1 inch, tapered to ⅞ inch at the ends, and a vertical thickness of ¾ inch. The apron is oak and has 3 inches of width of after face at the sheer height and 1½ inches of fore-and-aft thickness to the inner rabbet line at the stem head. The timbers, of steam-bent oak, are ⅝ inch wide and ½ inch in molded thickness, are spaced 7 inches on centers, and are continuous from side to side. The transom is teak, ¾ inch in finished thickness. The stern bench and thwarts are teak, ¾ inch thick. The seat riser is teak, ⅝ inch thick and 1¾ inches wide, tapering to 1 inch wide at the bow end. Floorboards are ¾ inch thick and fitted tight. They are screwed down to frames and to several floor strips across the garboards and keel batten, and are

painted. The center board is 8 inches wide amidships and has three 4-inch floorboards on either side. The floorboards curve and taper forward and aft to conform to the shape of the bottom. A sponge hole 5½ inches in diameter is located in the center floorboard under the middle thwart.

The upper surfaces of the thwarts and stern bench are 6⅞ inches below the sheerline. The stern bench is horseshoe-shaped and extends from the transom to join the after thwart, a distance of 4 feet. Side width is 1 foot. Each side of the bench is got out of a 15-inch-wide board. From the transom to the center of the horseshoe-curve cutout is 16 inches. Thwarts are 8 inches wide. From the forward edge of the after thwart to the after edge of the middle thwart is 28 inches. From the forward edge of the middle thwart to the after edge of the forward thwart is 27 inches. From the forward edge of the forward thwart to the after face of the stem apron is 15 inches.

There are two rowing stations. The oarlock pins are 12 inches aft of the after edges of the after and middle thwarts. The oarlock pads are 11 inches long and ⅝ inch thick.

There are 10 strakes of carvel planking finished ⁷/₁₆ inch thick. The top strake is teak, 3¼ inches wide at the bow, 4¼ inches wide amidships, and 3⅛ inches wide at the stern. Plank widths on the stem, except for the sheer plank and the garboard, are from 2⅛ inches to 2¼ inches. The bow end of the garboard is kept low so that the top edge of the garboard, viewed in place on the boat, appears straight or nearly so. The width of the garboard amidships is 4¾ inches. Planks are fastened with copper nails and riveted. Nails are small, about number 18, English standard wire gauge; burrs are about ⁹/₁₆ inch OD. The planks below the sheer plank are white cedar.

The outside sheer trim takes a standard cotton rope bumper and is hollowed from teak strips 1⁵/₁₆ inches wide by ⁹/₁₆ inch thick. The circular hollow is ¾ inch wide and ¼ inch deep. The center posts under the three thwarts are turned from 1-inch square stock.

Planking the Lawley Tender Carvel

For those familiar with clinker construction it would certainly be easier and less work to build the 12-foot Lawley tender lapstrake rather than to plank it carvel. Whether to plank clinker or carvel depends on a variety of considerations, some of which are discussed

This clinker-planked yacht tender is representative in its lines and interior layout of the fine 12-foot tenders built by Lawley and by Charles Lawton.

in connection with the Lawton tender, which is presented in the second part of this chapter. Some prefer the appearance of varnished carvel planking, and some claim that a boat so planked rows more easily, but this is a matter of opinion. The clinker boat is definitely stronger and will stand more hard use.

The novice who elects to build carvel will be well advised to adopt the procedure and order of work generally followed in commercial shops. He can start out by making molds for the four stations shown in the lines plan, and by making the transom. Next the pieces that form the backbone—the stem, apron, keel, deadwood, and sternpost—are got out and assembled with the transom. Bevels and rabbet are cut and stopwaters put in preparatory to setting up. This is done right side up on stocks, and high enough off the ground for convenience in fairing and planking the bottom. There are at least two good reasons for building right side up: One, it greatly facilitates bending in the timbers; two, it enables one person alone to do the riveting, although a helper who can hold the bucking iron makes things much easier.

In setting up, the molds must be centered, leveled, plumbed, and securely braced and shored. The transom is horned for perfect thwartships alignment. Substantial sheer battens running from stem to stern directly above the sheerline not only assist in fairing but help hold everything in place. At the bow these battens are fastened to untrimmed extensions of the apron and stem, which will be cut back later to their finished lengths. At the stern, temporary pieces rise above the inside face of the transom on either side to meet the sheer battens. Of course the molds are also made to extend high enough above the sheerline to take fastenings from the sheer battens.

The setting-up process is not complete until the molds have been thoroughly checked for perfect fairness throughout by fairing battens applied in various positions. These battens must run fair while touching all underlying mold surfaces at the same time. If high spots are found they are trimmed, and any low spots are brought up by shimming. When molds are carefully and accurately made, very little fairing is required.

Before the ribbands go on it is advisable to line out the planking, clearly marking the plank widths on the molds, stem, and transom. It will be a great help if the widths and lining can be taken off a scale half-model previously prepared—standard procedure for anyone building a particular type of boat for the first time.

Ribbands follow the lining operation. No ribbands are needed at the sheer, since sheer battens are already in place. Nor is a ribband needed in the garboard location. Ribbands should be about 1½ to 1¾ inches wide and ¾ to $^{13}/_{16}$ inch thick, and on the stiff side rather than being too limber. They should be straight-grained and without defects. They must bend fair, and they go on in one continuous length. If the upper ribbands are too stiff for the fullness in this tender's topsides at the bow—an especially handsome characteristic of the Lawley tender—their ends may be split with the bandsaw the necessary distance back, so that they can take the required curve. The ribbands line with the planking, and there is one for each plank, less the sheer plank and the garboard, as I have explained. Long flathead wood screws with washers under their heads fasten the ribbands to the molds.

Before the timbers go in, the garboards can be fitted and fastened in place. Their forward ends will need to be steamed or soaked in boiling water. Having the garboards in place helps when the timbers are bent in. The garboards are screwed to the stem and transom and riveted to the keel batten. Long, slim wood screws with washers under the heads secure the garboards to the molds temporarily. Later these screws are removed and the holes plugged.

Before the timbers are put in the steam box they are sanded and their inside faces are rounded very slightly. Also, the spacing of the timbers is clearly marked on the inside of the ribbands. Except for two or three pairs of timbers at the bow and a couple at the stern, the timbers run continuously from sheerline to sheerline. For best results, two persons are needed for bending in the timbers, one on either side of the boat. The timbers, hot and flexible from the steam box, are forced down inside the ribbands so that they lie on their station marks, and at the same time they are twisted as much as necessary to make them lie flat against the ribbands. This gives the correct bevels for attaching the planking. After the hot timbers have been clamped (not too tightly) to the sheer batten, their ends are tapped with a hammer. This drives the timbers down for a snug touching fit against all the ribbands. After that a nail is driven into the sheer batten through the timber head to secure the timber, and the clamp is removed.

With the garboards already in place, the second strake to go on will be the sheerstrake, directly under the sheer batten. As planking proceeds, the ribbands are removed one at a time and replaced with the corresponding plank; work proceeds from the garboard up and from the sheer down. Each plank is fastened in place as it is fitted. The last plank to go on, the so-called shutter, comes just above the turn of the bilge, where there is little or no twist or sny to worry about. When tapped into place, a properly prepared shutter should go in like a stopper into a bottle. Where plank edges need beveling, both meeting edges are beveled equally. The final operation before planks are hung on the boat is to burnish their edges by hard rubbing with a polished round of hardwood; this will compress their edges slightly. Later, when the planks take up moisture, these edges will swell back, tightening the planking immensely. Each plank as it goes on should be set up against the plank next to it as tightly as can be managed. A pair of chain clamps will be of great help for this. A boat of this sort, properly planked, will require caulking only in the garboard seam next to the keel and at the hood ends of the planking in the stem rabbet. When the boat is varnished, the planking seams can hardly be detected.

Once this tender is planked, no further special directions apply. Construction can be completed as for any other well-built small boat. The interior of the Lawley 12-footer is treated essentially the same as that of the Lawton 10-footer, which is detailed in the pages that follow.

THE LAWTON 10-FOOT TENDER

The first part of this chapter originally appeared in the *National Fisherman* in September 1977, and the response to it surprised me. I had expected interest, but not quite to the extent that developed. Several readers wrote that they had Lawley tenders that they would gladly permit me to inspect and measure. A Long Island man offered his for sale. A reader in Maine had worked as a young man in the Lawley boatshop helping Gus Deveau. There was also a letter from a yachtsman who remembered Lawley tenders from his boyhood, when they were numerous on Massachusetts Bay—particularly the 12-footer, "a splendid boat, easy towing and easy rowing, carvel planked, with a plumb stem and graceful sheer, the classic cutter of an earlier era when men of note were transported about their business in style."

Because of this interest, I decided to put into print for the first time the lines of a not dissimilar boat, the Lawton 10-foot tender, rechecked and redrawn for the occasion. These lines had been in my possession for over 30 years, awaiting disposition, and I felt it was high time they saw the light of day. Thus, they were published, together with explanatory and descriptive comments, in the January 1978 issue of *National Fisherman*, and are reprinted here.

I obtained the lines for the 10-foot tender from the builder, Charles Lawton, a man renowned for his fine tenders and whose reputation as a superlative craftsman is still green in Marblehead, Massachusetts. They came into my possession when Charlie and I were working together at the James F. Graves Beacon Street yard in Marblehead during World War II.

At that time Charlie, who was approaching 90 and had been working at the boatbuilding trade for close to 70 years, specialized in building these tenders. Except for legs that were a bit stiff, Charlie was still going strong and still turned out a good day's work with the best of them.

LAWTON 10-FOOT TENDER

HORIZONTAL STEM MEASUREMENTS FROM STATION A	SHEER	15" W.L.	12" W.L.	9" W.L.	6" W.L.
BEARDING LINE	0-10-0	0-10-0	0-9-5	0-8-5	0-5-5
RABBET LINE	0-10-6	0-10-6	0-10-4	0-9-5	0-7-1
OUTER STEM LINE	1-0-0	1-0-0	0-11-7	0-11-3	0-9-7

VERTICAL STEM MEASUREMENTS ABOVE B.L.	STATION A	STATION B
BEARDING LINE	0-3-7	0-6-3
RABBET LINE	0-3-2	0-5-3
OUTER STEM LINE	0-1-6	0-3-2

10-FOOT LAWTON TENDER - OFFSETS, FEET, INCHES, EIGHTHS								
STATIONS		STEM	A	1	2	3	4	TRAN.
HEIGHTS	SHEER	1-10-7	1-9-6	1-8-6	1-7-0	1-6-1	1-6-2	1-7-0
	BEARDING	—	0-3-7	0-2-5	0-2-0	0-1-7	0-2-6	0-5-5
	RABBET	—	0-3-2	0-2-1	0-1-5	0-1-4	0-2-3	0-5-2
	KEEL	0-1-6	0-1-0	0-0-4	0-0-4	0-0-4	0-0-4	
	BUTT. 6"	—	1-0-2	0-6-2	0-2-5	0-2-1	0-3-3	0-7-2
	BUTT. 12"	—	—	1-1-0	0-3-5	0-2-6	0-4-5	0-9-5
HALF-BREADTHS	SHEER	0-0-5	0-8-3	1-2-1	1-8-3	1-9-7	1-8-2	1-2-2
	15" W.L.	0-0-5	0-7-2	1-1-0	1-8-0	1-10-1	1-8-3	1-2-7
	12" W.L.	0-0-5	0-5-7	0-11-4	1-7-3	1-10-0	1-8-0	1-2-1
	9" W.L.	0-0-5	0-4-0	0-9-0	1-6-2	1-9-1	1-6-5	0-11-0
	6" W.L.	0-0-5	0-1-7	0-5-4	1-4-1	1-7-4	1-3-4	0-1-4
	RABBET	0-0-5	0-0-5	0-0-5	0-0-5	0-0-5	0-0-5	0-0-5
DIAGONALS	DIAGONAL A	—	0-7-4	1-0-5	1-8-0	1-10-5	1-8-4	1-3-0
	DIAGONAL B	—	0-8-1	1-0-0	1-5-6	1-6-6	1-4-6	1-0-1

LINES INSIDE PLANKING - OUTSIDE TRANSOM. HEIGHTS ABOVE B.L.

PLANKING 3/8". STEM AND KEEL SIDED 1¼".

DIAGONAL A, UP 17", OUT 22" ON 9" WATER LINE.

DIAGONAL B, UP 17", OUT 12" ON 3" WATER LINE.

These lines and offsets show a rounder, more cut-back forefoot than does the Lawton 10-foot tender donated to the Mystic Seaport in 1980, as will be discussed in the text. The tender from which the lines were taken more than 30 years ago may have been a slightly modified custom model, but the only change appears to have been in the stem.

Charlie and I got along well together. I made a point of lending a hand whenever he needed it for such jobs as bucking rivets and chasing stock in the mill downstairs, and Charlie appreciated it. Helping Charlie was a privilege and the kind of opportunity that doesn't come twice, and you may be sure I made the most of it.

When Charlie retired at 90, following the death of his wife, and went back to spend his declining years with his family in Saint John, New Brunswick, he left a sheaf of plans and drawings with me. I still have a box of boat molds that he used when he worked for Partelow in the canoe factory at Riverside on the Charles River in the 1890s. His shop notebook for recording special dimensions and directions for custom work started about that time.

The 10-foot tender was possibly his most popular boat and the one most in demand at the time I knew him. Even though yachting in Marblehead had begun to decline, there was still enough call for these tenders to keep Charlie busy most of the time in his corner at the head of the boatshop stairs; an occasional dory or other craft took up the slack.

Years afterward, following Charlie's departure to Saint John, Graves produced a fiberglass version of what purported to be the Lawton tender—taken, I presume, from Charlie's building molds remaining at the yard. What changes, if any, were made to facilitate the molding process I cannot say, though such changes often are made.

That some changes may have been made is suggested by reports coming to me that the performance of the glass tenders, at least the first ones, was inferior to that of Charlie's wooden ones. It was claimed that the glass boats were not as stable, possibly in part because of the excessive weight of the glass in the topsides.

The design of this tender is a critical one that will not tolerate much variation in the established lines. A slight departure here or there, though it might not be apparent to the unpracticed eye, could spoil the performance or at least damage it appreciably.

In a point-by-point comparison with Lawley tenders, those built by Lawton stack up favorably in all respects. Both have had their ardent proponents.

The perfected yacht tender of 60 years ago was the outgrowth of rigorous competition, a boat that excelled in both performance and appearance. Cost was not an overriding consideration. Yachtsmen were willing and able to pay for quality, and therefore workmanship did not suffer from drastic efforts to cut building costs.

These tenders had to row and tow well, be moderately good seaboats, carry heavy loads, yet shine like a piece of fine furniture. They not only had to be light in weight so that they would handle easily and row well, but they had to appear light, since delicacy of construction was aesthetically important.

Indeed, in one respect the heavy emphasis placed on appearance dictated a delicacy of scantlings that had an adverse effect on the lasting qualities of the tenders. Bent-oak timbers were shaved down so small—in some cases barely ½ inch by ⅝ inch in cross section— that almost invariably they broke much sooner than they should have. There are few old tenders that do not have cracked or broken timbers or frames, which have often been "sistered" and sometimes replaced. But the planking of such tenders, if not everything else apart from the frames, has lasted well.

The lines given here are drawn to the inside of the planking, so that either a carvel or clinker boat may be constructed on molds made from them. For a clinker boat with plank ¼ inch thick, however, the bearding line would need some readjustment. The bearding line shown is drawn for planking ⅜ inch thick, the recommended thickness for a carvel boat.

Building with clinker planking is easier, in my opinion, especially if the boat is to be varnished. Tight-seam carvel planking finished bright requires absolute precision of planking fit, but with clinker planking, some slight adjustment in the fit of the laps is possible without being obvious or apparent. Consequently, the same exacting precision is not required.

Clinker planking does not have to be hollowed or "backed out" on the inside to fit the round of the molds, and can be finished flat and sanded at the bench. Carvel planking, on the other hand, must be "backed out" precisely to fit the hull curves. After it is fitted and fastened in place, it must be planed and sanded to perfect curvature and smoothness without planing away the countersunk recesses for the rivet heads, which must be filled with facing tinted to match the color of the varnished hull.

Prior to 1980 I had few details to offer for the building of this tender. I could have worked out scantlings to go with the lines, but although they probably would have come very close, they would not have constituted the genuine article as built by Lawton—so I refrained. This is where things stood when, in the summer of 1980, a letter arrived from a yachtsman in Argentina who was seeking plans for a classic yacht tender. Donald M. Street, author of *The Ocean-Going Yacht,* had suggested that I might be able to supply them.

My correspondent informed me that he was considering extensive cruising in South American waters and needed a good boat—he'd had his fill of rubber dinghies and other modern substitutes. Having a tender built in Argentina offered no problem as far as skilled boatbuilders and materials were concerned, but he needed working plans to go by. So far, he had not been able to locate any that would do. Could I help?

My first thought was, "This is easy," but when I began to cast about for detailed drawings of wooden tenders I realized what a dearth of specific building information for such boats there actually is. Lines and offsets for tenders are not lacking, but lines and offsets are only the skeleton—to be fleshed out in building the boat. Until very recently, this was done by the boatbuilder in the boatshop according to trade practice, and little or none of it was written down anywhere. Building details remained largely in the boatbuilder's head and hands, but also, to a considerable extent, in various molds and patterns evolved by rule of thumb and passed directly from boatbuilder to boatbuilder, from shop to shop, and from one generation to the next.

Apart from the fact that the boatbuilding trade as formerly practiced had no real need for published manuals, the principal obstacle to getting the necessary information onto the printed page was the difficulties involved in recording uniquely curved shapes on a reduced scale in such a way that they could later be enlarged and precisely reproduced.

Lines and offsets are relatively easy to record, but this method, developed by naval architects to record the hull shape of large, carvel-built vessels, was not applied to boatbuilding until well along in the last century, and then only partially. Getting small-craft hull shapes from patterns—once the builder had the patterns—was quicker, easier, and just as accurate as getting the shapes from a laydown of lines.

For that reason boatbuilders were generally reluctant to switch from patterns, and some have continued to depend on them to this day. For instance, experienced builders of Adirondack guideboats—which are unexcelled by any small-craft type anywhere in fine workmanship, finish, and sweetness of line—produced their boats entirely from inherited molds and patterns whose origins have never been traced completely.

Charles Lawton not only built his famed yacht tenders largely from molds, but also turned out various other boats by the same method. He once told me that as a young man back in the 1890s (when he was working at the Partelow canoe factory) he was able to produce Saint Lawrence River skiffs at the rate of one per working week of 56 hours. He managed to complete a boat, except for painting, in this short time only because he had patterns or molds for every part.

In the summer of 1980, by happy coincidence, a 10-foot Lawton tender was donated to Mystic Seaport Museum's small-craft collection by Ray Burns, Jr., of Marblehead. This clinker tender had served the *Grenadier,* a 59-foot-10-inch-LOA auxiliary schooner yacht designed by John G. Alden and constructed in 1931 by the Lawley yard.

Built for Henry A. Morss, Jr., and Sherman Morss, the *Grenadier* was subsequently owned by John A. Magoon and then by George E. McQuesten. Her owners were prominent in Marblehead yachting circles. And it was from McQuesten that Burns acquired the tender.

Whether this is the *Grenadier*'s original tender from 1931 is not altogether clear, but it most probably is. The boat shows wear, although she has retained her shape perfectly. There are no broken frames, split planks, or failing joints, in spite of the extremely light scantlings characteristic of Lawton's tenders.

One thing is immediately obvious in comparing the profile shape of this tender with the lines in this chapter. The two stems are not quite the same. The curve of the forefoot in the lines on page 107 is rounder, fuller, and cut back more. It also rises somewhat higher. How this came about I cannot say. Perhaps the boat from which the lines were taken years ago was a custom job. But in other respects the lines of the two boats appear to correspond closely.

When Lawton retired from boatbuilding, he gave me a box of much-used boat molds, which, as I mentioned, I still have. Included are stem patterns for a number of different boats: Whitehalls, a Saint Lawrence River skiff, his Adirondack, and his 10-foot tender. In order to compare the shape of the *Grenadier* tender's stem with Lawton's molds, I carefully took off the lines of the former from the boat. The takeoff and the molds checked precisely. There can be no doubt that the stem of the *Grenadier*'s tender was built from these molds.

The shape of the rounded, cut-back forefoot in the lines in this chapter has some resemblance to the

Formerly tender to the 60-foot auxiliary schooner Grenadier, *this classic 10-foot Lawton boat was donated to the Mystic Seaport Museum's small-craft collection in 1980. Note the curve of the forefoot, sharper than that shown in the lines on page 107.*

forefoot shape of Herreshoff tenders built after the so-called Columbia lifeboat model, although it is less extreme. The upper stem has less rake than that of the Herreshoff model. According to L. Francis Herreshoff, his tenders towed better behind a yacht and did not tend to dart and yaw as much as the Lawley model with its straighter stem and deeper, more sharply curved forefoot, which was of Whitehall derivation.

The *Grenadier*'s tender is much closer in this respect to the Lawley/Whitehall model. To the best of my knowledge, however, no one has ever accused a Lawton tender of misbehaving in the wake of a yacht.

Although varying in size, rake, and curvature, all of the stem patterns Lawton gave me are for composite stems and are laid out in the same way. They are contrived for the assembly of a curved stem and forefoot from three pieces that are easily and economically cut from ordinary straight-grained oak plank.

Natural crooks of hackmatack or oak with the shape grown in are, of course, ideal for stems. These, however, are hard to come by, are expensive, and require much labor to shape and fit. A well-made pieced-up stem is amply strong and lasting, just as

handsome when finished, and much cheaper and easier to make. Rabbeting for the hood ends of the planking is greatly facilitated in the pieced-up stem because the joint between the apron and the outer stem falls on the apex line of the rabbet.

The three essential parts of this stem assembly are the main, or outer, stempiece; the apron; and the stem knee, joining the first two to the straight strip that forms the keel. By making the apron from a separate piece, one can easily make it wide enough to give ample back-rabbet support to the curving ends of the topside planking. Generally there was also a rabbet mold for marking the curves of the rabbet and bearding lines at the turn.

The stem shapes are not difficult. It would be easy to duplicate them exactly by carefully tracing around them on a thin board and cutting to the line. But when it comes to recording these shapes in print on a reduced scale, the job is not quite as simple or easy. And a high order of accuracy here is critical.

I believe an accurate duplication can be made from the accompanying diagrams. Should this appear at first glance to be something of a puzzle, requiring some patience and study, that is to be expected. All the needed information is here. Enlargement to blueprint

Stem patterns for the standard Lawton 10-foot tender. This stem shape with its more sharply curved forefoot could very easily be substituted for that of the lines given in this chapter when the full-size laydown is made.

size will not help. There may be a simpler and more direct way of presenting these data, but I have not found it.

Although the two stems are distinctly different, comparatively little adjustment would be required in the lines on page 107 if the stem shape of the *Grenadier* tender were substituted for the one shown there. This could be accomplished with no trouble at all when the necessary full-size laydown is made.

The amount of detail in this small and comparatively simple boat is all but staggering when it comes to getting down in print every precise detail required for duplicating it exactly, something no commercial boatbuilder would ever bother to do. Just how much detail there is will become clear from an examination of the sectional view through the boat at station 3, its widest part, as shown in the accompanying diagram.

1. *Frames:* White oak, ½ inch square, 6 inches on centers. Except for the two at the bow, the frames are continuous from gunwale to gunwale. The two bow frames are in two pieces joined across the stem-knee extension by small floors, and are canted slightly to conform to the curve of the sides at the bow, spreading at the top to about 7 inches on centers.

2. *Planking:* Ten strakes ⁵/₁₆ inch thick, northern white cedar, except for the mahogany sheerstrake. Lapped ⅝ inch. Laps copper-riveted every 2 inches. Widths of planks, including laps, measured at each station: garboard, 4¾ inches; broad, 3¾ inches; number 3, 3¾ inches; numbers 5, 6, and 7, 2¾ inches; numbers 8 and 9, 2⅝ inches; sheerstrake, 3¾ inches.

3. *Inwale:* Oak, sided ¾ inch, molded 1 inch. Inside face rounded very slightly for appearance.

4. *Middle thwart:* Mahogany, 8 inches wide, ¾

inch thick. Notched tight at the ends around two timbers and fitted snugly to the sides of the boat. Screwed to the riser and plugged. Sprung upward about ⅜ inch at the center by a supporting post. Under edges chamfered half the thickness of thwart for appearance of lightness.

5. *Keel strip:* Oak, sided 1¼ inches, molded 1½ inches.

6. *Keel batten:* Oak, 2⅛ inches wide by ⅜ inch thick.

7. *Bottom ceiling:* Cedar, ⅜ inch thick thinned to ¼ inch at ends to help twist. Outboard edges beaded a shallow ³/₁₆ inch. Middle strip is 7¾ inches wide, tapering toward the ends. Hollowed slightly underneath to correspond to the upcurve of the frames above the keel batten. Outside strips, two on either side, are 3¼ inches and 3½ inches wide. Screwed to every other frame, but not plugged.

8. *Mahogany trim strips:* Slightly thicker and shaped as shown.

9. *Seat risers:* Mahogany, 1½ inches by ½ inch (or a hair less). One-eighth-inch bead top and bottom. Risers run full length of frames. Fastened to each frame with a number 8 screw. Not plugged.

10. *Thwart knees:* Hackmatack, fitted tight to inside of planking and joggled around lap lands. Knees rise with a tight fit behind the inwale to come flush with the top of the sheer plank. Rivet-fastened through sheer plank and inwale. Knees are ⅝ inch thick, 7 inches long on the foot, and fastened to the thwart with three screws. Molded approximately 2 inches through

the widest part of the throat. Outer edges rounded slightly for appearance.

11. *Outwale strip:* One-inch-by-¾-inch oak, hollowed and shaped to take 1-inch-diameter cotton-rope bumper.

12. *One-inch cotton-rope bumper:* Sewed on with linen thread through ⅛-inch holes bored every 2 feet in outwale strip, top to bottom.

13. *Turned post:* From 1-inch-square mahogany.

14. *Socketed block:* One-half inch thick; secures post.

Anyone attempting to build this tender will be well advised to approach the job as a puzzle, for in some respects it is just that, and therein lies not a little of its appeal to the amateur builder looking for new worlds to conquer. Taking risks and resolving uncertainties add zest and incentive.

Building such a boat is no mere act of turning down so many nuts on so many bolts, or something equally cut and dried. Rather, it is an open-ended process from start to finish, one that makes exacting demands on the builder's judgment, eye, and aesthetic instincts.

There is simply no practical way to provide in printed words and diagrams the complete directions for the harmonious blending of all the subtle curves that enter into the fabric of this diminutive vessel. Here, deviating as much as the thickness of one thin shaving in a critical place is equivalent to singing out of tune or striking the wrong note on the piano.

After many years of publishing how-to directions for

Interior views of the Grenadier's *tender show the light scantlings and fine detail that make it a difficult boat to build.*

boatbuilding, I have found that a certain number of readers always write back asking for blueprints, even though they would be of little help and would contain nothing not already provided. Except for their size and color, there is nothing special about blueprints, nothing magical. Generally what is needed is close and careful study, plus some judicious extrapolation when gaps appear, as they inevitably will.

The two detailed drawings to be discussed next cover construction thoroughly from amidships aft. They are keyed, as above, both for easy reference and to avoid cluttering the drawings with notes and dimensions.

First, it would seem appropriate to make some

general observations on materials and fastenings. Five different lumber species were used for this boat: cedar, oak, hackmatack, mahogany, and pine. For planking, northern white cedar was the preferred wood, and because the boat was finished bright, absolutely clear cedar boards were required—lumber that was free of knots, sapwood, or other imperfections.

Cedar of this quality was not easily obtained in Lawton's time, and it is all but unobtainable now. This is what J. Henry Rushton had to say about such wood in his 1904 catalog:

Do not confound our white cedar, which grows only in the most northern states and Canada, with the white cedar of New Jersey and Virginia. The former is the lightest known wood of this or any country that is suitable for planks for small craft. One cubic foot, air seasoned (not kiln dried), weighs but 18 pounds, while the white cedar of New Jersey and Virginia weighs 28 pounds.

The northern cedar is soft, tough and durable. You can give it a vast amount of hard usage with but little injury, and time makes but little impression on it, as I have known cedar planking in a boat to be sound and perfect after 20 years' constant use every summer, and having such shelter during winters as may be found in a woods camp.

Thus, northern cedar is the preferred planking material for the Lawton tender, but it is not essential. Southern cedar—or juniper, as it is also known—is quite acceptable, even though it is slightly heavier and more prone to splitting. Lacking cedar, one may substitute other species as a last resort.

For ribs or timbers, inwales, keel, keel batten, outwale, sternpost, stem, apron, and stem knee, oak was used. For the keel, a piece of dense, close-grained red oak was sometimes preferred to white oak because of a tendency of the latter species to warp and twist in larger sections, thus pulling the boat out of shape. Builders characterized such oak as being too "strong." But for the steam-bent ribs or timbers, only the choicest white oak bending stock was considered. This was stripped from the butt logs of young, fast-growing trees cut close to the ground.

Only perfectly clear, straight-grained wood was selected. The wider the annual rings and the denser and heavier the wood, the better. With half an hour to an hour of boiling (or wet, low-pressure steam), such white-oak timbers can be tied in knots.

The timbers in the Mystic Seaport Museum's Lawton tender, only ½ inch square in section, must have been of the choicest select white oak, for despite the age of the boat, not one is cracked or broken. These days, prime white oak for timbers could be difficult or impossible to secure, necessitating substitutes that would need to be increased somewhat in section to ensure adequate strength. If bending stock of any sort is unobtainable, it would be possible to use glued-up, laminated ribs or timbers—if these were properly made.

Breasthook, thwart, and stern quarter knees in this boat are natural-crook hackmatack. Seasoned apple-limb crooks would make a handsome substitute, and were preferred by the old-time builders when they could get them. As a last resort, glued laminations would serve.

The mahogany used in the boat is high-grade Honduras with close, dense grain and rich, dark color. The stern transom, backrest, backrest cleats, stern bench, thwarts, supporting posts, risers, stretchers, oarlock pads, and sole trim or edging strips were all made from it. Pine was used for the end cleat under the bench and for the supporting crossbeam.

The screws originally used were brass, since this is what was obtainable when the boat was built. But bronze is far superior and should be used today.

Copper rivets through the laps and timbers are spaced on 2-inch centers. Precise spacing of the fasteners is critical for appearance in first-class work.

A cut nail of copper—parallel-sided one way and wedged-shaped the other—with a blunt, square end was used, but these are not generally available today. The square end punched through the hot oak timbers without the splitting that sometimes results when sharply pointed nails are not bored for first.

Boats were planked right side up, which permitted the builder to rivet the laps without assistance as the planking was put on strake by strake. After the planking was completed, holes for riveting the timbers were carefully located and bored in the laps, and the points of the nails were inserted. These were driven as the hot timbers were bent in. Set up in this manner, timbering could be carried out as a one-man operation.

Today, nails for riveting the laps should not be too large. A number 13 copper-wire nail and a number 14 burr will be about right. The burr should fit tightly, both to hug the nail and to hold it in place for riveting after it is driven down with the burr set.

A sloppy fit is no good. The larger, dished, European-type roves are unacceptable for this job because they produce a heavy, clumsy appearance.

Nailheads should lie flat and flush with the surface of the planking in varnished work. If necessary, they can be brushed with a flat file in finishing. Care must be taken in hammering to avoid denting the soft cedar, although sponging the wood afterward with boiling water will bring the dents back if they are not too deep.

Larger nails—number 12s or even number 11s—are required for riveting in the inwales, breasthook, and knees. Screws should be large enough, but not

oversize: ⅞-inch number 8s through the hood ends of the planking into the oak stem; 1¼-inch number 8s through the after ends of the planking into the mahogany transom; 1½-inch number 10s through the thwarts and stern bench into the risers and supporting cleats; ¾-inch number 6s through the sole into timbers; number 10s from the stretchers through the sole into the timbers; 1¼-inch number 10s through the keel batten into the keel; and number 10s through the stern transom into the sternpost, although number 12s could be used here.

Wherever the wood is thick enough to hold plugs without undue reduction of strength, screw fastenings in a bright boat should be plugged.

The following references are keyed to the accompanying diagrams.

15. *Mahogany posts supporting thwarts and stern bench:* Turned from 1-inch square stock. Delicate appearance desirable.

16. *Stern bench:* Mahogany, ¾ inch thick. Cut to curve as diagramed. Under edge chamfered as shown for appearance of lightness. The outside is brought flush with the inner surfaces of the timbers without notching around them as is done with the ends of the center and forward thwarts. Screw fastenings plugged.

17. *Beam supporting stern bench:* Lower edge cut to ornamental shape as shown. Pine, 3¼ inches by ¾ inch.

18. *Cleat strip supporting ends of stern bench:* Screwed to inner face of stern transom. Pine, 2 inches by ¾ inch.

19. *Stern transom:* Mahogany of ¾-inch finished thickness. Shape developed from the lines. Screw-fastened to the sternpost and plugged.

20. *Sternpost:* Oak, sided 1¼ inches. Fastened to keel with two ¼-inch bronze drifts.

21. *Stern quarter knees:* Hackmatack, sided 1 inch and molded as diagramed.

22. *Cleats to hold bottom of backrest:* Mahogany, fastened with number 8 screws and not plugged.

23. *Oarlock pads:* Mahogany, ¾ inch thick and beveled as shown. Space underneath, between inwale and planking, filled with solid reinforcement from timber to timber. Note that the ends are slightly curved for appearance.

24. *Oarlock sockets:* Set in flush with the top of the pads.

25. *Stretchers (foot braces):* Located 22 inches aft of the rowing thwarts' after edges. Mahogany, sided ¾

Lawton 10-Ft. Tender

inch, 1 inch high. Tapered and rounded at the ends. Screw fastenings plugged.

26. A 3½-inch-diameter hole cut through the sole for sponging out the bottom.

27. *Edges of the rowing thwarts and the stern bench:* Chamfered underneath to one-half full thickness and a 1-inch width for appearance of lightness.

28. Notches in stern quarter knees for backrest.

29. *Backrest:* Mahogany, ¾ inch, shaped as diagramed. Reinforcing strips on the back, held with ovalheaded wood screws.

Planking widths are measured on the outside of the boat, minus the width of the ⅜-inch laps, except at the sheer. Widths on the stem: garboard (8½ inches back from extreme tip), 3½ inches; number 2, 2¼ inches; number 3, 2¼ inches; number 4, 2 inches; number 5, 1¾ inches; number 6, 1¹³/₁₆ inches; number 7, 1⁹/₁₆ inches; number 8, 1½ inches; number 10, 2⅜ inches.

Planking widths on outside of planking, minus laps, measured amidships: garboard, 3⅝ inches; number 2, 3⅝ inches; number 3, 3⅝ inches; number 4, 3¼ inches; number 5, 2¾ inches; number 6, 2⅞ inches; number 7, 2¾ inches; number 8, 2⅝ inches; number 9, 2⅜ inches; number 10, 3¾ inches.

Planking widths on outside of planking, minus laps, measured on the stern transom: garboard, 3¼ inches; number 2, 3¹/₁₆ inches; number 3, 2¹/₁₆ inches; number 4, 2⁷/₁₆ inches; number 5, 2⁵/₁₆ inches; number 6, 2¼ inches; number 7, 1⅞ inches; number 8, 2 inches; number 9, 1¹³/₁₆ inches; number 10, 2½ inches.

These planking widths need not be followed precisely. Some slight adjustments may be necessary to secure fair planking lines. As a general rule for clinker planking, plank widths narrow as side curve increases, so that the laps may be closed.

9

Sea Bright Skiff

..................•......................

One of our most distinctive small fishing boats is the Jersey sea skiff, or Sea Bright skiff, as it is also called. It takes its name from the area where it originated: Sea Bright, New Jersey, on the southern half of the barrier beach that constitutes the Sandy Hook peninsula, just across the bay and south from New York City.

The surrounding waters have always been known for their abundance of fish. But it was not until the mid 1840s that a local fishing industry sprang up there and fishermen took up part-time residence in shacks and tents among the sand dunes of the barrier beach during the fishing season, which lasted from May through November.

In 1868, according to one account, "fifty-five men and boys—all fishermen..." were living at Nauvoo, as Sea Bright was first called. Twenty years later, due to the active demand for fresh fish from the expanding population of New York City, the Sea Bright fishery was flourishing. A guidebook printed in 1889 estimated that there were 250 boats with crews of two men each based at Sea Bright. The average "fare" of fish per day per boat was 150 pounds, making an aggregate daily total of 37,500 pounds, or 4,575,000 pounds from June 1 to October 1—by no means an insignificant part of burgeoning Manhattan's diet, even when these numbers are substantially discounted. "Sea Bright," the guidebook continued, "has been a fishing center for about fifty years. The population is a mixed one, nearly all nationalities being represented, among them Scandinavians and Negroes being prominent."

Fishing in small boats off exposed beaches where considerable surf is frequently encountered requires a special kind of boat. It must be burdensome yet buoyant, with ample "lift" and sheer at either end. Flat

JERSEY SEA SKIFF 18'-4" x 5'-8"

		STEM	1	2	3	4	5	6	7	T
HEIGHTS	SHEER	3-11-4	3-6-0	3-1-0	2-10-0	2-8-4	2-9-0	2-10-6	3-2-0	3-7-2
	OUTSIDE BOTTOM	0-8-1	0-8-0	0-7-0	0-5-6	0-5-0	0-4-0	0-3-1	0-2-5	0-2-0
	BUTT. 6"		1-1-0	0-7-0	0-5-6	0-5-0	0-4-0	0-7-7	1-0-5	1-3-4
	BUTT. 12"		2-1-6	0-10-3	0-7-0	0-5-6	0-6-1	0-10-3	1-3-0	1-7-1
	BUTT. 18"			1-4-1	0-10-3	0-8-6	0-9-6	1-1-4	1-6-4	2-1-2
HALF-BREADTHS	SHEER	0-1-2	1-3-0	2-1-1	2-7-0	2-9-6	2-10-0	2-8-0	2-3-6	1-9-2
	OUTSIDE BOTTOM	0-1-2	0-1-6	0-6-0	0-9-0	0-10-0	0-8-3	0-5-2	0-2-3	0-1-4
	W.L. 12"	0-1-2	0-4-7	1-2-1	1-8-5	1-11-0	1-9-3	1-3-2	0-5-1	0-1-4
	W.L. 18"	0-1-2	0-8-5	1-7-3	2-2-2	2-4-6	2-3-5	2-0-2	1-5-4	0-10-3
	W.L. 24"	0-1-2	0-11-3	1-10-1	2-4-7	2-7-4	2-7-0	2-4-4	1-11-2	1-5-1
	W.L. 30"	0-1-2	1-1-2	2-0-0	2-6-4	2-9-3	2-9-1	2-6-7	2-1-7	1-8-3
	DIAGONAL A	0-1-3	1-0-6	1-11-0	2-5-2	2-7-6	2-7-2	2-4-7	2-0-1	1-6-7
	DIAGONAL B	0-2-0	1-2-2	1-10-7	2-2-6	2-4-1	2-3-1	1-11-6	1-7-4	1-3-7

DIAGONAL A 2'-6" ABOVE BASE LINE. OUT 2'-0" ON 24" W.L. DIAG. B 2'-6" ABOVE B.L.

OUT 2'-2" ON B.L. OFFSETS MEASURED IN FEET, INCHES & EIGHTHS TO OUTSIDE OF PLANKING floors are required for the loaded craft to take the beach and to remain upright when the swells recede, leaving it high and dry.

The 1889 guidebook offers this description of the boats in use at Sea Bright at that time:

> Their fishing boats are fourteen and one-half and fifteen feet long, designed for two men, although there is a one-man boat of thirteen feet....The boats are all made by builders in the vicinity and cost eighty-five dollars. The frame is cedar, and the sheathing of oak [*sic*], with coppered keels. Each boat weighs about three hundred pounds and is easily handled by two men....The boat is rigged with jib and mainsail, and if there is any wind the fishermen sail out to the grounds. The boat is then anchored and the sails wrapped around the mast, which is unshipped.
>
> There are no ropes except the main and jib sheets, and no steering apparatus, the course being made by an oar. A primitive and simple centerboard, which is taken out when necessary, is dropped when the boat is sailed. The fishing grounds are by no means limited, and the fishermen go from one to fifteen miles away, as they deem best.

I believe whoever wrote this was not a boatbuilder. Surely, the frame was oak and the "sheathing"—that is, planking—was cedar.

A fuller and more informed description of these early boats is to be found in Peter J. Guthorn's *The Sea Bright Skiff and Other Jersey Shore Boats* Rutgers University Press, 1971. Guthorn makes the early skiffs about 15 feet long with a 5-foot beam and a U-shaped transom raked about 30 degrees.

Below the transom, the wide after ends of the garboards are twisted so that they stand vertically in order to fasten against the sternpost. This produces what has been called a *reverse chine,* which runs for several feet forward of the stern before gradually dying out toward the midsection in the normal rounded curve of the side.

Instead of a solid skeg or deadwood aft, the space between the after ends of the two garboards is hollow. Sometimes called a *hollow skeg,* this space is a feature that later facilitated the installation of the inboard engine. In the old skiffs, Guthorn states, the width of the plank bottom, which took the place of a keel, was commonly one-third the beam of the boat, although this was not always adhered to.

In the beginning, these boats were frequently referred to as dories. In fact, in shape and construction there was little difference at first between these Jersey shore boats and contemporary New England dories and wherries. The Maine salmon wherry, surviving down to the present time, has the same reverse chine and "planked-up," or hollow, skeg. There can be no doubt that all three of these 19th-century fishing work boats—Jersey beach skiffs, New England wherries, and dories—originated from a common source: the 18th-century Colonial bateau, developed for military use during the French and Indian Wars, when thousands were built.

When the gasoline engine became available around 1900, it was immediately adopted by fishermen along the Jersey shore, and the Sea Bright skiff underwent a marked change. In general, the shape and construction remained much the same, but power skiffs were considerably enlarged, and the sailing rig, including the centerboard, was discarded.

In August 1915, *The Rudder* published lines and a construction plan by Roger M. Haddock for a motorized skiff. These were taken from some skiffs then being built by Huff Brothers, Pleasure Bay, Long Branch, New Jersey. The following descriptive item accompanied the drawings:

> All along the coast of New Jersey, with a few on the Long Island shore and others extending well down the Atlantic Coast, where landings have been made on the sandy beaches, may be found the New Jersey or Sea Bright skiff. It is a boat better adapted to the use of fishermen in those particular localities than the dory or even the Norwegian pram, which it somewhat resembles. Their usual length is from 18 to 30 feet, with a flat floor slightly curving. Before the advent of the gasoline engine, they were equipped with single sprit sails or with a sail and small jib and, with a centerboard pretty well forward, would work to windward in very rough water and half a gale. In landing on the beach with fares of fish in a heavy swell, it is an unusual thing for a boat to get away from the willing hands of those who rush down into the surf to haul her out above the wash or reach of the next swell. Being very full aft, they are burdensome and lift with a sea.
>
> In no class of working boats has the gasoline engine been so willingly received as in the New Jersey skiffs. As usually installed, the flywheel is protected by a circular casing and the engine itself is covered by a removable hatch. The shaft runs low; a two-bladed wheel is used and so fastened that the blades are athwartship when the engine is on low center. When

landing on the beach the wheel is protected by being out of the way as much as possible. Engines of 2½ h.p. are used for the smaller sizes and for the larger, rarely over 5½ or 6 h.p.

The boat for which lines and offsets are printed in this chapter is very similar to this Long Branch boat, but it is not the same. Rather, it was built some years later and used in Great South Bay off the south shore of Long Island. Its length of 18 feet is at the lower end of the 18-to-30-foot range mentioned in *The Rudder*.

It would not be difficult to enlarge this boat, if so desired. In fact, it would be quite easy. The simplest way would be to cut the hull at station 4 and insert 2 or 3 extra feet between the two portions. The two end portions would not be disturbed or changed in the slightest. No fairing of the lines would be required.

Another way, which would require some fairing and a bit more manipulation of the lines, would be to enlarge the flat plank bottom by both lengthening and widening it, but retaining the same curved outline. The stem, transom, and sectional shapes at the various stations would not be changed, except perhaps to deepen the hull by 1, 2, or even 3 inches in the case of a much larger boat.

The lines given here are to the outside of the planking, although these skiffs were almost always clinker-planked. In clinker planking it is usual to give the offset measurements to the *inside* of the planking so that it will not be necessary to deduct the planking thickness when making the molds.

In a workboat like this the difference is not significant, as it would be in a racing yacht. Although the offsets here are to the outside, nothing would be gained by deducting the plank thickness, either for clinker or carvel planking.

All in all, because of its hull shape this is a relatively simple boat to plank, with the exception, perhaps, of the reverse chine at the after end of the garboard. There are various ways of handling this reverse chine, but I am suggesting that the seam between the garboard and the plank above be treated as a carvel seam; that it be beveled to fit tight; that it be covered with a 3-inch width of glass tape set in epoxy; and that it be finished smooth with a filet of epoxy and microballoons put on as a thick paste. This is simple and easy to do, and it makes a very strong, permanently tight joint in this critical place.

Above this the planking could be carvel, but not thinner than 11/16 inch, finished in order to hold the caulking. Conventional lapstrake planking probably would be easier and better. This could be done with ½-inch plywood, with the curved strakes gotten out of regular 8-foot panels and the short sections spliced to give the required lengths.

Splices are scarfed 12 times the thickness of the planking stock—in this case, 6 inches long for ½-inch plywood. Planed to make a tight fit and glued with epoxy, such splices are just as strong as the original ply, and if the required curves are laid out carefully on the 4-by-8-foot panels there is little waste. Considering the high cost and the difficulty of obtaining good-quality sawn lumber for planking stock, marine plywood used in this way could be the best and cheapest approach.

If good white-oak bending stock for timbers is available, such framing is certainly to be considered. A good framing job of steam-bent oak can hardly be improved upon. In some cases, however, suitable oak is simply not to be had. Should this be the case, I suggest making up laminated frames from thin strips of spruce glued with epoxy. Such laminated frames were used for the Herreshoff rowing boat built at Mystic Seaport in the spring of 1980, and the process is fully described in Chapter 1 of this book.

The process is not difficult, and the frames so made have proved more than satisfactory in every respect. There are several advantages. The frames can be made exactly to the required shape. There is no "pullback." Set up on the flat plank bottom, they take the place of molds, and the planking is fastened directly to them as it is put on. No ribbands, no fairing, nothing of that sort is needed.

Further, spruce is stiff and extremely strong for its weight. It also holds fastenings quite well—much better than pine, for instance. And because it is light in weight, a larger section can be used to get the equivalent strength of oak frames, without adding undue weight in the topsides. Finally, the numerous glue lines separating the thin laminates go a long way to prevent absorption of water, obviating much of the danger of rot.

The stem is like a dory stem: It is not rabbeted but rather is made up of an inner and an outer part. The latter consists of two pieces sawn out of straight-grained plank and scarfed together when they are put on, after the boat has been planked and the ends of the planking faired off to the curve of the inner stem. The inner stem can be sawn out of ordinary plank, but it could also be laminated like the frames.

The inner bottom is 1¼-inch oak, nearly straight fore and aft, with only a hint of rockered curve in the bow end. Somewhat more than 20 inches wide amidships, it will require two, and possibly three, planks pieced together. The edges are beveled to conform to the angle of the garboards, which cover them and are nailed to them, exactly as in dory construction. The projecting bottom edges of the garboard are planed off flat to conform to the underside of the bottom plank.

After this surface has been well painted with antifouling paint, and coated with bedding as well, the outer bottom of ¾-inch oak is put on with screws, which enable it to be removed easily should replacement because of beach wear become necessary. A layer of Irish felt between the inner and outer bottoms would not be a bad idea.

As shown, this boat is suitable for the installation of a small inboard engine. The hull has been given enough draft to get the propeller underwater even when the boat runs light, yet the propeller and rudder do not project below the bottom to interfere with beaching. This boat can be run up on a beach, will sit upright, and can be easily hauled up with rollers; no cradle is needed.

The engine will be located well aft under a small engine box and behind a thwart-high, watertight bulkhead. Although no fuel tank is drawn, it might best be located under the short section of deck forward. Narrow waterways and low coamings will run along the sides of the boat. Tiller lines leading from the rudder quadrant aft will run underneath to a small wheel or stick located against the coaming on the port side amidships.

Considerable room would be lost by the addition of a centerboard trunk. Because of that, if a sailing version is desired, some may want to lengthen the boat by 2 or 3 feet, as already suggested. There should be no hesitation in doing this, since it is easily accomplished and a better seaboat—as well as one of greater capacity—will result.

For an engine I have chosen a small diesel, in accordance with popular trends of the day. There are several makes now being distributed, any of which would be suitable. Some owners prefer one make, some another, but as far as I can determine, no brand has demonstrated overwhelming superiority.

I finally picked the smallest Yanmar, the 1GM 7.5 h.p. model. It is compact and light (dry weight 154.5 pounds), it is moderately priced as diesels go, and

Yanmar parts and service are widely available, an important consideration. I might have settled instead on a Norwegian Sabb, a fine engine of long-recognized superiority. For a time I toyed with the idea of installing an old-fashioned one- or two-cylinder make-and-break or jump-spark gasoline marine engine. But I gave that up when I found that engines of this type with power equivalent to the diesels were much larger and at least twice as heavy; that they require oversized propellers, which might present problems in a boat intended for easy beaching; and that they cost approximately as much. The safety of diesel over gasoline also influenced my choice.

Finally, let me repeat: One is not necessarily tied to Yanmar. Any of a number of similar small diesels could be installed with a minimum of alteration.

The closed engine compartment has several features that bear mentioning, since these are generally not found in small powerboats. This compartment is closed off from the rest of the boat by a ½-inch-thick plywood bulkhead extending from side to side and fastened to the bent-oak frames 11 inches forward of station 6. This bulkhead makes the compartment watertight up to the top of the sill of the slide opening. No water from the central portion of the boat can flow aft past this bulkhead into the after one-third (nearly) of the hull.

Ample (which is not to say generous) access to the engine is provided by a hatch opening through the bulkhead and deck that closes with a standard yacht-type "slide." When the slide is shut and the drop boards or closure boards are in place, the engine compartment is completely enclosed—and therefore impervious to the weather—and it can be locked. Having under lock and key the engine and such gear as one wishes to keep aboard the boat is increasingly desirable today because of the thievery and vandalism now plaguing the waterfront. I do not claim that access could not be gained with an ax or sledgehammer, but under ordinary circumstances security is assured.

If a tight bulkhead were to be raised forward just under the overhang of the deck and as high as the thwarts or slightly higher, all loose water taken over the side in heavy weather would be confined to the central portion of the boat for convenient bailing; at the same time it would be restrained in some measure from surging back and forth as the boat pitched. I have not shown this bulkhead in the drawings, but it is well worth considering. It would not be difficult to install, would provide dry storage under the deck in the peak, and would not be in the way.

Every aspect of boatbuilding has been hit hard by inflation, but none worse than fastenings. I like bronze wood screws, but their price, especially in small lots and at retail, is so ridiculous that I no longer consider them a possibility. In many places bronze annular (ring) nails are an acceptable substitute for bronze screws. They don't come cheaply, but they are still substantially less expensive than screws. My experience has been that their holding power diminishes markedly in water-soaked oak and probably in all thoroughly saturated wood. This suggests that wire size should be generous and that when bored for, holes should be no larger than is needed to prevent splitting. In soft wood, frequently, no preboring at all is needed.

If this boat is carvel-planked with $1^{1}/_{16}$-inch finished plank thickness on $1\frac{1}{4}$-inch oak frames, I suggest that $1\frac{1}{2}$-inch number 8 bronze ring nails be used, set below the surface deep enough to putty, although $1\frac{3}{4}$-inch nails could be used without breaking through the inside

of the frames. Certainly longer number 8s can be driven through the lower edge of the garboards into the inner oak bottom—$2\frac{1}{2}$ inches would be about right. If the hull is clinker-planked, copper rivets would be needed between the frames for the laps, with ring nails into the frames and bottom. A limited offering of copper clinch nails is now on the market.

Clinch nails are not as neat as rivets, nor do they have quite the same holding power as well-peened rivets, but they serve adequately for some construction. Unfortunately, copper has nearly attained precious-metal status, and how long we can continue to put it into boats if its price keeps rising is something to consider.

Old-fashioned hot-dipped galvanized iron or steel fastenings generously coated with honest-to-goodness zinc are not to be sneezed at, if they can still be found. The electroplated stuff covered with a wash a few molecules thick is worthless, despite being pretty to look at.

This is a small boat that will be out of the water, and therefore partly dried out some of the time. In addition,

SECTION B-B

SECTION C-C

SECTION A-A

SECTION D-D

STATION 6

BASE LINE

J.G. 4/81

there won't be all kinds of electrical equipment sending currents through the structure. Both factors should keep electrolysis from being a problem. Thus, I see no danger in a judicious combination of ferrous and nonferrous fastenings. Surely it is all right to use galvanized fastenings above the waterline, in the interior, and wherever the structure does not become thoroughly soaked. In fresh water, galvanized fastenings can be used throughout.

Glue is a great adjunct to metal fastenings, sharing much of the load with them and greatly strengthening the hull. Where it can be applied to joints and meeting surfaces, I highly recommend it—either a standard epoxy formulation or Aerolite 306 urea-formaldehyde. Avoid quick-setting epoxies. Too often they do not give the builder time enough to make desirable adjustments and to do the job properly.

The following numbered explanations correspond to numbers on the drawings:

1. *Planking:* Carvel, $^{11}/_{16}$ inch thick, finished. Northern white pine, white cedar, juniper, cypress, Douglas fir, or Port Orford cedar. Fastened with number 8 bronze ring nails. Alternate planking: Clinker, $^9/_{16}$ inch thick if sawn lumber and ½ inch thick if plywood.

2. *Frames:* Steam-bent oak, 1¼ inches by 1⅜ inches. The lower ends can be split a short way with a saw to facilitate their taking the sharp bend required to land on the bottom. Alternate: Glued laminated frames, 1¼ inches by 1½ inches. Spruce or Douglas fir.

3. *Plywood bulkhead:* Half-inch marine-grade fir plywood.

4. *Deck beams:* Oak, molded 1¾ inches, sided 1½ inches. Can be laminated spruce or Douglas fir. Camber: Rise amidships approximately 6 inches in 6 feet.

5. *Deck:* Half-inch marine-grade fir plywood. Ring-nail fastened.

6. *Coaming:* Steam-bent oak, finished ½ inch by 5 inches. Can be glue-laminated to shape using several thin layers of mahogany.

7. *Half-oval trim:* Oak, ¾ inch thick, 1¾ inches wide amidships tapering to 1⅜ inches at the ends.

8. *Thwarts and side benches:* White pine, ⅞ inch to ¹⁵⁄₁₆ inch thick.

9. *Thwart beam:* Pine, 1½ inches by ⅞ inch, nailed and glued to plywood bulkhead.

10. *Slide:* Top, mahogany or pine, ⅞ inch thick. Inside strips, 4 inches wide. Outside strips, 5 inches. Splined as diagramed, fitted tight, and glued. Screwed to slide beams. Holes plugged. Pine painted; mahogany can be bright.

11. *Slide beams:* Oak, 1⅜ inches molded, 1¾ inches sided. Camber: 1½-inch rise in 3 feet.

12. *Stiles for bulkhead opening:* Oak, 2 inches by 2 inches. Grooved as diagramed to take ends of drop, or closure, boards.

13. *Sill or stool:* Oak, shaped as diagramed and fitted tight at the ends to prevent leakage. Ends left long on inside to bulkhead to fasten to it for extra support.

14. *Drop, or closure, boards:* Pine or mahogany as diagramed. Should slip easily up and down in the stile grooves or channels without being sloppy. Edges are rabbeted as diagramed to shed rainwater when closed.

15. *Lock plate:* ⅛-inch brass as diagramed. Holed to receive brass padlock hasp when the slide cover is closed.

16. *Slide runners:* Oak, 1½ inches thick and shaped as diagramed. Must fit the deck perfectly; glued to deck and securely fastened from the inside through both decking and deck beams. First, the deck beams are installed full length across the boat. Next, the plywood deck covering is put on except for the aperture under the slide, but without cutting the deck beams extending across this aperture. These are not cut out until the runners are in place, fitted, and fastened.

17. *Brass end pieces:* ³⁄₁₆-inch flat brass, 3½ inches long by 1½ inches wide, fastened to the ends of the slide beams with two 1-inch number 10 or number 12 wood screws. These end pieces slide in the grooves in the inside face of the runners, holding the slide on.

They should slip easily without being sloppy. Both the fore and aft slide beams have them. To remove the slide, remove the end pieces on the forward beam. Push the slide cover back as far as it will go, lifting it enough to clear the slide end beam between the runners. The grooves in the runners are widened at the ends to permit this. You can then slip off and remove the slide cover without unscrewing the brass end pieces on the after slide beam.

18. *Padlock hasp:* ³⁄₁₆-inch flat brass or hardened stainless. Pivots on its bolt into the forward slide beam.

19. *Slide end beam:* Oak. Ends are let into the runners as the beam is screwed and glued to the plywood deck for a watertight fit. Otherwise there will be leakage at the after end of the slide. There are small limbers through the runners for drainage just aft of this end beam.

20. *Clamp:* Oak, ⅞ inch by 1½ inches. Nailed to the frames to support the ends of the deck beams at the fore and aft ends of the boat.

21. *Sheer filler pieces:* Pine, ⅞ inch by 2 inches. Fitted between the timberheads from the after bulkhead to the first forward deck beam. Nailed and glued to the inside of the sheer plank. These provide support for the edge of the side decking, which is glued and nailed to them.

22. *Coaming backup:* Pine, ⅞ inch by 2 inches. This can be in short lengths sawn to shape and spliced together. Must fit tight against the coaming, to which it is glued and nailed. Supports the coaming and also the edge of the decking, to which it is glued and nailed. Tight fit for watertightness.

23. *Side-decking supports:* Two thicknesses of ½-inch plywood decking (scraps) glued together. Ten inches long on the frames, to which they are glued and nailed. Notched as diagramed to take the coaming backup (see *22*).

24. *Forward thwart:* ⅞- to ¹⁵⁄₁₆-inch pine, 1 foot wide, located as diagramed. One foot ten inches above baseline.

25. *Side bench:* Pine, same thickness as thwarts and securely cleated to them on the underside. Supported on the outboard edge by the thwart riser (see *27*).

26. *After thwart:* ⅞- to ¹⁵⁄₁₆-inch pine, 1 foot 2 inches wide, 1 foot 10 inches above baseline. Glued to thwart beam (see *9*) and to plywood bulkhead for watertight fit.

27. *Thwart riser:* Pine, ⅞ inch by 1¾ inches. Nailed to the frames.

28. *Bottom cross cleats:* Oak, 1½ inches by 2

inches. Nailed to the bottom and positioned as diagramed. One foot six inches on centers the full length of the bottom.

29. *Inside bottom:* Oak, 1¼ inches thick, three boards wide.

30. *Floors under engine beds:* Oak, 1½ inches thick.

31. *Engine beds:* Oak, 2 inches thick.

32. *Engine:* Yanmar 1GM 7.5 h.p. marine diesel.

33. *After hatch:* Pine throughout. Keep as low as possible. Maximum height need not be more than 1¾ inches overall. Provides access to rudder quadrant and space aft of engine. Must be watertight and have secure closure.

34. *Rudder quadrant:* Ten inches/twelve inches.

35. *Rowlock base:* Slightly higher than the coaming, as shown.

36. *Forward bitt:* Oak, 3 inches square, tapering below the deck to 2 inches where it lets into the base of the stem; ½-inch bronze pin, 6 inches long.

37. *Inner stem:* Oak, sided 2½ inches and molded as dimensioned in the lines plan at the beginning of this chapter. Could be scaled with sufficient accuracy from the profile view printed herewith. Since the outer stem is put on after planking, as in dory construction, no rabbeting is required. Can be sawn from a straight plank, but one with some shape or curve is better.

38. *Outer stem:* Oak, in two pieces as diagramed. Should fit perfectly against the inner stem and the hood ends of the planking. To be glued and spiked in place.

39. *Outer bottom:* Oak, ¾ inch to ⅞ inch thick. Seams should overlap seams in inner bottom. Nailed in place with a nonhardening, antifouling bottom compound between the two layers. This acts as a shoe to take the wear from landing on beaches. Easily renewed when worn. Nails should have substantial heads to facilitate pulling.

40. *Blocking for bitt:* Oak, ⅞ inch. Fits tightly between deck beams and is glued to underside of deck.

41. *Breasthook block:* Oak, thick enough (1¼ inches to 1½ inches) to give solid fastening for the bow chocks. Glued to underside of deck.

The drawing on page 122 showing a profile and plan view of the construction should be accurate enough to scale. A more detailed dimensioning of the engine installation, rudder, steering layout, and so forth is provided below.

The sectional view at station 6, showing the after bulkhead, slide, and entrance into the engine compartment, was drawn before I decided to move the bulkhead forward one frame, or approximately 10 inches. The dimensional changes were so slight that I did not consider it necessary to redraw the sectional view.

One of the drawings on the opposite page shows a simple arrangement for steering, one much used formerly for small-displacement launches; the other gives sectional views through the hull in the way of the engine bed. These sectional views are intended to be self-explanatory. It may be worth mentioning, however, that while the engine-bed stringers *(31)* are let into the solid floor *(30)* at station 6, 10 inches forward of station 7 these stringers are notched to fit *over* the bent frames *(2)* without cutting into them.

In determining the height and the slope of the engine-bed stringers, I had to take a number of competing requirements into account and make adjustments to satisfy them all. If the boat is to be gotten on and off the beach easily, the propeller should not extend below the line of the bottom. Yet the wheel must be submerged when in operation, and the deeper the better.

Although the specification sheet the manufacturer furnished for the engine puts the maximum installation angle at 15 degrees, the American distributor recommends a 12-degree maximum. Here I have been able to keep it down to 8 degrees to provide for variations in the angle of trim under special or emergency operating conditions. Because of the sea skiff's hollow garboards at the after end of the engine-bed stringers, these stringers cannot be placed as close to the bottom as would be possible if there were more width here.

A number 2 10-inch standard wheel mounted on the port side as shown should be ample for easy steering. The bent tiller arm will drop the steering cable enough to clear the deck beams. Either a turnbuckle or a tension spring introduced at some convenient place in the steering-cable circuit is needed to take up any slack and to keep the cable taut. The bent tiller arm shown here replacing the tiller quadrant, as first detailed, is simpler, is easier to obtain and rig, and will work just as well, if not better.

The construction drawings presented earlier in this chapter do not show a fuel tank. The logical location would be forward under the foredeck. Depending on the shape and size of the tank selected, it might be necessary to replace the bitt *(36)* with a large deck

JERSEY SEA SKIFF 18'-4" x 5'-8"

WHEEL SUPPORT
OAK 1¼" x 6" – LENGTH TO FIT

10"

12"
3"

TILLER ARM

JERSEY SEA SKIFF 18'- 4" x 5'-8"

16   17   11   10

STATION 6

31
30
29
39   BASE LINE

1'-7"

5   16

7   20   4   2

10" FORWARD STATION 7

31
30   4"

1'-4½"

BASE LINE

cleat in the same location, bolted through the oak block *(40)* under the deck and between the two deck beams.

Hammond Power Dory

In our introductory consideration of the Sea Bright skiff's origins, we mentioned that early Jersey beach skiffs closely resembled New England fishing dories and were, in fact, called dories by the fishermen who built and used them. From their first appearance in the early years of the 19th century until the introduction of gasoline engines in fishing craft, beginning at about the end of the century, these beach skiffs changed very little. They remained small, open boats having flat, relatively narrow, longitudinally planked bottoms and slightly rounded clinker sides. Transom sterns that narrowed toward the bottom made them virtually double-ended on the water.

But motors brought rapid and radical change. Skiffs got wider and bigger in a hurry, and some of them, it must be admitted, suffered in appearance, although from the standpoint of utility and seakeeping ability they proved more than adequate. Despite the clumsy appearance of some of these early power conversions, others were more expertly modeled, earning excellent reputations both as working boats and as dependable pleasure craft, a reputation the type retains to this day.

What happened to Jersey beach skiffs after the gasoline engine appeared also happened to New England fishing dories, except that early power dories were far more numerous and more widely used. Between 1900 and 1920 or thereabout, thousands of these power dories were to be found throughout the Northeast and as far west as the Great Lakes. They were easily the most numerous class of small powerboats then in use. Quantity builders such as Emmons in Swampscott, Toppan in Boston, and the Atlantic Company, makers of the Gurnet Dory, in Amesbury, Massachusetts, advertised widely. Other well-known builders, such as Chamberlain in Marblehead and the Cape Cod Dory Company in Wareham, catered more to local demand. There were also many small shops turning out the new craft on a limited custom basis.

One such builder was Jesse Hammond of Danversport, Massachusetts, who in 1904 built a 28-foot power dory in his Endicott Street shop for George Whittier of the same town. This dory, said to be capable of 9 m.p.h., was considered a "speedboat" at the time, being equipped with a 6 h.p. two-cylinder two-cycle Essex gas engine produced in nearby Lynn, Massachusetts. Hammond, one of the first to put a gasoline engine in a dory, had built a power dory for his own use as early as 1899.

The dory built for Whittier proved so satisfactory that a number of others similar to it were built from the same builder's half-model. In 1951 I acquired this half-model from George Whittier and took from it the lines that were published in the *Maine Coast Fisherman,* October 1955. These lines were redrawn for publication in the *National Fisherman,* July 1981, accompanied for the first time by a table of offsets. They are reproduced here by way of showing the similarities between this dory and the Sea Bright skiff. The next chapter covers the New England powered fishing dories in more depth.

The 1955 article was the first in a series on "Low Cost Power and Easy Driven Hulls." This dory was offered therein as a boat having an easily driven hull form that for its size was exceptionally economical of power as long as no attempt was made to exceed the optimum hull-length speed for a displacement hull.

This is an exceptionally easy hull to plank: There are no difficult shapes or bends of any sort. As I stated in the 1955 article, "The model shows specialized development of dory design. The round sides, the very narrow bottom and the hollow sections aft are unusual (in classic dory hulls). Whittier recalled that the hull was planked lapstrake and dory fashion, but with more numerous and narrower planks than is usual in smaller, typical dories—a departure necessitated by the size and shape of the hull."

This hull could be planked carvel just as well as clinker, as some might prefer to do. Cape Cod dories built at Wareham were planked thus. In general configuration, this Hammond power-dory hull is not too dissimilar to the smaller Jersey beach skiff that we have been considering. In fact, the same construction details worked out for the beach skiff could easily be adapted for the Hammond power dory. At the same time there would be wide latitude for individual preference in such matters as stem construction—for example, whether to stay with the classic two-part dory stem or choose a rabbeted stem instead. Likewise, a rabbeted sternpost with some exposed deadwood would be an alternative to covering the sternpost with the hood ends of the planking, dory fashion.

Because of the easy lines of the Hammond hull, boats built from the half-model can be made shorter or longer by as much as several feet without altering the basic shape and performance of the hull—simply decrease or increase the spacing between the central

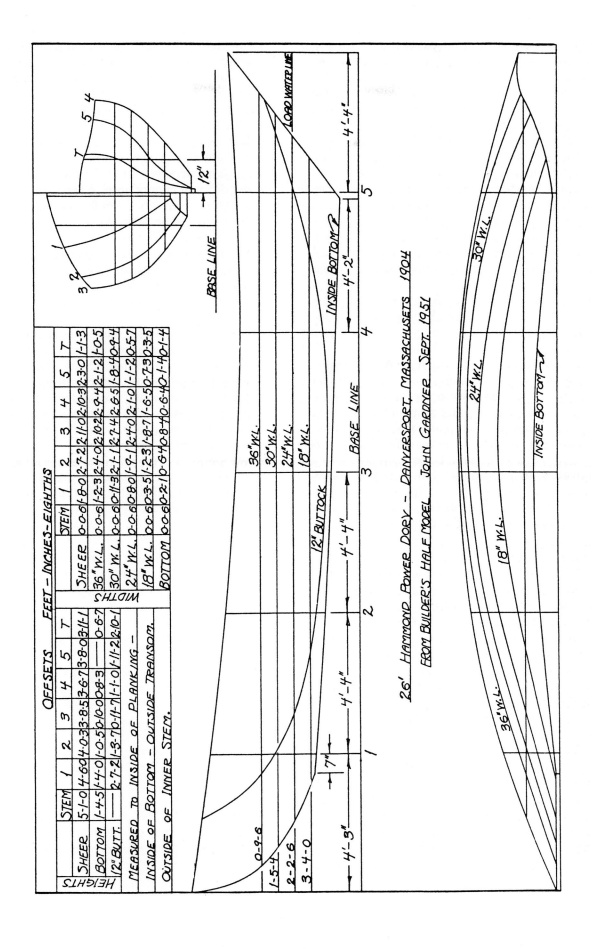

OFFSETS   FEET — INCHES — EIGHTHS

WIDTHS

	STEM	1	2	3	4	5	T
SHEER	0-0-6	1-8-0	2-7-2	2-11-0	2-10-3	2-3-0	1-1-3
36" W.L.	0-0-6	1-2-3	2-4-0	2-10-2	2-4-2	1-2-4	0-5
30" W.L.	0-0-6	0-11-3	2-1-1	2-7-4	2-6-5	1-8-4	0-9-4
24" W.L.	0-0-6	0-8-0	1-9-1	2-4-0	2-1-0	1-1-2	0-5-7
18" W.L.	0-0-6	0-3-5	1-2-3	1-8-7	1-6-5	0-7-3	0-3-5
BOTTOM	0-0-6	0-2-1	0-6-4	0-8-7	0-6-4	0-1-4	0-1-4

HEIGHTS

	STEM	1	2	3	4	5	T
SHEER	5-1-0	4-6-0	4-0-3	3-8-5	3-6-7	3-8-0	3-11-1
BOTTOM	1-4-5	1-0-1	0-5-0	0-0-0	0-8-3	—	0-6-7
12" BUTT.	—	2-7-2	1-3-7	0-11-7	1-1-0	1-11-2	2-10-1

MEASURED TO INSIDE OF PLANKING —
INSIDE OF BOTTOM — OUTSIDE TRANSOM.
OUTSIDE OF INNER STEM.

26' HAMMOND POWER DORY — DANVERSPORT, MASSACHUSETS 1904
FROM BUILDER'S HALF MODEL.   JOHN GARDNER   SEPT. 1951

molds. The bow and stern ends should be left strictly alone. Thus, although the half-model, which was made on a scale of 1 inch to 1 foot, is for a 26-foot boat, the boat built for Whittier, as mentioned, was 28 feet long. One 24 feet long might just as well have been built and would have proved a good model, I am confident, although less roomy and somewhat slower.

Much like the Jersey beach skiff, the Hammond power dory has deep, hollow garboards at the stern. This helps keep displacement low, making for excellent seakeeping performance. Because of the long, slim, easy lines of the Hammond hull, however, there is no abrupt transition in the lay of the planking above the hollow garboards aft, as there is in the beach skiff—one of the reasons the Hammond hull is easier to plank.

A principal reason for selecting a small diesel for the 18-foot beach skiff was its small, compact size and its comparatively light weight: only 154.5 pounds dry, with an overall length of 20.75 inches; height, 19.09 inches; and width, 16.14 inches. As I mentioned above, for the beach skiff, I had first considered installing one of the low-horsepower, slow-turning, old-type marine engines that originally powered such boats. Such engines are still produced in Nova Scotia and used by Canadian fishermen. The Atlantic two-cycle marine engine from Lunenburg Foundry and Engineering in Lunenburg, Nova Scotia comes to mind. Instead I decided on a lighter, faster-turning, modern small diesel in order to save weight and because it turns a smaller-diameter wheel.

For the Hammond dory, which was originally powered with a 6 h.p., old-style Essex engine, an old-type Canadian engine might be considered. Engine weight in a boat this size presents no problem, and there is ample depth of displacement for an 18-inch or even a 20-inch propeller.

The location of the engine in the larger Hammond boat is not as critical as it is in the 18-foot beach skiff. There is much more latitude for varying the placement to suit different interior arrangements. In the Hammond boat there is plenty of room for a small, closed cuddy with a couple of berths and even rudimentary cooking arrangements.

The 18-foot beach skiff is about as small as can be recommended for the installation of an inboard engine. A larger hull provides less economy but more options, and the superior qualities of the beach skiff's displacement hull become more apparent with some increase in size. As the need for fuel economy becomes more insistent, some people are certain to return to old-type, easily driven displacement hulls, which until very recently had almost passed from the boating scene.

Practically the only commercial builder of Sea Bright power skiffs who has managed to survive and who is still building in wood is Charles Hankins, 504 Grand Central Avenue, Box 7, Lavallette, New Jersey 08735. Although Hankins has adapted the beach skiff to meet his customers' demand for speed, he can still furnish the old-type, easily driven, economy beach craft.

1 0
Boston Fishing Power Dories

· · · · · · · · · · · · · · · • · · · · · · · · · · · · · · ·

At the beginning of this century, Boston was the largest fishing port in the United States. The city's fishing activity centered at T Wharf, where, according to an account in the *Fishing Gazette* of December 5, 1908, the local fleet of some 200 motorized Swampscott-model fishing dories tied up. Ranging in length from under 20 feet to nearly 30 feet, these dories were manned by hardy Sicilian fishermen, two and three men to a boat.

The Spartan requirements of power-dory fishing at the time tested both men and boats. An account of the risks and daily round of grinding toil was vividly reported in the *Gazette*:

> Hard, constant usage is the lot of the Boston motorboat fishing fleet. Nothing but a screeching gale keeps them in port. Starting out at daybreak or before, the boats go down the north and south approaches a

distance of 15 or 20 miles and set trawls for cod or haddock.

> They are exposed to the full force of the Atlantic, and nothing but a reliable outfit has any right to take the chance they willingly accept. Returning to the pier after 2 P.M., the catch is sold, and the crews begin to bait trawls for the next set. That completed, they go to their homes for a little sleep or turn in on the boats.

> During the flounder season, the trips are nearer home and the danger is not so great. For downright endurance, the torching of herring in the fall months tests motors most brutally. For 10 or 12 hours at a stretch, the machines are kept running, sometimes throttled to the slowest speed, then opened wide and as quickly shut down again, according to the movements of the schools of fish.

During the latter half of the 19th century, Boston's expanding immigrant populations of Irish and Italians

Above: *This photo taken in 1913 or 1914 shows the Sicilian powered fishing dory fleet at the head of South Dock, T Wharf, in Boston. (The Henry D. Fisher Collection, Mystic Seaport Museum)*
Opposite: *Another view of the "mosquito fleet." The fishermen are baiting their trawls. (Courtesy of The Society for the Preservation of New England Antiquities)*

required large quantities of fish. Fish was a large part of their traditional diet and was then both plentiful and cheap. Close by, abundant stocks of food fishes still frequented the waters of Massachusetts Bay.

For a time, the local fisheries that supplied the Boston market were dominated by Irish fishermen in their Paddy boats, sailing craft similar to the "hookers" they had been accustomed to in the old country. But toward the end of the century, as the new waves of Italian immigrants arrived, the Paddy boats succumbed to competition from Sicilian fishermen who, in the beginning, were not averse to rowing 15 to 20 miles a day in all kinds of weather.

These Sicilians adopted the round-sided Swampscott dory, developed in the town of that name on Boston's North Shore, and found these boats admirably suited to their needs. Eminently seaworthy and able, Swampscott dories both rowed and sailed well, could carry heavy loads, stood up to hard use, and were relatively cheap.

When the wind permitted, the fishermen sailed their dories; when it did not, oars came into play. Still, these craft were too dependent on the vagaries of the weather. Sometimes they did not make it back to port in time to command top prices for their fish, and in hot weather the lack of ice meant that the catch was not always in the best condition when boats finally did reach port.

Yachtsmen adopted the new gasoline motors first, and fishermen followed suit soon after. The changeover from sail was completed in a surprisingly brief time. Sails vanished from the Boston fishing fleet practically overnight. How this came about is described so well in the *Fishing Gazette* that I shall not presume to improve upon its narrative:

The first out-and-out motor fishing boat in Boston was a Swampscott dory fitted with a centerboard. It was a fast sailer and carried a crew of two men. Its owners got becalmed one day with a catch of cod and haddock, which spoiled on their hands when the market was high. As they tossed and pitched in the doldrums down by Boston light, a little motorcraft slipped by and was soon out of sight in the direction of the city wharves.

The occupant of the motor-propelled boat was a yachtsman with moorings at South Boston. Within a day or two, he was hunted up by the fishermen, who sought all manner of information about his motor, its make and cost, which was cheerfully given, and the fishermen were filled brimful of helpful suggestions before they quitted the club float. The fishing dory was taken to a yard in East Boston, and a four-horsepower, two-cycle motor of the make-and-break type soon followed it.

The boatbuilder was somewhat at a loss to decide how best to install the motor, but he finally spiked a block of wood to the transom, bolted a skeg to the dory bottom, so as to give the propeller plenty of room, bored the shaft-hole at what he believed to be the proper pitch, and then fashioned oak foundations on which to lag the engine.

Considerable squinting was needed before the motor could be got in line with the shaft, and lots of shim pieces of wood were tucked under the base of the machine to get a fit. Finally, when everything was declared to be right, and the exhaust pipe had been extended from a crude muffler through the side of the boat, the fishermen paid their bill of about $15, and the innovation was christened with Scotch as it splashed into the dock.

The older of the boat's owners grabbed the crank and essayed to start the motor. It didn't respond at first, so he got on his knees in front of it and began to spin the fly wheel with both hands. Suddenly it started and broke his wrist with the kick.

That modernized dory remained in the dock several weeks before an "expert" explained that it was the man's fault that he got hurt. He said the fisherman was altogether too reckless and ought not to have got on his knees to start a motor. He explained to the men the proper way to do the trick, got the engine running in fine form, gave a party of fishermen a spin down to the Graves, and from that day, makers of reliable gasoline motors have done a splendid business in supplying the Boston demand, and boats without number have been transformed from sail to motor in the same yard where the first craft discarded sail for an up-to-date pusher.

When the first motor fisherman got well into the harness, her owners' wives began to appear on the street in new dresses and wore smiles of contentment while promenading the North End of Boston, where

Old photographs of the dories at T Wharf give an idea of what the open cockpit (top) and decked-over (bottom) dories looked like from the outside; interior arrangements must be reconstructed from the few sources available. (The Henry D. Fisher Collection, Mystic Seaport Museum)

the Sicilians have their homes. The boat was a wonder in the way of earning money. She made two trips, sometimes three, while the sailboats were getting their fares to market.

A bigger success on a small scale never appeared in the harbor. It was no use for the old-fashioned craft to compete with the new-fangled boat. The immediate rush for motors sent manufacturers to their wits' end to keep up with the orders, and the same engine (Mianus) is in vogue today in larger sizes and with correspondingly more power.

Another contemporary publication, the *Nautical Gazette,* shows in its March 1, 1906 issue a photograph along with a lines plan and construction plan for a Camden Anchor–Rockland Machine Company power dory. The boat illustrated was 25 feet long and

The Nautical Gazette *of March 1, 1906 featured this 25-footer, ruggedly built of pine over oak by Camden Anchor–Rockland Machine Company of Maine.*

had a beam of 6 feet. A 4½ h.p. single-cylinder three-port Knox engine (manufactured in Camden, Maine) produced a speed of about 8 m.p.h.

The claim was made that as far as seaworthiness goes, these dories had no superiors. The *Nautical Gazette* explains:

> These boats are designed to withstand the severe weather they are subjected to on the bleak coast of Maine during the winter season. The keel, ribs, sternpost, stem, bottom board and engine foundation are made of native oak; planking, native pine, 1¼" [*sic*] thick; galvanized iron fastenings; deck, pine with oak frame; coaming, oak; fender rail, oak; decked over fore and aft to take in tank, muffler and batteries; bulkheads are of pine with doors fore and aft; ribs, steam-bent oak, 1" square, 10" on centers; fittings, galvanized iron. Many of these boats are finished with winch heads, which are driven by means of sprocket chains and are used for dragging scallops and hauling lobster pots.

Of course, dory planking 1¼ inches thick is out of the question. This has to be an error. The maximum plank thickness for a dory of this size would be ⅝ inch. Fore-and-aft bulkheads with doors indicate closed storage compartments under the decks at either end, yet the motor, lacking any covered engine box or compartment, seems to have been quite open and exposed.

This was an early installation. Quite soon after, the larger, powered fishing dories had closed engine compartments built into the stern. These were bulkheaded off from the rest of the boat and had a low trunk that rose above the stern deck, to which it was fastened. Entrance was through a companionway topped by a sliding hatch cover.

On the T Wharf 30-footers, the steering wheel was mounted on the inside of the engine-compartment bulkhead, and the helmsman stood inside the companionway with the slide pushed back to steer. His body filled the narrow companionway opening and served to keep out loose water in bad weather. Within reach was the pump, which would discharge a barrel of water in a few minutes, according to a 1912 *Power Boating* report.

The engine compartments varied considerably in size and arrangement, depending on the builder and the length of the dory. The accompanying illustration of a 30-foot Toppan fishing dory shows a large engine compartment built into the stern. Judging from photographs of T Wharf fishing dories as well as from contemporary descriptions, this one closely resembles the engine compartments favored by Boston's Sicilian dory fishermen. In fact, it is more than likely that a number of the dories then fishing out of T Wharf were Toppan-built.

According to its 40-page catalog for 1906, the Toppan Boat Manufacturing Company, "designers and builders of high-grade power dories, whaleboat launches, trunk cabin cruisers and special boats built

This 30-foot dory built by the Toppan Boat Manufacturing Company features a large engine compartment built into the stern, a configuration favored by Boston's Sicilian dory fishermen. (Courtesy Mystic Seaport Museum)

to order," had its factory, wharf, yard, and storehouse at Charlestown and its office and showrooms at 9 Haverhill Street, Boston, three doors from Haymarket Square. In 1906 Toppan was an established and successful company in a period of expansion and growth. Although it has long since been out of business, its dories are not forgotten. A fine example of one of the company's smaller power dories was displayed in 1982 at Boston's Museum of Transportation after having been restored by the museum's Skills Shop.

What the Toppan catalog had to say about its line of power dories was probably no great exaggeration:

These well-known boats need no description here. No better sea boat can be built.

We have shipped our boats to nearly every country in Europe, and our export trade is still growing. The same can be said in regard to our home market: still growing. The reader must surely know there is a reason, and if you are thinking of purchasing and want a good reliable outfit at a popular price, kindly read the testimonials at the end, and you will then see WHY the Toppan boats are in such demand.

The many pages of testimonials, all dated 1906, were submitted from all over the United States. There were also letters from Vienna; Genoa, Italy; and Quebec. The one from Canada reads:

Gentlemen: The 20-foot Toppan dory launch has given first-class satisfaction in every respect. The boat is a first-class sea boat and has both speed and

carrying capacity. The 3 h.p. Toppan engine gave fine results, and as I had *never even seen* a gasoline engine, let alone run one, I was more than pleased. Batteries troubled some, but when I put on a magneto, everything was fine. I have got nearly eight miles per hour. If you want to refer anyone to me, do so, and I will be more than glad to speak a good word. Yours truly, E.B. Blackwell, Manicouagan, P.Q., Saguenray Co., Canada.

The demand for the new power dories that had greatly expanded Toppan's business in Boston also made itself felt in Swampscott, where E. Gerry Emmons was the largest dory builder at that time. Boats from the Emmons factory were shipped to all regions of this country and to many other parts of the world. The Emmons Company had gotten into power boats early, marketing its own gasoline engines in 1, 2½, 5, and 6 h.p. sizes, and could well have been the first firm to install a gasoline engine in a dory.

A fisherman's power dory built by Emmons is shown here, reproduced from the company's catalog, which described the boat as

our 20-foot overall lobster and fishing dory, 5-foot beam, 21 inches deep. Has oak bottom, hardwood frame, pine planking, five strakes on a side, galvanized fastenings throughout, house and slide over motor, three cross seats, grating in bottom of boat, rudder and yoke, centerboard if wanted.

Boat is painted two good coats inside and out. Fitted with a 2½ h.p. Emmons motor, plain wheel and shaft, copper tank in bow, brass deck-plate in deck and tank, brass feed-pipe to motor, batteries, spark, coil,

The popularity of power dories in Boston carried over to Swampscott. There, E. Gerry Emmons built boats like this 20-footer. The lines appeared in an early 1900 issue of The Rudder *magazine, and the photograph was printed in an Emmons catalog of the time. Fitted with a 2½ h.p. motor, the dory sold for $275.*

muffler, etc., steering wheel, oars and rowlocks. Price, $275.

One thing to be noted here is that the engine compartment for this 20-foot dory, unlike that of the 30-foot Toppan model, is not topped by a trunk. The companionway slide is attached directly to the stern deck. Undoubtedly this is because a raised trunk aft in this 20-foot dory would be out of proportion to the rest of the boat.

Although Emmons produced a variety of other boats, both large and small, dories were the foundation and mainstay of his business. Pages 17–19 of the catalog (circa 1905) contain a historical sketch of the origins and development of the Swampscott dory. Several paragraphs apply to the new power dories, especially those for inshore fishermen:

The use of the dory for general purposes has greatly increased within the last decade, and with the

Oak Washboard 5/8 thick
Pine Deck 5/8"
Cedar Planking 5/8
Natural Crook Sawed Frames
Sheathing
Midship Section
Oak shoe

This 20-footer with carvel planking was designed and built by the Cape Cod Power Dory Company of Wareham, Massachusetts. The construction plan here appeared in the February 25, 1911 issue of Motor Boat. *The engine was a single-cylinder two-cycle 3½ h.p. Palmer or a 4 h.p. Ferro motor.*

marvelous growth of the manufacture of small power boats, the experiment was made of harnessing the dory with other than manpower. Even before this, the demand began to grow for a light dory for rowing and sailing, with more attention paid to comfortable fittings than in the fisherman's model, and the 16-foot and 18-foot dory, fitted with a leg-o-mutton sail, speedily became a favorite for pleasure boating.

But with the fitting of these dories—of all the models mentioned—with small gasoline engines, their pleasure-giving qualities and usefulness were greatly increased.

Shore fishermen began to look at them with interest, and now not a few of the Swampscott and other home toilers go out to their nets or lobster pots without the weariness of an "ash breeze," but instead may be seen of a summer morning standing erect with yoke lines in hand, scudding rapidly from one buoy to another, like veritable sea kings guiding their chargers.

Similar to the Emmons 20-foot power fishing dory is a 20-footer by the Cape Cod Power Dory Company of Wareham, Massachusetts. A construction plan for this craft was published in *Motor Boat,* February 25, 1911. Beam was 5 feet 6 inches. The engine was a single-cylinder two-cycle 3½ h.p. Palmer or a 4 h.p. Ferro motor.

As can be seen, this dory is carvel-planked rather than being lapped or clinker-built. Toppan also carried carvel-planked dories for those who preferred a boat with smooth planking, but these cost slightly more. Some fishermen believed smooth-planked dories lasted better and were tighter because they could be caulked. One of these early, smooth-planked 20-foot Cape Cod dories has survived more than a half century of service at Pine Island Camps in Belgrade Lakes, Maine, and is now preserved in the small-craft collection at Mystic Seaport Museum, Mystic, Connecticut.

The success of the Italian fishermen in Boston waters contributed directly to the early demise of the dory fleet. As soon as they acquired sufficient resources and could raise the required capital, they moved on in the expanding economy to larger vessels that could operate in more distant waters. Their catches became bigger and so did their profits.

In little more than 20 years, the power dory was obsolete as a working fishing boat and all but forgotten. But today, with the growing number of people considering small-scale fishing as a possible source of supplemental income, interest in the Swampscott dory is reviving. These boats appear to have most of the features and qualities that the small-scale fisherman requires.

None of the original dories have survived, and no detailed drawings of their construction details have ever been discovered. But we do have enough information about these dories, gleaned from a variety of sources, to be able to reproduce them fairly accurately.

We know almost exactly what these dories were like on the outside. What is less certain is just how they were built on the inside. How were the fish holds made? Did some have self-bailing cockpits? Did they have watertight bulkheads, and if so, where were they located? What were the cuddies like on the inside?

Few, if any, of these dories seem to have been exactly alike in all details. Their interior arrangements were constructed to suit their owners. I will try to make these arrangements consistent with what we do know and convenient for the duties this dory traditionally performed.

The lines shown here are typical Swampscott-dory lines, of which numerous authenticated examples exist. They are for a 28-foot-8-inch dory, the largest used by the Italian fishermen. I have given the keel a fair amount of drag at the stern to gain necessary depth for a slow-turning propeller of ample size.

The frames also serve as building molds; for this 28-foot-8-inch dory, they would be 30 inches apart. A smaller boat could be built by simply decreasing the frame spacing. The lower limit would be 24-inch spacing, which would give an approximate overall length of 24 feet. A 26-foot dory could be built by eliminating one frame spacing amidships but keeping the rest intact. If a reduction of this kind were made, the lines should be refaired by laying them down full size.

Swampscott dories were relatively inexpensive at the beginning of this century. They were clinker-built of the cheap white-pine boards that were then abundantly available in long lengths and extra-wide widths. Clinker construction is much quicker and requires far less labor than carvel planking. Today, white-pine lumber is even more expensive than some mahogany, and not to be had at any price in the wide widths of former times.

Nevertheless, marine plywood is an acceptable substitute. I have specified ½-inch marine fir. The strakes can be made of standard 8-foot and 10-foot panels in sections and spliced together when applied to the boat. Working in this manner (coupled with some planning and foresight) would virtually eliminate any waste of planking material.

The splices are made with 6-inch-long scarfs and put together with epoxy glue and nails. The 1½-inch-wide planking laps are also epoxy-glued, which produces a hull of great rigidity and strength. Plank splices are spaced to fall on the frames as shown in the diagram and are staggered to separate them as much as possible.

The details for splicing the planking are shown in the drawings and should be studied carefully until everything is clear and fully understood. A two-part clamp with a through bolt used for pulling the scarfed surfaces together until the glue hardens makes the splice as strong as the original uncut plywood itself.

Both the inside and outside pieces of this clamp are made of hardwood. A ⅜-inch carriage bolt is driven through a slightly smaller hole in the inside piece so that it fits tightly. A slightly larger hole through the splice allows the bolt to slip through easily. The hole in the outside part of the clamp should also be slightly larger for easy assembly.

A few turns with the wrench after the washer and nut are in place will apply sufficient pressure to bring the scarfed surfaces of the splice together and in firm contact. A tight pine plug fills the hole through the splice when the bolt is removed.

The surface of the scarf should be planed almost to a feather edge, but not quite, leaving an edge thickness of ⅟₃₂ inch or a hair less. A sharp smoothing plane is desirable for removing the bulk of the wood on the scarf surfaces. These surfaces should be finished and brought smooth and fair with a low-angle block plane.

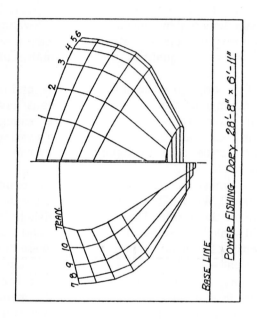

STATIONS		STEM	1	2	3	4	5	6	7	8	9	10	TRANSOM
								OFFSETS POWER FISHING DORY 28'-8" x 6'-11"						
HEIGHTS	SHEER	4-11-7	4-8-1	4-5-0	4-2-1	3-11-6	3-10-1	3-9-1	3-9-0	3-9-5	3-10-6	4-0-3	4-2-4
	KNUCKLE 1	4-8-0	4-3-6	4-0-1	3-8-5	3-6-1	3-4-3	3-3-6	3-3-5	3-4-3	3-6-0	3-8-0	3-10-1
	KNUCKLE 2	4-3-4	3-11-0	3-6-6	3-2-5	2-11-7	2-10-1	2-9-3	2-9-4	2-10-6	3-0-5	3-3-2	3-5-3
	KNUCKLE 3	3-11-0	3-6-1	3-1-4	2-9-1	2-6-1	2-4-1	2-3-5	2-3-7	2-5-0	2-7-3	2-10-2	3-0-3
	KNUCKLE 4	3-5-5	3-1-4	2-8-7	2-4-4	2-1-4	1-11-4	1-10-4	1-10-5	2-0-1	2-2-5	2-6-1	2-7-7
	BOTTOM	1-6-3	2-0-0	1-5-4	1-3-7	1-2-5	1-1-4	1-0-3	0-11-3	0-10-3	0-9-2	1-7-4	0-8-3
HALF-BREADTHS	SHEER	0-0-4	1-2-3	2-0-4	2-8-0	3-1-2	3-4-1	3-5-1	3-4-5	3-2-4	2-10-3	2-4-7	1-9-5
	KNUCKLE 1	0-0-4	1-1-7	2-0-0	2-7-5	3-0-6	3-3-5	3-4-5	3-4-1	3-1-7	2-9-7	2-4-5	1-10-6
	KNUCKLE 2	0-0-4	1-0-6	1-10-4	2-6-1	2-11-2	3-2-0	3-3-2	3-2-7	3-0-5	2-8-5	2-3-1	1-10-3
	KNUCKLE 3	0-0-4	0-10-4	1-8-0	2-3-5	2-8-5	2-11-3	3-0-3	3-0-1	2-10-1	2-6-0	2-0-2	1-8-1
	KNUCKLE 4	0-0-4	0-8-1	1-4-7	2-0-0	2-4-3	2-7-1	2-8-3	2-8-3	2-6-1	2-2-1	1-8-5	1-5-4
	BOTTOM	0-0-4	0-0-4	0-4-1	0-8-4	0-11-1	1-0-3	1-0-0	0-10-5	0-8-0	0-4-2	0-9-2	0-2-0

MEASUREMENTS IN FEET, INCHES AND EIGHTHS INCHES. HEIGHTS MEASURED ABOVE BASE LINE.

MEASUREMENTS TAKEN INSIDE PLANKING - INSIDE BOTTOM - OUTSIDE TRANSOM - OUTSIDE TRUE OR INSIDE STEM.

PLANK SPLICE — 6" — BOW →

TEMPORARY CLAMP →

FRAME NO. 4 — 2"

FRAME SIDED 1½"

FRAME SPLICE RIVETED & GLUED ½" PLYWOOD EITHER SIDE

2½" NAIL

⅜" BOLT   5/16" BOLT

3" NAIL   POWER FISHING DORY 28'-8" x 6'-11"

3"   1½"   2½" x 20

It is absolutely essential that both planes be as sharp as possible and in the best working order. Failure to make proper wood scarfs is due almost invariably to planes that are dull, set incorrectly, or used improperly—sometimes all three.

With seven strakes on a side, three or four splices in each strake, and two scarfs in each splice, almost 100 scarf surfaces have to be cut. This represents a lot of planing, but is not nearly the job that planing the outside of a carvel-planked boat of equal size would be. It might save time to make up a simple jig and cut these scarfs with a router.

Despite the scarfs and laps that have to be planed and fitted, this plywood lapstrake construction is one of the quickest and easiest methods I know. Furthermore, plywood is available almost everywhere, whereas other kinds of planking material frequently are not.

Plywood takes glue readily, and when the splices and laps are properly glued, a tight, superstrong product results. I recommend Chem-Tech's T-88 epoxy adhesive thickened with Cab-O-Sil, or an equivalent thixotropic agent. Mix them into a pastelike consistency that is stiff enough to stay in place in vertical joints until it hardens.

After the boat has been planked and the glue has had several days to fully cure, the dried-out interior of the hull should be completely saturated with several applications of linseed oil that is thinned about 20 percent with mineral spirits. The oil should be heated in a double boiler and applied boiling hot.

The strakes are nailed to the oak frames as shown in the diagram. The laps must also be fastened between the frames in such a way that their surfaces are held in contact until the glue hardens. The fastenings also add reinforcement to the glue.

In the past, galvanized chisel-point clinch nails were used as the standard glueless lap fastenings for dories, but these nails are no longer manufactured. Bronze nails that are soft enough to clinch readily make a good substitute. Copper rivets are neater and possibly stronger but are more trouble to put in.

The selection of fastenings for this boat presents some problems due to the high cost of copper and bronze and the poor lasting quality of galvanized steel. Here the builder will have to make a choice between how much money he wants to spend and how long a life he plans for his boat. The galvanized-steel nails and bolts used in a boat of this kind (galvanized iron is no longer available) can be expected to last reasonably well for about 10 years, providing no special electrol-

ysis problems develop. Because this boat will have an engine and some electrical installations, attention must be given to this possibility.

If the builder decides to use galvanized bolts, he might want to make the boat sturdier by increasing the size of the floor-through-bottom bolts to ½ inch in diameter and the floor-through-frame bolts to ⅜ inch in diameter.

Copper and bronze fastenings throughout should last almost indefinitely. However, the extra cost of nonferrous fastenings will be considerable.

Construction details and interior arrangements for a motorized dory such as this must be based on our best judgment from the few sources available. As stated above, none of the Italian dories have survived. No original construction plans were ever drawn, or at least none have come to light so far. About all we have are a couple of descriptive accounts by journalists, the one in the *Fishing Gazette,* December 1908, and one in *Power Boating,* April 1912. We can also refer to various photographs, especially those of Henry D. Fisher, which may be seen in Andrew W. German's book *Down on T Wharf.* These photographs are most informative and leave little doubt as to what the exteriors of these fishing dories were like. But they don't show the interior arrangements. Here we have to rely more on judgment and experience—even on plain, ordinary guesswork.

The original dory type had an open cockpit; the later model was completely decked over. The photographs we have show examples of both kinds. The decked-over model has a number of disadvantages, the combined effect of which might have been a deterrent to its wide adoption. Full decks are more expensive to build, requiring additional materials and extra labor. They add weight to the topsides, increasing the roll in a hull that tends to move a lot in any case. It is also difficult to make full decks tight and keep them so. If rainwater is admitted, it gets trapped in joints and between the decking and the deck beams, becoming a highly potent source of rot.

Due to the increased possibility of rot, decked-over dory hulls are likely to have appreciably shorter lives than hulls with open cockpits. If decks could be built flush, it would be much easier to make them tight, but some sort of low bulkheads are necessary to keep equipment, gear, and what-have-you from sliding overboard. This would mean fitting the waterways around the upper ends of the frames, which would serve as stanchions. Joggling the waterways to fit snugly around the frames is tricky, precise work.

These joints would then have to be caulked tight or "pined,"—that is, fitted with dry pine wedges driven tight. Furthermore, some scuppers of some sort would be required to allow any water that came aboard to drain quickly.

No hint remains of just how this was originally accomplished, but the simple construction shown in the drawing would work. Waterways of 1-inch-by-8-inch pine are fitted snugly against the inside of the top strake, just above its lap with the plank below.

The top strake is also thicker, $1\frac{3}{16}$ inch, for needed extra strength. A strand of cotton wicking set in thick oil paint (white lead if you can get it) is laid in the seam where the two planks come together. Three-inch galvanized wire nails spaced 4 inches apart are driven (from the outside) through the top strake into the waterways.

Scuppers measuring 1 inch high by 12 inches long are centered between the frames in each bay. The openings are cut through the top strake, level with the surface of the waterways.

The decked-over boats must have been less comfortable and not as convenient to work from as the older model with the open cockpit. The 1908 description from the *Fishing Gazette* specifies "a hatch amidships with a watertight, standing room forward, where the crew hauls trawls."

This seems to indicate a tight well of some sort forward, open at the top and large enough for two men to work from (most of the boats carried crews of two men). Without a cover, such a well, as distinguished from a hatch, would be bound to take on water in heavy and breaking seas, putting the boat down by the head and even endangering stability. It's possible the well was self-bailing, in which case it would need to have draining scuppers and perhaps be floored over above the load waterline.

In the accompanying drawing of a fully decked dory, I show a second covered hatch forward that opens into the fish hold below. The hold extends back to the watertight bulkhead at station 7, which separates the engine compartment and cuddy from the rest of the boat. The fish hold is tightly floored over on top of the frame floors with removable traps down the center, and it is tightly sheathed against the frames about two-thirds of the way up the sides.

Water taken in through the hatches is cleared by means of a large hand pump located just forward of the bulkhead at station 7. One of the crew can operate it by standing just inside the cuddy and engine compartment and reaching through the slide entrance. In 1912,

Power Boating described such a pump as "the galvanized barrel kind with spout and a wooden handle on either a wood or metal rod....The handle of the pump is within convenient reach of the man who steers and who operates the engine, and will discharge a barrel of water in a few minutes, taking care of a bad leak or deluge that gets below."

Large hatch covers can get in the way when they are taken off the hatches. To make them easier to stow they can be hinged in the middle with large piano hinges, which permits them to be folded to half their full size. Hinged in this way, covers will not be completely watertight. But what little water drips through, while intolerable in a yacht, is inconsequential here.

The open model I have drawn shows nothing distinctive or unusual. The cockpit is floored over, and the sides are sheathed partway up in the manner described for the decked model. From the bulkhead at station 7, the cockpit extends to station 2, where it is bulkheaded off partway up. This provides easily accessible dry stowage space under the foredeck.

The rather high coaming of steam-bent oak stands 6 inches above the narrow side decks or waterways. This is not so high as to make working difficult but is still high enough to keep out a lot of loose water. A canvas spray hood could be easily fitted, as could a snap-on canvas cover to keep rainwater out of the cockpit when the boat is lying at mooring. The pumping arrangement would be the same as for the decked model.

The combination cuddy and engine compartment is identical for both models. It provides dry shelter for both the engine installation and the two- or three-man crew. Extending as far forward as station 7, this section occupies approximately one-third of the overall length of the boat. It could be set back a foot or even more to give additional room in the cockpit or fish hold. Nonetheless, the frame at station 7 is convenient for locating the bulkhead, and ample room in the cuddy has much to commend it.

The cuddy trunk shown here rises 14 inches above the deck at its forward end, with the top crowned 2 inches or 3 inches. The forward end of the slide extends 6 inches above that, sloping back to 3 inches. This does not afford much space below, but there is plenty for sitting headroom above the low seats on either side of the boat, just aft of the bulkhead and abreast of the slide entrance.

The engine is set as far aft as efficient operation will permit, with skeleton transoms built on either side. These serve as low benches or berths with open-access

28'-8" POWER FISHING DORY
WITH TIGHT DECK

1	FRAMES OAK SIDED 1½" HEAD 2" FT. 2½"	11	CLAMP OAK 1¼" × 3"
2	FLOORS OAK SIDED 1¾" MOLDED 4"	12	HATCH LEDGES OAK 1½" × 3"
3	BOTTOM OAK 2" THICK	13	HATCH FRAME OAK 1¼" × 3"
4	PLANK WHITE PINE 5⅝ – 1½" THICK	14	HATCH COVER ⅞" PINE
5	TOP STRAKE WHITE PINE 1⅜" TH'K	15	WATERWAYS 1" WHITE PINE
6	INWALE OAK ⅞" × 2"	16	SHEATHING ⅝" PINE
7	CAP OAK SIDED ⅞" MOLDED 4½"	17	TRAP COVER 12" WIDE 1⅛" PINE
8	RUBBING STRIP 1½" OAK HALF-ROUND	18	LIMBER 3" × ¾"
9	DECK BEAMS OAK SIDED 1¾" MOLDED 2¼"	19	3" NAILS TOP STRAKE TO WATERWAYS
10	CARLINGS OAK SIDED 1¾" MOLDED 2¼"	20	DECK SCUPPERS 12" LONG 1" HIGH

CROWN 2" IN 7'

STATION 5

FRAME SPLICE. PLYWOOD
BOTH SIDES GLUED

FEET AND INCHES

TIGHT DECK LAYOUT

STA. 2

3'-6"

STA. 5

2'-10"

4'-1"

3'-4"

3'-1"

STA. 7

5'-0"

2'-3"

3'-0"

2'-0"

STA. 10

3'-7"

FEET AND INCHES

28'-8" POWER FISHING DORY
WITH OPEN COCKPIT

1	INNER STEM SIDED 3" MOLDED 4" SPLICED AS SHOWN	9	COAMING 3/4" OAK STEAM BENT 6" ABOVE WATERWAYS
2	OUTER STEM 1 1/2" THICK STEAM BENT	10	STEERING WHEEL 16" DIA.
3	TANK FOR DIESEL FUEL	11	TOP STREAKS 11/16" THICK
4	WATER TIGHT BULK HEAD 15" HIGH ON FRAME	12	RUBBING STRIPS TOP AND BOTTOM EDGES 1 1/4" OAK H.R.
5	COCKPIT FLOOR PINE 7/8" THICK	13	SKEG OAK SIDED 3 1/2"
6	THWART 1 1/4 PINE 10" WIDE WITH HOLE FOR MAST	14	STERN POST OAK SIDED 3 1/2"
7	WATER TIGHT BULKHEAD 3/4" MARINE PLY ON FRAME	15	INTERNAL SHAFT LOG OAK SIDED 3 1/2"
8	SILL, ENTRANCE THROUGH BULKHEAD TO CUDDY	16	RUDDER SHOE 1/2" X 2 1/2" GALVANIZED
		17	RUDDER GAL. 3/16" PLATG. SHAFT 1 3/8"
		18	TILLER QUADRANT 15"
		19	PORTS IN SIDES OF TRUNK. WOOD SLIDE CLOSURE
		20	TRUNK SIDES PINE 1 1/2" THICK

FEET AND INCHES

BASE LINE

storage beneath. Forward of the transoms enough space is left for the low seats just mentioned.

The first heavy, slow-turning gasoline engines installed in the fishing dories 75 years ago were much larger than the small diesels that would be the first choice now. Accordingly, they took up much more room.

For example, a modern 22 h.p. Sabb diesel (more than ample for these boats) is only about 40 inches long. When installed, more than 2 feet of clear space would be left forward of the engine—plenty of room for a crewman to stand at the slide opening to steer and to work the pump.

As the reporter for the *Fishing Gazette* put it, the body of the helmsman in his oilskins pressed into the slide opening makes this cubbyhole almost impervious to flying water. When both hands are required to work the pump, the wheel can be held by the pressure of the helmsman's thigh or hip.

Ventilation is obtained from square holes cut through the two sides and the end of the trunk. These can be closed when desired with simple slides of thin board.

Note should be taken of several features of the dory's construction, these being identical in both basic models under consideration. The bottom is rather narrow for a dory; it is nearly straight fore and aft, with only the slightest bit of upward curvature in the forward end.

If the bottom were made perfectly straight from end to end, without camber, the effect on performance, if any, would not be enough to matter. With such a straight, narrow bottom it is possible to have a good amount of drag in the keel, which is essential for getting the propeller deep enough to be fully effective. This is especially so with large-diameter propellers such as the 24-inch wheel shown in the drawing and specified for the 22 h.p. Sabb diesel.

Two-inch-thick oak for the bottom might seem to be larger and heavier than is needed, but it provides solid nailing for a tight garboard. Furthermore, establishing this weight so low in the boat has a positive stabilizing effect. Because the bottom has no fore-and-aft camber, it does not have to be bent and can be thicker than usual.

As reported in the *Fishing Gazette,* the sawn frames in the early Boston power dories were spaced 3 feet apart and had steam-bent frames in between. These bent frames were continuous from gunwale to gunwale and were nailed through into the bottom. I do not show

any bent frames in the drawings, since the sawn frames are spaced 30 inches on center.

Intermediate bent frames could be added for additional reinforcement if desired, but I doubt that they would be necessary. The substantial, well-fastened lapstrake planking and the internal sheathing that runs continuously from station 7 to station 2 would probably be enough.

Sawn frames are got out of ordinary straight stock, but if live-edge or flitch-sawn lumber is used, the builder should take advantage of any natural curvature in the planks. Frames are spliced as shown, and reinforcing plywood gussets are fastened on each side with both glue and nails. The stem can be spliced in the same way, with the splice located as indicated by the dashed line in the profile drawing.

The skeg, sternpost, and inside shaft log are all sided 3½ inches, which gives plenty of room for bolts on either side of the shaft hole. There is an easy way to bore the shaft hole and to get it right. First, the stern assembly should be laid out and drawn full size in profile so that molds can be made of the three component members.

These are cut precisely to the molds. The skeg is bolted to the bottom before setting up. Likewise, the internal shaft log, fastened to the transom, serves as a stern knee when the transom is set up. The sternpost goes on last, but before it is fastened in place it is bored for the shaft.

This is done on the bench with the post laid flat. The shaft line is transferred from the mold to the post, having previously been lifted from the laydown. Both ends of this line are squared down across the opposite edges of the block; centers are then marked on each of these lines, and the shaft hole is bored using the procedure for boring holes for shaft-log drifts or through bolts that is described in detail in Chapter 12.

When the shaft hole has been bored through the sternpost, the latter is fastened in place. It then becomes a jig for boring the rest of the shaft hole through the transom and the interior shaft log. To prevent any possibility of leaks at the bottom of the transom, a ⅝-inch-diameter pine stopwater is put in. It runs from side to side, as indicated in the drawing.

The shaft hole is lined with either lead pipe or annealed copper tubing. These are swelled at the ends to achieve a tight fit, as well as to properly seat the stern bearing and the inside stuffing box, which is made tight with flax packing.

11

Matinicus Peapod

....................•....................

The design for this 15-foot Matinicus peapod was based on a photograph taken at Matinicus Island in 1954 by Jerry McCarty, at that time editor of the old *Maine Coast Fisherman*. To a boatbuilder like myself who had made a close study of peapod lines, the overall shape and proportions of the fisherman's heavily built working pod were clearly revealed in the broadside view the photograph provided. The challenge of working out actual dimensions together with lines and offsets for a closely similar pod without straying beyond the limits imposed by the photograph was one I could hardly resist. The result was well received at the time by *Maine Coast Fisherman* readers. Several of the pods were built and got good reports. But then the pod faded into obscurity, so to speak, not to return to the public eye for nearly 20 years.

In 1973 Harold Kimber, a retired master boat-builder who for many years had operated a boatyard on the River Brue in Somerset, England, was invited to deliver the principal address at Mystic Seaport Museum's annual Small Craft Workshop. Afterward he was invited by Lance Lee, the director of The Apprenticeshop—which at that time was located in Bath, Maine—to come to Bath for a month to demonstrate clinker boatbuilding. Kimber was pleased to accept, and several different boats were considered for demonstration purposes, among them the Matinicus pod. Kimber liked the pod, and that was the one he finally selected.

This choice proved to have been well considered. The boat so built met every expectation, becoming the prototype of a stock model that The Apprenticeshop still continues to build for its customers. Although this pod was designed as a rowboat, since the lobster fishermen generally rowed their pods while tending

Above: *This photograph of a peapod taken in 1954 at Matinicus Island, Maine, served as the basis for the design in this chapter. (Jerry McCarty photo)* **Right:** *Boatbuilders at The Apprenticeshop, now located in Rockport, Maine, put the finishing touches on another 15-foot Matinicus pod. (Neal Parent photo)*

An Apprenticeshop-built Matinicus peapod with sailing rig. (David Lyman photo)

their traps, some of the pods built at The Apprenticeshop have been fitted with a spritsail and rudder and have been found to sail quite well for their type of boat. As long as the proportions and construction of the basic hull are not tampered with unduly, builders might experiment with a variety of simple rigs if they should be so inclined.

For amateurs with some boatbuilding experience or the equivalent, it would not be forbiddingly difficult to substitute a flat plank keel—say, 7 inches wide amidships, tapering to 2 inches wide at the ends, and 1¾ to 2 inches thick—for the beam keel of the original design. By mortising a slot in this plank keel, it would be easy to install a centerboard should the builder desire a thoroughgoing conversion to sail. In fact, numbers of working pods did have plank keels of this sort, although not for the purpose of installing centerboards. Most working pods were not fitted with centerboards, for a simple reason: If someone in a boat such as this is in a hurry to make a destination to windward, he can often make better progress rowing dead for it than he can tacking back and forth under sail.

The accompanying drawings contain the essential

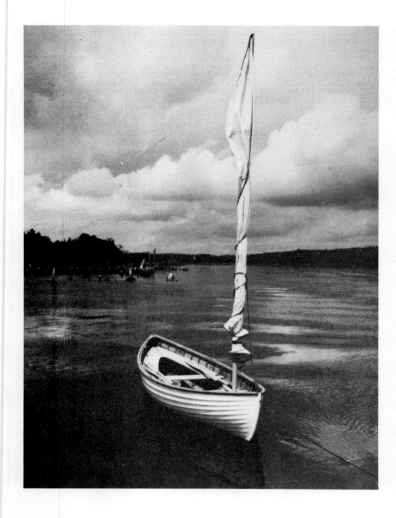

Another view of a Matinicus peapod built by the Apprentice-shop. This 15-footer is suitable for amateur construction. (Steve McAllister photo)

information required for building. What follows here is largely suggestions for procedures applying specifically to the building of this boat. Some basic boatbuilding experience—including some knowledge of the materials, the tools, and such essentials as laying down lines, steam bending, and lapstrake planking—is assumed.

Since the ends of this pod are exactly alike, the full-size laydown of lines need include only one half of the hull plus an additional station for assistance in fairing. One 4-by-10-foot panel of plywood is all that is needed. Molds are made for all stations except station 1. In other words, two station 2 molds, two station 3s, two station 4s, and one station 5 are made.

The keel, keel batten, two stem assemblies, and the molds are set up at a convenient height for working.

Two stout sawhorses will serve nicely. Stems and molds are plumbed, leveled, and secured in place with braces, shores, and stay-lathes. It is a good idea to secure the molds to the keel batten with short sections of angle iron bored for screws. When this is done, planking lines are marked on the molds. These lines locate the top inside edges of the eight clinker planks. The dimensions given for locating the planking lines are close, but a final trueing with a fair lining batten will be required. Such a batten, preferably of our native Eastern white pine, should be about 1½ inches by ⅜ inch in section, free of knots or other defects, and longer than the boat. This batten is tacked on the marks and then adjusted as required until it sights fair and true throughout, after which the marks are redrawn as necessary. Before the planking lines are

15-FT. MATINICUS ISLAND PEAPOD
LINES INSIDE PLANKING FINISHED ONE HALF INCH
STEM AND KEEL SIDED TWO INCHES

	15-FOOT MATINICUS ISLAND PEAPOD						
	STATIONS	STEM	1	2	3	4	5
HEIGHTS	SHEER	2-7-5	2-5-0	2-2-5	1-11-2	1-9-5	1-9-3
	18"BUTTOCK	0-0-0	0-0-0	0-0-0	1-0-1	0-4-7	0-4-0
	9"BUTTOCK	0-0-0	0-0-0	1-0-6	0-4-3	0-3-2	0-3-1
	BEARDING LINE	0-0-0	0-6-4	0-2-5	0-2-4	0-2-4	0-2-4
HALF-BREADTHS	SHEER	0-1-0	0-6-7	1-1-2	1-10-0	2-2-3	2-3-3
	17" W.L.	0-1-0	0-5-0	0-11-4	1-8-2	2-1-3	2-2-5
	14" W.L.	0-1-0	0-3-6	0-9-7	1-6-7	2-0-5	2-2-1
	11" W.L.	0-1-0	0-2-4	0-7-6	1-5-2	1-11-5	2-1-2
	8" W.L.	0-1-0	0-1-2	0-5-2	0-2-5	1-9-6	1-11-6
	5" W.L.	0-1-0	0-0-0	0-2-5	0-10-1	1-6-1	1-8-3
	BEARDING LINE	0-1-0	0-1-0	0-1-0	0-1-0	0-1-0	0-1-0
DIAGONALS	DIAGONAL 1	0-1-1	0-6-5	1-0-6	1-9-0	2-2-2	2-3-5
	DIAGONAL 2	0-1-1	0-4-4	0-9-7	1-5-5	1-10-7	2-0-4
	DIAGONAL 3	0-1-2	0-2-2	0-6-0	0-11-3	1-1-5	1-1-6
	DIAG. 1 UP 23" OUT 24" ON W.L. 14". DIAG. 2 UP 17"						
	OUT 24" ON W.L. 5". DIAG 3 UP 11" OUT 9" ON W.L. 5".						
LINES INSIDE PLANK IN FEET-INCHES-EIGHTHS. HEIGHTS ABOVE BASE L.							

STATION 2

SHEER

STEM OAK SIDED 2"

CLINKER PLANK 3/8" TH'K

23" W.L.

17"

14"

11"

8"

5" W.L.

OUTSIDE

RABBET
BEARDING
INSIDE STEM

UPPER HALF STEM

LOWER HALF OF STEM

FORWARD PERP.

4 1/4"

BASE LINE

+6"   +12"   +18"   +24"

9 5/8"

10 13/16"

5/16 BOLTS

3/8

3 1/8"

5 1/2"

STA. 1   STA. 2

5/16 BOLTS

3/8 STOPWATER

RABBET

1"

KEEL BATTEN 3 1/2" x 5/8"

STATION 3

1'-1"

KEEL

48"

STEM LAYOUT — FEET, INCHES, SIXTEENTHS					
	STEM	OUTSIDE	RABBET	BEARD	INSIDE
WIDTHS	SHEER	0-0-0	0-2-3	0-2-14	0-3-8
	23"	0-0-6	0-2-18	0-3-8	0-4-2
	17"	0-1-5	0-4-2	0-5-1	0-5-12
	14"	0-2-6	0-5-10	0-6-9	0-7-5
	11"	0-4-0	0-7-12	0-8-13	0-9-0
	8"	0-6-4	0-10-13	1-0-0	0-10-11
	5"	0-9-8	1-3-14	1-5-10	2-6-8
HEIGHTS	+12"	0-3-5	0-7-3	0-8-1	0-7-8
	+18"	0-1-0	0-4-3	0-4-14	0-6-4
	+24"	0-0-2	0-2-13	0-3-6	0-6-0
	+48"	0-0-0	0-2-2	0-2-9	0-2-9

WIDTHS MEASURED FROM FORWARD PERPENDICULAR

HEIGHTS MEASURED ABOVE BASE LINE.

STEM LAYOUT MATINICUS ISLAND PEAPOD

marked, of course, the molds themselves must have been tested for fairness.

Ribbands are now installed along the sheerline and the planking lines. These ribbands should be about 1¾ to 2 inches wide and 1⅛ to 1¼ inches thick, and should run the full length of the boat. They must be free of knots and weakening defects in order to bend fair. They are generally fastened to the molds using number 12 or 14 bright steel screws 2½ to 3 inches long with small washers under the heads. Ribbands can be fir, spruce, or pine and may be spliced if necessary, as long as they bend fair.

When the ribbands are in place, the location and spacing of the timbers are marked on the inside. Timbers are preferably of select white oak, free of weakening defects, air dried or still green but not kiln dried, 1 inch wide by 9/16 inch thick. Spaced 7½ to 8 inches on centers, they should be laid out to miss as many of the molds as possible. If possible they should be long enough to reach from gunwale to gunwale. When steaming has made them soft, they are bent in place as marked. By twisting them with a wrench applied to the timberheads and by driving down on the

ends with a maul after they have been hauled against the ribbands with clamps, the hot timbers are made to lie flat and touching against the inside of the ribbands throughout. To hold the timbers in place after the clamps are removed, the builder may nail through from the inside of each still-hot timber into the ribbands using long, slim, resin-coated nails with thick leather disks under the heads. These leather disks serve to apply pressure and to facilitate pulling the nails when the time comes. They are dinked out of scrap leather with a hollow punch about half an inch in diameter. The nails are removed as planking proceeds. Another method for securing the timbers to the ribbands is with twists of soft, strong wire. A pair of small "vise grips" is ideal for tightening these twists.

The boat could be planked upright. A particular advantage of this method is that riveting can be done plank by plank as the planking proceeds, and one person can do the whole operation himself, bucking the rivets on the outside while he peens them on the inside. The principal disadvantage of planking upright is that it is awkward and difficult to fit the bottom planks.

If the boat is planked in the bottom-up position, on

FLOOR JOGGLED TO FIT PLANK

STATION 2'-2"

3½"

OUTWALE 1¼ No. 10 W.S.

COPPER RIVET

KNEE JOGGLED TO FIT PLANK

JOG

2" RING NAILS

TOP STRAKE 1½" THICK

STATION No.4 MATINICUS POD

THWART

2½" RING NAILS

RIVETS

SPREADER BRACE UNDER THWART

COPPER WIRE NAILS CLIPPED AND RIVETED OVER BURRS

REMOVABLE FLOOR HELD IN PLACE WITH BUTTONS

1" No. 10 W.S.

LIMBER

WEDGE SHIM FILL-IN GLUED BETWEEN GARBOARD AND TIMBER

PLANKING WIDTHS 15'MATINICUS PEAPOD						
STATION	STEM	1	2	3	4	5
SHEER	3 3/8	3 7/8	4 1/4	4 1/2	4 7/8	5 1/8
2	2 3/4	3	3 1/4	3 1/2	4 1/8	4 1/4
3	2 3/4	3	3 1/8	3 3/4	4	4 1/8
4	2 3/4	2 2/8	3 1/8	3 1/4	3 1/2	3 7/8
5	3	3	3	3 1/2	4 1/4	4 3/8
6	3	3 1/4	3 3/4	4 1/2	5 3/8	5 3/4
7	3 3/8	3 1/4	3 3/4	5	5 5/8	5 3/4
GARBOARD		1 5/8	3 1/2	4 1/4	4 3/4	5
PLANK LINES TOP INSIDE EDGE OF PLANKING ADD WIDTH OF LAP 7/8" TO ALL PLANK EXCEPT GARBOARD. WIDTHS WILL VARY SLIGHTLY. FAIR WITH LINING BATTEN. W.PINE 5/16" x 1 3/8".						

① KEEL OAK, SIDED 2", MOLDED 2½". ② KEEL BATTEN, OAK 3¾" WIDE ½" THICK. ③ TIMBERS, WHITE OAK STEAM BENT 1" × ⁹⁄₁₆" THICK, CONTINOUS FROM RAIL TO RAIL EXCEPT LAST THREE TIMBERS AT THE ENDS. ④ SEAT RISERS PINE 2½" WIDE ⅝" THICK, TAPERED AT ENDS. ⑤ THWARTS 10" WIDE ⅞" THICK. ⑥ SPREADER CLEATS PINE 2½" × ⅞" TO FIT TIGHT BETWEEN THE SEAT RISERS. FASTEN THROUGH THWARTS AND BENCHES. ⑦ END BENCHES PINE ¾" OR ⅞" THICK. ⑧ INWALE OAK 1⅛" × ¾" THICK TAPERED TO 1" AT ENDS. ⑨ BREASTHOOK OAK, HACKMATACK, APPLE, GROWN SHAPES OR 2 PIECES PINNED AND GLUED TOGETHER. ⑩ SEAT KNEES OAK, HACK, APPLE, GROWN BENDS OR LAMINATIONS SIDED 1". 8-INCH FOOT. ⑪ OARLOCK PADS ⅞" OAK ⑫ FLOOR BOARDS ⅝" PINE. MIDDLE BOARD REMOVABLE FOR CLEANING. SIDE BOARDS SCREWED TO THE TIMBERS.

15-FT. MATINICUS ISLAND PEAPOD

the other hand, the garboards and broads will go on much more easily, but peening the rivets must generally be postponed until the planks are all on and the boat has been turned over. Then, although one operation can be made of the riveting, two persons are required to do it, one on the outside holding on and a second on the inside peening the rivets.

A variation of the upside-down method is sometimes used in production shops when building a stock model in quantity. The combined thickness of the ribbands and timbers is deducted from the molds before the ribbands are fastened in place, and the timbers are bent around the *outside* of the ribbands, permitting the planking to be fastened directly to the timbers as it is put on. When the planking operation

has been completed and the planked-up hull is lifted off, the form remains intact, ready to receive the timbers for another boat. This is an efficient method when a number of identical boats are built, but it would not pay to construct such a form for a single boat. Neither is it recommended when the plank fastenings are rivets rather than screws.

As an alternate method for planking a clinker hull, if only one boat is to be built, I'd like to suggest a combination of the right-side up and upside-down methods. After the timbers have been bent in and well secured to the inside of the ribbands with wire twists or leathered nails or both, the boat is turned over and the garboards and the next two planks above are fitted and fastened in place. The boat is then turned right side up

Though not a Matinicus pod, this boat being built at Mystic Seaport shows the standard peapod construction. The ribbands are on and planking is about to begin. (Mystic Seaport photo by Lester D. Olin)

A good interior shot showing the typical peapod seating arrangement.

One example of the many good peapods built by amateurs from the plans for a 14-footer in Building Classic Small Craft, Volume I. Construction methods are similar to those for the 15-footer offered here.

again. Whatever riveting is required for the planks already on is completed, and the remainder of the planking is fitted and fastened. This permits the builder to do whatever riveting is required for the upper plank without assistance. The bucking iron can be held against the rivet heads on the outside by pressure from some part of the builder's body—leg, side, or the like—while the burr is driven on from the inside and the rivet is snipped and peened.

In planking the topsides the ribbands are left in place as long as possible, removing them one by one as necessary to fit the planks. It will be easier to put in the seat riser, whose top edge is 7 inches below the sheer, before the topsides are closed in. In this way it will be possible to clamp it in place before fastening, by reaching through from the outside.

The following information supplements the accompanying drawings.

Stem and keel, white oak, sided 2 inches. Keel batten, white oak, 3¾ inches by ⅝ inch. Clinker planking, ⅜ inch thick, of cedar, white pine, or marine plywood. Timbers, steam-bent select white oak, continuous gunwale to gunwale, 1 inch by 9/16 inch. Inwales and outwales, 1⅛ inches by ¾ inch, tapered slightly at the ends. Seat riser, pine, 2½ inches by ⅝ inch. Thwarts, 10 inches by ⅞ inch, pine or Douglas fir. Thwart knees and breasthooks, grown crooks if possible; can also be glued laminates.

Fastenings through laps into timbers, screws or copper rivets. Screws, number 8, 1-inch or 1¼-inch bronze. Plank to stems, keel batten, and timberheads, number 8, ⅞-inch bronze screws. If rivets are used, cut copper nails would be first choice, but since cut nails are now largely unobtainable, copper wire nails are an acceptable substitute. Through laps and timbers, use 2-inch copper wire nails snipped to the correct length for riveting after burrs tight enough to draw have been driven on with a burr set. Through laps between frames, use two 1⅛-inch copper wire nails spaced equally, snipped and riveted, with burrs set down tightly enough to draw. Through wales, planking, and timberheads, use 2½-inch copper wire nails riveted over burrs.

1 2

Two Garveys

......................•......................

TWENTY-TWO-FOOT-FIVE-INCH WORKING GARVEY

Of all our native working craft, the type that occupies the bottom place on the totem pole in popular esteem must be the scow. Indeed, for many, *scow* is the lowest name they know for a boat. Although their scorn may be justified in some instances, it definitely does not apply to the many worthy, and even shapely, flat-bottomed, square-ended workboats that come within the generic classification of scow.

One such scow subtype that can hold its head high in any company of working craft—that is, when well built and properly designed—is the garvey, at home in shallow coastal waters from New Jersey to the lower Chesapeake. There is good evidence that the first New Jersey garvey was built about 250 years ago at West Creek by one Gervais Pharo, whose name in corrupted

form has passed down to us as the name of the workboat type he introduced.

Of course he did not originate the type. Flat-bottomed, square-ended scows of various shapes and sizes had been in use in Europe for many centuries before their appearance in the New World. As utilitarian craft they had much to commend them. Their simple construction made them relatively easy and inexpensive to build. Good carrying capacity was combined with shoal draft. Their wide, flat bottoms provided stable working platforms. And before conversion to power with the addition of skegs and deadwood, they beached easily and sat securely upright when grounded out.

On the debit side, the unmodified scow form is not suited to the open sea, although when properly designed and equipped with engines, some derivative scow forms have done quite well in rough water. One

WORKING GARVEY FOR INBOARD POWER
LENGTH INSIDE BOW AND STERN TRANSOMS 22'-5"
BEAM AMIDSHIPS 6'-8". INSIDE DEPTH AMIDSHIPS 2'-2"
LINES DRAWN TO INSIDE OF PLANKING.

OFFSETS 22' GARVEY				
STATIONS	HEIGHTS		WIDTHS	
	BOTTOM	SHEER	BOTTOM	SHEER
BT	2-4-2	3-11-6	2-0-0	2-0-0
1	1-10-3	3-8-7	2-3-3	2-7-7
2	1-4-1	3-6-2	2-8-1	3-0-7
3	1-1-4	3-3-6	2-10-4	3-3-1
4	1-0-4	3-2-1	2-11-2	3-4-0
5	1-0-1	3-1-2	2-11-1	3-3-2
6	1-0-5	3-0-6	2-10-0	3-2-1
7	1-1-7	3-1-1	2-8-1	2-11-5
8	1-5-3	3-2-0	2-5-1	2-8-7
T	1-6-7	3-2-4	2-4-4	2-7-5

such type was the Hickman Sea Sled, very popular and quite widely used for a time just prior to the Great Depression as a high-speed pleasure craft. The Sea Sled was not particularly easy to build because of its modified, inverted V bottom, which also lessened internal capacity to such an extent that the Sea Sled was of little use as a workboat.

Following the Sea Sled, a variety of less extreme modifications of the scow equipped with power and designed for speed have been tried with varying success, including a number of tunnel-stern garveys. By far the most popular modification of the powered scow for pleasure use is the Boston Whaler.

As long as gasoline was plentiful and cheap, powered scows, including garveys, were developed for speed, as were most other types. Needless to say, this has changed. Many small-craft fishermen are now finding that economy of operation is paramount, and that the fast, energy-intensive boat is something they can do without. As long as it is not necessary to commute great distances to offshore fishing grounds or race to a distant market with the catch, speed is proving a costly and unneeded luxury. The garvey, which formerly was modified by flattening and straightening its run aft to give it planing speed, is easily returned to slower, more economical operation by restoring some of the original bottom rocker and cutting down on horsepower. That is what we have attempted to do with the working garvey considered here.

In working out the following design for a 22-foot garvey fishing launch to be powered with a 12 h.p. Spanish Sole diesel, I have drawn quite heavily on a 26-foot New Jersey fishing garvey taken off by Howard I. Chapelle at Tuckerton, New Jersey, in 1925. This design was presented in Chapelle's "Some American Fishing Launches," a paper given at the first Food and Agriculture Organization (FAO) International Fishing Boat Congress in 1953 at Paris and Miami, and later included in the published proceedings of the congress, *Fishing Boats of the World*, Vol. 1.

Very few plans for working garveys have been published other than the two in Chapelle's paper—the one mentioned and a highly distinctive Virginia trap boat of 29 feet. Chapelle had a high opinion of the working garvey, which he thought compared favorably with another of his favorite workboat types, the New Haven sharpie, which is also cross-planked on the bottom.

One advantage the garvey had was greater working capacity in a given length. Chapelle promoted the type whenever he could, encouraging its adoption by fishermen. He felt that its good qualities had been largely overlooked outside the limited area on the East Coast where it first appeared, and that it deserved to be more widely known and adopted.

I am told that the garvey I have drawn upon in working out the details for the one shown here was powered with an old four-cylinder automobile engine and ran about nine knots with the throttle two-thirds open. My shortened adaptation, which has a somewhat more rockered bottom and a 12 h.p. diesel, is expected to run very economically at a maximum speed of six or seven knots. I am suggesting the Spanish Sole diesel manufactured in Barcelona and distributed in this country by Beacon Plastic and Metal Products, 50 Park Avenue, New York, New York 10016.

What appeals to me in particular about the Sole is its light weight and compact size—only 189 pounds with electric start, and approximately 2½ feet long by 22 inches high by 19 inches wide—and its good record in the Spanish fisheries for more than 25 years, where for some time fuel economy has been even more urgent than it is here at present. There may be other small diesels that would perform very well in this boat, in

particular the Norwegian Sabb, but I do feel the Sole, hardly known in this country up to now, deserves special consideration.

While I have used the 26-foot New Jersey garvey drawn by Chapelle as a model and as a control, so to speak, I have made the boat shown here 4 feet shorter, increased the curve of the bottom rocker at the stern slightly, and raised the height of the sheer by 4 inches. In his construction view, Chapelle did not show any bottom floors, any lengthwise stringers inside the cross-planked bottom, or any internal flooring for the working cockpit. I have added all three.

Cross floors at every frame station are bolted to the side frames with two 5/16-inch galvanized carriage bolts. In addition the chine is bolted through the bottom of each side frame. To further reinforce the cross-planked bottom, three stringers running fore and aft are let in flush with the bottom of the cross floors. This makes an exceptionally strong internal framing, and permits the use of ½-inch plywood panels for the side planking.

The 3½-inch-high cross floors support a tight sole or flooring of ¾-inch pine for the working cockpit, which is slightly more than 9 feet long by 5 feet wide. Sheathing on the sides and low, tight bulkheads at either end provide an enclosed working space, keeping dirt and water out of the bilge to a considerable extent. The center board is removable, permitting the removal of whatever water collects in the bilge. Limbers drain to the low point amidships.

The drawings reproduced herewith were plotted accurately to scale, and even in reduced size will yield reliable approximate dimensions by careful scaling. Where it has seemed that special explanation might be helpful, there are numbers keyed to the comments listed below. Altogether there should be enough information to provide a pretty good idea of how to construct this boat.

1. *Frames:* Oak. Spaced 16 inches on centers. Sided 1⅛ inches, molded 3½ inches at the bottom, tapering to 2 inches at the top. If Douglas fir is substituted for oak, siding should be 1¼ inches.

2. *Floors:* Oak. Sided 1⅛ inches, molded 3½ inches. Douglas fir, sided 1¼ inches. But see *28, 29,* and *52.*

3. *Sides:* Fir plywood, ½ inch to ⅝ inch thick. Marine grade or, if you are fortunate enough to find it, superior-quality exterior without internal voids. Put on as continuous panels. Can also be carvel-planked

with white pine, Douglas fir, Port Orford cedar, or equivalent finished ¾ inch thick.

4. *Chines:* Oak. Sided 1½ inches, molded 3½ inches. Sawn to the required curve, and got out in two lengths in order to minimize the width of stock needed to give the required curve.

5. *Bottom cross planking:* Northern white pine, Douglas fir, juniper, or Port Orford cedar, 1⅛ inches thick. Planks put on no wider than 6 inches; 5 inches preferable. Nailed with 3½-inch galvanized nails. Cross planks wedged tight on inside. Outside caulking seams ⅛ inch to 3/16 inch wide. Driven cotton caulking payed with red-lead primer and puttied with non-hardening bottom-seam compound. No synthetic-rubber caulk.

6. *Side decking and end decking:* Half-inch fir plywood.

7. *Deck gussets:* Oak or Douglas fir. Sided 1⅛ inches and bolted to the top of the frames with two 5/16-inch carriage bolts.

8. *Coamings:* Oak. Three-quarters inch by 6 inches.

9. *Backing strip:* Oak or Douglas fir. Three-quarters inch by 2 inches.

10. *Side sheathing:* Pine or fir. Five-eighths inch thick.

11. *Cockpit floor:* Pine or fir. Three-quarters inch

thick and 7 to 8 inches wide tongue-and-grooved except for the removable 8-inch center board.

12. *Removable center strip:* Gives access to the bilge for bailing.

13. *Middle stringer:* Oak. One and an eighth inches thick, 7 inches wide.

14. *Side stringers:* Oak. One and an eighth inches thick, 4 inches wide. In two pieces with open joint amidships to provide a limber so the bottom can drain to the center. Fastened together with a butt block on top over the open joint.

15. *Limbers in cross floors:* 1½ inches long by ¾ inch high.

16. *Engine box:* Removable flat cover. One side hinged to fold down part way to give convenient access to the engine. Watertight when closed.

17. *After bulkhead:* Seven inches above the cockpit floor.

18. *Forward bulkhead:* Same as *17.*

19. *Fuel tank:* Six gallons or larger.

20. Filler cap.

21. *Chine splice:* Located well forward to minimize the amount of curve in the forward section.

22. *Thwart:* Pine or fir. Twelve inches wide; ⅞ inch thick, or thicker. Eight inches below top of coaming.

23. *Sternpost:* Oak. Sided 3 inches, molded 6

inches. Extends up into the interior of the boat and bolts to a 6-inch-wide cross floor. This ensures that the deadwood cannot easily be wracked sidewise should the boat ground out hard. The sternpost should be laid out with the run of the grain so as to avoid cross grain as much as possible.

24. *Propeller:* Thirteen-inch-by-eleven-inch three-bladed wheel.

25. *Split shaft log for 1-inch shaft:* Sided 3½ inches and 8 inches when bolted together.

26. *Deadwood:* Oak. Sided 3½ inches.

27. *Tiller:* Pinned to the 1¼-inch rudder stock with a single ⅜-inch bolt, allowing the tiller to be raised and lowered easily.

For the most part, the construction of the 22-foot-5-inch working garvey is relatively simple, straight-forward boatbuilding, well within the capabilities of a nonprofessional who has some mechanical experience and a fair amount of woodworking skill.

Scantlings are fairly heavy, befitting a workboat, and construction is on the rugged side, because this is not a speedboat and hull weight is not a critical factor. This gives the builder more leeway and makes the job quite a bit easier.

One of the things that requires some special attention and study is the engine installation. Another is fitting together the deadwood–shaft log–sternpost assembly and attaching it to the cross-planked flat bottom.

For a workboat that stands some chance of being beached on occasion, the deadwood must be solidly attached. Otherwise there is a good chance of its being sprung to one side or the other, throwing the engine out of line, should the boat ground out hard. One measure taken to prevent this is to have the sternpost extend up into the boat and bolted to an extra-heavy cross floor (*29* in the accompanying drawings).

I have specified a split shaft log because it is not overly difficult to make with tools ordinarily available to the nonprofessional; the equipment needed to bore a solid shaft log of this size might be difficult to obtain. I have specified a heavy, 3½-inch siding for the shaft log and deadwood to make boring the ⅜-inch holes for the through bolts on either side of the shaft hole less critical.

The semicircular grooves in the two halves of the split log that form the shaft hole can be roughed out on an ordinary circular saw and finished with a gouge. A rounded molding plane with a blade an inch or so wide, if one can be had, will help.

The slots for the splines on either side of the shaft hole are also cut on the circular saw. The splines themselves should be dry white pine. They should fit snugly and be bedded in red-lead primer—not the synthetic nonlead substitute now being sold, but genuine red lead, the real McCoy. In fact, the whole bottom should be primed with red lead, especially the caulked seams of the cross-planked bottom. The cotton caulking, after it has been driven tight, should be thoroughly saturated with red lead for a lasting job.

Even though this is a simple, flat-bottomed workboat, it should be laid down full size before construction starts. This is particularly recommended for the nonprofessional, first-time builder. Not only will such a laydown make the work much easier, saving time in the long run, but without it the inexperienced builder is likely to find himself completely at sea as he gets into the job. Even if some initial study is required, it will be time well spent.

From this laydown, molds can be lifted for the several pieces that form the deadwood–shaft log–sternpost assembly. These molds are best made of ¼-inch plywood and should fit together precisely. With the molds as patterns, the pieces for this assembly are got out of 3½-inch oak. If this is done accurately, not only will these pieces fit together exactly, but the assembly will also fit into place in the hull structure.

It is best to drill for the bolts that will hold this assembly together before the shaft hole is put in. The location of these bolt holes is important, and drilling them is one of the most critical operations in the construction of this boat. If any of these long bolt holes deviate by even a small fraction of an inch, it will mess things up thoroughly.

Fortunately, there is a simple but reliable method

for drilling such holes accurately and safely. I have not seen it described in any of the boatbuilding books, although it may have been. In any case, it should be more widely known and used.

The several pieces to be bolted or drifted together are fitted together on a bench or some other flat, level surface at a height above the floor convenient for working. Then straight lines representing the centers of the drifts or bolts to be put in are marked across the upper surface of the assembly, which must be smooth and flat. The pieces are then separated so that the lines marked across their upper surfaces can be squared down across the edges on either side.

Next, an adjustable combination square is set to the required distance in from the upper surface to the bolts, and with the square as a gauge, this distance is squared down from the upper surface across each of the bolt lines, as marked on both edges. The intersections where these lines cross represent the precise centers of the bolt holes to be bored. Note that all measurements on the edges *must* be taken *only* from the upper surface.

Using a carpenter's spurred auger the size of the bolt holes to be bored, start shallow holes on both edges *exactly* on the centers that have been marked—¼ inch is deep enough, but no deeper. To bore the holes through from side to side, you can use either a long drill bit or a "barefoot" ship auger. The latter is best for this purpose. These are often extended by having a length of drill rod welded onto them. For holes ⅜ inch in diameter, most electric drills with ⅜-inch chucks will do, although one of moderate speed is to be preferred.

The procedure for drilling the bolt holes is as follows. The piece to be bored is clamped to the bench, its marked side up. A short straightedge of 1-inch pine board (or something similar) is laid across the upper surface exactly along the line marking the center of the hole to be bored. It is then temporarily tacked in place with a couple of small nails to prevent it from accidentally shifting.

One end of the straightedge should extend 8 to 10 inches, or thereabouts, beyond the piece and toward the drill. The operator inserts the point of the drill bit or auger into the shallow hole that's already been started and lines up his drill precisely with the edge of the straightedge in preparation for boring. This is readily done by sighting.

At the same time, an assistant, standing some distance to the side and at right angles, directs the operator to raise or lower his machine until the long shank of the drill is exactly parallel to the overhanging end of the straightedge. As drilling proceeds, the assistant watches closely to see that the drill shank remains parallel and is not raised or lowered in the slightest.

Drilling proceeds in this manner until the bit is *halfway* through the piece, but no more. The bit is then withdrawn, and drilling is started from the other side, following the same procedure as before. If care has been taken, the second hole will meet the first head-on in the center of the piece. If not, it will at least be so close that passing the drill through once from side to side will clear the hole, permitting the bolt or drift to be driven easily.

When all of the pieces have been drilled separately in this manner, they are reassembled—use the lines on the upper surface to realign them—and then clamped together so they cannot shift out of position while the bolts are being driven. A couple of strips of board nailed temporarily across the upper surface will serve for this. All the holes should line up, although it is just as well to pass the long drill bit through them before the bolts are driven.

This is a thoroughly tested procedure that cannot fail if care is taken and directions are strictly followed. I have used it for years in my boatbuilding classes, where it has been amply demonstrated that no experience or particular skill is required to do it successfully. It is the most trustworthy method I know for boring long holes through assemblies of several separate members in preparation for through bolting. This is particularly true when tolerances are critical—for example, when there is a double risk of the hole running off and either breaking through into the shaft hole or coming out through the side of the deadwood. This method is simpler, quicker, and easier than rigging a special boring jig, except possibly on a production job, and it's more accurate and dependable than any improvised jig I have ever seen.

Of course, a drill bit of the right size is essential, but that is another story. To make sure that the bit or auger you choose is neither too large nor too small, you should bore some test holes in the same timber before you proceed.

The boat is turned upside down for framing and planking. The bottom cross floors bolted to the side frames serve as molds, all except the floor at station 7 *(52* in the drawings), which is best fitted and installed after the deadwood assembly is in place and the boat has been turned back over. The recess in the upper half of the shaft log is not cut to receive this floor until it is fitted. The plan shows this floor fastened to the deadwood assembly with drift bolts on either side of the shaft hole.

These bolts could be through bolts whose holes were bored at the same time as those for the bolts through the deadwood assembly. This might be the better way of installing this floor. Holes through the floor *(52)* that connect with the already bored holes through the shaft log and deadwood should not be difficult to locate, and in doing it this way there would be no chance of hitting the shaft hole or breaking out through the side.

The engine beds are put in after the boat is turned over, when it will be most convenient to fit them over the bottom floor midway between stations 5 and 6

(55). They should be fastened to this cross floor with drift pins.

Lead pipe used to be the standard material for making watertight shaft-log liners, but it is often difficult to obtain today, so soft copper tubing may be substituted.

By carefully hammering well-greased turned and tapered wooden plugs of different sizes into the lead pipe, it is expanded so that it fits the ends of the shaft hole tightly. After being bedded with white lead, it is flanged over and nailed with copper tacks in the shallow recess cut for it to give a flat seat for the stern bearing. Soft copper tubing can also be expanded and flanged over in much the same way. To soften copper by annealing, bring it to a red heat and quench in cold water. It's just the opposite of steel in this respect.

The two stopwaters *(48)* shown for the deadwood

assembly are essential if the boat is not to leak. Obviously, the one in the way of the shaft hole cannot go all the way through and must be installed in two short pieces cut to the exact length before they are driven. They are located so the caulking in the seam at the ends of the short cross plank will make up tightly against them. Stopwaters should be made of dry soft pine or the equivalent.

Bore a hole the right size through a piece of oak board. Relieve the sharp edge of the hole on the upper side and apply grease. Plane or turn the stopwater to a diameter slightly larger than required. Drive it through the hole in the oak board with a heavy hammer or top maul. This will size the stopwater and compress it. When moisture strikes it, it will swell and become very tight.

Bottom boards are nailed to the chines and the cross floors with 3-inch galvanized wire nails, since cut boat nails probably are not available. The heads should be well set in for puttying. The bottom boards are fastened to the bottom stringers with 2-inch number 14 galvanized wood screws.

Construction Details

The following construction details relate to the numbered elements in the accompanying drawings.

28. The siding of these two oak cross floors is increased to 1¾ inches, molded 3½ inches, to beef up the bottom structure for support of the shaft log, deadwood, and engine beds.

29. *Oak cross floor:* Molded 6 inches, sided 1¾ inches. Supports the end of the sternpost, which projects through the bottom and is bolted to it with two ⅜-inch galvanized carriage bolts. This is a structural member of critical importance, carrying much of the weight of the shaft log and deadwood in addition to preventing the deadwood from being loosened and knocked sidewise should the boat accidentally strike an obstruction or ground out on a hard beach.

30. *Transom center frame:* Oak, sided 1⅛ inches and molded 7 inches to match the width of the middle bottom stringer *(13)*.

31. *Two knees:* Oak, sided 1⅛ inches and rising 7 inches against the transom center frame.

32. *Intermediate transom frames:* Oak. Sided 1⅛ inches, molded 4 inches.

33. *Engine beds:* Oak, sided 2½ inches. See dimensioned drawing for molded shape.

34. *Cross brace:* Oak, forward end of the engine beds. Sided 1⅛ inches. Fastened with 4½-inch galvanized wire spikes.

35. *Forward end of the engine box:* Pine, sided ¾ inch to ⅞ inch.

37. Limber through side stringers to drain to the center of the boat. Cut to leave a 1-inch gap between the ends of the two parts of the stringer. Joined with an overlapping block of the same material on top and fastened with 2-inch number 14 galvanized wood screws.

38. *Rudder stock:* One-inch diameter.

40. *Shaft line:* Fourteen degrees with the baseline and load waterline. This is well within the specified maximum installation angle of 20 degrees for the Sole diesel.

41. *Propeller shaft:* One-inch diameter. Propeller: Three blades, 14 inches by 11 inches.

43. Stern bearing.

44. *Inside stuffing box:* Flax packing.

45. Shaft coupling.

46. *Shaft log:* Upper half, oak, sided 3½ inches. See dimensioned profile layout for split shaft log.

47. *Shaft-hole liner:* Lead pipe or soft copper tubing, 1¼ inches inside diameter.

48. *Stopwaters:* ¾-inch soft dry pine. Located where the shaft line and the bottom of the split shaft log cross the caulking seam of the bottom planking.

49. *Drift bolts:* ⅜-inch galvanized drift rod driven through the floor at station 7 into the deadwood on each side of the shaft hole. Replacement by through bolts is optional.

50. Galvanized wire nails 3½ inches long spaced 5 to 7 inches through sides of the middle stringer into the sternpost–shaft log–deadwood assembly.

51. Three-and-a-half-inch cutout through the 7-inch middle stringer to admit the deadwood assembly.

52. *Floor aft of station 7:* Dimensions increased from 3½ inches molded height to 4½ inches.

53. *Shaft-log splines:* ³⁄₁₆-inch by ½-inch dry white pine set in red lead.

54. Lower half of split shaft log.

56. Three-eighths-inch galvanized bolts.

GARVEY 20'-3" x 7'-4¾"

	STATIONS	BT.	0	A	1	2	3	4	5	6	7	ST.
HALF-BREADTHS	Bottom	1-9-4	1-9-4	1-7-2	1-1-3	0-7-4	0-4-1	0-3-4	0-3-6	0-4-5	0-5-5	0-6-4
	Chine	2-4-5	2-2-6	2-0-2	1-6-0	0-11-6	0-7-7	0-6-0	0-6-0	0-6-7	0-8-0	0-9-2
	Sheer	4-2-2	3-11-3	3-10-4	3-8-0	3-5-6	3-3-7	3-3-0	3-3-2	3-4-1	3-5-0	3-6-3
HEIGHTS	Chine	1-4-3	1-5-4	1-7-0	1-11-0	2-4-0	2-8-0	2-10-6	3-0-0	3-0-1	3-0-0	2-11-3
	Sheer	1-10-3	2-3-4	2-5-1	2-9-2	3-1-6	3-5-1	3-7-2	3-7-2	3-6-4	3-5-6	3-4-4

OFFSETS   FEET-INCHES-EIGHTHS   MEASURED INSIDE PLANKING.

TWENTY-FOOT GARVEY

In designing this boat I have attempted to produce something that builders keep asking for every so often. Combined in this single vessel are as many as possible of the various features and characteristics specified by them for a workboat of small or moderate size.

Heading the list of requirements are the following: The boat has to be one that can be easily constructed without special boatbuilding skills or knowledge, which is to say one that is well within the capabilities of anyone with elementary carpentry experience and proficiency. Materials must be relatively inexpensive, although nothing is really cheap today, and readily available. So, instead of hard-to-get boatbuilding lumber, all that is required is standard construction lumber obtainable at most well-stocked retail outlets.

The materials list is short. Standard 2-inch Douglas-fir or hard-pine joists, net thickness about 1½ inches,

serve for framing throughout. One-inch boards (net ¾ inch thick) of northern white pine, southern hard pine, or Douglas fir in narrow or medium random widths will be used for the foundation of fore-and-aft stringers that underlie the ⅜-inch fir or hard-pine plywood covering the bottom, sides, and decks, and for the cockpit floor and side sheathing. For fastenings, hot-dipped galvanized wire nails in several lengths and epoxy glue will be used. Little else is required for constructing the bare hull, exclusive of the painting and the usual fittings to be added in equipping the boat for service.

After a lot of thought, we picked the garvey as the type of hull that would best meet the majority of our listed requirements. Twenty feet seems to be a popular and useful length, although this hull could easily be stretched out several feet or shortened to 18 feet.

The pram bow and the slight V forward should handle moderate seas without pounding the way a dead flat bottom would. Naturally this garvey will not prove as seaworthy as a boat like the St. Pierre dory, and is not recommended for offshore fishing in the stormy North Atlantic. Yet I am confident that it will be adequate for coastwise fishing under reasonable weather conditions. This hull has extra carrying capacity, can handle heavy loads, and provides a stable working platform. Although this hull is more or less a typical garvey hull, its construction is distinctly different, having been simplified to an extent not seen before, yet without any sacrifice of strength.

Power is supplied by an outboard motor. Much working room is saved by using an outboard instead of an inboard engine, and because there is no need for either shaft log or rudder there are significant savings of materials and labor.

A bare minimum of woodworking hand tools will suffice. All that are absolutely essential are two handsaws (a rip and a crosscut), a nail hammer, a plane (preferably a jack plane), a rule, a carpenter's square, a bevel square, and a couple of 6-inch C-clamps. A chisel would be handy but is not essential. Of course, an electric handsaw will speed up the operation greatly, and it might pay to get one if the time factor is important and power is available. And naturally a well-equipped woodworking shop will be even better.

Because the boat is a garvey, there is no stem or keel to rabbet. There are no difficult planking bends, no steam-bent frames or steam bending of any sort. No full-size laydown of lines is required, since dimensions and beveling for the frames that serve as molds are diagramed here.

It is recommended that the boat be set bottom up for planking on a ladder frame.

The pieces that make up the frame assemblies—that is, the side futtocks (*1* in the accompanying diagrams) and the bottom cross floors (*2*)—are cut out of 2-inch fir joists (1½ inches thick, net) as diagramed, and are beveled at the bench before they are put together. Beveling is much easier when the pieces are separated.

All the bevels are "under" bevels, as illustrated in the diagram. This requires that frames from station 5 forward be set on the forward side of the station lines with their beveled edges sloping forward, and that frames from station 6 aft be set on the after side of the station lines with their beveled edges sloping aft.

The exceptions are the transoms, which are set *inside* the ends. These are beveled "standing"—the opposite of under beveling. This requires that they be framed larger than the finished dimensions on the outside, to provide enough wood for beveling. See the diagram for the bow transom.

After beveling, the frames are assembled with plywood gussets applied to both sides of the chine knuckle. These are put on with epoxy glue and 1¾-inch galvanized nails spaced as shown.

It is recommended that the outline of the frame be accurately marked out on a flat, smooth surface—bench top, worktable, or floor. In assembling a frame, its pieces are laid out in conformity with this outline, beveled side up, and the gussets fastened on. Then the frame assembly can be turned over and the gussets put on the other side. When this has been done, triangular pieces of 1½-inch fir joist, previously marked and cut to shape, are inserted with glue into the two pockets on the inside of the frame assembly and are nailed through the gussets. The ends of these pieces are also nailed into the frame. Finally a cross spall for the ladder-frame setup is temporarily nailed in place. Double-headed staging nails work well for this as well as for setting up the ladder frame.

For this boat, the top edge of the cross spalls should be exactly 3 feet above the baseline. When the outline of each frame is laid out prior to assembly, it will be easy to locate the top of the cross spall 3 feet above the baseline.

In addition to the frames, assemblies of the bow and stern transoms must be made before the boat can be set up for planking. Both of these transom assemblies consist of internal framing of fir joist 1½ inches thick covered on the outer side with ⅜-inch plywood that holds them together and fastened with glue and galvanized nails. After the bottom and sides are planked, the projecting ends of the stringers and the plywood covering them are trimmed flush with the surface of the transoms, and an outer layer of plywood is put on with nails and glue, covering all. Finally the raw edge of this final layer of plywood on the ends is covered with fiberglass tape set in epoxy.

What is most distinctive and different about the construction is the planking, which is done in two layers. First is an under layer of fore-and-aft stringers ¾ inch thick nailed directly to the frames. These are covered by an outer layer of ⅜-inch plywood, which is nailed through into the frames as well as being nailed and glued to the stringers. There is only a minimum of fitting since many of the stringers are perfectly straight, as can be seen in the diagram of the bottom. Those shown are 5½-inch boards, but they could just

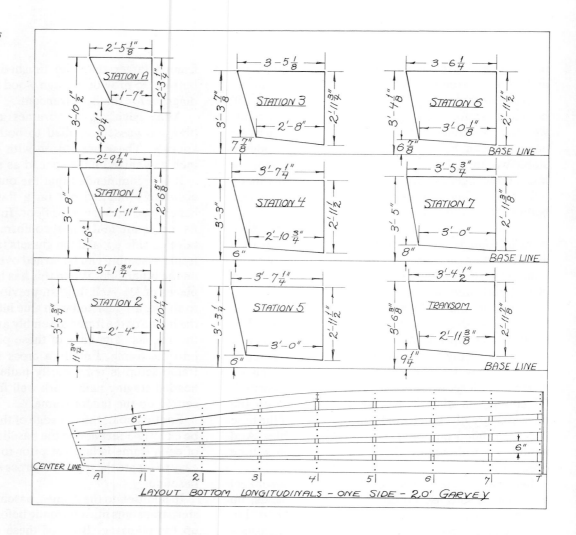

Above and opposite: *Dimensions and bevels as originally drawn for the frames and transoms of the 20-foot garvey. The stern transom rake was subsequently changed to conform to Outboard Marine Corporation recommendations (see page 172); if this modified rake is adopted by the builder, slight changes to the stern transom dimensions and bottom bevel shown here will be necessary.*

as well be narrower or wider, depending on what is conveniently available.

It should be noted that the middle stringers show a bit of curve at the forward end due to the deadrise of the V bottom. This will require some trimming to bring the two middle stringers together in a touching fit on the centerline, as well as some slight beveling of their inner edges on account of the V. Because of its curve, the outside stringer is made of two lengths spliced together.

All the longitudinal stringers in this 20-foot boat will most likely need to be spliced together from two or more shorter pieces. Joints in adjoining stringers

should be well staggered—that is, separated as much as possible. Joints may be butted on the frames provided they are well nailed, but short scarfs would be better, glued and nailed through into the frames. In any case, these bottom stringers are to be well nailed into the bottom cross frames with 2½-inch hot-dipped galvanized wire nails.

No time need be lost in measuring these longitudinals exactly to length. Any excess is allowed to project beyond the face of the transoms. It will be sawed off flush in one operation prior to adding the outer facing of plywood to the transom.

The recommended order of work in planking the

FRAME BEVELS GIVEN AS UNDER BEVELS

STA. A SIDE	69°	STA. 6 SIDE	90°
STA. A BOTTOM	69°	STA. 6 BOTTOM	88°
STA. 1 SIDE	73½°	STA. 7 SIDE	88½°
STA. 1 BOTTOM	72°	STA. 7 BOTTOM	88°
STA. 2 SIDE	76½°	TRANSOM SIDE	87½°
STA. 2 BOTTOM	78°	TRANSOM BOTTOM	85°
STA. 3 SIDE	81°		
STA. 3 BOTTOM	82½°		
STA. 4 SIDE	84°		
STA. 4 BOTTOM	86½°		
STA. 5 SIDE	89°		
STA. 5 BOTTOM	90°		

FRAMES FROM STATION 5 FORWARD SET FORWARD OF STATION LINES AND BEVELED FORWARD AND UNDER. FROM STATION 6 AFT FRAMES SET AFT OF STATION LINES AND BEVELED AFT AND UNDER.

SECTION A-A

SECTION B-B

BEVELED UNDER

INNER LAYER PLYWOOD

TOP BOW TRANSOM

SIDE BOW TRANSOM

BOTTOM BOW TRANSOM

EXPANDED SHAPE

BOW TRANSOM PLYWOOD
FIRST LAYER BEFORE BEVELING

BOW   TRANSOM

VIEW FROM OUTSIDE
FIRST LAYER OF PLYWOOD

20-FT. GARVEY

sides and the bottom is as follows: After the frames have been set up on the ladder frame and checked for alignment and fairness, as well as plumbed, the side stringers are nailed on. Next, the side stringers that follow the chine are trimmed to conform to the curvature of the bottom, so that the outside bottom stringers will cover their edges in a close fit. Third, the bottom stringers are nailed on, and the outside stringers that extend over the edges of the bottom side stringers are trimmed and planed to conform to the curvature of the sides.

The ⅜-inch plywood that covers the sides can now be put on. On each side there are two lengthwise panels that butt on the center of the middle side stringer. These side panels are glued with epoxy to the stringers underneath, nailed through them into the frames with galvanized wire nails, and nailed into the stringers between the frames with large wire ring nails 1 inch long and spaced about 2 inches apart.

If we assume that the plywood panels for planking this 20-foot boat will be got out of standard 8-foot sheets, two splices in each panel will be required. These splices can be made either off or on the boat. They should be 8 to 12 times as long as the plywood is thick, and glued with epoxy. For detailed directions for splicing plywood, see Chapter 13.

Exact fits in installing these plywood panels are not required, which makes the job a lot easier. If the panels do not butt together perfectly on the underlying stringers, the open seams may be filled with epoxy and microballoons, or epoxy and fine sawdust, to be sanded smooth upon hardening. Of course, an effort should be made to keep any seam openings reasonably small. When the lower side panel is put on, it can be a little wider than necessary, to be trimmed and planed fair with the bottom after the glue has hardened.

The plywood covering the bottom is installed in the same way. The diagram shows three lengthwise plywood panels on each half of the bottom. Two on each side would probably conform to the slight twist of this veed bottom without any difficulty. The number and width of the plywood panels on both sides and the bottom and the location of the stringers underneath can be varied considerably for economical utilization of materials available. A little attention given to planning in this regard can yield significant savings in materials.

Because the bottom plywood goes on last, the raw edge of the outside panels should be covered with fiberglass tape set in epoxy. This is covered in turn by the chine strip *(13),* which is glued and nailed in place. This makes a strong, lasting, perfectly waterproof joint along the chine.

Fiberglass tape and epoxy are also applied under the laminated keel *(12),* but first the raised V at the center of the bottom must be planed flat for a width of 4

inches to seat the keel strips. The first of these is nailed on over the strip of fiberglass tape before the epoxy has cured. The top strip is also put on with epoxy glue and should be well nailed with 3-inch galvanized nails.

A word about galvanized wire nails: These are the easiest and cheapest of all fastenings. No bolts, drifts, or screws are required. They are good for at least 10 years, by which time the boat should have paid for itself several times over and a new one is in order.

The following are keyed to numbers in the accompanying diagrams:

1. *Side frames:* 1½-inch fir or hard-pine joist.
2. *Frame bottoms:* 1½-inch fir or hard-pine joist.
3. *Bottom stringers:* One-inch boards (net ¾ inch), pine or fir.
4. *Bottom panels:* ⅜-inch fir or hard-pine plywood.
5. *Side stringers:* Same as bottom stringers.
6. Plywood side panels.
7. *Frame gussets:* ⅜-inch or ½-inch fir or hard-pine plywood.
8. *Deck beams:* 1½-inch fir or hard-pine joist.

9. *Deck stringers:* Same as side and bottom stringers.

10. *Plywood decking:* Same as bottom and side panels.

11. *Coaming:* Six inches by ¾ inch, pine or fir.

12. Two strips of ¾-inch pine or fir, 4 inches wide.

13. *Outside chine strip:* Pine or fir, 3 inches by ⅝ inch.

14. *Sheer trim:* Pine or fir, 2 inches by ¾ inch.

15. *Flooring:* Pine or fir, ¾ inch thick.

16. *Trap:* Same material as the flooring.

People who build their own boats are prone to making changes in the original plans. To discourage this tendency, designers often warn that if changes are made, they will not be responsible for the results. More often than not, this is no deterrent. Builders go right ahead with alterations according to their own ideas, sometimes with happy results, sometimes not.

The lesson is clear. Boats designed for amateur construction should be able to tolerate some alterations, because they are going to be made anyway. The ideal is a hull of proven lines and simple, straightforward construction with plenty of options left open to the individual builder. And this is what I have aimed for with this garvey—a general-purpose workboat hull with which there is considerable leeway for adaptation to a variety of needs.

The lines show a hull that is quite high-sided. When the boat carries no payload but only the motor, a couple of occupants, and miscellaneous equipment, the freeboard amidships will be about 26 inches, and the distance from the cockpit floor to the top of the coaming 32 inches. If this seems too high-sided, it would be the simplest thing in the world to lower the sheer by several inches. Merely subtract the desired amount while laying out the frame molds. No other alterations in the hull design would be required.

On the other hand, some will find the ample freeboard desirable if heavy loads are to be carried, a task for which the boat is well adapted. By raising the cockpit floor several inches and making it watertight, one could make the cockpit self-bailing, which is highly desirable for some fishing operations. And for extra-heavy loading, the scuppers could always be closed.

If a larger boat is needed, it would be easy to stretch this one out by inserting one or two additional frames amidships, setting them at the same frame spacing (27

inches) as the rest. This would not affect the ends of the hull, and no other alterations or adjustments would be needed. The hull could even be shortened, but caution is indicated here, for too much off the length could adversely affect performance. In shortening the boat, as in lengthening it, the excess should be removed amidships and the ends left alone.

Although the boat shown here is powered with an outboard motor, the hull is well suited for a small inboard engine. It would not be difficult to make the changes and additions that such an engine would require, though a considerable amount of extra work, as well as some extra expense, would be involved. But I see no design difficulties in adding a skeg, shaft log, rudder, engine beds, and engine box.

Where low or moderate working speeds would be satisfactory, any one of several small, light diesels now on the market would fill the bill nicely. A good example is the Sole, favored by Spanish fishermen and recommended for the 22-foot-5-inch garvey. This engine's comparatively low fuel consumption would soon cancel out the initial cost of conversion to inboard power, but the engine would never achieve anything approaching the speeds possible with large outboard motors.

If an outboard is to be used, there is much to say for the dry well recommended by the Outboard Marine Corporation for 1982 Evinrude and Johnson motors. Both companies make heavy-duty commercial motors that would be well suited to this boat; their 55, 40, and 25 h.p. models would all be appropriate. The size and dimensions of the well for the 20-foot garvey were adapted from five detailed sheets (numbers 21–25) obtainable from the Outboard Marine Corporation, 3145 Central Avenue, Waukegan, Illinois 60085. Although the diagrams for the well are fully dimensioned and explained here, it would be helpful to get these five sheets, which include instructions for a remote-control installation and arrangements for steering that I have not touched on here.

To conform to Outboard Marine's specifications, the angle of the transom is 14 degrees from the vertical, or 76 degrees from the horizontal. Note that the shaft length of the motor is 20 inches.

The motor mount *(17)* is a 2-inch-by-12-inch (1½-inch-by-11½-inch net) Douglas-fir plank built into the transom framing as shown in the diagram, which gives a view from the inside showing how it is made up. The mount could also be oak, if it were available.

In assembling the transom, the two side frames *(1),*

NOTE:

If transom cap strip is used, and extends beyond the transom more than 1/16'', make a plate the thickness the cap extends beyond transom to bring transom surface flush for engine mounting. The transom plate should be made to conform to transom mounting bolt pattern shown on Sheet 22. This will allow the engine to be raised and lowered on transom without interference with stern brackets of engine.

MOTOR HORSEPOWER	"A" THICKNESS		"C" COVER HEIGHT	"D" TRANSOM HEIGHT (VERTICAL)	"E" ✕ CUTOUT LENGTH MINIMUM
	MINIMUM	MAXIMUM			
UNDER 5-1/2	1-1/4''	1-3/4''	19-1/2''	15 ± 1/2 OR 20 ± 1/2	15''
5-1/2 TO 15	1-3/8''	1-3/4''	22-1/2''	15 ± 1/2 OR 20 ± 1/2	15''
16 TO 61	1-3/8''	2''	29''	15 ± 1/2 OR 20 ± 1/2	21''
62 TO 85	1-5/8''	2-3/8''	32-1/2''	20 ± 1/2 OR 25 ± 1/2	22''
86 TO 149	1-5/8''	2-3/4''	32-1/2''	20 ± 1/2 OR 25 ± 1/2	22''
150 & OVER	1-5/8''	2-3/4''	32-1/2''	20 ± 1/2 OR 25 ± 1/2	26''

✕ "E" DIMENSIONS PROVIDE CLEARANCE FOR OMC OUTBOARD ENGINES.

The dry well design recommended by the Outboard Marine Corporation for its 1982 outboards.

the bottom frame *(2)*, the short lengths of deck beam *(29)*, the motor mount *(17)*, and two upright filler pieces *(19)* are laid out to correspond with an outline of the transom drawn on some smooth, flat surface. Gussets *(7 and 20)* are glued on with epoxy and are well nailed with 1¾-inch galvanized nails.

Small, temporary gussets of plywood scrap are also tacked on to hold the two upright filler pieces *(19)* in place between *17* and *29*. The framing can now be turned over to receive its first outside layer of ⅜-inch plywood, which is put on with glue and nailed.

The framing is then inverted, and the two upright framing pieces *(18)* are bolted in place with ⅜-inch galvanized carriage bolts—one through the deck beam *(29)*, two through the filler piece *(19)*, two through the motor mount *(17)*, and one through the frame bottom *(2)*. This greatly reinforces the motor mount, which is the only place in this hull where bolts are called for. A bit stock and bit would also be useful in making the two freeing ports *(31)* through the motor mount.

After the sides and bottom are planked, the transom is covered with its second, outer layer of ⅜-inch plywood. This is glued to the inner layer and along the edges.

Before this is done, the spaces at the transom between the bottom and side stringers must be solidly plugged with ¾-inch strips of stringer stock, which are

glued in place with epoxy. Otherwise, there may be leakage here. I cannot stress enough the necessity of having a tight seal along the bottom edge and sides of the transom.

The plywood sides of the well extend forward to station 7, which is framed in the usual way but with the addition of two uprights *(21)* that receive the well sides. These uprights are lengths of 2 x 4 (net 1½ x 3½) whose ends are halved over the frame bottom and the deck beam and spiked to them. The framing diagram for station 7 shows *22* and *27* in place, but these do not go on until after the sides are installed.

The addition of the carlin *(30)*, which is halved into the upper end of *18*, completes the backing for the plywood side. No backing piece is required at the bottom. After the plywood side panel has been accurately scribed and cut to fit, it is set in place and nailed to the backing pieces.

Now the upright *(22)*, notched to halve over the deck beam *(29)* and the frame bottom *(2)* and to take the end of the bottom support *(23)*, is fitted and spiked to the deck beam and frame bottom and into the backing post *(21)*.

The bottom of the dry well is supported by *23* and *27*. The former is spiked to *18* and is let into *22*. It is glued to the plywood side and well nailed through from the back of the plywood. The bottom of the well *(24)*

CROSS SPALL
(33)
LINES AND OFFSETS TO INSIDE PLANKING

(35)
WATER TIGHT (34)
SECTION 2   LOOKING TOWARD THE BOW

TOP OF CROSS SPALL
3'-0"
1'-6"
1'-1"
18" W.L.
13" W.L.
BASE LINE
76"
1'-8"
0   1   2   3   4   5   6   7   T

consists of two layers, the first an under layer of 1-inch pine boards (net thickness ¾ inch). These run crosswise and are well nailed at the ends into *23*.

The outer layer of ⅜-inch plywood is glued and nailed to the under layer. In gluing around the edges care must be taken to prevent any possibility of a leak. Any water that managed to seep in between the two layers would almost certainly cause rot. The back of the well—actually its forward side—is made the same way as the bottom.

How the interior of the hull is finished out will depend on the needs and preferences of the builder or owner, so here we shall do hardly more than mention some general considerations in working out the interior arrangements.

The narrow side decks are important structural members that brace and stiffen the sides of the hull when there is a large, open cockpit. The forward deck, which we show coming back as far as station 2, also braces the hull, keeps out a lot of water, and provides dry storage space when combined with the watertight sill *(34)* that keeps water from surging forward from the cockpit. Because of its under layer of 1-inch pine

stringers fore and aft, the deck will be stiff enough without putting deck beams closer than the frame stations shown.

A self-bailing cockpit is a good idea. It keeps rainwater out of the bilge, and it makes for a clean boat, since it is easy to flush out any dirt that may find its way into the cockpit. And, as mentioned, the scuppers can always be plugged.

The following information will be useful in determining the height of a self-bailing cockpit. The weight of the boat when finished, provided it is built to the scantlings specified here, should be about 2,600 pounds, plus 600 pounds for the outboard motor, two occupants, and incidentals—or about 3,200 pounds total. On the waterline 13 inches above the baseline, displacement is approximately 3,200 pounds. At the waterline 18 inches above the baseline, displacement increases to 5,700 pounds.

It might be convenient to have one or more temporary cross thwarts, dory fashion. They would straddle the side frames and rest on a seat riser, added here especially for this purpose but also serving to brace the side. These removable thwarts would brace

A 20-foot garvey built in 1983 from the plans presented here. The builder, Warren Hatfield of Norfolk, Virginia, uses the boat for crabbing in lower Chesapeake Bay. A 60 h.p. Johnson outboard with a medium-power prop gives him a cruising speed of 12 to 15 m.p.h. and a top speed of about 20 m.p.h. Hatfield, an experienced builder, reported no problems in the construction, and he is impressed with the boat's strength. "One should loft the profile of the bow transom and the next three frames and include the ladder-frame building ways," he says. "That way a jig can be made with the correct angle to hold the bow in the proper position."

the sides too, but could be easily taken out and stowed when an open, unobstructed cockpit is desired.

A word of caution about turning the hull right side up after planking has been completed: This should not be attempted without plenty of help, and the procedure must be well thought out. This is fairly heavy construction for the home shop, and injury could result from carelessness. With the cross spalls in place on each frame to brace the sides, there is little chance of damage when the boat is rolled over.

Specifications for components are as follows. The numbers are keyed to the accompanying diagrams.

17. *Motor mount:* Two-inch (1½-inch net) Douglas fir or oak, 11½ inches wide.

18. *Framing for plywood sides of the motor well:* Two-inch-by-four-inch (net 1½-inch-by-3½-inch) fir or oak, bolted through deck beam, motor mount, filler piece, and frame bottom with ⅜-inch galvanized bolts.

19. *Upright filler piece between motor mount and deck beam and under the side framing piece:* Two-inch-by-four-inch fir or oak.

20. *Transom frame gusset:* ⅜-inch plywood, large enough to tie together side frame, motor mount, and frame bottom.

21. *Upright backing piece for plywood side of the motor well:* Two-inch-by-four-inch (net 1½-inch-by-3½-inch) fir or oak, halved at the ends to fit over frame bottom and deck beam and spiked to them.

22. *Upright to support the back of the motor well:* Two-inch-by-four-inch fir or oak, identical to *21* but

fitted and fastened in place after the plywood side of the well is in place. Spiked through into *21*.

23. *Support for the bottom of the motor well:* Two-inch-by-four-inch fir or oak. Installed after the plywood side is put on and glued and nailed to it. Let into *22* as shown and spiked to *18*.

24. *Under layer, bottom of well:* One-inch (net ¾-inch) pine boards laid crosswise.

25. *Under layer, back of motor well:* One-inch (net ¾-inch) pine boards.

26. *Liner, bottom of motor well:* ⅜-inch plywood. Glue around the edges to make completely tight. Leakage here will cause rot.

27. *Support for back of well:* Two-inch-by-four-inch fir spiked to *22*.

28. *Sides of well:* ⅜-inch plywood glued to *18, 21,* and *30*.

29. *Deck beams:* Molded 2½ inches, sided 1½ inches. Fir or oak. Camber 2 inches to 3 inches in 7 feet.

30. *Carlin:* Backs plywood sides of the motor well. Halved into *18*.

31. *Freeing ports:* Three inches by 1½ inches, to drain bottom of motor well.

32. *Outer layer of ⅜-inch plywood covering the outside of the transom:* Glued to the inner layer and along the bottom and sides. Nailed.

33. *Temporary cross spall:* One-inch pine or fir, 4 inches wide or wider.

34. *Watertight sill to keep water out of the storage space under the foredeck:* One-inch pine or fir 8 inches wide.

35. *Coaming, fore end:* Six inches wide.

1 3

Clamming Skiff

········●········

In the spring of 1982 I received an inquiry about clamming skiffs from a coastal town in the western end of Maine's Washington County. Considerable commercial clam digging is done in that area, and outboard skiffs are required to bring the clams ashore from the distant flats and remote coves of the deeply indented coast.

The boats now in use, according to my informant, are mostly home-built. They are heavy, crudely constructed, flat-bottomed skiffs that are wet and pound badly in a chop. They are about 16 feet in length, which is about as large as they can be for convenient transportation in a pickup truck, and are commonly powered with 35 h.p. outboards.

In casting about for ideas for an improved skiff, my correspondent had come across a 14-foot-4½-inch outboard flatiron that I designed for the *Maine Coast Fisherman* nearly 30 years ago. It was later included in my *Dory Book*. He was impressed with the

favorable report of a Great Lakes fisherman who had built one, and he felt the model might be worth adapting as a clamming skiff for use in Washington County.

The fact that this boat was constructed of plywood suggested that it might be built considerably lighter than some of the clamming skiffs now in use, a highly desirable feature when one must drag a boat off and onto distant stretches of flats or lift it on and off a truck. How would it be, he inquired, if the boat were to be enlarged by about 10 percent, bringing it up to 16 feet in length?

There is no reason this could not be done. But as I considered how these clamming skiffs are used, and the shortcomings described by my informant, it seemed to me that more was needed here than simply an enlargement of the old outboard flatiron, which is, after all, a more or less typical down-east flatiron except for its plywood construction. It would be

OFFSETS — FEET · INCHES · EIGHTHS								
STATIONS		STEM	1	2	3	4	5	T
HEIGHTS ABOVE B.L.	SHEER	3-3-0	2-10-0	2-7-2	2-4-7	2-3-5	2-2-7	2-3-2
	CHINE	0-8-4	0-8-3	0-7-0	0-6-0	0-6-5	0-8-0	0-10-0
HALF-BREADTHS	SHEER	0-0-3	1-10-0	2-5-0	2-8-1	2-9-1	2-9-2	2-7-7
	CHINE	0-0-3	0-1-0	0-10-2	1-5-6	1-10-4	1-11-5	1-11-5

MEASUREMENTS TO INSIDE OF PLANKING AND INSIDE OF BOTTOM

Outboard Clamming Skiff 15'-8" x 5'-8"

considerably lighter than a plank-built flatiron, but its wide, flat bottom would still pound in a chop, I fear, and it would be wet.

Certainly a wide, flat bottom aft was needed for carrying a heavy load, for supporting the outboard motor, for allowing a shoal draft, and for sitting upright on the flats. But couldn't the boat be made sharp forward so that it would have a soft entrance, and couldn't it be made with enough depth and flare at the bow to keep it dry? The result of some preliminary sketching and the construction of a scale half-model in soft, dry pine can be seen in the lines drawing reproduced here.

The long, raking stem coming all the way back to station or section 1, which is a sharp, widely flaring V, will give a soft, easy entrance with plenty of lift to keep the bow from dropping too low. A short length of bow deck extending back about 4 feet, together with a low, watertight bulkhead about a foot high under the after end, will keep the bow dry and provide a convenient storage space out of the weather. This will be fully detailed below.

The bottom has been widened aft, as has the whole after part of the boat, for greater capacity. Instead of making the bottom absolutely straight and flat fore and aft, a small amount of rocker—about 3 inches—has been added, but not enough to give much difficulty in shallow water. Six inches of level displacement figures to nearly 1,000 pounds; three more inches give an additional 700 pounds. How the boat trims will depend, of course, on how it is loaded.

Twenty-five horsepower is ample power, possibly more than ample. Certainly the boat could do with less. If the stern should show any tendency to squat, this could be offset by moving the load forward.

For lightness, fir plywood, ⅜ inch thick, has been retained for the sides. Three 4-by-8-foot panels will be required.

Each side will be spliced up from three sections: two full-length 8-foot sections and a small piece to finish out the tip of the bow. The two after sections (one for either side) can be got out of a single panel, as shown in the diagram. The bow sections will each require a panel, and there should be enough left over for frame gussets, for the low bulkhead under the forward deck, and for other small pieces.

Superior-quality exterior grade can be used if it is free from internal voids, thin veneers, and excessive patching. Otherwise, marine quality would be worth the extra cost. One alternative might be to sheathe ordinary exterior-grade plywood with a covering of fiberglass or Vectra.

Splices should be epoxy-glued. They are not difficult to make, and the method for doing so will be fully explained below. Epoxy adhesive will also be needed for gluing the chine strips to the plywood sides, as well as for the outwales and the frame gussets. If used economically, one quart will probably be sufficient for the whole job. For the parts listed, epoxy, in my opinion, is absolutely essential for good results.

The shape of the plywood sides was obtained by taking a thin poster-board template from the scale half-model. It should be quite accurate. However, the pieces should be cut oversize to allow for some variation and adjustment. They are easily trimmed when they are fitted on the boat.

The "matching line" shown on the separate sections should run perfectly straight for the entire length of the side when its sections are scarfed together. This is to ensure correct alignment when scarfing. Otherwise, the glued-up side might not fit.

Instead of using plywood for the bottom, I show cross planking heavy enough to take the hard use a working skiff gets. With fore-and-aft bottom stringers inside and out, through-nailed for added stiffness, inside gratings, which would be required with a plywood bottom, will not be needed.

Cross planking can be native pine or cedar, and it is not difficult to put on. A cross-planked bottom will weigh more than one of plywood, but not a great deal more if inside gratings are omitted. Considering the abuse this workboat must take, a little added weight can be tolerated.

This will not be a lightweight boat, but I believe it will weigh considerably less than some of the clamming boats now in use. After all, if a workboat is to withstand the conditions these clamming skiffs must endure, they cannot be built too lightly.

The shape of this skiff makes it an easy boat to build—easier, in fact, than it may appear at first glance. The plywood side wraps around the frames with no hard bends whatsoever, as became apparent when the shape of the plywood side was duplicated with poster board. Likewise, the chine strips have no bend to speak of.

The stem has such a slight curve that it can be cut out in one piece from a straight length of plank. Besides the plywood, lumber is pine, fir, and possibly cedar for the bottom, all from boards planed ⅞ inch thick. Oak can be used for the frames, chine strips, and fore-and-aft stringers, but it is not necessary and should not be used if weight is a primary consideration. If need be, every part except the plywood sides and the stem can be got out of white-pine boards planed to a finished thickness of ⅞ inch.

Fastenings are, for the most part, hot-dipped galvanized nails. If galvanized nails of this size and type are not available, ring nails, where specified, can be stainless or bronze without danger of electrolysis. Galvanized fastenings will last long enough, and then some, if they are hot-dipped with a generous coating of zinc. Electroplated fastenings are worthless.

The only place screws might be used to advantage is for fastening the plywood side to the chine strip. If ring nails of the right size cannot be obtained, 1-inch number 12 galvanized wood screws on 7- to 8-inch centers, staggered, should be used here to supplement and reinforce the glue joint.

The sectional diagram for frame 4 is keyed as follows:

1. *Side frames:* Molded 2 inches at the top, 3 inches at the bottom. White pine, oak, or Douglas fir, ⅞ inch thick.

2. *Bottom frames:* Molded 3 inches. White pine, oak, or Douglas fir, ⅞ inch thick.

3. *Frame gussets:* Fir plywood, ⅜ inch, both sides of frame. Assembled with epoxy glue and 1¼-inch number 11 or number 12 ring nails.

4. *Triangular filler piece between the two gussets:* Glued and nailed in place.

5. *Sides:* Fir plywood, ⅜ inch. Marine grade preferable; superior-quality exterior without internal voids, thin veneers, or excessive patching permissible.

6. *Chine strips:* Molded 3¼ inches to bevel 3 inches, sided ⅞ inch. Oak, white pine, or Douglas fir. Let into frames and fastened with two 2½-inch hot-dipped galvanized wire nails.

7. *Cross-planked bottom:* Plank ⅞ inch thick and 4 inches to 6 inches wide—and no wider. Cedar, white pine, or Douglas fir. Fitted tight inside; outside seams open ⅛ inch for caulking. Driven cotton caulking payed with red-lead primer and puttied with non-hardening seam compound. Bottom boards nailed to chine strips with 3-inch hot-dipped galvanized wire nails. Nailed to inside fore-and-aft bottom stringers with 1½-inch number 11 or number 12 ring nails.

8. *Inside bottom stringers:* Molded 3 inches and sided ⅞ inch. Oak, white pine, or Douglas fir. Cut into bottom frames and fastened with 2½-inch hot-dipped galvanized wire nails.

9. *Inside center bottom stringer:* Molded 4 inches, sided ⅞ inch. Oak, white pine, or Douglas fir. Cut into bottom frames and fastened with 2½-inch hot-dipped galvanized wire nails.

10. *Outside bottom stringers:* Molded 2 inches, sided ⅞ inch, fastened with 2½-inch nails.

11. *Outside center bottom stringer:* Molded 3 inches, sided ⅞ inch, fastened with 2½-inch nails.

12. *Hot-dipped galvanized wire nails, 2½ inches:* Must be hot-dipped; electroplated nails are worthless.

13. *Ring nails:* Number 11 or number 12 1½ inches.

14. *Seat riser:* Molded 3 inches before beveling, sided ⅞ inch. Oak, white pine, or Douglas fir. Fastened with 2½-inch hot-dipped galvanized wire nails.

15. *Outwale:* Molded 2½ inches amidships and aft. Tapers to 1¾ inches at the stemhead. Oak, white pine, or Douglas fir. Fastened into the frames with 2½-inch hot-dipped galvanized wire nails. Glued to the plywood sides and fastened through from the inside of the plywood with 1¼-inch ring nails, number 11 or number 12.

16. *Thwarts:* Ten inches wide, ⅞ inch thick. White pine or Douglas fir. Ends cut to straddle the frames like a dory thwart, for ready removal if desired.

17. *Ring nails:* 1 inch, number 11 or number 12, through ⅜-inch plywood side to chine strip, spaced 4 to 5 inches apart and staggered.

18. Two-inch hot-dipped galvanized wire nails through plywood sides into side frames every 3 to 4 inches.

19. Two-and-a-half-inch galvanized wire nails through inside fore-and-aft bottom stringers into bottom frames.

20. Three-inch hot-dipped galvanized wire nails through cross-planked bottom into bottom frames.

This is only a lowly work skiff. Nevertheless, a lot of thought has gone into its design, and every consideration has been given to making its construction as simple, straightforward, and easy as possible.

Despite its apparent simplicity, the dimensions must be maintained, the planned order of work followed, and accurate fits achieved, if the boat is to perform acceptably and stand up to the hard usage required of it. I'm not saying that this design and the recommended procedures for building it cannot be improved, but I must warn that unadvised and ill-considered changes here and there, even when they appear to be minor ones, could do much to spoil the boat.

Although the particular craft we are considering here is intended for use as a clamming skiff in Washington County, Maine, the construction and basic form are adaptable for other simple craft for a variety of uses. Built with considerably more bottom rocker, and fitted with a centerboard, rudder, and suitable rig, flat-bottomed boats of this general type will give a smart sail in semisheltered waters, although they are not suitable for venturing very far offshore in the open sea.

Small flats like this with the construction simplified still further make good, light tenders, shore-front workboats, and, because of their durability and great initial stability, good boats for children to play in on smooth water. Moreover, boats of this type make an excellent first boat for amateur builders. And they are comparatively inexpensive to build, to the extent that anything is inexpensive today.

No modern power tools are required, and in a pinch, a few basic hand tools can be made to do. The minimum kit would include a handsaw, chisel, plane, spokeshave, carpenter's square, level, chalkline, nail hammer, screwdriver, putty knife, and a pair of 6-inch C-clamps. Fastenings throughout can be hot-dipped galvanized common nails with the possible addition of some shorter galvanized ring nails of fairly stout gauge.

As previously mentioned, lumber can be limited to

BASE LINE

SECTION THROUGH SET-UP
TOP OF LADDER FRAME

CENTERLINE

DIAGRAM 1

⅜-inch plywood and ⅞-inch softwood boards. It is best to use marine-grade plywood, despite the expense, since ordinary exterior grade is so inferior today, with thin outer veneers and internal voids, that much of it is not worth putting into a boat. Boards may be northern white pine, Douglas fir, loblolly pine, or cypress. Western red cedar, redwood, northern white cedar, and juniper are too soft to hold nails well, except for bottom planking. Scantlings have been worked out so that boards of only one thickness—⅞ inch—are required. This permits the lumber to be purchased in one lot and planed at the mill at one time.

One thing we have that old-time builders didn't have is epoxy glue. I'm sure they would have used it had it been available. There are many formulations. My first choice is Chem-Tech, my second, Cold-Cure. Both are widely advertised in boating publications. I do not care for WEST System epoxy because I find it sets too quickly to give me unhurried working time, because it is too thin, and because I am concerned about the effect of the hardener on my health. These same considerations apply also to a number of other epoxy formulations. Cold-Cure, by the way, has a strong odor that I distrust.

Epoxy is used throughout the skiff. The stem

assembly is glued with it, as is the false, or outer, stem if it is laminated rather than steam-bent. The plywood frame gussets and the transom assembly are also epoxied, and the resin is used for scarfing the plywood sides and for gluing them to the stem, chines, and outwales. If used economically, one quart should do the job.

Once the boat has been set up it is more than half built, with only the preglued sides to be put on and the bottom cross-planked, caulked, and painted before the boat is turned over and the interior finished. Finishing involves little more than adding thwarts, oarlocks, and outwales, unless it is decided to add a short deck forward with a short, tight bulkhead under the forward end to keep the bilge water out of the bow.

Preparatory to setting up, however, a ladder-frame foundation and several subassemblies are built. These include the laminated inner stem; the outer stem, if it is to be glue-laminated from several thin strips; the five frame assemblies that also serve as molds, but remain in the boat; the full-length plywood sides scarfed together from three shorter pieces; and the glued-up composite transom. In addition, the middle bottom stringer should be cut out and fastened to the inner stem before the boat is set up. By fitting this into the recesses cut for it in the bottoms of the frame molds one can check their alignment before securing them in place.

The inner stem is built up in three layers of ⅞-inch-thick boards, each layer consisting of two pieces whose lengths vary so that the joints can be well staggered when they are glued and nailed together. Nails must be located where they will not interfere with the beveling. Don't cut pieces to the exact width

and shape before gluing. Instead leave a little extra wood for trimming to the exact shape after the glue has set.

The stem is beveled ahead of time for the plywood planking with the same bevel throughout, as shown in the diagram, and the lower end is notched for the middle bottom stringer. A glued-up softwood stem is plenty strong for this, since much of the strength of the bow derives from the full-width plywood sides glued and nailed to the stem. The outer stem adds further strength. This can be bent oak, steamed or boiled, but if it is glue-laminated from thin strips, these can be bent around the inner stem, which is used as a gluing form.

The five three-piece frame assemblies are held together at the lower corners with plywood gussets on either side, glued on and nailed with 1¼-inch nails. Frame assemblies are beveled, and are notched to receive the chines and the bottom stringers.

Temporary cross spalls, 4 inches wide, are screwed on the *after* side of the frames. These are located with their upper edges (their lower edges when the frames are bottom up on the ladder frame) exactly 2 feet from the baseline, as shown on the lines drawing. These cross spalls must be exactly level as well; special care is required because the accuracy of the setup and the final shape of the boat depend on them.

In setting up, the frame molds are all placed on the forward side of the station lines and spaced according to the lines drawing, with the cross spalls aft of the station lines and the ladder-frame cleats aft of the cross spalls. The sides of frame 5 require no beveling at all. The rest are all beveled forward. The amount of beveling will be diagramed below. So little beveling is required on the bottoms of the frames that this is easily taken care of with a few passes of the plane after the boat has been set up and the bottom members are being faired for the bottom cross planking.

Glue-scarfing the plywood sides is done quite easily if the following procedure is followed. Scarfs are laid out 4½ inches wide, or 12 times the thickness of the plywood. With a sharp plane and some care, the scarf bevels can be accurately planed. The outer edge of the scarf surface should be brought to something less than a feather edge, leaving it a scant 1/32 inch. The excess is easily sanded flat after the glue has set. The scarf surface should be perfectly flat but roughened somewhat with coarse sandpaper or a fine wood rasp so that a thin coating of epoxy glue may be retained in the joint. This is essential if the joint is to hold.

Since the width of ply to be glued is slightly more than 28 inches, two 30-inch lengths of 2-inch-by-6-inch fir construction lumber, the same lumber used for the ladder-frame stringer (actual dimensions 5½ inches by 1½ inches), will be required for a press. Plane one flat side of each to a slightly convex camber, not more than ⅛ inch of convex curve. Place one of these on the floor, cambered side up. Cover with waxed paper. Lay on this the scarfed end of one of the

pieces of plywood, scarfed surface up. Spread with a liberal coating of glue and cover with the scarfed end of the other, or mating, piece of plywood. Tack with a fine brad at each end to prevent the glue joint from slipping or shifting.

Cover with waxed paper, and directly over this place the other 2-by-6, cambered face down. Midway between the ends, a 3-inch two-headed staging nail is driven through the plywood and into the 2-by-6 underneath. (Later, when the nail is pulled through, the plywood is easily plugged.) Two more nails are put in, one on each side of the center nail and about 8 inches distant from it. These are set down hard. If staging nails are not to be had, ordinary nails can be substituted with a piece of leather under the head to make them easy to pull later.

Finally, the cambered crosspieces are pulled together tightly with a C-clamp at either end. If this procedure is followed step by step, a perfect splice should result.

One warning: It is easy for the two pieces of plywood to get out of alignment during gluing so that the side will not fit. One precaution against this already mentioned is to cut the plywood a bit large for exact trimming later. The most reliable is to make use of a "matching line," as shown above in the diagram of plank shape. When the splice is set up and after the glue has been applied, the matching line across both pieces should be checked with a chalkline or long straightedge to see that it runs perfectly straight. If it does not, it should be adjusted as necessary so that it does, before final clamping.

The ladder-frame setup has proved to be the easiest way of making an accurate form for building boats planked bottom up. The one diagramed here calls for stringers of 2-inch-by-6-inch fir construction lumber as the principal members of the platform. It hardly needs saying that these stringers must be perfectly straight.

The frame spacing is laid out on the two longer pieces, and cross cleats 2 feet long, 4 inches wide, and ⅞ inch thick are located ⅞ inch aft of the frame stations and nailed solidly in place. Since all of the frames bevel forward, they are set with their after sides on the frame stations and with the cross spalls aft of the frame stations. This brings the latter snugly against the cross cleats.

It is understood, of course, that the stringers must run parallel to each other with the cross cleats square to them. Short stringers spaced 14 inches apart

DIAGRAM 2

3"

4'

CROSS SECTION
LADDER FRAME
SET-UP

GUSSET
ON EITHER SIDE

FRAME STATION 2

CROSS SPALL

(23)

4"

3'—0"

(23)

LADDER FRAME CLEAT

(24)

LADDER FRAME STRINGER

HORSE

continue forward as the boat narrows. Finally, there is only the single plank that fits against the stem.

When the ladder-frame foundation is complete, a chalkline is stretched from end to end down the center, and a centerline is snapped. On this line the frame molds are located when they are set up according to the centerlines marked on their cross spalls.

The transom assembly is in three layers put together with glue and 1¼-inch nails. An internal core of ⅞-inch boards pieced together as shown in the diagram is held together by a partial covering inside with ⅜-inch plywood so that it can be set up on the building form. The outer covering of ⅜-inch plywood is not glued on until after the chines and the fore-and-aft bottom stringers have been fitted, nailed in place, and trimmed flush with the inner core.

This procedure makes the installation of these fore-and-aft members much easier and faster than if they had to be cut exactly to length to fit *inside* the transom. This way they start out a little long, their fore ends are fitted and pushed up tight, and what remains sticking out beyond the transom at the after end is sawed off flush to permit the outer covering of plywood to be glued on.

The exposed edges of the plywood at the top of the transom could be something of a problem. The only way to deal with this would be to saturate the edges with an oil-based paint to prevent the absorption of water as well as to harden the wood. Another method might be to bind with fiberglass tape set in epoxy.

Probably the best way is to stop the plywood about 4 inches below the top of the transom, replacing it with ⅜-inch-thick pieces of the same wood as the inner core, which are glued in place with epoxy as diagramed.

The diagrams illustrating the construction details just discussed are keyed as follows:

21. *Ladder-frame stringers:* Two-inch-by-six-inch fir.
22. *Transom support:* Two-inch-by-four-inch fir.
23. *Frame-mold cross spall:* ⅞ inch by 4 inches.
24. *Ladder-frame cross cleat:* ⅞ inch by 4 inches by 2 feet.
25. Transom.
26. Inner stem.

The side frames can be beveled at the bench before the frame assemblies are made. Frame bevels do not change over the length of the frames.

Frame 5 requires no beveling, and the bevels on the other frames are all cut sloping forward. However, the transom is beveled aft. That is, its after face finishes smaller than its inboard, or forward, face. Very little beveling is required on the bottoms of the frames, and this need not be done until the frames are set up on the ladder frame and the bottoms, chines, and edges of the plywood sides are faired to receive the bottom planking.

After the outer plywood facing of the transom has

been put on with epoxy glue and well nailed with number 11 or number 12 1½-inch ring nails, the plywood sides go on, having been spliced full length as previously described. The sides must be well glued to the chines and nailed with plenty of 1-inch number 11 or number 12 wire ring nails. Nails should be spaced closely enough to ensure that the sides are brought in contact with the glue-covered chine surface throughout for an optimum gluing job.

The sides should also be glued to the ends of the transom and fastened with 2-inch galvanized nails. Glue is also used on the stem, and 2-inch galvanized common nails are adequate for fastening the sides to both the stem and the side frames.

When the sides are on and the glue has set, the bottom framing, including the fore-and-aft stringers, and the chines with the plywood sides attached are ready to be faired to receive the bottom planking. For this a piece of straight, flat board somewhat longer than the maximum width of the bottom is used as a

straightedge. The upper surfaces of the various members upon which the bottom planking will rest are planed so that they are perfectly fair and true. The straightedge should touch them all wherever it is placed in an athwartships position. The bottom planking throughout must touch frame bottoms, stringers, chines, and the bottom edges of the plywood sides.

Putting on the cross-planked bottom is not quite as simple an operation as it might appear, which is to say there is a definite procedure to follow and standards of workmanship to be met. Accurate fits are essential. Planks must be neither too wide nor too narrow. Widths from about 4 inches to 6 inches will be about right. Planks that are too wide will shrink excessively when they dry out, which will cause the seams to open up too much. Likewise, there is the danger of planks buckling when they swell.

The seams between the planks are essentially expansion joints, and the more seams there are, the less seams open when the boat dries out. On the other hand, the narrower the planks are, the more there are of them and more labor is required to prepare and fit and, later, to caulk them. Besides, narrow planks are not as stiff, and if they are too narrow the ends may not nail securely.

There is one other thing to be taken into account. Slash-sawn boards—that is, boards cut from the side of the log—tend to cup toward the outside of the tree when they dry out and as they age. Thus, slash-sawn boards—boards most frequently used for bottom planking—should be put on the boat with the outside, or bark side, inside so that they will cup toward the inside of the boat, giving a smoother bottom with less drag. The wider the bottom planking used, the more important this consideration becomes.

When the bottom planking is fitted, the edges on the inside should be tight and touching for about the first one-quarter of plank thickness before beveling for the caulking seam starts. Caulking seams should be about ⅛ inch wide on the outside for each inch of plank thickness. Thus, for this boat with bottom planking ⅞ inch thick, the amount of bevel to be planed off each

edge for the caulking seam should be about 1/16 inch on the outside and die out to nothing about three-quarters of the way in. In planing the caulking seam when two planks come together, it is better to take wood off both planks equally rather than all off one.

These are general rules whose observation is likely to vary somewhat in practice. One thing may be depended on, however: Seams that are wider on the inside than on the outside will not hold caulking.

Planking starts at the stern with one of the wider planks securely nailed into the chines, transom, and bottom stringers. For nailing the plank ends to the chines, use 2½-inch 8-penny hot-dipped galvanized common nails spaced 2 to 2½ inches apart. If the chines are soft white pine, 3-inch 10-penny nails may make a more solid job. The second plank and those following are clamped in turn to the bottom stringers with a couple of C-clamps so that they are held down flat while being hauled up tight with a pipe clamp or door clamp against the plank previously fastened in place.

Lacking such a clamp, the builder can drive the plank up tight with just enough tension on the C-clamps to hold it snugly until it is nailed. A short piece of board should be used to pound against in order not to mar the edge of the plank.

After four or five planks are on and fastened, a space the width of a single plank is left vacant before the next plank is put on, and the planking operation is resumed as before. Observe that in the diagram this empty space tapers—that is, it is somewhat narrower at one end than the other. The plank that is later got out to fill it will be made to exactly the same taper but longer, and will be driven in place like a long wedge. There will be several of these wedge-shaped filler pieces the length of the bottom. They are all put in at the same time and set up together. The combined effect is to greatly tighten the bottom.

Note that the end piece at the bow runs fore and aft instead of athwartships and is made up of two lengthwise halves glued together, the grain on the outside running parallel with the outside of the boat. This brings the short grain inside where it is well supported. Left outside, the short grain could easily be split where the sides are nailed into the chine. Preparing the end piece in this manner may mean a little more work, but it makes for a much more dependable job.

After the bottom is planked, the plank ends are trimmed flush and are planed so that they fair with the sides. The seams are caulked with cotton set down tightly, but not tightly enough to strain the planks or break their edges.

The bottom edges of the plywood sides are beveled slightly before planking starts to provide a caulking seam after the bottom planking is in place. This must also be caulked. The tails of cotton driven into the ends of the bottom seams are brought all the way down and tucked into the seam between the bottom and the side planking. No opening anywhere that might cause a leak can be overlooked.

After the cotton is set in tightly it is saturated with a thin oil-based paint or primer. Red-lead primer is by far the best there is for this, but it must be thin enough to penetrate thoroughly. Several applications may be required for the best results. When the cotton has dried, the seams are filled with an elastic, nonhardening bottom-seam compound.

Before the boat is turned right side up, the bottom rub strips (that is, the outside bottom stringers) are nailed on, as previously diagrammed; 2½-inch 8-penny hot-dipped galvanized common nails are used for this. If they are driven on a slight slant, they will hold better,

and the heads can be set in ⅛ inch or so without danger of the points coming through inside.

The drawing on page 179 shows rub strips 2 inches wide that follow the outside edges of the bottom. These strips, bent on to conform to the curve of the sides, would go on without difficulty and would protect the ends of the bottom planking, but they would drag water behind their curved inside edges, making the boat harder to move and slowing it down somewhat. Bottom rub strips offer the least resistance to forward movement when their inside edges are straight and parallel to the fore-and-aft centerline of the boat. Such a rub strip for protecting the outside bottom edges of this boat is shown by the broken line, *39,* in the accompanying planking diagram. It extends only 6½ feet from the stern, but is nearly 6 inches wide at its widest part.

When the rub strips are on and the bottom has been given a priming coat, the nails through the cross spalls into the ladder-frame cross cleats can be drawn to allow the boat to be turned right side up. But before the cross spalls are removed from the frames, the outwales are put on. They are glued to the plywood sides and well nailed from the inside through the plywood with 1-inch number 11 or number 12 ring nails to ensure snug contact throughout the glue joint. The outwales are nailed with 2½-inch 8-penny hot-dipped galvanized common nails to the stem, frames, and transom.

With the outwales in place and fastened, the cross spalls are removed so that the side stringers, serving as seat risers, may be sprung in and nailed, which further stiffens the sides. But if this boat is to have a watertight bulkhead and foredeck, these should probably go in first.

The diagram shows that the bulkhead under the after end of the short foredeck is located 14 inches forward of station 2. It could just as well be at station 2 if more covered space forward is desired.

The frame for the bulkhead, including the after deck beam, is assembled first, with the plywood gussets and bottom strip on the forward side to hold it together. After being beveled and fitted, the frame assembly is set up in place and fastened through the sides and bottom.

The width of plywood that forms the watertight bulkhead or barrier is scribed and cut for a tight fit all around and is fastened in with plenty of nonhardening bedding compound to ensure that there will be no leaks. Deck beams located 14 inches on centers are cut to length with appropriate end bevels to fit tight against the sides at the sheer. They are nailed through the sides into the outwales.

The plywood deck is bent on and nailed to the deck beams and to the outwales over which its edges extend. If the edges of the deck are glued to the top edges of the outwales, the result will be tighter and stronger. The deck can be put on in two lengthwise halves, the seam down the middle supported underneath by blocks between the deck beams.

Outside, the seam is covered by a strip tapered for appearance. This is similar to the construction found on Adirondack guideboats and Saint Lawrence skiffs. The forward coaming, shaped as diagramed, is put on last.

A decked-over section at the bow sealed off at the bottom with a low barrier of watertight bulkhead not only provides dry storage space for clothing, lunches, and the like, but also strengthens and stiffens the sides of the boat.

At each frame station, removable thwarts like dory thwarts are fitted. When in place, these thwarts rest on the seat risers with their ends slotted to fit around the side frames. When in place they brace the sides, but they are easily removed when this is desirable.

A stern bench a foot or so wide braces the transom and the stern and is solidly nailed to cleats on the transom and to the ends of the seat risers. Quarter knees at the sheer level fasten through the sides and outwales, as well as through the transom, further bracing the stern. These knees are about 9 inches or 10 inches either way and are laid out so as to avoid short, weak grain.

Oarlocks are located 12 inches aft of the after edge of the thwart at station 3. If the thwart is 9 inches wide and centered on frame 3, that would bring the oarlock pins 16½ inches aft of station 3. Some might want to install another pair of oarlock sockets the same distance aft of station 2 so that the boat could be rowed from either of these two thwarts, depending on the loading or the weather. Pads for the oarlock sockets are located inside the topsides at the sheer and are fastened into the outwales.

No floorboards are needed. Limbers should be cut through the bottoms of the frames to enable the bilge to drain fore and aft. A final consideration: If oak is conveniently available, it might be well to use it for side frames. And if soft pine is used for this, it might not be a bad idea to increase the sided thickness of the side frames.

Construction details just discussed are keyed to the diagrams as follows:

30. *Bow end piece, bottom planking:* Glued up from two lengthwise halves, cut out so that the lengthwise grain runs parallel with the outside.

31. *Two-and-a-half-inch 8-penny hot-dipped galvanized common nails:* Ends of bottom planking to chine strip. Three-inch nails can be used in soft pine.

32. *Deck:* ⅜-inch-thick fir plywood. Marine plywood if possible.

33. *Deck beams:* Molded width 2½ inches, sided thickness ⅞ inch, crown 3-inch rise in 5 feet.

34. *Forward coaming:* Pine or fir ¾ inch thick.

35. *Gusset, deck beam, and frame:* ⅜-inch fir plywood.

36. *Bulkhead:* ⅜-inch fir plywood.

37. *Bulkhead stiffener:* Pine or fir, molded 2 inches, sided thickness ⅞ inch.

38. *Three-eighths-inch plywood strip:* Ties side frames to frame bottom.

39. *Bottom rub strip:* Inner edge parallel to the fore-and-aft centerline of the boat.

Sequel

I like to get feedback from builders of my designs, whether favorable or not, although I must admit to preferring the former sort. Except for such feedback I might never know if the boats performed as intended, or if they did not, in what way they fell short and to what extent. It is just not possible to build and test a prototype for every new design before it is published, although that would be the way to go if economics permitted. Thus, it is never possible to predict with complete certainty just how a new design will turn out in all respects, regardless of how closely known design characteristics successful in other configurations may have been taken into account. For these reasons I paid particular attention to a letter from Paul Rainey, a West Virginia builder of the down-east clamming skiff who followed the above plans and directions when they were first published in the *National Fisherman*. The letter follows.

West Virginia may seem a strange place to build a Downeast clam skiff, but I built your plan as published in May, June and July, 1982. My 15th boat and my third to build. Lots of fun and the plans were excellent.

Started construction on July 4th and launched on September 12th. I added strip planked decking around the sheer for trim as well as for strength.

Paul Rainey's skiff as originally built and with the center console installed later.

Now I have some running problems. With all possible adjustments on my 25 h.p. outboard and all loading arrangements she still porpoises at any more power than just enough to get on plane, and with the engine in any position except the most outboard, she sprays water up the transom. After numerous tests, I have taken out all the cross seats and am installing a center console with steering controls, etc., to get me out of the stern. I did not want to do this because I wanted simplicity. It also bothers me that I am losing cross bracing. But I can't see forward for safety with such a high-running bow. I am hoping to correct this problem with most weight concentrated in the center. I have considered trim tabs, wedges and extended planking. I would appreciate any advice.

From the photographs that accompanied Rainey's letter it was clear the builder knew what he was about. They showed a shapely hull attractively finished and fitted out. There can be no doubt that the skiff was well built, and built as designed.

There was no mention in the letter of pounding in a chop or taking water over the bow. From this it can be concluded that the sharp entrance and the long raking stem took care of what are often serious faults in heavily built flat-bottomed skiffs. But apparently the boat did squat by the stern under the conditions of loading to which it had been subjected, and then there was the "porpoising" complaint. How to account for this? Could the 3 inches of rocker built into the bottom be responsible to any significant extent for these undesired effects? Or was it something else that was chiefly amiss?

If this boat had been intended for use as a runabout

to be operated at planing speeds in a relatively light condition of loading, its after bottom would definitely have been designed without rocker. Instead, it would have run back dead straight from the midsection to the transom. But the boat was planned as a working skiff for clamming, to be used in shallow water around the clam flats while digging was in progress, where it would frequently ground out and have to be dragged about. Also it would be rowed part of the time in water too shallow for running the motor. For rowing and dragging about on the flats, a rockered bottom is advantageous. And when the skiff is on its way in from the flats, heavily loaded with clams, enough weight can be distributed forward to keep the bow down and the stern from settling unduly. If the stern does settle slightly, this is all to the good, for then the boat will run drier and pound less when heading into a chop.

Rainey's intentions for the boat were quite different. It is clear he wanted a smooth-running runabout that would plane and show a fair turn of speed with his 25 h.p. outboard. Quite correctly he sensed it would help to get the weight out of the stern and move it forward in the boat, and late that fall, following his September launching, he had begun to install a center console and steering controls. At the same time he was considering ways to modify the after bottom with such devices as trim tabs, wedges (shingles), or extended planking.

There things stood over the winter. Then in April another letter arrived from Rainey, this one a much more reassuring report, the jist of which follows.

> A few warm days in early March, and I turned the boat over, stripped the bottom, put on two coats of Chem-Tech L-26 and some hard bottom paint. Then I installed a center console and remote controls.... Wednesday's test run with all new rigging in place was a complete success. No sign of porpoising....Better visibility over the bow, a smoother ride in a chop, maybe best of all, my wife likes it better 'cause it drives more like a car. By the way the long bow and generous flare make for a very dry ride. She will run smoothly at full throttle.

No mention of trim tabs, wedges, or extended planking. No need to consider them anymore.

The first time around, Rainey ran out of lumber at the very end and left off the bottom rub stringers next to the chine. Might this omission have been "the key to the whole problem?" he queries. Definitely not for running performance, although the boat might have tracked better with the stringers in place.

What it all boils down to is weight distribution and trim. The weight of a large motor and the concentration of occupants in the stern of a lightly built 16-foot skiff are bound to make the stern settle, even a stern as wide as this one. A rockered bottom, especially in a boat as lightly built as this one, will add to this effect, but when there is only a small amount of rocker, as in this skiff, the prime cause has to be too much weight concentrated in the extreme stern. Unquestionably, the high-speed performance of this boat would be improved if the motor were mounted inboard in a well. This was not done, out of a desire to keep this ordinary working skiff simple and to not reduce its already restricted loading capacity.

As for porpoising, various factors are involved—not only trim and weight distribution but wave formation, running speed, and handling skill. Indeed, it is not uncommon for short, wide, lightly built outboard boats with heavy motors hanging over the stern, to start porpoising when driven at speed into certain wave formations. In fact, at least one of the most widely advertised and distributed small stock outboard runabouts of this kind has porpoised so severely as to flip over backward completely.

It hardly needs saying that the length of a boat has a lot to do with its performance. If this boat is not to be hauled about in a pickup truck—and there are no other restrictions on its length—I would recommend not only taking the rocker out of the after half of the bottom but also stretching the boat out to 18 feet, provided it is intended for recreation rather than use as a specialized work skiff. At 18 feet overall, and with a plywood bottom instead of cross planking, this skiff would be quite similar to the 19-foot Carolina dory skiff for which I made revised and expanded construction plans in 1979 for Texas Dory Boat Plans (P.O. Box 720, Galveston, Texas 77553). Some may recall the article in the September 1979 issue of the *National Fisherman* in which I described and commented on these revisions. These Carolina skiffs have since been built with gratifying success from the Arctic to the South Pacific, as well as here in the United States.

Although the Carolina skiff's motor is located in an inboard motor well, I do not recommend such a motor well for the clamming skiff lengthened to 18 feet. This is not because I do not think such an arrangement would give good results, but because it would require space and would add to the cost and difficulty of construction. I believe that if the motor is simply mounted over the stern, performance will be quite

BASE LINE

6" — 2'-3"
3"
STATION 6 & TRANSOM 1
5"
1'-8"
2'-2½"
4"
2'-9"

2'-3¾"
6"
1'-7"
FOR 20" SHAFT

TRANSOM 2
EXPANDED
2'-6"
1'
2'-9"

BASE LINE

1'-10½"
3" 5"
STATION 4
2'-3½"
2'-9¼"

6" — 2'-1½"
3"
STATION 5
CROSS SPALL
4" LADDER FRAME
1'-6"
2'-9¼"
2'-2¾"

FRAME REVISIONS

5/8"
TRANSOM

MOTOR DRY WELL – 15" SHAFT
MINIMUM DIMENSIONS
SHEER
1'-8½"
1'-9"
6"
2⅛"
1'-3"

7/8"
CROSS PLANKED BOTTOM
WEDGE OR SHINGLE
1'-2"
1"

REVISIONS CLAMMING SKIFF 15'-8" LOA & 18'-0" LOA

CLAMMING SKIFF REVISIONS 15'-8" LOA & 18'-0" LOA
LINES ALTERED FOR PLANING SPEEDS
FOR CONSTRUCTION DETAILS SEE NATIONAL FISHERMAN MAY, JUNE, JULY 1982

3 2 1
4
15'-8" LOA
1'-7"
5 T1

4
18'-0" LOA
1'-7"
5 T1&2

BASE LINE

OFFSETS – FEET-INCHES-EIGHTHS									
STATIONS		STEM	1	2	3	4	5	T1	T2
HEIGHTS ABOVE BL	SHEER	3-3-0	2-10-0	2-7-0	2-4-6	2-3-4	2-2-6	2-2-4	2-2-4
	CHINE	0-8-5	0-8-4	0-7-0	0-6-0	0-6-0	0-6-0	0-6-0	0-6-0
HALF-BREADTHS	SHEER	0-0-3	1-10-0	2-5-0	2-8-1	2-9-2	2-9-2	2-9-0	2-9-0
	CHINE	0-0-3	0-1-0	0-10-0	1-5-6	1-10-4	2-1-4	2-3-0	2-3-0
MEASUREMENTS INSIDE PLANKING and BOTTOM. OUTSIDE TRANSOM.									

CHINE
5" 5"
SHEER

OUTER EDGE
INNER STEM
1'
0·3·0
0·3·5
1'
0·2·4
1'
3-4-4

INSIDE BOTTOM
76°

BASE LINE
2-4-0 2-4-0 2-4-0 2-4-0 2-4-0 2-4-0
1 2 3 4 5 T1 T2

adequate. A motor with a long (20-inch) shaft will require hardly any cutout in the transom. A motor with a 15-inch shaft would call for a dry well of the type recommended by the Outboard Marine Corporation and detailed in the accompanying diagram.

The long, raking stem and sharp entrance of this skiff does much to eliminate one of the standing objections to flat-bottomed boats—the teeth-jarring pounding that occurs so frequently when they head into a hard chop. I don't believe the full benefit of this feature will be realized in a length of only 16 feet, which is one of the reasons I suggest increasing the length to 18 feet when work requirements or other imperatives do not dictate otherwise. Because of the 18-footer's increased length, and because it would have to take more of a pounding when driven at high speed in rough water, I would add narrow side decks (waterways) and coamings in order to strengthen and stiffen the topsides.

1 4

16-Foot Swampscott Dory

Every now and again I am contacted by prospective dory builders wishing to alter in some way the dimensions of the boat they are considering. Would it be possible to lengthen, shorten, widen, deepen, or otherwise change it without spoiling it? Generally the answer is yes, provided the change is not extreme and does not violate the basics of dory design. Dory design is more versatile, adaptable, and forgiving than most other small craft types.

Sometimes such a change turns out to be a distinct improvement, at least for the use for which the particular dory is built. That has been my aim in designing this modification of a proven rowing and sailing Swampscott dory. By moderately increasing the beam, the bottom width, and the size of the transom, I have significantly increased initial stability and stiffness, improved the dory's ability to stand up under sail, and added to its load carrying capacity.

This has been accomplished without detracting significantly from the craft's ability as a rowboat. In addition, there are alterations to the interior layout and the location of the centerboard that should improve performance and add to convenience.

The dory detailed here is descended from a typical Swampscott fisherman's 17-footer that I redesigned in 1974 for construction at the Mystic Seaport Museum. In late 1974 I reworked that design somewhat, shortening it to 16 feet, and I published plans and building instructions for the revision in a *National Fisherman* article and later in *Building Classic Small Craft, Volume I*. Both of these earlier designs have produced superior dories, including a fine 16-footer built by Dave Foster at The Apprenticeshop in Maine and the Mystic Seaport 17-footer that was rowed around Long Island by Dick Kohn, the Staten Island sailmaker, and two friends. On that trip, which took

OFFSETS 16' SWAMPSCOTT DORY		STEM	STA.1	STA.2	STA.3	STA.4	STERN
HEIGHTS	BOTTOM	0-5-0	0-3-4	0-2-0	0-2-3	0-3-4	0-4-2
	1	1-4-4	0-7-2	0-4-0	0-4-4	0-8-2	1-1-4
	2	1-8-1	0-10-0	0-6-6	0-6-4	0-10-4	1-4-6
	3	1-11-0	1-1-3	0-10-2	0-9-4	1-1-4	1-8-2
	4	2-2-0	1-6-0	1-3-2	1-2-5	1-5-4	2-0-1
	SHEER	2-4-5	1-10-6	1-8-6	1-8-5	1-10-5	2-3-5
WIDTHS	BOTTOM	0-0-2	0-6-1	1-0-0	1-0-2	0-4-7	0-1-1
	1	0-0-2	1-0-1	1-4-2	1-4-3	1-0-0	0-6-2
	2	0-0-2	1-4-0	1-9-2	1-8-4	1-5-0	0-8-0
	3	0-0-2	1-7-2	2-1-0	2-0-5	1-6-7	0-9-7
	4	0-0-2	1-9-6	2-3-2	2-3-7	1-10-1	0-10-4
	SHEER	0-0-2	1-10-4	2-4-0	2-4-4	1-10-7	0-9-6

MEASUREMENTS INSIDE OF PLANKING AND BOTTOM. OUTSIDE OF TRANSOM AND INNER STEM. HEIGHTS ABOVE BASE LINE. MEASUREMENTS IN FEET, INCHES AND EIGHTHS.

most of a week, the dory demonstrated its excellent seakeeping qualities by handling late-season winds and rough seas with no particular trouble.

Dories have long been recognized as fine seaboats, but their low initial stability and active response to wave action is apt to be disconcerting to the sailor unaccustomed to dories. Their quickness to heel under press of sail can be alarming. What we have here is a somewhat stiffer, steadier boat than the general run of dories, yet one that retains all the advantages of dory construction. I believe these revisions will produce a

boat more comfortable and less demanding when sailing, yet one that will still move easily and handle well under oars.

The true Swampscott dory, of which this boat is a good example, is essentially a round-bottomed boat, yet it has enough flat in its bottom to sit upright on the beach when it grounds out. For a boat that is to be beached frequently this is an especially desirable feature, particularly since it permits a double bottom, the outer layer of which is easily renewed when it wears thin from dragging over rocks.

These Swampscott boats are the aristocrats of the dory clan, and are not to be confused with their clumsier, more crudely built cousins, the heavy, slab-sided working dories of the Grand Banks fishermen. True, in some features of their construction Swampscott and Grand Banks dories are similar, but in performance there is a vast difference. Swampscott dories row and handle much more easily. Whether they are faster under oars remains open to argument, but certainly they are every bit as good seaboats. Their principal superiority over the Banks model for recreational use lies in their greater ease of handling. In normal conditions a youngster could manage the boat under consideration easily, but he definitely could not handle a Banks dory of the same size.

Yet this is by no means a small boat. With an inside depth amidships of 19 inches to the top of the railcap and a maximum beam of 59 inches, this boat could

easily take six men or an equivalent load without undue reduction of freeboard. And because of its ample beam and depth, this boat will do well under sail.

In adapting this boat for sail the interior arrangements have been somewhat altered. The seat riser has been raised 1 inch, leaving 6 inches between the thwarts and the top of the railcap. One inch may seem a trivial amount, but it adds needed width to the centerboard without detracting from the rowing qualities of the boat. It is still a comfortable boat to row. In addition, the height of the centerboard trunk has been decreased slightly, bringing the top of its cap in line with the surface of the thwarts. With the sail furled and the mast down and stowed out of the way in the boat, a single oarsman can row from any one of the three thwarts without interference; when two oarsmen are present, they occupy the forward and after thwarts.

The sailing balance of a small boat is affected by so many variables that it is difficult, and often impossible, to predict just how the boat will behave in the water. It is to be expected that adjustments will have to be made after launching and the first trial runs.

Charles G. Davis, who knew a great deal about small craft both as a designer and a sailor, believed that all too many small-sailboat designs locate the centerboard too far forward. As it happens, this is especially true for some of the sailing dories, which in consequence have wicked weather helms.

Loading also has a lot to do with the sailing balance. Shifting weight forward or aft in a small boat can make all the difference under certain conditions, as is demonstrated by the behavior of the St. Lawrence River skiffs, which are sailed without rudders. One steers simply by moving back and forth in the boat to alter the trim.

In laying out the rig for this dory several features have been incorporated that will allow adjustments to be made in the sailing balance. For one thing, the centerboard has been made rather longer and larger than is usual for a boat of this size, and it is located well aft. By dropping it to different depths, or by raising it in the same manner, it will be possible to shift the boat's center of lateral resistance back and forth to some extent. To facilitate this, the board has a lead insert to give it positive drop. The board can be raised by means of a rope pendant that belays to a cleat bolted on the side of the centerboard trunk.

The indicated sail area is a moderate one, and

provision has been made for reefing down in heavy weather. Since there are no shrouds or stays, the entire rig is easily and quickly lifted out of the step for stowing in the boat. The spars are short enough to stow at one side, out of the way of the oarsman.

If desired, one might have one or more replacement rigs, smaller or larger or both, for different weather. This was a common practice early in this century at Marblehead, Beverly, and other towns on Boston's North Shore. Some dory fishermen there had as many as three separate rigs—a large sail for summer racing, a medium working rig for the summer, and a small sail for winter fishing.

Construction essentials are shown in the accompanying drawings. Needless to say, these should have close and careful study. Parts have been keyed for

ready reference to the listed supplementary information that follows. Those familiar with dory construction should find it plain sailing. The inexperienced, however, would do well to consult *The Dory Book*, in which I give a thorough and detailed explanation of all aspects of dory construction.

Most Swampscott dories of this size, and some even larger—including the 17-footer built at Mystic Seaport—are intended to be planked with four strakes to a side. This requires wide boards, especially those for the garboards, where widths of 16 inches and more will be needed. Boards of such width are rarely found today, and when they are, they are priced out of reach.

Mainly because of this, I have increased the number of strakes on this boat to five, which narrows the individual strakes considerably. As a result, one-piece garboards for this boat can be got out of 12-inch boards, and if the garboards are glue-spliced amidships, 9-inch boards will suffice. If need be, all the strakes may be spliced, provided the scarfs are well staggered.

Actually, this has advantages, for it avoids the cross grain in strakes that are curved to any extent. Splicing curved strakes in this way to avoid the weakness of cross grain was standard practice in the construction of Adirondack guideboats, which required the ultimate in strength together with lightness.

In the northeastern United States, northern white pine is the standard material for the bottoms and sides of dories. Knots, if they are sound and not too large, are quite acceptable. In fact, a plentiful distribution of sound knots in the ⅞-to-1-inch-thick pine bottom is desirable; such a bottom is stronger and wears better thereby. Even some small, loose knots are not to be ruled out, for they can be bored out and plugged. "Spike" knots, which extend across the width of a strake, are not acceptable, but in the strakes, too, a moderate distribution of round knots, provided they're not too large and are well scattered, is quite all right.

This means that relatively inexpensive lumber may be used—even number 2 common pine in some cases—if the boards are carefully picked over and cut so that the worst defects are avoided. Here is where glue splicing and the judicious arrangement of scarfs can work wonders. Splices should be kept at the ends of the boat, except for the garboards, and out of the midsection as much as possible.

To a great extent the strength of this hull will depend on its clinker construction; good lap fastenings are of particular importance. Copper rivets should be used. In any case, old-type chisel-point galvanized dory nails are no longer available. I strongly recommend the heavier English dished roves. The dished roves have greater holding power and grip the wood with greater compressive force when the rivet is made up, and are in every way far superior to ordinary flat roves or burrs.

First choice for the stem, sided 2 inches and molded 2½ inches, is dry white oak. Red oak is almost as good. If a plank can be found with a run of grain that favors the curve of the stem, so much the better. If not, straight grain will do, but the stem should be laid out so that the cross grain is equally distributed and does not come all in one end.

If oak is not to be had, any lasting hardwood can be substituted, preferably one with a grain that favors the stem curve. Locust, although heavy, would be excellent, and should it be used, the stem could be molded slightly smaller—say 2¼-inch instead of 2½-inch. Apple would also be fine. In fact, there is nothing better for dory frames than sound apple limbs of the right bend or curvature.

In case suitable hardwood is not available, good-quality Douglas fir or even longleaf hard pine may be substituted. When these softer woods are used, it would be wise to increase the molded dimension somewhat in order to compensate, say to 2¾ or even 3 inches. The extra weight would be negligible. Also, if softer wood is used for the stem, the fastenings through the hood ends of the planking should be larger.

Another possibility is a stem glued up with epoxy adhesive. This can be made of smaller pieces fitted together if a single large plank of sufficient size cannot be found.

There are a number of ways of doing this. One is to use several thin strips bent to shape on a curved form and clamped until the glue sets. Another is to build up the stem in layers. Short pieces can be used, distributed so that the grain in each is reinforced by the grain in those next to it.

I have shown the hood ends of the plank fastened into the stem with 2-inch galvanized boat nails; 1½-inch or 1¾-inch number 12 screws could just as well be used.

The transom can be Douglas fir or hard pine as well as oak. If oak is used, it could be planed to 1⅛ inches thick to save weight. Red oak would be better than white, which is heavier and more apt to pull out of shape in wide widths.

The boat should be planked bottom up. A setup is made for this purpose over a strongback—a wide 2-inch plank (1½-inch net thickness) secured on edge at working height, its upper edge cut to the curve of the inner bottom and notched to receive the frames and bottom cleats. The ends of the strongback are likewise cut to receive the stern knee and the bottom end of the stem.

Thus the strongback supports the preliminary assembly of bottom frames (which serve as molds), stem, and stern transom during the planking operation. After planking is completed, the planked-up shell is lifted off the strongback and turned right side up, and the laps are riveted in one operation. Of course, all the nails were previously in place, having been driven as the planks went on. The planks must be carefully fitted and properly beveled when building in this fashion.

The boat could be built right side up and the laps riveted plank by plank, but it would then be much harder to bevel the bottom correctly to receive the garboards and to fit the changing lap bevels. The planking operation is far easier and surer when done bottom up over a strongback.

Plank splices could be fitted and glued on the boat as the planking operation proceeds, but I don't recommend this. It will be far better and easier to lay out the splices and glue them ahead of time. They can then be planed smooth and the full-length plank spiled and laid out in one operation. There is much less chance of error this way.

In making the bottom and frame assembly, prior to securing it in position on the strongback, the bottom is laid out first. It is cut to shape and cleated together. Its edges may be beveled to receive the garboard planks, but anyone building a dory for the first time probably should leave this beveling operation until the completed frame and bottom assembly is secured bottom up on the strongback. When the bottom has been cut out and cleated, the stem, the frames, and the stern transom and knee, which have been made up separately, are put in position on the bottom and fastened. All of these members will have to be beveled.

Bevels can be taken ahead of setup from the full-size laydown of the lines, which, according to good boatbuilding practice, should be made and faired before any woodwork is started. Again, however, beginners who may not trust completely the bevels they take from their laydown are advised not to cut the bevels all the way in to the bevel lines until the boat has been set up and the bevels are checked with a batten. Wood is easily taken off when necessary, but it is difficult to pad out bevels that were cut too deep. Besides, in almost all cases it will be necessary to fair the bottom and frame assembly more or less extensively after it is set up and before planking starts.

1. *Planking:* Northern white pine, ½ inch thick. For a boat intended for very hard use, a plank thickness of $\frac{9}{16}$ inch is recommended. The weight of the boat would not be greatly increased thereby. The sheer plank had best be $\frac{9}{16}$ inch in any case. It has considerable curve and might need to be spliced from three pieces.

Where suitable sawn lumber is difficult to obtain, the boat can be planked with strakes of ⅜-inch marine plywood. Strakes can be spliced from pieces cut from ordinary 4-by-8 and 4-by-10 panels, but even when plywood is used it would be desirable to make the sheer strake from sawn lumber $\frac{9}{16}$ inch thick. Increasing numbers of boats are now being planked in this way from marine plywood with satisfactory results. The use of plywood for planking is more fully treated in Chapter 1 and elsewhere in this book.

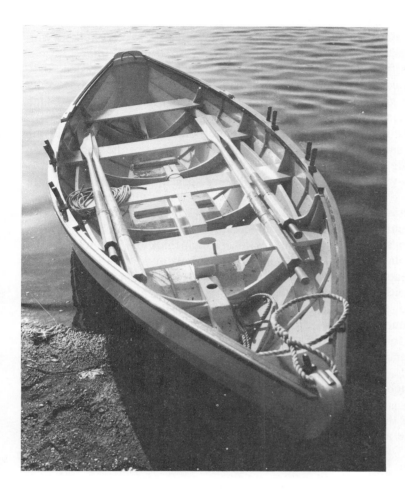

Three views of a 17-foot dory, forerunner of the design in this chapter, built at Mystic Seaport in 1974. **Opposite Page:** *Under construction, with stem, inner bottom, transom, and one frame clamped in place on a strongback.* **Left:** *The finished boat.* **Below:** *Under sail on the Mystic River. (Kenneth E. Mahler photos, Mystic Seaport)*

2. *Frames:* Oak, sided ⅞ inch, molded 2 to 3 inches wide, approximately 2¼ inches through the knuckles, tapering to 1½ inches at the top. While oak is first choice, substitutes such as Douglas fir can be used with a proportional increase in dimensions to give equivalent strength. As is shown here, the two sides of the sawn frames are joined and reinforced across the bottom by a strip or cleat set on edge of the same material as the side frames and 2¼ inches wide. If possible, sawn frames should be cut from lumber with grown crooks, to avoid cross grain.

There are a number of ways of making dory frames. They can be made in three sections that are cut out of ordinary oak boards and spliced where bottom and sides come together with galvanized-iron gusset plates located on either side and through-riveted. Instead of iron gusset plates, longer plywood gussets on either side of the frame, glued and screwed or riveted, are acceptable. It is even possible to laminate continuous one-piece frames from thin strips glued on a form. Detailed directions for framing dories can be found in *The Dory Book.*

3. *Frame bottom cleat:* Oak, ⅞ inch by 2¼ inches, set on edge.

4. *Bottom:* Pine, ¹⁵⁄₁₆ inch thick. To be not less than ⅞ inch or more than 1 inch. Three boards wide and solidly cleated together. Seams to be caulked with cotton and well payed with red lead primer.

5. *Outer, sacrificial bottom:* Pine, spruce, oak, elm, or other, put on with screws to be easily removable and replaced when thin from beach wear.

6. *Seat riser:* ⅝-inch pine, 3½ inches wide at the center and tapering to 2½ inches at the ends. Put on with 1½-inch number 12 wood screws.

7. *Thwarts:* Pine or spruce, ⅞ inch thick, three in number. Notched around frames and screwed to riser with number 12 screws. Center and after thwarts also fastened to the centerboard trunk, which they brace.

8. *Inwale:* Oak, ⅞ inch thick by 1½ inches wide, tapering to 1 inch at the bow and to 1¼ inches at the stern. Two different arrangements for installing it are shown. In one, the inwale is laid flat on top of the frame heads, which are cut so that the upper surface of the inwale comes flush with the top edge of the sheer plank, to which it is fastened. In the alternate construction the inwale is bent in on edge and riveted through the timberheads and sheer plank. Between the timberheads are filler pieces of ½-inch pine, glued in and nailed. The timberheads of the sawn frames are notched to receive the inwale, leaving ½ inch of wood against the sheer plank to line with the timberheads of

The 17-foot Swampscott dory built at Mystic Seaport in 1974 is shown here at the completion of a rowing voyage around Long Island in October 1980. This journey of 200 to 300 miles was accomplished by three men; when underway, one rowed, one steered from the stern sheets, and the man amidships bailed or slept. The boat proved seaworthy on this ambitious voyage. (Connie Marshall photo, Staten Island Advance)

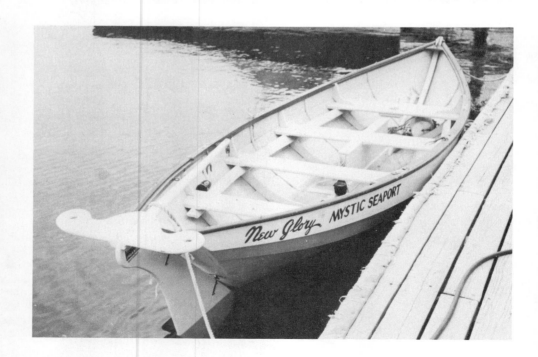

the steam-bent timbers. Through rivets are also put in here. Finally, this construction is covered and made watertight by the railcap of oak, ½ inch thick, well bedded and pulled down with 1-inch number 10 wood screws.

Of the two methods, the first is more traditional but the second is undoubtedly stronger.

9. *Cap:* Oak, ½ inch thick. Two inches wide to cover inwale and top edge of sheer plank. Sawn to shape, not bent. Extends from stem to transom. Put on in several shorter lengths, butted, well bedded, and fastened with number 10 wood screws.

10. Note that the bottom edge of the garboard is not beveled off in line with the bottom, but is left square or approximately square to provide a fit for the false bottom.

11. At the ends of the boat where the bottom bevel is not suited to riveting, the lower edge of the garboard plank is fastened to the bottom with 10-penny nails, spaced 2½ to 3 inches apart. Nails can be galvanized-iron common nails, bronze-wire, or annular.

12. *Limber to drain bottom of boat:* When metal gussets are used to join frame futtocks, the joint in the frame is here.

13. The planking laps between the frames are fastened with copper rivets spaced 2½ to 3 inches.

14. The laps are fastened into the sawn frames with 1¾-inch number 10 bronze wood screws.

This 17-footer is one of a number of dories built by amateurs from the author's 1974 design. Weston Keyes built her to be rowed from three positions or to be rigged with a leg-o'-mutton sail. "It was a good boat for me to start out on," he reported.

A 16-footer constructed from the plans presented in Building Classic Small Craft, Volume I. *Jack MacKay of Sacramento, California, built her in his garage over a seven-month period. She was his first attempt at building a boat from scratch. (Leilani Hu photo,* The Sacramento Bee)

15. Plank splices are made 12 times the thickness of the plank—½-inch-thick plank, 6-inch splice. Scarfs are not planed to a sharp or feather edge, but are left ¹⁄₁₆ inch thick on the ends. The splice clamps better this way, and the extra ¹⁄₁₆ inch is planed off after the glue has thoroughly set. Scarfs are planed fair and true with a sharp block plane or smoother. Either epoxy or resorcinol glue can be used, but epoxy is best by far. Pressure is applied with a piece of oak on either side of the splice, held by four C-clamps. Wax the oak pressure blocks to prevent sticking.

16. *Intermediate bent timbers:* White oak, 1 inch wide by ½ inch thick. Two equally spaced between each pair of sawn frames. Steam-bent into place and fastened through the laps with copper rivets.

17. *Cant frames:* Same as *16*, but bent in on a cant better to fit the narrowing curvature of the sides at the ends of the boat.

18. *Three bottom cleats:* Oak, ⅞ inch thick. Laid flat against the bottom. Equally spaced between the sawn frames and solidly fastened through the bottom from the outside. Width of forward cleat increased from 2¼ inches to 4 inches for extra bracing forward of the centerboard trunk. Center cleat cut in way of the centerboard trunk but recessed halfway into the bed logs on either side, and fastened to them.

19. *Transom knee:* Oak, sided 2 inches. Overall length 16 inches.

20. *Inner stem:* Oak, sided 2 inches and molded 2½ inches.

21. *Outer stem piece:* Oak, 1 inch by 2 inches wide. Steam-bent to fit over plank ends and nailed in place. Trimmed to fair flush with the hood ends of the planking.

22. *Transom:* Oak, 1⅛ inches thick. Maximum width inside face, 23 inches. Made up from three full-length boards drifted together with ⁵⁄₁₆- or ⅜-inch galvanized drift rod. Cleated inside (see *23* and *32*).

23. *Transom cleat:* Oak, ¾ inch thick, molded 4½ inches and curved to conform to the curve of the upper end of the transom. Fastened with number 12 or 14 wood screws. The after ends of the railcaps *(9)* land on it and fasten to it.

24. *Breasthook:* Oak, 1 inch thick. Width of 3 inches to the after face of the stem. Railcaps extend over it on each side and fasten to it. Number 10 wood screws.

25. *Oarlock pads:* Oak, 1 inch thick and 12 inches long. Fastened through railcap with number 10 wood screws.

26. *Filler pieces:* Pine, ½ inch thick. They fill in the space back of the inwale and between the timberheads when the inwale is bent in on edge.

27. *Rivets:* 2½-inch 8-penny copper wire nails through sheer plank, timberheads, and inwale, headed over roves.

28. *Nails:* 1½-inch or 1¾-inch galvanized common or ring nails through sheer plank, filler pieces, and into inwale.

29. *Sheer guard trim:* 1¼-inch half oval of oak, tapered to 1 inch at the ends of the boat. Put on with 1¼-inch number 10 wood screws.

30. *Stern sheets and side benches:* Pine, ⅞ inch thick. Same material as the thwarts. Side benches 10 inches wide at the widest part. Extend as far forward as the after thwart at station 3.

31. *Cleat:* Pine or oak, ⅞ inch thick. Set on edge to support the forward end of the stern sheets. Similar to a deck beam. Ends cut for a tight fit between the seat risers just aft of the frame at station 4.

32. *Cleat:* Oak, ⅞ inch thick and 4 inches wide. Fastened flat to the inside of the transom to support and fasten the after ends of the stern sheets and side benches. Nail and glue.

33. *Cleats:* Oak, ⅞ inch thick, 3 inches wide. They support the forward ends of the side benches where these join the after thwart. Fasten with number 12 screws and glue.

34. *Bottom gratings:* Pine strips ⅝ inch wide cleated together to make removable gratings to cover the bottom.

35. *Mast partner:* Oak, ⅞ inch thick and 8 inches wide. Grain runs fore and aft. Well fastened through the thwart with number 12 wood screws and glue.

36. *Knees:* Oak, hackmatack, or other suitable wood, preferably grown crooks, to brace the thwart at the mast location. Fasten through the side of the boat with number 12 wood screws. Riveted through the inwale and thwart.

37. *Mast step:* Oak, 4 inches wide and 3 inches thick. Fitted against the bottom cleat of the frame at station 1. Well fastened through the bottom from the outside.

38. *Head ledges or end posts, centerboard trunk:* Oak, 1¼ inches thick and 3 inches wide. The lower ends mortise through the bottom to allow caulking but are covered by the outer false bottom. The bed logs are

fastened through the end posts with ¼-inch bolts from side to side. The sides of the centerboard trunk are riveted through the end posts. Glue will help to ensure a tight job.

39. *Bed logs, centerboard trunk:* Pine, 2 inches thick and 4 inches wide. Logs are rabbeted to take the sides of the trunk and scribed to fit the curve of the bottom. They are set in glue and pulled tight with 3-inch number 16 screws spaced about 6 inches apart.

40. *Sides, centerboard trunk:* Pine, ¾ inch thick. Glued to the rabbeted bed logs; copper riveted through the end posts of the trunk.

41. *Cap, centerboard trunk:* Pine, same thickness as the thwarts. Screwed down tightly.

42. *Centerboard pin:* Bronze rod, ½ inch diameter. Tight drive fit through the bed logs.

43. *Centerboard:* Oak, ⅞ inch thick and approxi-mately 40 inches long and 12 inches wide. Two boards fastened together with ⁵⁄₁₆-inch galvanized drift rod. Weighted with lead insert.

44. Number 16 wood screws, 3 inches long.

45. *Lead insert in centerboard:* 4 by 8 inches, set flush with the sides of the board and weighing approximately 10 pounds.

46. *Rudder:* Oak, ⅞ inch thick, tapered thinner toward the after edge. Made up as diagramed from several pieces and pinned together with ⁵⁄₁₆-inch galvanized drifts as shown. Fitted for easy removal when the boat is rowed.

47. *Pintle.*

48. *Gudgeon.*

49. *Drifts:* ⁵⁄₁₆-inch galvanized rod.

50. *Tiller:* Ash or oak slotted to fit over the rudder head and pinned to hinge up and down.

15

Mower Dory

•

Blueprints for this 18-foot Swampscott sailing dory came to me in a roundabout way. Although I was familiar with Mower dories, I did not know that plans for this one existed, until the prints turned up in 1978 in a letter from Maurice M. Wiley of Newport Beach, California. Wiley wrote:

I purchased these plans from Mr. Mower many years ago (at least 40 or more) when I was searching for bank dory plans. At that time no one I contacted could give me any information as to where such plans might be available, if at all. I found out, not at all.

Mr. Mower told me that he had the lines for a Swampscott sailing dory, and that he was sure I could finish the hull for oars, and that it would handle well. I never did anything with the plans after I received them but laid them aside and forgot about them. The other day I came across these plans and thought they would be better off in your hands than anywhere else. I hope

they will be of interest to you, if not, the wastebasket!

As I hastened to inform Mr. Wiley, not only was this dory of great interest to me, but I expected that it would prove interesting to amateur builders, a number of whom would probably construct it. This dory will sail well and will be nice to look at. As *Yachting* magazine said in its tribute to Charles D. Mower in its February 1942 issue, "Mr. Mower in his long career designed many famous boats and it was always said of his designs that he never turned out a bad boat or one that was not pleasing to the eye."

This dory is not too large and not too small. With a length overall of 18 feet and a maximum beam of 5 feet, it is large enough to sail well and be safe, yet not too large for one man to handle, or to transport over the road on a trailer.

18' SAILING DORY by C. D. MOWER.
REDRAWN BY J. GARDNER

OFFSETS C.D. MOWER 18' SAILING DORY							
STATIONS	TRAN	4	3	2	1	A	STEM
HEIGHTS							
BOTTOM	0-7-0	0-6-0	0-4-3	0-4-5	0-6-4	—	—
1	1-0-5	0-9-5	0-6-7	0-7-1	0-10-0	1-2-2	1-5-1
2	1-4-3	1-0-3	0-9-3	0-9-5	1-2-0	1-5-7	1-10-4
3	1-7-2	1-3-4	1-1-0	1-1-4	1-5-4	1-9-0	2-1-4
4	1-10-0	1-7-0	1-5-6	1-7-0	1-10-0	2-0-2	2-4-4
SHEER	2-0-4	1-10-5	1-10-0	1-11-1	2-1-4	2-3-4	2-6-5
HALF-BREADTHS							
BOTTOM	0-0-0	0-2-0	0-6-0	0-6-4	0-2-4	—	—
1	0-4-0	0-9-2	1-1-6	1-2-0	0-10-0	1-4-6	0-0-1
2	0-6-5	1-2-7	1-8-7	1-9-0	1-3-4	0-9-1	0-0-1
3	0-8-6	1-6-3	2-1-4	2-1-5	1-7-1	0-11-6	0-0-1
4	0-10-4	1-9-4	2-5-0	2-5-0	1-9-2	1-1-1	0-0-1
SHEER	0-9-3	1-9-4	2-5-0	2-5-0	1-9-2	1-1-5	0-0-1

HEIGHTS ABOVE BASE LINE. MEASUREMENTS TO INSIDE BOTTOM & PLANKING, TO OUTSIDE TRANSOM & FORWARD EDGE OF INNER OR TRUE STEM. MEASUREMENTS IN FEET, INCHES & EIGHTHS.

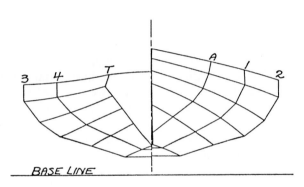

"Few naval architects who devoted their talents to yacht designing were better known during the past three decades, or will be more missed, than Charles D. Mower," declared *Yachting* in summing up Mower's career following his death in January 1942. From his New York City design office, established at the end of World War I, came such yachts as *Junius,* S. Morgan's Class M *Windward,* the *Ardelle* and the *Ardette* of the R class, and a number of successful 6-meter and Q class boats. Another of his larger vessels was the cruising schooner *Windjammer,* and still another was the centerboard schooner *Shellback,* for Commodore Crabbe of the Cruising Club of America.

Mower was a member of the Cruising Club of America, the Manhasset Bay Yacht Club, and the New York Yacht Club, for which, as official measurer in 1903 and 1904, he measured *Shamrock III* and *Reliance* for the America's Cup races in 1903. At that time he was design editor for *The Rudder,* then the leading yachting publication. Before he left *The Rudder* in 1910 to join Thomas Bowes in Philadelphia and form the design firm of Bowes and Mower, he designed a boat for the editor, Thomas Fleming Day. This was *Sea Bird,* the 25-foot yawl in which Day made his famous crossing to Europe in 1911.

To list all the boats and yachts, both large and small, designed by Mower, many whose names are now inscribed in American yachting annals, would far exceed the limits of this chapter. Yet despite all the celebrated yachts that came from his board, there can be no doubt that the Swampscott dory stood very high in Mower's esteem and affections.

Mower was born in Lynn, Massachusetts, and grew up on the beaches of Lynn and nearby Swampscott. If he did not learn to sail in a dory, it is clear that he knew the boats of the Swampscott fishermen, and he must have sailed in them as a boy, like all of his friends and neighbors. The centerboard sloop *Vitesse,* which he built as a teenager in his backyard, proved so successful that the following year, at the age of 20, he found employment as a draftsman in the design office of Arthur Binney, Boston naval architect.

In 1898 he left Binney to go to work for B. B. Crowninshield, one of the most eminent and successful naval architects of the period. That same year Mower designed a 21-foot racing dory for the Swampscott Club. This boat came to be known as the X-dory, a winner from the start and rivaled only by the Beachcomber dories of Marblehead and the Alphas of Salem, nearly identical craft from William Chamberlain's Orne Street shop in Marblehead. Scores of X-dories were built and sailed, and they continued to sail and to win races well beyond the 1940s.

Around 1900 the Swampscott sailing dories were about the hottest thing in small racing craft afloat. From Swampscott dory shops, of which the Elbridge Gerry Emmons dory factory was the largest, sailing dories were distributed throughout the Northeast, as far north as the Adirondacks and as far west as the Great Lakes. For the next two decades the Swampscott dory was easily the most popular small-craft type in the Northeast.

As far as we know, the X-dory was Mower's first commissioned design, and its outstanding success speaks well for the ability of the 23-year-old naval architect.

In 1899 Mower went to New York to become design editor for *The Rudder* magazine, which, under the distinguished direction of Thomas Fleming Day, had grown from a slim sheet that in 1890 was devoted to sailing canoes and printed at Watertown, New York, at the eastern end of Lake Ontario, to this country's most influential yachting and boating publication with editorial offices in New York City.

In 1895 the talented Charles G. Davis, *The Rudder*'s first design editor, had initiated a new feature that caught on immediately and added immensely to the magazine's popularity—fully detailed how-to-build designs for small craft of a size and kind that suited the desires and abilities of amateurs and backyard builders of the time. There followed designs for flatties, catboats, dories, and other craft by Edson B. Schock, Fred W. Goeller, and, when he replaced Davis as design editor, Mower himself.

One of Mower's boats is *Bonito,* the construction of

which is fully explained in his article in the May 1904 *Rudder,* "How to Build a Power Dory." At this time the gasoline engine for marine use was quite new. A powerboat like this, therefore, was a very advanced design—indeed, a daring innovation.

If you examine *Bonito*'s hull lines and then turn to those of the X-dory, you will see at once that both have what is essentially the same hull, except that *Bonito* is scaled down to 18 feet. This, of course, is the length of the dory under consideration here, whose basic hull is remarkably similar to the other two. Furthermore, the same similarity exends to another Mower boat, his Massachusetts racing dory, an advanced sailing dory the rig and construction of which he worked out in great detail.

In fact, it appears that Mower had one basic dory hull that he considered the ultimate Swampscott dory hull. In adapting it to a number of varying requirements he made some minor and superficial changes, but always without altering the fundamental characteristics of his original 1898 design for the Swampscott Club. The success of the X-dory was so outstanding that there was little incentive to attempt to improve on it, and good reason not to risk spoiling it, even to a minor extent.

Before making this 18-foot Mower sailing dory available to readers of the *National Fisherman* in January and February 1979, I consulted with Mower's son, Charles P. Mower, who graciously stated that he would be happy to have any of his father's designs published for unlimited use by anyone interested.

Maurice Wiley's blueprints, however, were not suitable for direct reproduction. It was necessary to redraw them before they could be printed. In doing so I adhered closely to Mower's dimensions but changed his layout and presentation somewhat in order to adapt the plans to the printed page and make them easier for the novice to follow.

I have made a few very slight changes in the widths and angles of the planks in order to make the planking operation somewhat easier, but none that could affect the performance of the boat in the slightest or change its appearance enough to be noticeable. This is what would have been done by most professional builders anyway. Such adjustment during the planking operation was always the builder's prerogative, and the architect expected him to make such minor adjustments in the widths and run of the strakes as the actual planking required.

Also, I have drawn in a line for the top of the

garboard, which Mower did not show because there is no knuckle in the deadrise where the garboard and the plank above it come together. The location of this plank line was one of the things left to the builder to vary slightly as he saw fit to suit the widths of the planking stock at hand. I thought it best to lay out an acceptable plank line here for the benefit of the inexperienced builder.

For those not used to working with the standard offset table, I have dimensioned the four principal frames that serve as molds and remain in the boat as a permanent part of the hull structure. Mower did the same in his blueprint. It will not be necessary to lay this boat down full size in order to build it, although the inexperienced builder might want to make a full-size laydown to be on the safe side, and could undoubtedly learn from it.

This 18-foot sailing dory is partly decked with narrow waterways along the sides and a low coaming. Having a maximum beam of 5 feet, it is 8 to 10 inches wider than the average fisherman's working dory of 18 feet LOA. This increased width greatly increases initial stability and the ability to carry a press of sail. Its side decking and coaming allow the boat to heel steeply in a puff of wind and still not take water over the side.

With foam flotation (not available when the boat was designed) placed under the forward and after decks and out of sight under the waterways along the sides, this dory can be made unsinkable, and would float right side up and only partly submerged when full of water. Hence, she would be a safe boat for children and an ideal boat for youngsters to learn to sail in.

Although this boat has essentially a round hull as far as its performance in the water goes, its dory shape can be planked much more easily than a round hull. For that reason it is better suited to amateur construction.

In supplying construction details for this dory, I followed the old prints closely. Mower included but one sectional view, and only a few basic dimensions. Apparently he expected that prospective builders would be familiar with standard dory construction, which hardly needed to be explained and dimensioned in comprehensive detail 60 years ago, about the time this dory seems to have been designed.

For the modern builder inexperienced in dory construction and considering building a dory for the first time, I recommend in particular my *Dory Book* (Camden, Maine: International Marine, 1978) and

FEET AND INCHES

BOTTOM RUDDER

OPTIONAL ROWING THWART

C. D. MOWER 18' DORY
REDRAWN J. GARDNER 1978

how-to-build dory articles by Schock and Mower, reprinted from early issues of *The Rudder* by Texas Dory Boat Plans, P.O. Box 720, Galveston, Texas 77553.

From these sources the prospective dory builder should be able to obtain answers to any questions that may arise. *The Dory Book,* a compilation of articles on dories and dory building published over the years in *National Fisherman,* was intended as a convenient, comprehensive, and authoritative source of information on dory building.

My principal departure from the original Mower blueprints has been to suggest the addition of a rowing thwart and the other minor changes that will make it possible to row this boat. If a boat is intended for general recreational use, and particularly if it is to be used by youngsters, there should certainly be provision for rowing it when the wind fails or becomes too strong, or on other occasions.

I have located the rowing position as far forward of amidships as the decking permits, to make it as easy as possible to keep the boat from blowing off when heading into the wind. When the rowing position is located too far aft, it is difficult and sometimes impossible to keep the boat on course when rowing into a head wind.

In order to locate the rowing thwart at a workable height, it was necessary to lower the forward end of the centerboard case. This in turn required alteration in the shape of the centerboard, but without any effective change in the area or location of its wetted surface. The shape resulting from lowering the forward end of the centerboard case may not be as aesthetically pleasing as what was drawn by Mower, but it is simpler and easier to build. If, however, one is not concerned about rowing and wishes a boat solely for sailing, it can be built as originally drawn.

As I mentioned, there is ample room out of sight under the decking along the sides and at the ends for the installation of foam flotation. The foam should be distributed so that the boat will float partly submerged, level, and on its waterlines, should it ever fill with water. Since the boat is built of wood and lacks outside ballast, it would undoubtedly float without foam flotation. But it would be better to have the foam, and the boat would float much higher with it. If the boat is to be used as a general-purpose family boat, and especially if it is to be used by children, I cannot recommend too strongly the addition of foam flotation attached inconspicuously to the underside of the decking.

The rig shown by Mower is the classic dory sailing rig, consisting of triangular leg-o'-mutton main with high-angled boom, and a small, loose-footed jib. The

18' MOWER SAILING DORY
REDRAWN J. GARDNER, 1978

MASTHEAD FLY
HEAD
SHEAVE IN MAST FOR MAIN HALYARD
BLOCK FOR JIB HALYARD
JIB HALYARD
LEECH 18'-4"
MAIN SAIL
HOIST (OR LUFF) 15'-0"
MAST
CLEW
LEECH 7'-0"
JIB
HOIST (OR LUFF) 8'-4"
MAST HOOP
FOOT OF SAIL 15'-0"
BOOM
MAIN SHEET
TILLER
TACK
FOOT 4'-6"
JIB SHEET

sail area is moderate, the mast unstayed. Such a rig is simplicity itself.

To lift up the boom and secure it and the bunched sail to the mast with a few turns of the main sheet, to unsnap the jib, and to lift the light mast out of its bury is but the work of an instant, and the whole thing stows easily in the cockpit. With the foot of the rig pushed up under the foredeck and the head tailing out over the cockpit's after coaming, the boat is ready to row with oars that are stowed conveniently under the foredeck.

Some may want more sail area, some less, depending on how the boat is to be used and who is going to use it. Many years ago in Marblehead some dory fishermen had as many as three rigs of different sizes, each with its own mast with sail and boom permanently attached to it: a small rig for winter sailing, a medium rig for summer fishing, and an oversize rig for racing.

No doubt there are others who will consider experimenting with other rigs. A sliding gunter mast might be more convenient to stow in the cockpit. Some might want to try a more modern high-aspect rig with fixed stays. There are many possibilities. Because of this dory's extra beam and its side decks and coaming,

it can safely handle more sail than narrower dories of the same length that are entirely open.

The construction views have been keyed wherever it seemed that detailed information would be required or helpful. The explanations and comments for the numbered references follow in order.

1. *Bottom:* The wood is pine. Mower indicated a thickness of 1 inch, which was slightly heavier than the ⅞ inch generally used. But the extra thickness is all to the good in providing ample wood for fastening the lower edge of the garboard, and it is insurance against leaks. Although the bottom is exceptionally narrow for a dory—only about 13 inches at the widest point—single boards of this width are not always to be had. When two boards must be used, they may be glued together. The location of the glue joint should be planned so that it is supported on the inside by bottom cleats and the bottoms of the sawn frames. White pine is the best bottom material. Acceptable substitutes are old-growth, rift-sawn Douglas fir, Port Orford cedar, southern longleaf pine, and Honduras mahogany, but not Philippine mahogany.

2. *Sawn frames:* Four sets of these serve as building molds and remain in the boat as principal

18' C.D. MOWER DORY
REDRAWN J.G. 1978

reinforcing members. Seasoned oak planed $1\frac{3}{16}$ inch to $\frac{7}{8}$ inch thick is the standard material. Ideally, such frames are cut to shape from flitch-sawn ("live-edge") boards, the builder taking advantage of any curvatures to avoid cross grain, which is weak. When frames cannot be got out full length with a good run of grain, it will be necessary to splice them from shorter pieces. This is what is generally required. The splices are glued and reinforced with overlapping pieces set in glue and fastened with nails or screws.

3. *Planking:* As shown, this dory has five planks on a side, the customary number for Swampscott dories like this one. However, instead of two planks to fill up the space between the bottom and the first knuckle, as shown, three narrower planks could just as well be used. More work is required to fit and fasten three planks, but there is little choice if wide boards cannot be found.

These early dories were planked with northern white pine. At that time wide pine boards were plentiful and cheap. Cedar was rarely used because it was more expensive, and because cedar boards wide enough for dory garboards and broads were usually not to be had. As a replacement for pine or cedar I do not hesitate to recommend ⅜-inch marine plywood. Standard 4-foot-by-8-foot panels can be used if the strakes are glue-spliced. With careful planning, the plank sections can be laid out on these panels and cut with very little waste.

Plywood for clinker planking has a number of advantages. On the whole, it is more widely and more readily available than good-quality pine or cedar planking lumber. It will not split through a row of lap fastenings, which occurs too frequently in aging boats planked with sawn boards of natural lumber. Plywood planking does not develop splits or "rents," as often happens with sawn lumber, especially in the wide ends of dory garboards. When boats are clinker-planked with plywood the laps can be glued, since the strakes do not move with changes in width from swelling and shrinking. In all cases the raw edges of plywood planking must be sealed. This is probably best accomplished with liberal applications of a thin, penetrating epoxy resin.

It would also be possible to plank up to the first frame knuckles with a single width of plywood instead of two or three strakes of sawn lumber. Actually, this would be the easier, quicker way, since it would eliminate considerable fitting, beveling, and riveting. The plywood would be lighter than the sawn lumber and just as strong, if not stronger. Directions for splicing wide, full-length plywood planks from standard 8- and 10-foot panels are given in Chapter 13.

4. *Bent timbers:* Mower called for bent timbers or frames 1 inch wide by ½ inch thick put in on the flat and spaced between the sawn frames 10 inches apart. White oak is the standard bending stock for this, but in places where good oak bending stock is not to be had, a substitute must be found. Laminated timbers glued up from strips of spruce or fir ⅛ inch to 3/16 inch thick are one possibility. They can be glued at least double width on a form of the right shape, and if they are made somewhat thicker than the required ½ inch, there will be wood enough for them to be cut to shape or "joggled" for a snug fit against the inside surface of the laps. This may require additional labor and careful workmanship, but it makes for an extra strong job.

5. *Decking:* ⅜-inch marine plywood. For an extra light deck ¼-inch plywood could be used, but in that case deck beams should be spaced more closely together.

6. *Deck beams:* Laminated deck beams glued to shape from spruce strips will be light but amply stiff and strong. Because of the slight curvature, strips ¼ inch or even 5/16 inch thick can be used.

7. *Coaming:* Standard material for this would be steam-bent oak about ½ inch thick. When suitable bending oak is not available, glued laminations may be substituted. The coaming is not put in in one continuous length, but is made up of four segments spliced together. Gluing it up in segments like this makes lamination a relatively easy process.

8. *Rowing thwart:* A pine or spruce board ⅞ inch thick and a foot wide. In case a board this wide cannot be found, two narrower widths can be glued together.

9. *Side benches:* Same material as the rowing thwart, although fir, Port Orford cedar, or mahogany might also be used.

10. *Post:* A strip of oak, pine, or mahogany with the lower end cut so as to shoulder on the sawn frame and lie flush against one side of the frame for most of its width. Should be glued to the frame at station 3 as well as screwed or nailed to it. The other end of the post should be fastened to the underside of the bench.

11. *Side-deck gussets:* These are made of plywood ⅜ inch or ½ inch thick and are glued and screwed or nailed to the upper ends of the sawn frames.

12. *Side-deck reinforcements:* These strips, 1½ inches by ¾ inch, are glued and screwed or nailed to the underside of the side decks to provide landing and fastening for the coaming.

13. *Sheer clamps:* These strips, 1½ inches by ¾ inch, must be glued and screwed or nailed to the top of the inside of the sheer plank. They take the deck fastenings and ensure a solid union of deck and topsides.

14. *Rowing-thwart risers:* These short risers, 3 inches by ¾ inch, span sawn frames 1 and 2 to provide support for the ends of the rowing thwart.

15. *Rowlock pads:* Oak or mahogany, 1½ inches high, 2 inches wide, and 10 inches long, positioned so the center of the oarlock socket is 12 inches aft of the after edge of the rowing thwart. The hole for the socket is limbered so that it drains outboard.

16. *Bed logs, centerboard case:* These should be pine, 1¾ inches thick and 4 inches high. They can be bolted through the bottom with 5/16-inch carriage bolts

or drawn tight with 4-inch number 16 or number 18 wood screws. Bed logs should be cut to fit the curve of the bottom perfectly. The joint with the bottom should either be glued or bedded with some nonhardening bedding compound.

17. *Sides, centerboard case:* ¾-inch pine, fir, Port Orford cedar, etc.

18. *After headledge:* Preferably oak, 1¼ inches by 2 inches, sawn to curve as shown.

19. *Forward headledge:* Oak, 1¼ inches by 2 inches. Extends above the centerboard trunk to meet the underside of the deck. The upper end is notched to receive the afterdeck beam, which lets into it flush on the after side. This is a neat arrangement that supports the deck and braces the centerboard case. Both headledges extend through the bottom to cut off flush with the outside at either end of the centerboard slot. In this way they can be caulked from the outside.

20. *Cap, centerboard case:* ⅝-inch pine, fir, or mahogany.

21. *Half-oval trim:* 1⅛-inch oak or mahogany tapered slightly at the ends for appearance.

Fastenings: Lap fastenings are number 11 gauge copper nails riveted over burrs or roves. The garboard is fastened to the bottom with copper rivets in the midships section and with 2½-inch annular nails (ring nails) at the ends. For detailed information on fastenings for this boat, see construction drawings for various dories in *The Dory Book*.

Glue: Glue joints greatly increase the strength of the hull structure.

1 6

Boatbuilders' Planes

········•········

The amateur aspiring to the art of wooden boatbuilding had best familiarize himself with boatbuilders' wooden planes, both as to their use and their construction. For if he would build craft worthy of the old-time craftsmen, he will require a number of specialized boatbuilders' planes that are not now, and never have been, available ready-made at the hardware store. More than that, he will find few directions for making them in boatbuilding manuals, nor are there many old-time boatbuilders still hanging on who can show him how.

Since Dr. Henry C. Mercer's pioneer work *Ancient Carpenters' Tools* first appeared serially in the late 1920s in the bulletin of The Society for the Preservation of New England Antiquities, a flourishing literature devoted to old tools has sprung up. A substantial part deals with planes, but there is little on the subject of the specialized planes used in boatbuilding and shipbuilding, and how they were made.

I believe that the first published information on boatbuilding planes was an article I wrote for the December 1952 issue of the *Maine Coast Fisherman*. Then in the *National Fisherman,* in November and December 1971 and in January 1972, I published three articles on boatbuilding planes and how to make them. Combined, revised, and extended, these articles appear here. Although they were written over 10 years ago, and despite the fact that the literature on 19th-century woodworking hand tools has proliferated since then, little or nothing has been done to rescue boatbuilders' planes from their undeserved neglect. There is just one exception, a notable one—the section on the making of boatbuilders' wooden smoothing planes in Kenneth D. Roberts's *Wooden Planes in 19th Century America, Volume II,* pages 22–28. Yet the growing revival of traditional wooden boatbuilding has brought an increased need for these old-time planes, and more and more builders have become interested in making the specialized planes they cannot buy. The directions that follow outline the essentials and provide enough information to enable the aspiring planemaker to proceed on his own.

But before setting out to produce the planes he requires, the builder of wooden boats can well afford to give some attention to the historical background of boatbuilders' planes. It is a fascinating story, and he will find himself in the company of craftsmen with whom he can identify. Planemaking by boatbuilders in bygone days was a craft within a craft. In some respects it was more than a craft, coming close to being an art and a means of creative expression.

Henry Hall, in his 10th census entitled "Report on the Ship-Building Industry of the United States," gives the average number of hands employed in the shipbuilding industry during the census year 1880 as 21,345. Not all would have used planes, it is true, but since it was not unusual for a boatbuilder to have 15 or 20 planes in his kit, while sparmakers and outboard joiners sometimes had 40 or more, it seems reasonable to assume that considerably more than 100,000 boatbuilders' and shipwrights' wooden planes were in active use that year.

During the 18th century, more than a million planes must have been made, used, and worn out. All but a few have disappeared, and even how they were made—or that they were ever used—is now largely forgotten.

In his chapter on small craft in *The Common Sense of Yacht Design,* L. Francis Herreshoff extols the old-time builder of wooden boats. The boatbuilder, he writes, is very much of an artist whose work is of a much higher order than that of the cabinetmaker, requiring an elaborate kit of tools, often numbering more than 100 items, some quite expensive, and others peculiar to his trade, most of which he had to make himself.

This last, of course, refers particularly to his specialized boatbuilders' planes. According to Herreshoff, the boatbuilder excelled over all others as a maker of wooden planes, often supplying the ship carpenter as well as himself, and sometimes the cabinetmaker. This is borne out by my own experience and observation and what I have learned from older tradesmen.

Many instances come to mind. Cap'n Perry, employed for the average working lifetime at the Lawley yard in Neponset as an outboard joiner, was still planing boats at the age of 80 in the Sims Brothers yard in Dorchester in the late 1940s. Sims was then building double-planked yachts of African mahogany and cedar for Sparkman and Stephens, Nielsen, and others.

Starting with the adze and finishing off with scraper and sandpaper, Perry did most of the work with planes, of which he kept a trunkful at hand to select from as needed. The result was as smooth as the proverbial bottle. It is impossible to achieve equivalent results with power sanders. The yachts that are finished with power tools today would never have been accepted when yachts were smoothed by planing.

Like most of the old-time outboard joiners, Cap'n Perry made his own planes. The most he ever made in one winter, he told me, was 40, some of which he kept for himself and some of which he sold. I used to watch him planing the difficult African mahogany, marveling at the way the shavings came away tissue-thin, leaving the surface smooth without ever once catching or tearing the difficult cross grain of the mahogany.

He was secretive about his trade, like most of the old boatbuilders. For a long time he would not tell me how he did it, but finally he relented. He honed the cap on the oilstone until it was sharp and fitted the surface of the plane iron perfectly. Then he turned down the edge with a burnisher as if it were a scraper. He then fastened the cap to the iron with its burnished edge set very close to the sharpened edge of the iron, within $\frac{1}{32}$ inch or thereabouts. A plane set in this manner is harder to push, but it will smooth the most difficult and treacherous cross-grain wood without catching, digging in, or tearing.

Another planemaker I have known was Charles W. Lawton, whose reputation as a boatbuilder still lingers in Marblehead. He worked until the age of 90 at the Graves yard on Beacon Street, building the finest varnished-cedar yacht tenders.

There was always a plane of some sort under construction at the back of his workbench, which he could turn to whenever he had a free moment. In this way, he kept up a more or less steady production of planes, providing relaxation as well as a minor source of pin money. I still have a couple of his planes—one a small spar plane with a quick radius, about right for boathook handles.

Planemakers who were gone before my time in Marblehead, but whose planes were prized by boatbuilders who had them, were Ed Howes of Essex and Jim O'Neil, the outboard joiner.

There was a mystique connected with planemaking

Two views of an assortment of boatbuilding planes made by the author. In the background are smoothers (flat sole), spar planes (concave sole), backing-out planes (convex sole), and a chamfer plane (third from right). In the left foreground are a wide Brazilian rosewood jointer, a normal-width jointer, an ironwood jackplane, and a lignum vitae jackplane. To the right of these (back to front and left to right) are a live-oak smoother, York pattern, angle of iron 60 degrees; a flat rosewood rocker; an ironwood rocker; a beech backing-out plane; a small ironwood rocker with sole curved both ways; and a large rocker. In the near foreground is a plane hammer for adjusting the set of the iron (or removing it from the stock) by starting, or loosening, the chip. (Mystic Seaport photos)

that is not easy to convey to anyone who did not work at the trade in days gone by. Wooden planes were not only valued for their utility, but were cherished as well for other reasons, some of which might be termed aesthetic or sentimental. Various kinds of fine and hard-to-get hardwoods were sought after as plane material. For example, the old Devereux Mansion in Marblehead was once enclosed by a great fence made of an extremely hard, dense, heavy tropical hardwood of a purplish red cast, which polished as smooth as marble and was known locally as "ironwood." This fence has long since been torn down, but pieces of it still live on in heirloom planes.

Junks of this fence that came into the possession of the true planemaker might be cherished for years under his bench or in some other safe, private place, until the time came for cutting it up into plane blocks. When this moment finally came, the prized balk was studied as carefully before the saw was put into it as if it had been a piece of gemstone.

Sometimes considerable stealth, not to say conniving, went into getting desired wood for planes. One of the shop floors at the Boston Naval Shipyard was originally laid with live-oak planks—the same material used to plank *Old Ironsides*.

Live oak (*Quercus virginiana*) has a dense, interlocked grain, is much heavier than other oaks, is highly resistant to checking and splitting, wears extremely well, takes a high polish, and is altogether ideal for making wooden planes. In times past, I have been told, when the planemaking urge reached a certain pitch at the shipyard, a suitable plank of live oak in the shop floor would be chosen. Then a substitute plank of ordinary timber, as nearly like the original in appearance as possible, would be carefully prepared. The switch was usually made late at night, and in the absence of foremen, snappers, and other supervisory personnel.

Junked-up blocks of the oak would then be parceled out to the conspirators, who would eventually transform it into planes. Thus planemaking at times was also a diversion, a means of relieving the tedium of the job and of outwitting the boss. Coups of this nature were always a favorite topic of conversation over the open dinner buckets, and no doubt were improved upon in the telling and retelling.

One such story, which I have heard more than once, took place on a large, expensive yacht under construction at the old Lawley yard in Neponset. A crew of joiners had come aboard to finish and fit out the interior. As the story goes, one of the crew took up quarters in the forepeak, where he improvised a workbench and proceeded to make planes for all hands. Signals were devised to give him ample warning when the yard foreman or the owner came aboard. He turned out the planes for weeks, and was never detected. Of course the crew enjoyed every minute of it hugely. Neither morale nor production suffered, I am sure. Planes made on the boss's time acquired a double value, and I'm not so sure he didn't know all the time what was going on.

If this seems like a long and roundabout introduction, it is because planemaking is something to be approached in the proper frame of mind in order to be savored and enjoyed. The true craftsman of former days, whether a boatbuilder or not, prized his tools and took enjoyment in them. In time, they came to be old friends, tried and trusted, familiar yet respected. But also, they brought him recurring pleasure just to touch and to look at, as well as to use. When Ed Perkins, the Essex ship joiner, was long past working, he would go into his shop for hours just to sit with his familiar and cherished objects around him. The modern tender of machines—who has neither tools of his own nor any need for them in his job—has been dispossessed of vastly more than he has any inkling of.

So we come to planes themselves: their shapes, sizes, and dimensions; the various woods from which their stocks are made; the tools used in their construction; the manner of laying out, shaping, and finishing; the procurement of suitable plane irons; their fitting, sharpening, and adjustment; and finally their use. There is more to making planes than some might think.

In general, boatbuilders' planes are slighter and better balanced than ordinary wooden bench planes. The reason, I surmise, is that the former are frequently used on the sides of vessels, overhead, or in other positions where ordinary planes would be clumsy and awkward. For the same reason, apparently, boatbuilders' jackplanes and jointers are razeed—that is, cut down aft of the bed to lighten them up and to bring the user's hand closer to the work for better balance.

The standard maximum width of irons for the boatbuilder's smoother is 1¾ inches, although many are narrower than this and some are only 1¼ inches wide. Jackplanes are also not infrequently made with 1¾-inch irons, but almost never with irons wider than 2 inches. As a general rule, boatbuilders' planes are from ¼ inch to ¾ inch narrower than the ordinary

A few of the author's planes, with stocks made of woods such as ebony, live oak, lignum vitae, osage orange, beech, and ironwood. A rosewood jointer is in the background, and two spar planes are in the foreground. Also shown are a float and a stiff, pointed saw, specialized planemakers' tools. (Mary Anne Stets photo, Mystic Seaport)

beech bench planes that were formerly factory-made and sold to house carpenters and cabinetmakers.

Boatbuilders' long planes divide roughly into two groups according to their length—jacks and jointers. I cannot recall having heard a boatbuilder use any terms other than these in referring to his long planes. Jacks run between 12 inches and 16 inches, with irons almost never wider than 2 inches. Jointers are rarely over 2 feet in length, with more irons 2⅛ inches wide than 2½ inches. The standardized sizes adopted for commercially made planes—jacks, trying planes, fore planes, and jointers—do not obtain among boatbuilders.

The planes we are considering here are those found in the northeastern United States and the Canadian Maritime Provinces. There are in this area fairly uniform norms or patterns for planes, apparently handed down within the trade for several generations at least. Just how far back these go, or how they developed, is very difficult to determine, for there is virtually no written record. It is extremely difficult to date boatbuilders' tools found in this area earlier than the first part of the 19th century.

Boatbuilders' shorter planes are by far the most numerous. In one sense these are all smoothers, although perhaps that term should be reserved only for

The author getting out a plank with a wooden jackplane. (Mary Anne Stets photo, Mystic Seaport)

SPAR PLANE

BACKING OUT PLANE

CHAMFER PLANE

ROCKER PLANE

Cross sections of three types of boatbuilders' planes, with a side view of the rocker plane.

planes with flat soles. In addition, there are planes with hollow or concave soles of various radii, commonly called spar planes; planes with convex or rounded soles, plankers' "backing-out" types being the most common; planes with their soles curved fore and aft, called rockers or rocker planes; chamfer planes, which are able to do most of the work of a rabbet plane; and others. The length of such planes averages about 8 inches, and is rarely less than 7 inches or more than 9 inches. Spar planes tend to be the longest.

Nothing can quite equal a sharp spar plane of the right curvature for bringing a newly made spar to its final uniform finish. The old sparmaker had them by the trunkful, of all degrees of curvature from sprit-size up, accumulated during a working lifetime.

Smoothing planes of convex bottom curvature called backing-out planes are indispensable for hollowing the inside of planking to conform to the round of the ribs. Three or four, all of relatively flat curvature, are all the planker requires, but similar planes of greater round are occasionally useful in boat work and are usually found in the first-class boatbuilder's kit.

Rocker planes for smoothing the inside curves of deck beams, covering boards, taffrails, railcaps, and other sweeps are useful and necessary to have. Boatbuilders much prefer their wooden rocker planes to the metal variety now available with the adjustable sole of flexible steel.

A variation of the wooden rocker plane, with its bottom also curved athwartships like a backing-out plane, is needed by the outboard joiner, for instance in smoothing around the tuck of a vessel where hollow planking curves run both ways. In fact, the outboard joiner at one time or another will need almost every shape and size of plane there is, including even an occasional spar plane.

It should not be hard to see how the old-time boatbuilder came to make his own planes. He made them to fit the job, and to fit himself as well. He required such a variety that he could not afford to buy them ready-made. Considering the wages he got, purchasing the irons alone often meant a sacrifice. For wood, he could often find around the wharves and waterfront pieces of tropical hardwoods brought back from faraway places.

In a pinch, beech and even rock maple would do, but far better to have lignum vitae, rosewood, cocobolo, live oak, "ironwood," Turkish boxwood, ebony, black mesquite, horseflesh, or some other hard, exotic species.

The maker of planes—who will want them to work well, last at least during his lifetime, give him pleasure, and do him honor as a craftsman—will take great pains, if necessary, to secure suitable wood for the stocks. The ideal wood for boatbuilders' plane stocks is hard, heavy, close-grained, and not susceptible to checking, shrinkage, or warping. In addition, a pleasing grain pattern and a rich color are usually looked for. Obviously, only fully seasoned lumber is to be considered. However, nothing is to prevent the collection of blocks of green or wet plane wood, whenever available, to be put aside until they are thoroughly seasoned and dry. The boatbuilder who makes his own planes will generally have a number of such blocks or pieces stashed away under his bench, or overhead on the rafters of his shop, or in some other secure place where they may lie for years, drying and seasoning until he gets around to using them.

Of course wood of the right sort is not to be found at the local lumberyard, and the few concerns that make a specialty of stocking tropical hardwoods for cabinetmakers may have trouble supplying it in the thicknesses required. Most plane blocks must be 2 inches thick or more.

Each species has its strong points, as well as its less desirable characteristics. Of the several species previously mentioned, I believe that live oak is the best. It is heavy, hard, and tough. It wears well, and when thoroughly seasoned it does not check, shrink, or warp. Not as hard as some of the more brittle woods, it has an interesting grain and, with age and use, acquires a marble smoothness and a rich golden-brown color. Rosewood—of which there are two somewhat different kinds, Brazilian and East Indian—is perhaps more handsome. Both kinds are excellent. They work well and wear well, but are not as tough as live oak. Cocobolo is somewhat similar to rosewood but harder.

Boxwood, when large enough blocks can be found, cannot be excelled for smoothness, but it is extremely brittle, and sooner or later it is apt to split out where the sides are cut thin for the slots that take the iron and the chip. Besides, when chiseling it, one requires goggles to keep flying chips out of the eyes. This is likewise the case with lignum vitae, which is nearly as hard and brittle as English boxwood. If it is not dried out thoroughly, lignum vitae is apt to check badly, and will shrink, twist, and warp. Some very fine planes have been made of lignum vitae, and, for want of adequate seasoning, some poor ones also.

Applewood that is the seasoned heartwood of large trees makes beautiful planes of a rich, reddish-brown color and a satiny texture. It chisels easily and wears quite well, but is only of medium weight, about the same as beech.

Beech, although not as heavy as live oak or lignum vitae, was adopted as the standard wood for commercially made planes. It wears well and becomes very smooth, cuts easily with sharp chisels, resists checking, and holds its shape well after seasoning. Formerly, beech lumber was plentiful in straight-grained, knot-free planks of any desired thickness, and was not expensive. Consequently beech was an ideal wood for the 19th-century plane factories. Good beech, if any can still be found, is not to be scorned as a utility material, but it is not quite in a class with the heavier tropical hardwoods.

Rock maple (not soft maple) can also be used. I have seen planes made of rock maple that worked very well, but like beech, it is not one of the heavier woods. Besides, it is not at all distinctive in appearance.

Well-seasoned cherry is not to be overlooked. About the same weight as beech and maple, it resists checking and holds its shape well. In addition, it has a pleasing reddish brown color.

Greenheart is a very heavy, hard wood, used for sheathing vessels against Arctic ice, which attests to its wearing qualities. In addition, it is a pleasing greenish golden-brown. But it has the serious fault of checking easily and badly, and so it is hardly to be recommended for planes.

Undoubtedly there are many more tropical hardwoods besides these that would make fine planes. One of the joys of planemaking is the search for materials.

Cherry, as well as applewood, is excellent for the totes of jackplanes and jointers, which require a firm, close-grained wood that resists splitting in short sections. Apple, it will be recalled, was long accepted as the standard wood for the handles of the best handsaws, which are quite similar to plane totes. Beech once furnished totes exclusively for commercially made planes, as it did for the stocks. Perhaps best of all would be rosewood, from which the wooden furnishings of the best iron planes were formerly made.

Shaping a plane stock, mortising it, and fitting the iron is not as difficult as it might appear to someone who has never done it—provided one goes about it systematically and has the right tools for the job. But before outlining the procedure, it will simplify the explanation to name the parts of the plane that we shall be considering.

Tote signifies handle. There are two kinds, open and closed. Only the latter is used on boatbuilders' planes. The *stock* is the body of the plane, exclusive of the tote and the chip. The bottom is the *sole*. The aperture in the sole through which the cutting edge of the iron protrudes and through which the shavings enter is the *mouth*. The shavings pass upward through the *throat* or the *escapement*. On either side of this opening through the stock are the *cheeks*. The incline on which the plane iron is seated is the *bed*: in iron planes it is called the *frog*. The angle of incline of the bed is the *pitch*. The after end of the stock is the *britch*. A *striker, button,* or *start,* as it is variously called, sometimes of

A standard boatbuilder's plane, showing positions of the iron, the cap iron, and the chip in the stock.

end-grain hardwood and sometimes of metal, is often inserted in the britch end of smoothers and on top of the forward end of jacks and jointers to take the impact of the plane hammer when loosening the chip to adjust the iron.

The iron is held firmly in position in the working plane by the *chip,* which is little more than a thin wedge the center of which has been cut away somewhat to facilitate the egress of shavings from the throat, leaving two narrow strips called *prongs* on either side of the chip at its lower end. These prongs fit into the shallow *slots* in the cheeks and wedge against the forward sides of the slots, which are called the *shoulders* or *abutments*. At the top, the slots are let in to a depth of ¼ inch or slightly more, tapering to nothing at the bottom (just above the mouth) to give as much room as possible for the shavings to clear. As planes are used, the prongs tend in time to reach too deep, and their ends have to be trimmed to prevent shavings from catching on them. They must not project beyond the slots into the mouth of the plane. In making the chip, the prongs should spread slightly wider than the side-to-side distance between the inside of the slots. This ensures a tight fit and prevents shavings from wedging behind the points of the prongs.

Diagrammatic view of a boatbuilder's long plane.

Plans for a smoother (top left), a jackplane (top right), and a jointer. Jackplanes and jointers are usually cut down aft of the throat to lighten them and to bring the user's hand closer to the work for better balance.

The wedge angle of the chip is critical, for if it is too great, the chip will not hold, popping up at the least jar or bump. But if the chip is made too flat, it will grip too tightly and will not loosen readily to permit adjustment of the iron. Ten degrees, plus or minus a degree, is about right for the angle of slope. To ensure getting this right is one reason for making a careful layout of the interior on the outside of the block, as will be described.

Undoubtedly there is more than one good method for making a wooden plane. The one we shall consider I have used successfully many times. I should not want to claim, however, that it cannot be improved, or that it should not be modified to suit different conditions or individual requirements.

First of all, and regardless of the kind of plane, the block is squared up to the desired size. It is necessary that its opposite surfaces be true and parallel to each other. After that, the ends are squared and cut to length. But other than this, the stock is not given its final shape until it has been mortised for the iron, and the iron and the chip have been fitted in place.

After the block has been squared, the position of the iron is located and marked on one side. Ordinarily, the iron is set at an angle, or pitch, of 45 degrees. This differs, however, for some specialized planes, such as the York pattern, used for planing cross-grained hardwoods, which has a pitch of 60 degrees. The line marking the seat of the iron against the bed is next squared across the sole, and also across the top. Then a line indicating the position of the iron is marked on the second side to correspond with the first.

Next the iron, in most cases composed of blade and cap, is laid along the seat line already marked on the side of the block, and the outline of the iron is carefully traced. Then the width and taper of the chip are laid out and the position of the shoulder or abutment marked, with care taken to make the wedge angle of the chip approximately 10 degrees. The layout of the interior is now outlined fully on the side of the block, and the mortising can proceed.

The mouth is cut in first. It is located by squaring across the sole from the layout on the side. To begin with, the mouth should be kept a little smaller than it will be in the finished plane. It is very easy to get it too large if this precaution is not taken. Later, it can easily be enlarged to the desired width with a fine wood rasp. However, should the mouth inadvertently be cut too large, this mistake can be rectified either by setting a graving piece into the sole ahead of the iron, or by padding the seat of the iron on the bed with a piece of leather to bring the iron forward. This last device is sometimes used to cushion the iron and to give it an even, firm bearing.

Cutting the mouth first serves much the same function as does the "stop-cut" in wood carving. If the internal mortising is carried all the way through from the top, there is a danger of splitting pieces out of the sole when the chisel breaks through the bottom. This is particularly likely to happen with brittle woods such as lignum vitae or boxwood. Furthermore, if the mortise is carried all the way through from the top, it may not come out precisely where it is supposed to, and in the course of attempts to rectify this, the mouth is apt to become too large.

The safest and really the easiest way to start is by chiseling into the sole about ½ inch deep, or whatever shows on the diagram of the interior previously laid out on the side of the block. Just as the fore-and-aft width of the cut across the sole is kept small (and enlarged later, if necessary), so the width of the cut across the sole is kept narrow enough at first to come inside the cheeks, if it were carried through to the top of the block.

After the mouth has been cut through the sole to the required depth, and while the block is still in the vise bottom up, a series of holes, as close together as possible, are drilled through the mouth out through the top of the block. The drill is kept far enough away from the outside to allow for the thickness of the cheeks. This operation is done most accurately with a drill press.

As soon as these holes are drilled, the block is turned over and cutting proceeds from the top. The row of holes also serves as a stop-cut, and with a stiff, narrow, sharp-pointed saw, it is easy to connect them and to make a continuous cut across the inside of the block to work against from both ends. Several sharp

chisels are required. The smallest is ¼ inch wide, and the widest is 1 inch or more, depending on what is available and the preference of the user. For working in very hard woods, chisels should be ground with a shortened bevel—that is, at a rather steep angle. Otherwise the edge may break under the blows of the mallet, especially if the steel is extra hard.

Several fine-cut patternmakers' rasps and riffles are desirable, with one or two narrow enough to fit into the side slots. If one of these narrow rasps has safe edges, all the better. One who intends to make a number of planes might consider converting an ordinary narrow rasp for this by grinding its edges smooth on the wheel. There are also specialized planemakers' tools called *floats,* which are finishing tools for leveling and smoothing hard-to-get-at places in the interior of the stock. These have rows of large parallel teeth running across one side. Some floats are quite narrow, no more than $\frac{3}{16}$ inch. Others are pointed at the end and widen toward the handle to resemble a triangular flat file. Floats are not manufactured for sale; they are generally made by planemakers for their own use. Often they are made from worn-out files annealed to saw hardness so that they can be filed to shape and the teeth cut in them with a three-cornered saw file. With such specialized tools it is much easier to clean out and to smooth the side slots in the cheeks for the chip and iron.

As already mentioned, a special saw with a stiff, narrow, pointed blade is well worth going to some trouble to obtain, even if one is obliged to make over a saw for this purpose. Such a saw can be seen in the photograph of tools required for planemaking. This one was adapted from a worn-out compass saw. Its blade is a narrow triangle, about 1 inch wide at the base where the blade joins the handle, and about 6 inches long, running to a sharp point at the end. It is filed crosscut with 10 teeth to the inch.

The blade was thick to start with, and before the teeth were cut it was filed to a tapering section from back to front, leaving the back edge quite thin and the front or cutting edge its original thickness. Thus, the teeth need no set, and the saw runs true, cuts smoothly, and does not bind. With its narrow, stiff blade and sharp point, it can be started in a space no wider than a single drill hole, and it is the perfect tool for making shoulder cuts in the cheeks when it comes to fitting the chip and the iron. Without such a tool, shoulder cuts can be troublesome.

After the side slots are cut and the iron is seated, a

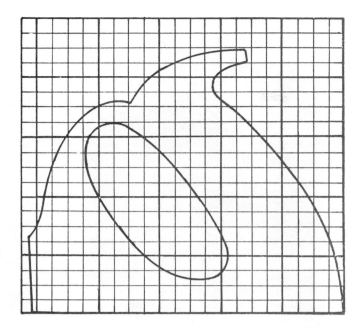

A pattern for a comfortable tote, or handle, of a jackplane or jointer. Cherry and applewood are fine materials for totes, which require firm, close-grained, split-resistant wood.

thin strip of pine is fitted in the tapered space between the iron and the shoulder to provide a template for making the chip, and also for checking to see if both side slots are the same size and slope. If they are not, one or the other must be trimmed to match. When the chip has been carefully fitted with the iron in place, and the throat has been smoothed and brought as near as possible at this stage to its final form, the outside of the plane is shaped and finished.

The sides of most boatbuilders' smoothers are cut on a convex curve so that the stock is narrow at the britch, somewhat wider at the fore end, and widest abreast of the mouth. It will be seen that this curved shape resembles a coffin, from whence comes the name *coffin plane* sometimes applied to them. This shape is traditional for boatbuilders' smoothers. The origin was clearly functional, for planes so shaped fit the hands better than if they were left straight-sided, and are easier to grasp and to push on the sides of a vessel, overhead, or in the other numerous awkward positions that occur in building wooden vessels. One exception, however, is that spar planes are sometimes left straight-sided.

Boatbuilding planes naturally vary in their shape, quality, size, and weight with the individual makers, yet for the most part they conform with remarkable fidelity to traditional patterns. As mentioned, the boatbuilders' long planes, the jacks and the jointers, are uniformly narrower and lower than the factory-made beech planes once supplied to house carpenters and cabinetmakers. But what particularly distinguished these long planes was their cut-down britch. This style of plane is often called a *razee,* the term formerly applied to ships whose upper deck was cut away.

Here again, the reason for shaping a plane in this way is functional. By lowering the tote, the force applied in pushing the plane is brought down more directly behind the iron, where it is most effective, improving both the balance and the efficiency of the tool. The tote can be shaped to fit the hand of the owner. Those formerly supplied on factory-made wooden planes are apt to be small and tend to cramp the user's hand. Not only is comfort affected, but also the control of the tool.

Not all planes are fitted with strikers or starts, but these are worth putting in. Smoothers that lack them are frequently disfigured and even split by continual pounding from the plane hammer in adjusting the iron. A small end-grain cylinder ¾ inch in diameter and about 1 inch long—of very hard wood inserted in a hole bored in the britch end of a smoother, with its end rounded over and protruding a little—makes a very good striking button. In a long plane, the striker is inserted in the top of the stock, near the forward end. Sometimes a metal pin is used, and occasionally a bronze carriage bolt, with the head serving as the striking button.

The blade of a wooden plane is properly called an *iron,* a name that has come down from antiquity. It is made principally of iron, except for the portion that does the actual cutting, which is a thin facing of the finest tempered steel welded on the inside at the lower end.

This type of iron, developed in Sheffield and standardized at the beginning of the 19th century, or perhaps even earlier, is not to be confused with the thinner, all-steel blade of the modern cast-iron bench plane. Such thin, lightweight blades are not well suited for wooden planes, being more apt than the heavier irons to jump and chatter when one is planing cross-grained wood.

The big problem facing the planemaker today is the scarcity of irons. These are no longer manufactured in this country, and old inventories on hardware shelves have long since been sold out.

Smoothers in various stages of construction, and the tools that made them. Left to right in the background are a block for a smoother with the mouth cut in; a block with completed mortise for chip and iron; a block shaped on the outside; a smoother cut away to show the interior; and a finished lignum vitae smoother. In the foreground are a wood carver's mallet; chisels; wood rasps and a riffle; the planemaker's special pointed saw; a Stanley block plane; a combination square; an Arkansas oilstone; and a back saw. In the near foreground are a plane hammer and a pattern-maker's vise. (Russell A. Fowler photo, Mystic Seaport)

Until a few years ago, a limited number of old-type irons by Marples and other Sheffield makers were obtainable from England, but that source has been exhausted. A few superior irons are still being imported from West Germany, notably Ulmia irons, and some apparently from Finland, but it is only a matter of time before these sources also dry up. At one time superior Swedish irons could be had—Shark Brand irons by Erik Anton Berg of Eskilstuna—but I have been informed that production has been discontinued.

There is another source of plane irons: secondhand ones, from old wooden planes, which are still to be found in considerable numbers. Only a few years ago such old planes, scorned and discarded by modern mechanics, were readily and cheaply available. The hockshops and secondhand stores were full of them, and many more found their way to the dump as attics and cellars were emptied and cleaned. More recently the antique industry has begun to take cognizance of the growing interest in old carpenters' tools, and the price of planes has gone up and will continue to rise.

Nevertheless, it is still possible to pick up an occasional bargain in secondhand plane irons. But don't delay, for these old irons are fast becoming

Planemakers' tools. In the foreground, left to right, are floats, rasps, chisels, a selection of double irons, and a plane hammer. Included in the background are the planemaker's saw (shown cutting an abutment) and two totes, one partly made and one finished. (Mary Anne Stets photo, Mystic Seaport)

collectors' items. Regretfully, what I am now writing can only hasten the inevitable.

In some cases the entire secondhand plane can be converted to boatbuilding use, even if it was not a boatbuilder's plane originally. A few simple changes or repairs to the stock may be all that is required, as I shall explain. But more frequently it is only the iron that is of interest.

Occasionally the stock will be so beat up and dilapidated as to appear next to worthless, yet it will contain a good iron. It does not matter if the iron is rusted, provided the steel facing is not pitted so deeply that the pits cannot be ground out without removing too much of the steel. Since the steel facing is generally about 1/16 inch thick, rust pits rarely go deep enough to spoil the iron. Unless all rust pitting is removed and the surface of the steel polished bright, however, it will be impossible to give the iron a perfect cutting edge.

Sufficient length of steel should remain on the iron to allow for enough grinding and sharpening to make it worthwhile to put the iron in a new stock. A new iron has about 2 inches of tempered steel, but even an inch of steel, provided care is taken to grind sparingly, will

last a long time in planes with special shapes that are used only occasionally.

Indeed, a mere half-inch of good steel is not to be scorned, for with careful grinding for occasional use it can be made to last for years. Should the steel be gone completely, the cap is worth having to match with irons missing their caps. Cap irons are also in short supply.

In reconditioning an iron that has rusted, there are a number of precautions to be observed. During grinding, the surface of the steel must be kept absolutely flat, and there should be no digging into it anywhere or lowering of the edges. The steel should not be heated to the point of drawing the temper. Grinding wheels coarse enough to leave deep scratches should be avoided. Such scratches are difficult to remove in the final polishing, which should result in a mirrorlike surface.

As previously mentioned, the width of iron most common in boatbuilders' planes is 1¾ inches for smoothers and jackplanes. Even in large jointers, an iron width of over 2 inches is rare. At the other extreme, a narrow smoother with an iron only 1¼ inches wide is one of the most useful tools a boatbuilder can have. I have one of this size in which I have worn out three irons during some 20 years of more or less continual use.

Wooden planes formerly used by house carpenters, joiners, and cabinetmakers were generally wider than boatbuilders' planes, and in adapting irons taken from them it is necessary to cut them down in width. If it is only a matter of 1/16 inch or thereabouts that has to be removed, grinding on a coarse power wheel is the answer. But a sharp hacksaw is recommended for cutting down oversize irons from either side of which as much as 3/16 inch or more must be taken.

Most of the iron—that is, what is actually iron—is soft enough to be sawn through readily. But the saw will not touch the tempered steel, which begins at about the base of the slot.

One way of handling this is to score the steel partly through on a thin, high-speed cutting wheel, and to complete the break by snapping off the nearly glass-hard steel in a machinist's vise. Care must be taken to score the steel deeply before clamping the iron, at the break line, between the jaws of the vise. Good contact the full length of the steel is essential. Otherwise there is a chance the break might not follow the scoring but instead run off into the center of the blade and spoil the iron. If this procedure is followed, including sawing through the soft iron backing of the steel behind where it is scored, a quick rap with a heavy hammer will snap the steel cleanly and instantly as if it were a piece of glass.

In grinding and polishing the steel facing of the iron after it has been cut down to the desired width, one must be careful not to overheat the steel to the point of drawing the temper. A buffing wheel is useful for bringing the steel facing to a bright polish. Afterward, the polished surface of the steel should be oiled to prevent further rusting, a critical precaution because in most cases the steel is not thick enough to stand grinding and polishing twice.

In sharpening the iron, the bevel of grind will be about 22 degrees, although for different work and different woods sometimes slightly more bevel, and sometimes slightly less, will be preferred. Unless the cap iron fits tightly against the face of the cutting iron it will be useless—and sometimes worse than useless, for shavings are sure to wedge themselves under a loose cap and become jammed there.

In his *British Plane Makers From 1700,* W.L. Goodman provides a check list of 48 British plane-iron makers, all but three of which were located in Sheffield. Many of these concerns exported plane irons to the United States; irons with various Sheffield marks are widely distributed in this country and constitute a considerable fraction of the secondhand irons. Sheffield names most commonly seen are William Ash, William Butcher, James Cam, Greaves, Graves, Hernshaw, Ibbottson, Moulson Brothers, William Marples, Newbould, Sorby, and Ward. Other Sheffield marks occasionally turn up. All such irons are of superior quality, as is any iron marked Sheffield and warranted cast steel. With enough steel left to justify putting it into a plane, such an iron should be considered a lucky find.

Irons by Moulson Brothers were highly esteemed by American boatbuilders and shipwrights, and must have been imported in quantity, considering the numbers to be seen in planes still in use. William Marples's irons were also popular and among the last to be sold commercially.

I have never seen a Sheffield iron that was not stamped *cast steel*. The unexcelled quality of Sheffield edge tools derived from the superior crucible cast steel produced by a process developed at Sheffield in the 1740s by Benjamin Huntsman for clock springs.

By the second quarter of the 19th century the forging of edge tools in this country was fast emerging from the local blacksmith shop to be carried on in mechanized factories. Tool manufacturing concerns founded by D.R. Barton at Rochester, New York, in 1832 and by L. and I.J. White at Buffalo in 1837 both produced superior plane irons faced with steel—although, for whatever reasons, they did not warrant their irons cast steel as most other plane-iron makers did.

White's irons were extra heavy, and in my judgment they were equal to any plane irons ever made anywhere. Buck Brothers, Sheffield edge-tool makers who removed to Millbury, Massachusetts, produced until about 40 or 50 years ago superior plane irons in great quantity, unquestionably a greater quantity than any other American concern. Their mark, a buck's antlered head, is still widely known and respected. One of the brothers, Charles Buck, left the original firm after a time, producing equally good irons under his own name.

On page 44 of his *Wooden Planes in 19th Century America,* Kenneth Roberts lists 32 concerns that formerly manufactured plane irons for wooden planes in this country. In addition to irons by Barton, White, and Buck, I can vouch from personal experience for

American irons marked Auburn Tool Company, Baldwin Tool Company, Chapin, Chapin-Stephens, Dwights French Company, Globe Manufacturing Company, Humphreysville Manufacturing Company, Ohio Tool Company, Providence Tool Company, Sargent and Company, and James Swan.

The would-be planemaker in search of irons will do well to familiarize himself with the lists by Goodman and by Roberts. Don't ask for these irons at the store. Chances are they wouldn't even know what you were talking about. Still, such irons in mint condition do turn up every once in a while in old tool chests, attics, dusty lofts, and cellars. Used irons with enough steel remaining to warrant consideration, while far from plentiful, can still be found. The places to look are flea markets, yard sales, tool auctions, and antique shops. Frequently, good irons can be salvaged from broken or wornout planes too far gone to be worth repairing. On the other hand, it is often possible to put worn or damaged plane stocks back in usable condition with only simple or minor repairs. Splits and checks are easily mended with epoxy adhesive. It is possible to renew the sole of a badly worn plane by gluing a new lift on the bottom. Sometimes a jack or a jointer is much improved by replacing the old loosened tote with a new one of improved design. Old beech planes are greatly improved in appearance by applying tung oil, Danish oil, or similar sealers or wood conditioners after they have been cleaned thoroughly.

Carpenters' or cabinetmakers' smoothers are readily converted to excellent backing-out planes for the use of the planker, merely by rounding the sole slightly from side to side and grinding the iron to match. In most cases a convex round of barely $1/16$ inch for a stock width of $2\frac{1}{4}$ to $2\frac{1}{2}$ inches is quite adequate. More than this will be too much for most planking operations. A convex round of $1/8$ inch in $2\frac{1}{2}$ inches of stock width is certainly the maximum for a backing-out plane, but even though one with as much curvature as this will rarely be used, the boatbuilder will do well to have one in his kit.

A simple but effective method for converting an ordinary flat smoothing plane to a backing-out plane is as follows. One side of a piece of soft-pine board about a foot long and 6 or 8 inches wide is hollowed out to the shallow curvature desired for the bottom of the plane. This can be done in various ways, one of which is to use a flat gouge followed by a slightly curved block and coarse sandpaper.

Next a sheet of coarse emery cloth is placed over the hollowed-out surface and secured along the edges of the board with tacks. This is now ready for trueing up the bottom of the converted plane after it has been planed freehand as nearly as possible to the desired curvature with a sharp plane set fine and a curved template of thin wood. Vigorously scrubbing the converted stock back and forth over the emery cloth will make its curved bottom perfectly smooth and true. The iron is now inserted in the plane and allowed to protrude slightly through the mouth to show how much should be ground off to produce the required curvature. This can first be done close enough by eye, after which the iron is reinserted in the stock, allowed to protrude through the mouth ever so slightly, and scrubbed back and forth over the emery cloth. This will shape the iron to the precise curvature required. It is now removed, carefully ground sharp, and honed to a keen edge on the oilstone. The cap iron must be slightly reshaped to fit the curve of the blade and made to fit absolutely tightly against the surface of the steel. This may involve some slight hammering, filing, and a final trueing on the flat surface of a coarse stone.

For most work, rockers should not have too much longitudinal curvature either. Among the rockers in my own kit, the one that has seen the most use has only a scant $\frac{1}{4}$ inch of longitudinal curve in a sole length of 8 inches. My most extreme rocker, and one I rarely use, has 1 inch of curve in a length of 8 inches. Most of the concave curves that call for smoothing in boatbuilding are long, relatively flat sweeps—the underside of deck beams, the inside of waterways or covering boards, and the like.

Spar planes require some explanation. The spar plane, so called, is a finishing plane used to give the final smoothing after the spar has been sized and shaped and brought to a nearly perfect round by the successive use of a variety of other tools, including ordinary jointers, jackplanes, and smoothing planes. Thus, a great deal of planing gets done on a spar before the spar plane is applied. Before abrasives came into use, spars received their final finish from planing rather than sanding.

Best results are obtained from a spar plane whose curvature fits the round of the spar as closely as possible. Thus, the professional sparmaker had a chest, or maybe two chests, full of planes of different curvatures.

The method of making a plane to fit a spar of given diameter is first to lay out the spar's largest circumference with dividers on a piece of thin board in order

Planing a small mast with a spar plane. (Mary Anne Stets photo, Mystic Seaport)

to make two templates of its curvature—one concave, the other convex. Thin pine does nicely for this. Using the concave template, a block of pine or other soft wood wide enough to clamp in the vise with 4 or 5 inches protruding, and about as thick as the plane, is rounded to fit. When this is smooth and the template fits, a sheet of rough emery cloth, grit side out, is stretched over the rounded surface and tacked on the sides. The tacks must be far enough down the sides to be out of the way.

The convex template is needed when the sole of the spar plane is hollowed. This is usually started with gouges and often continued using a plane with a rounded sole when one of suitable curvature is available. Such a plane is not essential, however, and patient gouge work is all that is needed before the hollowed sole is ready for final trueing on the emery cloth. From here the procedure is the same as previously described for finishing the backing-out plane. One item not previously mentioned: Before the sole of the spar plane is hollowed, the mouth should be cut in, because it would be more difficult to cut it later.

The mouth is slightly curved to match the circumference of the spar for which the plane is made.

An alternate way to make a plane for a small-diameter spar, such as a small sprit, is to turn on the lathe a short section of cylinder of the same diameter. One end of this cylinder is cut off square, and this squared end is applied against the sole of the plane to mark the curvature of the mouth. The other end of the cylinder is cut at an angle of 45 degrees, the same angle or pitch at which the iron is set in the plane. The end so cut provides an elliptical template for grinding the iron, the curve of the cutting edge of an iron set at 45 degrees being elliptical rather than circular.

Traditionally, boatbuilders' planes were mortised and shaped from solid blocks. Now that we have reliable glues, some find it easier to make planes from two lengthwise halves that are glued together after the internal cutting and shaping has been done, so to speak, from the outside. An old worn-out plane too far gone to recondition, such as one of those frequently found at flea markets, can be split lengthwise with the saw to obtain a pattern to go by. In choosing wood for this type of construction, it should be remembered that some of the heavier tropical hardwoods, such as lignum vitae and cocobolo, do not glue well.

From the standpoint of utility alone, these glued-up planes work quite adequately, yet for many who take pride in having fine tools, they lack something aesthetically.

Instead of wedge-shaped slots in the cheeks, some European planes have a different arrangement for holding the chip. A section of metal rod (about ¼ inch in diameter) extends across the throat from side to side with its ends embedded in the cheeks. Between the cheeks is a strip of metal, flat on one side, curved on the other, and about 1 inch wide, through which the rod passes. This turns freely on the rod, adjusting its flat surface to the angle of the chip wedged against it. A variation of this arrangement is to have a thinner strip of flat metal brazed or silver-soldered to a section of rod, the rod turning freely in the holes in the cheeks, which carry it. This arrangement is well adapted to miniature modelmakers' planes with single-bladed irons.

Both variations of this alternate method of wedging the chip hold the iron securely while allowing it to be adjusted easily. In addition, the planes clear their shavings easily and seldom clog up. Furthermore, by inserting backing strips of various thicknesses between the bed and the iron, one can move the iron forward to narrow the mouth when fine work or cross-grained wood makes this desirable. This cannot be done, of course, when the chip wedges in side slots cut in the cheeks.

The novice planemaker tends to make the mouth of his plane too wide. In extreme cases, it is advisable to correct this fault by setting a graving piece in the sole at the forward side of the mouth to narrow it. In restoring old planes worn from long use, a graving piece is frequently let into the sole in this manner to bring the mouth back to its original width.

Some of the simpler molding planes useful at times in boat work are rounds and hollows, beading planes, narrow rabbet planes, and a few others, but boatbuilders rarely went to the trouble of making molding planes of their own. The standard shapes were too easily obtained ready-made.

A plane included in the outboard joiner's kit is the chamfer plane. This is little more than an ordinary flat smoother, but one whose sides are cut away from the bottom in a long, easy chamfer that barely exposes the corners of the iron. With a chamfer plane it is possible to plane up to protruding parts, such as moldings or trim, much as with a rabbet plane. For fine planing on the outside of the hull, a sharp chamfer plane works better than a rabbet plane, in part because of its wood sole and in part because of its double iron that can be set for a fine, smooth cut.

Occasionally the professional boatbuilder has need for a plane with a lot of round in its sole. One use for such a plane, similar to what house carpenters call a gutter plane, is for smoothing the semicircular hollow in split shaft logs for large power launches. There is nothing special about making such a plane, except that reworking the cap iron for a tight fit against the cutting iron can be fussy and exacting.

This is not all there is to boatbuilding planes and planemaking by any means, but it is enough for a start. From here, the capable mechanic will be able to strike out on his own.

Bibliography

Chapter 1. Herreshoff Rowboat and Modified McInnis Bateau

Durant, Kenneth and Helen. *The Adirondack Guide-Boat*. Camden, Maine: International Marine Publishing Co., 1980.

Gardner, John. *Building Classic Small Craft, Volume 1*. Camden, Maine: International Marine Publishing Co., 1977.

Herreshoff, L. Francis. *The Common Sense of Yacht Design*. 1946. (Reprint: Jamaica, New York: Caravan-Maritime Books, 1974.)

Chapter 2. Pilot Gig

Hornsby, Thomas. "The Last Voyage of the *Thomas W. Lawson*." Nautical Research Journal, April 1955.

Larn, Richard. *Cornish Shipwrecks, Volume 3*. New York: Taplinger Publishing Co., 1971.

March, Edgar J. *Inshore Craft of Britain in the Days of Sail and Oar, Volume 2*. Camden, Maine: International Marine Publishing Co., 1970.

Chapter 3. Merrymeeting Bay Duckboat

Chapelle, Howard I. *American Small Sailing Craft*. New York: W.W. Norton, 1951.

Gardner, John. *Building Classic Small Craft, Volume 1*. Camden, Maine: International Marine Publishing Co., 1977.

Kunhardt, C.P. *Small Yachts*. New York: Forest and Stream Publishing Co., 1885.

Stephens, W.P. *Canoe and Boat Building, a Complete Manual for Amateurs*. New York: Forest and Stream Publishing Co., 1884. (4th edition, 1889, revised and extended, with 50 folding plates instead of original 30. Several subsequent editions.)

Chapter 5. Two 8-Foot Prams

Gardner, John. *Building Classic Small Craft, Volume 1*. Camden, Maine: International Marine Publishing Co., 1977.

Herreshoff, L. Francis. *Sensible Cruising Designs*. Camden, Maine: International Marine Publishing Co., 1973.

Chapter 6. Four Canoes

The American Canoe Association. "Sailing Canoes, a Brief History." June 1, 1935.

Crowley, William. *Rushton's Rowboats and Canoes: The 1903 Catalog in Perspective*. Camden, Maine: International Marine Publishing Co., 1983.

Kemp, Dixon. *A Manual of Yacht and Boat Sailing*. Fifth Edition. London: Horace Cox, 1886.

Manley, Atwood. *J. Henry Rushton and His Times in American Canoeing*. Syracuse, New York: Syracuse University Press, 1968.

Roberts, Kenneth G., and Philip Shackleton. *The Canoe: A History of the Craft from Panama to the Arctic*. Camden, Maine: International Marine Publishing Co., 1983.

Stephens, W.P. *Canoe and Boat Building, a Complete Manual for Amateurs*. Fourth Edition. New York: Forest and Stream Publishing Co., 1889.

Chapter 9. Sea Bright Skiff

Guthorn, Peter J. *The Sea Bright Skiff and Other Jersey Shore Boats*. New Brunswick, New Jersey: Rutgers University Press, 1971.

Chapter 10. Boston Fishing Power Dories

German, Andrew W. *Down on T Wharf*. Mystic, Connecticut: Mystic Seaport Museum, 1982.

Chapter 12. Two Garveys

Chapelle, Howard I. "Some American Fishing Launches." IN: *Fishing Boats of the World, Volume 1*. The Proceedings of the First FAO International Fishing Boat Congress, 1953. Ed. Jan-Olof Traung. Surrey, England: Fishing News (Books) Ltd., 1955.

Chapter 13. Clamming Skiff

Gardner, John. *The Dory Book*. Camden, Maine: International Marine Publishing Co., 1978.

Chapters 14 and 15. 16-Foot Swampscott Dory and Mower Dory

Gardner, John. *The Dory Book*. Camden, Maine: International Marine Publishing Co., 1978.
Mower, Charles. "How to Build a Power Dory." The Rudder, May 1904.
Schock, Edson B. "How to Build an Auxiliary Cruising Dory, *Fish Hook*." The Rudder, June 1904.

Chapter 16. Boatbuilders' Planes

Herreshoff, L. Francis. *The Common Sense of Yacht Design*. 1946. (Reprint: Jamaica, New York: Caravan-Maritime Books, 1974.
Mercer, Henry C. "*Ancient Carpenters' Tools*." Fourth Edition. Doylstown, Pennsylvania: The Bucks County Historical Society, 1968.
Roberts, Kenneth D. *Wooden Planes in 19th Century America*. Fitzwilliam, New Hampshire: Ken Roberts Publishing Co., 1975.
Roberts, Kenneth D. *Wooden Planes in 19th Century America, Volume II*. Fitzwilliam, New Hampshire: Ken Roberts Publishing Co., 1983.

Index